D0909590

THE RISE OF
PARTY
IN ENGLAND

THE RISE OF PARTY IN ENGLAND

The Rockingham Whigs 1760–82

Frank O'Gorman
Lecturer in Modern History, University of Manchester

London   George Allen & Unwin Ltd
Ruskin House   Museum Street

First published in 1975

© *George Allen & Unwin Ltd. 1975.*

ISBN 0 04 942135 2 hardback

Printed in Great Britain
in 11 point Baskerville type
by Unwin Brothers Limited
The Gresham Press
Old Woking, Surrey

To Annelise

Acknowledgements

The pleasure of exploring the world of Rockingham, Burke, Chatham, George III and Lord North has been enormously enhanced by the kindness and encouragement of many persons which I should like to acknowledge here. The staffs of many institutions have patiently borne an endless stream of visits and enquiries. That which displayed most fortitude was undoubtedly the Sheffield Public Library, where Miss Meredith and her staff always provided courteous and efficient service. I should also like to express my thanks to the staffs of the British Museum, the Public Record Office, the Berkshire County Record Office, the Essex County Record Office, the Hertfordshire County Record Office, the Leeds Public Library, the Middlesex County Record Office, the Northamptonshire County Record Office, the East Suffolk Record Office at Ipswich, the West Suffolk Record Office at Bury St Edmunds, the Warwickshire County Record Office and the North Riding Record Office at Northallerton, Yorkshire. Furthermore, a study such as this could not have been undertaken without the kindness of owners of manuscript collections. Among those who allowed me access were the Trustees of the Wentworth Woodhouse Estate, the Trustees of the Bedford Estate, the Duke of Devonshire, the Duke of Portland, the Duke of Grafton, Lord Spencer, the Marquis of Bath, Lord Bathurst and members of the Glynn family.

No historian can work in isolation and without inspiration. I share the debt of all scholars to Sir Lewis Namier and Sir Herbert Butterfield. I hope that I have managed to avoid blindly following or childishly attacking either. Further, recent work in the field of later eighteenth century studies has been extremely helpful to the present writer and I should like to single out the names of John Brooke, John Cannon, Ian Christie, Donald Ginter, Derek Jarrett, Peter Thomas and Derek Watson among others.

I cannot exaggerate the debt of gratitude which I feel towards particular friends and colleagues. They have helped me more than they know. John Woods has always been a patient, amusing and scholarly inspiration. Sir Herbert Butterfield and Derek Jarrett read the book in typescript, made pertinent suggestions and proffered invaluable advice. Richard Siddall and Wendy Howard also read the typescript and undertook the difficult task of helping me to say what I meant. To all of them I am sincerely grateful.

FRANK O'GORMAN
University of Manchester

Contents

Acknowledgements   *page*   9
Introduction   13

PART ONE: EMERGENCE (1760–5)

1 George III, Bute and Newcastle (1760–2)   25
2 The Young Friends of the Duke of Newcastle
   (November 1762–April 1763)   46
3 The Opposition to George Grenville (1763–5)   67

PART TWO: OFFICE (1765–6)

4 The Formation of the First Rockingham Administration   95
5 The First Rockingham Administration   110
6 The Repeal of the Stamp Act   136
7 The Decline and Fall of the First Rockingham
   Administration   157

PART THREE: RE-FORMATION (1766–72)

8 The Crisis of the Rockingham Whig Party
   (1766–8)   187
9 The Rockingham Whigs and the General
   Election of 1768   219
10 Party, People and Parliament (1768–70)   231
11 Edmund Burke and the Rockingham Whigs   258
12 Rockinghamites, Chathamites and the Failure
   of the Opposition (1770–2)   272

PART FOUR: EMPIRE (1772–80)

13 The Problem of Empire (1773–4)   297
14 The Rockingham Whigs on the Eve of the
   American Revolution   315
15 Reaction, Conciliation and War (1774–5)   325
16 The Problem of Independence (1775–7)   337
17 The Shadow of Saratoga (1777–8)   360
18 The War, The Empire and the Rockingham
   Whigs (1778–9)   379

PART FIVE: CLIMAX (1780–2)

19   The Rockingham Whigs and the Reform
     Movement (1779–80)   399
20   The Victory of the Opposition (1780–2)   426
21   The Rockingham–Shelburne Ministry (1782)   446

CONCLUSION   471

Appendix   478
Bibliography   483
References   495
Index   642

Introduction

Almost half a century has passed since Sir Lewis Namier effected one of the most remarkable achievements in the history of historical writing in Britain: the demolition of the Whig interpretation of eighteenth century politics. This achievement has been so dazzling and so compelling that historians are only now coming to realise that although Namier had demolished one building he had not constructed another. As Professor Christie recently remarked: 'Namier himself had provided only a few foundations and guidelines for the new historical reconstructions made necessary by the levelling of the old'.[1] Where Sir Lewis himself had not led, others did not follow. Indeed, 'Namierite' history appeared to rule out anything resembling general conclusions and wide-ranging interpretations. Its insistence upon the significance of local affairs reduced the body politic to a loose federation of country houses. Its assumption that material motives outweighed the importance of ideas drained politics of principle, of conscious human purpose and thus of any continuity. Under the rigours of Namierite analysis eighteenth century constitutional ideas withered and wilted; their validity, once questioned, crumbled into an incoherent jumble of myth, prejudice and misunderstanding. Professor Plumb complained that 'Concepts as methods of interpreting political history became totally unfashionable'.[2] But concepts, such as that of party, are essential to any meaningful interpretation of political history. They are not separate from events but arise out of them, acquiring their definition from the attitudes and prejudices, the principles and the rationalisations, the fears and the impulses of those involved in a series of historical situations. In the last decade, historians of both the early and the late eighteenth century have come to understand that some of the implications of the Namierite method, especially the redundancy of the concept of party, do not satisfactorily relate to their periods. After all, Namier's researches were confined to a narrow period. They offered a view of British society when its ruling order was united and when its customary divisions and discord had given way for a time to peace and tranquillity. The nature of politics at the accession of George III ought not to be regarded as *typical* of the eighteenth century as a whole. Indeed, the impossibility of depicting exclusively in 'structural' terms both the politics of the reign of Anne and the politics of the 1780s[3] leaves one in some doubt whether 'the Age of the American Revolution' could properly be understood without some reference to non-structural explanations and without reviving the concept of party.

It is only an extraordinary blinkered view of British history, none the less, which would lead any historian to contend that the party history of Britain absolutely and exclusively begins in any one decade. The present writer is not disposed to deny to his friends and colleagues who study the history of Britain in the seventeenth century the pleasure and privilege of acting as midwives to the sturdy if unpredictable and sometimes elusive child of party. Indeed, the party men of the reign of George III were so much aware of the seventeenth century ancestry of their party that to neglect it obscures the *continuity*, real or supposed, of party from the reign of Charles II to that of George III.

Parties had existed since the reign of Charles II, and the party names 'Whig' and 'Tory' had acquired national currency during the Exclusion crisis of 1679–81. Notwithstanding a persistent court–country distinction in British politics,[4] there had developed by 1688 first a Whig, then a Tory party, each held together not only by a set of political and religious attitudes but also by its ambitions and by a rudimentary party organisation based upon the territorial power of the aristocracy and gentry. In the 1690s when Parliament began to meet annually the goal of seeking executive power became a feasible political objective for parties. Whig historians mistook these party conflicts for significant manifestations of a two-party system of government and thus they exaggerated the role and the importance of party. Their claims were attacked by Namierite historians who, unfortunately, complicated what should have been a straightforward task of historical revision through their excessive concentration upon structural factors. Detailed analysis of a few division lists and selective examination of a few years of history will, if hung upon genealogical trees, bear Namierite fruit. In this case they did.[5] The political system was atomised. Historians abandoned parties in favour of 'connections', a concept almost unknown to contemporaries. The politics of the late seventeenth and the early eighteenth century became a bewildering mosaic of ephemeral connections held together by ambition as much as by family loyalty.

Fortunately, these tortuous permutations have in recent years given way to an interpretation of the politics of the period which is at once simpler, more traditional and a good deal more feasible. Historians have reaffirmed the prominent role played by organised Whig and Tory parties in these decades, questioning the importance of connections and bringing the court–country polarity into a proper relationship with the parties.[6] We have been reminded of some profound truths of human nature, that principles matter to men, that politicians seek power as well as place, that their conception of power need not be self-interested but may reflect a coherent political philosophy. In short, principles contributed largely to the cohesion of parties in this period. Members of Parliament voted with their parties with astonishing consistency, even on non-party issues. Party attitudes were, however, not confined to Westminster. The greater frequency of elections after the Triennial Act of 1694 aggravated party feeling in the constituencies. The 'rage of party' played itself out against a boisterous background of public participation, popular sentiment and eruptions of volcanic electoral violence.

The 'structural' interpretation of this period, nevertheless, has left us with some valuable insights into the workings of the political system which ought to safeguard us against a casual relapse into a 'Whig' interpretation. In a monarchical age, the ideal of service to the monarch during a period of national crisis was, in some ways, just as compelling to men as the partisan cries of Whigs and Tories. Furthermore, Members of Parliament represented their locality, their county and their region. Most parliamentary time was occupied in discussions of local matters and these could, and very frequently did, cut across party lines. Moreover, each party had a court and a country wing; it was not unknown for both country wings to unite in supporting Place bills, in resisting court 'corruption' and extravagance and in defending the independence of the Lower House. Party is not the only concept that historians should employ in their explanations of the workings of the political system in the age of William III and Anne.

We should also bear in mind that the parties of this age were not fixed and unchanging.[7] Soon after the Glorious Revolution the Whigs abandoned their political ideology of limited monarchy and foreswore their passion for religious toleration. The party of the freeholder and the shop-keeper became the party of the country house and the Bank of England. The Triennial Act was 'the last stand made by any Whig leader to secure major constitutional change on behalf of the independence of the legislature'.[8] Thereafter the Whigs ceased to attack royal authority and proceeded to exploit it. The Tories, once the upholders of passive obedience to an established church and a divine right monarchy, accepted the Glorious Revolution, a constitutional monarchy and religious toleration. The party which had defended the Stuarts now became the advocate of Place Bills, frequent elections and the purity and independence of the Commons. Those who had once favoured a policy of administrative centralisation now advocated the local independence of the petty squirearchy. The Tories were not a 'country' party—they sought power just as keenly as the Whigs—but they accepted many elements of country politics. Then, astonishingly, just when the parties seemed to have become part of the established conventions of British political life, after half a century of development, they vanished.

Historians explain this phenomenon not only as the engrossment of office and influence by the Whig 'Venetian Oligarchy', but also as the proscription of the Tory party. The Tories had lost the confidence of George I even before he came to England; their involvement in the Jacobite rising of 1715 and the subsequent discrediting of their divided leadership left them particularly vulnerable to the Whig purge which began their destruction. Once proscribed from office and influence the Tory party crumbled and disintegrated. The attractions of the Court persuaded some of them, especially some aristocrats, to become Whigs. The Tories rapidly became identified with the petty squirearchy, the permanent 'outs' of eighteenth century politics. Toryism survived, then, but not in the form of organised party. The old distinctions between Whigs and Tories continued to exist in the eighteenth century but they ceased to matter. The slogans of the party conflicts of the past echoed up and down the century, particularly to the constituencies where they marked ancient feuds and traditional family rivalries, but they no longer stirred the nation. In numerical terms, the Tories in the House of Commons declined from 370 in 1713 to less than 130 in 1727.[9] There were still slightly over 100 of them in 1760 but they had no policy, no organisation and no leader. After the failure of the rising of 1745 some Tories supported a cause that was somewhat more realistic than the restoration of the Stuarts, that of Prince Frederick, the heir to the throne. His death in 1751 dashed what little was left of Tory aspirations.[10]

Sir Robert Walpole was able to consolidate the rule of the 'Venetian Oligarchy' by resting his power upon the twin pillars of royal confidence and parliamentary support. Furthermore, his tenure of the Treasury enabled him to act as a party leader, providing him with patronage sufficient to maintain the coherence of his following. But there was never enought of it. By 1730 there were already nearly 100 dissident Whigs who had become disillusioned not only with the policies of Sir Robert but, more particularly, disappointed in their expectations of office.[11] The significance of their opposition should not be underestimated. As a systematic Opposition the dissident Whigs not only preserved the tactical and the organisational techniques of the old parties. They went much further in exploiting

the procedure of Parliament than they had ever done. These
dissident Whigs were prepared to carry their opposition to great
lengths to obtain revenge upon Walpole. They were prepared
to join the Tories and, later, to associate themselves with the
heir to the throne. The unity of the Whig oligarchy in the early
eighteenth century has frequently been exaggerated and
Walpole's departure from office in 1742 was by no means the
first chink in its armour. Furthermore, the failure of the '45,
leaving the Protestant Succession incontestably secure, deprived
the Whigs of their *raison d'être*.

Although they continued to dominate British politics until
the reign of George III the Whigs were no longer inspired by a
particular conception of party. Indeed, their unity was contingent upon certain tangible factors, all of them transient. The
personal and political arts of Henry Pelham and the Duke of
Newcastle had done much to soothe personal relationships and
maintain a reasonable harmony among the Whigs. Pelham's
death in 1754 was a real loss which left the aristocratic Whigs
vulnerable not only to their own divisions but also to William
Pitt. The exigencies of war kept the Pitt–Newcastle coalition
together until the end of the reign but it was an unhappy and
unstable partnership. There was, however, no alternative to it.
Politics in the 1750s were characterised, then, not only by the
evident relaxation in the texture of the Whig party—serving to
emphasise its constituent parts, the connections—but by the
near absence of any opposition to it.[12] The large and sprawling
federation of Whig connections had absorbed troublesome
groups. Domestic politics in the last three or four years of the
reign of George II were peaceful and opposition to the coalition
was weak and uninspired. George II had capitulated to the
Pelhams in the 1740s and to Pitt in the 1750s and he put up
little resistance to their political domination in the closing years
of his reign. George III succeeded to the throne at a time not
only when the monarchy was at its lowest ebb but when the
Whigs had lost their ideals and were losing their unity. It
was an unusual combination of circumstances and it would
occasion little surprise if he should take advantage of the
weaknesses of the Whigs to restore the role of the monarchy
in politics.

Toryism and Whiggism survived, then, but a two party system did not. Historians of the eighteenth century have frequently attributed this to a 'climate of opinion' which held party in low esteem, but even at the height of the party controversies of Anne's reign, party had been widely condemned.[13] Hostility to party was a slogan, a shibboleth, however widespread, rather than a fundamental element of constitutional theory. Indeed, hostility to party was neither so widespread nor so significant as historians often assert. Professor Foord has demonstrated convincingly how formed Opposition gradually became more acceptable to the mind of the eighteenth century[14] and Professor Robbins has shown that from the 1730s Englishmen, albeit reluctantly, began to accept the existence of party and to recognise its constitutional function.[15] Virtuous men might shake their heads but systematic opposition was practised whenever it was found to be convenient. Almost every First Lord of the Treasury from Newcastle to Liverpool, despite protestations to the contrary, went into a systematic opposition.[16] This being so, it is doubtful if historians of the reign of George III ought to take as established conventions of the constitution the anti-party slogans of the reigns of the first two Georges.

In 1760 party was a legitimate, albeit temporarily discredited, political contrivance. It is, therefore, possible to regard the claims of the Rockingham Whigs to a party status rather more sympathetically than Sir Lewis Namier was prepared to allow. It is no longer the fashion either to ridicule their constitutional pretensions or to vilify Burke's 'disordered imagination'. Mr Brooke has noted that around 1770 the era of 'personal parties' gave way to that of the 'political parties', a transition which the Rockingham Whigs, of all the political groups, were alone in making.[17] In other words, with the Rockinghams, the politics of place gave way to the politics of issues and conditions, of ideology and theory. Yet the story of the Rockingham Whigs has never been told; their claims to virtue have never been thoroughly tested. Were the Rockinghams merely seeking place or were they seeking power in order to implement a programme of measures which flowed logically from a coherent set of political principles? Many such controversial questions about the Rockinghams remain unanswered. The results of recent research now allow a modest and tentative attempt to be made to answer them.

These questions may, for convenience, be grouped under two headings: the problem of the uniqueness of the Rockingham Whig party and the problem of the continuity of party in the eighteenth century. The Rockinghams claimed to be unique and the validity of their claim was almost universally admitted by pre-Namierite historians. The unusual size of the Rockingham party, the abiding loyalty of its members to the Marquis of Rockingham and its unique structure enabled it to survive and to resist the allegedly insidious political and the disastrous imperial policies of the ministries of George III. Its proud defence of the principle of party and its formulation, in the hands of Edmund Burke, of a political theory which was recognisable to nineteenth century historians as an anticipation of the political system of Victorian England left the issue of the uniqueness of the Rockinghams in no doubt. Sir Lewis Namier and others began to question the truth of such assertions and to dispute the Rockingham's claim to a unique status. The Rockingham party was found to be similar to other eighteenth century connections. Its size was found to be much smaller than had been assumed by nineteenth century historians, its coherence and its commitment to the principle of party much weaker. The writings of Burke were found to be distortions of the true political state of Britain, his constitutional theory exposed as partisan rhetoric. George III and Lord North and not Rockingham and Burke were found to be the repositories of constitutional rectitude. This brutal turnabout of historical interpretation scaled down the Rockingham Whigs to the level of an ordinary faction. A detailed study of the history of the Rockingham Whigs will throw light on these questions and, perhaps, resolve some of the contradictions.

If this were not enough, Sir Lewis Namier scorned the idea of continuity between the Whig groupings associated with Walpole, Newcastle, Rockingham, Fox and Grey. The weak link in the chain was found to be that between Newcastle and Rockingham. Namier asserted that Newcastle, Hardwicke and the old Whigs 'had no conception of party government unconnected with the King, and hence of a constitutional Parliamentary Opposition'. He went on

> 'Newcastle, Hardwicke, etc., so far from being the spiritual ancestors of the Whig opposition of, say, 1780, were the direct forerunners of Lord North, who served his apprenticeship as the trusted young friend of Newcastle; and their own families, with a fine sense for realities, finished by joining North, while many so-called Tories of the reign of George II became radicals under George III.'[18]

And, indeed, how could men who had spent their political lives at Court have fostered a party which was to spend most of the first half century of its existence in Opposition and which vindicated its conduct on the grounds that a party in opposition had a useful and necessary constitutional function to perform?[19] The early chapters of this book attempt to resolve this problem.

Nobody now questions the existence in the 1780s of a well-defined Whig party with an elaborate organisational structure. Party organisation, however, is the effect, not the cause of party. It was the events of the early years of the reign of George III which both conditioned the attitudes of the Rockingham Whigs and established the conceptual framework which were essential pre-conditions of the institutional party developments of the 1780s. If the history of party in the eighteenth century is to be intelligible to us it must have an ideological dimension. The organisational developments of the 1780s were superimposed upon a set of mental attitudes, political traditions and constitutional ideas which go back to the beginning of the reign of George III. To their emergence, and to the subsequent development of the Rockingham Whig party, we now turn.

Part One

EMERGENCE
1760–5

Chapter 1

George III, Bute and Newcastle 1760–2

The pattern of political relationships which was to dominate the early period of the reign of George III began to form in the later years of the reign of his predecessor. It has its origins in the death of Henry Pelham, an event which removed from the political scene an enormous talent for conciliation, whose departure inaugurated a period of clashes of temperament and policy among the leading politicians of the day. The appointments of Newcastle to the Treasury and Robinson[1] to the Leadership of the Lower House in March 1754 provoked Pitt to launch himself into one of the most sensational and successful examples of aggressive opposition which the Hanoverian epoch had yet witnessed and which culminated in June 1957 when the Pitt–Newcastle coalition took office.[2] It was in the political stability thus established in response to the war and to the ambitions of Pitt that several of the problems which historians have found so controversial in the early years of the reign of George III have their origin.

The union of the politicians left the future George III isolated and powerless. After 1757 politicians could better serve their own interests by supporting the Pitt–Newcastle coalition than by concerning themselves with the young heir to the throne. The young Prince bitterly resented his neglect. Furthermore, Leicester House was tormented by the prospect of a

Regency. The Regency Bill of 1751 laid it down that if George II were to die before Prince George came of age (in 1756), then the country would be governed by a Regency Council in which the Princess Dowager (Augusta) would be Regent but over which the Duke of Cumberland would act as President and, undoubtedly, wield the greatest influence.[3] Even after 1756 Prince George and his mother continued to fear and to hate Cumberland. They believed that he would not respect the succession, that he would seize power and establish a military dictatorship. Although there was no foundation for their anxiety it was widely shared by the Prince's contemporaries who remembered how the 'butcher' of the '45 had earned his reputation. Neglected by the politicians, defenceless against Cumberland and fearing for the succession, the Prince and his mother found one man, and one man only, who had what the Prince took to be the loyalty and the courage to help them. That man was to become the Prince's 'dearest friend', Lord Bute.

John Stuart, third Earl of Bute, had been a hanger-on at Prince Frederick's Court since 1747 where he was noted more for his genius for amateur theatricals and his capacity for playing cards than for political finesse. He seemed, in short, destined for the political obscurity to which the mediocrity of his talents seemed likely to banish him. But the fact that George II detested him was a sufficient recommendation for Prince Frederick's patronage and in 1750 Bute became a Lord of the Bedchamber in the Prince's Household. The Prince's death a year later, however, threatened to terminate Bute's unpromising political career. Yet he remained on friendly terms with the Princess Dowager and this slender thread of loyalty was sufficient to salvage his sinking political fortunes.[4] Although the situation at Leicester House between 1751 and 1755 is obscure we know that by 1754 Bute had become the Princess's most trusted *confidante* and advisor and, more important, a year later he was in control of the future King's education. Prince George's friendship with Bute, which was to last for a decade and to have such disruptive effects upon the political life of Britain, had begun.

Bute owed his ascendancy over the youth not to his private

friendship with Princess Augusta but to the veneration and gratitude which the boy felt for his solemn and sententious tutor. Lord Bute reciprocated George's friendship but time found him willing to exploit it to satisfy his awakening ambition. Unfortunately for the future King and for Bute the latter's ambition was accompanied neither by strength of character nor political ability. Although his thirst for power grew with the years—in Shelburne's telling words 'He panted for the Treasury'—his abilities, his perceptiveness and his courage failed to mature.[5] Contemporaries found the most striking characteristic of Bute was his arrogance which, together with his unapproachability, amounted to haughtiness. It was this that prevented him either from understanding the motives or appreciating the emotions of other men. His concern for his own situation and his preoccupation with his own feelings inhibited what potential ability he may have had as much as it generated that cowardice which was his greatest single weakness. Yet many contemporaries were to be mesmerised by his relationship with George III, believing that he was both intent upon, and capable of assuming, dictatorial power. One of the few men to realise that this was not the case was William Pitt.[6]

In September 1755 Pitt, then Paymaster-General in Newcastle's ministry, had evinced his readiness to support the Prince in the new reign, to oppose Cumberland, if necessary, and to lead a Bute ministry in the House of Commons.[7] To what extent did Pitt really share the fears of Leicester House and the general dread of Cumberland? How far was he using the Prince for his own ends? It is doubtful if Pitt believed that Cumberland represented a real danger to the constitution of Great Britain and it is difficult to discern much sincerity beneath the obsequious praise which he lavished upon Bute and the Prince. Nevertheless, there are signs that Pitt felt uneasy, and perhaps guilty, when he accepted office in November 1756 and joined the coalition in May 1757. He made every attempt to ride two horses at the same time but he could not indefinitely protest his loyalty to the Prince while continuing in office with the old Whigs, prosecuting a continental war in defence of Hanover of which Leicester House increasingly disapproved.

By 1758 Bute and the Prince could no longer stomach the ministry's policy of sending troops to Germany. This was the signal for Pitt, now secure in the ministry and in the affections of the country, to reveal his true colours. By the end of the year he had let it be known that when Prince George succeeded to the throne Newcastle must remain at the Treasury. For his part, Bute proclaimed that he would not be prepared to work with Pitt in the new reign. The Prince's distrust of Pitt sharpened into anger and hatred; his dependence upon Bute correspondingly increased. Long before George II was in the grave, then, the prospects that the wartime coalition might endure the accession of George III without substantial disruption were already remote. George III's attitude towards William Pitt was to poison politics until 1766 and after.

Relations between Leicester House and the Duke of Newcastle in the last years of the reign of George II were rather less volatile than this but they lacked both warmth and mutual trust. Newcastle went out of his way to be obliging towards the heir-apparent. In 1756 when the Prince came of age he persuaded a reluctant monarch to allow Bute to become Groom of the Stole and head of the Household in the Prince's establishment, an action which recognised the increasingly powerful influence that Bute was wielding in politics.[8] There was nothing in the least surprising about Newcastle's behaviour. The old Whigs had co-operated for decades with the Hanoverian dynasty which they had done so much to establish and to maintain, and it was perfectly natural for Newcastle and his friends to ingratiate themselves with the heir and to attempt to give the new King an 'easy reign'. But Prince George and Lord Bute were already disenchanted with the old Whigs. In their view, they had enslaved the monarchy and tainted the political system of the country with their 'corrupt' methods of government. Until the new reign, however, they could do little to give practical expression to their hostility towards them. For the time being a sullen and uneasy spirit of co-operation (arising more from mutual convenience than mutual respect) characterised relations between the old Whigs and Leicester House.

It was during these years that Prince George and Bute were formulating their plans for the new reign. We now know enough about the education of the Prince to dispense with the old Whig legends that he was nurtured on 'Patriot King' ideas.[9] The Prince, far from planning to undermine the powers of Parliament and overthrow the constitution, was anxious to safeguard the constitution against the danger into which he believed it to be falling: the oligarchical domination of the old Whigs. It was not that he wished to reduce the importance of Parliament in the political system. On the contrary he wished to rid Parliament of corrupting influences and thus weaken the stranglehold over it which the old Whigs had enjoyed for so long. There was nothing unwarrantable in all this. The King was a necessary part of the executive and Prince George simply wished to restore the monarchy to what he considered to be its rightful place. But certain observations may be made about the Prince's intentions, however unexceptionable they may have been in theory.[10] *First*, if they were implemented they would alienate and offend the old Whigs and Pitt. In effect, the new King would be declaring war on the political leaders of the day, a risky and dangerous proceeding whose effects were impossible to foresee. *Second*, the Prince's intentions, however 'constitutional' they may have been, were really quite far-reaching. Not only was monarchy to be freed from its shackles. Faction would be destroyed, Government would be reformed and the war would be ended. These objectives were determined as much by personal antipathies, themselves conditioned by the traditional platitudes of Leicester House, as by a sense of the national interest. *Third*, these plans required the substitution of Bute for Pitt and Newcastle. If Bute were not at the Treasury the Prince considered that he 'should be in the most dreadful of situations'.[11] If it were not possible at once to place Bute at the Treasury—and even Prince George had some conception of the difficulties which he might encounter—because of the popularity of Pitt, the exigencies of war and the need to conduct a general election, the Prince still felt 'that some method may turn up of regulating affairs, which may still make the Treasury not unpalatable to you; if that should not happen, you will for all that be Minister, for all men will find the only method of succeeding in their desires will be by first acquainting you with what they mean to request'.[12] *Fourth*, it was not studied autocracy that pervaded the intentions of Prince George and Bute, but carelessness bordering on political irresponsibility. The nebulousness of their plans and their lack of detailed preparation for the new reign contrasts strikingly with the 'Great Outline' of Prince Frederick.[13] The steps by which their objectives were to be attained seem hardly to have been considered.

Thus, a change in the role of the monarch in politics *was* intended in 1760 although the means were left unclear. The new King, perhaps naturally, would wish to count for more in politics than his aged grandfather had done and when he came to the throne George III was anxious to participate in the daily routine of political and public business.[14] George III wanted to make it clear that he would select his servants from a wider circle than had been the case in recent years and he thus ended the proscription of the Tories. Insignificant this gesture may have been in terms of the number of Tories who came to Court but is was a significant and a symbolic departure from Hanoverian tradition.[15] Newcastle, at least, panicked and put the worst possible construction upon the new King's avowed determination to bestow his favours outside the charmed circle of the old Whigs. But George III was doing no more than assert his undisputed right to appoint his ministers. Although he was wildly mistaken in assuming that the old Whigs had deliberately enslaved his grandfather, he continued to nurse his resentment against them until the day would at last come when he might take his revenge on them.[16]

Notwithstanding the expectations either of the King or his contemporaries, however, the accession of George III effected little immediate political change. William Pitt continued in his office of Secretary of State for the Northern Department. His talents were necessary to bring the war to a speedy and successful termination.[17] Bute recognised Pitt's indispensability when, a few hours after the death of George II—and unknown to and unauthorised by George III—he took Pitt on one side to tell him that he had laid aside his ambitions of replacing Newcastle at the Treasury, preferring 'to hold the situation of a private man at the side of the King'.[18] Pitt was both unimpressed with Bute's generosity in withdrawing his claims to the Treasury and uninterested in accepting his offer of friendship.

Pitt disliked political connections with any man, preferring to retain complete freedom of action, but he was particularly unwilling to encourage the pretensions of a royal favourite. He was thus reluctant to associate himself closely with one whose position of influence with the King might threaten the continued prosecution of the war. The scant importance which the moody and unpredictable War Minister attached to securing the high esteem of Lord Bute was attested a second time by his reaction to the King's declaration in Council on 25 October 1760. It was not just that Pitt had the temerity to insist that a reference to the war as 'bloody and expensive' be changed to 'expensive, but just and necessary'. He remonstrated publicly with Bute (the author of the Proclamation) 'against the coldness of this declaration in respect to the King of Prussia', insisting on the insertion of some friendly reference to Frederick the Great.[19] Pitt had his way but the King was furious. 'I cannot help telling my Dearest Friend that my honor is here at stake. I therefore will certainly unless the great man entir'ly change his nature and conduct, show him that aversion which will force him to resign.'[20] It is not easy to see how Pitt could have entirely changed 'his nature and conduct' merely to suit George III and Lord Bute. As long as the war continued, however, George III was unlikely to translate his tantrums into action but the King's annoyance with Pitt is entirely understandable. The refusal of the Great Commoner either to serve under Lord Bute or to tolerate his political ambitions prevented the fulfillment of the ambitious plans of the Court. The King did not have the experience and Bute did not have the nerve to stand up to him. It is therefore easy to appreciate how Pitt's towering indispensability aroused occasional spasms of royal resentment. Early in the new year the King and Bute tried to remove Temple, Pitt's most reliable ally in the Cabinet, from the Privy Seal which he had held since 1757 to the fastness of the Vice-Royalty of Ireland. Temple, after consultation with Pitt, refused the offer. The affair was trivial but it aroused ill-will and suspicion on all sides. Although Pitt could afford to ignore the young King's petulance, he disliked the uneasy situation and particularly the ascendancy of Bute in the King's counsels.[21]

The Duke of Newcastle had rather less confidence than Pitt had in his own indispensability. He believed that the Court wished to dispense with his services at the forthcoming elections and his anxieties were not without foundation.[22] Bute refused to speak to him on the subject for some weeks and does seem to have entertained the notion that Newcastle's services might have been discarded. In the end, however, the Court asked Newcastle to manage the elections but this, together with his assistance in raising the loan from the City for the following year, was the extent of his indispensability. Bute was unfriendly towards him, ostentatiously kept him uninformed of the King's opinions and did nothing to discourage the growing rumours that the Duke's tenure of the Treasury must have a limited period.[23] Thoroughly unsettled, Newcastle sought some expression of the royal confidence. In so doing he merely irritated the King; George III was unwilling to allow Newcastle to force from him a promise of his indefinite tenure of the Treasury. In this way, uncertainty and mutual suspicion distorted relations between the Court and Newcastle. The Court, suspecting the old ministers of 'their usual insolence', feared lest they attempt to 'control the King as they shamefully did his father'.[24] Such fears arose, of course, from an exaggerated view of the unity of the Pitt–Newcastle coalition. Pitt wished to win the war against the Bourbons and to receive a grateful nation's thanks. Newcastle merely wished to remain in office and to serve his country and his friends. Neither found the atmosphere of intrigue and uncertainty conducive to the fulfilment of their respective political objectives.[25]

The unsettling factor was, of course, the situation of the King's favourite. As long as Bute had the ear of George III it was difficult for either Pitt or Newcastle to enjoy anything like a frank and confidential relationship with the monarch. And because neither Pitt nor Newcastle was the sort of man to mask his fears and anxieties the King found his mistrust of them borne out (and his affection for Bute correspondingly reinforced) by Pitt's abruptness and Newcastle's tiresome fussing. The *impasse* was broken by Newcastle, acting as the unwitting instrument of the Court. In January 1761 he adopted an idea put to him (at the Court's instigation) by Count Viry, the

Sardinian Ambassador, that he 'suggest' to the King that Lord Bute should be brought into the Cabinet. Although Newcastle raised no objections to this scheme his agreement was apparently insufficiently cordial to induce the King's favourite to overcome his cowardice and assume the responsibilities of public office. Perhaps Newcastle was simply too surprised by Viry's suggestion to respond to it with the warmth Bute expected.[26] It is more likely, however, that Newcastle was frightened of alienating Pitt. 'I repeated very strongly, That, If it was to be done, It must be in Concert with, & with the full Approbation of, Mr Pitt; Or he would suspect, That it was a Scheme of Mine either to Turn Him out; or to make Him a Cypher in.'[27] Nevertheless, Newcastle *did* approve of the idea. He never thought of trying to dissuade the King from raising the favourite to high office. Indeed, it dawned on Newcastle that he and his friends might improve their own political standing if they acquiesced in the Court's intentions. Bute, in fact, might be useful as a counterbalance to Pitt. The plan began to seem so attractive to Newcastle that by early March he was prepared not only to 'suggest' to the King yet again that Bute be brought into the Cabinet but to offer Bute a private assurance of his support and influence against that of Pitt.[28] Enjoying this unexpected bonus, Bute and the King accepted Newcastle's 'suggestion'.

The elevation of Bute to the office of Secretary of State for the Northern Department caused a political sensation but his appointment came as no surprise. Most contemporaries did not deny to the King the right to appoint Bute to the efficient Cabinet.[29] Indeed, the appointment did not violate any law, custom or precedent of the constitution. The political world was not divided in its view of the royal prerogative in 1761 and George III cannot be accused of unduly straining it.

Nevertheless, the appointment was to prove a disaster for the King and a misfortune for his country. At the very least, the appointment was unwise and unnecessary. To introduce into the Cabinet at the height of a war a royal favourite whose situation had already given rise to acute tension and mistrust between the King and his ministers marked a concern to gratify a royal whim with which it is difficult in the circumstances to sympathise. At all events, Pitt detested the appoint-

B

ment for two reasons. First, the Great Commoner thought of government in terms of the freedom of each departmental minister to approach the King whenever he considered it appropriate to do so and feared that Bute's appointment would jeopardise that freedom. Even before the favourite's appointment, messages to the King could only reach him with Bute's approval.[30] Second, Pitt was worried lest the appointment presage changes in foreign policy. Indeed, it was one of the intended consequences of Bute's appointment among Newcastle and his friends as well as the Court to weaken Pitt's control of foreign affairs.[31] Bute's appointment, then, threatened to interfere seriously with business. Inevitably, Pitt was angry with Newcastle whose little role in the affair he resented. The prospects for harmonious cabinet relations were already poor in March 1761; the appointment of Bute worsened an already difficult situation. It may be true that Bute's appointment did not provoke a difference of opinion on the constitutional issue of the right of the King to appoint him but it is, at the very least, wise to recognise that the King's action was not popular.[32] In offering a provocative manifestation of the prerogative of appointment George III was laying the foundations of future conflicts of opinion on its exercise. These could have been allayed only if the King's experiment succeeded and if it was seen to be operating in the national interest. But just over two years later the experiment in government by favourite lay in ruins. Between 1761 and 1763 it was to provoke discussion not only of the King's relations with his ministers but also of the relations between King, Lords and Commons. The old Whigs were always sensitive about any unrestricted exercise of the prerogative of appointment which violated the spirit if not the law of the British constitution[33] and their experience in these years was to bring them to re-examine the constitutional issues of the appointment of ministers and their relationship with the Crown. In March 1761, therefore, a difference of constitutional opinion did not surround the appointment of Bute but the events of that month were shortly to give rise to important divergences of view concerning what the King and Bute could and could not do.

All this, however, lay in the future when politicians in the spring of 1761 began to give serious attention to the problem of ending the war. Israel Maudit's pamphlet of the previous year, *Considerations on the Present German War*, had elicited an enthusiastic response from a British public which, satiated with military victory and accustomed to naval glory, perceived greater benefits from an early peace than from continuing a war whose objectives had been attained.[34] Notwithstanding this opinion, 'Peace', as Pitt had said in 1759, 'will be as hard to make as war'.[35] In some ways it proved to be harder. Although he had come to accept the view of the Court that peace negotiations ought to commence he differed with Bute over the terms which Britain ought to extract from the French. Newcastle's position was invidious because he agreed fully with neither. In June 1761 Pitt's view of the most contentious of the several problems standing in the way of a peace settlement was that France should not be allowed fishing rights off Newfoundland. Newcastle thought that she should. It was Bute who thought of a sensible *via media* and this was adopted: to try to exclude the French from the Newfoundland waters but not to insist upon her exclusion as a *sine qua non* of a treaty. In this way, the unity of the Cabinet was preserved for a time but it was to be maintained less by the moderation of Pitt, Newcastle and Bute than by the apparently intransigent attitude of the French. Choiseul was unable to agree to the terms which the British demanded and he played for time until the signature of the Franco-Spanish alliance.[36] When the news of the Family Compact was made known in mid-August the Cabinet decided that peace was preferable to war and made one last attempt to reach a compromise with the French. At Cabinets on 19, 20 and 24 August the Cabinet conceded the French claim to fish the Newfoundland waters, only Pitt and Temple dissenting. This did not impress Choiseul who was now determined to prolong the war. In September he ordered home the British envoy in Paris. The war was to continue. The lingering question was: by whom was it to be conducted?

William Pitt's characteristic eagerness to prosecute the war against the Bourbon powers vigorously now found less favour at Court than it ever had done.[37] Although the King and Bute realised that the breakdown in the negotiations with the

French completely vindicated Pitt's belligerent attitude towards the Bourbon powers they feared that if the war were to be prolonged then Pitt would become more indispensable than ever and, seemingly, for an indefinite period. George III would have none of it. During September he began to show unmistakeable signs of his 'aversion' for his great minister.[38] Although these differences between Pitt and the Court were of the highest importance we should certainly not overlook the fact that the political disagreements between Pitt and Temple, on the one hand, and Newcastle and his friends, on the other, would have made Pitt's continuance in office embarrassing at the very least. Nevertheless by the end of the month it was well-known that his services were no longer required by the King.[39] On 2 October Pitt and Temple were alone in the Cabinet in advocating a pre-emptive strike against Spain. On 5 October Pitt resigned and four days later Temple followed his example.

Within twelve months of coming to the throne George III had succeeded in placing Bute in the Cabinet and was now presiding over the disintegration of the war-time coalition. Although it had not been systematically planned by George III, he nevertheless welcomed—and did something to encourage— Pitt's resignation when his continuance in office became politically unacceptable to him, and did nothing to persuade him to stay. On the other hand Pitt was behaving with characteristic obduracy on the Spanish issue. It was not his opinions but those of the King and of Bute which found most support in the Cabinet and which most accurately reflected public opinion.

Yet without the great War Minister, the King and Bute found themselves in considerable difficulties and Pitt seems to have realised it. After all, there was still a war to be won and a peace to be negotiated. In September Bute had been unhappy at the prospect of governing without Pitt and it was not without a certain timorous realisation of the daunting difficulties of his situation that Bute made him the offer of either the Governor Generalship of Canada or the Chancellorship of the Duchy of Lancaster. Pitt refused lest his acceptance be taken to imply any sort of approval of ministerial policy, but he welcomed some mark of family advancement. His wife, Lady Hester Pitt, received a peerage and a pension of £3,000 per annum. Bute was annoyed at Pitt's neat avoidance of the trap which had been set for him. 'These unusual marks of royal approbation', he wrote to Pitt on 8 October, 'cannot fail to be agreeable to a mind like yours.' Pitt retaliated, thanking Bute for 'The same royal benevolence which showers on the unmeritorious such unlimited benefits'.[40] The Court was playing a dangerous game in provoking Pitt. He was not a man to shed his grudges lightly and his antipathy to Bute was now considerable. The King and Bute were hanging their political futures upon their success or failure in bringing the war to a speedy, successful and popular conclusion. Success, and only success, in this undertaking would vindicate their judgement and discredit that of Pitt.

The Court still had to take into consideration the position of Newcastle and the old Whigs. The Duke, in fact, was now almost completely at the mercy of Bute and the King. An earlier quarrel between Bute and Newcastle over patronage was resumed when Bute refused to accept the Duke's nominees to the offices vacated by Pitt and Temple. Newcastle began to feel uneasy, realising that he was to be edged out of favour and influence, while Bute 'was to get the whole power and disposition of business, as well as employments to himself'.[41] On issue after issue Newcastle's advice was ignored, his opinions unheeded. He whimpered in pain when he found he had no voice in the appointment of Egremont and Bedford, who succeeded Pitt and Temple, and he was hurt to find that he was ignored in the selection of a new Speaker. Finally, the reconstruction of the ministry—Newcastle's ministry—was concluded when George Grenville undertook the management of the House of Commons at the end of October. Newcastle's misery was complete when he found that the unpopularity of the war and the popularity of Pitt were threatening to endanger the raising of the loan for the coming session in the City.[42] Ironically, although Newcastle was too preoccupied with his own difficulties to notice, Bute was coming to realise the weaknesses of his own position and, in particular, his political isolation. Not even the King's favourite believed that the confidence of the King was itself sufficient to maintain him in office with any real security. Bute saw that if his own position were to be strengthened then that objective must be attained at New-castle's expense. But that was a long-term ambition. For the present, the favourite was prepared to suffer Newcastle in office for a year or two, to try to win over his most talented followers and then to engineer his resignation. For the time being, as the King rather nastily put it: 'a little seeming good humour from me and your telling him things before he hears them from others are the sure maxims to keep him in order'.[43]

Kind and honied words could not possibly conceal from Newcastle not only the neglect of himself and his friends but also the drift of court policy, the projected abandonment of the continental war (a war which Newcastle had always advocated) and the growing talk of war against Spain. He declared: '*if we think to out-war Mr Pitt, we shall find ourselves greatly disappointed. But if our real view is peace . . . by that only shall we get the better of Mr Pitt*'.[44] His position was both difficult and embarrassing. When raising the loan for 1762 he had given the City to understand that the ministry was not contemplating war against Spain.[45] But on 2 January 1762 the Cabinet issued a formal declaration of war on that country. His situation weakened with the spread of rumours that the Court intended to reduce the subsidies to Frederick the Great. Such an action would amount to a repudiation of a policy of which Newcastle had always been the foremost champion. When the issue came before the Cabinet on 27 and 30 April, Newcastle was unable to dissuade the other ministers from reducing the subsidy. Only Hardwicke and Devonshire supported him.[46] At one level the conflict was a personal one between Newcastle and Grenville, the Leader of the House of Commons, but on another it was a symbolic and complete rejection of Newcastle by the Court. Had Newcastle's opinions on the Prussian subsidy carried the day then not only Grenville but also Bute and the King would have seen the frustration of their fundamental strategic objectives. They were not prepared to make their enemy the unchallenged master of the Cabinet and thus they were quietly pleased at the Duke's discomfiture. Newcastle was forced to offer his resignation and, much to his chagrin, the King accepted it. With a heavy heart, and with a dignity for which he has never been given credit (at Cumberland's suggestion he spurned both a pension and honours) he resigned formally on 26 May after thirty-eight years in public service.[47]

Newcastle had crossed his political Rubicon but he crossed it without an army, for he instructed his dependants to stay in their places. His resignation was, characteristically, partly accidental, more the effect of the fears and doubts which tormented him rather than the consequence of a rational decision, but it may also be seen as the culmination of a succession of personal and political differences between himself and the Court which rendered doubtful his continuance in office. Indeed, his removal from office had been rumoured for some time.[48] Newcastle, in short, was weary at what he considered his constant ill-usage at the hands of the King and his favourite. He was angry when he discovered that members of his Treasury Board had been passing secrets to Bute without informing him; 'a plain declaration of the little regard and confidence which His Majesty's ministers have in me'.[49] He was in no doubt that on the Prussian subsidy the Court had decided to strike against him. 'It was certainly determined to drive me out. My great crime was my resolution not to abandon the war in Germany this campaign, and that has drawn this immediate ill-usage upon me with regard to my own office.'[50] Yet the humiliations to which he had been subjected at the hands of the Court did not embitter him and he felt no anger against the King. In any case, in the weeks after his resignation, Newcastle was preoccupied with the problem of his new and unaccustomed political condition out of office.[51]

The difficulty of his situation was that his friends might look upon his resignation 'as lying down and dying without any hopes of a resurrection',[52] but all possible lines of action which were open to him were attended with some disadvantage. But unless his friends were given a lead, they might gravitate towards what was, after all, their natural home, the Court. Yet what sort of a lead could he give? If he attempted to persuade his friends to resign, his call might fall on deaf ears. In any case, this was a course of action from which his habits of service to the monarchy deterred him. The idea of resigning from politics occasionally drifted across his mind but his longing for peace and rest and his desire to be free from all of his political worries were not as strong as his incurable and overpowering sense of curiosity. Newcastle was not the man to quit the political arena at the moment of his greatest humiliation. One further possibility was to support the ministry from without. But to have done so would have been to demonstrate publicly his approval of policies over which he had resigned. Not only would such a proceeding have been ludicrous; it would have been dangerous. It would have left his friends in office at Bute's mercy and have allowed them to drift over to the Court. There was nothing for it for Newcastle but to wait on events—especially the peace terms—and to allow the King and Bute the initiative. He would consult the opinions of his friends but, meanwhile, he advised them to 'keep themselves clear as to any engagements for their future behaviour'.[53] There was little else that he could do. The main business of the parliamentary session was over and there were no issues to hand upon which he could have mounted a credible opposition campaign. The line he adopted appeared, in the circumstances, to be not unreasonable. It had at least one merit, that of flexibility, which, to a bewildered Newcastle who was trying to find his bearings in a new political world, had much to commend it. Having reached this decision Newcastle was determined to play the political game for all it was worth. On his resignation he grandly announced to the King that he would feel himself 'at liberty to act as his conscience shall guide him'.[54]

The Court gradually came to understand the implications of Newcastle's enigmatic pronouncement. The King and Bute were already concerned at his continuing influence in the City.[55] They were worried about his rising influence in another quarter, too. In the weeks after his resignation Newcastle began to ingratiate himself with the old enemy of Leicester House, the Duke of Cumberland.[56] What this was to mean in practice was not yet clear but it was enough to worry the Court. The King, moreover, had worries of his own. The lack of foresight and the stumbling improvisations which had characterised the conduct of the Court since the beginning of the reign once more vitiated its plans. Bute, as had long been intended, replaced Newcastle at the Treasury but at their moment of triumph the King and Bute had omitted to consider a simple, yet ultimately a crucial, question: who was to fill the vacancy left by Bute? The obvious candidate for his Secretaryship was Grenville, but although his considerable talents were much needed by Bute, Grenville was closely related to the other Secretary, Egremont, and they were likely to present a united, and possibly obdurate, front to Bute on some issues. Bute's attempts to demote Egremont from his Secretaryship to the Vice-Royalty of Ireland offended Grenville and Bute soon found that he had alienated both his Secretaries. Thereafter, the rising star of George Grenville proved to be a troublesome and unsettling influence in the Cabinet.[57] In particular, he favoured a strong line against the French and one which made the conclusion of a peace treaty much less likely. There was only one thing for it. The King and Bute agreed that Newcastle would be a useful counter against Grenville and at the end of July Bute, through Hardwicke, intimated that the Duke might have almost any office he chose. Without much hesitation he rejected the overtures and it is not difficult to understand why he did so. Perhaps he suspected that Bute intended to use him for his own purposes. Certainly, the Duke had no desire to experience a repetition of his recent ill-treatment at the favourite's hands.[58] But not content with rejecting the Court's advances, Newcastle went further, first declaring his dissatisfaction and disapproval of the progress of the peace negotiations—especially the proposal to restore St Lucia to the French—and then proceeding to rally his City friends, presumably to prepare them for opposition on the peace.[59] His distrust of Bute, his ripening friendship with Cumberland, his rejection of ministerial overtures and his growing tendency to oppose the peace terms were all combining to widen the rift between Newcastle and the Court. Indeed, by October his friends had begun to discuss the prospect of overthrowing the favourite. He proposed to replace him with 'such an Administration, and such a Treasury settled, as might protect our old Friends, without laying them under Difficulties'.[60] It is astonishing that one who had for so long lived at Court and sat in Cabinets could in less than six months adjust his political attitudes to accommodate his new and still unfamiliar situation in Opposition. The sentiments of earlier months when he had protested his eternal refusal even to contemplate systematic opposition did not now lie heavily upon him.[61]

The peace preliminaries had been agreed by the Cabinet on 22 October but only after long and bitter wrangling between Bute and Bedford, on the one hand, and Grenville and Egremont, on the other.[62] Bute had now to obtain the approval of Parliament for the peace preliminaries (which were signed on 3 November). Defeat on this issue could not even be contemplated. If the preliminaries were rejected then Bute would almost certainly resign and the King would find himself with either Pitt or Newcastle (or both) in his Closet. In short, the monarchy would have sunk back into the depths from which George III ardently believed himself to be rescuing it. If defeat could not be contemplated, it could not and must not be risked. Bute lacked the experience to manage Parliament effectively and Grenville had proved himself to be an unreliable instrument. It was to ensure a majority for the peace that in the middle of October Henry Fox was prevailed upon to accept the Leadership of the Ministry in the House of Commons. Without his assistance it is doubtful if Bute would have remained at his post, so weary was he of cabinet conflicts with Grenville and Egremont.[63] Bute, in sending Grenville to the Admiralty and promoting Fox, was thus not only preparing to fight Pitt, and perhaps Newcastle as well, but attempting to strengthen his administration.[64] It was the first confession of a failure on Bute's part, an indication that he was not able to discipline his Cabinet without the assistance of Fox. In the weeks before the opening of Parliament on 1 December Fox proceeded to rally the friends of the ministry and to woo the Tories as they had never been wooed since the Hanoverian succession. Bute co-operated with him as far as he could. As the ministerial supporters fell into line, Fox even terrified Cumberland's leading dependents into supporting the peace.[65] It was now up to Newcastle to save his connection from these ravages. At the very least it was absolutely incumbent upon him to give some guidance to his friends on the line they were to take on the crucial issue of the peace. Were they to support it or oppose it?

What instructions was Newcastle to give to his friends? And who were those friends? The growing weakness of his parliamentary position is revealed by the lists which Newcastle himself drew up at this time. Between September and early December he watched his following shrink to a derisory forty-four votes in the Upper House, less than one quarter of the whole.[66] In the Commons, things were not much better. The most optimistic assessment of his strength on the eve of the new session showed that he would be able to rely on much less than one half of the Members.[67] It was a stark fact that Newcastle now could not hope to attain a majority at the meeting of Parliament. Henry Fox had realised as much as early as July 1762 but it had taken Newcastle four months longer to reach the same conclusion.[68]

Newcastle's party might have continued to melt away had not George III been responsible for a personal slight which was to have important consequences. Ever since Newcastle's resignation, the Duke of Devonshire's membership of the Cabinet had been anomalous. Because of his personal regard for Newcastle he had refused to attend its meetings. Originally, the King had not been much concerned at Devonshire's irregular behaviour and he permitted him to retain his staff as Lord Chamberlain of the Household. Devonshire explained away his absences from the Cabinet on grounds of ill-health.[69] For some months the matter rested until Devonshire began to voice his criticisms of the ministry and of the peace which it was negotiating.[70] When his formal assent to the peace preliminaries was demanded he refused to attend the Cabinet on the grounds of his ignorance of public business.[71] The King interpreted Devonshire's refusal as a personal affront and refused to grant him an audience on 28 October. Not allowing him to resign, George III paid the Duke of Devonshire the twin insult of summarily dismissing him from his offices and of striking his name off the list of privy councillors on 3 November.[72] Amidst the outcry of an affronted aristocracy—or, at least, part of it—Newcastle and Cumberland agreed on 2 November to 'punish' the Court by depriving it of the services of some of their friends. They believed that the high-handedness of the Court was a symptom of its insecurity and an indication of its fear. If the Whig lords were to teach the favourite an unpleasant lesson then he might not be able to continue in office. This was the reasoning behind

Newcastle's attempts to persuade thirty-three of his closest friends and connections to resign their offices. This was to be the aristocratic riposte to the political influence of Bute and the crude threats of Henry Fox.[73] It was indicative, however, that only seventeen of the thirty-three did resign their offices and many of these with extreme reluctance. The reasons for this were simple. To resign, as Newcastle was suggesting, on a personal matter was factious. Furthermore, resignation was futile. It would not restore Devonshire to favour at Court and it would deprive the office-holder of his political livelihood. No wonder, then, that Newcastle was disappointed at the response to his clarion call. Yet it is not easy to see what he might have realistically hoped to achieve. Devonshire's conduct had not been beyond reproach and the whole affair was a test of the loyalty of Newcastle's friends to Devonshire rather than to Newcastle. The Devonshire affair was the first manifestation of a new and punitive campaign waged by the Court against the friends of Newcastle. The war had begun although it was not clear what was at issue. Newcastle's obsession with an insidious court plot, however, bore as little relation to reality as the Court's fear of a concerted aristocratic plan to enslave the monarchy.[74]

As the month of November wore on it became apparent that the Court was winning the war it had lately declared upon its enemies. Further disasters were staring Newcastle in the face when he saw his estimated parliamentary support decline at an alarming rate. Between 15 and 25 November, for example, his own lists showed a reduction from 238 to 142 in the numbers of Members who would support him in the Commons.[75] It was not just that the threats and persuasions of Henry Fox were having some effect. Newcastle was still unable to give his followers a lead. Even on the eve of the meeting of Parliament Newcastle had issued no instructions to his followers on how to vote on the peace. This he had not done because he was torn with indecision and wracked with doubt over the best course of action to adopt; because of his inability to provide any sort of leadership his connection was wasting away with every day. Six months earlier he had believed that his influence with the office-holders was sufficiently strong to maintain his political following intact even though he was out of office. Since then, the attractions of power and his own vacillations had begun to weaken the loyalty of many of his adherents. To prevent further defections from and the dissolution of his connection, therefore, Newcastle had to resolve his indecision over the peace preliminaries. The political futures of Newcastle, his connection and the old Whigs were to be decided in the early days of the forthcoming session of Parliament and in a manner which none could have foreseen and with consequences that none could have anticipated.

Chapter 2

The Young Friends of the Duke of Newcastle November 1762–April 1763

Towards the end of his great work, *England in the Age of the American Revolution,* Sir Lewis Namier uncovered the existence of a group of young men at the very centre of the Newcastle connection. The book ends before these 'Young Friends' began to play any considerable role in the politics of the time but Sir Lewis left his reader in no doubt that 'the Rise of Party' in the later eighteenth century has its origin in the attitudes and the activities of these men and that it is to them that the party later to be known as the Rockingham Whig party owed its foundation. This conclusion reinforced Namier's contention that between the Pelhams and the Rockingham Whigs there was little, if any, continuity. To the emergence of the 'Young Friends' as a group within the Newcastle connection, therefore, there attaches considerable historical significance.

Their emergence can only be understood by carefully examining the position of Newcastle as the date for the discussion of the peace preliminaries approached. If the Duke wished to prevent the destruction of his connection there seemed to be two alternatives open to him, neither of them inviting, both of them distasteful. The first was to close ranks with Pitt in Opposition. Hardwicke was the prime advocate of this policy. 'No opposition could be formed with any probable hope of success without joining Mr Pitt in it.'[1] This was certainly true but Charles Yorke,[2] Hardwicke's son, saw the real difficulties which would accompany any future coalition with Pitt; 'Mr Pitt must be the Minister. In measures he was so before; and Lord Bute being laid out of the case, he would be so in everything; for the Duke of Newcastle would not have strength enough, either in the King's personal inclination or natural temper, to resist as he had in the last reign, especially after having offended in opposition and proved the main instrument of bringing Mr Pitt back again'.[3] In any case, Pitt had not forgiven Newcastle for his part in bringing Bute into the Cabinet in March 1761 and he had not forgotten his refusal to resign with him in October 1761. Why should he now spring to Newcastle's rescue and resolve his political difficulties for him? Newcastle sought him out and arranged a meeting between Pitt and Cumberland on 17 November only to find that although Pitt disliked the peace and the regime of Bute ('Favour and Honour might be allowed but not within the walls of the Treasury') he would neither co-operate with Newcastle's friends nor promise to oppose the peace in Parliament.[4] Newcastle's remaining alternative was to commit himself and his friends to oppose the peace terms and to act in systematic opposition to the ministry. There was something to be said in favour of such a view. For one thing it might be a way back to power. 'As to the present administration, if my Lord Bute cannot make a peace that can be supported in the nation, there must be an end of him.'[5] For another, there were aspects of the peace preliminaries which might reasonably be attacked, especially those which had been agreed after Newcastle's departure from office—the articles relating to Spain and the West Indies. Newcastle even went so far as to say 'that there is scarce one Article in it which ought to stand, or which we may not oppose with the utmost consistency with ourselves . . .'.[6] Newcastle seems sincerely to have believed that the acquisition of Florida was inadequate compensation for the restoration of Havannah and, like Cumberland, worried over the fact that the peace left France the dominant power in the West Indies.[7] He was perfectly clear in his own mind of the importance of the decision he had to make but he shied away from making it. 'We must soon come . . . to some determination, or we should lose all our friends by default, and they will afterwards alledge in their justification that they knew nothing of our determination; and this already begins to be the case.'[8] Newcastle could not, even now, commit himself to a line of action which might have appeared factious and of which the rank and file of his supporters might not have approved. On the eve of the session, then, he was tantalised with uncertainty and overcome by doubt and indecision.[9]

Newcastle was not helped by his friends and advisers at the summit of the Whig hierarchy. None of them seem to have understood the urgent need of giving a lead to the Members of both Houses who were drifting back to town for the opening of Parliament on 25 November. Devonshire's advice was almost meaningless: 'Let us weigh the terms well, and act consistently with ourselves . . . the first time we attempt to shew our strength, it shou'd be upon some point where we are well founded and that we shall be strong upon'.[10] Devonshire was trying to have it both ways, to preserve his own consistency but yet to enjoy the fruits of a successful opposition ambush. Cumberland, too, was whistling in the dark, unable to offer any constructive advice except 'to keep quiet till some point arose and some leader and some plan'.[11] But what point, what leader and what plan? These were precisely the questions that Newcastle wanted to answer. Even Hardwicke, Newcastle's usually reliable right arm, was unable to help him. His earlier opinion had been that there was nothing in principle wrong with opposition to the peace but when the peace terms were published he shrank from opposing them on the grounds that Newcastle's friends would be influenced by public opinion to support them.[12] His own indecision and the inability of his friends to help him disabled Newcastle from giving a clear lead to his followers. The old Whigs had proved themselves incapable of producing a plan for the session and for their failure they were to pay dearly.

A group of Newcastle's younger supporters were weary of the Duke's vacillations and yearned for the clarion call of Opposition. George Onslow, Newcastle's nephew and one of their number, told him roundly 'that if nothing else can be found out, *they* will attack the Peace, which, they think, the most popular point they can go upon'. They estimated that, given effective organisation in the Commons, they could secure the attachment of 180 Members but unless they were allowed to organise in a club *'they must and will go elsewhere'*[13] presumably to Pitt. There was no holding them. On their own initiative they assembled for dinner at the Duke of Grafton's London residence on 30 November. It was on this occasion that the fateful decision to oppose the peace was taken. Although they did not wish to 'throw things more than is to be wish'd into the hands of Mr Pitt' their decision to oppose the peace preliminaries was taken because 'without it, we lose all our ground, all our popular cry'.[14] In the early days of the new session, therefore, the 'Young Friends' had announced a distinctive strategy while the party grandees were still fumbling and floundering. This strategy amounted to a systematic opposition to the ministry of Bute, a publicly declared opposition to the peace preliminaries, independence of Pitt and the revival of the Newcastle connection. The next two weeks were to demonstrate if this programme was realistic but the initial move which the 'Young Friends' made was an absolute disaster. The day after the dinner at Grafton's and buoyed with their new found determination they went down to the Commons and divided upon a procedural motion fixing the date for the formal discussion of the preliminaries. It was a defiant and symbolic gesture of their opposition to the ministry and recognised as such but the 'Young Friends' could only muster 74 votes against 213.

Who were the 'Young Friends' and to what extent do they represent a breach with the political traditions of the Pelhams? Those who attended the dinner on 30 November at Grafton's may, together with three others, be regarded as the leaders of the 'Young Friends'.[15] After their age, the most remarkable thing about them is their relationship to Newcastle. They were not only his 'Young Friends' but his relatives, too. (Although they assembled initially under the auspices of the Duke of Grafton, that unstable nobleman's failings of character deprived the group of the only potential leader which might have organised the 'Young Friends' into anything like an anti-Pelhamite force.) Onslow was Newcastle's nephew, Pelham his cousin and Villiers a nephew of his wife. Both Tommy Town-shend and Thomas Walpole were sons of close friends of the Duke while the Cavendish brothers inherited their father's intimate loyalty to Newcastle. These were men who wished to revive and strengthen the Pelhamite connection and to do so they were prepared to declare their opposition to the ministry of Lord Bute. They wished to save the Pelhamite connection from extinction because they were themselves Pelhamites.[16] The 'Young Friends' do not, therefore, represent a new political ideal, still less do they aspire to political ob-jectives which contravened those of the Pelhams in any way. Their call for vigour through organisation and opposition was a means of *preserving*, not of transforming, the political connection of the Duke of Newcastle.

The peace preliminaries were to be debated in both Houses on 9 December but Newcastle's friends, both young and old, were inadequately prepared for the debates. Tactics for the Lords were discussed in some detail to accommodate different sections of opinion, and, to some extent, a formula satisfactory to all was found: the Newcastle connection would oppose the peace verbally but not with its votes. Astonishingly, however, the Whig lords neglected strategy for the Lower House, possibly because Pitt's intentions were not known in any detail.[17] Newcastle thus failed to take sufficient care to ensure that the precipitate and damaging division of 1 December would not be repeated.[18] When the day of the debate arrived, then, Newcastle was *still* unable to provide a lead for his friends on the peace issue. What is even more astonishing, however, is the fact that the 'Young Friends', determined as they were to oppose the ministry and force a division did not trouble to organise themselves, failed to prepare a plan for either House and neglected to seek support.

The debates on the peace preliminaries of 9 and 10 December 1762 were nothing short of a catastrophe for the friends of Newcastle. The debate in the Lords was something of an anti-climax. It was carried on in a low key by Newcastle and Hardwicke; only Grafton violently denounced the peace. There was no division. In the Commons the debate stretched over two days. The first was dominated by Pitt's three and a half

hour *tour de force*. His speech was a carefully measured performance which must have disappointed Newcastle's friends for
Pitt condemned systematic opposition, announced his independence of all parties and proceeded to criticise several
aspects of the peace which Newcastle had agreed to in office.
After he was done he swept from the House, itself a significant
gesture of his refusal to lead or to be drawn into a systematic
opposition to Bute. Charles Yorke did not even bother to speak
and, like Pitt, left the House. These developments created a
sensation and caused Newcastle to instruct his friends against
forcing a division in such unpropitious circumstances. Many of
them—at least thirty—had already left but Newcastle's
message arrived too late to prevent a division. The result was
an enormous victory for Fox, Bute and George III; the figures,
319–65, were an adequate commentary upon the indecision
and disarray of Newcastle's friends. Even the 'Young Friends'
seemed to have been incapable of any exertion. On 9 December
they furnished no more than a couple of speakers but on the
second day of the debate they took a more active part in
proceedings. Lord John Cavendish, Lord Middleton, George
Onslow, Tommy Townshend Junior and Thomas Walpole
were 'Young Friends' who joined with other colleagues of
Newcastle, Sir George Armytage, H. B. Legge, James Shelley
and John White in opposing the peace but it was all to no
avail. The division on 10 December was 227–63.[19] Speeches
were no substitute for effective organisation and whipping.
Indeed, so wretched was the planning of the Opposition's
campaign that many of the leaders of the 'Young Friends' did
not themselves divide. Charles Yorke made an equivocal
speech on the second day and then, as on the first, he left the
chamber taking several with him and this may have influenced
the behaviour of some members. No doubt the opposition to
the peace was discouraged by Pitt's remark that he was an
independent man—a public avowal of his refusal to co-operate
with the friends of Newcastle—but for their sorry showing in
the divisions of 9 and 10 December the friends of Newcastle
were themselves responsible.

Division lists for 1, 9 and 10 December survive and happily
enable some rough computation of the size of the Duke of

Newcastle's connection to be made together with some assessment of its structure.[20] Altogether a total of 96 Members voted against the peace on 9 and 10 December. Analysis of these divisions together with that of 1 December reveals the uncertainty of political relationships and the fluidity of political groupings. Of the 74 Members who had voted in the minority on 1 December the names of 68 can be retrieved. Only 43 voted in the minority on either 9 or 10 December. Amidst this uncertainty, nevertheless, the identity of the Newcastle connection was slowly becoming clear. Altogether a total of 123 Members are known to have opposed the ministry on 1, 9 and 10 December. Of these, just under 70 can be classified as Pelhamites. To the 37 Pelhamites who voted on 1 December can be added a further 32 who can be identified in the division lists for 9 and 10 December. This 'inner core' of the Pelhamite connection was to be so important in the later history of the Newcastle party that it deserves close analysis. The overwhelming (and quite unsurprising) conclusion which emerges underlines the ubiquitous influence of the Duke of Newcastle over his connection. His group included some relatives, his nephews, the two Onslows, Shelley and Ashburnham, Sir Francis Poole and the Thomas Townshends (Senior and Junior). It also embraced his dependants, John Butler, Nathaniel Cholmley, John Norris and Andrew Wilkinson. A further five men can best be described as Newcastle's City friends. These were Sir William Baker, Bartholomew Burton, John Calvert, Sir Joseph Mellish and Thomas Walpole. There follows a long list of men who can only be described as friends of the Duke. To men whose relationship to him was both long-standing and intimate—men like H. B. Legge, John West, Jack White and John Offley—to these can be added men whose connection with him was of more recent origin but yet cordial. They included Lord Middleton and John Plumptre, Spanish Charles Townshend and John Roberts, Wenham Coke and John Dodd, Brice Fisher and Brooke Forester, Lord Gage and Lord Winterton. The above thirty names illustrate the extent of Newcastle's domination of his connection. There were no rivals for the leadership. Rockingham's friends, men like Armytage and Savile, were of too independent a stamp to be easily led and the only close friend whom the Marquis appears to have shared with Newcastle was Sir George Metham. Rockingham's day was yet to come and he was still in his political apprenticeship. The Cavendish family connection was already well-established (including Lords Frederick, George and John, Richard Cavendish and T. L. Dummer) but remained, like the head of the family, the Fourth Duke of Devonshire, completely loyal to Newcastle. The only conceivable 'cave' within the Newcastle connection was the group around the Duke of Grafton. Its members included Charles Fitzroy, Sir Alexander Gilmour, Hugo Meynell, Charles Fitzroy Scudamore and Lord Villiers. At this time Grafton, the most eminent in rank if not the most gifted in abilities of the 'Young Friends', was politically ambitious. 'By the figure he makes (he) will probably soon be the head of the Opposition' wrote Horace Walpole of the Duke of Grafton, but he added significantly, 'if it continues.'[21] Thus statistics confirm what common sense suggests, that in December 1762 the most significant fact about the Duke of Newcastle's connection was his supremacy over it. The 'Young Friends' of Newcastle may have succeeded in forcing his real friends to declare themselves but they remained a small, isolated, and, after 10 December, a discredited group.

With this in mind we can better understand the reaction of Newcastle to the disastrous events of early December. Sir Lewis Namier suggests that Newcastle and the old Whigs disapproved of the 'Young Friends' and their policy of systematic opposition to Bute's ministry and that they only accepted them after the overthrow of Bute had seemingly demonstrated their utility.[22] But it was not the 'Young Friends' who brought Bute down and it is only partially true that the Whig lords disapproved of systematic opposition. Kinnoul, for example, quoted by Namier, may well have disliked the blundering initiatives of the young men and feared a challenge to the aristocratic leadership of Newcastle's connection but had Sir Lewis' quotation of the letter in question been somewhat more extensive it would have appeared that Kinnoul did *not* oppose the principle of opposition at all. Indeed, provided that the principle of aristocratic leadership was recognised and supported by the young men then opposition should be encouraged. 'If any Thing unconstitutional, any Thing manifestly injurious to the Welfare of the Country be proposed, To Such Points Opposition should be made upon strong Grounds and solid Principles.'[23] Devonshire, normally the most cautious of men, was coming to much the same sort of conclusion: 'if we can get Leaders & a tolerable Corps of Troops I am for Battel, but I am against appearing in a weak opposition as we shall make an insignificant figure, prejudice our Friends & do no good'.[24] What Devonshire opposed, therefore, was not the notion of opposition but the prospect of a humiliatingly weak Opposition. What he wanted was an Opposition based on constitutional grounds: 'I am against factious Opposition, but the time is come for us to be very watchful that these People, to secure their Power, shou'd not endanger our excellent constitution, & that we should transmit that invaluable blessing whole & entire to our Posterity'.[25] The old Whigs, as well as the 'Young Friends', accepted the principle of opposition.[26]

In the political circumstances which existed at the end of 1762, however, opposition was to cost them dear. Officeholders sitting in Parliament were traditionally allowed some discretion in the disposal of their votes, especially on matters of conscience, but they were not allowed in any circumstances to vote against the ministry on important issues of confidence such as the peace. In December 1762 some office holders not only failed to support the ministry but voted against it in an attempt to destroy the favourite. Having failed, they could expect nothing but punishment and retribution. (Newcastle saw it coming and retired to Claremont after the disastrous divisions of 9 and 10 December, waiting for the axe to fall.) Bute was perfectly justified in depriving them of their offices. Indeed, the Court had been planning since the Devonshire affair to discipline friends of Newcastle who did not support Lord Bute. On top of that, Fox had already promised Bute that he would dismiss anyone who voted against the Peace.[27] He was as good as his word and thus December brought extensive dismissals. Those dismissed even included several of Newcastle's friends who had resisted his call to resign over the humiliation of the Duke of Devonshire.[28] In many ways, however, the punishment meeted out to members of the Upper House—which had *not* divided on the peace preliminaries—was more drastic and more far-reaching than that rendered to members of the Lower House. Newcastle, Rockingham and Grafton lost their Lord Lieutenancies and dragged many of their dependants down with them. In some places the 'Massacre of the Pelhamite Innocents' became annihilation. In Yorkshire, for example, the effects of the 'Massacre' upon local life and administration were considerable. Rockingham lost his Lieutenancy of the West Riding, the offices of Custos Rotulorum of the North and West Ridings, his Lieutenancy and his office of Vice-Admiral of the City of York. At the same time, Devonshire resigned his Lieutenancy of the East Riding. These changes affected the Deputy-Lieutenancies, the Justices of the Peace and lesser office-holders. Many men in offices, loyal to the families and the persons of Rockingham and Devonshire, resigned *en masse*. So widespread and so numerous were the changes and the disruptions in local administration that Rockingham confessed himself worried at their effects upon the functioning of the local judicial system.[29] The pattern was repeated elsewhere. The number of 'Innocents' massacred in Sussex, for example, extended to exceedingly trivial offices.[30] Newcastle was heartbroken. Politics was politics, but for him the 'Massacre of the Pelhamite Innocents' was a collection of personal tragedies: 'But why should Mr Fox turn out all those unhappy men to starve, who have no Demeritt of their own, are in office incapable of a seat in Parliament, and who have been, at any time, put into those offices by the Duke of Newcastle'.[31] The extent of the dismissals was something which Newcastle could neither forgive nor forget. Three years later, during the first Rockingham ministry, he laboured with considerable success to restore to their offices those friends who had lost them in 1762–3.[32]

Newcastle might weep but it was among the 'Young Friends' and not the old Whigs that some modest signs of vigour appeared, directed towards saving the shattered connection. Within a fortnight of the peace debates the 'Young Friends' had taken some steps to improve the organisation of Newcastle's party. On 21 December at a dinner at George Onslow's at which Newcastle was present they decided to establish a political club and to hold regular meetings.[33] In spite of Newcastle's misgivings,[34] the club was launched and thereafter met fairly frequently. The formation of this club has been judged by Namier and other historians as an event of cardinal importance. Namier was in no doubt that with this club he had unearthed the origins of 'the Rise of Party' while Professor Foord stated categorically that 'The establishment of a regular "dining club" on 23 December 1762 marks the formal beginning of the Rockinghamite party'.[35] Such a view is seriously misleading. *First*, it over-estimates the importance not only of the club—it was, after all, only a convivial wining-and-dining arrangement—but also of the 'Young Friends' as a distinct group within the Newcastle connection. Even though they had a coherent identity and a distinctive approach to politics they remained very much secondary in authority and prestige to Newcastle and the old Whigs. They were, on occasion, more vigorous, and sometimes more rash, than their seniors but their schemes rarely met with success. Consequently they were not highly regarded by the old Whigs. When the Opposition, for example, was making its preparations for the session of 1764 Newcastle consulted Hardwicke, Devonshire, Legge, Charles Yorke and Pitt. The 'Young Friends' were not approached. In any case, as we have seen already, they were not a force apart from Newcastle but his friends, relatives and dependants.[36] *Second*, the view of Namier and Foord gives a misleading impression of what actually happened. It was not, in fact, until December 1763, a year later, that a club with a formal organisation was established which was to have a continuous history. This was Wildman's club in Albermarle Street.[37] The so-called club established at Onslow's in December 1762 was not a club at all. It is not at all clear how frequently it met or how distinct its activities remained from the normal round of social intercourse. Like Dr Watson, I have found no evidence that before late 1763 the 'Young Friends' had a club with a formal organisation, which met frequently and which had a continuous history.[38] There occurred no disruptive break, then, in the history of the Newcastle Whigs in 1762–4 and the establishment of the so-called club in December 1762 does not mark the beginning of a new departure in the history of Newcastle's party. And even if it had done, the fact remains that the 'Young Friends', club or no club, were unable to help Newcastle solve the daunting problems which he faced at the end of the year as a consequence of the peace debates and the 'Massacre of the Pelhamite Innocents'.

The first necessity was to keep together what was left of his connection in the Commons. But who was to lead it? Newcastle approached his old friend, H. B. Legge but that venerable politician wisely refused Newcastle's offer on the grounds that he did not adequately understand 'the rules of business and forms of the House of Commons'.[39] It may have been fortunate for Newcastle and his friends that Legge refused but when Charles Yorke and Charles Townshend[40] in turn rejected Newcastle's overtures then the prospects for his parliamentary following began to look decidedly dim. Newcastle, indeed, could not afford a repetition of his party's indecisive and ineffective posturing but he was unable to make any constructive suggestions for its future conduct. On the trivial question of opposing the estimates, for example, he refused to commit himself, looking to Hardwicke, Devonshire, Kinnoul—even Grafton and Rockingham—to decide his policy for him. Should they decide 'that any Opposition at present is Impracticable and Unadviseable *Let them say so*; and . . . I shall acquiesce—with great Pleasure and Satisfaction'.[41] No agreement was forthcoming, nothing was decided and the opportunity was lost. All that can be said for such timidity was that Newcastle's party was spared further embarrassments before the holidays. Nevertheless, there was a lesson here for Newcastle's party. If Newcastle were not able, and if the 'Young Friends' were not allowed to provide effective leadership of the Opposition then it was time to make contact with one who might provide just the energy, the vigour, and perhaps the popularity which the Newcastle Whigs so conspicuously lacked.

Out of public office and out of the royal favour, William Pitt remained the extraordinarily magnetic figure who had captured the imagination of his countrymen during the war. As a parliamentary orator he was unequalled in his day. He still enjoyed some, though by no means all, of his former considerable influence in the City.[42] His recent opposition to a popular peace had left him temporarily under a cloud but the peace was no longer an immediate issue. In short, it was more than likely that Pitt would shortly leap back into public favour. If Newcastle could establish some grounds for co-operation with him then he might solve the problems of finding a suitable leader for his connection in Parliament, of establishing his party upon a more respected footing in Opposition and, not least, of controlling his 'Young Friends'. For the pathetic inaction of Newcastle could not indefinitely satisfy Grafton and his circle which was still anxious for a systematic opposition.[43] To the old Whig Lords, however, an appeal to Pitt was something less than a means of bringing about a systematic opposition. His co-operation might stimulate the Opposition to greater vigour and unity but it might also restrain the 'Young Friends' from an ill-calculated rush into a systematic opposition. Newcastle did not object to attempts to improve relations with Pitt so long as they were guided by the Whig lords and not by the 'Young Friends'.[44] Yet to achieve success would be a daunting undertaking because Pitt had not manifested the slightest glimmer of friendship towards Newcastle and his friends for over a year. He had done nothing to support them over Devonshire's removal and he had ostentatiously declared his independence of them during the peace debates. He still professed to be angry at what he regarded as Newcastle's desertion of him in October 1761 and he had even declared that he did not wish to see Newcastle hold public office again.[45] A further source of discord between them was Newcastle's relationship with Cumberland, of whom Pitt had always been suspicious. There also remained the problem of Charles Yorke. Hardwicke's son had failed to obtain his desired office, that of Attorney-General, during the war-time coalition ministry mainly because of Pitt's preference for Pratt.[46] The conflict between Newcastle's loyalty to Yorke and Pitt's fondness for Pratt was to bedevil relations between them for the next three years.

Prospects for an accommodation between Pitt and Newcastle were thus dismal but the need for one was urgent from Newcastle's standpoint. Temple, at least, was not discouraging, avowing his wish for 'a connection with the Pelhams' and asserting that he expected his brother-in-law to attend Parliament (and presumably act with the Opposition) during the remainder of the session.[47] Pitt himself was cordial with Tommy Townshend who visited him on Christmas day although he stated that he was not ready to associate himself with the Newcastle party.[48] Newcastle was not easily deterred. By the end of January he had come to believe 'That Nothing can be done, without putting Mr Pitt at the head of us, to a degree'.[49] Furthermore, Pitt was finding that his olympian isolation was having a negligible impact upon the political situation. His hostile attitude to the overtures of the Newcastle Whigs began to soften. In early February he told Devonshire that he was prepared to co-operate with Newcastle's party but not to enter into a formal alliance or connection.[50] Newcastle fastidiously refrained from doing anything to offend Pitt. As the weeks passed their differences over the peace came to seem less important after the formal ending of the war in February. When Devonshire saw Pitt shortly afterwards, he found him, although still unwilling to attend Parliament regularly in a systematic Opposition, friendly towards Newcastle and contemptuous of Bute.[51] In the interests of co-operation with the Great Commoner, therefore, it was the least that Newcastle— and Cumberland—could do to swallow their distaste for large military establishments in deference to Pitt's support of them and thus Newcastle's friends remained silent during the debate on the Army Estimates on 4 March.[52] Their restraint was rewarded by a cordiality on Pitt's part which was not the less pleasing for being unexpected. The Great Commoner attended an Opposition dinner at Devonshire House on 8 March, a symbolic event at which the opportunity cannot have been missed to concert strategy for an attack upon the ministry over the issue of the Cider Tax.[53]

On this issue Newcastle's party appeared to be in a strong position. Just when Bute had appeared to be at the very summit of his power the Cider Tax provoked an upsurge of hostility towards the administration which was reminiscent in many ways of the excise crisis of 1733. Newcastle and Pitt were agreed in their opposition to the tax and they were supported by members from the cider counties of the south west (whose constituents in certain cases instructed their members to vote against the obnoxious excise). The Cider Tax, moreover, turned against the ministry just that section of opinion which had applauded the peace and which had been firmly behind Bute, the independent country gentlemen.

In spite of all these advantages, the performance of Newcastle's party in the Commons during the Cider Tax debates was an anti-climax. On 11 March Newcastle's men were in a minority of 74 against 116; on 14 March 81 against 139. On what should have been an excellent opposition issue Newcastle was unable to bring to town more than about sixty of his friends. It was not that his connection was wasting away,[54] but that attendance in the House in general was low and Newcastle's members were not whipped in. It was significant, for example, that it was none of Newcastle's friends but William Dowdeswell[55] the Worcestershire Tory, who spearheaded the attack upon the Cider Tax. The 'Young Friends' were scarcely in evidence in the Commons. There is a most revealing list of Newcastle's party drawn up by the Duke himself in which the 'Young Friends' are labelled as 'Young Speakers of Consideration in the House of Commons', but he adds the significant rider that they must be led either by sober and weighty members of the connection, such as Savile and Legge, or by Pitt.[56] Newcastle, then, was probably glad of their absence from the Commons but he could not prevent their attendance in the Lords. Although he told Hardwicke that 'Tho I may differ a little in Opinion, as to the prudence of the Measure, I cannot avoid going with my Friends', in reality he shuddered at the very thought of opposing a ministerial finance proposal in the Upper House. His younger colleagues there insisted upon a trial of strength with the ministry. On the commitment on 28 March they mustered 39 against 73 and on third reading, two days later, 32 against 68. This was failure—not upon the scale of December, it is true, but manifest failure all the same.[57]

In some ways, the Cider Tax was not a favourable issue for Newcastle and his party. Perhaps the Duke disliked co-operating with Tories (although he had always done it in the past whenever he had found it expedient). In any case, the Cider Tax was essentially a provincial issue. It did not affect, directly or indirectly, the interests of Newcastle and his party.[58] The West country was not and never had been a Pelhamite stronghold. Furthermore, there can be no escaping the fact that Newcastle's opposition to the Cider Tax was muted for another reason. Hardwicke, although he disliked the Cider Tax, recalled that he and his friends had concurred in the comparable excise proposals of 1733 and he argued that on grounds of consistency they ought not to oppose the Cider Tax.[59] Legge objected to the Cider Bill because its clauses authorised a loan and a lottery (thus levying two different taxes in one bill), but Hardwicke, once again, found that precedents for raising money in this fashion existed in the time of Walpole.[60] Clearly in opposing the Cider Tax the Newcastle Whigs were treading on dangerous ground and leaving themselves vulnerable to charges of inconsistency and faction. It was only on Pitt's insistence, indeed, that Newcastle agreed to encourage any opposition to the tax in the Lords at all.[61] Newcastle had been pressing for an understanding with Pitt for three months and he was not prepared to allow the delicacies of political consistency to stand in the way of achieving his aim. His single-mindedness received almost at once the most pleasing and unexpected reward which he could ever have imagined. Just as the storm which the Cider Tax had whipped up was subsiding, the political world was astonished when Lord Bute resigned.

Although Bute had succeeded in placing the Cider Tax upon the statute book he had been unnerved by the hostility which the measure had aroused in the country and worn down by the pressure of ridicule and aversion to which he had been continually subjected. Lord Bute, by this time, had done much for his King. Not only had he persevered with the Cider Tax when both George III and Fox had advised him to abandon it[62] but he had banished the old Whigs and freed the monarchy from its chains. He had been as much responsible for the peace as any other individual. This was achievement enough for one of such modest talents and tender temperament. He had defied the Opposition for most of the parliamentary session but now he was unable to bring himself to endure any longer the often totally unjustified public ridicule and criticism which was directed against him. In some ways it is surprising that Bute stayed at his post for as long as he did. He had seriously contemplated resignation before the beginning of the session and only the blandishments of the King had persuaded him to stay.[63] In the quiet weeks between the debates on the peace and those on the Cider Tax his spirits had for a time risen. 'This most triumphant peace . . . will silence faction and baffle all the arts of implacable, designing men.'[64] Such bursts of confidence could not indefinitely allow him to ignore the weaknesses of the ministry and the fissures in his Cabinet. (He was hardly on speaking terms with Egremont.) The clouds had begun to darken in January when Henry Fox had intimated his own intention of resigning. Much though he may have disliked the man and despised his methods, Fox was indispensable to Bute. Only he could lead the ministerial team in the Commons and stand up to Pitt; the only alternative to him was George Grenville whom Bute hated and with whom he could not work. In February and March Bute began to show all the symptoms of nervous illness, sleeplessness, pessimism, loss of confidence and irritability. Fox ignored his desperate appeals for him to remain in the ministry.[65] Bute's decision to retire had thus already been taken for some weeks when it was made public on 8 April 1763. Once the peace treaty had been ratified (on 18 March) Bute was desperate to leave office, feeling that he had accomplished for his master what he had set out to achieve. The storm over the Cider Tax, therefore, coincided with and perhaps confirmed Bute's decision to retire.

Bute delayed the announcement of his resignation so that he could organise a new ministry, appointing men of whom the King would approve. At first he hoped that Fox would replace him, but, to the King's relief, Fox turned the offer down, preferring the calm waters of the House of Lords to the taxing responsibilities of the highest political office in the land. Nevertheless he suggested that George Grenville be approached and took it upon himself to proceed to recommend to other cabinet posts.[66] Bute took care with his appointments. He agreed with George III that 'the only means of supporting the King's independency' was to ensure that the members of the new ministry should have had no previous political connections with each other.[67] At all costs, the King must be protected from faction.

Bute succeeded in forming a Cabinet which seemed to meet these requirements. He was assisted by the fact that George Grenville's ambitions got the better of his political sagacity. After Fox, he was the obvious candidate for the Treasury but he was so anxious to attain the high political prize for which he yearned that he was careful to make no difficulties with the King. Consequently he made no demands of his own, made no recommendations to offices. (He was not even consulted on the composition of his own Treasury Board.)[68] Thus it was not Grenville but George III who insisted on the exclusion of Newcastle's friends because they were 'men who would have ruin'd my D. friend, if they could'.[69] Nevertheless, a ministry which excluded not only the friends of Newcastle but also Pitt could not, in the opinion of many contemporaries, survive for long.[70] The resignation of Bute and the circumstances of the appointment of Grenville appeared to many contemporaries to be puzzling and unusual. To the Newcastle Whigs, however, they had a sinister meaning.

In the later history of the Newcastle–Rockingham party the attitudes of the Newcastle Whigs towards Bute were to be of fundamental importance. Their suspicion of him was to provide the origin of their belief in secret influence, the double cabinet system and the King's Friends. Ian Christie has traced their obsession with Bute back to 1765, but their weird fascination with the court system and its corruption existed at least two years earlier.[71] Although the King's favourite had naturally attracted considerable attention, jealousy and suspicion there had been little serious objection to his appointment to the Cabinet in March 1761. As Henry Fox said: 'The H. of Commons has a right, & has sometimes exerted it, to accuse a Minister, & make it very unadviseable for a Prince to retain him in his favour. But I do not remember that they ever undertook to say who should succeed him'.[72] Xenophobic hatred of his nationality, together with wildly exaggerated stories of his

Jacobitism, account for the popular hostility which existed towards him, but there was in 1761 nothing resembling a constitutional issue surrounding Bute's appointment. Newcastle himself admitted to Devonshire: 'In this Reign, I own, I did, in Concert with Your Grace, and My Friends, prefer My Lord Bute to Him (Pitt), & was an Insignificant Instrument to bring My Lord Bute into the Secretary's Office'.[73] It was only when the old Whigs themselves began to suffer the effects of Bute's appointment that they began to criticise it. As early as May 1762 Rockingham had written to Newcastle: 'I have long thought that the determination of Ld B[ute] was to act without Controul & that Your Grace was look'd on as rather a Check in his Career'.[74] By the end of 1762 Newcastle had come to agree with Rockingham's observation but he objected to Bute because he was 'haughty', 'absolute' and 'ignorant of business', not because his behaviour was unconstitutional.[75] Similarly, Pitt's objection to Bute's situation ('Favour and Honour might be allowed, but not within the walls of the Treasury')[76] did not question the King's right either to appoint Bute or to maintain him in office. The humiliation of the Duke of Devonshire gave rise to a good deal of aristocratic resentment but nothing of a constitutional issue was made of it. What it taught the old Whigs was that the Court had now declared open war on them. Newcastle thought 'That no Violences would be omitted, which could tend to & establish, The Sole Power of the Minister'.[77] Personal hatred of an overbearing minister gave way after the Massacre of the Pelhamite Innocents to a belief that from the very outset of the new reign the court had planned to humiliate the Whig aristocracy and to destroy its political power. This was why Newcastle had been pushed out of office in 1762 and why so many innocent dependents of the Whig lords had been attacked and 'massacred'.[78] The King, of course, was not held to be responsible. Devonshire wrote: 'I am very sorry that the King, who I am sure has good sense and good nature can be so governed and blinded by any one as to pursue such measures'.[79] Bute was the culprit then and George III the innocent victim of circumstances. Newcastle's friends were supported by a strident element of public opinion which denounced Bute as a

Tory, as a Jacobite, and as a Stuart. Few men can have been so hysterically persecuted by a public which seeks and finds a scapegoat for its grievances and Bute attracted criticism, ridicule and hatred like a magnet.[80]

By early 1763 a constitutional issue had been made out of Bute's position. As Almon described it in *The History of the Late Minority*: 'The Whigs, in reply to the Tories, or partizans of the minister . . . said they could not admit a minister to be a servant of the King only; he was servant of the nation likewise, and accountable to the people as well as to the King'.[81] Thus when Bute fell from power in April 1763, his situation became more, not less, suspicious in the eyes of Newcastle and his friends. For Bute was now the Minister behind the Curtain, responsible and accountable to no one. The Grenville ministry thus appeared to be 'an experiment to see whether he can govern this country in this mode as it was plain he cou'd not long maintain himself at the head of the Treasury'.[82]

This was the customary political language of all oppositions in the eighteenth century. Charges of secret influence and accusations of monopolising power had been directed against Walpole and the Pelhams by successive dissident groups. Furthermore, the Newcastle Whigs were wide of the mark in their charges against Bute. There was very little factual basis to their imputations. Simply because their charges rested upon rumour, gossip, fear and exaggeration, the Newcastle Whigs found them so compelling. Myth bred myth. Fantastic systems of corruption and secret influence lodged themselves into the minds and found a ready home in the imaginations of the friends of Newcastle at just that time when they perhaps needed a simple and plausible explanation for their recent set-backs and humiliations. But this does not mean that the attack of the Newcastle Whigs upon Bute was devoid of significance. On one level, they gave expression to their anxieties in terms of a constitutional theory which attacked Bute because his position as a Minister behind the Curtain violated the traditional responsibility of ministers to Parliament.[83] This was respectable enough but it does not go to the root of the matter. The 'Bute Myth' can only be properly understood if its function in the minds of the Newcastle Whigs

C

is grasped. They were in need of a relevant criterion of constitutional theory and practice during the Bute and Grenville
ministries and they did not have far to look. What can only
be described as the 'Whig tradition' provided a ready made
set of assumptions which proved to be remarkably relevant to
the political problems of the 1760s. Although the Pelhams had
always maintained the prerogatives of the crown they had
always insisted that a minister had rights independent of the
Crown, duties to the public and to his political dependents.[84]
In other words, the Pelhams had always been loyal both to the
Crown and to the Constitution. In 1762–3 these two loyalties,
for so long over-lapping, now came into conflict. It was this
transmutation of certain aspects of the Whig tradition into the
'Bute Myth', then, rather than the activities of the 'Young
Friends' of the Duke of Newcastle which was the most important
development in opposition politics between the debates on the
peace preliminaries and the establishment of the ministry of
George Grenville.

Chapter 3

The Opposition to
George Grenville
1763–5

The years of Grenville's ministry were arduous and perplexing for the friends of Newcastle. Their attempts to adapt themselves to the routine of opposition were rarely successful. They remained uncertain and divided among themselves when a vigorous and enthusiastic attack upon Grenville's ministry might have enjoyed some chance of success. Occasionally they were stirred from their lethargy either by the 'Young Friends' or, more usually, by a blunder of the Government but they were unable to fashion an effective political strategy of their own. The 'Massacre of the Pelhamite Innocents' had built up their suspicions of Bute into an embryonic political issue of the appointment of ministers; the role that they imputed to him during the formation of the Grenville ministry suggested that he intended to be 'Minister behind the Curtain' and thus arose their conviction that he was a dangerous influence over the King. Newcastle's connection was united in its wish to destroy Bute and his advisors but the Duke discovered that the undertaking was fraught with overwhelming problems. He found it difficult to rally and maintain the coherence of his connection, to provide it with decisive leadership on the political issues of the time and thus to mount an effective assault on the ministry of Grenville, to say nothing of administering the *coup de grâce* and of routing out Bute and his evil influence—and all without appearing to encroach upon the prerogatives of the King. It was a tall order and Newcastle lacked both the nerve and the skill to fill it.

Aware of his own failings, it was natural for Newcastle to look to others to help him. For the next three years, then, it was Newcastle's consistent aim to achieve an alliance or, at least, a working agreement with Pitt. As for Pitt, his anti-Bute feelings did not go very deep. What he really wished was to replace the Grenville ministry with one of his own choosing, one whose members would defer to him and to the King, who would allow him the freedom of action which he always craved and whose relations with the King would not be distorted by the aristocratic cliqueishness of the Newcastle Whigs. In short, Pitt did not intend to be the tool of Newcastle. It was not for him to resolve the old Duke's difficulties and this he constantly refused to do. The opposition to Grenville was thus frequently disunited although when it was capable of co-operating on an important issue the ministry could be severely embarrassed, as in February 1764 over the issue of General Warrants. During the Grenville ministry, then, the Newcastle Whigs began to receive their education in the routine of opposition politics and they began to understand some of the difficulties of working, or trying to work, with Pitt. It is worth emphasising, however, that even by the end of the ministry they had not yet come to see themselves as a self-contained party which might be able to form a ministry entirely and exclusively from among their own number and to maintain themselves in office independently of the Crown or of Pitt. In essence, the situation was that Newcastle was seeking to liberate the Crown from the influence of Bute so that the 'Revolution Families' might return to their traditional role in Government but that they needed the assistance of Pitt to do so. Pitt, not unreasonably, refused to collaborate too closely in such a risky undertaking of which the friends of Newcastle rather than himself would be the chief beneficiaries. The conflict over the affairs of John Wilkes was to provide the first example of the working of this pattern of opposition politics in the ministry of Grenville.

In the history of Britain it has usually been the case that in those historical episodes in which public opinion has played a powerful role the timing of events has proved to be an all-important factor. Number 45 of *The North Briton* was published on 23 April 1763, on the eve of the parliamentary recess. The lethargy which usually afflicted politicians in Opposition during the summer months was thus avoided and such impetus and cohesion as the friends of Newcastle had tenderly cultivated during the eventful session of 1762–3 was not squandered by the customary retreat of the aristocracy to their palladian mansions in the country. The Wilkes issue enlivened politics and embarrassed the ministry, but most of all, it appeared to provide new and sensational proof of that sinister influence in the ministry and around the Court which was threatening to undermine the constitutional liberties of Englishmen.

John Wilkes, MP for Aylesbury since 1757 had been publishing *The North Briton* since Bute had come to power as a counter-blast to the loyalist platitudes of Dr Smollett's *The Briton*. Wilkes' newspaper had been scurrilous, amusing and un-expectedly successful in the metropolis where it focussed the hostility of mercantile and financial elements towards the ministry. The intensity of *The North Briton's* attacks upon the Scottish favourite steadily rose to a calculated crescendo in April 1763. There is no truth in Almon's assertions that the newspaper had fallen upon hard times and that Number 45 was intended to be the last issue.[1] Wilkes, in fact, was waiting for his opportunity and it was the speech from the throne closing the session on 19 April which provided him with materials enough to launch into a comprehensive indictment of the personnel and policy of the late ministry. He castigated the peace of Paris, ridiculed Grenville and the Cabinet as 'wretched tools' of Lord Bute and—most offensive of all—attacked the Speech as the composition of ministers, lamenting 'that a Prince of so many great and amiable qualities, whom England truly reveres, can be brought to give the sanction of his sacred name to the most odious measures, and to the most unjustifiable public declarations, from a throne ever renowned for truth, honour, and unsullied virtue. . . .' On top of every-thing else, to call the King a liar and publicly to denounce him as a tool of Lord Bute was too much for George III. No one could have expected the new and unproven ministry to ignore such an offensive challenge. The Secretaries of State obtained from their law officers an opinion that Number 45 was a seditious libel, whereupon Lord Halifax, Secretary of State for the Northern Department, procured on 26 April a General Warrant for the arrest of the author.[2] A General Warrant provided no legal protection for the subject in that there was no restriction upon the powers of the law officers to seize persons and papers. On 30 April John Wilkes was consigned to the tower.[3]

As always, Newcastle disliked issues where public opinion and political responsibility combined but his reluctance to make the slightest gesture of support for John Wilkes is perfectly understandable. His hesitation to do so arose partly from his personal distaste for the unsavory reputation and the scurrilous publications of the reprobate journalist. But, more important, Newcastle was no stranger to General Warrants. He had occasionally used them during his long years in office. He now contented himself with the view that the arrest of Wilkes contravened the immunity which he derived from parliamentary privilege.[4] Furthermore, few of his friends were sympathetic to Wilkes and most of those who were did not wish to give public expression to their private views.[5] Cumberland, the much respected patron and protector of Newcastle's party, always refused to admit that important political principles were at stake in the case while the Duke of Devonshire committed himself to the view that the party should do nothing in order to 'show that we are firmly united & not to be divided, & not in a hurry to get ourselves in. . .'.[6] As for Hardwicke, Newcastle's mentor played a curious role at this time. He had already suggested to his son, Charles Yorke, that an earlier number of *The North Briton* (Number 39) should be prosecuted[7] and after the issue of the General Warrant in Wilkes' case he advised his son and helped him to search for precedents.[8] It is no surprise to find Hardwicke counselling Newcastle against 'the discourse of the Zealous Young Gentlemen' and reminding Newcastle not only of his past complicity in the issuing of General Warrants but the remarkable resemblance which the present one bore to those issued by Newcastle![9] Newcastle's own inclinations coincided, therefore, with those of most of his friends and advisors. They also coincided in time with the addresses which were raised during the summer congratulating the King upon the peace. Newcastle needed little reminding that the country had no use for a factious Opposition at the conclusion of a successful war, especially an Opposition which might condone attacks upon the King's honesty by scribblers of slight repute. Newcastle's tactic of refusing to make political capital out of the Wilkes' case, therefore, had much to commend it and it carried the day. In any case, if the ministry were to be provoked by the Opposition, it might choose to legitimise its actions by placing General Warrants upon a statutory basis. After the public outcry over the Wilkes affair it was unlikely that General Warrants would ever again be used. The best line of action for Newcastle to adopt was to allow ministerial powers to remain undefined and to resist the temptation of taking factious advantage of the unhappy Grenville. All this is understandable enough but to allow the Wilkes case to go by default was not likely to lead either to an improved relationship with Pitt or to the overthrow of the Government. For the sake of his personal consistency Newcastle was neglecting his major political objective, the establishment of closer relations between his connection and William Pitt.

Newcastle still clung to the hope that the assistance of Pitt, whose personality and ability he so much respected, would enhance his own situation, maintain, perhaps augment, the size of the Newcastle connection, strengthen its cohesion and thus quieten, the 'Young Friends'.[10] Newcastle believed that the foundations for such an alliance had been laid during the Cider Tax debates in March and he was further encouraged by the fact that over Wilkes the position which he had taken up did not appear to offend Pitt or to differ from his luke-warm attitude towards Wilkes.[11] Newcastle's optimistic expectations of achieving a working relationship in Opposition with Pitt were raised to their highest point when Pitt received Yorke at Hayes on 7 June. For once, Pitt did not choose to labour the persistent difficulties which stood in the way of co-operating with Newcastle. He thus overlooked the position of Cumberland and his own much-vaunted fear of being isolated in a future Pitt-Newcastle ministry. Pitt even went so far as to concede that Charles Yorke deserved promotion in his profession as much as Pratt did.[12] How far Pitt was sincere in thus raising Newcastle's hopes is difficult to determine. His behaviour about this time suggests that he was testing the opinions of some of the politicians of the day but it is impossible to prove that Pitt was deliberately misleading Newcastle. Nevertheless, in the following weeks his attitude towards Charles Yorke perceptibly hardened. In early August he was insisting that Pratt's claims to the Woolsack were superior to those of Charles Yorke and he had come harshly to condemn Yorke's part in the issuing of the General Warrant used in the Wilkes case.[13] Nothing that Newcastle and his friends could do seemed to succeed in mollifying Pitt. Although Newcastle did not expect him to engage in a systematic Opposition he believed that 'the whole Machine must be directed by him' whatever part he chose to take himself.[14] Unaccountably, Newcastle thought that Pitt might be open to persuasion not only if Devonshire but, more astonishing, Cumberland were to add their expostulations to those of Newcastle himself to beg Pitt 'to enter into a proper Concert, not for a General Opposition to what may be right but to consider what should be opposed and what not, and what Steps should be taken to deliver the King, and the Nation, from the Arbitray-Arrogant & Incapable Ministers'.[15]

As the opening of the new session approached and as Pitt's interest in the political game quickened, his hostility to Charles Yorke increased. Yorke, of course, stoutly defended his actions in the Wilkes case and refused to retract the official advice he had publicly given in office simply to please Pitt.[16] Charles Yorke had thus become the symbolic barrier standing in the way of co-operation between Pitt and Newcastle. Newcastle attempted to remove it by acting upon a hint dropped by Pitt which might well have appeared to the Duke as a brilliant political manoeuvre. If he and friends could persuade Charles Yorke to resign from office they would at one and the same time deliver a harsh blow at the ministry, embarrassing it on the Wilkes issue, while demonstrating to Pitt their willingness to go to any lengths to please him. Charles Yorke thus came under considerable pressure from Newcastle's circle. The tragic circumstances of his death in 1770 were now curiously antici-

pated and with startling similarity. After a dinner at Rockingham's on 20 October the conflict in Yorke's mind grew. On the
one hand, he wished to help gratify the political interests of his
friends (to conciliate Pitt). On the other hand, he wished to act
consistently with his own opinions and thus to further his own
career (by staying in office). He resolved the conflict by decid-
ing that friendship came before consistency. On 2 November
he submitted his resignation. Charles Yorke had been deliberately sacrificed by Newcastle upon the altar of co-operation
with Pitt.[17]

How effective was the resignation of Charles Yorke in assuring
Pitt of the friendly intentions of the Newcastle Whigs on the
eve of the new session and in persuading him to act with them?
It did not for a moment soften Pitt's anger against what he
now regarded as the unconstitutional use of the General
Warrant in the Wilkes case and Yorke's resignation could not
change his mind.[18] He remarked, rather unfeelingly and
flippantly, 'the ministers were not to be removed that way'.[19]
Pitt could not even begin to appreciate the agonising personal
decision which Charles Yorke had made. He lacked the
capacity for understanding the feelings of others and the fact
that their opinions, however much he might disagree with them,
were held just as sincerely as his own. In these personal defects
lie some of the reasons, at least, why Pitt's career after 1761
was one of continuous failure and constant frustration. For the
present, Newcastle's sacrifice of Yorke left the Great Commoner
scornfully indifferent towards the prospect of their mutual
co-operation. Newcastle reported on 2 November, 'that Mr
Pitt was in a violent fury, would do nothing, would concert
with nobody, expected that everybody should follow him and
his measures, without vouchsafing even to give his reason for
his opinions'.[20] Amidst the ruins of Newcastle's policy of
alliance and co-operation with Pitt, then, the new session of
Parliament opened.

As for the ministry, everything that had happened to the
unfortunate George Grenville since Bute had decided to resign
the Treasury appeared to give some foundation to the fears and
suspicions of the Newcastle Whigs about the peculiar political
situation which existed in the new reign. Although George III

disliked Grenville for the obstructive part he had taken against Bute in the previous year he had much to commend him. He had no following and no policy to impose upon the King. He was an able parliamentarian and a competent administrator. He was, moreover, willing to attempt to defend George III from the Newcastle Whigs and from William Pitt and to rally the gentry around the throne.[21]

Grenville, in fact, was to step into Bute's shoes, to represent the interests of the King, and, with the two Secretaries, Egremont and Halifax, to maintain the continuity of government.[22] There can be no doubt that George III intended from the outset to remain a real power behind the throne. 'The Grenville ministry was intended as a mere facade.'[23] But a facade for Bute was what Grenville and the other two members of 'The Triumvirate' obstinately refused to be. The First Lord and the Secretaries from the outset resented Bute's presence behind the scenes and tried to restrict the King's access to him. Within weeks of entering into the King's service they were threatening to leave it. And because 'The Triumvirate' refused to be manipulated by King George III, the monarch did not rest easy with them and within a few months was desperately seeking to remove them. There was, after all, a kernel of justification for the exaggerated suspicions of the Newcastle Whigs that Bute occupied a position of influence after his resignation.[24]

The instability of the ministry was made clear for all to see when in early August the King, wishing to deliver himself from Grenville, turned to the old Whigs. Hardwicke was sent to but he refused to enter the ministry as an individual. He would take office only as part of a wider plan which included the old Whigs.[25] When he heard of these soundings Grenville expostulated with the King and told him roundly that he had better send for the Opposition if he were not prepared to support his ministers. George III asked for ten days in which to make up his mind but it is doubtful if he seriously intended to spend ten days in contemplation. He was desperately seeking advice and assistance. He took advice from Bute whereupon he decided that Hardwicke's terms were inadmissible.[26] At the same time he sounded Bedford and Pitt for assistance. As for Bedford he ruined any prospect of coming to an agreement with the King when he demanded the exclusion of Bute from his counsels. The King was back where he started, in chains to George Grenville; but the chains had scarcely been fastened when he was given a reprive. Just after the failure of the discussions with Bedford the death of Egremont on 27 August plunged the political situation once more into confusion. It was not just that there was a vacant Secretaryship to fill. Granville's office of Lord President had been unoccupied since January. There was every likelihood of extensive ministerial changes. Bedford and the old Whigs had excluded themselves from serious consideration by the stringent terms which they had recently tried to impose upon the King. William Pitt had made no such demands of his monarch and it was, therefore, to Pitt, that George III turned expectantly in late August. Perhaps he was at last beginning to see that Pitt might be his best ally in 'his crusade to restore the independence of the monarchy, destroy faction and to inaugurate the reign of virtue.

Pitt had already spoken to Bute on 25 August and two days later he met the King when he outlined his conditions for taking office. His cabinet list included some of Newcastle's friends, both old and young, but Temple was to have the Treasury, Pitt himself a Secretaryship, Hardwicke the Privy Seal, Newcastle the Lord Presidency of the Council, Rockingham the Admiralty and Devonshire his Chamberlain's stick returned to him. Pitt demanded a peerage but not the Woolsack for Pratt where Northington would remain. Pitt refused to make any concessions about the ministerial posts but he indicated to the King that he would look favourably upon his desire to retain particular persons. Pitt wished to proscribe those responsible for the peace, a proscription which would involve the dismissal of office-holders appointed by Bute or by the King, dismissals which would be a public confession that his hand had been forced. At a second audience on 29 August, the King declared that to dismiss his servants and to accept the old Whigs back into office would amount to a public breach of his honour. He could agree to neither course of action and thus the negotiations concluded. In short, Pitt's proposals amounted to something which bore a striking resemblance to the wartime coalition, which the King had come to the throne intent upon destroying. George III hurriedly repaired his relationship with Grenville and gave him full assurances of his support, public and private. The problem of ministerial reconstruction he resolved simply if expensively. He bought the Bedford Whigs who, with Grenville, stipulated that Bute must retire from all involvement in politics.[27] The King had thus obtained men of some talent,[28] reduced his dependence upon Grenville and protected himself from the possible resurrection of a Pitt-Newcastle alliance. He had, in the circumstances, extricated himself from a difficult situation as well as he could reasonably have expected.

One question mark hangs over these events, that of the sincerity of Pitt. There are grounds for suspecting that he was less than completely sincere in professing to desire a successful outcome to his discussions with the King and Bute. The changes he proposed *were* extensive and there was never any chance that George III would accept them. It was not Pitt's way to impose a cabinet list upon the King. It was not Pitt's way to insist either upon a sweeping exclusion of office-holders or of those who had supported the peace—the latter when made public lashed the Bedfords into such a fury of indignation that they were willing to enter the ministry. His conduct in 1765 and 1766 was to be very different. It may have been the case that he was testing the water, beginning a lengthy and complex manoeuvre to return to office, pitching his terms so impossibly high at first that a later retreat from them would have the appearance of moderation and unselfishness. In any case his little diplomatic excursion did him no harm with the King. For the first time George III began to look favourably upon Pitt as both of them came to realise that now the divisive issue of the peace was passing their mutual detestation of party might at some future date ripen into a formal arrangement. The seeds of the Chatham administration were being sown, although they took many months to ripen and to grow. This new-found cordiality was signified to the world at the levée on 31 August when the King singled out Pitt and Temple for particular attention. At the same time, Pitt was building up a store of goodwill with the Opposition. He kept Newcastle and his friends informed of what passed between himself and the

King and wrote to Devonshire asking him to come to town 'to give' as Devonshire excitedly wrote to Rockingham 'my concurrence in forming a System of Administration, to be compos'd of the *Great Revolution Principle Families of the Kingdom*'.[29] Was this merely Devonshire's exaggeration? That it was not can be confirmed from what Pitt had written to Devonshire. He went so far as to say that he could not take office 'unless the System be so formed that the great Revolution Principle Families of the Kingdom shall return to where They ought to be, about the Throne, and in the Councils of His Majesty'.[30] Can it be seriously maintained that Pitt believed all this? Is it not more likely that he was both amusing himself by wrapping the Newcastle Whigs around his little finger, improving his relations with them whilst using them to further his own objectives? Pitt's behaviour was none other than a well-timed and nicely executed exploration to test the opinions and the ambitions of the leading politicians of the day, including the King. Perhaps this is to credit Pitt with excessive predetermination but it is surely to misread the entire negotiation to believe that Pitt meant everything that he said. Finally, was there not an element of theatre in his lavish disappointment at the failure of the overture? 'As to the Country, it is lost beyond the possibility of being restored; the Moment thrown away was, in my Judgement, the Last which offered the smallest Gleam of Hope. May it never be my fate again to hear anything of taking a share in the affairs of a nation devoted to confusion and ruin'.[31]

Meanwhile, by bringing the Bedfords into office, the King may, and probably did, have it in mind to establish in the Cabinet an influence to balance the political power of Grenville. He could have been none other than delighted with the result. At once quarrels and dissensions wracked the Cabinet. Bedford made it plain that he would not tolerate the monopoly of offices which Grenville claimed, insisting that all ministers should share patronage equally. Grenville, of course, had come to office without a party of supporters and he needed patronage to create one. Bedford's obstructiveness, therefore, threatened to make him a cipher inside his own Cabinet.[32] Grenville was never able to work smoothly with the Bedfords. He could both vindicate his own personal reputation and also strengthen his

Cabinet situation only through success in Parliament, and, especially, the House of Commons. Political failure would have left George Grenville at the mercy of the Bedfords and he knew it. The parliamentary session was to open on 15 November. Grenville spent eight weeks preparing for the day, whipping in supporters[33] and preparing his programme of measures to deal with the lingering issue of John Wilkes.[34] In view of the fact that Parliament was opening at such an early date, an attendance of about 250 supporters of Government at the Cockpit on the eve of the opening of the session augured well for George Grenville.[35]

Newcastle, too, had begun after a fashion to consider his tactics for the coming session but he obstinately ignored the lessons which the events of the recess ought to have taught him. Although the Duke had come a long way along the road to systematic opposition during the previous year and now understood the need for active and vigorous opposition, he and, it must be admitted, his colleagues and the 'Young Friends' continued to assume that they could only succeed with an alliance between themselves and Pitt. But the recess should have taught Newcastle that Pitt, of all men, could not be relied upon to come to the aid of the old Whigs. As far back as September he had disappointed the Newcastle Whigs by refusing to be drawn into any 'Plan of General Opposition' and by even refraining from commenting upon the ideas and suggestions for the forthcoming session with which they plied him.[36] His refusal dismayed Newcastle for the Duke had now come to relate the Wilkes issue to his notion of Bute's situation and he feared it was Grenville's intention 'To affect the most Essential Points of the Constitution; & establish a Power in Ministers entirely destructive of it'.[37] For Newcastle, then, opposition was legitimate when the constitution was in danger, but he shrank from taking any action to defend it. For example, to oppose the Address from the Throne, in the view of Pitt and some of the friends of Newcastle, might easily be construed by the public as unqualified support for Wilkes.[38] Furthermore Newcastle was paralysed by the expectation that there were likely to be angry disputes between Pitt and Yorke in which Newcastle's friends were themselves at odds. For example,

Newcastle agreed with Pitt's opinion that seditious libel did not constitute a breach of the peace and that, therefore, Wilkes should enjoy the immunity afforded by parliamentary privilege. But Rockingham, burning with resentment at Pitt's high-handed treatment of the affair and full of pity for Charles Yorke, violently disagreed with him.[39] Newcastle was committed to Opposition but it seemed that any positive act of leadership he might provide would inevitably create fissures which might damage the delicate unity of his connection. Newcastle, astonishingly, even failed to come to the help of his City friends. The autumn of 1763, found Europe—and Britain—shaken by a series of financial crises 'which led to fears of bankruptcies and, a serious credit crisis in the City of London as well'[40] but Newcastle completely failed to mount any sort of convincing attack upon George Grenville's handling of the crisis. Newcastle was reduced to vapid platitudes of hope 'That some Solid Union, upon real Revolution Principles, & an Assertion in Earnest of the Freedom of the Constitution' might somehow unite the Opposition.[41] Newcastle had failed to win Pitt and he had proved himself incapable, for the second year in succession, of preparing his friends for the session. He did not even send out attendance notes to his followers. He failed to revive the one promising issue of the previous session, the Cider Tax. To have attempted to wipe the unpopular measure from the statute book might have attracted some support from independent Members. Hardwicke dissuaded him from adopting such a popular line of policy and the opportunity was missed.

Newcastle's connection, unprepared and unaware of what was in store in the new session, found itself helpless to prevent Grenville's masterfully engineered plans to discredit Wilkes and to expel him from Parliament. In the Upper House on the first day (15 November) Sandwich's unexpected attribution of the *Essay on Woman* to Wilkes stunned Newcastle's friends into silence. Only Temple ventured to reply and he could do little more than attack the ministers' methods. The peers voted the *Essay* both a blasphemy and a breach of privilege.[42] In the Lower House on the same day, a more comprehensive vindication of the ministry's actions in the Wilkes case was approved overwhelmingly, by 300–111.[43] The Commons proceeded to vote Number 45 a seditious libel. The way was now clear for Grenville's clearly thought out strategy to be implemented step by step. The first great matter to resolve was the question of privilege. On 23 November the Commons determined by 243–166 to consider the case further in Wilkes' absence.[44] The following day, Lord North's important motion that seditious libel was not covered by parliamentary privilege was carried by 258–133. Pitt came to town for this debate. He distinguished carefully between the personality of Wilkes which he abhorred, and the constitutional issues at stake in the Wilkes case, on which he attacked the ministers' abandonment of privilege. Nevertheless, he made it clear that he was independent of all groups yet solicitous to defend the Constitution. He disapproved of certain legal aspects of what the ministers had done but thought that Wilkes deserved punishment for, if nothing else, insulting the monarch.[45] On 29 November in the Lords a similar motion was passed by the overwhelming majority of 114–35.[46] The ground was now prepared for the fateful decision of the Commons on 19 January 1764 to expel Wilkes from the Lower House. On that date Grenville's attempt to obtain parliamentary approval for the actions of his ministry against Wilkes reached its climax in a triumphant victory when motions for the adjournment of the Commons were lost by 225–64 and 227–57.

The first part of the session of 1763–4, then, was almost as much a disaster for Newcastle and his friends as the events of December 1762 had been. The differences between Pitt and Yorke had now become public knowledge for on 15 November Charles Yorke had defended his part in the Wilkes case, to be followed the next day by Pitt's bitter recrimination, his ridicule and his boast that he stood independent of any faction or group. Pitt could hardly have made himself clearer to Yorke, Newcastle—or to the King.[47] By the new year Newcastle was increasingly coming to seem a broken reed, his policy a mass of contradictions. He continued, in spite of everything, to believe that it was possible in a reconstructed administration to reconcile the claims of Yorke and Pratt to the Woolsack. He wanted the best of all worlds and to obtain it he followed too many policies simultaneously. Because he was anxious that none should fail, none succeeded. For example, he sought the co-operation of Pitt but supported the pretensions of Yorke and basked in the friendship of Cumberland. He attacked the ministry yet did not support Wilkes. Within his own connection he neither encouraged nor condemned the 'Young Friends'. Newcastle's friends hardly knew where they were because Newcastle scarcely followed a coherent policy. In the circumstances, perhaps, the opposition to the ministry and the turn-out of Newcastle's friends in both Houses were better than he had a right to expect.

It was as a natural consequence of these early failures that the Opposition sought to strengthen its proceedings through placing its organisation upon a more formal and institutionalised basis than had hitherto prevailed.[48] The 'club' activities of the previous year had attained neither the continuity nor the effectiveness which their initiators had anticipated; it was the transparent and continuing indecision of the old Whig leadership, combined with the constitutional questions which the Wilkes case provoked, which gave rise to the formation of Wildmans club. Only those who seek a superficial continuity in the history of the 'Young Friends' and who claim that there existed an ideological polarity in the Newcastle party between the old and young Whigs can depict the establishment of Wildmans as anything other than the response of some of Newcastle's friends, old as well as young, to the opposition catastrophes of the early weeks of the session.. The establishment of regular meetings at premises in Albermarle Street in January 1764 marks a further development in the history of the Newcastle connection. Wildmans was largely the work of the younger men in the party who longed for unity and a constitutional crusade against Grenville but it should not be inferred from this that the older Whigs were hostile to the establishment of Wildmans. There is considerable evidence to show that men like Legge and Newcastle, if not initiators of Wildmans, were kept informed, and did not disapprove of proceedings there.[49]

Our modern affection for the organisational criteria of institutional development should not allow us to exaggerate the importance of Wildmans and it should not prevent us from placing in its correct perspective the role of the club in the opposition politics of the time. For one thing, formal political business was forbidden at the club. Wildmans was *not* a political club. Although it acted inevitably as a discussion centre for Newcastle's friends (and even provided a reading room of pamphlets and books) its main business was the mundane yet convivial one of providing food and drink.[50] Nevertheless, Wildmans did enjoy a moment of glory in February 1764 when it acted as the focus of the Opposition's whipping-in campaign during the great debates on General Warrants.[51] On particular occasions, then, the club could meet the Opposition's need for improved communication, organisation and co-operation during the session but that was not its original function.

Some measure of the influence and the importance of the club may be gained by examining lists of its membership, two of which survive.[52] In February 1764 23 peers, 98 MPs and 27 others were paid-up members of Wildmans. Of the peers, only 2 had not divided in the minority on 29 November.[53] Of the 98 MPs, 85 had already voted in opposition to Bute and Grenville and only 4 of the 98 appear to have had no previous connection with Newcastle and his followers. Non-political it may have been, therefore, but Wildmans was able to provide the Opposition with a solid block of about 100 members during the session. Of its ninety-eight MPs, for example, only H. B. Legge (who was ill and shortly to die) and John Offley failed to support Opposition in at least one of the three divisions against General Warrants in February.[54] On the other hand, we should resist the temptation to ascribe organisational miracles to institutional factors alone. Most of these men, no doubt, would have voted with the Opposition in February if Wildmans had never existed and the club failed to attract more than a thin trickle of new converts to the cause of Newcastle. Finally, its influence, reaching dizzy heights in February, rapidly declined thereafter, and never again enjoyed the importance of those hectic weeks.[55]

The founding of Wildmans, nevertheless, heralded something of a revival of the Opposition after its failures in the early weeks of the session, a revival which began seriously to embarrass the ministry when the repeal of the Cider Tax was at last brought forward in the Lower House on 24 January 1764. The Cider Tax had, in the minds of Newcastle's friends, at least, been the occasion for the hounding of Bute from office and it was tempting for them to believe that the same issue might prove to be the cause of the downfall of Grenville. The tax had caused widespread complaint and even popular rioting but it had also elicited a number of respectable petitions. It was an ideal issue, therefore, for the opposition, attracting the support of exactly those members who might have been offended by Wilkes' behaviour and by the Opposition, however tepid, which the friends of Newcastle had raised to the ministry's handling of the Wilkes issue, that is, the independent country gentlemen. On this issue, too, the opposition could count upon Pitt's unreserved support. Furthermore, the Worcestershire Tory, William Dowdeswell, spearheaded the protests against the tax, as he had in the previous year. So effective was the Opposition's onslaught that Grenville only managed to save the Cider tax by persuading the Commons by 167–125 to agree to the establishment of a committee to inquire into the operation of the tax. Indeed, Dowdeswell's proposal of 31 January that the tax should fall on the retailer rather than the manufacturer was lost only by the slender margin of 172–152 but thereafter Grenville was safe. On 10 February a motion for repeal was lost by 204–115. But the run against the ministry was already gathering momentum on a very different topic, the most sensational constitutional aspect of the Wilkes case and the one which best avoided raising the more unsavoury aspects of the personality of Wilkes himself, the issue of General Warrants.

Grenville knew what was in store for him but he was unable to do more than postpone the Opposition's assault on 6 February by deferring a full discussion of General Warrants by 217–122.[56] The debate was to take place on 14 February and Wildmans was the scene of frantic activity; ten of its leading Members undertook to whip in ten Members each while Newcastle undertook to exploit his own extensive network of contacts.[57] Significantly, the culmination of these elaborate preparations took place at the home of the 'independent' friend of Rockingham, Sir George Savile. At this meeting on the eve of the debate a motion condemning General Warrants was drawn up.[58] On 14 February the matter was deferred yet again, however, the ministers defeating Savile's motion by the excitingly narrow margin of 207–197. The minority included, as Grenville noted in his report of the debate to the King, some defections.[59] The crisis of his ministry was at hand. The fate of George Grenville was to be decided on 17 February and for this occasion both sides strained their organisations to the limit as they strove to bring to town all their supporters.

The debate on General Warrants on 17/18 February was one of the great parliamentary occasions of the eighteenth century. The House was one of the fullest of the century and the atmosphere was electric. It disappoints the historian, then, that the accounts—usually sketchy—of the debates which survive are tedious and legalistic. It is not only impossible to recapture the accuracy of the speeches but also the atmosphere of the occasion. As might have been expected Pitt and Charles Townshend were the most prominent and most effective speakers for the Opposition, outshining the friends of the Duke of Newcastle. Grenville and Charles Yorke struggled to defend themselves from these attacks. The issue was decided in the early hours of the morning of 18 February when the division was taken. George Grenville received approval of his conduct by 232–218, a majority of 14.[60]

He had managed to weather the storm and, in spite of this extraordinarily narrow majority, his administration was safe for the remainder of the session. The high minority division figure should not obscure the fact that many members who had voted against Grenville were men who felt that even though Wilkes had received his just deserts there were aspects of the case where administration had blundered. In short, General Warrants was exactly the sort of issue on which independent country gentlemen liked to demonstrate their independence of the executive. They, no doubt, enjoyed the orations of Pitt and Townshend (indeed, they may have influenced their votes) but they did not wish to vote for a Pitt–Newcastle ministry. They did not think it was their business to impose ministers on the King. Furthermore, Grenville was made of sterner stuff than Bute. He was ambitious and intended to cling to office, refusing to be deflected from his purpose by a few close divisions. He was able to stand up to the big guns of the Opposition and he had not the slightest qualm about the prospect of a running fight with them. Such a fight would, at least, tell him who his friends were.[61] As it happened, however, such a conflict did not materialise and within a few weeks he was congratulating himself: 'The state of the House of Commons appears much more favourable to His Majesty's administration and the minds of men seem to be much less heated than they were.'[62] For his part, although the King disliked George Grenville, he would not have allowed the House of Commons to force a ministry to resign simply because of a narrow majority on just one aspect of the Wilkes case. Even if Grenville had been defeated it is not at all clear that he would have offered to resign or that he constitutionally ought to have done. If he had been defeated, Grenville could have proceeded to test the confidence of the House in his ministry and it is probable that he would have comfortably survived on such a vote of confidence.

History might have been different if Newcastle had been able to harass the ministry further. Taken together, those who voted *against* the ministry on 6, 14, and 17 February outnumbered those who voted *for* it.[63] The materials existed for a protracted attack on Grenville but Newcastle, partly to please Cumberland, relaxed his pressure on the ministry. He had laid no plans for a long campaign and he had nothing in reserve with which he might have followed up his challenge to the ministry on General Warrants. He well knew that the success of the Opposition depended upon its ability to find another issue on which to attack the ministry. He suggested that Grenville's budget and American policy might be contested but he was unable to persuade his friends to agree.[64] And to be fair to Newcastle, the death of his old friend and mentor, Lord Hardwicke, on 7 March left the Duke without the political support of a life-time and he became pessimistic and lethargic.

At the same time, there were more promising straws in the wind. The death of Hardwicke, in fact, was a significant indication that the old order was passing. Moreover, William Pitt was on the point of abandoning anything like a regular attendance in Parliament. He was disillusioned, gloomy at his prospects of returning to office, unwilling to commit himself to systematic opposition: 'let George Granville do right, He would support him'.[65] The weakening of the power of the old guard and the decline of Pitt left the field of opposition open to the friends of Newcastle and promised to end their infatuation with Pitt.

Already in the session of 1763–4 the Opposition had come near to overthrowing Grenville's ministry while the size of Newcastle's party had continued to grow.[66] These positive and practical aspects of the achievement of the Newcastle Whigs in the session were paralleled by a profound conviction of the righteousness of their cause. This was best expressed in Temple's pamphlet, *A Letter from Albemarle Street to the Cocoa Tree.* The *Letter* was not only an attack upon the ministry for its use of General Warrants but a general statement of the Opposition's hostility to Bute and an expression of its belief that since the beginning of the reign the Court had adopted a policy destructive of the liberties of Englishmen. Temple refuted the charge that the Opposition was motivated purely by faction,[67] and claimed that the Opposition wished not merely to remove Grenville but to establish a different system of politics. These ideas received a wide circulation and were coming to be accepted even outside the confines of the Newcastle party.

What grounds now existed for the widespread belief in the continuing influence of Lord Bute? Although Bute went to Harrogate when the Grenville ministry had been installed it soon became apparent that the Opposition's conviction of his continuing influence with the King was shared by those best qualified to judge, by Grenville and by Egremont. Indeed, George III had always had every intention of keeping up his intimacy with Bute. Mr Brook has pronounced: 'If ever King George III can be accused of behaving in an unconstitutional manner it is during the first few months of the Grenville ministry'.[68] The King had freely chosen George Grenville as his First Minister but he chose to place his confidence in Bute, even allowing him when he returned from Harrogate on 1 June 1763, to meddle in politics. (Bute was, of course, behind the approaches made to Hardwicke and Pitt in August.)[69] No wonder Grenville complained of the King's 'want of confidence and communication, the evident marks of that superior influence to which it is owing'.[70] After the failure of the negotiations, Grenville demanded as a condition of remaining at his post that Bute's political influence should cease. The King obligingly assured him that 'Lord Bute wished to retire absolutely from all business whatever'.[71] That retirement began formally on 5 October 1763 when Bute was banished to Luton Hoo where he remained until the following March.

It was unfortunate for both men and for the country that during this period neither man learned to understand the other, the King to appreciate Grenville's sense of insecurity and Grenville the King's fear of being dominated and dictated to. The minister's suspicion of Bute's continuing influence with the King[72] together with endemic patronage disputes ruined his relationship with George III.[73] The King, of course, thought himself perfectly entitled to take counsel of anyone he chose but it is not clear that he was justified in allowing his relationship with Bute to go far towards weakening the authority of a First Minister whom the King had freely chosen. Of course, Newcastle and his friends wildly exaggerated the extent of Bute's influence[74] but there was a kernel of truth in what they were saying for Bute *did* have influence with the King. His situation *was* anomalous, unsettling and unnecessary. The friends of Newcastle undoubtedly exaggerated Bute's power and misread the intentions of the Court but they had grasped a real political issue when they protested against the system of government by favourite.

It was not in the least surprising, then, if Newcastle and his friends should ascribe to Bute's influence a provocative act hostile to the Opposition. Conway's dismissal from his regiment for voting against General Warrants became the most important *cause célèbré* of the year.[75] If soldiers were to be punished in this way for their political conduct then who in public life could afford ever to question the judgement of the Court and the policy of the ministers? The Newcastle Whigs at once blamed Bute for this action as they had blamed him for the political setbacks they had experienced since the winter of 1762–3. The 'Bute Myth' was unfolding. In 1762 Bute had tried to destroy the Whigs and had succeeded Newcastle at the Treasury. In

1763 he had become the Minister behind the Curtain. In 1764 he had apparently begun to use the influence of a young and gullible king to subvert the ministry and to attempt to silence opposition to the Court.

Newcastle bewailed the sinister influence of Lord Bute but he could think of no plan which might in the medium or long term strengthen the Opposition. Charles Townshend, however, suggested a two-fold plan. First, he recognised that the Newcastle party alone was too weak to reduce the influence of the favourite and that it had not proved possible to negotiate an alliance with Pitt. Townshend advocated, therefore, an alliance with either Temple or with Lord Holland or, even with Bute. He believed that if they were to remain in Opposition the Newcastle Whigs could achieve nothing. They must use every means available to them to force themselves into office and thus put themselves in a situation in which they could achieve their ends. Second, Townshend suggested an ambitious measure of political organisation to enable the Newcastle party to become a more effective political force. There would be a party newspaper, a party secretariat in London and a network of clubs in the towns and in the counties. The whole would be presided over not by a group of languid aristocrats but by a committee which would, for one thing, keep the party alive in the summer.[76] This was too much for the party grandees. Alliance with Bute, the diminution of the political influence of the old Whigs, an appeal to public opinion—all of this was completely unacceptable to them.[77] Townshend's schemes were far more radical than anything the 'Young Friends' had ever dreamed of and they were decisively rejected.[78]

The rejection of Townshend's interesting scheme could not silence the mutterings of dissent and dissatisfaction. The Second Lord Hardwicke had only just succeeded his father when he began to speak of the hopelessness of Opposition, the impossibility of breaking up the ministry and the need to make overtures to Bute, or at least, to Bedford.[79] Even the loyal Henry Bilston Legge, a few months before he died, warned Newcastle that unless a more decided opposition line were forthcoming 'the patience of the public will be worn out and we shall grow contemptible and unpopular'.[80] Newcastle's suggestion that there ought to be a meeting at Wildmans before the opening of the next session, however, was hopelessly insufficient to satisfy the young men of the party. One incident in particular infuriated them. Newcastle furthered the nomination of Dr George Hay to the office of Dean of the Arches, a ministerialist, a Lord of the Admiralty and a Member of Parliament who had supported the use of General Warrants in the February debates. This Newcastle did simply to please Charles Yorke, a friend of Hay's. To the young men, however, Newcastle's renewed attempts to conciliate Yorke and his family were as irrelevant and as fruitless now as they had proved themselves to be in the past. To extricate himself from these complex problems Newcastle, yet again, turned to Pitt for if, at least, his co-operation could be obtained then Newcastle would simultaneously reinvigorate his connection and compose the divisions within it.

Time after time Pitt had made it clear to Newcastle that no lasting alliance could be negotiated between them, although they might co-operate in Parliament when their opinions coincided. In June, for example, Pitt explained: 'That all Opposition was to no Purpose; that for one, He never would force Himself upon the King; That however, He would oppose all Measures he thought was wrong.'[81] As late as October the tireless Newcastle was still hoping that Pitt would join him in the coming session of Parliament. Pitt had to make it clear to Newcastle once and for all that he had 'no disposition to quit the free condition of a man standing single . . . under the obligation of Principles'. He intended to attend Parliament when an issue arose upon which he could give a free and honest opinion, appealing to the nation and not to a party to recognise 'the Soundness of his Principles and the rectitude of his Conduct'.[82] The political strategy which the Duke of Newcastle had pursued for two years was now seen to have failed absolutely. It may have been as well for Newcastle that it was so. For few of his friends now shared his enthusiasm for a coalition with Pitt. Rockingham had never been keen on the idea, had never accepted the assumption that Opposition could only succeed with Pitt's assistance and he believed that the Newcastle party would have greater freedom of action if it acted independently.[83]

Cumberland, and even Grafton, one of the original 'Young Friends', believed that a coalition with Pitt would alienate the supporters of their party.[84]

The blows were now beginning to rain upon Newcastle. Just a few weeks after Pitt's abrupt note shattered his political dreams Charles Yorke entered the ministry as Master of the Rolls.[85] As if this were not enough, Charles Townshend also declared formally his independence of Newcastle's party.[86] These political disappointments came on top of a series of personal tragedies. The loss of Hardwicke in the spring had been a great blow to him, his own health was poor and that of the Duchess in the summer gave grounds for alarm. Then, in August, his old friend Legge died. The final blow was the death of the Duke of Devonshire in October.[87] This was all too much for Newcastle. His political ambitions lay in ruins and his private life left him lonely, broken-hearted and incapable of shouldering public responsibilities. Except for a few weeks at the beginning of the First Rockingham Ministry he was never the same again. Personally and politically he was no longer fit to lead his followers.

The 'Young Friends' rushed to fill the vacuum of leadership left by Newcastle's incapacity. The new parliamentary session opened on 10 January 1765. By then they had, without reference to Newcastle, determined to adopt a systematic opposition for the session no matter what Pitt's opinions were.[88] Newcastle was quite unable to stop them. In December and January, Wildmans revived as the focal centre of the Opposition.[89] Attendance notes were sent out from its premises and plans for regular meetings and for effective communication for the session were decided there.[90] The great plan of the young men at Wildmans was to revise the issue of General Warrants early in the session. The fact that Pitt was absent did not trouble them. On 29 January 1765 Sir William Meredith moved that General Warrants were illegal and he was supported by the 'Young Friends'. The motion was lost by 224–185.[91] The ministry appeared to be vulnerable on the issue but it would be difficult for the young men to reduce Grenville's majority much further.

Although they had captured the Opposition, the 'Young

Friends' found that the problems of leadership were unexpectedly complex. After their defeat on General Warrants, indeed, some of them began to look longingly towards none other than Pitt for assistance! They decided to await his arrival in town before raising the other issue which they intended to bring forward during the session, the dismissal of Conway. The early weeks of the session were thus quiet and uncontentious. On Grenville's Stamp Act there was little discussion. In British parliamentary circles at this time there was near unanimity over the right of the imperial Parliament to lay taxes upon the colonies and, unlike the questions relating to Wilkes and Conway, America was not a party—indeed, it was hardly a political—issue at this time. There were some differences of opinion in commercial circles over the Stamp Act but these were not reflected in the world of politics.[92] There was little opposition to Grenville's budget and only a clause in the Mutiny Bill permitting private quartering roused the Opposition.[93] Newcastle and Rockingham continued to hope that if Pitt came to town then the Opposition would find the inspiration which the 'Young Friends', for all their enthusiasm, could not arouse. Rockingham swallowed his former opinions and went to see him at Hayes to discover his opinion on Conway's dismissal. Pitt was as unhelpful as ever. Rockingham found him resolved on 'determined inactivity'.[94] Horace Walpole sarcastically put it: 'Mr Pitt, whom we begin to know only by tradition, was lai'd up with gout; so he is still, which postpones any further questions from the Opposition'.[95]

When Parliament recessed for the Easter holidays on 4 April 1765 there could be no disguising the fact that George Grenville appeared to be in an impregnable position. The Newcastle Whigs were too weak to bring him down alone and their obsessional hatred of Bute's influence rendered them unacceptable to George III. Pitt treated them with undisguised contempt and withering indifference. The future political prospects of the Newcastle Whigs seemed bleak and gloomy. And then, suddenly, an unexpected series of astonishing changes utterly transformed the political scene. Nobody in British politics would in early April have believed that within three months the Grenville ministry would lie in ruins, that a ministry of the

Newcastle Whigs, without Pitt—a possibility that had scarcely even been contemplated by the friends of Newcastle—would have replaced it, that Newcastle would have found himself relegated to playing a secondary role within the ministry and that he would have surrendered his pre-eminence in his own connection to the Marquis of Rockingham.

Part Two

OFFICE
1765–6

Chapter 4

The Formation of the First Rockingham Administration

The sequence of events which led to the establishment of the first Rockingham ministry had its origin in the illness suffered by the King which incapacitated him from the normal routine of public business from 25 February to 10 March 1765. The illness was not serious, but it alarmed the King who decided to make arrangements for the government of the country in the event of his death. His very natural desire to make some provision for the Regency brought up the whole question of the succession. From George III's sense of responsibility, then, arose what is known to history as the Regency Crisis of 1765, a confusing and complicated affair in which the motives of participants were either unstated, misunderstood or misrepresented. If the pieces of this puzzling jig-saw are to be fitted together it is absolutely necessary to understand the motives of George III and to be clear that he hoped to achieve a dual objective. His preoccupation with the succession may have been uppermost in his mind but he also wished to use the crisis to rid himself of the unbearable Grenville.

The most authoritative historian of the Regency Crisis is inclined to accept the sincerity and the good faith of George III.[1] He did not wish to bequeath a legacy of partisanship and bitterness to his people and he may, perhaps, have dreamed of reconciling the old Whigs, led by Newcastle and Cumberland, to the Court, to Princess Augusta (the King's mother) and to Bute.[2] More immediately, he sought to regulate the succession by means of a Regency Bill. In early April he instructed an astonished Grenville to prepare a Regency bill reserving the choice of Regent to the King, a bill, moreover, which George III wanted passed into law before the end of the present session of Parliament. Why did George III wish to reserve to himself the nomination of the name of the Regent? And why did he feel such a sense of urgency? His reserving the name of the Regent went far towards creating suspicion and mistrust of his motives among men as far apart as George Grenville and Horace Walpole. Yet to have named a Regent would have provoked divisions and dissensions among the royal family, exactly the sort of divisions and dissensions which had made George III's life as a boy such a misery. To have nominated the Queen, the obvious candidate, would have been the most straightforward course of action but she was not yet of age and, as Mr Brooke points out, the Duke of York, the King's brother, 'stood in 1765 precisely where the Duke of Cumberland stood in 1751—the nearest adult male in succession to the throne'.[3] To have named a Regent, then, would have divided the royal family, something which throughout his life King George III attempted to avoid. Furthermore, there was nothing sinister in his desire for haste in securing the passage of the Regency Bill through Parliament. He feared a recurrence of his illness. He wanted the matter settled quickly while it was on his mind and there was plenty of time left in the session. At the same time he decided to take this opportunity of ridding himself of his present ministers and to this end he sought the assistance of the Duke of Cumberland. The *raison d'être* of the Grenville ministry had, of course, been that it kept at bay the Newcastle–Cumberland party. Now that the King wished to reconcile that party to the Court, George Grenville became redundant. After an initial reconciliation between the King and Cumberland on 7 April negotiations for a change of ministry proceeded.[4] Meanwhile, the ministers were preparing a Regency Bill while the King allowed himself to indulge his spiteful hatred of his minister. He treated him with undisguised contempt and kept him ignorant of his plans.[5]

What were the reactions of Newcastle and his friends to these curious proceedings which within a few weeks had transformed the political situation? It is essential to realise that although Cumberland was in the confidence of the King he and Newcastle did not inform Newcastle's followers of the King's private motives until the middle of May,[6] that is, *after* the Regency Bill had passed through both Houses. Although it may have been necessary for the King to maintain secrecy in order to rid himself of his minister, that same secrecy caused the friends of Newcastle to misunderstand and completely to misjudge what was happening. The surprising speed with which the Regency bill was produced and rushed through Parliament, the reserving to the King the naming of a Regent, and, later, the sudden search for a new ministry could only have one explanation, that Lord Bute and his sinister friends were at work again. In particular, the withholding of the name of the Regent suggested strongly that the King would nominate his mother, Princess Augusta, and by doing so perpetuate Bute's evil influence. Initially, therefore, some of Newcastle's supporters were prepared to join in the opposition to some of the bill's more disquieting features. At a dinner at Newcastle's London residence on 25 April, Newcastle and the 'Young Friends' proposed to name the Queen as Regent and also to insert the names of the three royal Princes as Councillors.[7]

Newcastle and his party had thus committed themselves to opposing the Regency Bill and the policy of the King, a policy of which they might well have become the beneficiaries. They performed unimpressively during the debates as they failed either to co-operate with other groups or to grasp the basic realities of the situation. Opposition to the bill first manifested itself in the Lords on second reading on 30 April when Lord Lyttleton, a friend of Pitt, asserted that reserving to the King the right of nominating the Regent was unconstitutional because it derogated from the status of Parliament and undermined its function of advising the King. Although he was supported by Newcastle, Grafton, Shelburne and Temple the motion was lost by the derisory figures of 120–9, partly because Newcastle and his friends left the House before the division was taken.[8] On the following day a similar motion received rather

D

better support (89–31) when the Duke decided to remain in
the House.[9] This, of course, only encouraged further opposition
to the bill. To the fury of the King, the Duke of Richmond on
both 1 and 2 May demanded to know whether the Princess
Dowager was eligible for the Regency. Now the King had no
intention of naming his mother to the Regency. This had never
been in his mind and it appeared to him that Richmond and
the young bloods in the Lords were attempting both to stir up
trouble in the royal family and to raise unnecessary public
discussion of the Princess Dowager's public status. Richmond's
question required a judicial pronouncement, however, and on
3 May the judges reported that the Princess Dowager *was*
eligible to act as Regent. The Lords thereupon added a clause
excluding her. When George III realised the offensive construction which might be placed upon this amendment and the
personal distress it might occasion his mother he instructed
Grenville to reinsert the Princess Dowager's name when the bill
went down to the Commons.[10] It was Cumberland's wish, that
Newcastle's followers in the Lower House should neither vote
nor speak. Newcastle was prepared to allow a more rigorous
opposition in the Lower House—and one which would be less
embarrassing to himself—but the attendance was low, the
dignity of the throne at issue and thus the minority division
figure rarely climbed above forty, a total which included
Tories and Independents. It was only when his 'Young Friends'
took matters into their own hands that opposition to the Court
appeared to revive slightly. In spite of their efforts, a motion to
name the Queen as Regent had been rejected by the House on
9 May. An attempt by the Opposition to reverse this decision
on the following day was defeated by 258–67.[11] The bill easily
passed through its remaining stages in the Commons. In spite,
therefore, of the paltry opposition offered by the friends of
Newcastle, the first stage of the King's plans had been successfully accomplished.

The King now had a Regency Bill which reserved to him the
sole right of nominating to the Regency Council without further
reference to Parliament. It remained to complete his plan by
removing Grenville and substituting for him a ministry including friends of Bute and Cumberland. George III was willing to

forgive the Newcastle Whigs for their opposition to the bill because the ministers had blundered in the House of Lords and allowed himself and his mother to be embarrassed. The King wanted more than ever to be rid of Grenville. This ought not to have been a very difficult problem but the King had his own ideas on how a new ministry ought to be constituted. On 14 May Cumberland was able to talk with Newcastle about the outlines of a new ministry. Northumberland, whose son had married a daughter of Bute, was to have the Treasury, Pitt and Charles Townshend were to be the two Secretaries, Newcastle and Temple were to have the offices of Privy Seal and Lord President of the Council between them while Egmont was to have the Admiralty.[12] Much of this was unobjectionable but the nomination of Northumberland to the Treasury was not. Although the King may have regarded Northumberland's occupancy of the Treasury as a necessary means of self-protection he reluctantly dropped his insistence on the point 'when it was shewn to him to be inconsistent that so near a relation of Lord Bute should hold so great a post of business'.[13]

This was not the only drawback to this 'Butal–Ducal' arrangement.[14] Pitt, as always, was a problem. He, or rather, his friends had recently demonstrated their independence of mind by opposing the Regency Bill in both Houses. He had his own conditions to impose before he would agree to serve in a new ministry. He demanded the restoration to their places of those dismissed for their votes on General Warrants. He demanded promotion for Pratt, guarantees on the future use of General Warrants, amendments to the Cider Tax, and, inevitably, the revival of the Prussian alliance.[15] These were very substantial demands indeed. As in the summer of 1763, however, Pitt may not have entertained serious expectations of taking office at this time, and while willing to discuss his terms and make his position clear to the King it is doubtful if Pitt felt that this was the time for him to come into office again. For one thing, he disliked the intervention of Cumberland in the negotiations between himself and the King. Relations between Pitt and Cumberland had never been cordial and Pitt's distaste for the Duke's militaristic propensities was exaggerated by the prominent role played by Cumberland in putting down the

silk riots of May 1765, a fortuitous event which revived fears in
many quarters of his military reputation. By a curious twist of
fate, none other than Northumberland happened to be Lord
Lieutenant of Middlesex and thus he, too, took some part in the
suppression of the riots.[16] Pitt was not merely suspicious of a
reviving militarism in court circles. Neither he nor Temple
could even begin to understand why the King wished to remove
Grenville. The ministry stood in no danger of losing its parliamentary majority. Lord Frederick Cavendish may not have
been far from the truth when he observed that Pitt 'drew a
conclusion from the situation of the present ministers, that if
they were turned out for no other reason than supporting the
measures they advised, it *augured* ill for him, and therefore he
must know why they were turned out'.[17] As the Court's desperation for an agreement with Pitt grew, so did the liberality of its
offers to him. Indeed, on 20 May Cumberland, with the inevitable uniformed military guard, visited Pitt at Hayes, informed
him that the King accepted his conditions and offered him
something approaching *carte blanche* in appointments. Pitt was
uneasy, feeling in his bones that something was wrong, and
therefore extricated himself from the negotiation.[18] There was
little prospect of him coming into office during May, therefore,
and such prospects as there may have been were finally shattered
by the news of the reconciliation between Temple and Grenville
on 22 May. Temple, and thus Pitt, would be unlikely to scheme
to bring down George Grenville now. The negotiation was at an
end. The second part of the King's plan had utterly failed.
Cumberland persuaded the King to send for Grenville and,
wearily, George III submitted to his demands.[19]

Grenville was in good, if mistaken, company in believing that
the recent, mysterious events had their origin in the circle
around Bute. It was inevitable, then, that he should impose
upon the King stringent conditions for continuing in office and
he was in a sufficiently strong position to force George III to
agree to them. The King had to promise that Bute would be
banished from politics and to agree to important office changes.
Thus the King was forced to accept the dismissal of Lord
Holland from the Pay-Office, of Stuart Mackenzie from the
Scottish Privy Seal (and control of Scottish patronage) and the

immediate replacement of Northumberland as Lord Lieutenant of Ireland by Lord Weymouth. The only change which Grenville was unable to force upon the King was the replacement of Cumberland as Captain General by the Marquis of Granby.[20] The King had lost the final battle but he could rest reasonably content with his achievements. The Regency was provided for,[21] the schism in the royal family had been healed, Pitt had been sounded and the hostility of the Newcastle Whigs neutralised. Although he had failed to rid himself of Grenville at least George III had ensured that something had been done to lay the ground for the future accomplishment of that objective. For his part, too, Grenville had cause for congratulation. He had retained his self-respect, he had defeated Pitt, Cumberland, Newcastle, the King, and, he imagined, Bute.[22]

The Regency Crisis of 1765 has a profound significance in the history of the Newcastle Whigs even though they had only played a secondary role in it. It is clear that the King expected Newcastle and Rockingham to take positions in his projected ministry subordinate to those of Pitt and Temple. Neither Newcastle nor Rockingham uttered a word of protest at this prospect.[23] They quietly accepted the superior claims of Pitt and Temple to leading positions in the new ministry. Their attitude is caught by Newcastle in the lists of probable office-holders which, inevitably, he painstakingly began to compile during the Regency Crisis once he had begun to smell the scent of office. Not only was he prepared to defer to Pitt but *he was even prepared to allow the Buteite Northumberland to take the Treasury.*[24] Newcastle and his friends constantly affirm that Pitt's participation was necessary to the successful negotiation of a new arrangement. No doubt they looked to Pitt to guard against Bute's influence in the closet. Furthermore, Newcastle shrank from laying names before the King. He accepted the negotiating role of Cumberland and believed that between them, the Duke, Pitt and Newcastle, could work out a general arrangement satisfactory to everybody which could then be placed before the King.[25] Newcastle's lists show how far he was prepared to go in conceding to Pitt and his friends the right to the major offices. Temple might take the Treasury, Pitt and Charles Townshend were to be the secretaries, Pratt might receive a peerage, Charles Yorke the office of Attorney-General and Rockingham, amusingly, the Chamberlain's staff. The Newcastle Whigs were willing to defer to Pitt but they were prepared to treat Bute very much as George Grenville did in May. Bute was to have nothing to do 'directly or indirectly, in the conduct of the Administration, and in the management of publick affairs'. Indeed, 'some persons known to depend entirely upon my Lord Bute' must be excluded from office, including Stuart Mackenzie.[26] These, he assumed, were also the sentiments of Pitt. In general, then, Newcastle must have been greatly encouraged by the political situation after the Regency Crisis. His party was in safe hands, those of Cumberland and himself, rather than those of the young men. Although the ascendancy of Cumberland in the party ('Cumberland House is the great place now')[27] was likely to offend Pitt, the King was beginning to look more kindly upon Newcastle's party than he had hitherto done ('worthy men . . . who have principles and therefore cannot approve of seeing the Crown dictated to by low men').[28] But it is important to remember the King's own priorities. He would have best preferred a ministry formed of 'the few persons that have zealously stood by me'.[29] If that were to prove impossible then his next preference would have been for a ministry led by Pitt, perhaps supported by Newcastle and his friends. The prospect of a ministry led by Newcastle and his friends, if it ever occurred to George III, must have come a poor third in his list of priorities. Indeed, the King looked upon the Newcastle Whigs with some slight favour less because of their 'principles' than because they might be useful to him in his burning quest to rid himself of the hated Grenville.

Nobody expected that Grenville's ministry could survive the Regency Crisis for long. His relationship with the King had deteriorated to such an extent that the normal routine of business could scarcely continue.[30] Most observers assumed that it was only a matter of time before Pitt replaced Grenville. After the failure of the negotiations with Pitt in May the King had, in fact, tried in vain to form a ministry without Pitt led by Lord Lyttleton at the Treasury and Charles Townshend at the Exchequer and including the friends of Bute as well as 'the

Duke of Newcastle's party'.[31] But neither Lyttleton nor Townshend would serve unless Pitt and Temple joined the ministry and, in view of Temple's reconciliation with Grenville, there was no prospect of them doing so.[32] Newcastle heard of these overtures. There is nothing to suggest that Newcastle would have refused to enter such a ministry, a ministry, it may be said, which would be little more than a stop-gap for Pitt and whose only *raison d'être* would have been the King's hatred of Grenville. Its ephemeral existence, moreover, could presumably have been terminated by the King whenever he wished. For the moment, however, George III had, perforce, to receive back into his closet the autocratic devil whom he utterly detested. His only escape lay in direct negotiation with Pitt. This he was unwilling to concede not because he had any qualms about going behind the backs of his ministers— George III never hesitated to resort to that strategy whenever it suited him—but because he believed that the honour of the Crown might be sullied if a further negotiation with Pitt came to nothing.[33]

Further negotiations between the King and Pitt became virtually inevitable, however, when the tension between the ministers and the King sharpened to breaking point. On 12 June the Duke of Bedford sought and received an audience of the King at which he accused him of befriending enemies of the administration and chastised him for allowing Bute to interfere in politics. In no uncertain terms Bedford told him either 'to permit his authority and his favour and countenance to go together' or 'to transfer to others that authority'.[34] The King was unwilling to do the former and thus he chose to do the latter. Through Cumberland he ascertained that the opinions of Newcastle's friends remained unchanged. They would still welcome the opportunity of delivering the King from George Grenville but Pitt must first be sounded.[35] Cumberland saw that the King must swallow his dislike for personal confrontations and grant Pitt an audience. This, at least, would remove one barrier which had stood in the way of Pitt co-operating with the King, his distaste of Cumberland. Pitt, in fact, insisted upon a personal meeting with the King. Reluctantly George III agreed.[36]

On 19 June there occurred the first of two famous interviews between Pitt and his King. That the King regarded the interview as an event of the highest importance is attested by the fact that he prepared in considerable detail what he wished to say to Pitt. According to his notes[37] the King wished to 'heal all jealousys' and to that end Pitt might satisfy any suspicions he might entertain against the King's friends by taking them under his own wing, to lead and to discipline them as he thought fit. The King pledged his support for Pitt, made professions of friendship for him and assured him (untruthfully) that for the last two years Lord Bute 'has been earnestly wishing these Two years to see You the Minister of this Country'. For his part, Pitt must accept the modest terms which the King laid down. These amounted to Pitt accepting Northington as Lord Chancellor 'who will soon indeed think of retreat' (a proviso which promised an early opportunity for Pitt to bestow the Great Seals upon Pratt) and to the reinstatement of Stuart Mackenzie. The King told Pitt: 'You can name no Whig familys that shall not have my Countenance; but where Torys come to me on Whig principles let us take them'. This was what the King meant by the phrase 'heal all jealousys', that politicians should support himself and Pitt, forget their political differences (with him as well as with each other) and accept his conditions respecting MacKenzie. Charles Yorke was not far wide of the mark when he described the King's ambition as attempting 'to restore the Harmony of the beginning of this Reign, to restore Popularity and consequently Peace to the King and his Favourite'.[38] Indeed, much of this chimed in well with Pitt's own views. He did not share the fears of men like Newcastle and Grenville that Bute was still a power behind the throne and he agreed with the King that parties must be broken. At the interview on 19 June, therefore, Pitt spoke more of measures than of men, assuming that few if any difficulties existed in that area. He agreed to the continuation of Northington in office and to the reinstatement of Mackenzie. In return, George III agreed to Temple taking the Treasury and Newcastle the Privy Seal. All seemed set fair for an accord between the two men, the King's only worry concerned Pitt's vision of a Northern alliance against the Bourbon powers.[39]

His worries were perhaps mitigated by Pitt's willingness to accept Stuart Mackenzie in a prestigious office. On 22 June they met a second time. Pitt insisted that if the King accepted his foreign policy then he would attempt to form an administration. The King agreed and although the details of offices had not yet been worked out both Pitt and the King appeared optimistic that an agreement was at hand.

At the eleventh hour and with almost no forewarning these agreements and understandings were dashed to pieces. Temple refused to have anything to do with them. On 24 June he visited Pitt at Hayes to tell him so. On the following day he told the King of his refusal. This had been unexpected but what happened next was sensational. On 26 June William Pitt informed the King that without Temple in the Cabinet, he could not serve him.[40] The political situation had been plunged into greater confusion than at any time since the beginning of the reign. These events are, even now, enveloped in a shroud of mystery. Why did Temple refuse to co-operate with the King and with Pitt? More difficult still to understand is why Pitt found Temple's refusal a sufficient reason for him to withdraw his services.

These questions are of considerable importance because it was Temple's refusal to serve the King which made the first Rockingham ministry possible. Temple told George Grenville that two motives swayed him.[41] First he believed that the House of Commons would be difficult to manage from the Lords, especially when Pitt's ill-health made his regular attendance in the Lower House impossible. It is, no doubt, true that the leader of a successful ministry in the eighteenth century usually sat in the Commons but it was precipitate, to say the least, for Temple to decide that the Commons was too difficult to manage when he did not even know who was to be in the Cabinet and did not know who was to be *the Leader of the Commons*. His second motive was, ostensibly, a private reason of a 'tender and delicate nature'. Historians have speculated for two centuries on what this obstacle may have been. One possibility is that the recent reconciliation between Temple and Grenville may have left him reluctant to scramble into office over the ruins of his brother's ministry. (It is interesting that both before and after his interview with the King on 25 June Temple was with Grenville, the First Lord of the Treasury and surely the most interested spectator of these proceedings.) This, no doubt, counted for something, but what drove Temple more than anything else into open mutiny against his brother-in-law was, quite simply, Pitt's high-handed treatment of him. Pitt's tactless and inconsiderate behaviour aroused resentment and jealousy on the part of Temple. So far as can be discovered, Temple had shown remarkably little interest in the conversations between Pitt and the King. He had even ignored an urgent appeal to come to town sent, not by Pitt, of course, but by James Grenville.[42] The reason for this may have been that he had taken umbrage because Cumberland had not thought fit to summon him to take part in them (as he had done a month earlier). Surprisingly, Pitt did not even seek Temple's consent to what he was doing on his brother-in-law's behalf until after the second interview with the King. He had not thought fit to keep the future First Lord of the Treasury informed of the possibility that there might exist an administration for him to lead. Grafton had every reason to suspect that Temple might prove difficult.[43] Well might the proud and touchy Temple refuse to tolerate his brother-in-law's effrontery and thoughtlessness. As the events of July 1766 were again to illustrate, Temple was unwilling to be a cipher in an administration dominated by Pitt. Although Pitt would receive the honour of leadership and enjoy a close personal relationship with the King, others would be left to take responsibility and to bear the burdens of routine administration. Finally, ever since his involvement in the Wilkes case Temple had been one of those members of the Opposition who were almost hysterically obsessed with the influence of Bute. Temple might well have been amazed at Pitt's seeming generosity to the friends of Bute. As George Grenville wryly noted: 'almost all Lord Bute's friends were to have been continued in their employments'.[44] Temple's refusal to take part, then, arose from a recent and rapidly growing antipathy towards his brother-in-law, which the events of mid-June had apparently confirmed and strengthened.

Pitt's refusal to launch his administration without Temple at the helm is rather more difficult to fathom. There can be no doubt that Temple's blank refusal was a bitter and unexpected blow to him and his pride.[45] Without Temple, he confessed, he would 'not have one person, whom he could trust to convey to His Majesty his thoughts upon any occasion'.[46] Pitt may well have been guilty of some overstatement but it may have been the case that if he took office without Temple he might have found himself dependent, in the Lords as well as the Commons, upon the friends of Cumberland and Newcastle, men he had for years distrusted. Furthermore he well knew that his own ill-health might prevent his own regular attendance in the Lower House. He was not worried if the 'Young Friends' were closer to him on certain issues than they were to Newcastle. He held them in scant regard for they were unreliable and inexperienced and in 1765 they had not been particularly active as a group.[47] He may have felt that for one of his advancing years and ill-health it would have been difficult to take a leading day-to-day role in a ministry, many of whose members were likely to annoy the King by their obsessional hatred of Bute. To the opposition of the Grenville and the Bedford Whigs, then, might be added the hostility of Bute and his friends. These were not the conditions in which Pitt wanted to assume political responsibility. It was, in his eyes, much too risky an undertaking. Newcastle and Rockingham, much less perceptive and more inclined to rush into the King's service, failed to understand the weaknesses of their situation. Pitt's policy of 'safety first' was the most sensible approach to adopt in the circumstances.

The King by this time was desperate to rid himself of the Grenville ministry. On two occasions, in May and now in June, his attempts to do so had been frustrated not by Grenville himself but by the inability of other politicians to agree among themselves. On this occassion, however, there was a crucial difference. George Grenville had now no wish to continue in office. He had left town in the middle of June for ten days and showed himself indifferent to the urgent letters from his friends begging him to come to town to attempt to save his collapsing ministry.[48] At last, the King was free of Grenville but who was to take his place? Between 26 and 28 June the King was hesitant and uncertain about the few alternatives that remained open to him. He toyed with the idea of a ministry led by Egmont and including some friends of Bute.[49] To prevent the political catastrophe towards which George III appeared to be moving, the Duke of Cumberland brought the Newcastle Whigs into the front line. He interviewed its leaders and found them willing, if reluctant, to take office in the King's service.[50] On 28 June the King sent for Cumberland and begged him to form a ministry 'out of such as would serve him'.[51] Cumberland conveyed this message to Newcastle and the Whig lords, who decided to sound the entire leadership of the party to ascertain if they would agree to form a ministry.

The dinner that was held at Newcastle's London residence on 30 June is customarily, and rightly, held to be the crucial occasion on which the Newcastle Whigs decided to embark upon the uncertain life of ministerial office but because the first Rockingham ministry occupies such an important place in the history of the Newcastle-Rockingham party it is important to recognise that many of the *characteristics* of that ministry were already determined *before* 30 June. Newcastle had already decided to take a back seat, 'For my own part, I never will be a responsible Minister myself; or be in any responsible office whatever. Let those young men, and others, who may be found, take it; I will give them my assistance. . . .'[51] It was already evident that a ministry which hoped to avoid the active opposition of Pitt would have to follow his measures fairly closely. For Newcastle and his friends, however, this meant that their taking office was conditional upon the King's agreement to those terms. He must also agree 'to the removal of such persons as shall be necessary, to convince the world, that My Lord Bute has not the power to protect his friends. . . .'[52] Nevertheless, the important dinner witnessed a crucial vote of 12–6 in favour of taking office even though Pitt would not be in the Government.[53] As a condition of taking office Stuart Mac-Kenzie was to be sacrificed to the prejudices of the Newcastle party as were certain other friends of Bute, who would lose their offices as an indication of his complete eclipse.[54]

According to Newcastle, who saw Cumberland the next day, the existence of the dissident 'Young Friends' group at the meeting persuaded the latter to advise the King to break off the negotiations for an administration. Newcastle began to realise that if his friends wavered now, if Pitt refused to serve, and if the King refused to have Grenville, then there was no alternative but for the King 'to fling himself entirely into the hands of My Lord Bute, and the Tories'. The cessation of negotiations, in Newcastle's view, would mean 'an end of the Whig party, and all our poor suffering friends for ever'.[55] He still dreamed of reversing the results of the 'Massacre of the Pelhamite Innocents' and he begged Cumberland not to end the discussions. On 1 July, therefore, Cumberland advised the King to allow Newcastle's friends time to attempt to form an administration. On 10 July, although many minor offices were still to be disposed of, the new ministers kissed hands and received their seals of office. Against all expectations—not least those of the untried Marquis of Rockingham himself—the first Rockingham ministry was born and with it a new era in the life of the Newcastle-Rockingham Whigs.

Chapter 5

The First Rockingham Administration

The first Rockingham ministry did not, in the eyes of the watching political world, have a very auspicious beginning. Everyone knew that men were reluctant to serve even in the most senior positions of the new administration. Everyone recognised that the ministry rested upon a dangerously narrow foundation. Everyone saw that almost all of the established political figures of the day would not, or could not, be drawn in to support it. The new ministry faced the prospective opposition not only of Grenville and Bedford and their friends but also of Pitt and Temple. It was no wonder, then, that men could scarcely be found to fill vacant posts. In so far as the Rockingham–Newcastle connection had expected to take office in the summer of 1765 it had been as junior partners in a coalition led and dominated by Pitt. The leaders of the connection had never for one moment anticipated that they might be called upon to lead a Government whose members would be drawn substantially from among their own following. Time was thus needed and time was certainly taken by Newcastle and his friends in forming their ministry. But this delay, together with the accompanying vacillations, hesitations and interminable discussions, could not have made a very favourable impression upon the King. On 5 July, when Cumberland met Rockingham, Newcastle, Grafton, Conway and others at

Cumberland House, some of the major posts were still unfilled.[1] Cumberland saw that procrastination was dangerous to the reputation of his friends, and it was in response to his entreaties that the remaining cabinet offices were filled during the next few days. The formal kissing of hands took place on 10 July.

The most sensational of the new appointments was undoubtedly that of Rockingham to the Treasury and, in the long run, it was to prove the most significant. The leadership of the Newcastle party and the responsibility of leading the new ministry were now thrust into the hands of a young and inexperienced figure who had hitherto been a secondary figure in the opposition politics of the reign of George III. His sudden appearance on the political stage has always puzzled historians.[2] It is absolutely vital, therefore, if we are to understand the man, the ministry, his career and that of his party to consider his life up to 1765 and the manner and significance of his rise to power. During the reign of George II Rockingham had been a perfectly conventional politician but even before the old King was dead, three aspects of Rockingham's career tended to separate him from the ordinary run of aristocratic politicians.

First, he was a very rich man, even by the standards of his time and of his class.[3] Second, he was friendly to and much admired by the Pelhams.[4] Third, Rockingham had local political ambitions which were perhaps unusual in their scale even for a member of the English aristocracy. His first electoral venture was a disaster. He tried to intervene in a county seat in Yorkshire but suffered a humiliating reverse when a county meeting in July 1753 refused to accept his candidate, Sir George Savile.[5] Yet success attended his more modest exertions at York later in the same year. Although his father had never dared to intervene there, Rockingham effected the return of one member without putting the city to the inconvenience of a contest.[6] It was to consolidate his interest at York that the famous Rockingham Club was established later in the same year. It was thus not difficult for Rockingham to maintain his position in the city in the by-election of 1758. The fact that in the same year he was at last able to bring in Sir George Savile for the county consolidated both his power and his reputation.[7] In the general election of 1761 Rockingham took the second county seat despite objections that he was dominating the representation of the county.[8] But as Newcastle put it: 'Your Lordship's credit in the first and most considerable county in all the King's dominions seems now to be fixed beyond dispute'.[9]

Rockingham's 'credit' in Yorkshire, however, should not be measured simply by the number of members whose return he influenced. Rockingham's Yorkshire background injected an element of 'country' politics into the Pelhamite traditions of aristocratic Whiggery and service to the Court. There are, indeed, very good reasons for calling Rockingham a 'Country Whig'. It is significant that he attracted to him men like the independent Sir George Savile and the Tory, William Dowdeswell and, in the West Riding, at least, a large number of 'Whig Dissidents and Old Tories'.[10] This is *not* to argue that Rockingham obtained the support of *all* such men. Many of them were infatuated with Pitt and later rallied to the Yorkshire association. It is enough simply to appreciate 'the widely divergent standpoints and tendencies in politics over which Rockingham's mantle was thrown'.[11] The basis of the old Whiggery was being widened. Rockingham's monopoly of power in his Yorkshire kingdom enabled him to enjoy the support of dissident Whigs, Tories and Independents. Rockingham's Whiggery, then, was 'popular' in the sense that his electoral influence was based upon opinion as well as upon the ownership of boroughs and the deference of tenants.

In this manner, Rockingham's wealth, his connections with the Whig establishment and his influence as a Yorkshire magnate prepared him for the part he was later to play on the national stage. It should be said, at once, however, that this was more the intention of his friends than of the Marquis himself. Notwithstanding his local influence Murray told him, 'You are born, I hope, to figure in a larger and nobler sphere'.[12] But in 1753 this was not Rockingham's ambition and this was why he refused the entreaties of both Murray and Newcastle to move the address in the Lords at the beginning of the session of 1753–4.[13] Newcastle, who had been friendly with the first Marquis, was determined to allow nothing to come between himself and the rising star of Wentworth Woodhouse. The Duke's ministerial colleagues treated Rockingham with unusual delicacy[14] while Newcastle himself even refused to take umbrage at Rockingham's electoral incursions in the county of Yorkshire which went against the ministerial interest.[15] Despite the friendly gestures of Whig ministers Rockingham kept his distance, reinforcing his reputation for independence, disinterestedness and integrity. It is true that he supported Newcastle and Murray during the political crisis of 1756–7[16] but he declined a place in the King's household.[17] Newcastle wished to reward his young friend with a garter, much to the annoyance of Temple, who valued his own pretensions to the honour above those of Rockingham. More important, Pitt threw his weight behind Temple. Newcastle stood firm for a time but it was Temple who received his garter first, in November 1759, while Rockingham had to wait a little longer, until January 1760.[18] The incident, trivial though it was, showed that whatever the nature of Rockingham's 'independence', the Marquis thought himself to be closer, personally and politically, to the Newcastle rather than the Pitt wing of the Pitt–Newcastle coalition at the end of the reign of George II.

Events in the early months of the new reign threw Rockingham more decidedly into Newcastle's camp. An unimportant and almost farcical dispute in the Bedchamber[19] over procedure in August 1761 elicited Newcastle's support for the Marquis. 'If you was my son, I could not love you more than I do or be more solicitous that you should do everything for your own honour and credit.'[20] More important things were shortly to be at stake. Like Newcastle, Rockingham had not initially regarded Bute with unwarranted suspicion.[21] When George III had been on the throne only for a year, however, Rockingham had already begun to talk of the 'injustice and inhumanity' of the Bute system. It was natural that he should support Newcastle after his resignation in May 1762. For his part, Newcastle wished 'to act in the most perfect concert' with Rockingham.[22] 'I hope you will not forsake me, tho' many others do', he wrote in August.[23] Rockingham did not hesitate when the Duke of Devonshire was attacked by the Court later in the same year. He resigned all his offices and went into Opposition with the other Whig aristocrats. This, of course, he did partly from motives of friendship and Whig solidarity but there were at least two further considerations which help to explain his resignation. One was the increasing unpopularity of Bute in the country and especially in Yorkshire. As he told the King in no uncertain terms—'the alarm was general among his Majesty's affectionate subjects'.[24] More important, however, for Rockingham, the humiliation of Devonshire was not just an isolated incident in which one of his aristocratic friends had been slighted. Rockingham saw it as the culmination of a systematic attack by the Court upon the aristocracy, a scheme in which the elevation of Bute and the appointment of Fox to lead the Commons had been the essential preliminary steps. Rockingham complained to the King that 'those persons who had hitherto been always the most steadily attached to his royal predecessors and who had hitherto deservedly had the greatest weight in this country were driven out of any share in the Government and marked out rather as objects of His Majesty's displeasure than of his favour'.[25] In short, Rockingham adopted a typically Pelhamite attitude towards Bute and Fox at the end of 1762. He could not, and did not, accuse them of acting unconstitutionally. In adopting these views Rockingham was, no doubt, sincere but he was reflecting opinion in Yorkshire and, to a lesser extent, in the City of York. The general reaction in Rockingham's northern kingdom to the resignations and dismissals of the winter of 1762–3 reinforced his conviction that the natural leaders of the country were being set aside in the interests of a court favourite and that rank, station and virtue were being ignored in favour of obsequiousness to the Court.[26] The readiness of their friends and dependants to resign their offices in support of Devonshire and Rockingham alarmed the two Whig grandees, who advised their followers not to disrupt the administration of the country but to serve their new masters until the normal state of politics could be re-established.[27]

The parliamentary session of 1763 saw the consolidation of Rockingham's political importance on both the national and the local level. After the 'Massacre of the Pelhamite Innocents' he became the intimate friend and trusted confidant of both

Newcastle and Devonshire.[28] His growing importance was revealed by the fact that it was he who was sent to interview Pitt at the end of January 1763.[29] During the session he stayed in town and kept Newcastle informed of political affairs whenever the Duke was at Claremont and, at his request, relayed information and instructions to their friends. Although he joined in the round of dinners which was part of the social life of the Opposition it would be seriously incorrect, however tempting, to regard Rockingham as a 'Young Friend'. His youth and his popularity might lead one to include him in their number but he was never closely associated with them. He had not been of their original number in November–December 1762 and, for example, he had supported Newcastle's efforts to prevent the 'Young Friends' from going to extremes during the Wilkes affair.[30] Rockingham—and this was the vital fact about his political role in the first half of the 1760s—straddled both wings of the party of Newcastle. He was not only close to Newcastle, Cumberland and Devonshire but also friendly with Grafton, Baker and Onslow. Both wings would unite behind him, however, when the occasion required. The death of Lord Egremont in August 1763 created a vacancy among the Governors of Charterhouse. George Grenville, ever greedy for offices, wished to fill the vacancy himself whereupon his candidature was challenged by Rockingham. This symbolic struggle between Government and Opposition ended when Grenville found himself unable to obtain promises of a majority of votes and had to withdraw from the contest leaving Rockingham triumphant.[31] His growing importance was recognised when proposals for reconstructing the administration were proceeding in August 1763 and he was offered a cabinet post, the Admiralty.[32]

Rockingham was rapidly becoming an important voice in the counsels of the Newcastle party but he was not the sort of man to accept blindly the ideas of his seniors. The Marquis had never shared Newcastle's conviction that the first objective of their connection was to obtain the support of Pitt. Rockingham believed that to wait upon Pitt was both futile and unnecessary. Towards the end of the year he became sharply critical of Pitt's obdurate refusal to work with the friends of

Newcastle and the nauseating relish with which he dismissed
their gestures of friendship. Rockingham felt the sacrifice of
Charles Yorke to Pitt's whims to have been particularly unfortunate. Rockingham was learning more quickly than his
colleagues that their connection would find strength and
coherence less in dependence upon others, particularly the
unpredictable Pitt, than in dependence upon themselves,
independence of Pitt, and all-out war upon Bute and his
influence. He was the beneficiary of the failure of Newcastle's
plan to negotiate an alliance with Pitt. Once that failure
became apparent, Rockingham's suspicions of Pitt might be
seen as far-sighted statesmanship.

The decisive period of Rockingham's life was now approaching. In the session of 1764 he began to long for a more sustained
and a more vigorous Opposition, and on more than one occasion
he tried to galvanise Newcastle into life. But this was not the
season of Newcastle's activity. The beginnings of his political
decline were becoming visible as the friends of his political
generation left the political stage. The deaths of Hardwicke,
Legge and Devonshire in 1764 deprived Newcastle of trusted
friends and advisors and created something of a political
vacuum in the leadership of Newcastle's party. It is tempting,
as well as tidy, to conclude that Rockingham rushed to fill it.
He did nothing of the kind. During the months of Newcastle's
sorrows, Rockingham sought to console the old man rather than
to displace him from the leadership of his connection.[33] Nevertheless, the most striking characteristic of the opposition to
Grenville during that session was neither Newcastle's decline,
nor Rockingham's rise but Cumberland's emergence during
the Regency Crisis as the leader of Newcastle's connection. In
short, Cumberland and not Rockingham filled the political
vacuum which the deaths of Hardwicke, Legge and Devonshire
created. Cumberland acted as the focus of the unity of Newcastle's connection, acting as its spokesman in the closet,
counter-balancing the influence of Pitt and preventing the
'Young Friends' from assuming undue political influence.
Newcastle was glad to be deprived of the worrying responsibilities of party leadership and both during the Regency Crisis
and after, he deferred to Cumberland, almost completely

abdicating to him the leadership of his own connection.[34] Cumberland it was who negotiated with the King the first Rockingham ministry after the refusal of Pitt and Temple to take office. Given Newcastle's refusal to take the Treasury, there was only one obvious alternative choice, the Marquis of Rockingham. Thus was born the first Rockingham ministry and the party known to history as the Rockingham Whigs.

It was Rockingham's position rather than his talents which won him the Treasury. The only other feasible candidates were Charles Yorke and the Duke of Grafton. The former was an impossible choice because to place him at the Treasury would bring forth terrible wrath from Pitt. Moreover, Yorke's part in the Wilkes case weakened any pretensions he may have entertained to the leadership of the party which had fought the heroic fight against General Warrants. In any case, he had contributed little to the activities of the Opposition and had never settled down outside the ministry.[35] Grafton had been very active politically in 1763 but he had become so closely identified with the 'Young Friends' and then with Wilkes that he would have been unacceptable to many members of Newcastle's party as well as to the King. In any case, in the last year he had gone into something like political retirement while he consoled himself for political misfortune with his mistress.[36] Rockingham had several positive qualities which made him an acceptable candidate for the Treasury. He was on reasonably good terms with George III. He possessed the rank, the personal character and the dignity which the old Whigs preferred and he was popular with them. Having made very few political enemies he might reasonably hope to unite and to reconcile friends both young and old.

Rockingham succeeded directly, therefore, to the leadership of the followers of the Duke of Newcastle, a leadership which he was materially to confirm by the power and influence which was his to command at the Treasury. But Rockingham was not Newcastle and it is not surprising that within a few years of his succeeding to the party leadership the complexion of the party was changing but without at the same time, rejecting or discarding the cardinal precepts of the Pelhamite inheritance. The Rockingham party remained an aristocratic party, desirous of office, longing to serve and to liberate the King and to remove from his circle those who despised both the constitutional principles of the Glorious Revolution and the families which had safeguarded those principles since the Hanoverian Succession. As a Yorkshire magnate, however, Rockingham brought into the Newcastle party a sensitivity to opinion in the provinces and an appeal to the independent sort of gentry with whom Rockingham was popular in his native country and who were represented among his friends by Sir George Savile. In short, Rockingham maintained the essential qualities of Newcastle's party but he mixed 'country' elements into it and thus he broadened its base and its potential appeal by laying less emphasis upon its traditions of court Whiggery. This is not to say that Rockingham adopted any such objectives deliberately. There is no evidence that he *intended* to lead a party which was different in nature to that of Newcastle. There is no evidence, for example, that he did other than welcome the position which the Duke of Cumberland enjoyed within the Rockingham ministry. Nevertheless, Rockingham's leadership was to effect considerable changes which were, in July 1765, still in the future.

Rockingham was an attractive figure with many personal qualities—especially his integrity—but there is no reason to exaggerate the qualities of the man. His political and electoral achievements in Yorkshire had been remarkable but to reconcile local factions, to preserve family and proprietorial power, to dominate the representation of one county and a few boroughs was not the same thing as leading a party or running a government. The essential fact to remember about Rockingham in 1765 is that he lacked administrative experience. He was undoubtedly one of the least well qualified of all eighteenth century Prime Ministers. Almost as serious was the fact that, however rapid his rise to power had been, he had yet to demonstrate both competence in Government and application to business. The Marquis was, by nature, lethargic, preferring the turf to town, enjoying the leisurely management of his estates and the occasional incursion into a borough. Full-time political involvement was something that was not likely to come easy to him. Furthermore, his somewhat inflexible arrogance and his touchy pride indicated a fundamental lack of confidence in himself and in his own judgement. To an extent which has been underestimated, Rockingham lacked trust in other men, confining his confidences and placing his loyalty in a small group. He was always ready to blame others as bitterly as he blamed himself for his own failings. He could be neurotically suspicious of those he regarded as his enemies, first Bute, then Pitt and the King, and then Shelburne. He tended to concentrate on the immediate problem and, on the whole, neglected to take a long-term view of affairs. He was usually satisfied if he could exist from day-to-day without serious embarrassment. And now, Rockingham had to run a government and come to terms with the King, with Pitt and with many who would not wish to make the going easy for him. The first Rockingham ministry was thus bound to be of the highest importance not only in the history of the Newcastle–Rockingham party but also in the life of the Marquis of Rockingham himself. He had weaknesses in plenty and faults in profusion, when he reached, completely without effort, the highest political office in the land. The experiences of his first administration were likely to leave a deep impression upon him and to go far towards determining his future political attitudes, attitudes which for the most part were in July 1765 taken over unquestioningly both from the aristocratic traditions of the Pelhams and the 'country' and more independent Whiggism of Rockingham's native county.

The fact that Rockingham rather than Newcastle occupied the Treasury during the ministry of 1765–6 bristles with significance for the future of the Newcastle party. As First Lord of the Treasury Rockingham became the prime dispenser of patronage and it was to him rather than to Newcastle that the members of the connection began to pay court. As early as 11 July loyal followers of the party—and others not so loyal—sat down to write their begging letters.[37] Inevitably, many applicants were disappointed but Rockingham's position was not thereby weakened. For a time the Duke of Cumberland took a serious interest in appointments[38] and this effectively protected the authority of the Marquis. Men might grumble at his inattention but they would think twice before they actively pursued a complaint against a member of the royal family. In any case, the number of places at Rockingham's disposal was limited and the Marquis apparently did not intend to be unduly lavish in his distribution of pensions.[39] As the months passed, then, Rockingham came to replace both Newcastle and, after his death on 31 October, the Duke of Cumberland, as both the effective head and titular leader of the party. The history of the Rockingham Whigs was beginning.

Rockingham's star rose into the ascendent as Newcastle's continued to decline. The Duke's refusal of the Treasury amounted to a withdrawal from the leadership of what had hitherto been very much his own party. His action clearly requires some explanation. It was not just a dread of assuming responsibility which filled Newcastle with alarm. He may well have been conscious of his age and failing health. Further, public motives strengthened the force of these private considerations. Newcastle knew that his acceptance of the Treasury would destroy any prospect that existed of bringing Pitt into the ministry. Why, then, did Newcastle not exclude himself from the Cabinet entirely and why did he accept the Privy Seal? First, he wished to come to the rescue of the King, so cruelly enslaved by George Grenville and so treacherously deserted by Pitt. Newcastle recognised his own political limitations but he saw also that the traditional Pelhamite nostrum of service to the monarchy was relevant in the political crisis of the summer of 1765.[40] Second, Newcastle yearned, as he had been yearning for two and a half years, to reinstate those dismissed during the 'Massacre of the Pelhamite Innocents'. Only by taking office himself would he be in a position to achieve this long-standing objective. Finally, Newcastle wished to take office because he was, as much as ever, incapable of removing himself from the political stage upon which he had acted throughout his life. His incurable desire to meddle together with his overpowering inquisitiveness drove him, inevitably, into the Cabinet for the last time in his long and distinguished life.[41] It was to be an unfortunate and unhappy ending to his career. He had to endure the agony of neglect and the pain of indifference. Although he was given ecclesiastical patronage to dispose of, this was insufficient to keep him from interfering in the patronage of other ministers. When Grafton found Newcastle distributing his offices for him he had to speak very sharply to him before the Duke promised to mend his tiresome ways.[42]

The appointment of Grafton as Secretary for the Northern Department was effected readily enough and no significant problems occurred. It was less his talents than his contacts which won for such an unpretentious and unassuming man such a senior position. For Grafton had a foot not only in the Rockingham but also the Pittite camp. It is significant that the only two Rockingham Whigs to appear in Pitt's list of ministers in his projected administration were Newcastle and Grafton.[43] Grafton's indispensability as a bridge linking the ministry with Pitt was recognised by the senior men of the Rockingham party from an early date.[44] Grafton had no great desire to serve. He played little part in the negotiations and attended neither the Claremont meeting nor the regular assemblies of senior Rockinghamites which occurred thereafter. Like so many other politicians of the decade Grafton was chronically unable to assume responsibility and to take decisions, and he looked to others to provide the political courage and personal character which he lacked. He had idolised Pitt for two years and, lacking faith in Rockingham,[45] agreed to take part in the new ministry on the understanding that it was 'our desire to receive Mr Pitt at our lead, whenever he should see the situation of affairs to be such as to allow him to take that part.'[46] Grafton was ideally suited to be the tool of Pitt, a role which he was to fill for the next three years. Something of the measure of the man and his attitudes can be gleaned from his frank confession to Pitt. 'I only wish for that hour in which I could resign the Seals, and stand forth the loudest supporter of the measures of you, my successor.'[47] In short, Grafton regarded Rockingham as nothing more than a *locum tenens* for Pitt. Grafton's cabinet colleagues, however, under-estimated the strength of Grafton's attachment to Pitt. This was a mistake which was to cost them dear.

The appointment of the other Secretary was attended with much greater initial difficulties. From the outset Newcastle and Rockingham both wanted Charles Townshend for the office but a fortnight of persuasion failed to induce him to accept.[48] The reason for his refusal probably lay in the close relationship which then existed between Charles and his brother, Lord Townshend, who had a long-standing grudge against Cumberland. The early weeks of July were a struggle between Rockingham, on the one hand, with some help from George III[49] and Lord Townshend, on the other, for the political allegiance of Charles Townshend. In the end, Charles' own feelings decided the issue and he refused to take office. Thereupon, Cumberland persuaded Conway to take the Secretaryship. With it, however, went the Leadership of the Commons, an enormous political responsibility for one whose claim to political office was less that of ability than of service to the old corps and martyrdom in its cause. These were likely to be insufficient qualifications for coping with an Opposition strong in speakers in the Lower House and for dealing with the unpredictable Pitt. Conway proved to be a conscientious and well-meaning Leader of the Commons but he was wholly inadequate in that situation and the ministry's weakness there was an open invitation to the growth of a formidable Opposition.

The uncertainty surrounding Conway's Secretaryship was surpassed only by the indecisive behaviour of Charles Yorke in particular and the problems of the legal offices in general. It was essential, as most reasonable people recognised, to retain Lord Northington as Lord Chancellor. His removal would have offended the King and created fresh political difficulties. If Charles Yorke replaced him, then Pitt, continuing to champion the claims of Pratt, would have been offended. If Pratt had received the office then Yorke would have been alienated. Yorke was offered the post of Attorney-General. He had already held that office between January 1762 and November 1763, when he had resigned at the request of Newcastle and his friends. Was this how the martyr of the Opposition was now to be rewarded? Although there is much to suggest that the Court sincerely wanted Charles Yorke to enter the ministry, Yorke was unwilling to take an office other than the Lord Chancellorship. He was stung by Pratt's elevation to the peerage and made every objection which a man in his position could raise to accepting the offers and promises which the

King, Cumberland and Egmont dangled before him day after day in July and early August.[50] One by one, however, his objections were overcome. Yorke professed reluctance to drive from office the existing Attorney-General, Fletcher Norton, an old friend; after Norton had been dismissed, however, such scruples were irrelevant. If Yorke did not take the office, some-one else would. Even George Grenville urged upon him the wisdom of accepting.[51] As the days passed Yorke's resistance gradually crumbled. His excuse that he would be unable to attend Parliament regularly began to seem increasingly selfish and shallow. Finally, Yorke's basic complaint against the ministry could in part at least have been overcome by his own adherence to it. Yorke disliked its narrow basis and the partisan attitudes of the Rockingham Whigs. He believed that the King ought to overrule 'the personal warmth and passions of particular men and connections' and teach 'different de-scriptions of Persons to know their due bounds'.[52] There was nothing in this to distinguish Charles Yorke from any 'King's Friend'. It was this attitude which ultimately brought Yorke, albeit reluctantly and hesitantly, into the ministry on 8 August, but only when George III had promised him free access to the closet and the reversion of the Lord Chancellorship within a year. Yorke had played for high stakes for five weeks and his gamble had won him some significant concessions. Charles Yorke's political future was now closely bound up with that of the Rockingham ministry itself.

The closer the scrutiny to which the coming to power of the first Rockingham ministry is subjected, therefore, the less truth there is seen to be in the old Whig interpretations of the nature of the ministry. Far from anticipating the nineteenth century's notion of a 'liberal' and ideologically coherent administration, the ministry appears to be a jumble of all sorts of conflicting, contradictory and incompatible men and ideas. The remaining Cabinet places, for example, went to Lord Winchelsea, a seventy-six year old friend of Newcastle, and to Lord Egmont, an able, honest, if eccentric King's Friend. To complicate matters further, just outside the Cabinet as Chancellor of the Exchequer stood the Tory, William Dowdeswell.[53] The ministry was led, then, by some men, such as Northington and Egmont, whose primary loyalty was to the King, by others who looked to Newcastle, by others, who looked to Rockingham and by still others, especially Grafton and Conway, who looked to Pitt. It is difficult if not impossible, to ascertain the existence of any single 'ideological' factor which united the administration. Hostility to Bute was widespread but it did not extend to Northington, Egmont, Yorke and perhaps others. Professor Butterfield once drew attention to the ministry's 'refusal to make any compromise with the party of Bute',[54] but its hostility towards the Buteites was carefully measured. It is true that Lords Despencer and Northumberland were removed from their offices of Keeper of the Great Wardrobe and Lord Chamberlain, respectively, and that Stuart Mackenzie was not restored to the Privy Seal of Scotland. But this was scarely a constitutional revolution. Moreover, Egmont and Northington remained at the centre of political affairs and the Buteite Lords Talbot, Huntingdon and Lichfield were not removed. The Rockingham ministry can only with severe reservations be depicted as an anti-Bute crusade. There was no purge of the Buteites because the ministry was too divided and too weak to have carried one out. In any case, such a tactic would have offended the King and recalled the worst days of George Grenville's domination of the Closet. Finally, any idea of an anti-Bute crusade soon appeared to be irrelevant to the day-to-day business of running the Government.

Indeed, the Rockinghams seemed far less determined to destroy the influence of Bute than to ingratiate themselves with Pitt. Newcastle expressed what many felt when he wrote that 'the plan of administration should in general be made as palatable to Mr Pitt and as agreeable as possible to his notions and ideas'.[55] The plan of elevating Pratt to the peerage (as Lord Camden) came from the Rockinghams and was not suggested by Pitt. Indeed, Newcastle attached such importance to the move that he worried himself greatly when the King delayed the arrangement; 'if Mr Pitt is not kept in good humour, nothing will go well'.[56] It was for this reason, too, rather than for any reason of policy that moves were set on foot to revive the Prussian alliance. Pitt and his friends were not impressed. Significantly, with the exception of Nuthall, who became Treasury Solicitor, not a single friend of Pitt could be tempted into the ministry. Lord Shelburne, Lord Lyttleton, James Grenville, Isaac Barré and Tommy Walpole all refused to serve under Rockingham. The grounds for their refusal were summed up by Shelburne who professed ignorance at the measures Rockingham intended to pursue and declared that 'Measures not Men' would be the rule of his conduct.[57] More seriously, Pitt himself was not impressed by the extravagant gestures of self-abnegation made by the ministers. It was all very well for Grafton to return from his visits to Hayes, convincing himself that Pitt really did approve of the conduct of ministers, but Pitt, in reality, did not think highly of the arrangement, mainly, he claimed, because it included Newcastle. 'Claremont could not be supposed an object to me of confidence and expectation of a solid system of measures according to my notion of things.'[58] Furthermore, he probably became irritated to find his name constantly linked with the ministry in an advisory capacity. More than ever, Pitt chose to keep his own counsel and to safeguard his independence. He saw no reason to lend his approval to the actions of a ministry which had been formed without his advice and over whose deliberations he neither had nor wished to have the slightest connection or influence.

One of the most coherent and powerful attitudes which informed the early actions of the Rockingham ministry, in fact, could have done little either to impress Pitt or to lead him to think that the Rockinghams were anything other than a factious clique. Among the lower office-holders the scale of removals in the summer of 1765 was larger than anything seen since the 1720s. The removals were designed to reverse the Massacre of the Pelhamite Innocents, a reversal which Newcastle had consistently had in mind for two and a half years. Newcastle certainly assumed that Rockingham and his friends would not take a single step 'with regard to measures or men without previously consulting me or knowing my thoughts'.[59] In spite of his reluctance to take an efficient office he assumed that he had 'some pretensions to be the first in His Royal Highness's confidence in every thing relating to Administration or publick affairs' and he was certain that he could be of more use to Cumberland 'than all the young men whom he may consult'.[60] He proceeded to deluge Rockingham with a veritable flood of lists and letters, constantly and ceaselessly reminding him to dismiss incumbent office-holders in favour of Newcastle's old friends.[61] All this was far more than an idiosyncratic reaction by Newcastle. What was in question was not only the possession of office but the effectiveness of Rockingham's tenure of the Treasury. Newcastle completely failed to see that his suggestions, however well-meaning, would have been far more proper and would have carried far more weight had he taken the Treasury himself and thus acquired the undisputed right to nominate to the offices in question. Treasury patronage, however, was now in Rockingham's hands and thus the issue reduced itself into a struggle between Rockingham and Newcastle for its bestowal.

What degree of success did Newcastle enjoy in these endeavours? Some indication may be obtained from examining the extent of office restoration in Newcastle's own county of Sussex. There Rockingham acted upon no fewer than forty-six of the sixty-six separate suggestions made by Newcastle, forty-three of them within a fortnight of the kissing of hands.[62] Newcastle was not seeking power for its own sake or power to rival that of Rockingham. He was trying to maintain his interest in Sussex, and, in so doing, to reward faithful friends who had supported him during two and a half years of Opposition.[63] Indeed, it was not only personal loyalty on Newcastle's part but a question of political common sense to restore these men. Some of them, such as Edward Milward at Hastings and Thomas Snooke at New Shoreham could be of considerable electoral use to the Rockingham party. Rockingham presumably took Newcastle's advice over appointments because he saw both the justice and the expedience of Newcastle's suggestions. Furthermore, there is evidence that Newcastle played a significant role in the distribution of offices in the Central Government as well as in local Government. Although it is certainly true that he had his failures—he was unable, for example, to obtain places for James West, Capel Hanbury and Rose Fuller—the lists of ministerial offices and removals with which he bombarded Rockingham and the King between 2 and 9

July bear a remarkable resemblance to the final shape of the ministry. Most of the Duke's suggestions were complied with. Most of those which were not were at least attempted.[64] It was surely this substantial success enjoyed by Newcastle over appointments which awoke Rockingham to the need to watch Newcastle and to deprive him of influence over future appointments—and policy—for the Duke's interference might seriously compromise the newly established leadership of Rockingham himself. Therefore, in spite of Newcastle's experience, his essential loyalty to the Marquis and his genuine eagerness to help him, Rockingham ostentatiously shunned Newcastle, refusing to allow him his friendship, his confidence and even regular communication.

Newcastle's delicate feelings were hurt at the neglect which was his only reward for maintaining the Whig interest in Sussex and for offering to advise the young and inexperienced ministers. He complained bitterly to Cumberland of 'the total want of confidence, and communication'[65] and felt that he had deserved better. '*These young men* do not know the world; and what *Ministers* must do, and ought to do, to be able to serve the publick, and support *themselves*.'[66] Shortly after the death of Cumberland at the end of October the Marquis and his old mentor enjoyed something of a reconciliation. This touched Newcastle very deeply. 'I honor, and love Your Lordship; and have ever done so, since our first acquaintance'.[67] Within a week, however, Newcastle was drawing up a list of 'Considerations to be laid before My Lord Rockingham only'.[68] These included '*Confidence, Communication, and Previous Information*'. It should not be thought that nothing more was in question than the pride of an old man. Newcastle was alarmed at the position of Egmont and Northington and wanted Rockingham to keep their influence in check. In spite of the Duke's public spiritedness Rockingham was determined to be master in his own house and leader of his own ministry. The first casualty of Rockingham's determination was, unhappily, the Duke of Newcastle. On Christmas day 1765 he sadly drew up a memorandum about 'My own situation in the Ministry—To know My Lord Rockingham's own thoughts—No confidence, no friendly concert or previous communication'.[69]

As if these were not troubles and difficulties enough, the first Rockingham ministry suffered from the consequences of its tepid relationship with George III. In later years the Rockinghams were to look back upon the events of 1765–6 and to ascribe their misfortunes to the King's untrustworthiness. It is important, therefore, to investigate the origins of the King's alleged hostility towards them. In July 1765 George III had only two priorities. These were to escape from Grenville and to establish a stable administration. The Rockingham ministry proved to be the only means of effecting the former in the short term and perhaps the latter in the long term. It was surely in the King's interest to support it rather than to undermine it. Indeed, he advised King's Friends like Egmont, Elliot and Oswald to support the ministry.[70] Furthermore, he told Bute (truthfully) in January 1766 that he did not wish to have the ministry overturned because he had pledged his own support for it.[71] As we have seen, he lent his own good offices in its support when the ministry was desperately trying to procure the assistance of Charles Yorke and Charles Townshend. On the other hand, although there is no evidence that George III ever plotted against his ministers, he never entertained feelings of warmth or cordiality towards them. It is true that on occasion he could be kind to old Newcastle—he made a great fuss of him at the levee on 10 July, for example[72]—but he never seems to have thought highly of Rockingham. His letters to him are invariably formal, brusque and almost tetchy; they are those of an irritated schoolmaster to an indolent and sluggish schoolboy. It was not just that the King despised Rockingham's inexperience. He was suspicious of his intentions. George III bitterly resented the antagonism towards Bute which several of the ministers displayed. As he confided to himself: 'necessity not choice has made Me take several Steps that cut Me to the Soul'.[73] He thought that they had taken unnecessary advantage of his own straits to indulge their spiteful prejudices. The King reasoned that not only had Bute been excluded from political influence for the past two years but 'in addition to this on the formation of the present Ministry produc'd also Ld B. (a) very handsome letter wherein He gives me back my word with regard to the promises I made his

Brother, & added that He would not meddle either as to persons or measures in the Closet'. The King must have been infuriated when he was made to agree not only that Bute should have no contact at all with him during the ministry but also that office-holders should be removed if they voted against the Government.[74] George III had no alternative but to accept these obnoxious conditions. At the time, the Rockinghams thought that he would keep them. It was when he broke his word that their suspicions of a system of secret influence became almost paranoic.

In the summer of 1765, however, these unhappy disputes lay in the future. Newcastle virtuously congratulated himself that this ministry was not 'liable to the trite common objection of forcing the Crown—coming in without the King's approbation—being not sure of the King's support etc. His Majesty was the first proposer'.[75] We have already noticed that the attitude of ministers towards Bute did not materially affect the distribution of offices. Rockingham, for example, was perfectly prepared to accept Northumberland in office because his support would have been useful to the ministry while Elliot ought not to be removed because he 'brings in two or three members'.[76] The Claremont meeting of 30 June had decided that 'Some steps should be immediately taken, by removing some of My Lord Bute's principal friends; and by such other method, as may be proper, to convince the world that My Lord Bute will not be permitted, either directly or indirectly, to meddle in publick affairs, either at home or abroad'.[77] This sounds provocative enough until we recognise that nothing approaching an exclusion of the Bute party was considered—Cumberland would not have allowed it—and that any serious attempt to prevent Bute from meddling in politics 'either directly or indirectly' would have required the ministry to have imitated George Grenville's unfortunate attempts to restrict the monarch's personal freedom of action. It was the latter, of course, from which the ministry was supposed to be delivering the King! According to some observers, indeed, Pitt and Temple were anxious at the degree of tolerance shown by ministers towards Bute.[78] Nevertheless, in the early days of the ministry there arose a rumble of protest from some prominent Buteites

E

at the complexion of the administration and this was enough to prevent the Rockinghams from burying once and for all their prejudices against Lord Bute.[79] Finally, ministers had little in the way of policy to impose upon the King. They did not yet have an American policy because America in July 1765 did not appear to be a serious problem to Englishmen. Such policy as they did have arose from two considerations, the need to vindicate their past conduct and the need to conciliate Pitt. Consequently, their policy consisted of repealing the Cider Tax and declaring the illegality of General Warrants, promising to restore to their regiments army officers dismissed from them for voting against General Warrants in 1764 and, for Pitt's benefit, pursuing the Prussian alliance. George III may have disliked these measures but two things may be said about them. First, they amounted to a reversal of many of George Grenville's policies and this fact might have mitigated the King's hostility. Second, they did not represent and were not intended to represent a new system of government which would damage the authority of the monarch. For these reasons, then, George III accepted the policy of the first Rockingham ministry.

The Rockingham ministry, inexperienced as its leaders were, divided in its attitude towards the King and towards Pitt, lacking the support of either and led by a young man who was almost completely untried in politics, limped into the first few weeks of its unhappy existence. How did its young leader react to the mountain of problems which now faced him? From his private memoranda it is possible to reconstruct his thoughts at this time and curious thoughts they were. Rockingham assumed that Pitt would not oppose the ministry (although Pitt had never promised his support) and that 'The New Administration may therefore rest assured of their being *Popular*, to the utmost extent of their wishes'. Such misplaced optimism persisted when he surveyed the parliamentary scene.

'Nor can there be any Fear of not having a Majority large enough to carry on Business. The Experience of the last Two Years will evince the contrary. Nor can there be any the least Danger in undertaking it especially as Mr Pitt will, I am convinced, be proud of being consulted, and glad of advising the conduct of Foreign Affairs, in which there cannot be the least difficulty, except in his Favourite Point of Prussia. When the Treasury &c is in your hands, the inferior Part of the *Bedford* and *Holland* Party will soon apply to You for such terms of composition as Your attention to Your friends will permit you to give them, whereas whilst they held the Staff, they expected you should offer conditions to Them.

The same will happen with the *Bute* party, if you will be cautious not to speculate any precise Engagement in their favour beforehand. Upon the whole, it is evident that Lord Bute is now so much press'd, that, as an accomodation with the Bedford Set is desperate, he must give way to Your own Terms, and throw himself entirely upon your generosity'.[80]

This is what is meant in political terms by the inexperience of the Marquis of Rockingham. He made every miscalculation that it was possible to make. Not only did he take for granted the unswerving protection of the King (never realising that the support of George III had to be earned, not assumed) but he greatly over-estimated the goodwill of Pitt. He neglected to consider the seriousness of the Opposition which threatened from the Bedford–Grenville group, assuming that that formidable coalition would be ready to treat on almost any terms. Most curious of all, after years of warning his friends of the dangers of the influence of Lord Bute, he now dismissed as unimportant the threat to the ministry from that quarter. Rockingham's basic mistake was in his assumption that possession of the Treasury was itself the solution to his political problems. In fact, of course, it was only the beginning of them.

During the long parliamentary recess the ministry was fortunately able to conceal its weaknesses from public scrutiny. At this time the continuing protection afforded by Cumberland to its leaders gave the ministry not only the stamp of dynastic approval but also prestige and, perhaps, confidence. Cumberland was no mere figure-head. He was consulted on almost all matters and attended the cabinet, over whose deliberations he normally presided. His relationship with the ministry has, in fact, for long been the subject of much discussion. His position

was a natural consequence of the pattern of political relationships which obtained within the Newcastle connection after
the Regency Crisis of 1765. There is no doubt that his support
was of great assistance to ministers. As Horace Walpole put
it, Cumberland 'understood the Court so much better than
the Ministers, and could dare to hazard language in the closet
which their want of authority and favour forbade them to use
. . . he could have interposed on their behalf, or could have
bent them to a necessary submission to the Crown'.[81] Yet
Cumberland possessed no responsible cabinet office and
although he sat in the House of Lords, custom would have
prevented him from speaking in support of the ministry. His
anomalous position makes it difficult to sustain unwarranted
claims of constitutionality which may be advanced on behalf
of the Rockingham Whigs at this early stage in their history.
The Rockinghams were not consciously pioneering a novel
constitutional theory or practice. They were simply taking
advantage of a set of circumstances which offered to strengthen
their weak political position. There was nothing in the slightest
degree improper about their doing so. The King never complained about Cumberland's position and, indeed, seems to
have welcomed his uncle's leadership of the ministry. Furthermore, Cumberland appears to have performed a very real
service both to the King and to the ministers. He made
Newcastle's friends hold in check their distaste for Bute although
he was unable to persuade them to reinstate MacKenzie.
Furthermore, it was he who put a stop to the unsettling talk of
an early election for the purpose of disciplining the place
holders. He was wise to do so for there was absolutely no need
and no justification for an early election. It was far more
urgent for the ministry to seek the co-operation of the Court and
administration group than to threaten to 'discipline' it. Finally,
Cumberland played a crucial role in the internal struggles
within the ministry. Newcastle always wished 'to be *first* in the
Duke's confidence'.[82] But Cumberland refused to take Newcastle's complaints of neglect too seriously and threw his
weight behind Rockingham.

On 31 October Cumberland died and the ministry had lost
its indispensable focus of unity, its spokesman and its protector

in the closet. Rockingham wrote to his wife a few hours after the tragic event.

> 'Prepare yourself for what will affect you—but yet it was what has long been probable to happen—The Poor Able & Respectable Duke of Cumberland is no more. . . .
> It must not be suffered to depress us in that Public Situation which we are now in. The Enemy will rejoice, but I hope the same Zeal & Spirit with which we undertook, will & must now carry us through.'[83]

A few days later he reported to Lady Rockingham the attitude of his colleagues. 'The wish on the whole was that administration would not be dispirited and they will not find us deficient in spirit, when and while, the same motive which made us undertake, would prompt us to go on. It seems like vanity to put that we are well in the Closet—and therefore on that subject it may be decent to be silent—events and circumstances will fully evince *we are so*.'[84] Such optimism contrasted strongly with the opinions of others who thought that disunity would now prevail and that the influence of Lord Bute would revive, thus driving the ministers to seek the support of Pitt.[85] Indeed, the meeting of Parliament was only a few weeks away and the disturbances in America were beginning to look ominous. Decisions on important questions needed to be taken and as November advanced Rockingham himself began to realise how useful Pitt would be as a parliamentary ally against a dangerous Opposition led by the Bedford and Grenville Whigs. For the first, but not the last time during the first Rockingham ministry, relations with Pitt became the crucial hinge upon which events were to turn. Although the King had no intention of changing his ministers at this juncture, the death of Cumberland had removed a useful link between the Throne and the Cabinet. Ministers became nervous: they tried to obtain an accession of strength but succeeded only in persuading Lord George Sackville to accept a minor office.[86] Events were thus driving the ministers into an attempt to obtain the co-operation of William Pitt.

There was a certain logical simplicity in this line of proceeding, but it had at least two disadvantages. First, nothing could

have been better calculated to affront the King. At this time
George III did not believe that Pitt was a free agent, assuming,
as did others, that he had fallen under Temple's influence.
How else could Pitt's refusal to take office in June be explained?
Moreover, Temple had effected a reconciliation with Grenville
in May. In hoping for Pitt's co-operation, therefore, the
ministers were unwittingly terrifying the King into believing
that Grenville was to return to haunt his· Closet. In short, the
ironic situation existed where the King believed that the
Rockingham ministry, whose *raison d'être* had been to deliver
the King from Grenville, now threatened to make overtures
which might result in his political restoration.[87] It was all the
more necessary, then for George III to swallow his resentment
at the Rockinghams' attitude towards Bute and to endeavour
to keep them in office. Second, there was not the slightest
chance that Pitt would be prepared to assist Rockingham. He
had no intention of abandoning his much prized independence
of action to support a ministry whose dependence upon the
Duke of Cumberland Pitt had deplored. He was careful to
allow no action of his to be construed as support for the
ministry and was quick to advise his friend, George Cooke, MP
for Middlesex, to refuse the ministry's invitation to second the
Address at the meeting of Parliament. Pitt saw, or thought he
saw, that Newcastle was trying 'to hold out to the public an
appearance of connection *where* he knows he has none, and I
know he never shall have any'.[88]

In spite of all this, Rockingham and Newcastle were more
determined to establish some sort of working agreement with
Pitt than they were to conciliate the King by abandoning their
offensive proscription of Stuart Mackenzie. Although Rockingham had never been among those who worshipped at Pitt's
feet he had agreed with Newcastle and Conway even after the
Claremont meeting that Pitt should be sounded[89] and some
time in late 1765, almost certainly in November, he penned the
following private memorandum. 'The time is critical. Might I
wish to know whether Mr Pitt sees the possibility of his coming
and putting himself at the head of the present Administration.
I can say with very sufficient grounds that Mr Pitt has only to
signify his *idea*.'[90] Fortuitously, while Rockingham was reaching

this conclusion, his wife, taking the waters at Bath, found a fellow visitor there in Pitt himself. Rockingham wrote to his wife on 23 November:

> 'I shall trouble you to present my Best Respects to him & to return him Many Thanks for his Politeness to You & to convey to him the enclosed Minute of the Treasury which I believe is in itself Correct & may be Serviceable. . . .
> If your Communication to Mr Pitt is by note or Conversation—don't ask his Approbation—as that might lay him under difficulties—but represent it only as some matter of attention to him in communication of Affairs of some Consequence to the Commerce of the Nation.'[91]

The Treasury Minute in question was that of 15 November which admitted Spanish bullion into the American colonies. This was the first reversal of any part of George Grenville's American policy and it may well have been this fact which decided Rockingham to seek Pitt's opinion. Lady Rockingham dutifully conveyed the Minute to Pitt who 'highly applauds the Contents'.[92] Characteristically, Rockingham read too much into what must have been intended by a rather amused Pitt as a stone-walling response to a clumsy stratagem: 'his approving the Minute is to me as Strong Confirmation of the Minute's being right & proper as any of the letters of thanks with which some of the great manufacturing and trading towns have honoured us at the Board of Treasury on this occasion'.[93]

Whether it was or not would, however, shortly be revealed as members came to town for the meeting of Parliament. The death of Cumberland had left the ministry stranded between the two greatest political leaders of the decade, William Pitt and George III. Furthermore, it faced a well-organised and competent parliamentary opposition. Just when domestic political problems were beginning to exercise the First Rockingham ministry, the Empire in America suddenly seemed to crumble away in rebellious uproar. Just when the political relationships which had obtained since the ministry had taken office were beginning to dissolve, the question of Empire came along to subject it to still greater stresses. The age of the American Revolution was beginning.

Chapter 6

The Repeal of the
Stamp Act

The greatest work of the first Rockingham ministry was indisputably the repeal of George Grenville's Stamp Act. If it was not quite the case that the ministry would stand or fall by its handling of imperial problems, it remains true that on the American issue Rockingham and his colleagues were faced with the stiffest political test imaginable. We would do well in considering their achievement, however, to avoid the temptation to ascribe to the Rockinghams a conscious, 'liberal' pro-American sympathy. The ministry of 1765–6 was responding to a unique situation, one for which it had not prepared itself and for which there was no ready answer in the traditional principles of its members. The Rockinghamite solution to the American problem in 1766 was a pragmatic recognition of the fact that the Stamp Act was unenforceable. It was not informed with an ideological sympathy for the American colonists and it was not reached without many hesitations. At the same time, we ought to avoid personalising politics and political problems. It is thus misleading to interpret the American policy of the Rockingham ministry simply as a reversal of that of George Grenville. When he came to office Rockingham had no intention of carrying out a repeal of the Stamp Act. It is perhaps more fruitful to remember that politicians like Rockingham and Grenville were called upon to restructure the Empire after decades of neglect and that they had to undertake this immensely complex task at break-neck speed and against a background of vociferous opinion both in the colonies and at home.

The Rockingham Whigs came to power with no American policy. They had no preconceived ideas on the subject and they had never taken the trouble to interest themselves as a party in American affairs before they assumed the responsibilities of office. On the whole, they had accepted unthinkingly the American legislation of George Grenville.[1] His budget of 1764 had imposed no new domestic taxation and the friends of Newcastle did not oppose it. Sir William Baker, by this time emerging as a semi-official spokesman of the Newcastle Whigs on economic matters, attempted, it is true, to reduce the Molasses duty to 2d per gallon but he was in agreement with George Grenville on the fundamental issue, that the British Parliament had the *right* to tax the colonies.[2] Thus, like his friends, he approved of the proposed Stamp tax.[3] Grenville had been careful in his budget to balance competing economic claims and to conciliate both the West Indian and the American interests; it was thus difficult for the friends of Newcastle to oppose the budget without offending one or the other. There was a further reason why the Newcastle Whigs did not make an issue of America. William Pitt's opinions were not yet known and they did not wish to commit themselves to a line of proceeding of which he might disapprove.

These same considerations, lethargy, reluctance to offend one of the great commercial interests and fear of offending Pitt determined the behaviour of Newcastle's party in the session of 1765. When the Stamp Act came before Parliament Rose Fuller and Sir William Meredith questioned the expedience of imposing the tax at that time but neither questioned Parliament's right to do so.[4] Even those of the Opposition who divided in the minority of forty-nine on 8 February did so for commercial rather than for political reasons. Predictably, the Opposition, a little later in the session, launched an attack on a clause in the Mutiny Bill which permitted private quartering in America but this was a characteristic opposition ploy. On the whole Newcastle's party upheld the Grenvillian conception of Empire and agreed with most of the policies which flowed from it. They stood by his defence of the rights of Parliament and of the crown, the right to tax and the right to regulate colonial commerce. Those who took office, then, in July 1765, had done practically nothing to oppose Grenville's policies. On the other hand, they were not closely identified with them either. Politically, they had nothing to lose by adopting a different policy should the need arise.

In so far as the new ministers had any American policy at all, it was initially to enforce the Stamp Act.[5] They shrank from taking immediate action and chose to ignore the Virginia Resolves and it was not until mid-September that the ministry declared its hand. On 13 September a Treasury minute required Governors to co-operate in the execution of the Stamp Act.[6] Opposition to the Act in America was dismissed as the factious and irresponsible work of a small minority of hotheads. Ministers assumed that firmness tempered with fairness on the part of the troops and the Governors would ensure the smooth working of the Act. The Duke of Cumberland, furthermore, strongly supported the Stamp Act and adopted an authoritarian attitude towards the dissident colonists. During October the ministry came to accept the necessity to enforce the Stamp Act with the use of troops.[7] The Rockinghams were just as determined to enforce the Stamp Act as George Grenville could have been.

The Stamp Act, however, was simply unenforceable. Stamp distributors were forced to resign their offices and anyone who had any connection with the operation of the act was subject to social ostracism and, frequently, physical persuasion.[8] The 'Sons of Liberty' were in control everywhere. Only, perhaps, in Georgia might the act have come into force. Ministers did the sensible thing and abandoned the tax. Rockingham saw at quite an early stage that it could be nothing more than an enormous embarrassment to his administration and foresaw that colonial disturbances might disrupt English trade.[9] His ministry came under pressure from several sources. The colonial agents in London (who had exerted some influence over the formulation of Grenville's policy in 1763–4) had resumed their lobbying when the new ministers had taken office and they now intensified their activities. It was, however, to be the extra-parliamentary voice of the provincial merchants which was to persuade the ministers that an alternative to the Stamp Act must be sought.

Merchants trading with America were directly affected by the dislocation of trade occasioned by the Stamp Act troubles. Led by Barlow Trecothick they made contact with the ministry in early November.[10] Arising out of the discussions which followed, the Treasury Minute of 15 November permitted the importation into the colonies of Spanish bullion. This was the first hint of any change in Grenville's imperial system.[11] Thereafter, the ministry kept up its contacts with the mercantile community. It collected evidence of the interference with trade from specially organised meetings of merchants. Then, on 6 December a circular letter, drafted by Rockingham and Trecothick, was sent out to thirty provincial towns to collect still more evidence on the state of trade. By this time the merchants were well organised and led by a central committee of twenty-eight of their number. It would be easy but almost certainly incorrect to leap to the conclusion that the merchants were a 'pressure group' which ultimately persuaded the Rockinghams to repeal the Stamp Act. For one thing, the ministers were by no means acting as passive instruments of the trading community. Rockingham was astutely aware of the advantages which might accrue to the ministry if the situation were handled carefully, and it did not require the agitation of the winter of 1765–6 to teach Rockingham the importance of mercantile opinion. There were, after all, plenty of merchants in the West Riding and Rockingham had consistently shown himself sympathetic to their interests. He could see the virtues of conciliation with the colonists even if conciliation required a change of policy. Rockingham was not blind to one further consideration. If he played his cards skilfully he might not only endear his ministry to the merchants but also to a wider public, perhaps to the King and to Pitt, and he might also discredit George Grenville. There was a coincidence of interest, therefore, between Rockingham and the merchants in the winter of 1765–6. He was anxious to gather the widest possible representation of mercantile opinion and, at the same time, the best possible advice. Rockingham was using the merchants as much as the merchants were using him. The best possible proof of this proposition is that the merchants, in their replies to the circular of 6 December[12] did not clamour for *repeal* of the Stamp Act. Rather, they protested at the interruption of trade and did not much care how the ministry brought about a resumption of normal conditions. Nevertheless, there cannot be the slightest doubt that in December repeal was being discussed between Rockingham and Trecothick and between Rockingham and some of his cabinet colleagues.

In the Cabinet, Northington and Yorke were opposed to a repeal of the Stamp Act. Rockingham and Conway probably favoured repeal while Dartmouth, Grafton, Newcastle and, of course, old Winchelsea were likely to agree with the decision of the others.[13] One of the reasons, therefore, why the working out of an American policy took so long was that the Cabinet was sharply divided. In the circumstances Rockingham did perhaps the wisest thing possible: he saw that, at the very least, some amendment to the Stamp Act would be required, and throughout December and into January sat with like-minded colleagues such as Conway inside the Cabinet and Dowdeswell outside in a committee to study the American problem. It was with this ministerial committee that Treco-thick's committee dealt. It seems impossible to avoid the conclusion that the American policy of the Rockingham ministry was decided in committee rather than in Cabinet, where dissensions would have wrecked the fragile coherence of the ministry and whose deliberations would have been reported by Egmont and Northington to the King. All that can be said with certainty, however, is that by the time Parliament met for the new session on 17 December ministers were talking about repeal but that they had not yet decided upon it.[14] Most of them had come to recognise, none the less, that the Stamp Act was unenforceable and required amendment.

Ministers had begun to make preparations for the new session towards the end of October. Rockingham had begun to scout for support at that time[15] while Newcastle was including in his interminable 'Points for consideration with My Lord Rockingham' on 28 October questions about the King's speech.

'Who is to prepare it? The Subject matter of it' and 'Who are to move the Addresses?'[16] They were wise to make early preparations. Grenville had as good as promised George III in July that he intended to go into Opposition and, together with Bedford, was likely to defend the Stamp Act with all of his considerable abilities.[17] Furthermore, the ministry stood low in public esteem, had gained little credit for its apparent inaction during the recess and had not recovered from the blow which it had received when the Duke of Cumberland died. Because of the ministry's state of indecision on a policy for America nothing definite could be proposed in the Speech from the Throne. Rockingham was well aware that many supporters of administration would bewail its reluctance to use coercive measure against the Americans. As he wrote to the King on the eve of the session: 'The Address originally proposed for the House of Commons had been somewhat altered in order to accommodate it more to some Persons in his Majesty's Service, but it is now thought that the Alterations made will not be thought sufficient by them'.[18]

In the event, the debate on the Address on 17 December was something of an anti-climax. For one thing the Grenville–Bedford coalition was by no means as united as many observers, particularly in the ministry, had expected.[19] Nevertheless, the debate was sharp and contentious. Grenville moved an amendment deploring the disturbances in America and demanding the enforcement of the Stamp Act. Angrily though he spoke, he found little support and had to withdraw his amendment.[20] In the Lords on the same day a similar amendment was lost by 80–24.[21] On the following day Rigby and Grenville called for papers relating to the American disturbances but this time-honoured opposition play was easily repulsed in a thin house by 70–35.[22] Having established that they enjoyed a comfortable numerical majority the ministers were not seriously troubled again before the holidays.[23] These had merely been skirmishings and the Government had come well out of them. Rockingham derived precious little joy from that fact. He was beginning to wonder how thoroughly he enjoyed the King's confidence; he even allowed the predictably slight opposition in both Houses to trouble him unnecessarily. The

American issue loomed over the political scene and until it
was satisfactorily dealt with, the fate of the ministry must
remain uncertain.

Events in Parliament did not affect the reconsideration of
imperial policy which continued during the Christmas recess.
Regular meetings at Rockingham's London residence between
Rockingham himself, Conway, Dartmouth, Dowdeswell,
Trecothick and representatives of the provincial merchants
were beginning to move slowly but surely towards accepting
repeal.[24] It may be plausible, however, but it is just not true
to argue, as a consequence, that the merchants were 'for
repeal' and that these meetings 'converted' Rockingham. A
unanimous and monolithic 'mercantile lobby' did not exist.
Opinion within it was not always united. Some of the merchants who were most strongly opposed to the Stamp Act
were often the same men who had joined in the scramble to
obtain administrative posts in the Stamp offices for friends and
relatives, Trecothick among them. These meetings continued
to impress upon Rockingham the damaging economic consequences of the Stamp Act and the difficult economic situation
of several of the colonies. He learned with surprise, for example,
that in many places there was insufficient specie available to
pay duties.[25] On the other hand, Rockingham was becoming
firmly convinced that whatever may have been the temporary
injustices of imperial policy, whatever the hardships caused
by the Stamp Act, the rights of the British Parliament over the
Empire must not be weakened. It could almost be argued that
as the dramatic events of the autumn unrolled, Rockingham
become more of a declared supporter of the rights of the imperial Parliament than he had ever been before. There was
therefore no gradual shift in Rockingham's opinion from enforcement to repeal. Rockingham was facing up to the crisis
of imperial relations and working out his own response to the
crisis. Sheer realism led him to shy away from enforcement.
But still he was reluctant to go quite as far as repeal.

As late as Christmas day, the Duke of Newcastle could
write, in one of those interminable memoranda:[26]

'Stamp Duty.   Q. What is to be done about it?

What mention of it in the Speech?
Who is to be consulted upon it? Whether
to be repealed, or some modifica-
tions. . . .'

In short, Rockingham and his advisers could not make up
their minds. The Marquis knew that a repeal would be
politically dangerous and he was prepared to consider almost
any other policy rather than face up to its political consequences. Rockingham would have done anything, reduced the
Molasses duty further or even replaced the hated Admiralty
courts rather than face the explosion of an angry public opinion
and the hostility of the King which repeal might arouse. 'I
am sure the variety of opinions of what is right to be done is no
very easy matter to reconcile and I for one shall heartily
rejoice when a real concerted plan can be agreed upon', he
wrote to Newcastle on the second day of the new year. To
guard against the political consequences of repeal, Rockingham
realised that 'the legislative right of this country over the
Colonies should be declared,' . . . although this declaration
ought to be accompanied by an offer to the colonists of 'every
possible relief in trade and commerce'. That was only Rockingham's view. It did not yet represent the opinions of a majority
of the Cabinet. '*All* would agree to various amendments and
curtailings of the Act—*some as yet* not very many to a suspension
and *very few* to a repeal'.[27] Early in the new year, then, Rockingham had almost come round to defining what was later to be
the policy of the ministry. As yet his colleagues had not come
so far.

There was one final puzzling problem to be solved. Pitt's
views on America were likely to be of the greatest interest to
the ministry. But what were they? Everybody knew that he
disapproved of Grenville's policy but he was prepared to
commit himself to nothing very definite before Parliament
reassembled after the Christmas holidays. He refused to explain
himself to the ministers, preferring to launch his thunderbolts
in public rather than in private. And in private he was already
coming round to those views which were to shake the political
world when Parliament met on 14 January.[28]

Because ministers were still divided on America, the speech from the Throne was ambiguous and allowed Pitt to make a dramatic pronouncement of his imperial philosophy which was to be of crucial significance in the history of the repeal of the Stamp Act. He once more asserted his independence of ministers and Opposition alike, condemned the vacillations of the ministry and laid down the astonishing doctrine 'that this kingdom has no right to lay a tax upon the colonies'. He acknowledged 'the authority of this kingdom over the colonies to be sovereign and supreme, in every circumstance of government and legislation whatsoever'. By this he meant that Parliament had the right to lay an external tax upon the colonies, that is, to regulate their commerce but that it had no power to levy an internal revenue tax. Towards the end of his speech he gave some very significant advice to the ministry as to the policy it should adopt. 'It is, that the Stamp Act should be repealed absolutely, totally and immediately. . . . At the same time, let the sovereign authority of this country over the colonies be asserted in as strong terms as can be devised. . . .' Pitt's great speech made a deep impression upon his contemporaries and not only on account of its immediate political implications. In a few sentences he had separated the power to tax from legislative sovereignty. In a few words he had cast doubt upon the theory of virtual representation, arguing, with the Americans, that it was unjust to tax those who were not represented. In a few moments the greatest politician of the age had encouraged the American colonists to rebel against the mother Parliament. 'I rejoice that America has resisted', he pronounced twice.[29] There was much in Pitt's speech, it goes without saying, that Rockingham could not accept. It may be true that Pitt's attack upon the Stamp Act enabled Rockingham to repeal it but, at the same time, much of what he said struck at the basis of Rockingham's approach to imperial questions and opened up a wide gulf of opinion between them. This was now added to their earlier differences. For the moment, anyway, the Rockinghams could forget their nervousness about repeal. They were assured of the support of the Great Commoner. Even if Pitt had never made the speech that he did, the Stamp Act might have been repealed by the

Rockingham ministry (it would certainly have been drastically modified) and a declaration of parliamentary supremacy would certainly have been forthcoming. But there can be no doubt that the extraordinary events of 14 January precipitated the ministry's final decision on American affairs from which it had hitherto shrunk. As Lord George Sackville not unjustly put it: 'I conclude the ministers intend to direct their future proceedings by what he then declared.'[30]

After a meeting at Rockingham's on 19 January Rockingham wrote to Charles Yorke to inform him of the fateful decision which he had reached after discussion with Townshend, Conway, Dowdeswell and Grafton: 'That is, a *Declaratory Act* in general terms, afterwards to proceed to *considerations of trade*, and final determination on the *Stamp Act*, a *repeal* of which its own demerits and inconveniences *felt here* will justify'.[31] A policy of declaring parliamentary sovereignty over the colonies was manifestly necessary if a majority were to be obtained for the repeal. It was also necessary to appease the King and to appease Charles Yorke, who had supported the Stamp Act but who would have to guide the repeal through the Lower House.[32] Nevertheless, when Charles Yorke drew up the Declaratory Act taxation was not specifically mentioned. Such ambiguity was necessary to reconcile the Americans to repeal. Declaration was necessary for one final and much underrated reason: it satisfied Rockingham's conscience. It is quite clear from his private memoranda that he believed the resolutions of the colonial assemblies passed in 1765 against the Stamp Act with their specific rejection of the rights of the imperial Parliament required some reaffirmation of parliamentary right.[33]

The Rockingham ministry had found its formula to deal with the American crisis. Dr Watson is surely right to stress the dependence of Rockingham upon his mercantile connections, but he wisely warns against accepting the view that the ministry 'was pressurised into repealing the Stamp Act through mercantile agitation'.[34] One may add that much of this 'mercantile agitation' far from being a spontaneous demonstration of opinion in commercial circles was a carefully and deliberately arranged procedure for the raising of petitions by men connected to Trecothick and Rockingham. In general, the ministry acted upon the most detailed information available, went to great pains to obtain it, and the ministers, in spite of their inexperience, worked unusually hard to investigate all aspects of the American problem. That it took the speech of Pitt on 14 January to shake ministers out of their indecision should not conceal the praiseworthy and conscientious industry which went into the formulation of the American policy of the first Rockingham ministry.

The American policy had been decided by the middle of January, but it was several weeks before it was embodied in a form suitable for the consideration of Parliament.[35] These were tense and uncertain weeks for ministers. They realised that they were by no means certain of Pitt's friendship. On 28 January, for example, Conway opposed the request of George Cooke for permission to present a petition from the Stamp Act Congress. Characteristically, Conway dithered and gave the impression that the ministry was uncertain and undecided on the matter, appearing to be persuaded to reject the petition by the Buteites Jeremiah Dyson, Charles Jenkinson and Fletcher Norton.[36] Pitt happened to be present and poured scorn both upon Conway's refusal and his manner of proceeding.[37] This unpleasant scene could hardly have encouraged the ministers to count on Pitt's support during the repeal debates yet to come. But an even bigger shock was in store for them. On 31 January Alexander Wedderburn[38] presented an election petition which the Government wished to throw out but its majority dropped alarmingly to nine in a division of 148–139.[39] This augured none too well for the ministry's ability to carry a major and contentious piece of legislation such as the repeal. Although it had not been an issue of confidence there appeared to Rockingham to be something sinister about the sudden alliance between the friends of Grenville and Bedford and those of Bute. Rumours about a revolt of the office-holders had, in fact, been floating around for some time. The events of 31 January seemed to confirm the Rockinghamites' fear that an organised plot was on foot.[40] In fact, it had been an organisational failure on the part of the ministers in the Commons which had been responsible for the narrow division. Nevertheless, ministers feared the worst and their anxieties contributed to the atmosphere of nervous uncertainty which poisoned the political climate just at the moment when the great American business of the session was to come before Parliament in February 1766.

On 3 February, Conway moved the first of five resolutions upon the acceptance of which the American policy of the first Rockingham ministry was founded. In their original form the resolutions had been so strongly worded that Newcastle doubted whether the repeal would make any impact. In spite of violent opposition from Yorke the resolutions were given a milder wording in their final form[41] The first resolution claimed that parliament enjoyed 'full right and power to bind the Americans in all cases whatsoever', the principle underlying the Declaratory Act. Conway claimed that internal taxation was 'false in its principle and dangerous in its consequences.' His opinion was contested by several speakers who argued that 'enacting Laws and laying taxes so entirely go together that if we surrender the one we lose the other'. This was dangerous ground for Conway, who retracted his former view and proceeded to argue that: 'I have no doubt on the Right because I cannot distinguish between internal and external cases but I doubt of the Justice, Equity, and Expediency.' Burke took a much more liberal position than Conway and, in making his first considerable impression upon the House, declared that:

> 'The British Empire must be governed on a Plan of Freedom for it will be governed by no other. . . .
> I shall vote for this motion because I know not how to fix bounds to the coercive Powers of the British legislature.'

Pitt's opinion was more liberal still and he seconded Barré's amendment to strike out the words 'all cases whatsoever', stating that 'It is absurd to vote the Right in order not to exercise it'. Pitt repeated his denial that the financial right was integral to sovereignty. His arguments, mainly historical, were impressively challenged by Sir Fletcher Norton. There were too few Members present who sympathised with Pitt's novel ideas and Barré withdrew his amendment. Nevertheless, it had been a bad day for ministers. The contributions of Conway and Dowdeswell were insignificant compared with those of Grenville and Norton on the one side, and Pitt and Barré on the other. Ministers obtained the Commons' approval of the first resolution but precious little credit.[42] On 5 February Conway moved the second resolution (that 'tumults have been carried on').[43] Dyson mischievously attempted to insert a clause complaining that the Stamp Act remained unenforced but Pitt came to the rescue of ministers and Dyson was forced to withdraw his amendment.[44] The third resolution ('that the votes of the assemblies are illegal') was not contentious. On the fourth resolution (to punish the rioters) the ministry crumpled before Pitt's onslaught and acceded meekly to his demand that the motion be withdrawn. On the fifth and last resolution (to compensate the victims of the riots) a close friend of Grenville, Lord Nugent, 'proposed the word require instead of recommend'. Pitt deplored the amendment and was attacked by Grenville but who, nevertheless, was able to bring forward a form of words acceptable to Pitt and there the matter rested.[45] Ministers had managed to obtain the approval of the Lower House for the principles of their American policy but they had been dwarfed in debate by Grenville and Pitt. No wonder that on the following day, 6 February, George Grenville chose to stage a full-scale assault on the ministry and he chose the most favourable ground possible. He asked the House to address the King demanding that the laws in America be executed.[46] On this occasion the ministers could be sure of the support of Pitt but the star of the occasion proved to be Burke who argued that to enforce the law would bring it into disrepute and remedy no grievance. 'Nothing can hurt a popular assembly so much as the being unconnected with its constituents'. At Pitt's insistence a division was taken—the first important one of the ministry—and Grenville was decisively defeated by 274–124.[47] In the end, all had come right for the ministry in the Lower House. They had a new star in Burke. Pitt, if not cordial, had at least been helpful.

Yet the sweetness of their success was immediately soured by events in the Upper House. On 3 February the five resolutions passed the Lords 125–5[48] However, on 4 February,

Lord Suffolk, one of Grenville's senior colleagues, moved that American governors should be *required* rather than *recommended* to compensate victims of the American disturbances. Astonishingly—and this was perhaps to be a turning point not only in the first Rockingham ministry but in the attitude of the Rockinghams to George III—the ministry was defeated by 63–60.[49] There was more to come. Two days later (6 February) the ministry was once again defeated on a formal motion of thanks to convey gratitude to those American officials who had remained loyal to the British Government. This time the division was slightly worse, 59–54. 'The great event was that Lord Bute voted with the Opposition in both questions, and drew after him very many Lords in employment.' And in the second debate, Bute declared: 'that he should not be satisfied with supporting the legislative authority of Great Britain by resolutions only, and that if the ministers of the Crown acted upon other principles he was resolved, notwithstanding his duty and affection for the King, strenuously to oppose them . . . and the two Lords who applauded him most were the Duke of Bedford and Lord Temple'.[50] In later years it was to be incidents such as these which gave Rockingham and his colleagues what they considered to be positive proof that sinister influences were at work trying to weaken the authority of the ministry. Indeed, Rockingham professed no surprise at all at what happened. 'It is the Fullest Proof of what Ld Rockingham has in duty been obliged to inform his Majesty what was to be Expected.'[51] No time was wasted in calling a meeting of the leading Rockinghamites in the ministry and the possibility of resignation was discussed. Newcastle overrode Grafton's arguments in favour of resignation.[52] The ministry was to continue but with its reputation severely weakened, its confidence sapped and amidst an atmosphere of rumours of changes and resignations. It is surely worth investigating, in just a little detail, the reasons for the defeat of the ministry in the House of Lords.

It scarcely needs to be pointed out that it was essential to have the largest possible attendance of friends of the ministry when contentious business came before Parliament, but there appears to have been no systematic whipping of peers on

this occasion. The division taken on 3 February revealed that
a large number of peers had come to town but the Government
had done nothing to organise them and it can only be assumed
that ministers believed, after the satisfactory result of the
division on that day, that no trouble was to be expected in the
Upper House. We should recognise, however, that the division
of 3 February gave a deceptive impression of the opinions of
the peers, and a vote favourable to the Government on that
occasion by no means precluded peers from voting against it
on a future, perhaps more particular, and controversial matter.
Moreover, in spite of the enormous majority enjoyed by
ministers on 3 February, much Government support yet
remained untapped. Over twenty peers who had customarily
supported the Newcastle–Rockingham connection did not
attend. Had Rockingham bothered to procure their attendance
he need never have suffered the embarrassments which he did
in early February. The weight of culpability resting upon
Rockingham himself is very great indeed. He did not even vote
on 4 February! Furthermore, of the peers who had attended
and voted with the Government on 4 February, at least
twenty did not vote two days later and nine of those who did
voted against the ministry. There was thus no leadership
and hardly any organisation from the ministry. The Opposition's *coup* was a spectacular success because there was chaos
and shameful negligence on the ministerial side. It is well
known that Lord Northington voted against his ministerial
colleagues on 6 February. There was probably nothing that
Rockingham could have done about the Lord Chancellor,
but he did absolutely nothing to avert a second disaster. He
was not well suited to the task of organising a following and
ought, perhaps, to have allowed Newcastle to have performed
this service for him. Rockingham's lists show a good deal of
uncertainty as to who his own friends were, and he knew even
less about his enemies. Even after the divisions, Rockingham
was only able to list forty-four peers who had voted against
the ministry twice and he confessed complete ignorance of
twenty peers. For Rockingham, therefore, to have shifted the
blame for his reverses onto anything other than his own
disregard of proper organisation was uncharacteristically

evasive. It may have been the case that parties were much less developed in the Upper than the Lower House, their membership much less well defined, but for their setbacks in February 1766 the ministers themselves were responsible.[53]

Meanwhile, the ministry's plans for dealing with the American issue in the Commons were working with a smoothness which contrasts completely with the bungling of its organisation in the Lords. On 29 January the Commons had gone into Committee on the American papers and it was from the evidence presented to this Committee that the Declaratory bill and the bill to repeal the Stamp Act derived. It was essential that what had the appearance of an impartial investigation should nevertheless produce the results which the ministry wanted. The Committee met on thirteen occasions between 28 January and 21 February and interrogated twenty-six witnesses. (For good measure, the ministers had a further twenty-eight witnesses in reserve but they did not need to call on them.) The ministry stage-managed the whole proceeding extremely efficiently. One half of the witnesses had connections of one kind or another with the ministry and many of them had been rehearsed to give the answers which led the Committee to recommend the repeal of the Stamp Act. By comparison the witnesses brought forward by Grenville were inexpert and inarticulate. Most of the evidence went to demonstrate that the Americans were financially incapable of paying the Stamp Act and that the disastrous effects which the disturbances had had upon the Atlantic trade could only be mitigated by repealing the tax. The Committee made repeal seem not only possible but almost inevitable.[54]

It remained to negotiate a safe passage through Parliament for the repeal. On 21 February Conway moved for leave to bring in a bill to repeal the Stamp Act. Closely following the impact of the Committee's hearings he refused to enter into discussion of political principles, preferring to rest his case upon the distress caused to the mercantile community at home. The debate which followed[55] was something of an anti-climax. The issue had now been long in contemplation and the arguments on both sides were familiar to all. Jenkinson's amendment—'to amend and explain' rather than to repeal the Stamp Act—seemed particulary well designed to produce a tedious and legalistic debate in which only Burke shone. The speeches of Grenville and Pitt were completely undistinguished. In the end ministers won their severest test by 275–167.[56] It is at this point in time that the great myth of the popularity of the Rockingham ministry has its origin. There can be no doubting the very real enthusiasm which was felt in commercial circles for the repeal and the exultation and sense of achievement which swept through ministers. Here, at least, was one great moment of victory after months of political uncertainty, worry and weakness.[57]

Nevertheless, Rockingham found something to worry about even in the hour of his greatest triumph. The size of the minority gave him grounds for disquiet. He wrote to Newcastle describing his audience with the King on 22 February.[58]

> 'His Majesty seemed to think the majority very great. I told him I expected it to have been even larger. We had 12 Members shut out and 2 miscounted. I remarked to His Majesty how strong the torrent of opinion in favour of the repeal was and is—when notwithstanding the checks of seeing so many persons in his Majesty's service voting against it and notwithstanding the great combinations there were in the House of Commons against it and ultimately the knowledge that had lately been given of His Majesty's own sentiments being for modification . . . ended with lamenting that His Majesty had not adhered to the repeal.'

Rockingham's jubilation clouded his judgement. When he went on to demand that the King smooth the bill's passage in the House of Lords by advising peers who frequented the Closet how to use their votes, the King might have been forgiven for believing that Rockingham was beginning to act like Grenville. Rockingham was perfectly secure in the Commons, and, if he went about things properly, in the Lords, too. If the Marquis had any fears about the Commons he must have been relieved when the next important division, permitting ministers to bring in a bill to repeal the Stamp Act, was won by 240–133. From the reports of the debate which survive, however, it seems clear that it was Isaac Barré rather than the ministers who shouldered the burden of defending the repeal.[59]

In the Commons, thereafter, ministers were safe and they were able to push their measures through with great speed. The first and second readings of both the Repeal and De-claratory bills were taken on 26 and 27 February, respectively, through an apathetic House.[60] Opposition was waiting its opportunity for the debate on the third reading of the repeal bill on 4 March. Even then, ministers were scarcely troubled by a division of 250–122 and the debate was remarkable only for Pitt's affirmation of his 'total dissent' from the Declaratory Act.[61] That act passed its third reading without a division and attention once more switched to the House of Lords.

Ministers appeared to have learned some lessons from their embarrassment in that chamber earlier in the month, perhaps because they suspected that the King's support of repeal was at best half-hearted. Friends were brought to town and persuaded to attend.[62] Newcastle settled down to compiling one of his states of the House and concluded that there were eighty-eight peers for the ministry, seventy-two against it and thirty-two doubtful.[63] Although we know little about pro-ceedings in the Lords, in these weeks there was a lengthy debate on the second reading of both bills on 7 March.[64] The main confrontation occurred on 11 March on the committment of the Repeal bill. The opposition moved up to a formal assault upon the ministry and savaged the unhappy Newcastle and Grafton in debate.[65] Lord Coventry declared that 'You have come into a Resolution asserting your Right and at the same time you're doing an act by which you give up that Right'. Sandwich could not resist repeating what Grenville had been saying for months, that to repeal the Stamp Act would encourage the Americans to demand further concessions. Lord Halifax took up the same point: 'it is not the Stamp Act that is opposed but the Authority of this Legislature'. Lord Suffolk refused to regard the protests against the Stamp Act as a true reflection of American opinion. 'I consider her as an Unfortunate People misled by factious Judges and Seditious Lawyers.' Finally, the tetchy Northington damned the ministry.

He was prepared to accept the repeal through necessity but he looked forward to the day when a strong administration would administer the law of the Empire with a powerful force of police. It was all that Newcastle and Grafton could do to argue the case for repeal from the commercial chaos which the Stamp Act had occasioned and they demanded to know the consequences of persevering with the act. Grafton, in particular, leaned heavily upon the Declaratory Act and the taxing power. 'If however America is not sufficiently taxed, there are other Means by which they may be taxed—don't tax them universally. By that means you join them when you should keep them asunder.' The poor performance of the ministerial speakers—among whom Rockingham was not included—was reflected in the division. Ministers won by 105 to 71. It would have been a much closer thing if ministers had not taken the trouble to collect proxies, of which they had a majority of 32–10. The Opposition followed up the debate by entering thirty-three protests against the repeal. On the third reading of the repeal on 17 March twenty-eight peers signed a protest but there was no division. The following day both the Declaratory and the Repeal Acts received the royal assent.[66]

Although the great work of the administration was done, imperial and commercial matters continued to fill the time and engross the attention of Parliament for the remainder of this busy session. The work of historians in recent years had demonstrated that the Declaratory Act and the repeal of the Stamp Act were not isolated measures but rather part of a thoroughgoing and ambitious overhaul of colonial and commercial affairs. In early March Burke wrote that with the Stamp Act out of the way 'We now prepare for a compleat revision of all the Commercial Laws, which regard our own or the foreign Plantations, from the act of Navigation downwards; it is an extensive plan'.[67] The plan, as it later emerged was the result of co-operation between the ministers and the merchants but, more important, of co-operation and discussion between the respective committees of West Indian and the American merchants to which, as Lucy Sutherland has written, 'business in the house tended to become merely the sequel'.[68] Indeed, after the committees had reached agreement they then began discussions with the Board of Trade and with the Treasury. Out of these discussions emerged a comprehensive scheme which included the further reduction of the duty on foreign Molasses from 3d to 1d. The interests of American distillers would be safeguarded by excluding imports of rum from the colonies, although imports of British raw sugar would pass duty free. A Free Ports bill would open Free Ports in the West Indies to revive Caribbean trade. This last proposal originated with the American merchants and was supported by a wave of petitions in early April.[69] It was, however, too much for the West Indians who felt their interests to be threatened by the opening of a Free Port. Northington and Egmont thoroughly disapproved of the scheme and Grafton, following William Pitt, was lukewarm. Dissension led to uncertainty and thus to delay.[70] It was not until 9 May that proposals were placed before the Commons to establish a Free Port on Dominica and to make Kingston, Jamaica, a Free Port, to reduce the Molasses duty to 1d and to lower duties on cotton and sugar. Grenville and his friends opposed the bills and castigated the ministry (not unjustly) as the tool of the merchant interest but the bills passed through empty Houses to receive the royal assent on 6 June.

The Rockinghams pushed an impressive amount of imperial and commercial legislation through Parliament and could fairly claim to have restructured and reshaped the Empire. It would be idle, however, to claim too much for them. Their policy fell short of statesmanship because no coherent view of Empire informed their policy. It could hardly be claimed that the Rockingham ministry did much more than improve and streamline the old mercantilist structure of the Empire. The interests of the colonies had still to be subordinated to those of the mother country and the political status of colonists remained inferior to citizens of Great Britain. The Rockinghams lacked an imperial vision. They wished merely to deal with existing problems with the benefit of the advice of those most closely concerned. It must also be added that much of their policy was limited in its success.[71] In America the Vice Admiralty courts remained, as did restrictions upon the issuing of credit bills. In spite of the repeal of the Stamp Act the ministry was unable to entirely satisfy the demands of the colonists and the American problem remained to torment the Chatham and Grafton administrations. Although the Declaratory Act affirmed parliamentary sovereignty, the Repeal seemed to confess the inability of Parliament to exercise that sovereignty. Perhaps the Rockingham ministry succeeded in compensating for some of the harm which Grenville's policies had effected, but its measures did not represent a complete solution to the basic problems of Empire. Americans disregarded the Declaratory Act and continued to behave as though the colonial legislatures were sovereign assemblies. After all, the Repeal had demonstrated that Britain was unwilling to enforce her sovereignty. The British Government still had to face up to the problem of raising money to finance an army for America. In so far as the Empire in North America was concerned the British Government was back roughly where it had been in 1763.

Chapter 7

The Decline and Fall of the First Rockingham Administration

The passage of its imperial legislation did not effect a trans-formation in the fortunes of the Rockingham ministry. Indeed, the greater the degree of success which attended its exertions over the problems of Empire the weaker the position of the ministers became. This unusual predicament arose from a tactical error. The ministers ostentatiously shunned the friends of Bute. At the same time, they assiduously cultivated William Pitt. From these two basic and consistently held attitudes flowed a whole series of complex problems which the Rocking-hams never succeeded in understanding, still less resolving satisfactorily.

The fundamental error of judgement which afflicted the Rockingham Whigs was a belief that they could afford to indulge their distaste of Bute. Although there was, indeed, some justification for the widespread suspicion that Bute still maintained some contact with the King,[1] the Rockinghams exaggerated his influence and depicted him as a sinister power behind the throne.

The fact that so few of the friends of Bute were displaced in July 1765 only appeared to annoy ministers and led some of them to continue to express quite openly their deep seated resentment against his alleged influence and that of his friends. Such behaviour was unbelievably short-sighted.[2] Not the least important of its effects was that it infuriated the King.[3] Even more damaging, however, it diverted the ministers from at least one pressing political need—to unite behind the ministry the Court and Administration group. After the Grenville ministry had fallen it was uncertain how many of that group would continue to support him in Opposition. The Rocking-hams should have sought to rally to themselves the allegiance of this body. Instead they chose to snarl at some of its leaders, to do practically nothing to endear it to the ministry and then to explode with anger when the group greeted with less than enthusiasm the American policy of the Rockingham ministry, which effectively reversed the policies which these men had supported during the Grenville ministry. The Rockinghams assumed that the Court and Administration group would automatically support the ministry, however. Had not the King given Cumberland his word at the beginning of the ministry that he would remove those who refused to do so? How far the King would keep his word, however, only time would reveal. Paradoxically it was not the friends of Bute but the loyal servants of the Court who had suffered from the effects of the Rockinghams coming to power in 1765. As we have already noticed, few Buteites were affected but the removal of men like Welbore Ellis, the Secretary at War, Lord Hillsborough, at the Board of Trade, and George Hay and Hans Stanley at the Admiralty Board deprived the ministry of the services of loyal servants of the Crown and appeared to be a declaration of war upon the Court and Administration group.

The alienation of the Buteites and the failure of the ministry to unite and lead the Court and Administration group could only be sustained by the weak Rockingham ministry if it succeeded in obtaining the co-operation of William Pitt. Ministers realised this but proceeded to annoy him by engaging in public expressions of his support for the ministry and its policy which were completely unwarranted.[4] The death of Cumberland at the end of October 1765 had two effects. It removed one enduring obstacle which had stood in the way of persuading Pitt to co-operate with the Rockinghams. His suspicion of Cumberland went back to the middle of the 1750s and it may well have been his concern at an apparent revival in the royal Duke's influence in the spring of 1765 which had led Pitt to bury the hatchet with Grenville and which persuaded him to keep his distance from the Rockingham ministry. With Cumberland gone, at least one formidable obstacle to co-operation between the Rockinghams and Pitt had disappeared. In so far as the death of Cumberland weakened the prestige of the ministry and its weight in the Closet, Pitt was 'more wanted than ever'.[5] Further, the need for the ministry to deal with the disorders in America together with its fear of the combined Grenville–Bedford Opposition decided its leaders to seek out the help of the Great Commoner. Rockingham decided to follow-up his smoke signals to Bath[6] with something a little more substantial, especially after Shelburne's speech in the Lords on 20 December. That speech dashed Rockingham's hopes of Pitt. He knew that Shelburne had been to Bath to visit him just before the opening of the session and, like many contemporaries, took Shelburne's opinions to be a reflection of Pitt's. Shelburne's reiteration, therefore, of the principle of 'Measures not Men' was, to Rockingham, an alarming assertion not only of independence on Pitt's part but a possible warning of his future opposition on particular measures. The Marquis reacted sharply and intimated to Shelburne that the ministry was prepared to make itself acceptable to Pitt 'as he pleased'.[7] Shelburne passed these manifestations of good faith on to Pitt but the Great Commoner wanted nothing of them. For one thing Pitt stated that he would negotiate only with the King and not with ministers. For another, he pronounced darkly upon Newcastle. For some reason best known to himself, and which he continued to conceal, he proclaimed that 'the country is undone' in Newcastle's hands, a remark which no doubt would have surprised the old Duke who had been complaining for months of his exclusion from business.[8] In fact, these two conditions need not have been insuperable. The King might be persuaded to open a negotiation with Pitt and Newcastle was the first to declare that he would not allow his own situation to stand in the way of an accommodation with Pitt. But the Great Commoner made another stipulation. This was that 'many other things' would have to change before he would consider entering the ministry. What could this enigmatic pronouncement mean?

The ministers decided to try to find out. On 2 January 1766 Tommy Townshend was sent to visit him at Bath, ostensibly to ask his advice about American affairs but with the purpose of sounding him out with a view to his joining the ministry.[9] Pitt was polite but his response was forbidding. His opinions on imperial matters he reserved for the King and for Parliament. He reiterated his condition that Newcastle must resign but now added a new demand, that Rockingham should surrender the Treasury to Temple.[10] Rockingham discussed these proposals with his colleagues at cabinet meetings on 5 and 7 January. Grafton thought Pitt's terms worth serious consideration and had the courage not only to tell the King on 8 January but to threaten resignation if the opportunity of gaining Pitt were lost.[11] Conway wanted Pitt in the ministry almost as much as Grafton did but he was not prepared to go to the lengths of that impetuous nobleman. In particular, he was not prepared to sever his ties with Rockingham and Newcastle. Newcastle would have been the first victim of an arrangement with Pitt but he gallantly offered to step down.[12] The fact that Rockingham thought Pitt's terms too stiff will occasion no surprise. He did not believe that Pitt seriously intended to assist the ministry at all, exhibited no desire to have him do so and was perfectly prepared to soldier on without Grafton if necessary. In short, he was not prepared to humiliate himself unnecessarily simply to please Pitt. George III supported Rockingham's refusal to negotiate with Pitt. He doubted if 'so loose a conversation as that of Mr Pitt and Mr Townshend' was a sufficient basis for a negotiation and thought that it would only serve to unsettle the public.[13] He told Grafton roundly that even though his own private desire might be for Pitt that in itself was an insufficient reason for remodelling the administration.[14] George III was prepared to discuss affairs of state with Pitt but he saw no reason to embark upon a negotiation which even Pitt was indicating would be distasteful to him. This appeared to be enough to bring Grafton into line. Rockingham wrote to the King on 10 January that 'the idea of writing to Mr Pitt immediately is laid aside'.[15] That was not quite the end of the matter, however. Grafton and Conway went to see the King on the same day to beg him to consult Pitt at least on American affairs but Rockingham and the King squashed this suggestion, too.[16]

For a few days the situation hung, but Pitt's sensational speech on 14 January once more demonstrated his indispensability and revived the yearning in some Rockinghamite hearts to attach him to the ministry. Even Rockingham's confidence that he could continue without Pitt's support was severely shaken. He advised the King that the ministry 'will be shook to the greatest degree' unless Pitt took 'a cordial part'.[17] In short, Pitt's speech of 14 January converted Rockingham to Grafton's view of the desirability of including him in the ministry. Rockingham persuaded the King to allow Grafton to visit Pitt and to put two questions to him. As the King recorded them in a memorandum these were:

1. 'Whether He is disposed at this time to come into my service.
2. Whether Ld Temple's declining would prevent his accepting.?'[18]

Pitt's response was predictable. He completely dashed Grafton's hopes by reiterating his condition about Newcastle and by stating that Temple must have the Treasury. He can have been sincere about neither of these two conditions, especially the latter, coming, as it did, after Temple's refusal to serve with Pitt in the previous June.[19] Pitt had no intention of coming to the rescue of Rockingham and therefore he demanded impossible terms which he knew must be rejected (paradoxically, these terms amounted to a demand for a new administration). The King and Rockingham could not accept his demands and on 21 January Rockingham told Pitt that the negotiation was at an end. This decision left the Rockingham ministry to fight its battles over America without the aid of the Great Commoner. But something had been achieved and neither Rockingham nor Grafton noticed it. Pitt had conveyed to George III his willingness to take office when the situation was ripe for it and there is evidence that the King understood Pitt's gesture.[20]

F

It is worth underlining the unintended consequences of these attempts by the Rockinghams to seek Pitt's support. No one could blame the King for believing what his ministers were always telling him at this time, that they could not go on without Pitt. Once it had proved impossible to obtain his support, then George III naturally sought to provide for the contingency of ministerial resignations by scouting after loyal friends who would serve him in a future ministry. He always intended that Northington should be the centre-piece of such a ministry. 'I expect that those of the Ministers who remain, will open their Eyes, & act with You in particular & others in a more liberal and open manner than they have heretofore & not to be continually squinting to a quarter from whence they have met with such personal contempt.'[21] By the middle of January something resembling a new administration had been drawn up by the King, probably with the assistance of Egmont. Northington was to replace Rockingham. Egmont and Charles Townshend were to be the new Secretaries and Northumberland was to take the Privy Seal. Conway was to be relegated to the Ordnance. Lord Townshend was to become First Lord of the Admiralty and Lord Hardwicke Paymaster.[22] It was fortunate for the King that he never had to trust his political fortunes to such a ministry. Nevertheless, these were the straits to which he would have been reduced had the Rockinghams resigned. No wonder that he was keen to keep them in spite of all their weaknesses. This state of affairs was the consequence of the fragmentation of the great connection of the Whigs and the inability of the King to replace the regime of Pitt and the Pelhams with a coherent and stable system. It was not the King who was particularly to blame for this situation (though he was as much to blame for it as any other individual) but the mistrust which prevailed among politicians. Indeed, many of them distrusted the Court and for this the King must bear his share of the blame. In January 1766, however, there is no evidence to suggest that the King was plotting against his Ministers. It would be doing George III a grave injustice to affirm that his 'reserve' Cabinet, such as it was, represented a Cabinet which the King actually *wanted* to take office. George III's loyalty to the ministry—and thus the security of the ministry—arose from the fact that as long as Pitt remained reluctant to serve the King then the alternative to the Rockinghams was the hated George Grenville.

There were, however, strict limits to the extent of the King's support for his ministers and this was demonstrated by his refusal to discipline office-holders. Towards the end of January Rockingham began to worry about their loyalty, especially that of those placemen who had *supported* the Stamp Act in 1765.[23] Newcastle went so far as to assume that the repeal would be lost in the Lords unless the King would 'signify to his Lords of the Bedchamber and his servants . . . that His Majesty wishes the repeal and thinks it for his service that it should be done'.[24] Moreover Newcastle and Rockingham always understood that Cumberland had received assurances from the King at the outset of the ministry 'that if those of his friends who might remain in office did not vote with, and by speaking support the present administration, His Majesty promised to remove them the next day'.[25] How far King George III considered himself bound by these assurances was now to be revealed.

The defeat sustained by the ministry in the Lords on 31 January on an election petition was a warning shot cast across the bows of the ministry by friends of Bute and courtiers anxious about the ministry's treatment of them.[26] Rockingham tried to ignore it. But he could not ignore the defeats suffered by the ministry during the next few days in the Upper House. They arose not only from the lack of organisation of ministers but owed something to the fact that peers who had been in favour of the Stamp Act a year earlier now refused to contradict their opinions. Thus the Government was defeated on an American question on 4 February by 63–60. The tension of the last few weeks proved too much for Rockingham who now chose to blame the King for his political difficulties. He threatened to resign unless the King disciplined the Household Lords who had voted against the ministry. George III's refusal to do so was not without some justification. The ministry's defeat was humiliating but it did not touch the substance of its American programme and George III had no intention of allowing a nervous and near hysterical Rockingham to bully him into a Bedchamber revolution.[27] In any case, he did not think it reasonable to punish loyal servants of the Crown for adhering to their political beliefs simply to calm the fears of the Marquis of Rockingham.[28] But after Bute's speech attacking the repeal on 6 February Rockingham decided to take matters into his own hands. He took it upon himself to spread among Members of the Lower House before the debate on the following day the news that George III was for repeal.[29] (In a sense he was, but only because *modification* of the Stamp Act was impossible.)[30] In short, Rockingham was using the King's recognition that enforcement of the Stamp Act was not practicable for his own political purposes and to sway the votes of Members. In so doing he distorted the King's real opinions. It is important to be clear that the King was for enforcement if possible, then for modification if possible and only for repeal if the other two alternatives were not feasible. For Rockingham to broadcast around Westminster the fact that George III was a friend of the repeal was, to say the least, an exaggeration. Furthermore, Rockingham's attempts to persuade the King to honour his promise to dismiss Members for their votes in Parliament, however understandable, surely contradicted the stand he had taken earlier over the Massacre of the Pelhamite Innocents and, more recently, the dismissal of Conway from his regiment in 1764 for his vote on General Warrants. Rockingham no doubt thought himself to be in a desperate situation which required desperate stratagems, but there can be no doubt that his behaviour, however understandable, was unfortunate.

That of the King is almost inexplicable. On 10 February Lord Strange, the independent MP for Lancashire and Chancellor of the Duchy of Lancaster, warned George III that ministers were spreading the word that the King was for repeal. George III explained to Strange that his original preference had been for *modification* of the Stamp Act rather than for repeal and 'I therefore authoriz'd him to declare to whoever declar'd that to be my idea, the very words I now acquainted him with'.[31] Strange was full of his new-found importance and at once began to tell everyone that the King's preference was for modification and not for repeal. Rocking-

ham was horrified at this weakening of the position of the
ministry in the eyes of the public and on 11 February insisted
that the King interview Strange.³² Rockingham took the
trouble to be present at the audience the following day and
heard the King state his opinions quite fairly: that he was for
modification but that if modification without repeal would
lead to violence then he was for the repeal. Rockingham's
suspicions were now thoroughly awakened and he determined to
leave no room for possible misunderstandings in the future
about the King's opinions. He made the King sign a statement
'*That Lord Rockingham was on Friday allow'd by his Majesty to say,
that his Majesty was for the Repeal*', although George III insisted
upon appending in his own hand '*The conversation having only
been concerning That or Enforcing*'.³³

Just when the tedious matter had been straightened out to
everyone's satisfaction, exactly the same problem arose again.

A few days later Lord Denbigh³⁴ 'came down to the H. of
Commons and went about to the Members assuring them that
the King disapproved of the Repeal'.³⁵ The piece of paper
which he was showing around stated that 'his Majesty never
was for the Repeal—that he had been misrepresented to the
Publick'.³⁶ It must have been with wearied resignation that
Rockingham once more went to the King to declare that he
'hoped his Majesty w'd not let an impression rest on him, as
if he (Ld R) had deceived his Friends but that the King would
so far justify him as to admit that in the last conference they
had held on the subject his Majesty had acceded to the
repeal'.³⁷ The King was compelled to commit his opinions to
paper. 'Ld Rockingham's question to the King was whether
he was for enforcing the Stamp Act or for the Repeal: the
King was clear that Repeal was preferable to Enforcing and
Permitted Ld Rockingham to declare that as his opinion.'³⁸
These curious incidents gave rise to mutual suspicion and
mistrust between the King and Lord Rockingham and provoked generations of historical legends of George III's attempts
to undermine the authority of his ministers. It is clearly
important to place them in their correct perspective.

The King's pertinacious insistence upon exercising his
freedom to express in public his provocative opinions upon the

most controversial topic of the day overrode his loyalty to his ministers. There was an element of premeditation about it. According to Professor Christie 'the King's well-known nervous volubility had betrayed him into an unintentional indiscretion'.[39] Nevertheless, what the King actually said to Strange does not bear the mark of spontaneous enthusiasm still less of carelessness. 'I therefore authoriz'd him to declare to whoever declar'd that to be my idea, the very words I now acquainted him with.' This was a specific and intentional authorisation and not a loveable piece of garrulousness. Furthermore, the King believed that so long as he affirmed that he was for repeal he could nevertheless continue to tell his courtiers that he thought modification preferable. His continued attachment, moreover, to a policy of modification which by the middle of January had become utterly obsolete is difficult to explain. His behaviour is difficult to defend and the Rockinghams, not unnaturally, put the worst possible construction upon it. But the King was not the only one at fault in all this. His ministers had used his name for their own political purposes. The ministry was in no danger in the Lower House and his opinions were unlikely to affect the outcome of the parliamentary struggles over repeal. Was he to allow himself to be muzzled and his name to be used by his ministers? He did not wish to do so but, as we have seen, there was no alternative to them and, at this time, there cannot be the slightest doubt that much though the King disliked repeal he wished to continue the Rockinghams in office.[40] Nevertheless, the King was prepared to give voice to his opinions on repeal and refused to keep silent for the convenience of the ministers. He was not prepared to plot behind their backs because it was too dangerous to do so and, in spite of a fatuous eleventh-hour intervention by Bedford to undermine the policy of repeal,[41] the King realised that it was now too late.[42] His insistence, however, upon publicly expressing his own opinions had the predictable effect of upsetting the ministers who were already unsettled. They now proceeded to watch his every move with Grenvillean suspicion. This, in turn, annoyed the King and must have encouraged him to hope that as soon as the American business was over Pitt would step forward. Ministers seemed to sense the King's rapidly ebbing confidence in them and this realisation itself contributed to their own demoralisation. That curious state of indifference to the future of the ministry which was such a marked feature of the dying months of the Rockingham ministry had its origin in the middle of February. Nevertheless the ministry continued to carry out its legislative programme and although much weakened in spirit persisted faithfully with the task in hand. It was somehow typical of the state of the ministry, however, that it neither handled all these measures well nor received for them any of the credit which it might have deserved.

It had, for example, been one of the principal conditions of the formation of the ministry that General Warrants would be declared illegal by resolution of the House of Commons. On 23 April the resolution was carried, but on the previous question by the hairsbreadth majority of 173–171. Just as they were recovering from the shock of the nearness of the division ministers had the glory whipped from under their noses. 'Mr Pitt then moved to extend it to all cases whatsover. As well as Libells. Agreed to.'[43] The following day the astonishing prospect of a Pitt–Grenville union confronted ministers. Pitt and Grenville went much further than the Government was prepared to do over General Warrants.

> 'Mr Pitt proposed the declaring to morrow either by Bill or otherwise the illegality of General Warrants in all cases whatsoever, and their being a Breach of Privilege in the case of a Member of Parliament, except in Treason. And also the seizing of papers. Mr Grenville seconded him, declared he had *ever* been of that opinion and that the Resolution came into two days ago was in diminution of the liberty of the Subject, as it was confined to libels only.'[44]

On 25 April, therefore, Pitt made his motion. Sir William Meredith and Sir George Savile moved to strike out the words 'in all cases whatsoever'. But Pitt, having made his point and having made the ministers appear half-hearted in their commitment to the liberty of the individual, did not press the subject to a division.[45] Ministers obtained their resolution, but in doing so demonstrated an almost uncanny ability to fail to exploit their opportunities whilst they paraded their weaknesses for all to see. It was on occasions such as these that the Government really felt the absence of a group of talented speakers in the Commons. Finally, it may well be doubted whether the resolution of one chamber had the slightest effect upon the legal status of General Warrants. It is not excessively unkind to the Rockinghams to point out that their concern to declare the illegality of General Warrants was a symbolic but quite pointless and, in the execution, a botched endeavour.

What ought to have been not only the most popular but the most straightforward undertaking of the Rockingham ministry, the repeal of Lord Bute's Cider Tax, proved to be equally problematical.[46] The Chancellor of the Exchequer, William Dowdeswell, who had led the opposition to the tax since its imposition in 1763, had not the slightest difficulty in obtaining parliamentary approval for the repeal of the tax, a fact which is perhaps a little surprising in view of the attitude of some of the Court and Administration members to the repeal of the Stamp Act and their former support of the Cider Tax. Everything so far had gone smoothly but the ministry's genius for bringing problems upon itself was once again revealed when, to make good the loss of revenue from the Cider Tax Dowdeswell plunged into the deep waters of controversy when he imposed a tax on windows. The principle of the tax was agreed on 21 April by the comfortable majority of 162–112,[47] but the remaining stages of the bill found the majority weakening.[48] Although the tax was approved and incorporated into the budget in June Dowdeswell had stirred up a hornet's nest of hostility and the ministry was constantly pressed and harassed in parliament until the very end of the session. If ministers had ever believed that after the repeal of the Stamp Act tranquillity and popularity would reward their well-meaning endeavours then they were sorely disappointed.

But it was William Pitt who made their lives a misery during the last few months of the ministry. By April he had decided, there can be little doubt, to drive the Rockinghams from office. In January he had never seriously wished to connect his fortunes with theirs and as the months passed he considered the floundering ministry to be little better than a lost cause.

In addition to those which he had raised against the ministry earlier in the year he now brought forward further objections. He must surely have been offended by the ministry's apparent failure to endear itself to Frederick of Prussia. It cannot be claimed on Pitt's behalf in this matter that he was merely using the issue for his own purposes. It is certain that he continued to embrace the vision of an Anglo-Prussian alliance and his enthusiasm for Prussia drove the Rockingham ministry into serious efforts to establish friendly relations with the great German power. That it was unable to do so arose less from its own incompetence, as Pitt would have it, than from the simple fact that Frederick was no longer interested in an alliance with the country which had deserted him in 1762. The lynch-pin of Prussia's foreign policy in the mid 1760s was an alliance with Russia against Austria. England was irrelevant to Frederick's plans, as Pitt himself was to discover less than six months after he came into power.[49] On top of this, Pitt disliked the imperial policy of the ministry. It was not just that he disapproved of the Declaratory Act. He even disliked the further imperial measures of the ministry such as the Free Ports bill. As Mr Jarrett has trenchantly described his attitude: 'Pitt had conquered an Empire for the sake of the old commercial system, with colonies serving as sources of raw materials and as markets for manufactured goods, and he intended that it should remain that way.'[50]

During the spring Pitt gradually dropped any lingering pretence of friendship for the ministry and proceeded with ruthless calculation to attack and to undermine it. As early as 10 March, indeed, he had already proclaimed his wish in the Commons 'to see a good administration formed to the liking of the King and the approbation of the people' from which even Bute's friends need not be proscribed. To the astonishment of those present he went on to praise Lord Bute and to affirm that he had been generally ill-treated and unfairly criticised.[51] In the following weeks his attacks upon the ministry became almost hysterical. He was out to drive the Rockinghams from office and to this end to drain them of confidence. Although he 'confided' to Tommy Walpole in mid-April[52] that his displeasure with the ministry arose from the appointment of Lord George Sackville in December 1765 and that he had been neglected by ministers since January, little credence can be attached to these excuses. He had said nothing about the appointment of Sackville at the time, and he was almost certainly using the appointment as a convenient excuse in the circumstances of the spring of 1766. Furthermore, he, more than anybody else, had been responsible for the break-down of negotiations in January and again in February.[53] Pitt wanted power and influence on his own terms. Thus on 17 April he attacked the Ministry for its inattention to the militia. He stated that he would 'go to the farthest corner of the island to overturn any ministers that are enemies to the militia'.[54] And in the last speech that he made in the session before he went to Bath for the recess

> 'he wished, for the sake of his dear country; that there might be a ministry fixed, such as the King should appoint, and the public approve: that men might be properly adapted to the employments they were appointed to, and whose names were known in Europe, to convey an idea of dignity to this Government both at home and abroad; that if ever he was again admitted, as he had been, into the Royal presence, it should be independent of any personal connections whatsoever; with plenty of recommendations to unanimity, virtue, etc.'[55]

The effects of his attack upon the ministry were not slow to make themselves felt. During April, Conway's resolution to continue in office began to weaken. Grafton's failed.[56]

Grafton, more than anyone, had been deceived by Pitt's ability to play a double game and had regretted bitterly the breakdown of the January negotiations. It is possible that he never quite lost touch with Pitt between January and April.[57] It is certain that he never ceased to yearn for his inclusion within the ministry. On 26 March he told the Lords that he 'expresses the wishes and hopes of all the companies he went into and of the whole nation that Mr Pitt should come into the King's service'.[58] During April when the rift between Pitt and the ministry was widening, Grafton became desperate and he begged Rockingham at least to attempt a rapprochement with Pitt. Rockingham, by now, had had his fill of the Great Commoner: '*he would never advise his Majesty to call Mr Pitt into his closet, that this was a fixed resolution to which he would adhere*'.[59] This was a clumsy declaration for Rockingham to make. It could do no other than upset Grafton. Little would have been lost had he expressed himself a little less strongly and allowed time to reveal Pitt's tactic of undermining the ministry. Rockingham did Pitt's work for him. He precipitated the resignation of Grafton.[60] The King persuaded Grafton to defer his resignation for a week until a replacement could be found for him. His determination to resign wavered during the week and Conway tried to persuade him to reconsider but Pitt's speech of 24 April must have clinched the matter. On 28 April he formally resigned.[61] That it took so long to find a replacement for him revealed that the downfall of the Rockingham ministry seemed to be at hand.

In fact, the astounding situation had been reached where few of the ministers had any enthusiasm for carrying on. The only possible way of strengthening the ministry now that Pitt had turned against it was to attempt a reconciliation with the friends of Bute, but the prejudices of Rockingham and Newcastle ruled this out. Nevertheless, they were prepared to make a gesture of friendship towards them. They would tolerate the restoration of Stuart Mackenzie to his offices but they would go no further.[62] Their reluctance to do so, in the long run, ruled out any possibility that the ministry might survive. It was to be merely a *locum tenens* until the King could put together an administration on a broader basis. Ministers knew this so they went about the task of finding a successor to Grafton with little enthusiasm.[63]

The King, for his part, was angry with the ministers for passing up their last chance of strengthening the administration and went as far as to contact Bute, wondering if 'I cannot form something out of that chosen band that will stand by me' but Bute decided that he could not.[64] The Rockingham ministry would have fallen at this time if George III had had an alternative ministry to hand. This he did not have. In any case, there were two advantages which he enjoyed from keeping the Rockinghams in office. They kept the Grenvilles at bay and, because of the weaknesses of the ministry, allowed the King considerable freedom of action. The King was afraid that if the ministers resigned then they might lay the blame for their resignation on him. He preferred that the ministry be replaced when it had shown itself incapable of continuing and when an alternative to it became available. That time had not yet come. The much-weakened ministry, therefore, was able to stagger on for a further two months but not, it should be stressed, through any strength or virtue of its own but simply because there was no alternative to it. The reluctance of the ministry to approach the Buteites was driving into opposition the only group of men who could have saved it.[65]

The Rockinghams attempted to put the best possible face upon the dilemma in which Grafton's resignation left them and attempted to achieve an overall cabinet and ministerial reshuffle. This the King would not have, and nor would other politicians.[66] Therefore it was not until 23 May that a replacement for Grafton could be found. This was the third Duke of Richmond. He was appointed simply because no one else could be prevailed upon to serve. Both Lord Hardwicke and Charles Yorke refused the vacant Secretaryship, a sure sign that they realised that the ministry was doomed.[67] Rockingham was keen to have Richmond but the more experienced Newcastle was much more sceptical about the wisdom of forcing the young Duke upon the King. George III disliked Richmond's youth and inexperience and it took threats of ministerial resignation to place him in office.[68] Rockingham was now almost indifferent about maintaining good relations with the King. He revived his old demand that the best method of stabilising the ministry was to discipline the placemen. He contemplated trying to force from the King a written declaration that the King's friends must support the ministry, but he was dissuaded from this foolish and futile course of action by the ever-present Egmont.[69]

Having offended the King by their refusal to behave in a conciliatory manner towards the friends of Bute, having annoyed him by insisting upon the appointment of Richmond, the Rockinghams proceeded to infuriate him by offering him a political and personal insult. George III wanted to settle the late Duke of Cumberland's estate upon his two brothers, the Dukes of York and Gloucester, in the present parliamentary session. Rockingham, Conway and Richmond, as well as others in the Government and even some in the Opposition, felt that it was too late in the session to bring in an important financial matter touching the royal family.[70] There was much to be said for this view. Most Members had gone home and the ministers had endured a long and tiring session. The Rockinghams may also have feared that had they acted upon George III's request then they might very well appear as handservants of the King and the dynasty. On the other hand, ministers had promised the King that they would do his bidding on this matter some months earlier although details of the arrangement had not been settled. Newcastle was horrified at Rockingham's obstinacy and his indifference to the opinion of the King.[71] The King was angry because he had promised his brothers that the matter would receive attention before the summer recess and he felt morally obliged to fulfill his promise. His anger was insufficient to shift Rockingham. By the end of May George III had decided that there was no time to lose in ridding himself of a ministry which was becoming increasingly obstructive and obnoxious to him.[72]

That was not the end of Rockingham's insulting behaviour towards the royal family. On 3 June, Jeremiah Dyson, MP for Yarmouth, a Lord of Trade and one of the most prominent Buteites in the ministry, embarrassed the Government by dividing the Commons against a message from the King asking a dowry for Princess Caroline for her forthcoming marriage. Dyson was a distinguished administrator and a prominent speaker but he had, moreover, ostentatiously opposed the repeal of the Stamp Act. On this occasion, he lost his motion, 118–35.[73] Dyson's action, however, stimulated a lesser Buteite, Colonel E. Harvey, to divide the House on the issue of an immediate settlement upon the princes of the Cumberland legacy. This was likewise defeated, by 109–31 but it was exactly the sort of action on the part of office holders which infuriated Rockingham. The next day he expostulated with the King and demanded that he dismiss Dyson. George III temporised and suggested that Rockingham interview Dyson.

This Rockingham did on 5 June, but he obtained no satisfaction from the discussion.[74] The King, however, with Northington's encouragement, flatly refused to dismiss Dyson and told Rockingham that he would create no more peerages.[75] This symbolic withdrawal of the royal confidence could have only one meaning, that the days of the ministry were numbered. The point was underlined when the Lord Chancellor began to absent himself from the Cabinet until, on 6 July, he resigned, ostensibly because of the 'tedious tho' trifling counsels' of the ministry and its reluctance either to strengthen itself by negotiating with other groups or to fill vacant offices.[76] Northington's resignation was the signal for George III to send for Pitt and although the Rockinghams did not formally resign their offices until 30 July, to all intents and purposes the first Rockingham ministry was at an end.

In recent years, the weaknesses of the first Rockingham ministry have tended to obscure its many legislative achievements, especially on imperial matters. The old stories about a constitutionally 'progressive' Rockingham ministry suffering ill-treatment at the hands of the King and desperately defending itself against a revolt of the friends of Bute which figured prominently in Whig mythology are no longer accepted by historians. They prefer to point out that the Rockingham ministry suffered from chronic internal divisions which were compounded by the inexperience of so many of the ministers. There can be no question that they failed to impress the King and that they treated him clumsily. After the death of Cumberland they made the mistake which Newcastle had been making for the last three years. They were prepared to surrender everything to Pitt. When he refused to help them they then blamed him as well as Bute rather than themselves for their problems and their removal from office.[77] All of this leads to one conclusion. The Rockinghams were not yet a party in any developed sense. It was their lack of constructive strategies, at least as much as their inexperience and lack of ability, which was responsible for their psychological dependence upon others. Indeed, their misfortunes and their miscalculations themselves became vehicles for the later exposition of party attitudes. Almost from the very day of Northington's resignation the Rockinghams began to place into the context of the myth of Bute's secret influence the erratic behaviour of the King, his reluctance to dismiss recalcitrant placemen, the mysterious proliferation of notes and messages purporting to express the King's opinions on the repeal of the Stamp Act, and the strange circumstances surrounding the last weeks of the life of the ministry. The first Rockingham ministry appeared to provide unchallengeable proof of the validity of their complaints and protests. So, too, in rather a different manner, did the coming to power of the Chatham administration and the mysterious question of the Court's purposes in replacing the ministry of the Rockinghams with that of the Great Commoner.

It was during the Rockingham ministry that Edmund Burke first made his impact upon the political scene in England. Burke had been born in 1729, one year before Rockingham, of an Irish Anglican family, one of four children who survived from a litter of over a dozen infants. The first hint of intellectual distinction came during the years he spent at Trinity College, Dublin. His father had in mind for him a legal career and it was to pursue this that Edmund came to London in 1749. But his heart was never in his legal textbooks and he put them aside in 1750. He chose the career of a writer but it was not until 1756 that he made his first mark upon the London literary scene. In that year were published both his *Vindication of Natural Society* and his *Essay . . . on the Sublime and Beautiful*. Both of them concentrated upon the same theme albeit in different ways, his distrust of the prevailing belief in abstract reason. These and subsequent less theoretical writings[78] gave Edmund a modest reputation which enabled him to mix in the fashionable literary circles of the capital. In 1758 there began his connection with the *Annual Register* for which Burke received £100 for editing each issue. Together with Robert Dodsley Burke ran the *Register* at least until 1764 and there is evidence, more tenuous it is true, of a continued connection thereafter. But Edmund had already discovered the harsh fact that the income of a writer was insufficient to sustain his ambitions. To supplement that income he became secretary to William Gerard Hamilton[79] with whom he went to Ireland from 1761 to 1764 but from whom he parted in the following year. In July 1765 through the good offices of Lord John Cavendish Edmund became private secretary to the Marquis of Rockingham. Burke, no doubt, respected the elevated political and the unblemished social position of the Marquis but it was the security of employment—and the pension—which he offered which must have impressed Edmund rather than any distinction of character, virtue or ability which Rockingham possessed.[80] There is, indeed, evidence that Burke, who entered Parliament in December 1765 for Lord Verney's pocket borough of Wendover, was, by the summer of 1765 quite desperate, and that he regarded his employment with Rockingham as his last chance to make a name for himself in politics. 'I came into Parliament not at all as a place of preferment, but of refuge; I was pushed into it; and I must have been a Member, and that too, with some *Éclat*, or be a little more than nothing.'[81]

It would be misleading to claim too much for Burke. It is true that his early speeches made a considerable impact upon the House of Commons but he was as yet very far from being Rockingham's mentor. The idea that Burke 'educated' Rockingham politically cannot withstand even the most cursory examination of Burke's behaviour in the ministry of 1765–6, in particular, his advocacy of alliances which must have been anathema to Rockingham, with Grenville and with the Butes.[82] In 1765 Burke had no carefully thought-out political principles which it was his historic destiny to impart to the Rockingham Whigs. In particular, he had no conception of party government. There is no evidence that Burke exercised decisive influence over the formulation of the ministry's policy of Declaration and Repeal. (To expect that a newcomer could ever have done so is surely to credit Burke with superhuman talents of perception and persuasion which he did not possess.)[83] He was still inferior to men like Dowdeswell in the Marquis' counsels and estimation and was to remain so for some years. Furthermore, there is evidence to suggest that Burke's political loyalties were not yet quite finally determined. In July 1766 Grafton offered Burke a post in the Chatham administration— a move indicative in itself—and it was not without some hesitation that Edmund refused Grafton's offers.[84] On the other hand, we should recognise that he brought to the ministry a deep conviction of the need to obtain popular support, especially from the commercial circles of the provincial towns and the metropolis, for its measures.[85] Furthermore, there can be no doubting the extent of his work in obtaining the support of the mercantile community for the American policies of the ministry. In this, however, he was not alone and it would be wildly misleading to credit Burke with sole responsibility for establishing links between the Rockingham ministry and the mercantile community in the country. What matters, in the long run, is that Burke learned a good many lessons from the Rockingham ministry—the need for unity, the need for popular support and a deep-rooted distrust of William Pitt. In the accumulated experiences of Burke and the Rockingham Whigs, the downfall of the Rockingham ministry and, still more, the curious circumstances in which the Chatham administration took office, were to be of outstanding importance.

In the weeks after Grafton's resignation, the fate of the Rockingham ministry was sealed. The King had to seek an alternative administration and the only feasible alternative left open to him was to have recourse to his old enemy, William Pitt. In May, Camden had reported to Northington that Pitt 'was ready to come if called upon, that he meant to try and form an Administration of the best of all partys and an exclusion to no description'.[86] This coincided well enough with the intentions of George III. These were 'to try through Mr Pitt to build an Administration on as general a basis as the times will permit, to see as many of those gentlemen who were contrary to my inclinations remov'd reinstated, particularly Mr Mackenzie'.[87] The King was not prepared to stretch his principles as far as to allow George Grenville to return to office but he was willing to accept some of his followers.[88] The King, in fact, had no very great ambitions left after nearly six unsettled years on the throne. He merely wanted to establish a stable ministry under Pitt which was prepared to govern the country efficiently, and to treat the monarch and his friends with a little consideration. His motives were just as much personal as political. As he had written to Bute on 3 May: 'if I am to continue the life of agitation I have these three years there will be a Council (of) Regency to assist in that undertaking'.[89] How far the King, together with Pitt, were to succeed in their fairly modest ambitions will shortly appear.

On 6 July George III sent for Pitt, who came to town on 11 July.[90] He saw Northington that evening and the Lord Chancellor reported to the King that Pitt's language was reasonable. (He was insisting upon the inclusion of Temple in the arrangement but not that of Grenville.)[91] All seemed to be set fair for a successful negotiation when Pitt met George III at Windsor at noon on 12 July. The King must have been delighted with what he heard. Pitt affirmed that even if Temple refused to take a part it would not deter him, and he declared that Mackenzie and other friends of Bute could be restored to their offices. Furthermore, Pitt stated that 'the only means of carrying on affairs with any degree of utility' was 'as far as possible to dissolve all factions & to see the best of all partys in Employment' although time would be needed to achieve that objective. This last condition was to be crucial. Pitt did not think it was feasible to implement the plan of his administration immediately and he had perforce to 'recommend taking the Subsisting administration as the basis & making such alterations in it as would give it more stability'.[92] Perhaps Pitt felt that with the Bedford and Grenville Whigs in Opposition he could not very well afford to offend the Rockinghams. Whatever the explanation, one thing was clear. The establishment of the Chatham administration was to be founded upon necessity and not upon the armchair aspirations of a young King and an aged statesman.[93]

Much, though by no means everything, would depend upon Temple's willingness to take office and on 13 July Northington summoned him to town.[94] The King saw him on the evening of the 15 July and was dismayed not only by the fact that Temple was not prepared to base the new ministry on the existing one, but also because he held notions 'very heterogenius to My and Your ideas' as he wrote anxiously to Pitt.[95] An interview between Pitt and Temple on the following day ended in an angry exchange, a point blank refusal by Temple to take the Treasury and the ending of a political friendship of many years.[96] Temple was unwilling to play second-fiddle to Pitt as he had done for so long. If he had taken the Treasury in a ministry led by Pitt and dominated by the Rockinghams 'At the head of this I might have stood a capital cypher, surrounded with cyphers of quite a different complexion, the whole under the guidance of the great Luminary, the great Commoner, with the Privy Seal in his hand'.[97] This statement not only throws light upon Temple's refusal to take office in July 1766. It illuminates his behaviour a year earlier when his refusal to take office had made the first Rockingham ministry possible. Then, as now, he was angered at being kept uninformed. On this occasion, he was summoned to town by Northington and told nothing of what had passed between the King and Pitt.[98] It must be confessed, however, that neither Pitt nor George III were much distressed at his refusal to take part and Temple suspected as much.[99] Northington went to see Pitt shortly after the altercation between Temple and the Great Commoner and found the latter 'very settled I think to proceed at all events'.[100] As for the King, he might have looked with pleasure upon the refusal to take part of the brother of George Grenville and the patron of Wilkes.[101] The refusal of Temple to take office was thus not wholly distressing to George III and William Pitt, but it had at least two important consequences. First, it destroyed any chance that may have existed that the Grenville Whigs would take office, thus violating the ideological basis of the ministry, to take the best men from all parties. Further, Temple's refusal led to a number of cabinet appointments which were to prove disastrous, to Pitt, to George III, to the nation and to the Empire.[102]

In spite of the grand intentions of the King and Pitt, the distribution of the major offices was determined less by the ideological beliefs of those appointed than, more simply, by the need to put together some sort of ministry. Both of them had put at stake so much of their prestige that they could not now draw back from the 'experiment' in government upon which they were embarking. After Temple's refusal to take the Treasury, Pitt offered the post to Grafton. To regard that amiable Duke as one of the 'best' men from the parties is, of course, nonsensical. Pitt offered him the Treasury, calculating correctly, that if Grafton came in then Conway probably would and thus the hostility of the Rockinghams to his ministry might be neutralised. Pitt was thus anxious to persuade Grafton and he did not stop short of a little moral blackmail, telling the alarmed Grafton that the success or failure of the whole arrangement depended upon his accepting Pitt's offer.[103] Grafton agreed so long as Charles Townshend could be prevailed upon to accept the post of Chancellor of the Exchequer. Pitt found this a bitter pill for he mistrusted Townshend but he was forced to swallow it.[104] The fact that he did so made Conway's retention of his post of Leader of the Commons absolutely essential in view of the need to provide a counter-weight of stability to Townshend's unpredictability. This Conway agreed to, as well as a transfer from the Southern to the Northern Secretaryship.[105] Pitt bestowed Conway's old department upon Shelburne in spite of the King's lack of enthusiasm for him. Other offices were likewise distributed through necessity rather than design. Pratt, predictably, went to the Woolsack and Northington became Lord President. Egmont vacated the Admiralty and Pitt offered it to Gower, one of the leading, though by no means most able, Bedford Whigs. Lord Granby, an old friend of Pitt, became Commander-in-Chief. These were the major offices, then, of the Cabinet which George III and William Pitt intended to spearhead the crusade against party.

This Cabinet can only by the remotest stretch of the imagination be depicted as the best men of all parties. It was not unusually talented, even by the less than stringent standards of eighteenth century cabinet competence. Its members were united only by their prospective readiness to obey Pitt passively. The Cabinet was an uneasy collection—the words 'alliance' and 'combination' seem inappropriate—of men who were close to Pitt, like Camden and Shelburne, of men who were close to the King, like Northington, and those whose loyalties were divided between Pitt and Rockingham such as Grafton and Conway. This was hardly the ministry of the best of all parties, and, indeed, some parties were not represented in it. 'The plan will probably be, to pick and cull from all quarters, and break all parties, as much as possible'.[106] But the parties remained in existence. Pitt had been unable to obtain the best men from all parties and break faction. He had not even been able to put together a stable ministry, still less one which was united on matters of policy, for example, on America. The real question hanging over politics towards the end of July 1766 was not whether Pitt would be able to destroy faction but whether his ramshackle ministry would be able to survive at all. The only measure of success which the ministry had, indeed, was in reconciling Bute's friends to the Court. Mackenzie was restored to his office and Northumberland was given a Dukedom. How easy it would have been for the Rockinghams to have won over this office-hungry group! The Chatham administration was to face almost every conceivable kind of political difficulty but it was not to face the kind of office holders' mutiny which had so distressed Rockingham.

The fact that Pitt accepted the Earldom of Chatham is a fact both more widely known and its consequences better understood than the fact that *even during the days when the ministry was being negotiated* his health, which had not been robust for several years, now began to give grounds for serious concern. His journey to London had been enough to confine him to his bed. Between 15 and 22 July Pitt was down with fever.[107] As for the peerage, it was not until the formal kissing of hands on 28 July that the ministers learned of Pitt's elevation. As Camden put it: 'Our conception of the strength of the Administration had been, till that moment, derived from the great advantage he would have given to it by remaining with the Commons'.[108] As Lord Privy Seal, Pitt's administrative energies were already lost to the ministry. Now, the ministry's greatest single asset (and of these it had remarkably few), Pitt's personal domination of the Commons, was thrown away and its authority there left to rest with the inadequate and uncertain Conway and the irresponsible Townshend.

Pitt saw his grand role as that of a general ordering his army to march in a general direction but he failed to provide it either with a route or with supplies. His inattention to major matters of administrative and parliamentary management was to prove fatal to the success of his ministry in achieving its loftily proclaimed objectives. The first attempt of the reign to destroy party in 1762–3 had collapsed because of the timidity of Lord Bute and the unyielding character of Grenville. It was not until the Chatham administration that George III was able to repeat his attempt. It was to be still-born because of Chatham's ill-health and bad judgement. Both men, for different reasons, wanted to destroy party; the King desired independence of action and Chatham wished to rally the country in a patriotic revival directed against the House of Bourbon. Before the ministry was even formed, however, the disappointment of the intentions of both was evident.[109] In the event, the Chatham administration was not much unlike the other ministries of the 1760s although George III and Chatham would have had it otherwise.

The Rockinghams, meanwhile, were concluding that the downfall of their ministry and the curious circumstances surrounding the formation of the Chatham administration vindicated their constant preoccupation with the evil influence of Lord Bute. They were agreed that there was a coherent plan behind these puzzling events. On the day that Northington resigned, however, Rockingham agreed with George III that his ministry was too weak to go on. He did not believe that there was a sinister plot. 'I rather think there is no plan—a few days must show it.'[110] Richmond, on the same day, however, thought that Northington's resignation 'looks very like a break, and not of our bringing on'.[111] Things moved quickly. By the following day Newcastle believed that a plan to remove the ministry existed. 'The great point is to know, whether the step of the Chancellor is in concert with the King, Ld Egmont, or any body else.'[112] Inevitably, the finger of suspicion began to point in one direction. Hardwicke wondered where the decision for Northington's resignation had originated. 'I presume from that *quarter, which has and will have the real interior* influence and weight, which turned out the last Ministry, and will the present, let the outward instruments, and actors change ever so often.'[113] These rumours were confirmed by others to the effect that Bute had been to Kew to see the King.[114] In short, the Rockinghams were compelled to interpret the events of July within the context of the Bute myth. In

Newcastle it reached its most extreme exposition. 'To be sure, the Princess of Wales, & My Lord Bute were the Movers, & must be the Finishers of this great Work. But how far they may agree with Mr Pitt, or Mr Pitt with them; And what Part My Lord Temple, Mr George Grenville, the Duke of Bedford, & His Friends, are to have in this New Administration, may be the Cause of Difficulty & Delay.'[115]

By this time, too, what was left of Rockingham's laconic indifference to the fate of his ministry was beginning to disappear. Until as late as 9 July he put a brave face on everything, avowing that the Chancellor's resignation need not bring down the ministry so long as Charles Yorke was allowed to replace him and, as always, that intransigent office-holders were punished.[116] This was whistling in the dark and Rockingham began to realise it. A man with Rockingham's pride and the first victim of the King's desire to destroy the parties could hardly be expected to take his misfortunes lightly. Dwelling and brooding upon the slights administered to him by George III and by Pitt during the last three years, he concluded that the union of the King and Pitt in July 1766 was a declaration of war upon his own party, and proof that intrigue and plotting had for months past been undermining the foundations of a ministry which had striven unselfishly to serve the public interest for the credit of the Empire and of the King himself. Furthermore, Rockingham was not mollified by the fact that several of his friends were retained in office. He found far more significant the fact that Temple was Pitt's first choice for the Treasury and Grafton his second.[117] Rockingham was offended that his advice had not been sought on the composition of the new ministry. He was angry at Pitt's silence and the King's secretiveness and, above all, he was infuriated at the approaches made to his friends without the King or Pitt informing him.[118] It was for this reason that Rockingham refused to receive Pitt when the latter called on him on 27 July, a childish piece of retaliation for previous insults, yet one for which Pitt was as much to blame as Rockingham, for he had undoubtedly transgressed the boundaries of courtesy in entirely ignoring Rockingham for so long.[119] Nevertheless, it was a petty and spiteful action on Rockingham's part and Conway, who had persuaded Pitt to make this little gesture of conciliation, was understandably annoyed with the Marquis.

In view of the revival of the Bute myth and the worsening of relations between Rockingham and Chatham it is, on the face of it, surprising, that almost all of Rockingham's friends remained in office and did not resign with Rockingham and Newcastle. So far from the Chatham ministry breaking parties it seemed to owe its very existence to the fact that it was built upon the Rockingham ministry. Because the Government was staffed with so many men upon whose loyalty Rockingham thought he could depend, he believed that he might still retain some leverage over Chatham and George III. There was no reason why Rockingham should call out his men to go into a declared opposition to a ministry which had not yet announced any matters of policy which it intended to pursue, and upon which an opposition might have been launched. Newcastle saw as early as 12 July that in view of Pitt's difficulties in filling posts the Rockinghams ought to remain in office.[120] On the Government side, too, there was no talk of a purge. Camden believed that 'The D. of N. and . . . the Marquess must give way: but I do not believe Mr P. will wish to remove the rest in office, unless they in a pique shd scorn to hold on under his appointmt'.[121] This suited Newcastle and Rockingham well. There was no need to go into Opposition. It was, moreover, better to watch over he constitution from within rather than from without. Had they sounded the clarion call to Opposition how many of their friends would have resisted the blandishments of the Court, the glamour of Pitt and the magnetic pull of service to the King? Furthermore, to oppose Pitt would be to endanger that support amongst the mercantile community of the metropolis which the Rockinghams had so carefully cultivated in the winter of 1765–6. Furthermore, to declare a systematic opposition to Pitt might only drive him into Bute's arms and under his influence. The only way of thwarting the plan of the Court was to keep the Rockingham party sound and entire and this could best be done by keeping its followers in their places.

Part Three

RE-FORMATION

1766–72

Chapter 8

The Crisis of the Rockingham Whig Party 1766–8

During the parliamentary recess the attitude of the Rocking-hams towards the ministry hardened but their leaders remained content to maintain the position decided upon in July. Their friends in office were to remain there and those outside the ministry were not to enter into a systematic opposition to it. As the weeks passed, however, the feeling grew among the Rockinghamites outside the ministry that Chatham and Bute were hand in glove and that the only way to defeat them was for all supporters of the late ministry whether in office or not to remain united. Rockingham summed up his position:

> 'The only thing I fear is a real disunion amongst those *with whom I had the honour to be called into Administration.* Our private, personal friendship, is the greatest security against that event; and, I am sure, politically speaking, nothing can gratify Lord Chatham or Lord Bute half so much as our disunion, or in future will be a severer check upon them both than keeping in good humour those I call ourselves.'[1]

The theme of the next two years was to be Rockingham's limited success in achieving this objective and thus preserving the existence of his party in spite of the fact that the drift of men to Chatham proceeded upon a scale which at the end of

1766, at least, seemed to presage the destruction of the Rockingham Whigs.

Throughout this period the most important psychological reality in the minds of Rockingham and his friends remained their belief in the revived influence of Bute in the guise of the Chatham ministry. It was not just the restoration of Mackenzie's office and the granting of a Dukedom to Northumberland which seemed suspicious to them. It was the granting of offices to men like Harcourt, Jenkinson and Despencer and the general rallying around the Court of the friends of Bute in the autumn of 1766 which worried them as the Buteites returned to their natural home after their unfamiliar and uncongenial spell in Opposition in 1765–6.[2] The Rockinghams were not alone in entertaining these fears. Indeed, 'the polemic conducted between the Rockingham and Grenville groups between 1765 and 1767 was dominated by the attempts of both sides to convict the other of complicity with Bute'.[3] Even if the fear of Bute's influence had not been so widespread, the friends of Rockingham who remained inside the ministry could not lightly cast aside the political loyalties and beliefs of the last four years. Although the evidence is scanty there is enough to show that George Onslow (who was in the ministry), the Cavendishes, Tommy Walpole and Sir William Meredith, among others, were dining regularly together on the eve of the session in an informal club arrangement.[4] It is quite likely that sooner or later the Rockinghams would have come out in opposition to Chatham but that time had not yet come. Rockinghams from within and without the ministry alike attended the meeting at the cockpit on the eve of the session, the only party not in Government to do so.[5]

As was so frequently the case in eighteenth century politics, however, momentous events were to spring less from ideological conflicts than from clashes of personality. It was the characteristic tactlessness of Chatham which forced the Rockinghams to reconsider their position and ultimately to declare their opposition to the ministry. The ministry had not been in existence for more than a few weeks before Burke was complaining of the scanty treatment meted out to office-holding Rockinghamites by Chatham.[6] Thereafter, continued slights and offensive gestures gradually alienated the Rockinghams. The first really significant case occurred when Chatham required Chief Justice Monson, a loyal Rockinghamite, to surrender his Justiceship in Eyre, North of the Trent. Grafton saved Chatham from himself. Chatham hardly considered the storm which Monson's dismissal would arouse and it is to Grafton's credit that he saw the need to offer Monson a post of at least equal status. Monson's honour should have been satisfied when an Earldom was found for the Chief Justice.[7] However, although the offer was not ungenerous, the language in which it was couched was extremely discourteous and Monson rejected Grafton's gesture.[8] Chatham seemed to be unable to treat the Rockinghams with any respect. His offer to promote Lord Scarborough to the office of joint Paymaster-General, for example, was expressed in arrogant terms which offended even the mild Conway.[9] The Rockinghams, naturally touchy, became over-sensitive at these continued slights and at the uncertainties surrounding the situation of those in office. For twice during the first six months in the life of his ministry Chatham attempted, without success, to come to terms with the Bedford Whigs. The first of these occasions came in August when Gower was offered the Admiralty.[10] In October further negotiations floundered when Chatham was unwilling to pay the price in offices and patronage which the Bedfords were demanding.[11] These soundings unsettled the Rockinghams in office for the support of the Bedfords could only be bought at the expense of themselves. It was surely the fact, then, that their fears had been already aroused and their sensitivities already pricked which explains the howls of anger which went up from the Rockinghams when one of their leaders was publicly humiliated.

The parting of the ways between the office-holding Rockinghamites and Chatham came in November when Lord Edgecumbe, Treasurer of the Household and a considerable borough owner, was informed that he was to be replaced by John Shelley, a nephew of Newcastle, but who had been estranged from his uncle for some years. It was a symbolic appointment. For Shelley, a Chathamite and ex-Rockinghamite, to replace the loyal Edgecumbe was an insult of the most direct kind not to Edgecumbe alone but also to Newcastle and Rockingham. Conway saw at once that this unnecessary irritant could have far-reaching consequences and he attempted to soften the blow of Edgecumbe's dismissal in an effort to avoid bringing the already frayed relations between Rockingham and Chatham to a head. But these attempts only made matters much worse. Edgecumbe was offered a Bedchamber post but understandably refused to acknowledge what was in effect his own demotion. To Conway's intense annoyance, Chatham then dismissed Edgecumbe.[12] The Rockinghams saw in all this not merely an attempt by Chatham to humiliate an individual but a comprehensive plan which had for its objective the crushing of the Rockinghamites and the further enhancement of Lord Bute's influence.[13] On 19 November the leaders of the Rockingham party met to decide upon a tactical riposte. Of those present, Rockingham, Richmond, Newcastle, Albemarle, Dartmouth, Bessborough, Grantham, Lord John Cavendish, Jack White, Dowdeswell and, significantly, Burke, none had a good word to say for Chatham. It was agreed that of those in office, Portland, Scarborough, Bessborough and Monson should resign.[14] This was intended to provoke the resignation of other loyal friends culminating in the *coup de grâce*, the resignation of Conway, which would leave Chatham in such dire straits that his ministry could not survive. Not wishing to appear guilty of factious behaviour, however, the Rockinghams decided to give Chatham one last opportunity of redeeming himself. Portland saw Conway on 21 November to convey his party's ultimatum: Edgecumbe was to be restored and the Rockinghams in the ministry were to be given an increased share of patronage otherwise the resignation plan would be put into effect.[15] Chatham was not the man to be bullied into changing his mind by the threats of a few aristocrats whom he despised and on 27 November the Rockinghams implemented their stratagem.[16]

The outcome was disastrous for Rockingham. In addition to Portland, Monson, Bessborough and Scarborough very few Rockinghamites wished to martyr themselves for the sake of Lord Edgecumbe. Saunders and Keppel, both at the Admiralty Board, and Sir William Meredith came out. The rest stayed in.

This was a supremely important moment in the history of the Rockingham Whig party. Just when it was beginning to achieve something of an independent existence, and just when its former dependence upon men like Cumberland and Pitt was beginning to decline, it lost both its ministerial and its Chathamite wing. In numerical terms the Edgecumbe affair was part of a larger process in which the Rockingham Whig party declined in size in the House of Commons from 111 in July 1766 to only 54 on the eve of the general election of 1768. It can be calculated, nevertheless, that at least 18 members of the House of Commons failed to respond to Rockingham's call to resign.[17] Late in 1766, therefore, the Rockingham Whig Party changed its character. It was no longer a sprawling confederation of groups of every description, Pelhamite, Chathamite, ministerialist, Country and Tory. The Edgecumbe affair may have weakened the Rockinghams numerically in the Lower House, but it enabled a coherent, identifiable and reasonably united party to emerge, dedicated no longer to the destruction of the power of Lord Bute alone but now also that of Lord Chatham. The effects of the Edgecumbe affair upon the history of the Rockingham Whigs were thus far-reaching and fundamental.

The Rockinghams were now in Opposition, where they were to remain for almost sixteen years. Mr Brooke is quite justified in reminding us that whatever the consequences of the Edgecumbe affair, the Rockinghams did not go into Opposition on a matter of constitutional principle.[18] Differences of personality and the culmination of months of jealousy and distrust led to the breach. It was not quite the case, however, that the Rockinghams declared their opposition on 25 November when they opposed the ministry on the motion for a committee to inquire into the state of the East India Company. Although they did oppose the ministry on that occasion,[19] there were several abstentions among the Rockinghams. It was only later, in December, that their opposition became both thoroughgoing and 'systematic'.[20] On 5 December, for example, the Rockinghams divided *with* the ministry on the Indemnity bill for the embargo on corn.[21] But it was to be on the East India Company question, the most important issue of the session, that the Rockinghams were to come out consistently against the ministry. Their systematic opposition was never announced. It was made evident and then accepted as a matter of routine during the early weeks of the session.

The departure of the Rockinghams and their drift into systematic opposition left the Chatham administration not only with some vacancies to fill but also with the prospect of a tough parliamentary session ahead. It was thus natural for the ministers to resume their earlier courtship of the Bedfords. In late November and early December Chatham indicated that he wished for an accession of strength from that quarter. But he made the incredible mistake of trying to win the avaricious Bedfords on the cheap.[22] He offered them a handful of offices of paltry political weight. In return, Bedford listed over ten of his friends who needed to be provided for. Chatham would not go so far and there the matter ended. Somehow, Chatham had, within a matter of days, managed to drive into Opposition two parties neither of which had wanted to go into Opposition at all.

It can, at least, be said for Chatham that he and the King refuse to accede to the rapaciousness of Bedford's demands, because to have done so would have offended against the fundamental principles upon which the ministry had been constructed. The King told Chatham that

> 'this hour demands due firmness, 'tis that has already dismade all hopes of those just retir'd, & will I am confident shew the Bedfords of what little consequence they are; a contrary conduct would at once overturn the end propos'd at the formation of the present Administration; for to root out the present method of banding together, can only be obtain'd by a withstanding their unjust demands, as well as the engaging able Men be their private connections where they will.'[23]

In other words, the King would not have the Bedfords as a party and the Bedfords would not come in on any other basis. Nevertheless, there was evident a certain weakening in the moral position of the King and Chatham. It was not so much that the Bedfords were unacceptable because they were a party, but because they were too greedy. This was the impression that Bedford derived: 'That the King did not design to proscribe particulars of any denomination, and consequently that there would not be room at present for a full reinstatement of my friends.'[24] Bedford, at least, believed that the day would come when the Bedford Whigs might take office as a party and time was to show that he was right.

The way was now open for the Rockinghams and the Bedfords to try to come to some sort of working agreement. Rockingham, indeed, had been willing on more than one occasion since July to consider an arrangement with the Bedfords but never with the Grenville party. It is, of course, true, as Mr Brooke has argued, that Rockingham's preference for a Bedford alliance had much to do with the fact that the Bedfords 'had no candidate for the Treasury and dominant personality in the Commons'.[25] Rockingham's distaste for a Grenville alliance, furthermore, had little to do with their differing views on America. The Bedfords had been just as determined as Grenville to have the Stamp Act enforced. Nevertheless, it may be argued that Grenville was no longer a serious contender for the Treasury in view of the King's hatred of him. Furthermore, for Rockingham to have allied himself at this juncture with Grenville would have affronted George III. The Rockinghams had saved the King from Grenville once. It seems most unlikely, having done so, that they should immediately try to force him upon George III as soon as they were once more in Opposition.[26] An understanding with the Bedfords would not be subject to these disadvantages. Nevertheless none was reached. Portland was completely opposed to the idea and Rockingham himself was never more than lukewarm.[27] The Rockinghams had therefore to fall back upon the only line now open to them and one which was already popular with some of the younger men in the party, to oppose the ministry of Lord Chatham from a position of independence.[28]

The Rockinghams were alone now, but they were quick to congratulate themselves that they had not been contaminated by the influence of Bute. As for Chatham, he 'openly shakes hands with My Lord Bute . . . and He depends upon the

G

Corruption of the Times, and upon the Instability of our own Friends . . . for the success and support of himself and his measures'.[29] There now appears for the first time in the history of the Rockingham party what is to be commonplace a year later—the notion that the Rockinghams were better off in Opposition and much more likely to preserve their virtue and consistency in opposing the corruption of the Court than in staking all their fortunes upon the attainment of office.[30]

Virtuous and innocent ideas were one thing; the organisation of a vigorous Opposition was quite another. The Rockingham party was at this stage of its history in such a state of flux and change that improved organization came low on the list of its priorities. It was not just that the Edgecumbe affair had effected a drastic change in the nature of the Rockingham party itself. There was also a transition to be achieved in the leadership of the party. Newcastle's influence was steadily declining while that of Burke and Dowdeswell had not yet reached their apogee. Rockingham still smarted from the failures of his ministry and from the slights to which he and his friends had been subjected since July. There was not yet in the Rockingham party the cohesion, the direction and group feeling which were later to be such pronounced characteristics. In the session of 1767 which was just opening, inexperience, incompetence and confusion were to lead to despair and demoralisation. The Marquis of Rockingham confessed to his wife at the outset: 'As to politics, I am bereft of all ideas. Under the present divisions, Lord Bute and Lord Chatham are very safe. And there appears, to me at least, no prospect of union.'[31] There, in fact, lay the clue to the activities of the Rockingham Whigs in Opposition in the session of 1767. The Rockingham party was as yet too weak to expect to launch an effective Opposition and too inexperienced in the routine of systematic opposition to engineer the destruction of Chatham. Political salvation was to be found not in party but in a union of the opposition parties. Much of the year 1767 was to be spent searching for this elusive chimera. Rockingham had already shown himself to be unwilling to co-operate with Bute, Chatham and Grenville, and his attempts to work with Bedford had not advanced beyond the discussion stage. On the other hand, although the prospects for Opposition were poor the ministry was weak and divided. How far the Opposition would be able to make life difficult for the Chatham administration in the session depended upon the effectiveness of its challenge on the great domestic, foreign and imperial issues of the day.

Already before the opening of Parliament the reputation of the new ministry had fallen catastrophically because of its handling of foreign and domestic policy matters. Chatham seemed completely incapable of recalling his sure touch in foreign affairs. He was unable to realise that the diplomacy of the middle of the decade was no longer the same as that of the Seven Years War. He might think of recreating the Prussian alliance and, ultimately, of building up a great alliance of the northern powers against the Bourbon powers of France and Spain but, as Frederick the Great wanted to know, what dangers were to be expected from the Bourbon powers, particularly in their current state of financial weakness and, in the case of Spain, political instability? He could see no virtue in arousing suspicions among the great powers by forming an unnecessary alliance against imaginary dangers. Frederick had no intention of associating himself closely with England. His own diplomatic objectives—especially in Poland—could perfectly well be attained with a Russian alliance. Frederick the Great may once have had some regard for William Pitt, the Great Commoner, as a loyal friend to his country at a time of military crisis. But he felt that he owed little to the Earl of Chatham and, indeed, feared lest Prussia be dragged into conflicts in Western Europe, fomented by the treacherous Court of St James and the sinister Earl of Bute, which were no concern of Prussia. Chatham would not swallow the bitter pill at once; it was some few months later before England ceased her fruitless representations with Prussia, but Chatham must have been shocked to find that his most treasured scheme of all, the reshuffling of the diplomatic cards of Europe, was now completely out of the question.

The domestic policy of the new ministry was as unfortunate as its foreign policy was irrelevant. Chatham's return to office was greeted with widespread rioting over the food shortages

which were a consequence of the poor harvest of 1766. Chatham
dealt with the situation in a characteristically abrupt manner.
Through an order in council of 24 September he placed an
embargo upon the export of corn. This was an unusual
exercise of the royal perogative. The status of his high-handed
action was not clear to constitutional purists and it came under
attack at the meeting of Parliament on 11 November. 'Lord
Northington, and Lord Chatham went so near the old prerogative doctrines of Chas. Ist, of the *salus populi suprema lex*,
and *necessitas lex temporis*, and then making the King the judge
of the necessity, and that necessity superseding law, you at
once establish the doctrines which were held by the judges in
the case of ship money, and give in to King James's notions of
suspending laws.'[32] Lord Mansfield's considered view was that
ministers had acted illegally and that they ought to have
procured a bill of indemnity to protect those responsible for
enforcing the proclamation. This, in fact, was what Conway
admitted in the Commons, but the debates on the Indemnity
bill only allowed ministers in both Houses further opportunities
for tangling themselves up in constitutional doctrines better
suited to the seventeenth than the eighteenth century. No
one can accuse the ministers of evil intentions. It was confusion and incompetence which accompanied their actions
but their total effect was devastating. It was something of an
achievement for the Chatham ministry in the first few days of
the session to bring about one of the most startling alliances
of the century, however short-lived, that between the friends
of Bute and the Rockingham Whigs. 'Sir G. Elliot, Mr Dyson
and that set of gentlemen spoke strongly against the legality
and the doctrine of a power in the King to dispense with it,
so did Mr Burke, Lord Rockingham's late secretary, and Mr
Dowdeswell, and for the necessity of a Bill of Indemnity to
vindicate the constitution.'[33] In the early days of the session,
the ministry had been discredited by the collapse of its foreign
policy and by its farcical mishandling of the Corn Embargo.
All this had been accomplished before opposition to the ministry
had even had an opportunity of organising its forces. On the
affairs of the East India Company which were to dominate the
session, Opposition was likely to be far more formidable.

The Indian problem required an urgent solution. The Indian territory governed by the East India Company had been enormously increased by the late war. Its defence, security and prosperity could no longer reasonably be entrusted to a trading company whose activities went almost entirely unhindered by government interference. Chatham took the view that the right and the responsiblity for the Government of the Indian Empire rested with the British Parliament, although the Company might be permitted to administer it and to take some revenue at the discretion of Parliament. Chatham assumed no deep-rooted philosophical position on the issue. He may well have shared in the prevailing antipathy towards the alleged vast profits of the company, the distaste for its speculations and the widespread concern over the effect of Indian fortunes upon British politics.[34] He intended that a far-reaching reoganisation of the Government of the subcontinent would follow a parliamentary enquiry into the affairs of the Company. Conway and Townshend[35] were far more cautious. Not wishing to antagonise the Company, they were prepared to negotiate about the right and responsibility of Parliament as a preliminary to discussions about the revenue. Although Chatham believed that the right and responsibility were non-negotiable, he was unable to impose his views upon the two Secretaries because of his absence from London during most of the session.

At first the Rockinghams knew little of these divisions and opposed the ministry for no reason other than their desire to embarrass it. They were largely spectators of the parliamentary discussions of the end of the year which led to the establishment of a committee of enquiry. By the time the enquiry opened, after interminable delays early in March, Rockingham was aware of disagreements in the ministry and he knew of Conway's unhappiness with the enquiry. Had Rockingham at this point been more perceptive and perhaps more ruthless, he would have brought forward motions in the Commons which might have forced Conway, and perhaps even Townshend, to declare themselves. He might, at least, have prepared his parliamentary ground with a little care. For example, on 6 March, the Commons debated Beckford's motion to continue the enquiry. Townshend and Conway disapproved of the enquiry and, according to Townshend himself as reported by Newcastle to Rockingham: 'we should have amended, or turned Beckford's question as to have got himself and Conway with us upon a division.'[36] This they did not do. In fact, they did not even express a clear opinion upon the need for an enquiry. They doubted the propriety of it 'but did not make any opposition to it, only threw out reflexions . . . (on) the weakness of the argument which had been used for it'.[37] It seems to have been only as late as the end of March 1767 that the Rockinghams first began to champion the Company's case with any great enthusiasm. It was from the pen and tongue of Burke that the defence of the chartered rights of the Company became equated with resistance to a conspiracy of secret influ- ence designed to subvert property and expand hugely the influence of the ministry. The Bute myth was at last being depersonalised. The theory of secret influence was about to take its place.[38] It was perhaps no accident that the newly found ability of the Rockinghams to discuss the affairs of the East India Company in terms of court conspiracies and secret influence tended to reinvigorate their activities. On 14 April Sir William Meredith's motion to abandon the enquiry was lost by the very respectable figure of 213–157.[39] Just at the time when the Rockinghams were beginning to bestir them- selves the affairs of the company embarrassed the ministry still further. Early in May the Company announced an increased dividend of 12·5 per cent compared with the pre- vious 10 per cent. The ministry wished to prevent the pay- ment by introducing a Dividends Bill but it was no more united on this matter than it had been on the inquiry. Charles Towns- hend did not wish to see his East Indian stock depressed, and he opposed Chatham's attempt to restrict the dividend in his 'champagne' speech on 8 May. On 26 May he even voted with the Opposition against it.[40] In opposing the dividend limitation, the Rockinghams were not unconcerned with the restriction of dividends to 10 per cent but their major pre- occupation was to uphold the traditional Whig principle of the sanctity of property and chartered rights against the encroaching influence of the executive. They protested against the Government's infringement of the prescriptive right to its territories enjoyed by the Company. No party had delivered a claim against that prescriptive right, and the Company had been found guilty of no crimes. If the ministry were to be permitted an unrestricted right to interfere so closely in the affairs of the Company so as to regulate its dividend, then no bounds could be set to the expansion of the influence of the Crown.[41]

The opposition of the Rockinghams on East India Company affairs was languid, ineffective and elevated only by a certain ideological concern. That on the Land Tax was to be short, sharp, successful and marvellously factious. It was easy for the loosely connected opposition of Rockinghams, Grenvilles and Bedfords to work together to ambush the ministry on a proposal to reduce the Land Tax from 4s in the pound to 3s in the pound, a measure, moreover, which was almost certain to enjoy the support of the country gentlemen who were sick and tired of a land tax at war time rates after four years of peace. At the same time, the 1761 Parliament had almost run its course. An election was beginning to seem a distinct possibility and a Member anxious for his seat was unlikely to vote for a high Land Tax. It was an almost perfect issue for an Opposition. It is not surprising, then, that the idea had been mooted almost every year since the ending of the war, most recently by Grenville in October 1766.[42] The Rockinghams were alive to the political and electoral advantages which might accrue to them for lowering the Land Tax. On 11 February a meeting of Rockinghamites agreed, although not unanimously,[43] to press for the reduction in Parliament. Dowdeswell would seem to have been the leading spirit. He had been Chancellor of the Exchequer in the Rockingham ministry and was now able to work out a budget for the coming year, calculating that even with a reduced Land Tax of 3s no less than £1m debt could still be paid off.[44] Filled with jubilation at the prospect of defeating the ministry and of snatching Grenville's cup before it reached his lips,[45] the Rockinghams deployed their forces with unaccustomed efficiency. Rockingham and sixteen friends set themselves to contact seventy-five members while Newcastle, in his element drawing up lists and compiling 'States', contacted friends, and the friends of friends. On 27 February in the Committee of Ways and Means Dowdeswell, supported by the country gentlemen, carried his amendment for a reduction of the Land Tax by 206–188.[46]

It is important to be clear that this was not entirely, nor even largely, a Rockinghamite victory. The reduction of the Land Tax was a classic example less of an Opposition ambushing a ministry than of the country gentlemen turning against one. The victory was theirs rather than the Rockinghams'. Furthermore, the Rockinghams were not even able to console themselves with the reflection that they had 'led' the country gentlemen. A coalition of parties had done so. As Burke correctly described the situation: 'The whole Bedfords, and Grenvilles, reinforced by the almost compleat Corps of the Tories, came united into the field.'[47] Even in one of their few hours of triumph, therefore, the Rockinghams found that they could only succeed in a union of the Opposition. Nor were Rockingham and his friends naive enough to believe that the ministry ought to resign after its defeat.[48] At the same time, they could attribute its continuance in office as a sure sign of the abiding system of secret influence which grew strong as ministries grew weak. And in general they must have been rather disappointed at the lack of public rejoicing in the measure and taken aback at the unpopularity which it met with in the City and in other quarters.[49]

On the affairs of the East India Company the Rockinghams had been pathetically unable to influence events; on the reduction of the Land Tax they had only been able to succeed in a factious opposition ploy through co-operation with other groups in a blatant appeal to the prejudices of the independent country gentlemen. On the affairs of America, they were to cut a strikingly different figure from that of the previous year. Then they had triumphantly succeeded in settling the affairs of the continent in spite of what seemed to be insuperable odds at home. In the session of 1767 they were to find themselves lacking a sense of direction and buffeted by events over which they had no control. The repeal of the Stamp Act had failed to settle the problems of America. The repeal agitation had brought to the fore popular leaders in Massachusetts determined to seize control of the provincial governments and there were issues aplenty on which they could rouse the colonists.[50] Moreover, the issue of taxation had only been shelved, not solved by the repeal of the Stamp Act. 'The Rockinghamites planned to lay import duties upon fruits going to America and create a colonial currency, the interest from which would be applied to the support of the army.'[51] In these circumstances, it was extremely doubtful if the coming to power of Chatham and Shelbourne, with their so-called liberal ideas towards America, would be sufficient to quieten the colonial situation.[52] In fact, it had absolutely no effect whatsoever and did nothing to stem the rising tide of American protests.[53]

On 26 January in the Committee of Supply, Charles Townshend, the Chancellor of the Exchequer, agreed with a remark of George Grenville's that the colonists ought to pay for their own defence, and undertook to bring forward measures to secure that objective before the end of the session.[54] Historians have often described Townshend's bombshell as an engaging and unpremeditated slip of the tongue, a dramatic example of how the destiny of empires is sometimes contingent upon the idiosyncracies of personality.[55] On the other hand, there can be no doubt that the Chatham administration had from an early stage been studying the problems of raising a revenue and that Townshend had for many years been interested in raising a colonial revenue and had consistently supported attempts to do so.[56] Indeed, by December 1766 what history has come to know as the Townshend duties were already in existence. Furthermore, there was no resistance, even from Chatham and Shelbourne, to Townshend's schemes. Although it remains true that no one gave him active help and positive assistance no one attempted to stop him, not Grafton, nor Conway, nor even Chatham. It was easy for Chatham in Opposition to attack the Rockingham ministry for even asserting the right of the British Parliament to tax the colonists. But in office he found the American resistance to the British Government in the summer and autumn of 1766 a sufficient reason for reaffirming the need to pacify the colonists through taxation and through force rather than through conciliation. Nevertheless, there can be no doubt that it was Townshend who took the initiative and who must bear a large share of the responsibility for introducing them. The notion, however, that Townshend dragged his cabinet colleagues unwillingly into a support of irresponsible policies haphazardly thrown together simply will not bear examination.

Correspondingly, it did not need George Grenville to remind Townshend that something would have to be done about America. Nevertheless, Townshend could not have wriggled out of his promise to tax the Americans after the events of 18 February. On that day Grenville resumed his campaign against the cost of keeping troops in America and Townshend assured him that scruples against 'internal taxation' would not prevent him from doing his duty.[57] On 12 March he threatened to resign unless the Cabinet *continued* to support him in his taxation proposals. These, in fact, were by now beginning to include some of the ideas of none other than Grenville! Inland troops were to be moved nearer to the coast and the colonists were to pay the cost of defence against the Indians. The other ministers were content to allow Townshend to work out the details of a policy for America by himself, and even made public commitments of their support for policies which would discipline the Americans once and for all. Events were leading inexorably to the fateful implementation of Charles Townshend's policy for America.[58] The tragedy about the Townshend duties was that although they would make almost no impression upon the financial problems of the British Government, they infuriated and frightened the colonists. The cost of American defence was about £750,000 per annum. The duties would bring in perhaps £40,000. Yet this meagre sum was *not* to defray the costs of defence but to fund a civil list for the colonial Governors, threatening to make them independent of the colonial assemblies. In effect, Townshend was weakening their control of the purse, their most important constitutional safeguard. Yet the political consequences of the duties were so distasteful and so thoroughly unacceptable to the Americans that within a year the right of the British Parliament to impose any taxes at all came to be questioned.

In view of the consequences which the Townshend duties were to provoke, it has always seemed more than a little surprising that the Rockingham Whigs, the champions of the colonists in 1765–6, should not on this occasion have leaped to the defence of their colonial brethren. The problem becomes even more acute when we take into account that on 13 May when a discussion of the recalcitrant colony of New York was proceeding, the Rockinghams attacked Townshend for bringing forward proposals for disciplining the New Yorkers which were too mild, and they supported George Grenville's motion that New Yorkers pay for their own defence.[59] In the circumstances, it is, unbelievably, Charles Townshend, and not the Rockinghams who stands forth as the man of moderation.[60] What explains this dramatic turnabout on the part of the Rockingham Whigs?

They did not oppose Charles Townshend's early assertions of his intention to tax because they did not contravene the Declaratory Act which, it will be remembered, contained nothing to forbid the raising of an American revenue. Townshend brought forward no detailed proposals for revenue raising until early June. How could the Rockinghams oppose a plan which had not been made public and the hints of which did not appear to be inconsistent with their own past policy? By that time, public attention had swung away from the American problem and focussed upon the ministry's desperate fight for survival in the House of Lords. Furthermore, throughout the session of 1767 the Rockinghams constantly hoped to detach Charles Townshend from administration and desired him to take a prominent part with them.[61] To shout and bluster in opposition to a scheme which he had not even yet fully worked out was scarcely the best method of attaining that objective. At the same time, they were hoping to gain the support and the assistance of other groups in opposition, notably the Bedfords. Their co-operation was unlikely to be forthcoming if their differences on American affairs were to be constantly agitated.[62] Finally, nobody in Britain foresaw the disastrous consequences which the Townshend duties were to have in America. The Rockingham Whigs would, indeed have looked inconsistent, if, having recognised the inexpediency of the

Stamp Act as a prelude to repealing it, they had proceeded to oppose what little they knew of Charles Townshend's duties, before knowing if they were expedient or not. Nevertheless, the Rockinghams have been blamed for not understanding what later generations were to have no hesitation in asserting to be the inevitable fruit of the Townshend duties.

If not inconsistent, then, on American affairs, the Rockinghams had been uninspired and ineffective, relying heavily upon the assistance of other parties in Opposition. Indeed, not only on the Land Tax but also on American and especially, East India Company business, the political groups had begun working together. Separately, they had no chance of overthrowing the ministry. Although Rockingham clung to the view that if Townshend and Conway could be prised out of the ministry, it might collapse, leaving the Rockinghams to pick up the pieces, Newcastle and most of the other leaders preferred to co-operate with the other groups, especially the Bedfords.[63] The prospects of the groups working cordially together, however, were never high.[64] The Bedfords, indeed, insisted that any connection with them must also include Grenville.[65] Was it the case that nothing more than personality separated the groups, and that the Rockinghams were no different in their office-seeking objectives from the Bedfords and the Grenvilles? The simple fact, nevertheless, that all the three groups in Opposition were willing to effect a union does not itself imply that they entertained identical objectives in so doing.

All politicians in the 1760s agreed that *union* not *exclusion* was the ideal to be achieved in political relationships. Chatham wanted to draw the best men from all groups into his ministry so that he could destroy opposition parties. Grenville wanted a great coalition of all the parties in an almost co-equal relationship with each other.[66] Rockingham wished to bring about a coalition led and dominated by his own party with himself at the Treasury and excluding the Buteites. Diversity of purpose, then, rather than uniformity of aim characterised the ambitions of political leaders in their desire to achieve a union of the parties. It is no accident that the Rockinghams refused to hurry into an alliance with Grenville in March and

April.[67] Not only was such a course of action likely to offend some of the Rockinghams. It was certain to offend the King. In any case, the feasibility of a union of the parties might best be demonstrated if the Opposition could achieve its immediate purposes, that of destroying the Chatham administration.

The final attack launched by the Opposition on the ministry in the session of 1767 came excitingly close to success. As in the first Rockingham ministry, the Government was more embarrassed by proceedings in the Upper than in the Lower House.[68] Rockingham and Newcastle did everything that they knew to bring the divided ministry to its knees. On issues relating to North America they acted with the Lords of the Bedford and Grenville parties. On 6 May, Gower's motion for papers relating to an Act of pardon for Massachusetts rioters was defeated by only 52–43. Exactly fourteen days later the ministry was afraid to divide upon Richmond's motion for papers relating to Canada and tamely granted his demand.[69] Two days later Gower contested the validity of the Massachusetts pardon but his attack was repulsed only by the very narrow margin of 62–58. The stage was now set for the final act in this peculiar little drama. On 26 May the Chatham administration survived by only three votes, by 65–62. The great experiment in non-party government had saved itself in the House of Lords by a handful of bishops, although if the ministry had lost its majority there it is doubtful if a resignation would have followed. The survival of the ministry was to lead to attempts to strengthen it. In strengthening it, however, the ministry became not a means of destroying party but a means of preserving it. In other words, George Grenville's conception of a union of co-equal groups now became the objective of the Court and of Grafton.

The dramatic events in the Upper House terrified Grafton into threatening to resign, something which Conway, in fact, had been contemplating for some time.[70] If either of these men resigned, the ministry could not go on. Without Conway the Commons would be left open to the wayward ambitions of Charles Townshend. Without Grafton there would scarcely be a competent, regular defender of the ministry in the Lords. If either of them were to resign then the King might become the prisoner of a ministry including Grenville, Bedford and Rockingham. George III, at this time, was extremely worried about Chatham.[71] Neither the King nor the First Lord of the Treasury could engage him in business. Although both he and Grafton were desperate for his advice and begged his assistance in June he would give none. He made light of the difficulties under which Grafton and Conway were labouring. The ministry could continue, he assumed, so long as Grafton, Camden and Northington remained at their posts and he had nothing against finding support from other groups, especially the Bedfords.[72] Chatham at least permitted Grafton a fruitless interview. Armed with this enormous complement and the Great Man's permission to negotiate with other groups Grafton agreed to remain in office. The document formally recommending negotiations with the Opposition which Grafton and Northington presented to George III on 2 July marks the conclusion of what may be termed the 'ideological' period of the Chatham administration. In this document the credo of seeking out individuals is expressly *rejected* and it is implied that the only way of forming a stable ministry was to bring in one or more groups *as groups*.[73]

The nature of the involvement of the Rockinghams in the negotiations of 1767 arose from differences of opinion among ministers. Grafton's own wish was to bring in the Bedfords; Conway's (and the King's) to bring in the Rockinghams. To resolve the conflict Grafton approached both parties simultaneously, a ploy which unhappily succeeded only in arousing general suspicion. Grafton found Gower and the Bedfords unreasonable and over-confident, insisting even upon the inclusion of Temple in the ministry. As for the Rockinghams, Grafton and Conway found the Marquis willing to negotiate only on condition that the present ministry be considered at an end. Rockingham believed throughout these negotiations that a new ministry was to be constructed. He reasoned that Conway and Grafton were on the brink of resignation, the ministry thus on the verge of collapse. Rockingham might be forgiven then for jumping to the conclusion that the present ministry was as good as finished and that a new one was to replace it.[74] For the new ministry, moreover, Rockingham had conditions of his own to lay down. The Treasury must be in his hands, Grenville was not to be allowed a cabinet place and, inevitably, the friends of Bute were to be excluded from office. These conditions arose from a very natural and very proper desire to make the most of his bargaining position, a position whose strength, albeit very real, he nevertheless tended to exaggerate. Rockingham did not wish to repeat the mistakes of his first administration. Thus he wished to place the projected administration upon a broad basis by coalescing with the Bedfords and to use his power over appointments to scatter the Buteites and to reward his followers. No difficulty was anticipated from the Bedfords. Rockingham believed that they would accept his supremacy. As for his differences with them over America, a few verbal formulas would satisfactorily compose them. Rockingham heard that the Bedfords were not averse to his terms. In particular, they did not contest his wish to have the Treasury and they did not insist upon a cabinet place for Grenville. Rockingham tended naturally to assume that the political game was as good as won. A Rockingham–Bedford ministry led and dominated by the Rockinghams must be formed. The present ministry must be declared to be at an end and the King must in person declare his assent to the new arrangements. Rockingham would be content with nothing less.

The Marquis viewed the political situation too casually and he over-simplified what he saw. He was too confident and by stages his negotiating ground collapsed under him. First Conway announced that he was not going to resign. This was as good as saying that the present ministry was to continue. Second, the Marquis had underestimated the Bedfords. On a visit to Woburn on 20 and 21 July Rockingham learned not only that they had been kept informed about the progress of his own discussions with the ministry but also that they had conditions of their own to put forward before they would take part in a joint administration. These were two-fold; they wanted some guarantee that parliamentary sovereignty over the colonies would never be surrendered and they demanded the removal of Conway from the Leadership of the House of Commons. Third, Rockingham had taken for granted that the

King approved of the general drift of the negotiations and their manifest purpose of replacing the present ministry with a Rockingham–Bedford coalition. At an audience on 22 July Rockingham found that the King had no intention at all of moving Grafton from the Treasury. After Conway decided to remain in office Grafton withdrew this threat of resignation. The King therefore saw no need for a new and comprehensive administration, simply the strengthening of the old. Rockingham's sublimely confident assumption that the Treasury was his for the asking stemmed from the fact that he had been negotiating with the Duke of Grafton. George III at once dispelled the prospects that the Rockinghams could take office on terms acceptable both to the King and themselves.

The July negotiations, despite their failure, mark a significant step in the internal development of the Rockingham Whig party and, in particular, of Rockingham's own place within it. Although he made serious errors of political judgement, Rockingham's leadership was accepted without question. He kept his men together, consulted with his friends, and could always be confident that he spoke for his party. Some might disagree with one aspect or another of his political tactics but, in the last analysis, his leadership was unquestioned. Richmond wanted Rockingham to increase his pressure upon Grafton and Conway, prise them out of the ministry and recreate, as it were, the ministry of 1765–6. Rockingham was perhaps wise to ignore such advice (although there was much to be said for Richmond's argument that the King would never accept happily the extended administration for which Rockingham yearned). For his part, Newcastle was unhappy at Rockingham's cold attitude towards Grenville. The Duke feared that if Grenville were alienated then he might fall into the arms of Bute. And then: 'This *Bute* Administration must last; and will grow too strong for you all.'[75] But Rockingham was probably wise on the whole to keep his distance of Grenville if he seriously wished George III to summon him to form a new administration. Rockingham was willing to listen to different views and opinions but in the end he made his own decisions and was prepared to accept the responsibility for them. The July negotiations mark the emergence of the Marquis of

Rockingham as an opposition leader with lofty ambitions and indisputable control of his party. Rockingham might now hope to arrest the erosion of his own following and the decline of his party whose weakness had been such a pronounced feature of the session of 1767.

The negotiations, moreover, induced Rockingham to define his attitudes and to prepare himself for future soundings with the King and other parties. Rockinghamite tactics were in future to stem less and less from expedience and necessity, and more and more from adherence to principle. We have already noticed that Rockingham was not at this stage thinking in terms of anything resembling an exclusive party administration. He wanted a union of parties, led by his own, to form a ministry so broadly based that the King would find it irresistible. He did not wish to repeat the mistakes of his narrowly based first ministry. The influence of Bute could only be destroyed by an alliance of parties.[76] How to achieve these ends and how to respond to future ministerial soundings were problems to which William Dowdeswell now lent his attention. His *Memorandum* was drawn up immediately after the failure of the negotiations.[77] It laid down two conditions before the Rockinghams would in future consent to take part in an administration. First (with the events of July very much in mind) the offer must proceed from the King and not from a minister. Second, Rockingham should not hesitate to make it clear to the King that his party was out to destroy the system 'which says that the power of the Crown arises out of the weakness of the Administration' and the Rockinghams, in a future ministry, must demand their 'necessary weight in the closet'. The Bedfords and Grenvilles would be junior partners in a projected ministry (although Grenville would be allowed no influence over its construction) and the bulk of offices would go to the Rockinghams. If the ideal of an extended administration could not at present be achieved, then the Rockinghams ought to resist the temptation to enter the present ministry and remain in an honourable Opposition.

The idea of single party Government, therefore, is entirely absent from the Dowdeswell *Memorandum*. This is not to say, however, that the *Memorandum* is of no account in the history of party. Dowdeswell was laying down strategy for a party to enable it to achieve its objectives better in the future than it had in the past. At the same time it indicated that the Rockinghams were far from being an unprincipled clique. They could certainly have had office in 1767 if Rockingham had watered down his demands but this he steadfastly refused to do. There was nothing shameful in co-operating with other groups. The first Rockingham ministry had been proof enough that the Rockingham party alone could not stand and by itself destroy the influence of Bute. Furthermore, Rockingham's claim to pre-eminence and superiority was restated in uncompromising terms. The *Memorandum* laid it down that the Leader of the House of Commons should be a person in whom Rockingham had confidence. Indeed, Rockingham *himself* was to appoint to all offices. (Although it is not mentioned in the *Memorandum*, Rockingham was absolutely resolute that in his next ministry office-holders who refused to support the ministry would be dismissed.)[78] Had the ideas of the Dowdeswell *Memorandum* been implemented in 1767 the royal prerogative of appointing ministers would have been severely curtailed.

To the charge that all this infringed the royal prerogative, Rockingham and his friends would no doubt have replied that, far from attacking George III, they were striving to save the monarchy and the constitution from the unhappy consequences of the political instability and turmoil to which the influence of Lord Bute had given rise.[79] To act consistently with this precept became a cardinal principle of the Rockinghams. They 'should constantly look back . . . and adhere to the same lines in future'.[80] And this they should do even if by so doing they damaged their prospects of office. Unwittingly, the Rockinghams were preparing themselves for a long spell in Opposition. Perhaps Rockingham glimpsed the prospect when he confessed that he 'rather wished that our old friends who were in, would come out to us than chuse to go in with our friends to them; that if we did we must still be subject to the same power as we had been to before'.[81] In other words, the Rockinghams could contemplate their virtue more safely in Opposition than in office. The more that the Rockinghams set about establishing their own identity and outlining their principles the more

they marked their own exclusiveness and the harder it would
be for them to fit into a union of the parties. Indeed, for a
young idealist like Burke, it was utterly unthinkable for the
Rockinghams to take office except as a party in a ministry in
which Rockingham would be the undisputed leader and in
which the interests of the individual would be severely curtailed in favour of those of the party.[82] Thus the failure of the
chimera of a united Opposition to materialise made possible the
growth of the independent political party of the Rockingham
Whigs.

Although much was said even after the July negotiations
about the desirability of a united Opposition, especially by
interested parties like Rigby and Albemarle, the prospects of
achieving it were poor. It is true that Grenville and Bedford
were always willing to allow Rockingham the Treasury in a
reconstructed administration but they were unwilling to act or
to let their friends act as ciphers in a ministry over whose
measures they might have little or no responsibility. In particular, they steadfastly demanded the removal of Conway from
the Leadership of the Lower House. Although during the
autumn scarcely any contacts passed between Bedford and
Grenville, Rockingham must have thought twice about an
alliance even with Bedford alone. To have entered into any
such agreement would be a prelude to a formal parliamentary
assault upon Grafton and Conway, his erstwhile friends. If that
assault succeeded and the Rockinghams and Bedfords came
into office then Rockingham would have to turn out those
friends (or, at least, some of them) who had remained in
office after the Edgecumbe affair. The Bedford alliance might
be Rockingham's best—indeed, his only—immediate means of
returning to office but it was accompanied by many problematical considerations. Even the staunchest advocates of the
Bedford connection were troubled by some of its implications.
Newcastle remarked 'I think the Duke of Bedford &c are very
desirous of a union with us, but in some of the suggestions, I
think I see a little of the Grenville and Temple school'.[83]
Others believed that the salvation of the party would be found
in a unilateral accommodation with the ministry and they
included such respectable and influential figures as Lord John

Cavendish and the Duke of Richmond. Between these two positions Rockingham reached a compromise. He believed that neither policy at that time was realistic and the Marquis decided, therefore, to wait upon events because to have done otherwise might have damaging and divisive effects upon his party.[84]

The Bedfords now made their peace with the Court. It was clearly impossible for them to come into office as part of Rockingham's 'comprehensive administration' and the Duke of Bedford, who had kept his party together for two and a half years, was determined to do his best for his friends. Now old and going blind, he had acted a not dishonourable part in politics. The Rockinghams had enjoyed many opportunities of showing their willingness to work with the Bedfords and they had thrown them away. Other methods of seeking office having been exhausted there was now nothing for them but to approach the Court unilaterally. At the eleventh hour, however, the Rockinghams swung back once more towards the Bedfords. In late October they decided once and for all to have done with their futile expectations that Conway might leave the ministry and they decided to open a negotiation with the Bedfords.[85] It was now too late. The Bedfords were weary of Opposition. In any case, Rockingham allowed precious days to slip by and failed to persuade the Bedfords to revive the united Opposition of the last session which, with all its weaknesses, had caused the ministry some difficulty. His failure to do so had immediate repercussions. On the first day of the new session (24 November) and again on the second, George Grenville blasted any remaining prospects for a united Opposition when he delivered withering attacks on the American principles of the Rockinghams.[86] The Bedfords, not surprisingly since they agreed with Grenville, failed to leap to the defence of the Rockinghams. This was enought to convince the touchy Rockingham that Bedford was now in league with Grenville.

The Duke of Grafton was ready to receive the Bedfords with slightly extended if not quite open arms. Although his situation was incomparably stronger in November than it had been in June and no immediate crisis faced him his Cabinet badly needed reinforcement. Northington was desperate to retire,

Conway was unwilling to face another exhausting session as Leader of the Lower House and Camden and Shelburne felt very little enthusiasm for Grafton.[87] In the last days of November the Bedfords approached the Court and after several weeks of more or less secret negotiations they received the generous terms for which they had always hoped and Grafton the Cabinet reconstruction which he so badly needed. Gower replaced Northington as Lord President and although Conway remained in the Cabinet as Master General of the Ordnance his Secretaryship went to Lord Weymouth. A separate Secretaryship for the colonies was carved out of Shelburne's Southern Department and this went to Lord Hillsborough. In addition to these offices the Bedfords received two other important posts. Richard Rigby became a joint-Vice Treasurer of Ireland and Lord Sandwich a joint Postmaster-General.[88]

These important and significant changes had far-reaching consequences. They ended months of uncertainty about the ability of the ministry to survive in the absence of Chatham. Now it clearly could. They dashed the hopes of Rockingham and Grenville, men whose former differences promised to render difficult their future co-operation. The new Cabinet, furthermore, could be expected to be much harsher towards America than the old one had been. The Bedfords, after all, had been partly responsible for the Stamp Act and had bitterly opposed its repeal. Furthermore, the character of the ministry changed. The ministry of the Duke of Grafton in effect commences with the entry of the Bedfords. The Chatham administration was over. Grafton had been able to save the ministry not by destroying party but by bowing to one of the parties. The Bedfords, moreover, had been George Grenville's allies during the King's 'captivity' in 1763–5 and George III must have disliked having to turn to them on this occasion. As Grafton delicately put it: 'for some time His Majesty observed a shyness towards our new allies'.[89] Grafton, in fact, acted an indispensable part at this point, gradually easing the Bedfords into the ministry, making them as acceptable as possible to the King and playing the role of mediator.[90]

The strengthening of the ministry was an exceptionally bitter blow for the Rockinghams and for Rockingham himself.

He had by now squandered almost all of the political advantages which he had enjoyed during the summer. Grafton was no longer desperate to have the Rockinghams in office; Conway was now a broken reed and could no longer be expected to act either as a vehicle for easing the Rockinghams into office or for easing Grafton out. By now Rockingham had to surrender any lingering hope that he might yet be able to revive his dying influence over the friends who had remained in office after the Edgecumbe affair a year earlier. Furthermore, a General Election would be held during the next few months, and it was imperative for his party to impress the public with its vigour and energy. Furthermore, it would not be pleasant to attack Conway and Grafton and other former friends, to say nothing of the uneasiness which Rockingham might feel if his men launched an attack against their former allies, the Bedford Whigs. The co-operation of George Grenville in this unprepossessing Opposition was neither to be expected nor encouraged. There was, finally, a dearth of issues to hand upon which anything like a successful Opposition might be mounted. Inevitably, the morale of Rockingham's men slumped. Richmond, greatly disappointed with the sorry outcome of what had once seemed a shining opportunity for his party, retired from politics for over a year. Rockingham, however, put a brave face on all his mistakes. Recent events, he claimed, vindicated the purity of the party and its independence of the corrupting influences of the Court.[91] Newcastle swallowed his disappointment and joined this chorus.[92] The accession of the Bedfords was seen to be only the latest instalment in the long story of intrigue and corruption which had commenced with the elevation of Bute. The Bedfords were only the latest dupes of the secret advisors of the Crown, and they would go the same way as Chatham, Grafton and Conway.[93] The Rockinghams, on the other hand, had done well to resist their blandishments. Political isolation was made somewhat more palatable and acceptable to them than it might otherwise have been by their willingness to believe that for their political misfortunes they were not themselves to blame and that their own weaknesses could be ascribed to the secret influence of the Crown.

The lack of contentious issues together with the approach of

a General Election rendered the brief session of 1768 unin-
teresting to contemporaries and attendance at Parliament was
correspondingly low. This and the weakness of the Opposition
was reflected by the division figures on the Dividends bill of
the last session which had to be renewed before the dissolution.
On second reading on 16 December the ministry prevailed by
128–41, and on third reading on 25 January 1768 by 131–41.
These figures speak both for themselves and for the rock
solid security of the administration.[94]

There was only one issue which provided the Rockinghams
with a little encouragement before the dissolution. The *Nullum
Tempus* affair had all the ingredients required to rouse the
Rockinghams from the glum lethargy into which they sank
after the accession of the Bedfords. In the first place, one of the
great Whig lords had not only his personal rights and his
property but also his electoral influence threatened by a
relative of Bute. Nothing could have been better calculated
than this to bring the Rockinghams to town. The affair, in fact,
had been simmering for some months. In July 1767 Sir James
Lowther, a son-in-law of Bute, claimed Inglewood Forest and
the Socage of Carlisle from Portland, on the grounds that these
parts of Portland's estate had not been included in the original
grant to the Bentinck family in the seventeenth century, and
that they thus reverted to the Crown. Far from being a manifestation of the lingering medievalism which charmed the
English law of property, the affair was a deliberate attempt on
the part of Lowther to undermine Portland's control of the
county of Cumberland. If his claim were recognised Lowther
might well expect to rent the estates concerned from the
Crown with the intention of influencing the voters of Inglewood Forest against Portland's candidate in the forthcoming
elections and thus determining the election Lowther's way.[95]
The ministry showed where it stood on the matter by acceding
to Lowther's claim on 28 December 1767. Two days later
Portland challenged the grant and the slow process of litigation
proceeded upon its lengthy course. The Rockinghams were
determined to make their opinions on the matter known before
Parliament rose, and this they proceeded to do.

The Rockinghamite reaction to Lowther's presumption was

far more than a matter of personality. The Rockinghams interpreted his action, and the condoning of it by the ministers as an extension of the system of secret influence which was now manifestly directed against the rights of aristocratic and private property. That their attitudes should not be thought to relate solely to Portland's problems can be shown, since Sir George Savile, in bringing forward his *Nullum Tempus* bill (which stated that possession of property for sixty years or more rendered void any claims to ownership by the Crown) rendered the operation of the bill non-retrospective, that is, it could not relate to Portland's case. It was not so much the defence of Portland, then, as hostility to Bute, the defence of private property and the preservation of the independence of 'the Landed Interest in England . . . against the Odious Revival of *long dorment* Claims of the Crown or Duchy of Lancaster on Private Property',[96] which motivated the Rockinghams. In the debate on Savile's bill on 17 February the Rockinghams stressed these constitutional principles and did so with some effect. The fact that their opposition was neither negligible nor factious was illustrated by the division figure. Savile's motion for leave to introduce his bill was lost by only 136–116, a more than respectable performance by the Rockinghams. There were also other factors to take into account. They did well because the defence of property rights was a popular platform on which to stand and because they had the support of Grenville in defending those rights. The ministry, furthermore, had almost been ambushed, as on the Land Tax a year earlier. Notice of motion was only given two days before the debate and until then the Opposition's attack had remained a closely guarded secret.[97] In the last few weeks of the 1761 Parliament, therefore, when the fortunes of the Rockinghams appeared to have slumped to their lowest, a modest yet significant revival had been staged and further opposition in the new Parliament on this promising issue could be expected.

In truth, the ministry was not quite as strong as its recent reconstruction might have led observers to expect. Already, by the end of January, Grafton was begging Chatham to come to town because his assistance and advice 'were never of more importance to the King's service than at this moment'.[98] The

King added his royal expostulations to Grafton's pleas: 'for though confined to your house, your name has been sufficient to enable my administration to proceed'.[99] Why were Grafton and the King so worried? At this stage the Opposition had not attacked the ministry on the revival of dormant claims of the Crown and nothing was to be feared from that quarter. Moreover, the coming elections did not promise any undue difficulty. The problem was, of course, the situation of the Bedfords. The friends of Chatham in the ministry, Shelburne and Camden, and those of Rockingham, Grafton and Conway, now found themselves in strange and not entirely congenial company. The Bedfords were clannish and determined to mould the ministry to their ways of thinking. They were, in short, unwilling to act the part which Grafton and the King expected them to. They had come in not to give Grafton their support but, so it appeared to Grafton and the King, to dominate the Government. Chatham was now needed to save the King from faction but this time a faction within his own ministry! On this occasion he was too ill to provide any assistance and Grafton had to soldier on in uneasy alliance with the Bedfords, to accept the disgrace of the Opposition's near-success on Nullum Tempus and to fight the election of 1768.

The parliament of 1761 was dissolved on 11 March 1768 by a King who had experimented with almost all possible combinations of politicians in office, but who seemed as far as ever from establishing the stable administration of which he, and by now the country, dreamed. George III must have felt that everything turned to dust in his hands since every expedient that he had tried had failed to procur that political stability and harmony for which he yearned. For the time being only Grafton stood between him and the Bedfords and Grenville and Rockingham. The King's hatred of party had ensured that after eight years none of the parties in existence trusted him and he had had of necessity to have recourse to a series of individuals to maintain his independence, first Bute, then Grenville, then Cumberland, then Chatham and now Grafton. The King had kept the parties at bay but the price the country had to pay for this was the succession of short-lived ministries which characterised the 1760s. The election of 1768 was now to inject into the politics of the reign novel and alarming popular forces which were to make the King's ambitions far more difficult to achieve than they had yet been but which were, at the same time vastly to complicate the already perplexing problems which the emerging Rockingham Whig party was facing.

Chapter 9

The Rockingham Whigs and the General Election of 1768

By the time that Parliament was dissolved in 1768 the Rockingham Whig party had acquired the character which it was to retain for at least a decade and a half. Its size, its structure, its attitudes and its ideas had all emerged with some clarity by 1768. What relationship did this party bear to the connection of the Duke of Newcastle and to what extent had the latter changed or 'developed'? How many of the Newcastle Whigs who had been in opposition to George Grenville remained loyal to the Marquis of Rockingham and to what extent was the Rockingham Whig party a 'new' party? To what extent did the Rockingham Ministry and its downfall effect the composition of the Rockingham party? According to Mr Brooke 'the party Rockingham built up had to be formed on different principles and with new men' while most of Newcastle's supporters had gone over to the Court by 1768.[1] To understand the Rockingham Whig Party in 1768 clearly requires this verdict to be examined and the above questions answered.

By the end of the debates on the peace preliminaries in December 1762, 69 Members of Parliament can be identified by their votes and speeches as followers of Newcastle who remained loyal to him. By the end of the session of 1762–3 this number had increased to 75. By November 1763 the number had increased further to 90. By the end of the session of 1764 109 Newcastle Whigs had publicly demonstrated their loyalty to their leader.[2] By the date of the formation of the Rockingham ministry 4 of these men had left Parliament.[3] During the life of the Rockingham ministry 8 of the remaining 105 left Parliament, in most cases through death,[4] but the accession of 14 new supporters more than made good the loss.[5] It is important to recognise the implications of these figures. Rockingham, as we have observed earlier, took over the leadership of the party of the Duke of Newcastle. The Rockingham Whigs were not a 'new' party in 1765. Furthermore, it certainly cannot be maintained that the Rockingham Whig Party was created by the Rockingham ministry. Indeed, there is a surprising consistency about the size of the Newcastle–Rockingham party which stabilised at slightly over 100 between 1764 to 1766. In May 1764 it numbered 109, in June 1765, 105 and in July 1766, 111. In terms of numbers, then, the ministry of 1765–6 had very little effect on the development of the Rockingham Whig party.

Thereafter a catastrophic decline overtook the party. Between the fall of the Rockingham ministry and the General Election of 1768 the number of the Rockingham Whigs declined from 111 to 54. The loss of 4 members leaving Parliament was more than made good by the entry of 6 new Rockinghamites,[6] but during these eighteen months Rockingham failed to maintain the loyalty of no fewer than 18 members.[7] Not that these men joined the Chatham administration; most of them either became less active politically or more independent of the Marquis than they had hitherto been. Finally, and most important of all, the Edgecumbe affair gradually cost Rockingham the support of 41 members, 18 of whom were office holders.[8] In less than two years the size of the Rockingham Whig party had been halved.

It is not altogether surprising, therefore, to find that during this period of rapid changes in membership, the party leaders themselves sometimes had difficulty in realising just what was happening. Both Rockingham and Newcastle drew up lists of their supporters in the Commons at about the same time, the former in December 1766 and revised in February 1767, the latter in March 1767. After analysing these lists Mr Brooke concludes:

> 'more than one third of Rockingham's list of friends was rejected by Newcastle, and about a quarter of Newcastle's list was rejected by Rockingham. . . . Yet the two lists were drawn up within three months of each other. Here, then, are the leaders of a party unable to agree upon who were their followers. What value can be given to their lists of the other parties if they did not know their own. And what kind of a party was it whose leaders did not know their own followers.'[9]

Yet these apparent inconsistencies do not render the concept of party superfluous nor do they make nonsense of the party pretensions of the Rockingham Whigs. For one thing, the inconsistencies can to some extent be accounted for. Strictly speaking, the lists are not comparable. They were drawn up at different times during the crisis following the Edgecumbe affair, exactly at the time when it would have been most difficult for any kind of leader of any kind of party to know the precise details of party loyalties. Furthermore, Rockingham's 'Whigs' are not quite the same thing as Newcastle's 'Friends to the Last Administration'. Rockingham's mistakes, moreover, reflect his inexperience and the difficulty of categorising some members who rarely attended. Some discrepancies between the lists are thus to be expected but exactly how extensive and how serious are they? Let us take Rockingham's list of 121 names and discover how they are dealt with by Newcastle. The number can immediately be reduced by 1 because Lord George Lennox appears twice. Of the remaining 120, 76 appear in Newcastle's list of 'Friends'.[10] How does Newcastle deal with the outstanding 44? He places 16 of them in the 'Doubtful or Absent' column[11] but a further 14 in the 'Administration' column. Yet of these 14 an asterisk accompanies the names of 6 of them, former friends of the Duke.[12] Another 8 names[13] appear as Whigs on Rockingham's list and as Tories on Newcastle's but half of them are asterisked, again men whom Newcastle clearly recognised as *quondam* friends but whom he had now to place in another category. Newcastle placed 4 names in the Bedford–Grenville category[14] and 2 others are unidentified.[15] Thus, in attempting to calculate the extent of the discrepancy between the lists we can include 8 names assigned by Newcastle to Administration, the 4 non-asterisked Tories and the 4 names placed in the Bedford–Grenville group. Of Rockingham's 120 names, then, only 16 are categorised by Newcastle in a contradictory manner, a discrepancy of slightly more than one eighth. Given the peculiar state of politics at the end of 1766 and the early months of 1767 it is the similarities rather than the discrepancies between the lists which impress the modern reader. What is more significant than these discrepancies, however, is the fact that Rockingham's list was too *optimistic*, placing his support much higher than the situation warranted. But, again, in view of the almost constant size of the party in the previous two and a half years and without the benefit of hindsight, Rockingham can hardly be blamed for failing to predict the extent of the desertions which gradually affected his party in the session of 1767. These desertions showed that the loyalties which an opposition party leader could command were still less powerful than the conventions of loyalty to the court and service to the monarch, the attraction of office and the magnetism of Chatham.

After the unstable period with which these lists deal the size of the Rockingham party gradually stabilised and it is possible to estimate not only the size but also the structure of the Rockingham party on the eve of the Election of 1768. Its fifty-four members can, of course, be grouped in a variety of ways but the structural nature of the party can best be understood by subdividing its members into family or personal connections.

Rockingham	10
Newcastle	7
Cavendish	6
Portland	4
Albemarle	4
Verney	3
Richmond	2
Yorke	2

In addition, there are sixteen members who do not fall into the above categories, most of whom brought themselves into Parliament.[16]

This brief analysis reveals that the Rockingham party had acquired a structural framework which was somewhat different from that of the Newcastle Whigs of the early part of the decade. The Rockingham Whig party was not so much the party of one man as Newcastle's had been. The Rockingham party was an alliance, and on the whole not an uneasy one, of connections, grouped around the growing Rockingham and the declining Newcastle connections. It is unwise, however, to erect artificial barriers between these sub-groups. Edmund Burke, for example, was of the Verney connection yet his first political attachment was to Rockingham. The Cavendishes were not a family apart from Rockingham. Since the death of the Fourth Duke in 1764 they had no leader and were prepared to follow Rockingham. As for the Portland connection, it was linked to the Cavendishes by marriage. As one would have expected, then, the great Whig families were interlinked by marriage and by friendship. Around these family connections moved a number of men, almost one third of the party, like independent yet related satellites whose connection with them was voluntary and based neither upon material factors nor family relationships. Already the Rockingham party was characterised by the twin features of interlinked aristocratic connections and voluntary attachment based upon personality and principle.

Who were these Rockingham Whigs? If we compare the members of Newcastle's party in May 1764 with that of Rockingham's on the eve of the General Election of 1768 some significant facts emerge. Of the 109 members of Newcastle's party 16 were no longer in Parliament. What had happened to the remaining 93? As we have noted, 18 of them had abandoned the practice of systematic opposition and of the remaining 75 no fewer than 41 supported the Chatham administration. The remaining 34 were Rockingham Whigs, whose number was made up by the allegiance of no fewer than 20 new members. Dr Langford has obtained a similar impression in his analysis of the MPs who were members of Wildmans in 1764. In 1767, 45 per cent of them voted with the Chatham administration, only 42 per cent supported the Rockingham Whigs.[17] About two-thirds of the members of the party in 1768 had been attached to Newcastle four years earlier and about one third received their political education at the hands of Rockingham. That there existed a substantial element of continuity between the parties of Newcastle and Rockingham cannot therefore be doubted. The Rockingham Whig party grew and developed from its unpromising Pelhamite origins in 1762–3 and survived both the misfortunes of the ministry of 1765–6 and the disastrous Edgecumbe crisis of 1766. The fact that only thirty-four of the ninety-three original Newcastle Whigs still active in politics continued to support the party is not altogether surprising. By 1768 the Rockingham Whigs had developed a fondness for certain political priorities which were not likely to endear themselves to every Pelhamite. Their detestation of Bute was not sufficient to outweigh the alarm aroused by Rockinghamite American policy and by the mistrust of Chatham which sharpened into hatred and mistrust between 1766–8. Its unpromising situation in Opposition as well as its increasingly well defined political attitudes no doubt provide a further explanation of its reduced size.

If there ever existed the danger that the Rockingham Whig party might have declined still further in numbers then the fortuitously timed General Election of 1768 might have translated that danger into reality. Yet few elections in the eighteenth century generated much interest in politics and that of 1768 was no exception. No one could then have predicted that the Parliament elected in that year would have to confront imperial and domestic questions more complex and more critical than any the country had faced since the days of Anne. There were, in 1768, few issues to excite an electorate whose attention was still fastened on to local problems and it scarcely seemed to matter that on the ministerial side this was the least efficiently managed of all the elections of the second half of the eighteenth century. This was only partly Grafton's fault. There was no pressing reason for extensive management of the election as was to be the case, for example, in 1780, and especially in 1784. In short, the Rockinghams were unlikely to be faced with a full scale attack launched by a determined administration. The contests in which they became involved consequently turned upon local rather than upon national issues. The

Rockingham Whigs did not fight the election of 1768 on a party basis. There was no need for them to do so. It was sufficient that each patron should protect his own.

The election was a resounding success for Rockingham himself. If his leadership of the declining party needed vindication then it received it during the spring of 1768. It was the personal friendship among the great Whig Lords which provided the structural backbone of the Rockingham party but it was to Rockingham that they looked to provide a lead. He was thus the necessary focus of unity and loyalty which linked the whole together. His party, made up of sub-groups, some of which stubbornly retained their own identity, could not be bullied and led arbitrarily. It needed all the arts of conciliation which Rockingham could muster and his readiness to make sacrifices in the interests of his party to keep his men together in the dark years of Opposition.[18] After the election of 1768 the size of Rockingham's own connection stood unchanged at ten. Sir George Savile was returned unopposed in the Yorkshire county seat, as were Lord Downe and Savile Finch at Malton and Frederick Montagu at Higham Ferrers. Rockingham's influence was decisive in bringing in William Weddell at Hull and F. W. Osbaldeston at Scarborough. Due more to good luck than good management, the Marquis picked up an extra seat at York, where he already controlled the return of one member.[19] The corporation usually returned the second member but at the last moment its candidate declined the poll. Rockingham had a replacement to hand. Lord John Cavendish, smarting from his failure to carry Lancaster, within a few days was found to be acceptable to the gentlemen of York. Rockingham's following was completed by three independently minded men, N. Cholmley, who moved from Aldeburgh to Boroughbridge, George Dempster at Perth and Sir William Meredith at Liverpool.

The elections reflected the continuing decline of the Duke of Newcastle and his influence. It was only the supineness of the Treasury which allowed him to continue dominant at Rye and Seaford. At Lewes, Newcastle's candidate came bottom of the poll[20] while at East Retford old John White lost his seat, a particularly bitter blow for Newcastle. Thus the last remnants

H

of Newcastle's once mangificent empire were on the point of disappearing.

While Newcastle's power continued to wane, that of Portland waxed. He increased the numerical size of his own group from four to seven. He helped his brother-in-law, Lord Grey, to enter Parliament as MP for Staffordshire. He brought George Byng and Beaumont Hotham in at Wigan. (He had been nursing Callington for some time but was unable to bring in David Hartley.)[21] Although Portland was not directly involved in the Westmorland election, Thomas Fenwick, one of the victors, attached himself to Portland in the new Parliament. Furthermore, Portland won a famous victory against Lowther. He carried both seats at Carlisle, returning Lord Edward Bentinck and George Musgrave. To crown his triumphs in the north, he won both Cumberland seats. Henry Curwen led the poll and Sir James Lowther was unseated on petition in favour of Henry Fletcher.[22] It was a great year for Portland and one which established him as one of the leaders of the Rockingham party. Electoral success together with his marriage connection into the Cavendishes—he married Lady Dorothy Cavendish in November 1761—were sufficient credentials. Less proud and haughty than Rockingham (though no less indolent), but less dashing and restless than Richmond, Portland has had a bad press at the hands of historians. He was a conscientious politician, full of integrity and loyalty, thrown by events into responsibilities after the death of Rockingham with which he found it difficult to cope. For the moment, however, all that lay in the future. The General Election of 1768 was Portland's great hour of triumph. It was he, in fact, rather than Rockingham who seemed to be the heir of Newcastle. Portland had electoral interests up and down the country, in London, Buckinghamshire, Nottinghamshire, Lancashire, Cumberland and Westmorland.[23] Rockingham's electoral interests, by comparison, were far more localised.

It was a reflection of the electoral structure of the country and of the lack of interest in the election which allowed other Rockinghamite patrons to maintain their positions with little difficulty. The size of the Cavendish connection eased notionally from six to five when Richard Cavendish left Parliament but the other groups continued unchanged. Albemarle returned the same four Members without a contest. Richmond returned Lord George Lennox and Thomas Connolly at Chichester 'without a dissenting voice'.[24] The two Yorkes came in again as did the two Burkes and their patron, Lord Verney.

There were eighty-three contests at the Election of 1768 but only nine Rockinghamites were involved in seven of them. There was nothing particularly significant about the nature of these contests. The Rockinghamites were not concerned in those constituencies where radicalism was a factor, those in and on the verge of the metropolitan area. They were not, on the whole, representative of 'mercantile' opinion nor did they seek deliberately to express or to represent it at the Election.[25] Of the nine Members who faced contests four were taken up with the Portland–Lowther dispute: Lord Edward Bentinck and George Musgrave at Carlisle and Henry Curwen and Henry Fletcher in Cumberland. Harbord Harbord endured a contest at Norwich and William Weddell at Hull. Of the newer Members, Sir Edward Astley had an expensive contest at Norfolk, Thomas Hay won at Lewes and Lord Ludlow won Huntingdonshire.

The Rockingham Whig party included in its number a large proportion of men of Independent standing. Thirteen such Independents from the old parliament came in: W. A'Court, T. Anson, C. Barrow, Sir W. Codrington, Sir G. Colebrooke, W. Dowdeswell, Sir M. Fetherstonehaugh, H. Harbord, J. Hewett, W. Plumer, J. Plumptre, J. Murray and J. Scawen. Six new Independent Members must be included with the Rockinghamites after the election of 1768. Sir R. Clayton, R. H. Coxe, Sir Edward Astley, Thomas Hay, Lord Ludlow and Beilby Thompson. To the 38 members from the connections, therefore, a further 19 Independents must be added to provide a total of 57 Rockingham Whigs after the election of 1768, a gain of 3. Of the old friends 9 were not returned but 12 new members attached themselves to the party.[26]

The Election of 1768 was thus a modest success for the Rockingham Whigs. Well might Edmund Burke claim 'we keep our Union and our Spirits',[27] while Rockingham could justly write: 'Many election events have happened most

honourably & most successfully on our side, & I flatter myself
you will not find that we are lowered in the Estimation of the
Publick'.[28] Yet the modesty of their success could lead Sir
George Savile to ruminate sadly that the new Parliament would
be just as 'base servile dependent profligate infamous wicked
mean prostituted & obedient as the last'.[29] If it were to be so
then the fortunes of the Rockingham Whigs looked bleak. The
Rockinghams believed in 1768 that they and they alone could
save the constitution and restore it to its original principles. To
what extent is the Rockinghams' claim to uniqueness justified?

Only the wildest admirer of the Rockingham Whigs would
attempt to argue away their manifest weaknesses. It is true that
the party included several men of great talent like Savile,
Burke, Dowdeswell and Yorke but there was aristocratic dead
wood aplenty in the party. It is not at all clear either that the
Rockinghams were better organised than other parties or that
they were more constitutionally correct in their attitudes than
the friends of Chatham, Grenville and Bedford, or even of the
King. Furthermore, Rockingham with all his attractions, was
less experienced than the other party leaders and more indolent
than most of them.

The Rockinghams' claim to uniqueness, however, is borne
out by a combination of circumstances. Their party, although
aristocratic in leadership, was both larger and more broadly
based than any of the other parties. It had appealed, not
without success on occasion, to non-aristocratic opinion in the
country and was to do so again in the near future. It is significant
that the party of the great Whig aristocracy sought to be
popular and was prepared to welcome within its ranks the
allegiance of men of Independent standing in their counties.
In other words, the Rockingham Whig party represented the
political traditions of the Pelhams. These can be described as
ideals of service to the monarchy combined with the group
solidarity of the old corps in office and fidelity to the principles
of the Glorious Revolution and the Hanoverian Succession.[30]
These it united to the principles of 'country' Whiggism, that is,
distaste for 'corruption' and wasteful expenditure and perhaps
the advocacy of Place bills or other expedients for securing the
independence of the Commons. There can be little doubt

that in formulating their own version of Whig principles the Rockingham Whigs were consciously seeking to relate their own activities to the Whiggism not merely of the age of the Pelhams and of Walpole but also to that of the Revolution era. In doing so they were beginning the process of creating a fresh synthesis of Whig principles.

The reformulation of Whiggism at the hands of the Rockingham Whigs was one of the consequences of the political instability of the 1760s.[31] For their failures and disappointments in that unpredictable decade the Rockingham Whigs, in common with many others,[32] made Bute the scapegoat. Yet the very real political and constitutional issues which arose from the vexed question of the favourite, especially those concerning relations between the King and his ministers[33] did not die with the passing of his influence and the waning of popular belief in the influence of Lord Bute. For in 1769 Bute went abroad and did not return to political life.[34] The myth of Lord Bute's secret influence was ready to give birth, in the womb of Edmund Burke, to the theory of secret influence and the principle of party government. But that was still in the future in 1768. Yet already the materials and the men from which Burke was to fashion his theory were in existence. Already, for example, there lay to hand the myth that the key to the failure of the Chatham administration was to be found in the Great Commoner's misguided alliance with Bute. Already, the Rockingham Whigs regarded themselves as the sole vehicles of constitutional recuperation. Only they were free from the contamination of the Court. Only they retained their virtue, their independence and their public spiritedness. In vindicating their own isolation in this manner the Rockinghams were making it difficult for themselves to take office, even in the broad based and tolerant regime of North after 1770. They were erecting powerful psychological barriers which stood in the way of their participation in the consensual politics of the 1770s.

It is necessary, at this point, to divest oneself of the notion that there is or ever has been in British history such a thing as an 'ideal type' of party. It is not clear, for example, why a party has to be a 'mass' party in order to be regarded as a legitimate party.[34] Since the seventeenth century, British political history has to a greater or lesser degree turned upon the conflict which has usually, though not always, been institutionalised via the medium of political parties. Thus, although there have been periods when bi-polarity has not existed (the early-mid eighteenth century, for example, and the 1930s), and occasional tendencies towards a multi-party development have made themselves felt, these have been the exceptions rather than the norms of British political development. The *nature* of the political conflict, the political party and political issues have changed out of all recognition during the last three centuries and to regard those centuries as a period of preparation for the 'perfect' parties of the twentieth century is clearly a travesty of history. In resorting to party and the claims of party the Rockingham Whigs were acting within the traditional patterns of British political life.

This they did because the aberrational politics of the mid-eighteenth century could not withstand the accession of George III, the Seven Years War and the popular 'issues' in politics. The politics of principle and conflict began to weaken and to undermine the traditional eighteenth century ideals of un-animity, co-operation and service to the monarch. In political terms, as Professor Foord has shown, the notion of 'opposition' was becoming increasingly respectable in the 1760s.[35] Most contemporaries would admit that opposition was not only permissible but that it had a useful constitutional purpose to serve within the existing political framework. It still remained, however, to reformulate the tools, the practices and theories of opposition and of party. It was to be the historical significance of the Rockingham Whigs that they were to achieve these objectives, although in 1768 their achievement still lay in the future. The new issues of radicalism and America weakened rather than strengthened the Rockinghams and thus retarded rather than facilitated the growth of party. The Rockingham Whigs owed far more to the traditions of the Pelhams and the ideals of country Whiggery than they owed to the new issues of the 1760s for those issues were superimposed upon existing attitudes and habits of thought. In 1768 the Rockingham Whig party owed more to the past than it owed to the issues of the future.

Chapter 10

Party, People and Parliament 1768–70

The revival of the career of John Wilkes and his uncanny ability to raise constitutional issues of the gravest significance was undoubtedly the most important and most abiding single legacy of the General Election of 1768. In the months immediately after the Election, however, political circles were less preoccupied with Wilkes than we might assume. It was not until the following year, with the ministry's ill-fated attempts to unseat the demagogue, that 'Wilkes and Liberty' became the greatest political issue of the day. In the months after the Election the situation of the ministry and the problem of America were the two subjects of greatest political interest.

Although thé Election had not endangered the Government's majority the ministry was in a sorry internal situation. There was no unity in the Cabinet. In Chatham's absence, Grafton soldiered conscientiously on supported by nobody but the King and the ineffective Hawke.[1] North and Hillsborough looked to George III rather than to Grafton, Camden and Shelburne to Chatham. Weymouth and Hillsborough remained attached to Bedford, unable to sink their separate identities in a ministry which lacked one. In spite of his proven ability at least to survive and the failure of the Opposition to take advantage of his difficulties, Grafton's future was the subject of considerable discussion in the summer of 1768.[2] Nothing seemed to go right for him. Richard Rigby persuaded the hapless nobleman to honour an earlier promise that he should have the reversion of the office of Joint-Paymaster-General after the death of George Cooke. To achieve this, Grafton was forced to shuffle Thomas Townshend into Rigby's old office, the Vice-Treasurership of Ireland. Not only did Grafton handle the matter clumsily but Townshend felt, not without some justification, that this was a manifestation of the growing supremacy of the Bedfords within the ministry as well as a grave personal insult to himself. The unhappy affair ended with Townshend surrendering his office.[3] Grafton was not only in trouble on account of the Bedfords but he fell foul of one of their greatest opponents inside the ministry, Shelburne, when he encroached upon the patronage of Shelburne's department. The resulting disputes were not kept secret. 'I hear of nothing like, ministerial alterations', wrote Lord George Sackville to General Irwin on 10 August 'any farther than that the general opinion is that Lord Shelburne is to be removed.'[4] Trivial such as these disputes were, they upset Grafton and demonstrated the miserable situation into which Chatham's arrogance and ill-health had brought the ministry. They also indicate that nobody in administration was able to compose its internal differences. The ministry drifted without purpose and plan. In this state, it had to tackle once again the problem of America.

American reaction to the Townshend duties, however vociferous, was perhaps more moderate than the British Government had a right to expect. In John Dickinson's *Letters of a Pennsylvania Farmer*, published in February 1768, for example, as well as in the 'Massachusetts Circular' which went round the colonies in 1768–9, the supreme legislative authority of the imperial Parliament was respected. Objection was raised to the principle of taxation without representation and against the uses to which the revenue raised by Townshend's duties was to be put, but judicious handling of the problem might yet have saved the situation. Prospects for some sort of accommodation were dashed when Boston and parts of Virginia erupted into violent demonstrations against the duties in July 1768.

Reflecting the frustrated annoyance with the colonists which many Englishmen felt in 1768, the Government hurriedly despatched troops to maintain order.[5] Thus a further twist was given to the upward spiral of events which was to end on the field of Lexington. The colonists reacted by joining together in the Non-importation agreements which had sprung up in the autumn of the previous year, but which by early 1769 had spread throughout every colony except New Hampshire. The only gesture of conciliation which the British Government made was in appointing a resident Governor of Virginia. Sir Jeffrey Amherst's non-residence had always been a source of grievance to the colonists. The appointment to the Governorship of Lord Botetort may have gone some little way towards conciliating them. At the same time, it aroused the suspicions of the Rockingham Whigs for in years past Botetort had been associated with Bute. Rockinghamite heads shook gravely as they reflected at this further instance of the favourite's apparently continuing influence over the ministry.[6]

The Rockingham Whigs were now in a position to make a real effort to come to terms with the situation in America. The Marquis had decided to have no future dealings with the ministry, suspicious as he was of the influence of Bute and the predominance of the Bedfords.[7] At the same time, he was determined to have nothing to do with George Grenville, believing that it was impossible to improve relations with him appreciably.[8] Nothing would have been easier for the Rockinghams in this situation than factiously to have opposed or indolently to have approved the ministry's American policy, but with commendable public spirit the Rockinghams chose to do neither as they embarked upon a fairly wide-ranging review of the American problem. Mr Brooke has heavily underlined the thinking of William Dowdeswell on the American problem and suggested that it was a well-intentioned, reasonable and courageous attempt to come to grips with the realities of the American situation.[9] With great perception, Dowdeswell saw that the disorders in America were likely to spread, their cause being the principle rather than the weight of the Townshend duties. Thus to repeal the duties would shelve rather than settle the question of sovereignty which had now arisen. There were, for example, many other revenue measures whose repeal the Americans might be encouraged to demand if the Townshend duties were surrendered. Dowdeswell's solution to the dilemma was to recommend the repeal of the Townshend duties provided that the thorny question of sovereignty was not touched. At the same time, Dowdeswell recognised that the imperial question was not merely one of theory but one of maintaining law and order. Ministers should therefore be supported in their attempts to restore order and protect property. Like almost all of his contemporaries, Dowdeswell was unable to envisage some intermediate form of association of Britain and America, between full political and economic integration, on the one hand, and independence, on the other. Rockingham's view was similar. For him the Declaratory Act had been a manifestation of constitutional wisdom, whereas the Repeal of the Stamp Act had been a matter of expediency. This did not mean that Rockingham supported the policy of the British Government in 1767-8. He rejected 'The new Ideas of making the colonies an Object of Increase of Revenue', because Britain would assist the cure of her budgetary problems less by taxing and harrying the Americans than by trading with them. Yet Rockingham always shrank from encouraging the colonists to resist British rule. He condemned the 'Misfortunes of opinions entertained here by Various Great Persons; Some *Nurse* America in the Follies of Speculative Propositions. Others keep constantly continuing the Terror of raising large Revenues on them'.[10] Rockingham wished to do neither. Compromise and moderation were the essential characteristics of his position on American affairs. The extent to which he unreservedly embraced the cause of the colonists should not, therefore, be exaggerated.

These contemplations were dramatically interrupted by events within the ministry which left the advocates of repressive measures against America enormously strengthened. During the summer, tension between Shelburne and the Bedfords had reached intolerable proportions. Their desire to rid the ministry of Shelburne was shared not only by Grafton but even by the King.[11] It says something for Grafton's skill that he was able to remove Shelburne in October without provoking the resignation of his closest friend in the Cabinet, Camden. It seems impossible (though it has been suggested) that Grafton was engineering the resignation of Chatham. But Grafton was fearful of taking responsibility. It seems incredible that he should have deliberately sought it. Perhaps with the intention of learning Chatham's intentions for the coming session, Grafton arranged a meeting with Lady Chatham on 9 October 1768. Hearing that Chatham's indisposition was likely to prevent his participation in politics in the near future, Grafton informed her of the dismissal of Amherst and the forthcoming resignation of Shelburne. This was the last straw for Chatham. His wishes had been ignored on almost every matter of policy for the last two years, and now his political friends were to be removed. At the same time, Grafton's communication may have been nothing more than an excuse for a resignation which Chatham had by now decided upon. On 12 October he wrote to the King professing his desire to resign. George III begged him to reconsider. 'I think I have a right to insist on your remaining in my service, for I with pleasure look forward to the time of your recovery when I may have your assistance in resisting the torrents of faction this country so much labours under.'[12] But Chatham had had enough of this by now. His ill-health came before the ideological crusade of which George III was still dreaming. He clung to his resolution. The Chatham administration was at an end.[13]

The Grafton administration had come into being but in circumstances which actually weakened Grafton's own position. Although Chatham's Privy Seal went to the Chathamite Lord Bristol,[14] Shelburne's Secretaryship went to the Bedford Whig, Lord Weymouth. In the Cabinet only Camden was likely to support Grafton in adopting a moderate line on America and Grafton was becoming more of a prisoner of the Bedfords.[15] By accident then, and against the wishes of the third Duke of Grafton himself, the Grafton ministry arose like a phoenix from the flickering embers of the Chatham administration. Grafton's immediate problem was nothing so elevated as to work out a policy for America. It was that of survival. The ministry was weak in leadership, ability and organisation and the meeting of Parliament was only a few days away.

Nevertheless, the Opposition was too weak either to stop or to modify the American policy of the ministry. When Parliament met on 8 November 1768, Dowdeswell moved an amendment to the Address to take American policy into consideration. But the Opposition was divided. Grenville and Dowdeswell spent more time and energy attacking each other than they did their opponents and the feeling of the House was against Dowdeswell's wish to debate the ministry's policy. Humiliatingly, he had to withdraw his amendment.[16] The Opposition was obviously well advised to turn its attention to the issue of Corsica. That island had been conquered by the French earlier in 1768. Very sensibly, the ministry had not regarded the annexation of Corsica as a threat to British interests. Nevertheless it was a useful opposition ploy to arouse the country against the alleged designs of Bourbon expansionism. On 17 November Henry Seymour moved for the papers and the diplomatic correspondence relating to Corsica. Ministers pleaded secrecy and threw the motion out by the comfortable majority of 230–84.[17] Clearly, the Opposition was unable to shake the ministry and, in spite of its weaknesses and divisions, Grafton appeared to be safe for at least some time to come.

These last few weeks of the year were dispiriting for the Opposition not only on account of their unsuccessful attack on the ministry but also because of the death on 17 November of the old Duke of Newcastle. His influence within the party had long been declining, but especially since he had suffered a stroke a year earlier, and his death made little practical difference to the Opposition. There is little need to defend Newcastle from the old-fashioned charges that he was a weak-minded and ridiculous fool. A man with those qualities could not have remained at the centre of the political stage for half a century and few men left such a mark upon politics in the eighteenth century as Newcastle did. In striving to serve what he sincerely believed to be the public interest and to protect the constitution he contributed largely to the stability of the eighteenth century political system. It was, perhaps, no accident, that his fall from power in 1762 heralded a period of uncertainty and instability unknown for decades.

Newcastle's death coincided with renewed talk of a 'union of the Opposition'. At least, George Grenville, while sticking to his opinions on America, was making some gestures of friendship, promising, for example, to support the Duke of Portland over

Nullum Tempus.[18] More significantly, at the end of November a suddenly reinvigorated Chatham received Temple at Hayes on 25 November and a reconciliation between them followed.[19] Although Grenville did not go so far, he also signified his readiness to forget his past quarrels with Chatham.[20] The basis was being laid for the union of the Opposition of 1769. Rockingham welcomed it, although he desperately wanted to know the answer to 'the *Grand* Question whether Ld Chatham *did* or *did not authorize*'.[21] Nevertheless, the Opposition was preparing itself for a session which saw the rise of novel forms of political organisation and an upsurge of opinion in the country, all of which seemed to present a heaven-sent opportunity for destroying the Grafton ministry. Until January 1770, the future not merely of Grafton but also of the Grenville and Rockingham parties was at stake and remained in doubt. And all this because John Wilkes, once more, began to wreak his havoc upon British politics.

Since his escape to France in 1764 Wilkes had been careful to maintain his contacts with politicians in Britain, including the Rockingham Whigs. He had expected the first Rockingham ministry to absolve him from all the charges laid against him but this it had not done (although it had paid his debts and allowed him a small pension, presumably to avoid the embarrassment which would surround his homecoming).[22] Chatham and Grafton, in their turn, were no more ready than the Rockinghams to lift a finger to help a political charlatan who had apparently outlived his usefulness. Financial necessity drove Wilkes back to England but as an outlaw he was still liable to imprisonment. The only way of avoiding a sentence was to become a Member of Parliament and thus acquire immunity from the processes of the civil courts. Long before the dissolution of 1768, then, Wilkes had decided to contest a seat at the General Election.[23]

Wilkes' first candidature was a pathetic failure. He came last of seven candidates for the four seats of the city of London.[24] At what appeared to be curfew of his political career, Temple stepped in to provide Wilkes with some land in the county of Middlesex, thus qualifying him for the election there. Within a few days a hitherto uncontested election became a sensation.

Wilkes overnight emerged as a local hero and something of a champion of the people. Working astutely upon the materials to hand—especially the high prices and low wages which afflicted the labouring poor in the winter of 1767–8—Wilkes roused the people and swept to an astounding victory over two competent and, in normal times, fairly popular sitting members.

John Wilkes	1292
George Cooke	827
Sir William Beauchamp-Proctor	807 (25)

Ministers were left with two agonising decisions to take. What were they to do about Wilkes himself, and what measures were they to take to deal with the rioting and looting which had accompanied the Middlesex election and which continued into the spring?

On the first of these problems it was Wilkes himself who took the initiative and gave the unfortunate ministry of Grafton no alternative but to persecute him if it wished to avoid political disgrace. He chose to compound his popularity with martyrdom. On 27 April he surrendered to the courts for his outlawry only to find that the charge against him was dropped on technical grounds. Thereupon he manfully refused to shirk the outstanding charges of blasphemy and seditious libel. In the middle of June he was sentenced to twenty-two months imprisonment on these charges. As a Member of Parliament he would normally have been protected by privilege but ministers had already decided in April to expel Wilkes from Parliament on the grounds that he had been technically an outlaw at the time of the Middlesex election. To have done otherwise would have been to bow to Wilkes' victory and this the ministers of George III could not do.[26] The expulsion had to be delayed, however, until the next session of Parliament because the attention of ministers was taken up with the preservation of order and stability in the metropolis amidst scenes of growing disorder and mob violence.

In spite of allegations of high handedness and authoritarianism levelled against the Government in 1768–9 we should remember that the authorities had very few powers at their disposal for dealing with the rioters. The Government's determination to expel Wilkes must be seen as an attempt to impress the frightened propertied classes with its vigour. Something of the helplessness of the authorities may be grasped when we recall that so great was the enthusiasm of the crowd for Wilkes in the early stages of the Middlesex election that all the peace officers from London were required to control its enthusiasm, thus leaving the capital entirely defenceless.[27] Even the magistrates realised that the suppression of violence owed more to the good sense of the Wilkites themselves—who would not wish their candidate to acquire a reputation for rabble rousing—than it did to their own efforts.[28] The precariousness of peace and order was perhaps most effectively demonstrated by the activities of the organised Wilkite mob when Wilkes was surrendering himself as an outlaw. With great good humour they kidnapped him from the coach in which he was travelling whereupon Wilkes voluntarily gave himself up.[29]

Both the authorities and the Wilkites tried to avert violence but their efforts could not succeed indefinitely. Rioting had continued in a desultory fashion for over two months when it culminated in the Massacre of St George's Fields, an event which instantly captured the popular imagination and entered into radical mythology. On the day of the opening of the new Parliament, 10 May 1768, the authorities stationed about 100 men, some on horseback, near the prison where Wilkes was held in custody. Predictably, these precautions attracted like a magnet the crowds they were supposed to discourage. As the size of the crowd grew in the afternoon, perhaps to 20,000, violence broke out. The reading of the riot act served only to aggravate the disorder. The troops panicked and at least a dozen citizens were killed.[30] The Massacre convinced the mob that the troops were acting on orders from the ministry to murder some civilians as an example to others.[31] It also provoked rather than prevented further rioting and underlined the growing belief of the propertied classes that the Government was incapable of keeping the peace. The Wilkite riots, in short, presented a quite new and frightening force in politics which few contemporaries were able to understand.[32]

Although the Opposition was secretly rather pleased that the ministry found itself in such straits over the affairs of Wilkes, its members did nothing to encourage either him or his friends.[33] Rockingham's party might have been glad to see the Court humiliated in public but it did not wish to lift a finger to stoke the fires of the radical movement in 1768. Rockingham believed that the Wilkes affair would be forgotten within six months and he was careful to avoid public pronouncements on it. His friends might casually reflect that the spontaneous eruptions of sympathy for Wilkes were a manifestation of the Englishmen's love of liberty, but they regarded such demonstrations as an unpleasant and transitory phenomenon. As Burke put it: 'The plan of our party was, I think, wise and proper; not to provoke Administration into any Violent measure upon this Subject . . . besides we had not the least desire of taking up that Gentlemans Cause as personally favourable to him; he is not ours, and if he were, is little to be trusted'.[34] In the session of 1768 the Rock-inghams refused to champion the cause of Wilkes and Liberty. Rockingham, indeed, was loth even to ask his friends to come to town.[35] Like Grafton, he was waiting for the case of John Wilkes to go away.

In the following months this obstinately refused to happen. During the long summer recess Wilkes and his movement went from strength to strength. His birthday on 28 October was celebrated throughout the capital with noisy jubilation. Furthermore against an alliance of the Court and the interest of Newcastle, the Wilkite John Glynn won a by-election at Middlesex in December. Glynn obtained 1542 votes against Sir William Beauchamp-Proctor's 1278. Wilkes increased his prestige when he secured election as an Alderman of the City of London after his unopposed return in the ward of Farringdon Without on 27 January 1769. The creation of the Bill of Rights Society on 20 February placed the radical movement upon a solid, institutional basis and left it perhaps less dependent upon the personality of Wilkes than it might otherwise have been. The immediate purpose of the Society were to retrieve Wilkes' desperate financial situation, but within a few months it had acquired broader political objectives. Both the man and the movement were incomparably stronger early in 1769 than they had been six months earlier.

The Government could no longer afford to ignore Wilkes. The final provocation to its waning prestige and sinking authority came when Wilkes published and denounced a message sent by the Secretary at War, Lord Barrington, which appeared to congratulate the troops responsible for the Massacre at St George's Fields.[36] The ministers were now goaded beyond endurance, and pushed and prodded by the King they decided finally to seek parliamentary approval for the expulsion of John Wilkes.[37] This they attempted to obtain on 3 February, a date which marks the end of anything resembling a common attitude of Government and Opposition towards Wilkes.[38] The Rockingham Whigs openly opposed the expulsion. They protested because the seditious libels, which were the basis of the resolution to expel Wilkes, had already been punished in the previous Parliament. Burke, however, went much further: 'you have put an end to the liberty of the press; you have put an end to the franchise of the country; you have put something into the hands of the minister, that will enable him to oppress you'.[39] The subsequent re-elections of Wilkes and expulsions by the House confirmed Burke's fears. The seating of Wilkes' defeated opponent, however, Henry Lawes Luttrell, was far more sensational to contemporaries than the expulsion of Wilkes. For Wilkes, whatever his faults, laboured under no legal incapacity with might have warranted the seating of Luttrell and, as Grenville pointed out frequently at this time, a resolution of the Commons alone could not make or declare law either in election or any other matters. That Wilkes could not be incapacitated by a Commons resolution was to be the constitutional ground upon which the Opposition stood in the Wilkes controversy. Here was an issue which transcended personality and faction but which could conveniently be within the framework of Rockinghamite ideas. The expulsion of Wilkes and the seating of Luttrell appeared not only to violate the independence of Parliament from the executive but also to violate the rights of electors. Those rights may have been more honoured in the breach than in the observance in the unreformed Parliament but when they were breached it was usually at the hands of local patrons and local men rarely by the Government. It was easy for the Rockinghams, once they had been drawn into the Middlesex election controversy, to believe that the system of court influence over the Commons was now extending its dangerous tentacles to touch the hitherto sacrosanct rights of electors. Once the Government, then, had moved against Wilkes, the Opposition leapt to his defence and was quick to raise the constitutional issues at stake in the affair.

The popular and parliamentary protest against the expulsions of Wilkes dominated politics until January 1770 and in the summer and autumn of 1769 drew the country into a spate of political activity more widespread and better organised than anything the century had seen since the Hanoverians had come to the throne. Although Grafton's parliamentary position remained strong,[40] the expulsion of Wilkes brought together different elements in opposition to the Court. As Professor Rude has shown, Wilkes drew his electoral support from the urban parishes of Middlesex to the north and east of the City from men who though lower in wealth and status than those who supported the ministerial candidate, were nevertheless not negligible. They were middle-class types of tradesmen, merchants and respectable workers. Moreover, the freemen in the counties might well have interpreted the expulsion of Wilkes as a threat to the security and power of their franchise. There was little question that these men might wish to 'reform Parliament'. They wished to protect one of the few valuable, proprietorial commodities which they owned. At the same time, given the absence of political consciousness and political organisation in the country at large, it would be unwise to regard the Petitioning Movement of 1769 as a spontaneous eruption of freeholders' indignation. Their revolt required the organisation and the leadership which only the great county and territorial families could provide. The parliamentary opposition to Grafton therefore joined together to unite the Wilkite movement in the city and the freeholders of the counties in a great national protest against the expulsion of Wilkes, designed to destroy the present administration. We should not exaggerate either the extent or the cohesion of the movement. Only one quarter of the electorate signed petitions in 1769, a substantial figure but one which suggests that the vast majority of the population was not reached by the movement. Furthermore, the movement was never united. Professor Rude chooses to divide it into three elements, the metropolitan radicals, the Rockingham Whigs and the Chatham–Temple–Grenville triumvirate.[41] But even these categories disintegrate on close examination and it is possibly more helpful to think of each town and county as part of a bewildering mosaic of different local situations. Moreover, it is, in retrospect, fanciful for Rockingham and others to have believed that they could have come into office as supporters of Wilkes. It was unlikely that George III would choose to employ them, and apart from frightening Grafton out of office it is not at once clear what the Opposition hoped to gain from the petitions. One result of their attack was completely unexpected. The Cabinet rallied behind Grafton and the ministry was consequently more united in the summer of 1769 than at any other time in its unhappy history.[42] Exciting and perhaps unprecedented the Petitioning Movement of 1769 certainly was, but it would be a mistake to exaggerate its monolithic qualities or to liken it too closely to the radical movements of the 1790s and the nineteenth century.

The Rockingham Whigs were involved in the Petitioning Movement from the very beginning. On 17 April 2,000 Middlesex freeholders gathered at Mile End and resolved to prepare a 'Bill of Grievances and Apprehensions'. What followed is not entirely clear but owing to the influence of Rockingham, Burke and Dowdeswell the terms of the original 'Bill' (or Petition, as it became) were changed and restricted to the single issue of the Middlesex election and the seating of Luttrell, thus avoiding the more contentious radical issue of parliamentary reform.[43] Sir George Savile presented the Middlesex petition to Parliament on 29 April, but there was no debate upon it until 8 May when the Commons upheld their earlier decision to expel Wilkes by 221–152.[44] The stage was set for the Petitioning Movement of 1769. On the face of it, it seems surprising that the city radicals should seek out the aristocratic, Rockingham party to present their petition to Parliament. After all, Rockingham had never been greatly interested in city politics. Unlike Newcastle, he rarely exerted himself in attempts to establish influence there. Indeed, his failure to do so—especially his inactivity when Trecothick was up for re-election as Mayor in 1770—could drive his advisors to distraction.[45] It was the Chathamites who were actively concerned with city affairs and who seemed to be the obvious parliamentary allies for the Wilkites. But this was not the case. The Chathamites were potential rivals to the Wilkites for influence in the city, and it was natural for the Wilkites to seek the assistance of the non-Chathamite section of the parliamentary Opposition.

Rockingham and his friends threw themselves into the Petitioning campaign with greater vigour than they had ever exhibited hitherto. The Marquis began to acquit himself with some little oratorical success in the Upper House, something to which their Lordships were not accustomed.[46] To some extent this was the natural reaction of an Opposition party whose prospects of office seemed unpromising but it would be unjust to conclude that the Rockinghams wished merely to make short-term political capital out of the Middlesex election issue. They found in that issue not only a stick with which to beat the Grafton ministry but also confirmation of the suspicions which they had entertained first against the Chatham administration and now its successor. These flowed directly from their earlier suspicions of Bute and their fear of the operations of a sinister court party. Rockingham summed up this view, later to receive its classic exposition at the hands of Burke, when he wrote that the Grafton ministry was 'an Administration without the Confidence of the People & supported by nothing, but from their obtaining the support *of a Party* whose views are arbitrary everywhere & to whom the Administration pay almost implicit Obedience'.[47]

To avert the acquiesence of Parliament in these sinister designs it was necessary to take advantage of the fact that the people appeared to be awakening to the danger just in time. If their voice could be channelled into appropriate political activity there might be time to save the constitution. The Rockinghams believed themselves to be sufficiently strong to defeat the crusade of the court party against the constitution. Not only were they the most numerous party in Opposition

but they enjoyed extensive territorial influence. Their leadership would be indispensable for the organisation of a national
campaign on behalf of the rights of electors. That same leadership might also be necessary to prevent such a campaign
running to extreme lengths and diverting public attention
from the main issue of the rights of electors. Tactical expedience
and political consistency combined to stimulate the Rockinghams into action as a party in an appeal to the nation on a
scale which they had not hitherto even contemplated.

To achieve this objective, it was necessary for the Rockinghams to concert their plans and strategy with other political
groups. For this reason William Dowdeswell arranged a dinner
at the Thatched House Tavern on 9 May which was attended
by seventy-seven members of Opposition groups in both
Houses.[48] The meeting decided to co-operate with the metropolitan radicals if they would drop their demands for parliamentary reform. To prepare the ground for the reinstatement
of Wilkes, the parliamentary Opposition would ally with the
radicals in raising petitions confined to the single issue of the
Middlesex election. If sufficient petitions could be raised to
demonstrate the opinion of the country then Parliament would
have to restore Wilkes to his seat and the rights of electors
would be safeguarded. An enthusiastic participation in what
Temple called the 'one great constitutional cause' was conceivable in the euphoria of Westminster a few hours after an
exceptionally good Opposition division figure[49] but success
or failure in this enterprise would depend largely upon the
extent to which the political groups were able to co-operate
with each other, with the radicals and with the freeholders.

Men on all sides of the Opposition seem to have recognised
the pressing need to work together but this recognition was
expressed more frequently by the 'men of business' such as
Burke and Whately, rather than by the party leaders.[50]
Although Burke met Whately in September and went to Stowe
in November there were few contacts between the Rockinghams and the other parties. At bottom, the Rockinghams were
chronically suspicious of the other leaders. Burke said of their
allies: 'they are never fair and direct; they have a thousand
underplots and oblique views; one of them always reserves

himself while another acts'.[51] Although the Rockinghams had no reason to love Chatham they were prepared to accept him in a union of the Opposition. Indeed, they could hardly do otherwise. His personality was still a factor in politics. Though his reputation had been damaged by the administration of 1766–8 his name would doubtless lend weight to the Opposition's efforts in the country. It must be said of Chatham that he did what he could to dispel Rockingham's hostility. 'He says that he is body and soul united to Ld Rockingham & Sir George Savile in this measure. . . . That he will go hand in hand with Ld R. and his Friends who are, & who have proved themselves to be the only true Whigs in this Country.'[52] According to another report, Chatham said of Rockingham: 'He & He alone, has a knot of *spotless friends*, such as ought to govern this Kingdom.'[53] Rockingham and his friends were not impressed with Chatham's effusiveness. In particular, the Marquis understood that it would be easier to unite in opposition then to form a coalition ministry with Chatham and Grenville. Although he respected the talents and experience of the other Opposition leaders Rockingham believed the claims of his own party to be superior to those of others. 'I mean The Constant Uniform and Invariable Conduct—which *we* have held in all situations from the first Rise of Confusions—on Ld Bute's Accession to Power—down to the Present moment.'[54] It followed then: 'we & *we only* of all the Parts now in opposition are so on System & Principle. That we ought to avail ourselves of other Parties now in opposition, in order to effectuate good Purposes, but that we should be cautious not even to throw the appearance of *Leading* into Hands—whose Principles we have no reason to think similar to our own—& whose Honour we have no reason to confide in'.[55] Rockingham was demanding the *support* of Chatham and of Grenville *on his own terms* in a new ministry. How his attitude to Chatham had changed since the ministry of 1765–6 when the Marquis had done almost everything except to humiliate himself in his desire to obtain Pitt's support! The only sort of ministry which the Rockinghams were prepared to consider was not simply a party ministry but a party ministry formed out of 'a Negotiation thrown into our Hands'. The Rockinghams were prepared therefore to co-operate in opposition with other groups so long as such co-operation did not imply an equality of status in Government.

Rockingham was always anxious to confine the petitions to the single issue of the rights of electors. In his view, the radical demands, particularly that of parliamentary reform, had no place in the petitions. The petitions, in fact, were to be little more than a means of propagating the first Rockinghamite commandment: 'that the great and continual increase of the power and influence of the Crown in the course of this century (if the Crown should unfortunately be led by weak—wicked and arbitrary ministers and surrounded by evil counsellors) would operate most dangerously to the Constitution'.[56] The Rockingham party was eager to place its proceedings in 1769 upon this constitutional basis. Dowdeswell, in his *The Sentiments of an English Freeholder on the late Decision of the Middlesex Election* demonstrated how the constitution was endangered. He attacked the status of Parliament's action in expelling Wilkes, asserting that a resolution of one House was an insufficient, non-statutory basis for effecting a drastic constitutional innovation. Wilkes could by no stretch of the imagination be included among the categories of persons (such as aliens and idiots) who were incapacitated from sitting in Parliament. Sir William Meredith wrote in much the same way in his *The Question Stated, whether the Freeholders of Middlesex lost their Right by voting for Mr Wilkes at the Last Election*, arguing that the legal right to elect could not be taken from freeholders by the arbitrary whim of one House of one Parliament. The right of the freeholders to vote, moreover, was equivalent to a property right and to deprive the freeholder of his *right* was at the same time to deprive him of his *property* by virtue of a law which was unknown to the constitution. In defending the rights of electors in 1769, then, the Rockinghams were not merely out for place, nor even merely out to maintain the consistency of their political attitudes of the 1760s. They were also deeply concerned to defend the fundamental rights of property and the traditional Whig ideal of a mixed constitution, the consent of all members of which was necessary for the making of law.

How far were the Rockingham Whigs able to influence the course of the Petitioning Movement? At first the metropolitan radicals kept up their early pressure. A second Middlesex petition, signed by 1,565 freeholders, was ready for presentation to the King by 24 May. There had evidently been some reduction of Rockinghamite influence since the first petition because the second raised a number of grievances totally unrelated to the rights of electors, such as the violence of the militia and the repression of the American colonists. A month later, however, a petition was raised in London which would have pleased Rockingham, exposing the influence of Bute and the plan of the Court in the new reign.[57] Although its two Members were inclined to the Court, a meeting was held at Bristol on 18 July to organise a petition modelled upon that of London. By 25 July, 2,445 people, over half the electorate, had signed it.[58] The only petition at this time which could be regarded as an absolute victory for the Rockinghamite formula came from Surrey. The petition there confined itself to the issue of the Middlesex election and the committee was crammed with Rockinghamites.[59] Within two months the movement had made an effective start. There now came the first petition from Rockinghamite territory. In Dowdeswell's Worcestershire, a petition was presented to a freeholders' meeting on 9 August which confined itself to the issue of the Middlesex election. By September 1,475 signatures had been appended to the county petition, 650 to the (similar) city petition.[60] Elsewhere the Rockinghamite formula was not always observed. Although Buckinghamshire housed Edmund Burke and Lord Verney the county was dominated by Temple and Grenville. The Buckinghamshire petition is worthy of attention because, following the Westminster petition formula, it was addressed to the King, demanding him to dissolve Parliament. The earlier petitions had not carried this plea for a dissolution.[61] In spite of the rather lethargic pace set by the parliamentary politicians in organising the petition there, no fewer than 1,800 freeholders signed the petition at a county meeting at Aylesbury on 7 September.[62]

We should resist the impression that the raising of a petition was a straightforward matter which involved a handful of noblemen in snapping their fingers at a line of obedient freeholders. As men like Burke and Dowdeswell found to their cost, the petitions involved heavy work, weeks of planning and of organisation. Many gentlemen and freeholders would be just as wary of disturbing the peace of the county (or borough) over the Wilkes issue as they would be at election time. Even when a movement to raise a petition was set on foot it rarely embraced half the freeman. The fact that the issue was so closely bound up with the personality of Wilkes himself, moreover, must have deterred many respectable freeholders from lending their support to the petitions. Furthermore, it was not at all difficult for supporters of the Government to arrest the progress of the petitions. Whenever they were prepared to bestir themselves, moves to launch a petition were quickly blocked, as happened at Essex, Norfolk, Cumberland, Lincolnshire and Northampton-shire, and perhaps elsewhere. It is well to remember that there was more than one opinion abroad in 1769 about the Middlesex election. Had ministers and their friends set up a vigorous counter-petitioning movement, they might well have exposed the Opposition's claim that on the Middlesex election issue it spoke for the country. But even without ministerial intervention the Petitioning Movement lost its impetus during the summer. The trickle of petitions dried up thanks to the lethargy of most members of the Opposition who saw little point in raising petitions during the recess. By the end of August the Movement clearly required a stimulus to activity and a dramatic example of success. Eyes naturally turned to the largest, most populous, most independent county of all, Rockingham's county of Yorkshire.

At the outset, however, the Marquis' earlier readiness to take up the gauntlet which the Court had thrown down over the Middlesex election had atrophied in view of the very real difficulty of forcing the notoriously independent Yorkshire freeholders into any particular line of conduct. Rockingham's views, while not exactly equivocal, did not smack of vigour. At the end of June his position was that he wished the Grand Jury at the summer assizes to address the county Members.[63] Rockingham was also inhibited for a time about petitioning the Crown for a dissolution of Parliament. Only when Sir Anthony Abdy, MP for Knaresborough and a close confidant of Rockingham at this time time, satisfied him that there was nothing improper in such petitions did Rockingham decide to proceed.[64] Abdy was not the only man in Rockingham's confidence at this time. Burke was among those who tried to persuade the Marquis that a petition from Yorkshire was necessary if the Petitioning Movement were to have any prospect of success.[65] Dowdeswell was likewise full of warnings that 'Yorkshire should set the example'. Furthermore, it was he who insisted that the Yorkshire petition should demand a dissolution.[66] Even as late as September, however, Rockingham was still unhappy at the prospect of calling a county meeting in Yorkshire, and it was only at the instigation of some of the Yorkshire gentry that he agreed to the holding of a meeting at York on 24 September.[67] He need not have worried. The meeting was distinguished both for its large attendance and for the respectability of those who attended. There was not a breath of Opposition to the moderate petition moved by Sir George Armytage and seconded by Sir Cecil Wray and which had the influential support of Sir George Savile. Ultimately, no fewer than 11,000 freeholders signed the petition in York-shire, a staggering tribute to the efficiency of Rockingham's political machine.[68] In the end, despite all his hesitations, Rockingham had been ready to defer to his advisors and to follow the wishes of the gentry of his county. In doing so he maintained the unity of his party and of his county, kept the petition to the single issue of the Middlesex election and gave encouragement to the Petitioning Movement elsewhere. Here, if anywhere, is a perfect demonstration of Rockingham's ability to lead from behind.

The Yorkshire petition ultimately roused other counties to activity. Its more immediate effect was to provoke from the western counties a spate of petitions which, however, owed little to Rockinghamite influence. The Herefordshire county meeting of 4 October owed more to the spontaneous enthusiasm of the county than to the Rockinghams; it accepted a petition however, which concentrated upon the single issue of the rights of freeholders. By the time it was presented to the King on 5 January 1770 about 1,800 signatures had been appended to it.[69] In Hereford itself Rockinghamite influence was rather more apparent. John Scudamore, MP for the City, did much to facilitate the passage of a petition very similar to that adopted by the county, and between 5 and 10 December it attracted 400 signatures.[70] In Devon, on the other hand, supporters of the Bill of Rights society were in evidence at the county meeting on 5 October. In spite of their activities the petition which was approved was perhaps the most moderate of all the petitions— it did not even mention the Middlesex election and the seating of Luttrell—and possibly for this reason 2,800 freeholders signed it.[71] At the Exeter meeting of 24 October, however, radical efforts were more successful and the petition approved was much more contentious than the others. It obtained 860 signatures out of a maximum 1,000, a remarkable demonstration of political consciousness in a normally apathetic area.[72] The most theoretical petition of all, however, came from Cornwall, voted at a county meeting at Bodmin on 6 October and signed by 1,500 people.[73] The North of England was more thoroughly infected with the Rockinghamite spirit of the Yorkshire petition but, even there, much depended upon local circumstances. Sometimes, the Middlesex election conflict was superimposed upon older feuds. Such was the case in Liverpool where the Rockinghamite, Sir William Meredith, was confronted with a loyalist corporation. It took pressure from his supporters to persuade Meredith to lend his approval to a petition, even one which clung tenaciously to the single point of the rights of electors. Although 1,100 Liverpudlians signed the petition voted at a meeting on 8 October, at least 450 signed a counter-petition.[74] In Derbyshire, on the other hand, there were no such feuds to divide the freeholders. Out of deference to Chatsworth almost 3,000 of them obediently signed a petition which confined its complaint to the rights of freeholders. Most of the other Northern petitions bear signs of Rockinghamite influence.[75] Similarly, in other parts of the country, the petitions confined themselves to the subject of the rights of electors. Essex, Southwark and Kent went a little further, demanding a dissolution.[76] In general, in only four of the fifteen petitioning counties was there no significant Rockinghamite influence. Among the twelve petitioning boroughs, that influence was much less. This does not mean that in most of the counties (and some of the boroughs) Rockinghamite influence was paramount.

The degree of Rockinghamite influence evident in Yorkshire and Derbyshire was not matched elsewhere. In several places friends of Rockingham had to co-operate with other groups, as in Buckinghamshire, Middlesex and Surrey, for example. Considering the variety of local situations and established local interests, however, there can be no escaping the conclusion that the Rockingham Whigs, in their attempt to mount a national campaign on the subject of the rights of electors, were able with the assistance of other groups, to go far towards succeeding in their objective.[77] Given the state of the country, the nature of communications, the local political concerns of most freeholders and the divisions within the Opposition, the degree of cohesion and unity which was achieved is all the more surprising.

If it was the case that the Rockinghams made a significant impression upon the Petitioning Movement of 1769, then, it is just as important that the Petitioning Movement made a significant impression upon the Rockingham Whigs. Unlike the County Movement of 1779–85, the Petitioning Movement of 1769 actually strengthened the cohesion of the Rockingham party whose size and membership had been so recently defined. With the exception of Richmond, who spent these months in France, all the Rockingham leaders seem to have plunged into the movement with varying degrees of enthusiasm and success. Even Portland, who does not figure very largely in the standard accounts of these events, took some part in Liverpool and in the unsuccessful attempts to launch petitions in Cumberland and Westmorland.[78] Furthermore, it was one thing for the Rockinghams to indulge in theoretical attacks upon the court system. It was a distinct advance upon this for them to harness their local influence to their national campaign to protect the rights of electors and to rid the country of a ministry which seemed so patently to be bent on undermining the traditional liberties of the country. Rockingham, once so timid of petitions, became a strong advocate of them.[79] But to what extent the Petitioning Movement would succeed in removing Grafton would only be seen with the meeting of Parliament, fixed for 9 January 1770. At the turn of the year, then, attention swung back from the counties to Westminster.

At first sight, it appeared that the winds of public opinion aroused by the Petitioning Movement would brush the ministry aside. If it was no weaker during the autumn of 1769 than it had been during the spring, then it was no stronger. Grafton had no suggestions for repelling the assault of the Opposition and he was unable to make any arrangements for strengthening the ministry.[80] He had little or no contact with the Bedfords. His position became impossible when his friends in the ministry, Camden and Granby, a few days before the opening of the session decided to obey Chatham's call to resign.[81] As the ministry began to collapse from within, the public abuse to which it was subjected rose to heights unprecedented in British politics. It was not merely the humiliating paragraphs of *Junius* which tortured Grafton but almost all sections of the British press united in castigating him. It was no longer the case merely that he had no policy, no tactics and no friends. He had no reputation. In attempting to retrieve it, Grafton transformed farce into tragedy.

He approached Charles Yorke and begged him to replace Camden on the Woolsack. Yorke was at once in an intolerable dilemma. If he were to accept Grafton's offer he would, of course, satisfy his own and his family's long-standing ambition, but he would be acting as the saviour of a ministry which his colleagues in the Rockingham party seemed to be on the point of destroying. This was not the only dilemma in which he stood. Whether he decided to accept or not, he would divide his family. His elder brother, Lord Hardwicke, urged him to accept while John Yorke, his loyal younger brother, urged him to refuse. No wonder Charles Yorke responded to Grafton's offer of the Great Seal on 12 January by asking for time to think. Rockingham saw him on the night of the thirteenth and advised him to reject the Court's approaches. Convinced that his friends would disapprove of his acceptance and, no doubt, familiar with the risk he would be running in boarding a sinking ship, Yorke saw Grafton on the following day and rejected his offer. But even now, he was unable to rest his mind. He thought over his decision, took advice from a variety of quarters and gradually wore away first his determination to refuse, and then his determination to reach any decision at all. He decided to accept, then to decline and once more to accept.

But on 16 January he told George III that he must decline. The King saw that Yorke's refusal would presage the disintegration of his ministry, and began to use all his arts of persuasion upon the unfortunate man. By the end of the day Charles Yorke once more was to be Lord Chancellor of England. If left to himself, he might just have been able to reconcile his fears with his ambition. But in the hysterical atmosphere of these weeks, and with so much depending on his ultimate decision, Yorke could not be left alone. Rockingham, Hardwicke and now John Yorke interviewed the Lord Chancellor and drained him of his resolve to accept. If he were just to be patient, they told him, he could have the same post in the next administration. Charles Yorke morbidly dwelt upon the possibility that he was being used by the Court for its own sinister purposes. Within a couple of days he was struggling to summon up sufficient courage to resign. Charles Yorke died on 20 January 1770, a victim of his own torments of conscience and of the political hysteria which whipped viciously around the lunatic administration of Grafton. It has never been established whether or not Yorke died by his own hand. On the one hand, he had both the motive and the opportunity. Suicide, indeed, would have been a likely solution for a man like Yorke to have chosen in the impossible position in which he found himself in January 1770. On the other hand, attractive though the suicide theory is, there is no evidence to support it. Yorke's health had long been poor; in the weeks prior to his death it had been rapidly worsening. The balance of probabilities tilts towards the conclusion that Yorke died a natural death, precipitated by the mental anguish to which he was subjected in January 1770.[82]

It was against this personal and political drama that the parliamentary conflicts of January 1770—so important in their long-term political implications—were to be played out. Everything seemed to favour the Opposition. Rockingham was well aware of the fissures within the ministry and wished to make as much political capital as he could from the paralysis which numbed its activities. To this end it would be necessary to concert forces with other opposition groups to bring Grafton down as a prelude to a new ministry led and dominated by the

Rockinghams. The need for unity was paramount. Dowdeswell had always been in favour of securing the largest possible degree of co-operation on the petitions.[83] Rockingham really believed he had the whip-hand. 'In every respect it strikes me, that *we* should keep to ourselves—for indeed should Ld Chatham be sent for & really should wish to form a solid Administration it is to *us* who he or any man with such intentions must come.'[84] Yet Rockingham concealed these determinations from Chatham and Grenville, and thus the precious union of the Opposition was preserved at least until the opening of the session. Rockingham, however, had not the slightest intention of allowing the union of the Opposition to become an equal union in Government.[85]

The Opposition came to town with rising spirits and great expectations. In spite of its preparations, however,[86] the opening of the session was something of an anti-climax. The King's speech was so devoid of content that it became known as the 'Horned Cattle' speech because an outbreak of cattle distemper seemed more important to the ministry than either the Petitioning Movement or America. On 9 January Burke and Dowdeswell furiously attacked ministers for their venality and corruption, for their wasteful and extravagant expenditure of public money and for their reluctance to heed public opinion. This was all very well, but all the petitions in the world were unlikely to weaken a ministerial majority. The fact that Dowdeswell's amendment to the Address was lost by 254–138 left Rockingham and Chatham with the uncomfortable feeling that the great opportunity might be lost and that the petitions might not be enough to persuade the King to dissolve Parliament.[87]

It was the death of Charles Yorke which destroyed the ministry of Grafton. The Petitioning Movement and the parliamentary harangues of Dowdeswell, Burke and Chatham were much less important.[88] On the day that Charles Yorke died, Grafton began to bleat of resignation. Three days later, on 23 January, Lord North was invited to replace Grafton at the Treasury. George III was absolutely desperate. 'You must easily see that if You do not accept I have no other Peer at present in my Service I could consent to place in the Duke of

Grafton's employment, whatever You may think do not take any decision unless it is one of instantly accepting without a further conversation with Me.'[89] The King wished to be enslaved neither by the Bedfords nor by the Opposition. North was to be the instrument of maintaining his freedom of manoeuvre. In retrospect, North's success in clinging to the Treasury for twelve years appears to be almost inevitable, but in January 1770 his chances were not rated highly. He had been MP for Banbury since 1754 and a Lord of the Treasury between 1759–65. Thereafter he had risen to the Exchequer in 1767. He had many weaknesses—ugliness of appearance, lack of reputation, of stature and of a political following—but he was a solid and experienced administrator, loyal to the King, wished to impose nothing upon him and was ready to defend his cause in Parliament. In the Lower House, North was an effective debater although he was never a great orator. Hitherto a second rank politician, North was now hurried into the highest office in the land at one of the great crises of the monarchy of George III. The King identified his fortunes so closely with those of Lord North that if North were to be defeated then the monarchy would suffer a shattering reverse.

North replaced Grafton on 28 January although the change was not announced publicly until two days later. What probably persuaded North to take the Treasury was the outcome of the debate on 25 January. On the Opposition's pet topic of the Middlesex election the ministry beat off the Opposition's attack by 224–180. It was just enough. Indeed, it was unusual in the eighteenth century for the fate of a ministry to be decided in the House of Commons and in this instance a vote against Grafton was tantamount to dictating to the King who his ministers should and should not be. The majority of forty-four was dangerously low but it was twice as large as had been anticipated. The bulk of the placemen had remained loyal to Grafton and the King and might be relied upon to be loyal to North.[90] On 28 January North finally agreed to replace Grafton and at once began to whip in supporters of the ministry.[91] The culmination of the political drama came on 31 January. On that day, William Dowdeswell's motion that only statute can incapacitate a member from taking his seat was lost by 226–186.

North had held his majority together, narrowly, it is true, but safely. He had, in short, established a *prima facie* right to govern.[92] The day after the debate, Rockingham wrote sadly to Chatham that the majority might as well have been 226 because 'it is neither men nor measures, but something else, which operates in these times'.[93] As if to underline the fact, when the issue was tried in the Lords on 2 February, North triumphed by 96–47.[94] The final test came on 19 February when the ministerial majority in the Upper House rose to 69.[95] The Opposition even with the support of the Petitioning Movement had been unable to dislodge the minister of the King's choice.

As the crisis of 1783–4 was also to demonstrate, the general acceptance of the King's right to choose his ministers was one of the most powerful facts of eighteenth century political life. The events of 1769–70 illustrate that even a union of the Opposition which included Chatham, Granville and Rockingham was unable to bring down Grafton.[96] In early 1770 Parliament supported the ministers and although it would be rash to say that North was secure, he had, at least, bought precious time. The Opposition knew that they had lost. They made things as difficult as they could for North but the ministry had won a decisive moral victory. Within a few months it became plain that the ministry enjoyed the confidence of the King, of Parliament and of the public. By its attack on North and the King in the early weeks of 1770 the Rockingham Whigs condemned themselves to years of opposition and the outcome of the conflict between the King and the Rockingham party was deferred for over a decade, and the American Revolution perhaps became inevitable. Certainly, had the Rockingham Whigs come to office in early 1770 then Edmund Burke's *Thoughts on the Causes of the Present Discontents* might never have been published and the theory of party might never have come to prominence.

I

Chapter 11

Edmund Burke and the Rockingham Whigs

The political career of Edmund Burke embraced many of the controversial national and international problems during the the later eighteenth century so that it is extremely difficult for historians to reach anything like an agreed assessment of the man and his career. Indeed, many aspects of Burke's life have been neglected by his biographers. Further research is needed to illuminate key areas of his work. This is especially true of his philosophy, including his philosophy of party. For too long, philosophical and political commentators have endowed Burke's thought with grandiose explanations and sweeping theories which, far from making it intelligible, only serve to inject into discussions of his ideas meanings which Burke never intended to use and concepts which were unknown to him. In these circumstances, we ought to adopt a more modest approach, contenting ourselves with relating Burke's party thought to the circumstances of his political career.[1]

By the end of 1766 Burke had come thoroughly to identify himself and his fortunes with the Rockingham Whig party.[2] Indeed, it must have been at about this time that he wrote *A Short Account of a Late, Short Administration* (1766) which recounted with curious brevity the achievements of the first Rockingham ministry.[3] Burke was perhaps glad to act as its propagandist. We should remember that when he entered

Parliament Edmund was thirty-seven years of age. He needed the Rockingham party not only for the security which it offered to him but for the opportunity of playing a leading role on the political stage. He needed the Rockinghams more than they needed him. It is true that his industry and his resolution were vital qualities in which Rockingham was personally deficient. It is also true that he rather than William Dowdeswell, was the effective party propagandist. (Dowdeswell's writings and speeches are dry, legalistic and narrow by comparison with Burke's.) Yet his talents and his industry went unrewarded by the highest political posts in the land. He was never considered for—indeed, he never petitioned for—a cabinet office. He was the servant of the great Whig lords not their master. The highest positions in the land were not for the likes of an Irish adventurer around whose family there hung distinctive traces of financial opportunism.[4] His oratorical abilities never won him the leadership of his party in the Commons. That position was held by Dowdeswell from 1766–74, then by Lord John Cavendish, 1774–6 and thereafter by Charles James Fox. In the same way, the task of electoral management was for the great lords of the country and Edmund never attempted to establish an electoral interest independent of Rockingham. Burke never resented his exclusion from the innermost counsels of his party. He was content to serve as Rockingham's dogsbody because he knew his place and he idealised and loved his leader and patron. Rockingham treated Burke with respect and kindness but their relationship was one of master and servant, not one of equals.

In some ways, Burke brought little that was new to the Rockingham party. He was more than ready to repeat the Rockinghamite catch-phrases, for example, about the Chatham administration. 'Lord Bute, to be sure, is uncertain and unquiet in his Nature; but who *will* do more, who can do more to satisfie him, than the present Minister.'[5] The party's hostility to Bute was a product of events in which Burke had not been a participant. They could not possibly have left upon him the kind of impression which they made upon Rockingham. Nevertheless, he was prepared to adopt the Rockinghamite belief in secret influence. In this he was by no means alone.

There were many who found the collapse of the old political cer-
tainties in the 1760s unintelligible without reference to some
such theory. The apparent failure of the Whig constitution to
function efficiently was inexplicable unless blame was laid
upon hidden and sinister forces. The type of political language
used by Burke in his party writings was therefore not
unusual.

In the same way, it is hard to say that Burke exerted any
considerable influence upon the policy of the Rockingham
Whig party between 1765 and 1770. In the early days of the
Chatham administration he was in favour of opposing the
ministry, but he fell in with Rockingham's decision that his
followers should remain in their places. He ostentatiously
excluded himself from Dowdeswell's factious scheme for
reducing the Land Tax in 1767, and although he took an
active part in the debates on the East India Company's
problems during the same parliamentary session, he cannot by
any stretch of the imagination be said to have 'imposed' a
policy upon his party. Furthermore, in the negotiations of
July 1767 it was not Burke but Rockingham himself who
decided policy. Burke took little part in the discussions, preferring to watch from the side-lines and to congratulate his
master upon his every move.[6] He was a little more adventurous
in the autumn when he tried to dissuade Rockingham from
attempting to come to a better understanding with the Bedfords, but Rockingham chose to ignore his advice and proceeded to act completely contrary to Burke's wishes. In 1768
Burke played an insignificant part in the General Election.
The great lords of the party may have found Burke's assistance
and advice useful, but there are precious few instances of their
seeking his help. Burke is sometimes claimed to have played a
significant part in the Petitioning Movement of 1769 and to
some extent this claim is true. Although it was not he but
Dowdeswell who organised the dinner at the Thatched House
Tavern which sparked off the movement Burke, together with
Dowdeswell, Abdy and others, was responsible for overcoming
Rockingham's reservations concerning the raising of a petition
in Yorkshire.[7] He was of rather more importance in the drafting
of the Yorkshire petition. He took the drafts of Wedderburn

and Lee and fashioned them into the final version which was voted at the county meeting.[8] Burke was also partly responsible for the wording of the Buckinghamshire petition.[9] There are hints of his influence elsewhere—especially in the Burkeian style of some of the petitions (of Liverpool, Derbyshire and Surrey, for example)—but nothing more definite. He played some part in the Petitioning Movement, then, but no more than several other individuals. As we have already observed, much depended upon local circumstances and the Petitioning Movement was not 'master-minded' by Burke or by anyone else. In general, it can hardly be maintained that from 1765–70 Edmund Burke was the dominant influence in the Rockingham party. He was not responsible for *any* important decision taken in these years either with respect to other groups (Dowdeswell, and not he wrote the *Memorandum* of 1767) or with respect to political issues. Burke was a rising man but he had not yet risen very far. He was the first to admit that he was 'slow, backward and irresolute'.[10] On one occasion in 1771 he specifically denied the truth of a friend's assertation that he occupied a dominant role in his party: 'I am no Leader my Lord, nor do I ever answer for the Conduct of anyone but myself. If your meaning be that I commonly make the Motions; or am forward in laying the grounds for opposition, your Lordship is certainly misinformed.'[11] The notion that Burke was the sole confidante of and the dominant influence upon Rockingham, therefore, must be abandoned. It was not Rockingham's way to rely upon one man. He preferred to sound all his friends and to take a course of action which he believed to combine the best of all the proposals set before him. Furthermore, to an extent which is often overlooked, Rockingham tended to look for advice from different men and sets of men. In 1766, Newcastle and Albemarle were in the ascendant, in 1767 Dowdeswell, in 1768 and over *Nullum Tempus* Portland and Savile and in 1769 Dowdeswell and Burke. In short, everything depended upon the issue, the circumstances and the geographical position of the party leaders. Burke was very much one among several of Rockingham's advisors, the Marquis very much the leader of his party.[12]

Yet Burke's unique contribution to his party is the philosophy of party which he bestowed upon it. What was the political genesis of Edmund Burke's idea of party, from whence did it arise and what influences shaped its character?

It would be a mistake to imagine that Burke, having made his decision to attach himself to the Rockingham party, was, in 1766, or for some time afterwards, a 'party man' in anything but the most general manner. He did not come to the Rockinghams with a ready-made theory of party to impose upon them. Between 1765 and 1769 he *learned* from the political experiences of the Rockingham party that not only its problems but also those of the nation could only be resolved through the agency of party. The principles of the Rockingham party, as we have seen, were defined by circumstance and through necessity. Party principles were enunciated by Rockingham and not by Burke.[13] They derived from political conflicts which antedated Burke's connection with Rockingham. It was from the starting points of hostility both to Bute's influence and to Grenville's policy that Burke had to begin to construct his theory of party. It was from the experiences and conflicts of the Rockingham Whigs that his theory of party derived. Burke, in his role of party propagandist, created a political theory out of a set of existing attitudes and assumptions and thus gave them enduring worth and value.[14]

Nevertheless, Burke expresses this theory of party in such general terms that it is at first not at all obvious that he had in mind the situation of the Rockingham Whigs. In his *Short Account of a Late Short Administration* (1766) Burke had made no pretensions to philosophical enquiry. The same cannot be said for the second of Burke's party writings, his *Observations on a Late Publication intituled The Present State of the Nation* (1769), Burke's reply to a Grenvillite publication by William Knox. Nevertheless, many of the general themes of the *Observations*— that politics and morality are inseparable, that party government is an inevitable consequence of a mixed constitution and a free state, that honour and 'principle' must be restored to politics through party—many of these are commonplace ideas in the party writings of the eighteenth century.[15] What is significant is the juxtaposition of these themes and their reference to the Rockingham Whigs and their experiences in the 1760s. As many commentators have noted, the idea of party is to a greater or a lesser degree a response to and a rationalisation of the political difficulties and attitudes of the Rockingham Whigs. In the *Observations*, Burke professed his rejection of Grenville's politics. In the *Thoughts on the Causes of the Present Discontents*, published in April 1770, Burke gave utterance to the deep-rooted distrust of Chatham and his principles felt by the Rockingham Whigs. Burke loftily proclaimed the value of *party* against *popularity*, of the permanent, settled and landed interest against the transient abilities of one man. The idea of party was thus an attack upon Chatham's anti-party crusade, a rebuttal of any claims he may have had to the leadership of a united Opposition in 1769 and 1770, and a confident reassertion of aristocratic Whiggery against the 'Patriot', non-party loyalism of the Great Commoner.

But the *Thoughts* were far more than a defence of the aristocratic cliqueishness of the Rockingham Whigs. Harvey Mansfield Junior has shown that the *Thoughts* were a theoretical counter-attack upon those pamphleteers who volunteered either royalist or Chathamite solutions to the problems of the day.[16] In undertaking such a counter-attack, Burke consciously affirmed his party's committment to traditional Whiggism, vindicating the purity of its Whig doctrines over and against those of Chatham. In the *Thoughts* Burke argued the traditional case that the executive ought to be separated from the legislative power and that the legislature ought to be properly representative of the wishes and protective of the rights of electors. One of Burke's objectives in the *Thoughts* was therefore to restate the fundamentals of the Whig creed, of which the Rockingham Whigs were the only legitimate heirs and which their recent actions had done much to protect. Burke's Whiggism was not, however, a stereotyped reiteration of old platitudes. The Rockingham Whigs had already succeeded in uniting to the traditional proprietorial concerns of the great landed aristocracy[17] an intimation of newer, radical currents of opinion. Burke, in short, was the spokesman of this new synthesis of Whig attitudes and his great achievement was to fashion a Whig theory of the constitution which both embraced and transcended the immediate political objectives of the Rockingham Whigs.

At the same time, the *Thoughts* were directed against Lord Bute and his secret influence. They were, therefore, a natural weapon in the Rockinghamite struggle against the court system. The *Thoughts* expressed the deep-seated conviction of the Rockingham Whigs that the constitution was still in danger.[18] But now, it was no longer the man but the system which the Rockinghams attacked. The answer to the power of Lord Bute would have been to remove *him*. The only solution to the system of secret influence, double Cabinets and King's Friends was to establish party government. Lord Bute, therefore, makes few appearances in the pages of the *Thoughts*.[19]

It cannot be argued, therefore, with any conviction that in the *Thoughts* Burke was self-consciously formulating the principles of a two-party system to which the British constitution was obediently to conform in the nineteenth century. It cannot even be maintained that Burke's defence of party was a particularly novel undertaking. Certainly, his contemporaries found nothing surprising in it.[20] Notwithstanding what later commentators have attributed to Burke, there can be no doubt that during the nine months when Burke was composing the *Thoughts*[21] he and his friends had it continuously in their minds to justify the activities of their party and of the Opposition in general. Furthermore, they wished to set out Rockingham's claim to predominance in a future ministry by asserting the superiority of their principles over and against those of Chatham.[22] It cannot be maintained that the *Thoughts* was a rarified philosophical treatise written in isolation from political reality. The drafts of the pamphlet were circulated among the party leaders for their approval until, after some redrafting, a form satisfactory to everyone was found.[23] Rockingham, at least, believed that one of the functions of the *Thoughts* would be to define the principles of his own party and thus to encourage its coherence.[24]

The *Thoughts* contains political, historical and moral justifications for party government. Burke commences by stating that the country stands in a perilous situation. The 'Discontents' he defines in a wide-ranging manner to include the instability of ministries, the weaknesses of government, the maladministration of the law and even the disturbances in America. Significantly, Burke alludes to the fact that 'Disconnexion and confusion, in offices, in parties, in families, in Parliament, in the nation, prevail beyond the disorders of any former time'. In other words, the Discontents are not exclusively political in nature and origin. In particular, they are not the product of parties because 'the great parties which formerly divided and agitated the kingdom are known to be in a manner entirely dissolved'. The *raison d'être* of the old parties has disappeared. But the need for party has not disappeared with them. Burke adduces arguments from history in support of party. Between 1689 and 1760 the Crown was too weak to govern the country without devolving its power upon 'connections', whose landed wealth and social position underpinned the workings of the constitution. 'The influence of Government, thus divided in appearance between the Court and the leaders of parties, became in many cases an accession rather to the popular than to the royal scale'. Party was thus a proven instrument of Government which had helped to secure the fruits of the Revolution Settlement and the Hanoverian Succession.

Burke next adduces arguments from political necessity in favour of party. In the reign of George III a new scheme of government was introduced. Not only were the great parties entirely dissolved. 'The power of the Crown, almost dead and rotten as Prerogative, has grown up anew, with much more strength, and far less odium, under the name of Influence.'[25] Burke adverts to the failure of the Bute ministry when the court had to abandon its plan of overtly gaining control of the Government. Its new plan was to form a party 'in favour of the Court against the Ministry' on the basis of the rewards distributed and emoluments granted by the Crown. The crucial condition for the success of the plan of the 'double Cabinet' was that Parliament had to be brought to heel. To this end connections were to be destroyed and future ministries were to be composed of men who had none of the usual qualities for such high office, 'rank, influence, abilities, connexions and character'. This amounted to a declaration of war upon the Whig aristocracy. The court faction had reason enough to fear William Pitt for his talents and popularity, but the Whigs 'possessed a far more natural and fixed influence. Long possession of Government; vast property; obligations of favours given and received; connexion of office; ties of blood, of alliance, of friendship . . .; the name of Whig dear to the majority of the people; the zeal early begun and steadily continued to the Royal Family'. Consequently the Whigs were placed under a general proscription. Burke dismisses as nonsense the claims of court propaganda that it was imperative for the monarchy to liberate itself from aristocratic tyranny. On the contrary, it was the designs of the Court which threatened to disrupt the constitution, to weaken the powers of Parliament and to undermine the rights of electors. The Court was seeking to arrogate political power to itself by splintering the connections, by detaching their leaders and by thus leaving their followers at the mercy of the Court. Burke condemns the system of administrations 'composed of insulated individuals, without faith plighted, tie or common principle', in which ministries rested upon court favour rather than upon public support. He could not, however, claim that the court system was unconstitutional, for it offended against no statutory law of the constitution. He therefore had to take refuge in asserting that 'the discretionary powers which are necessarily vested in the Monarch . . . should all be exercised upon public principles and national grounds, and not on the likings or prejudices, the intrigues or policies, of a Court'. Similarly, he attacked the Court system because Parliament no longer fulfilled its traditional responsibility of refusing to support governments which had lost the confidence of the people. But this was not an 'argument from precedent' but an idealised recollection, and an incorrect one, of the role of Parliament in the political system of early and mid eighteenth century Britain.

He proceeded to consider possible solutions to the problems confronting the nation, and by process of elimination reached the conclusion that only through party could salvation be found. He first rejected the nostrums of parliamentary reform. More frequent elections or a wider franchise would simply provide the Court with more frequent opportunities for practising corruption than it enjoyed already. He next considered some of the traditional slogans of the 'country party'. He rejected Place Bills as he believed governments ought to have some influence with the legislature. To remove that influence would tend to a damaging separation of executive and legislature. Burke believed that it was not the structure of the constitution that needed to be changed. Indeed, it needed to be restored and consolidated. What needed changing were the beliefs and attitudes which informed political practices. Party would effect not only a reinvigoration of action but of attitude. For men could not act an honourable public part when they 'are not acquainted with each other's principles, nor experienced in each other's talents, nor at all practised in their mutual habitudes and dispositions by joint efforts in business'. Party had, therefore, not only an historical vindication but an immediate relevance to the politics of the day.

There is, however, a further dimension to Burke's party theory. It cannot be understood without some appreciation of his moral, 'When bad men combine, the good must associate'. It was not just that it was a moral obligation upon politicians to uphold the Revolution Settlement, which represented 'the ancient and tried usages' of the country and the 'Ancient Constitution' which human action must preserve, not violate. On the level of the individual man, combination in party was just because it was natural. They were 'essentially necessary for the full performance of our public duty'. Burke thought it extraordinary that some men would not act in party. Because most public business depended upon 'some great leading general principles in Government' men of the same party would be able to agree on the course of action they should pursue nine times out of ten. Party thus existed for Burke as a principled union of men: 'united, for promoting by their joint endeavours the national interest, upon some particular principle in which they are all agreed'. Although this moral aspect of party was not new with Burke it was, nevertheless, an immensely important element in his political thought, reinforcing the historical and political arguments for party which we have already considered.

That Burke's description of the 'Present Discontents' was a superficial and rhetorical polemic, that his assessment of the Court's intentions was little more than the prejudices of the Rockinghams erected into a suitably embellished philosophical system, that his explanation of the political system of the eighteenth century was absurdly inaccurate—all these, and other criticisms of Burke need to be made. It does no good at all to claim for him not only more than is warranted by the evidence but to credit him with ideas which he specifically rejected. For example, he did not think in terms of a two party system, assuming that if the Rockingham Whigs came to power it would be in alliance with other groups. At the same time, it is equally misleading to reject Burke's party ideas as worthless simply because later generations have seen the shortcomings of the arguments which he used to support them.

Edmund Burke sincerely intended to justify the principle of party at a time when it appeared to be under attack and, in so doing, to define the nature of party and party attachments. It does not follow that Burke attempted to inject 'principles' into the Rockingham Whigs and, with the wave of a wand, transform them from a faction into a party. As we have noticed, the principles of the Rockingham party owed little to Burke. Although the *Thoughts* were a plea for a party acting upon principle, Burke does not define the nature of the principle. How can this apparent dilemma be resolved? Two possible approaches may help us to unravel the nature of Burke's principles. First, we should remember that Burke did not accuse the Court of behaving unconstitutionally and he was led to embrace the view that the court system contravened not the law but 'the spirit of the whole constitution'. It was Burke's objective to restore the practices and principles of the constitution to those which had existed before 1760. At one level, then, Burke's principles were *what he thought* the constitutional principles of the age of Walpole and the Pelhams to have been. To restore the constitution upon these principles was the objective of the Rockingham party. Nevertheless, we should not rest satisfied with this partial explanation. We cannot evade the fact that when Burke defines party he alludes to the desirability of party men being united on 'some particular principle' but he does not say what that principle is. It is essential to realise, however, that Burke wished to assert the value of principles in public life for their own sake. In an age of corruption and inconsistency honest politicians were needed to restore trust, virtue and consistency. Party was thus a vehicle for harnessing men of principle in a crusade to oust evil men from secret positions of influence. Party should seek 'To bring the dispositions that are lovely in private life into the service and conduct of the commonwealth'. Burke's 'Principles' then, derive partly from his moralisitic pre-occupation with corruption and partly from his wish to identify the Rockingham Whigs as the heirs of the Whig tradition.

Edmund Burke wished to restore a polity which he imagined had existed in the past. He did not wish to invent a new one. He did not describe that polity in any detail for he assumed that it was so familiar to his contemporaries that he did not need to do so. Nor did he waste words discussing *how* that polity could be re-established. The coming to power of the Rockingham Whigs would magically achieve that objective. We should notice that Burke wished to cure '*Present* Discontents' not future ones. He believed not that party should be a permanent part of the British political system but rather an occasional refuge to which recourse might be had in exceptional times of difficulty.[26] Because he did not conceive of a *permanent* party he did not advocate the *institutionalisation* of party. He wished to compose differences in the state, not to polarise them. He wished to restore the ancient constitution of the country, not to change it by making its organisation more democratic. He wished to right a constitutional wrong, not elaborate a manifesto of measures which a future Government might transact. Once this had been achieved, party would disappear. There would be no further need of it. Once the Rockinghams attained power, the 'Present Discontents' would be cured and the ancient constitution re-established. How the party would sustain itself in office for a sufficient period, what measures it ought to pursue, how it would deal with a monarch who was almost certain to be hostile—to all these questions Burke had no answer. Government by party was the end of Burke's argument, not the beginning.[27]

Many of the limitations of Burke's theory of party are thus characteristic of the mental climate of his age. Burke's theory is rooted in the practice and thought of the eighteenth century. He dared not, for example, contest the prerogative of appointing ministers. He probably did not even realise that the logic of his own argument was leading him to divest the Crown of the free exercise of the prerogative of appointing ministers. His modest conception of the role of legislation in politics prevented him from grasping the notion that a party in power might carry through a programme of measures. So powerful was the ideal of Independency that he never seems to have believed that a party might ever achieve a majority in the House of Commons. In short, it is to do Burke a serious mis-service and to misunderstand his ideas to uproot him from the assumptions and attitudes of the century of which he was so clearly a part.

The immediate effect of the enunciation of Burke's party ideas was to widen the gulf which separated his party from Chatham and to open a gulf between the Rockinghams and the metropolitan radicals. Indeed, hostility to Chatham and his principles had coloured the writing of the *Thoughts*. Chatham believed that the publication of Burke's pamphlet did great harm to the united Opposition.[28] What Burke had done was to claim that the principles of the Rockinghams were the only true Whiggery. No wonder that Chatham was affronted for he had always despised the aristocratic cliquenishness of the Rockinghams which Burke had now erected into a philosophical theory. Nevertheless, the *Thoughts* were a symptom of the difficulties of co-operating with Chatham which had existed since the beginning of the decade. The *Thoughts* did not create them. In the same way, the pamphlet epitomised rather than caused the difficulties which the Rockinghams had already found in their dealings with the radicals. The Wilkites and their supporters had recently rediscovered the radical ideas of the seventeenth century. No sooner had they recovered from the ecstacy of their discovery than Burke was challenging their beliefs. The radicals thereupon castigated Burke as a tool of the aristocracy. Their response was enshrined in the work of Catherine Macaulay in her *Observations on a Pamphlet entitled, Thoughts on the Cause of the Present Discontents* (1770).[29] Burke, therefore, registered rather than moulded the narrow and distinctive ideological ground upon which the Rockingham Whig party stood.

It would be misleading, however, to conclude that Burke's theory of party, in spite of its weaknesses, had no more constructive effects. He provided his party with an impulse to ideological unity which was to become one of the most prominent characteristics of the Rockingham Whigs. He fused the ideas of Pelhamite and country Whiggery into a political theory. He, almost as much as the Marquis of Rockingham, gave the Rockingham party an identity which it retained for many years. He did much to revive confidence in party and Opposition after a generation which had known relatively little of them. And even if his party theories had their weaknesses (and who could deny it?) then those ideas were flexible enough to be adapted by others in the future so that party could become a developing, integral part of the British political system. Burke related party and Opposition to traditional Whiggery and enabled the Rockingham Whigs to become the vehicles of the rise of party.[30]

Chapter 12

Rockinghamites, Chathamites and the Failure of Opposition 1770–2

The ministry of Lord North seemed unlikely to survive for long. But by the middle of February it had achieved a certain stature and security which left observers in no doubt as to his ability to govern.[1] By the end of the month Chatham had slunk away from town, conveniently 'betaken himself to the gout', as Horace Walpole nastily remarked, while Rockingham a few weeks later was hoping that the extent of North's success might drive some of the Independent members into Opposition.[2] North crowned his success in April with a budget which won him widespread applause. Richmond wrote to Rockingham on 18 April hoping 'that you would all think it best to give over Opposition for this year, as many people will be like myself very unwilling to go to town, nay more so, for I am persuaded that many very good friends would not attend'.[3] North had inflicted a crushing defeat upon the united Opposition. This achievement is, in retrospect, easy to explain. He was the first leader of a ministry since Grenville to sit in the Commons but, unlike his predecessor, he enjoyed the confidence of the King. North brought with him to the Treasury no hungry mouths to feed and no political principles to impose upon George III.[4] Indeed, his transparent weaknesses, his isolation, his lack of reputation and his lack of a following, did him no harm at all. On the contrary, he was not likely to be attacked as a domineering minister, monopolising power for his own ends. The political world was thus prepared to take North at his own estimation, as a simple and sincere servant of the King. North wished to consult the national interest, flatter the Independents and keep the political temperature low. He was aided by what can only be described as a minor loyalist reaction in 1770. People were yearning for political stability; they were weary with Wilkes and tired of petitions. North offered them unspectacular and uncontentious government, moderate yet firm leadership. For these reasons he was able to survive in 1770.

North also seemed to be something of a magician. With one wave of his wand he apparently succeeded in settling the troubles of America. On 5 March he brought forward a motion to repeal all the Townshend duties except that on tea.[5] Governor Pownall moved an amendment to abolish the Tea duty as well. North responded by affirming that tea, because it was not, like the other goods, manufactured in Britain, fell into a different category. Pownall, supported by the votes, though not the speeches, of the Rockinghams, lost his amendment by 204–142.[6] North appeared at once firm and yet moderate, conciliating the colonists yet not surrendering the fundamental powers of Imperial taxation to them. His policy enjoyed the advantage of dividing the Opposition. The Grenvilles were in utter disarray. They did not vote because Grenville found that he could support neither North nor Pownall. The Chathamites were for total repeal of all the duties, the Rockinghamites still for the 1766 formula. Well might North taunt the Opposition for its glaring differences of opinion on America. Well might he ridicule the Rockinghams for the dogged persistence with which they seemed determined to *claim* rights in America without ever *enforcing* them. North's American policy may not have been perfect but at least it was a policy. The Opposition were not able to agree upon a policy at all.

The Rockingham Whigs had by this time come to judge American affairs almost exclusively in terms of the domestic political situation, in particular in the context of secret influence. On 9 May, for example, Edmund Burke in moving for an enquiry into the American situation, complained that the disorders in America were the consequence of ministerial paralysis and the rising influence of the Crown.[7] Yet this belief in the existence of a constitutional malaise, however sincerely and passionately it may have been held, was no substitute for imperial statesmanship. Although a Rockinghamite like Sir William Meredith could consistently demand a repeal of all the Townshend duties on the grounds that the Declaratory Act adequately safeguarded Parliament's right to tax, such a view ran perilously close to expediency. It appeared to advocate taxation whenever it could be enforced, to remove it whenever it could not. It also ignored the fact that the Americans no longer respected the Declaratory Act. And, indeed, what was North doing in 1770 which the Rockinghams had not done in 1765–6? North was bowing to representations of American grievances by repealing the heaviest and most obnoxious burdens, much as Rockingham had done in repealing the Stamp Act. What was the duty upon tea if not a token acknowledgement that the Declaratory Act still existed? The Rockinghamite line on America arose less from any determination to uphold the cause of liberty in America than from domestic political considerations which rendered their American policy at once factious and unconvincing.

Yet the events of 1769–70 could have no other affect than to underline the belief of Rockinghamites that Burke was right, that there was on foot a sinister plot to undermine the constitution and to exclude them from office. This belief must have been powerfully confirmed by the fact that it was not confined to the Rockingham Whigs. In the session of 1769 the Opposition had been able to unite in its attack upon the Grafton ministry's attempts to persuade Parliament to pay off the debt of £300,000 which had accumulated on the Civil List since the beginning of the reign.[8] This attack was renewed in the session of 1770 for here, if anywhere, lay to hand an opportunity for the Opposition to probe the muddy waters of corruption which allegedly lay at the heart of the court system. On 28 February 1770, Grenville moved to have the Civil List expenses for 1769 laid before the House. Although his motion was rejected by 262–165 the division figures showed that on these fascinating matters touching corruption, the Opposition could divide more than respectably.[9] The attack was followed up in the Lords on 14 March by Chatham who, in an extravagant and powerful speech, unsuccessfully moved for a committee to enquire into the Civil List.[10] This was not quite the end of the matter for on 2 April William Dowdeswell provocatively moved an address to the King, which demanded that the monarch run up no further debts on the Civil List.[11] Although such motions and addresses were doomed to failure, they show that the Rockinghams were moving away from their earlier vapid generalisations about secret influence towards a direct attack upon wasteful and extravagant expenditure and in this there lay the seed of economic reform.[12]

In the session of 1770 the failure of the Opposition was compounded by its internal divisions and dissensions. The Marquis found Chatham a tiresome and unreliable ally. He found it difficult to work with one whose attendance in the Lords was as unpredictable as his gout. When the great man condescended to appear in town, he expected Rockingham to obey his instructions and adhere to his own time-table.[13] Nevertheless, both men realised the importance of their mutual co-operation. Chatham's main objective in the session of 1770 was to secure the passage of a bill to limit the powers of the Commons over elections, and in this he had Rockingham's support. The Marquis favoured a bill which simply declared illegal the recent pretensions of the House to allow expulsion to create incapacity.[14] Chatham largely shared this view and it was thus with a considerable measure of common ground that Chatham, supported by Rockingham, introduced on 1 May a bill to reverse the Commons resolution of 2 February which had justified the proceedings of the Lower House on the Wilkes case. In defence of the rights of electors, Chatham and Rockingham advanced the claims of the House of Lords to act as an arbiter in the constitution between the claims of the Commons and the Crown. They proclaimed the doctrine that the aristocracy held power in trust for the people.[15] Chatham demanded a dissolution of Parliament, because he believed it to be an 'Illusion, little short of Infatuation, to imagine that this House of Commons, the Violaters of the

People's Rights cou'd ever become the Safe Instrument of a System of Administration founded on the reparation of the violations, and on a total extinction of the Influence which caused them'.[16] Rockingham disliked reviving once again the demands of the previous year but in the interests of opposition harmony he did not allow his disagreement with Chatham to prejudice the prospects of their working harmoniously to-gether.[17] Until the end of the session, then, the union of the Opposition was maintained, although the failure of its strategy left both Chatham and Rockingham with no great respect for the other.

Indeed, as time passed, a new issue was coming to act as a wedge between the two sections of the Opposition. Chatham's adoption of parliamentary reform in January 1770 was a significant rejection of the Rockinghamite thesis, laid down by Burke, that the ills of the state had their origins in a corrupt court system. As Chatham told the Lords on 22 January, they stemmed from the inequalities of the representative system.[18] To remedy them, Chatham advocated an increase in the number of county Members. It was, however, because of the persuasions of Temple, rather than any consideration which he may have felt for the Rockinghams which led Chatham to reject more frequent Parliaments.[19] When to all this is added differences of temperament,[20] then it becomes clear that although the union of the Opposition survived the session of 1770 there were very few prospects indeed of its indefinite continuation.

In any case, the Opposition would have found it difficult to have withstood with equanimity the shocks, blows and disappointments which showered upon it in the recess of 1770. They had lost the battle for place. Fate now began to deprive them of some of their most talented, leading figures. Temple announced his retirement from politics. Camden, unsure of his political line, wavered uncertainly between action and inaction, frozen by indecision.[21] Lord Albemarle was ill and went abroad in the autumn.[22] Most important of all, George Grenville died in November. His colleagues in Opposition had not always appreciated his talents during his lifetime. They were sorely to miss him in the debates on the press and the judiciary in the coming session. From every other point of view, things looked grim for the Opposition. The publication of Burke's *Thoughts* had been little more than a damp squib and had done little to raise the spirits of the defeated Rockinghams in the session of 1770.[23] Furthermore, the Petitioning Movement had passed its zenith and it was Chatham's view that without support in the country the Opposition was doomed.[24] To judge by opinion in the country, it was. Remonstrances against the Court's bland responses to the petitions of 1769 were set on foot in Buckinghamshire and Kent but the impetus for such movements was now gone. The last hope for the Petitioning Movement was Yorkshire. But a county meeting of 25 September was attended by only 300 people and was torn by divisions.[25] Thus the Petitioning Movement was laid to rest. At the same time, Rockinghamite influence in the metropolis was declining almost to vanishing point.[26] By the autumn of 1770, then, the Opposition was much weakened owing to its loss of support out of doors, to the growing divisions between Rockingham and Chatham, to the retirement of several of its leading members and to the success of North. To these factors was now to be added the absence of Rockingham.

When the new session opened in November 1770, Rockingham was at Bath where his wife had been stricken with a severe attack of jaundice. At one point it was thought that she was close to death. Personal considerations required that the Marquis should remain with his wife until her recovery (in February 1771). How far the absence of its leader affected the Rockingham party is an interesting and significant theme of the first half of the session of 1770-1. The Duke of Richmond acted as Rockingham's deputy, a man whose independence of judgement, honesty and perceptiveness had endeared him to the Marquis, and whom he regarded as one of his ablest lieutenants.[27] His own opinion was that North was safe and that further exertions by the Opposition were a futile gesture, but he swallowed his opinions and came to town for the new session.[28] His relationship with the Marquis during the latter's absence illustrates Rockingham's unique place in his party. He ensured that he was kept informed of events not only by Richmond but also by Dowdeswell and Burke. Richmond assured the Marquis: 'All I wish of you to do with Regard to Politicks is to acquaint me with your wishes if you have any respecting the H. of Lords, and you may be certain that I shall be happy to be of any use to you & the Party, or if you cannot attend to Business and would have us make the best shift we can without troubling You, I shall be ready to meet our Friends and concert matters for the best'.[29] Occasionally Richmond would summon a party meeting to which Rocking-ham might send instructions. Usually Richmond in the Lords and Dowdeswell in the Commons attended to matters of detail in their respective Houses. Yet Rockingham always remained the master. In spite of Richmond's expostulations, for example, Rockingham refused to make any concessions to Chatham in the 1771 session. On the issues which arose in that session Rockingham's opinions could not be ignored. Richmond knew his place. He wished to avoid the imputation, as he told Rockingham, 'that in your absence I am setting up for myself & endeavouring to draw the lead into my own hands . . . I have no ambition to supersede you. The little I see of it, makes me think it no tempting situation . . . '.[30] Richmond did his best to supply the deficiency which Rockingham's absence created. He held frequent dinners and consulted with colleagues, as was Rockingham's way. He resisted the temptation to try to impose a policy on others. On the whole he rose to the occasion at least as well as any alternative deputy leader would have done.[31]

There was perhaps one area where Rockingham's presence might have made some difference. After the death of George Grenville in November 1770 his supporters drifted leaderless until they were offered places or the prospect of places in the ministry.[32] Had Rockingham made a direct attempt to secure the allegiance of these men, then he might have achieved some success. Rockingham, at least, believed as much.[33] The loss of the Grenvilles was a disaster for the Opposition. In particular, Wedderburn, tempted by the office of Solicitor General, had been a crucial link between Rockingham and other sections of the Opposition. Wearily, Richmond declared: 'All this reduces greatly our line of battle, but nevertheless I am for persevering in our Fight'.[34] But what tactics would

Richmond and others advocate? As Burke realised, the plight of the Rockinghams at the end of 1770 was desperate. The Grenvilles were drifting over to the Court, Shelburne and Chatham were dominant in the City. As he told Rockingham: 'The Court is irreconcileable to you, and professing itself so; and *the sober, large—acred part of the Nation, whom you have most studied to please, and whom it is the most reputable to please,* either entirely indifferent about us, or of no considerable weight in the publick Scale'. Burke, at least, had some ideas for remedying this situation: he advocated constant activity based on the principles which he had recently outlined in the *Thoughts.* 'We lost much of the advantage of the Last Pamphlet, because the Idea was not kept up by a continual succession of papers, seconding and enforcing the same principle. . . . The more you are confined in your operations, by the delicate principles you profess, the more necessary it becomes to push with the utmost Vigour the few means that you have permitted to yourselves.'[35] In one sense, of course, the Rockinghams *did* need to attack, to attend to business and to show themselves to be a keen and conscientious Opposition party. Yet—and this was the great weakness with Burke's plan—the Rockinghams were not entirely free agents. They needed to consider Chatham. The logical conclusion of Burke's argument was to ignore Chatham, indeed, to embrace conflict with him and his principles. Rockingham, however, would never allow it. Much though he disliked Chatham, he recognised the necessity of co-operating with him in Opposition if North were ever to be defeated. Rockingham's adherence to the old concept of the united Opposition was long to prevail over Burke's emerging ideas of party exclusiveness.[36]

Even when relations with Chatham were still tolerably cordial and, more important, contacts with him fairly regular, the Rockinghams benefitted little from them. On the most important and promising issue of the 1770–1 session, the Falkland Islands crisis, when the ministry was reeling from internal disagreements, resignation and the threat of war,[37] the Opposition was unable to present anything more than routine resistance. Although Rockingham and Chatham co-operated from the start in the Lords, the Duke of Richmond's motion for papers on 22 November 1770 attracted only twenty-one supporters.[38] In the Commons on the same day, Dowdeswell's similar motion was lost 225–101.[39] Indeed, it was less the problem of numbers than that of ministerial morale which worried the Government. North's careful handling of the situation within the Cabinet and the negotiation of a solution to the dispute with the Spanish Court, announced on 22 January, left the Opposition little room for manoeuvre.[40] Indeed, the preservation of peace, in the last analysis, dashed any lingering hopes that the Opposition may have entertained that North might be brought down. Peace and economy bolstered North's administration. War would have destroyed it. Therefore, although they enjoyed Chatham's co-operation,[41] the Rockingham Whigs were unable to attack the ministry very convincingly. In the debate on 25 January 1771 they were reduced to moving for papers (to which the ministry agreed) and to demonstrating 'the defenceless State this Country was in—in Septr: and to show how highly culpable the Administration have been in having neglected taking earlier Precautions'.[42] Fortunately for the Opposition in the Commons, there was no division. On 4 February, however, Dowdeswell returned to a charge which he had levelled against the Government on 25 January, that the negotiation had been dictated by France. There was no truth in the charge and no evidence to support it.[43] The united Opposition mounted its final assault upon the administration on 13 February when Dowdeswell divided the House on an Address of Thanks to the ministers for their handling of the dispute. In a full House the Opposition was defeated by 275–157, a more than respectable minority figure but one which left the Government incontestably secure.[44] This was a symbolic failure for the united Opposition. On a good issue lasting several weeks, which had a considerable measure of potential popular support, with an Opposition that was as well organised as it was united, it had been unable to come within 100 votes of Lord North.[45]

The rest of the session was dominated by issues concerning freedom of speech. These were not only intrinsically important. They went far to destroying what was left of the union of the Opposition. The first, the rights of juries in libel cases, had been simmering for some time before it broke the surface of politics in the session of 1771.[46]

The issue had arisen with the publication of Junius' infamous, insulting and libellous letter to the King of 19 December 1769. The anonymous author could not be prosecuted but the publishers Henry Woodfall and John Almon could. They were brought to trial and, as was perfectly normal in such cases, the judge, Lord Mansfield, instructed the jury to find solely on the *fact* of publication and not on the *matter* of libel. Such was the popularity of the two men with the metropolitan radicals, and so intimate their connections with the parliamentary Opposition that the matter could not end there, especially as, in Lord Camden's opinions, there lay conveniently to hand an alternative interpretation of the law of libel, and one which would allow the jury to determine if a publication was or was not libellous.

Burke even toyed with the idea of including this subject in the petitions of 1769.[47] In the session of 1771 the issue was raised by the Rockinghams who wished to legislate to provide juries with the right to pronounce upon the matter of libel as well as the fact of publication. Rockingham told Chatham in December 1770 of their intention to bring forward '*a Bill to remove doubts and controversies* over the rights of juries in libel cases'.[48] In theory, Chatham's view was not very different. He too, was completely dissatisfied with the prevailing law of libel and saw the need to legislate. Chatham wanted a parliamentary committee of enquiry to investigate the administration of the law of libel. Upon its conclusions he desired Camden to prepare a bill declaring *as existing law* the rights of juries in libel cases.[49] The Rockinghams were unwilling to follow Chatham's lead tamely. Their preparations were proceeding when Chatham tried to pre-empt their campaign. On 6 December 1770 his followers in the Commons moved for an enquiry into the conduct of libel cases. The Rockinghams were in something of a dilemma. They did not want an enquiry but it would have been politically damaging for them to have opposed it. They realised that they would have to tread with caution and that any reform of the law must proceed cautiously. And, of course, to have opposed the enquiry would have put an end to the union of the Opposition. Burke and his friends, therefore, supported the enquiry but with no great enthusiasm. Only seventy-six members divided in the minority.[50] Chatham continued his little campaign by prompting the obliging Camden to quiz the eminent if controversial Mansfied in the Lords on 10 December on the law of libel. Mansfield had the wit to evade his catechising.[51] Rockingham's reaction was interesting. He thoroughly disapproved of this clumsy attempt to embarrass Mansfield, but not because of that lord's legal eminence and expertise and not, as Horace Walpole claimed, because Mansfield's wife was Rockingham's aunt.[52] Rockingham knew that Mansfield could take care of himself. Although 'Lord Mansfield backed by the Kings Bench Judges—and many others of the Judges—and many authorities dead and living— may be opposed and controverted by Lord Camden and others'. Rockingham knew that Mansfield could stand his ground upon the unimpeachable fortress of precedent. Rockingham was less interested in arguing legal technicalities than in placing legislation on the statute book 'to check and Controul the Wantonness of Power, & hang *in Terrorem* over those who should even think of Using them'.[53] Strongly supported by Dowdeswell and Burke, Rockingham was prepared to go ahead no matter what Chatham or the public—thought of his plans.[54] 'I do not expect any great Good being carried *into Effect* in *either Houses of Parliament* in These Times, but what I think is very material is, that our Friends should shew that in their Endeavours, the *Publick Advantage* is their object.'[55] Inevitably, the Rockinghams interpreted the apparent attacks upon the rights of juries as a further manifestation of the system of the Court to undermine the liberties of Englishmen.

> 'It is much too probable that the power and influence of the Crown will increase rapidly. We live at the period when for the first time since the Revolution, the power and influence of the Crown is held out, as the main and chief and only support of Government. If we, I may say emphatically *we* do not exert now, we may accelerate the abject state to which the Constitution may be reduced.'[56]

In the present instance it was necessary to attempt to place legislation on the statute book. So long as precedent remained the arbiter of law, then the influence of the Court might prove sufficiently powerful to persuade those responsible for the law to administer it in the interests of the Court. Notwithstanding Chatham's fury, then, the Rockinghams were prepared to proceed with their own plan of legislation. Indeed, they had to endure his active opposition to their measure, although they continued up until the last minute to show every respect for him and to seek his approval.[57] On 7 March 1771 Dowdeswell moved for leave to bring in a bill setting out the rights of juries but leave was refused by 218–72, a result which delighted not only Lord North and the King—that was only natural— but even some of the friends of Chatham.[58] Such was the atmosphere in which the union of the Opposition declined and disintegrated.

The collapse of the Opposition was delayed rather than prevented by the Printers Case which occupied public attention in February and March 1771. On 5 February 1771, a ministerial supporter, Colonel George Onslow,[59] demanded that the Government enforce the law against the printing of debates, a practice which was still technically illegal but which had rapidly spread since 1768. For his pains he was ridiculed in the press and singled out for public mockery in *The Middlesex Journal* and *The Gazetteer*. The House determined not to ignore this challenge to its authority and, after a division of 90–55 on 8 February 1771, summoned the offending printers.[60] The summons was ignored; the printers disappeared into the radical fastness of the City and the Government offered a reward of £50 for their arrest. The Government had thus direct responsibility for what had initially been the campaign of a private member. Like Grenville in 1763–4 and Grafton in 1768–9, North was in some danger of taking things too far. It proved to be impossible to arrest the printers short of violating the independence of the City and all that the ministry could achieve was the imprisonment of the City magistrates who stoutly defended the printers.[61] Against an apparent revival of the rioting mobs of former years, the ministry wisely abandoned its futile claim to punish the printers and to maintain the secrecy of debates.[62]

On this issue, of course, the Opposition believed that it was necessary once again to fight the good fight for the liberties of the subject, and it was possible, on the issue of free speech, to recapture something of the spirit of the united Opposition of 1769. Not surprisingly, however, the Rockinghams were unwilling to become closely identified with the radicals, wishing to confine their criticisms of the Government to the single issue of the rights of free speech. Not just the leaders of the Whig aristocracy, but also Dowdeswell and Savile, refused to support the City magistrates in the division lobbies. Nevertheless, Rockingham and some friends did make the symbolic, public gesture of visiting them in the tower.[63] And they did keep up, night after night, in alliance with some of the Chathamites, an enthusiastic parliamentary campaign in defence of the rights of public debate. Characteristically, the Rockinghams did *not* question the *right* of the House of Commons to enjoy secrecy of debate. They were more concerned with the expediency of exercising that right either in the present instance or as a matter of course. Their view was that only if the freedom of the press turned to dangerous licence ought the House to enforce its right to secrecy of debate. Chatham's opinions were very similar to these and, as long as the issue lasted, he remained on speaking terms with the Rockinghams.[64] But Chatham did little to support the printers. He was sulking at the reluctance of the city reformers to follow his lead. He might agree with the line taken by the Rockinghams but he refused to lift a lofty finger in defence of the liberties of the subject.[65]

As the session drew to a close and as North's ministry was seen to be securely established, the curfew began to sound for the united Opposition. In late April Chatham approached Rockingham, reviving his idea of the previous session for a motion in the Lords for a dissolution of Parliament. The Marquis politely declined to co-operate and left Chatham to move his motion on 1 May when it was overwhelmingly negatived by 72–23.[66] By the end of the session the ministry had triumphed and the campaign of the Opposition was beaten off with ease. The Opposition, furthermore, had lost whatever unity it had ever possessed. The union of the Opposition was at an end.

At one level, the failure of the united Opposition to endure may be put down to personal conflicts and ascribed to jealously and mutual suspicion. On 29 December 1770, for example, Burke wrote to Rockingham to warn him that Chatham was busy 'endeavouring to discredit you with the people, and what is worse, to weaken you within yourselves'.[67] Rockingham had never liked Chatham. He attributed Chatham's rejection of Dowdeswell's Juries bill to personal pique and pride. 'He can not assent to *our Friends* getting the Credit with the Publick which on this and All occasions they have deserved.'[68] Yet the decline of the united Opposition was far more than a question of personalities. Those conditions which had in 1769 encouraged the union of the Opposition and its co-operation over the Petitioning Movement no longer existed. Now, that movement was gone and the radical movement in the country was fragmenting, splintering and dying. Not long after the Printers Case, for example, the Wilkite wing broke off from the Bill of Rights Society to form the Constitutional Society. The Opposition had been able to sink its differences only when the incentive of public opinion enabled it to strive for office with some real hope of success. Now, that incentive had disappeared and the hope had not been realised.

Indeed, the differences between the Rockinghams and the Chathamites had always been too great to compose. For they amounted to fundamentally different conceptions of government and even of politics. It seemed that the more frequently and the more harmoniously the two wings of the Opposition worked together, the more they came to realise how widely separated they were in their basic beliefs and attitudes. In February 1771 Richmond, who was of all the Rockinghams, the one most inclined to sympathise with Chatham, had two conversations with him in which he summarised the Rockinghamite *credo*.

'That the Treasury carried with it the Government of this Kingdom. That my principles were, that the Court had adopted a system destructive of the constitution viz., to have the Minister depending solely on the will of the Crown and not on the opinion of the Publick for his situation weight and

Consequence . . . and therefore to remedy it, the only way was
to reunite in Party, to hold steadily together, and by acting
upon true Whig principles, to recover the weight and Party
of the Whigs. Upon these grounds I said we were a Party
and should stick together. That since we had been glean'd
of some rotten Limbs we were sound all over and I believed
nothing could detach a man from us. That reduced as we
are, we were still the most numerous corps in either House
of Parliament and in the nation, indeed we were the *only*
Party now left, and were very respectable by our numbers,
Fortune, rank, and especially by our Characters. That for
these Reasons, we thought our party ought to be the foundation of any good administration, that you (Rockingham)
was the Head of our Party and as such the Man to be Minister. . . . That we did not confine our Pretensions here, for we
should expect to have the Majority of the cabinet from our
Corps and the efficient offices the Admiralty, Plantations,
etc., that in short we meant to be the Ministers to govern the
Country by the Corps of Whigs. . . . That we did not mean
to proscribe any man or set of men provided they would join
us upon our own principles. That the larger our Party was
the better it would answer to our idea of what a party should
be, but we look'd upon ourselves as the only Party at present
subsisting. That we should be happy to reckon Lord Chatham amongst us, and as many more as would act with us
upon our own principles.'[69]

The whole of the above is significant, the last nine words
particularly so. Fundamentally, the Rockinghams were willing
to have Chatham in a future ministry (and perhaps some of his
friends, too) so long as the bulk of offices and influence were to
be lodged in Rockinghamite hands and so long as Chatham
accepted Rockingham's leadership within the context of a
united, party administration. As we have observed already, the
Rockinghams treated the union of the Opposition as a means to
the end of a *party* administration and not a *united* administration. Chatham's personality, his belief in 'Not Men but
Measures', indeed, his whole career arose from principles
glorifying the role of the individual in politics which were quite

different from those propounded by Richmond. The demise, therefore, of the union of the Opposition should occasion no surprise. To the Rockinghams it had been a temporary expedient whose efficacy had not been borne out by events and whose uselessness had became apparent by the end of the session of 1771.

It is certainly true that in 1770 and 1771 the conditions required for the overthrow of a ministry did not exist. There were no urgent domestic or foreign crises which North could not deal with. The ministry enjoyed the confidence of the King and large majorities in Parliament. North had survived in office and demonstrated political abilities which were now beginning to commend themselves to the large number of uncommitted members. He proceeded to consolidate his administration. He had, as we have seen, the good fortune to win the support of the remnants of George Grenville's party. In June 1771 he captured an influential political prize in the shape of the Duke of Grafton, who came back into the Cabinet as Lord Privy Seal.[70] Both this appointment, and that in August 1772, of Lord Dartmouth who became Secretary of State for the Colonies, enormously strengthened North's own position in the Cabinet because both men could be relied upon to support North (and moderation) against the Bedfords (and severity) should the American problem revive. After the death of Charles Yorke, the Hardwicke family had lapsed into political apathy. North coaxed them into soporific contentment with the ministry by the grant of an occasional favour.[71] Lord George Germain, an important link with Chathamite opinion, was in the summer of 1771 about to come to Court, while the Rockinghamite Sir William Meredith was shortly to make his own peace with King George III.[72] Lord North, in short, was succeeding where Chatham had dismally failed in 1766. Men from all parties were drifting into the ministry.

The Rockinghams were beginning to despair. Already in February 1771 Rockingham had felt the ominous chill of popular apathy: 'I fear indeed the Future struggles of the People in defence of their Constitutional Rights will grow weaker and weaker'.[73] At about the same time Burke declared that the court system was fastening itself more and more firmly on to the country. 'Lord Bute is no longer the advisor . . . his System is got into firmer and abler hands'.[74] The Rockinghams found it easy to read a sinister meaning into what was in reality a perfectly explicable political situation. They interpreted their failure as an effect of the deliberate proscription of the Court. Burke used much the same arguments against North as had been used against Bute a decade earlier with the significant addition that Lord North was not a party man. Burke declared that 'he is a single man, no body. That as such I thought he ought not to be the minister of this country, for that as such a man did not depend upon the opinion of the world for his consequence but merely upon the King's pleasure, he could not follow his own opinions or those of the nation, & must be in too literal a sense the *servant* of the Crown'.[75] All this was, perhaps, predictable. But what did the Rockinghams propose to *do* about the North administration, and what was left to them as an opposition party after the failure of the united Opposition?

Much thought was given to these unpleasant questions during the recess of 1771. The Rockinghams proceeded from the assumption that systematic opposition was bound to be a daunting undertaking. Richmond put his finger on the central issue: 'We have long lost all hopes from Numbers. Character alone must support us, and that will give us great inward satisfaction, but never bring us into Power; I confess I despair of that, but I do not lament it, for I do not think, all things considered, it is to be wished'.[76] In other words, if Opposition were bound to be weak, there was no point in opposing actively. Even if the Opposition triumphed, the Rockinghams might so easily lose their character and their reputation by becoming the dupes of the Court that it was perhaps dangerous even to seek office. But there was a logical absurdity in what Richmond was saying, for only by coming to power could the Rockinghams put an end to the influence of the Crown. More sensible was the advice proferred by the Duke of Manchester. He argued that the Rockinghams should secede from Parliament until a measure was brought forward by the ministry which threatened to increase secret influence. It was unnecessary to oppose systematically 'trifling questions unfollow'd by any vigorous measures' as long as the party remained constantly on the watch, ready to spring to the defence of the constitution. Burke agreed with Manchester, approving of 'a total secession on proper ground', provided that secession was not simply a convenient excuse for Members to avoid attending Parliament.[77] Many Rockinghamites, including Rockingham himself, came to accept and, to some extent, to approve of the idea of secession during 1771 and 1772. Attractive though the idea might have been to an exhausted and defeated Opposition party, its members did not in fact decide to make such a public admission of their political failure.[78] Indeed, there was no need for it. The 1772 session was one of the quietest of the eighteenth century in which two measures only were of sufficient significance to warrant the exertions of the Rockingham party.

The first issue directly concerned the monarchy and was thus bound to be the focus of attention and controversy. Two of the sons of Frederick, Prince of Wales, the Dukes of Gloucester and Cumberland, had contracted morganatic marriages. The King, not unreasonably, and with the health of the constitution and the harmony of the royal family very much in mind, wished Parliament to pass a bill requiring the marriage of members of the royal family to be approved by the monarch. Characteristically, George III exaggerated the urgency of the matter, insisting to North that the bill must be rushed through Parliament in the 1772 session, and demanding 'a hearty Support from everyone in my Service'. In other words, the King was threatening to punish defaulters.[79] The Rockinghams thought the speed with which ministers acted was suspicious. Furthermore, they observed with grave foreboding a bill which seemed both to augment the royal prerogative and to effect a constitutional innovation. The month of March 1772, therefore, witnessed a flurry of political activity as a series of legalistic debates on the powers of the monarchy within the constitution signalled the gradual progress through Parliament of the Royal Marriages Act.[80]

The Opposition did surprisingly well. For one thing, it was joined on this occasion by recruits from unexpected quarters. No less a figure than the Speaker himself, Sir Fletcher Norton, took a prominent part on the Opposition side and did so with such effect that ministers were sorely embarrassed. More

K

important in the long term, however, was the attitude of Charles James Fox. On the issue of the Royal Marriages Act he resigned from his post as a Lord of the Admiralty which he had held since 1770 and joined the Opposition.[81] Indeed, it was during these debates that Fox made his first dramatic impact upon the House of Commons. Furthermore, the Opposition moved so swiftly and with such effect that ministers were almost taken off guard. On 13 March, for example, Dowdeswell's motion denying the ministerial argument that the crown had always enjoyed the power to approve of royal marriages was lost by only 200–164. Rose Fuller's motion on 23 March to confine the duration of the bill to the lifetime of George III was lost by the breathtakingly narrow majority of 150–132. Frantic Opposition whipping was endangering the majority of the ministers and the King had to speak sharply to North to encourage him to bring his men to the House before his majorities recovered.[82] To some extent the Opposition must have been assisted because this did not appear to be a party issue. Grave constititional questions usually crossed party boundaries and, although the history of this issue has never been written, it is clear that there were at least two different opinions within the Opposition. The first entirely rejected the bill. Its adherents included a handful of Rockinghamites, Sir William Meredith, Sir George Savile, the Chathamites and Charles Fox. The second group, including the bulk of the Rockinghams, was willing to accept the bill provided certain amendments could be effected.[83] On 11 March, indeed, the second group voted with the ministers against an attempt by the first to throw the bill out.

The second matter on which the Opposition was able to attack the ministry was that of religious toleration. The issue surfaced twice in this session of Parliament. On the first occasion, some clergymen of the Anglican church drew up a petition (known as the Feathers Tavern petition, after the name of the place where it was drawn up) asking to be relieved from the embarrassment of subscribing to the 39 Articles.[84] Richmond seems to have been the mainspring and initiator of the Rockingham's support of the petition. He begged Rockingham to approve a relief bill 'founded on Reason good Policy and the true Principles of Whiggism and toleration'.[85] Lord North did not wish to make a party fight of it and allowed the bill to pass through the Commons in April, leaving it to the bishops in the Lords to throw it out. This they did on 14 May by 102–39. It was now too late in the session for the weak and divided Opposition to make further headway with a measure which touched the religious establishment. Rockingham was unwilling to bestir himself to make further exertions and allowed the issue to lapse.[86] On the second occasion on which religious toleration became a political issue in the session of 1772, a group of Protestant Dissenters produced a bill which would have granted them relief from subscription to the 39 Articles. This was a classic 'Whiggish' measure, reflecting the traditions of dissenting support for Whiggery and the Whigs' cardinal precept of liberty of conscience. As Burke put it: 'The dissenters do not desire to partake of the emoluments of the church. Their sole aim is to procure liberty of conscience'.[87] Consistency was not the only motive which persuaded the Rockinghams to support the bill. Richmond told Rockingham that 'your giving it a warm support will greatly recommend you to that weighty body of men, the Dissenters, who all over England are very powerful, and who stick pretty much together . . . their religious principles and our political ones are so very similar, and most probably will make us generally act together'.[88] Expedience thus chimed with conscience in dictating Rockinghamite policy on religious toleration. Yet the Rockinghams were successful in securing the passage of this bill neither in 1772 nor in the following session when it was reintroduced. On both occasions it was greeted with a mixture of apathy and hostility.[89]

Although the session of 1772 had not been entirely devoid either of issue or of incident, the Rockinghams had done little more than mark time; they had not a single constructive achievement to their credit.[90] The most that can be said is that the party avoided serious internal conflict, and, significantly, that talk of a 'united Opposition' was no longer heard. Nevertheless, the party's desperate situation of hopeless and seemingly permanent Opposition provoked in the recess of 1772 renewed discussion of the principle and practice of secession. Burke was

a warm adherent of a secession of the right kind. He believed
it to be advisable because the ministry enjoyed an impregnable
majority in Parliament and while the public seemed deaf to
the forlorn cries of the Rockingham Whigs. Only a secession
might awaken the public to some understanding of the danger
in which the constitution stood.[91] But by a secession he did not
mean a casual lapse of attendance, nor did he mean a complete
withdrawal. Secession might be justified on those occasions
when 'the house is mortgaged to the Court', but 'The attendance on other points will mark the distinction we mean to
keep in view, the more strongly'.[92] Dowdeswell agreed with
Burke that a partial secession could do nothing but good. 'We
have great difficulties now which We should not have upon
such an event.'[93] Richmond thought a partial secession in-
finitely preferable to 'a poor weak attendance and a despicable
opposition'. However, a secession should be throughly concerted: 'we should all agree to attend & give a warm opposition,
or all agree to stay away'.[94] The Marquis had originally favoured
a limited secession, perhaps during the pre-Christmas session
until full details of the business for the session became known.[95]
But by mid-November 1772 it was widely known that the
session would be an active and interesting one. Rockingham
discovered that the major business promised to be the reorganisation of the Government of India, a major imperial
concern which a responsible Opposition party could not
ignore.[96] Furthermore, there was much hostility to a secession
within the party. Sir George Savile was strongly against one[97]
and, according to Burke: 'Your Lordships Northern Friends
are generally adverse'.[98] The case for a partial secession had
been extremely powerful in the summer and early autumn.
Towards the end of the year it was much less so. Rockingham,
characteristically, chose to consult the leaders of his party as to
the best course of action to be pursued. At a party meeting in
mid-November the leaders inclined towards some kind of
secession but they could not agree upon its extent. To preserve
harmony where differing opinions prevailed the only course of
action left open to Rockingham was to defer a final decision
and to wait upon events. Time and a healthy expediency would
dictate how far to carry the secession.[99]

Time and expediency, indeed, seemed to be the major consolations which the Rockingham Whigs might find for their political disappointments. Three years earlier they had been on the point of toppling Grafton's administration, in alliance with Chatham and Grenville, and backed by considerable sections of public opinion. Now, constant failure had worn down their morale as they languished in isolation in the political wilderness of a hopeless Opposition. That they could not even agree how far, if at all, they should continue active in the political life of the nation only serves to illustrate the paralysis which was spreading throughout the Opposition. Yet the pace of politics was soon to quicken and the stakes to rise, for in the next three years the existence of the British Empire appeared to be at issue. A critical turning point in the history of the Rockingham Whigs was fast approaching.

Part Four

EMPIRE

1772–80

Chapter 13

The Problem of Empire 1773–4

The feebleness and the failings of the Rockingham Whig party in the parliamentary sessions of 1771 and 1772 should not be judged out of their political context. Although for many of their weaknesses the Rockinghams were themselves to blame, it is nevertheless the case that these *were* unpropitious years for an Opposition. Essentially, the political tension of the later 1760s had relaxed. As Lord North went from success to success, building his broad based regime, the instability and the excitement of previous years gave way to general contentment. Englishmen basked in the dull and unimaginative security which Lord North gave them. The Rockinghams, furthermore, found few issues on which they could excite either the public or Parliament (or even themselves). But in 1773 and 1774 the problem of the British Empire came to the centre of the political stage. Although it would be wildly exaggerated to claim that the problem of Empire in any way weakened the North administration in these years, it provided the Rockinghams with a series of opportunities to demonstrate their loudly proclaimed virtues, their much vaunted statesmanship, their consistency (for all these problems arose from earlier disputes in which the Rockinghams had declared their principles) and their integrity. We most now consider how far the Rockinghams succeeded in living up to their own estimation of themselves.

The first of the imperial questions to which politicians turned their attention in the parliamentary session of 1773 was that of India. Indeed, financial necessity had forced the East India Company to request government assistance in the previous years,[1] and it was generally expected that in the new session the ministers would bring forward far-reaching proposals for establishing the Government of the sub-continent upon a stable financial and political basis. Its proposals (known to history as North's Regulating Act, but in fact a series of bills) provided the East India Company with a loan of £1,400,000, restricted its dividends to 7 per cent for the duration of the loan and reformed the administration of the country. This was to be done by placing the Government of Bengal in a Governor, a Council and a Supreme Court of Judicature. (Madras and Bombay were placed under the direction of the Governor of Bengal.) The Governor General and Council would be nominated for five years by Parliament, thereafter by the Company with the approval of the Crown. Corruption was tackled by provisions forbidding senior officers from engaging in trade, and junior officers from accepting presents. All of this amounted to a massive extension of the area of state intervention over the Company and over India. Indeed, some such extension was inevitable. To continue blindly defending the chartered independence of the Company, and to assert, as the Rockinghams did, that it could continue unaided, was palpable and factious nonsense. The Regulating Act was eminently reasonable and flexible. Contemporaries recognised it as such and, as had been expected by George III, it enjoyed an almost unhindered passage through Parliament.[2]

The Rockingham Whigs were in a sorry state at the beginning of the session of 1773. The general confusion which prevailed over the policy of secession had to be cleared up before an effective Opposition to the Regulating Act could be mounted. On the eve of the session Rockingham fell ill. The thankless burdens of party leadership devolved upon the slender shoulders of the Duke of Portland until his recovery in January.[3] Although full of pessimism for the future of his party Rockingham ended the secession and sent his men to town.[4]

Yet they still needed to evolve an Indian policy and under the least auspicious of circumstances.

The attitude of the Rockingham Party to India derived from its suspicion of the Crown and its desire to maintain the independence of Parliament. The Rockinghams defended in 1773, as they had defended in 1767, the chartered independence of the East India Company not as an end in itself, but as the defence of one of the last bastions of independence against the rising tide of secret influence. However, the Rockinghams did not believe that the Company should be completely free from parliamentary scrutiny. 'We considered [*sic*] it as the Duty of Parliament to see, that the Company did not abuse its Charter Priveleges, or misgovern its Asiatic possessions.'[5] But they disapproved of parliamentary interference in the routine affairs of the Company. Still more, they trembled at the prospect that the Government might lay its hands upon Indian patronage.

Rockingham feared that if North's proposals were implemented:

'The Lucrative offices & Appointments relative to the E.I. Company's Affairs, will virtually fall into the Patronage of the Crown, such an addition to the ways & means of corruption, which is at least equal to all the Appointments of the Crown—in Army—Navy—& Revenue, Church, etc., must be felt, when already what the Crown possesses in Patronage have nearly over-balanced the Boasted Equipoise of this Constitution, which consisted in the Equality, & Independence of the three separate Estates of King— Lord & Commons. The danger to the Constitution is imminent, I fear unavoidable.'[6]

Two comments need to be made about this statement. First, Rockingham's extraordinary, though widely shared and tenaciously held, opinion that Indian patronage 'is at least equal' to all other patronage surely explains the Rockingham party's morbid fascination with the affairs of the sub-continent. Second, his reference to the theory of a balanced constitution which was in danger of being upset was a characteristic Rockinghamite reaffirmation of a traditional Whig idea.

In this way, both the ideas and the political language of the past were employed and used by the Rockinghams to inject meaning and significance into the political events in which they played a part.[7] The Indian policy of the ministers, in short, sharpened Rockinghamite fears for the constitution. By now, the Rockingham Whigs were deeply committed to the idea that to reduce royal influence by means of party was a principle worth fighting for, and even remaining in Opposition for. Since the middle of the previous decade, the Rockingham Whigs had been conscious of the prospects of such a situation. By 1773 the issue was writ large for all to see. As Richmond put it:[7]

'We have not been able to succeed in destroying that System of Government which has prevail'd almost constantly during this reign, the grand Principle of which, is to make the King govern by his own Power and the weight of His Influence, instead of the old system of governing by that Party or Set of men who had the most personal influence in the Country. The obvious Difference of these two Systems is this, that by the old, the leading men were obliged to consult the Good of the People and court them as deriving their power from them: but by the new, the ministers court only the Crown from whom alone they derive any Consequence. This evidence tends to despotism and the more so as those who are laid aside, the whigs, were united upon principles of Freedom and Liberty.'

At the same time, it is possible to establish a link between the newer, humanitarian principles which were just beginning to affect politics and the Indian attitudes of the Rockingham Whigs. Many of them shared a very real and compassionate concern for the welfare of the Indians. Frequently, such humanitarian assertions may have been the rhetorical accompaniments of political calculation, but they were not always so. Rockingham once confided to his private Memorandum references to 'provinces in that Empire . . . in a State of the most dreadful Disorder. . . . That the Country at both ends of it is afflicted with the Famine & in one part of it utterly desolated'.[8] Thus the basic attitudes of the Rockingham

Whigs towards India were informed not only by a suspicion of secret influence, nor by a desire to protect the chartered rights of the East India Company as a means of maintaining the balance of the constitution but also by a genuine humanitarian impulse.

Yet this reasonably coherent set of ideas failed to inspire the Rockinghams to work out anything like a viable policy for India. At first Rockingham suggested that the Company ought to reduce its dividend to 6 per cent, and at the same time suspend the payments due to the Government under the 1767 arrangement. This had at least the merit of being simple and straightforward. It was also childishly superficial in that it ignored most of the questions urgently facing the Company and the Government, which included the administrative reorganisation of the sub-continent. Burke, similarly, was so obsessed with the ideological aspects of the Indian problem that he gravely underestimated its political complexities. He advocated a loan to the Company of £1,000,000 which would enable the dividend to be kept to $12\frac{1}{2}$ per cent.[9] Dowdeswell with characteristic common sense, believed that the intricacies of Company finance ought to be left to those best fitted to deal with them, the senior personnel in the Company itself. Parliament ought not to dictate the rate of dividend.[10] There was one common weakness with all of these 'solutions' to the Indian problem. They all presupposed that state intervention was both unnecessary and undesirable. The Rockinghams could not see the realities of the Indian situation on account of their preoccupation with secret influence. Burke thought that 'Next to the grand object of the destruction of Wilkes, the leading object in the Politicks of the Court, is to seize upon the East India Patronage of Offices'.[11] So long as they allowed such considerations to obscure the need to provide constructive and coherent alternative policies to those of the ministry, the Rockinghams were inhabiting a psychological world of their own, increasingly divorced from political realities.[12]

One further aspect of the Indian question in 1772–3 deserves mention, and it is a matter which may throw some light upon the inability of the party to delay or amend the Regulating

Act. This was Rockingham's deliberate decision to have nothing to do with Chatham.[13] The union of the Opposition was now quite dead and the Rockinghams were the main casualties of its death. Nothing had gone right for them since they had begun to act independently. In any case, there could never have been agreement between the Rockinghamites and the Chathamites on the Indian issue. Chatham and Shelburne supported the Government against the Rockinghamites. Chatham conceded that the Government had 'a fixed right to the territorial revenues between the state and the Company . . . the State equitably entitled to the larger share, as largest contributor in the acquisition. . . . Nor can the Company's share, when ascertained, be considered as private property, but in trust for the public purposes of defence of India and the extension of trade. . . .'[14] Although the Chathamites disliked certain aspects of the ministry's proposals, especially the Crown and the Government's large discretionary powers of patronage, they gave them general support. And, of course, in supporting the principle and practice of State intervention over the affairs of the Company, Chatham was only acting consistently with the line he had followed in 1767.[15] Thus he objected to those aspects of North's proposals which allowed parliamentary nomination of the Governor General, because he regarded this as a violation of the principle which allowed *the Crown* to nominate to public offices. Thus Chatham, while retaining his distaste for secret influence and corruption, neatly reaffirmed his commitment to the defence of the royal prerogatives, leaving the Rockinghams to their own interpretation of the powers of the imperial Parliament.

Events were isolating the Rockingham Whigs, leaving them with few remaining areas of co-operation with other opposition groups, confirming their stubborn adherence to their theories of secret influence both at home and in the Empire. The next imperial problem to capture the attention of the political world did little more than confirm their growing isolation, and underline their somewhat inflexible attachment to a belief in court plots and cabals.

A stability of sorts in Anglo-Irish relations existed in the first half of the eighteenth century, but it was founded neither upon equality nor conciliation. In short, the Irish had been battered into submission in the 1690s. The peasantry enjoyed no legal or property rights, still less rights over education and the franchise. Yet the Irish problem slept in the first half of the century and awoke only when the British system of controlling the country began to show signs of strain. An Irish Parliament existed to cloak British domination with respectability. To perpetuate it, that Parliament had to be managed. The local parliamentary managers (the 'undertakers') were thus in a position of great potential influence should they choose to exercise it. In 1768 Whitehall demanded an increase in the Irish military contribution to the defence of the country. In view of what had happened in America in the 1760s this was, perhaps, a dangerous policy to pursue. To avoid trouble before it started the British tried to conciliate the Irish political establishment by agreeing to its demand for an Octennial Act. The prospect of regular elections of course, made the 'undertakers' more important to the British, and thus more powerful than they had ever been before.[16] The Octennial Act was accompanied by a new interest in Irish affairs in London and, consequently, the first resident Lord Lieutenant, Lord Townshend, who held his office from 1767–72, did well to keep the situation in Ireland in check. Yet there was one problem which he could not overcome, the Irish public debt of about £1,000,000. If this could be extinguished, then the Lord Lieutenant would to a large extent be freed from his dependence upon the 'undertakers'. Under Lord Townshend's successor, Lord Harcourt, who was appointed in September 1772, the matter came to a head. His secretary, Sir John Blaquière, discovered an answer to the nagging problem of Irish finance. Increased taxation of the peasantry would have raised a popular cry and aroused unpleasant social and nationalist sentiments. It would moreover, have been ineffectual. But a tax on absentee landlords would be popular in Ireland because it was easily enforceable. The beauty of Blaquière's proposal was that it did not affect most Englishmen, and affected no Irishmen at all. He proposed a rate of 2s in the £ on the rents of landlords in Ireland who resided there for less than six months in a single year. There

304 *The Rise of Party in England*

can be no doubt that this proposal would hit the absentee landlords hard. The loss of 10 per cent of their rents threatened to disrupt the financial structure of their estates. There were ministerialists like Hertford and Hillsborough who drew something like £10,000 per annum from their Irish estates. But it was the Rockinghamite leadership which would be most damagingly affected by the tax. The Marquis himself drew £15,000 per annum, the Devonshires drew £12,000, Lord Bessborough drew £9,000 and even Sir George Savile drew £1,500.[17] Although the tax was not directed against the Rockingham Whigs, and was not intended to be a party measure, it magically roused the Rockinghamite leadership to furious protest. That the Rockinghams' activities over the absentee tax were self-interested is as blindingly apparent as it was natural and inevitable. It seems less useful speciously to attempt to defend Rockingham from the charges from which he would not have sought to defend himself, than to probe the relationship between Rockingham's stand on the absentee tax and other aspects of his imperial ideas and attitudes.[18]

It must at least be said for Rockingham that his attitude to the Absentee Tax did not contradict the imperial ideas which he and his party had expounded earlier. Although he opposed the tax, he did not question the *right* of the Irish Parliament to impose it.[19] He questioned its expediency. He believed that the tax might interrupt commerce and separate the two countries because it would force absentee landlords to reside in Ireland. As Burke put it, the security and the integrity of the Empire could only be maintained so long as its constituent parts did not 'assume to themselves the power of hindering or checking the resort of their muncipal subjects to the centre or even to any other part of the Empire (or) arrogate to themselves the imperial rights, which do not, which cannot, belong to them'.[20]

How seriously may one take these solemn protestations? Rockingham does seem to have believed his own rationalisations of his self-interest and Burke seems to have adopted his opinions. But Richmond, for one, was altogether cynical of these posturings. His objection to the tax was its partiality, not its constitutionality. He pointed out: 'When once a system of partiality is established, when one part of our dominions are excluded from any advantage for the benefit of another part, one must expect retaliation when in their power'.[21] Only Richmond, perhaps, really sympathised with the great problems of the Irish people, and only he, of all the Rockinghams, really wished to alleviate them. It was easier for him to take this view than it was for Rockingham because he had no land in Ireland, but to his credit, he refused to become involved in what appeared to him a factious proceeding.

Indeed, even Rockingham seems to have understood that his opposition to the Absentee Tax could not be effectively vindicated on grounds of imperial security. He insisted 'that it is not a mere personal oppression, which affected individuals who had estates in Ireland, but also that every man in England would be a sufferer by it'. By this he meant 'that it would be a violation of the Liberty and freedom with which every man in this constitution has a right to the usufruct of his own property'.[22] But the Court did not intend to destroy liberty and Rockingham knew it. Furthermore, although he asserted that 'It may be the policy of a weak Court to strike at opulence in order to restrain independency', the tax had never been designed by the Court to reduce its political opponents to penury. And although Rockingham insisted that 'our property is our own; we have a right to spend it where we please',[23] he was unable to show that the rights of property could not be restricted by statute.

Whatever the merits of Rockingham's case, he argued it with great vigour. Urged on by Burke and by Bessborough, he stumped up to town, drafted four different circulars, and proceeded to distribute them to absentee landlords likely to be affected by the tax. The first of these he issued on 16 October 1773. It met with such a warm and enthusiastic response that the Marquis was encouraged to persevere in his efforts.[24] The culmination of those endeavours came when Rockingham sent to Lord North a remonstrance[25] signed by himself, Bessborough, Devonshire, Lord Upper Ossory and Lord Milton. North, by this time, was worried by the mounting opposition to the tax. Lord Upper Ossory had hitherto been a firm ministerialist. Even Lord Hertford, the Lord Chamberlain, a

Cabinet Minister, was in touch with the Rockinghams. More-over, George III was worried at the sight of friends deserting the ministry and he began to have second thoughts about the tax.[26] Tactically, Rockingham had succeeded in making a non-party attack upon the tax which was beginning to cause the ministry and the King serious concern. Furthermore, Rockingham's timing was beautifully calculated. 'The Early apprizing Lord North at this Time will have one great Conse-quence, as it affords him the opportunity of directing the King's Servants in Ireland that they should divide this tax from the general Supply bill.'[27]

By November the ministers and the King were beginning to wish they had never heard of the tax. It raised a stir in both countries, among the followers of Government as well as the Opposition, and constitutional issues of great complexity as well. By mid-November North was instructing the Castle to delay the measure. By the time it was introduced into the Irish Parliament—by Blaquière—on 25 November the ministry—and certainly the King—wished the bill to be defeated.[28] Probably because it received only lukewarm official support, the tax was thrown out by 120–106 and no more was heard of it.

Rockingham, flushed with success, could not leave well alone. He contemplated bringing in a parliamentary resolution to prevent the imposition of an absentee tax in the future.[29] Either his good sense or his lethargy saved him from almost certain political embarrassment. He gave up the idea and went up to Yorkshire for the Christmas recess, convinced that his efforts had contributed exclusively to the failure of the ministers to obtain their tax.

To some extent, of course, the defeat of the Absentee Tax was a famous victory for Rockingham. He had personally led the campaign against it and could fairly claim some of the credit for its rejection. In particular, the stimulus which he gave to the Irish Opposition[30] and its augmentation by other Members dependent upon absentee landlords was a potent weapon to use against the ministry. Furthermore, the ministry must have been troubled by the attitude of the City, many of whose institutions—especially the liveried companies—owned extensive tracts of land in Ireland.[31] The Rockinghams, through Burke, tried to stir up opposition in that quarter.[32] Although the defeat of the Absentee Tax was not exclusively a party victory, it was certainly a moral victory for Rockingham. It was fortunate, however, that he knew when to stop. Had he persisted with his idea of preventing the future imposition of such a tax, he would have risked taxing severely the support which he had mustered in the last few weeks.

On this, as on so many issues of these years, the Rockingham-ites and the Chathamites were at variance.[33] Chatham's attitude to the Absentee Tax was, in short, that of Richmond taken to its logical conclusion. Chatham did not accept the view that the tax was unjust. If they had accepted the tax, the Members of the Irish Parliament would have been 'acting in their proper and peculiar sphere, and exercising their inherent exclusive right by raising supplies in the manner they judge best'.[34] How consistent this is with Chatham's line on the American issue, and how clearly it derives from his imperial ideas, with their insistence on the rights of local legislatures. Chatham overlooked, however, the fact that the tax was not a spontaneous action of the Irish legislature. It was the policy of the British Government. In fact, Chatham's argument, taken to its logical conclusion, would have allowed the British Government the right to lay internal taxes upon any part of the Empire it wished, so long as the local legislature could be cajoled into agreement. It also implied that opposition to such taxes should legitimately proceed in the local legislature rather than in the Imperial Parliament at Westminster. Notwith-standing these strictures, Chatham not only disagreed with the Rockinghams on the justice of the tax. He thoroughly condemned their methods. Under Poynings' Law, Irish money bills had to be approved by the Privy Council. There was no need for them to be ratified by the British Parliament. Rockingham had proposed to oppose the Absentee Tax in Council. Chatham's opinion of such a proceeding was scathing. 'This power of the purse in the Commons is fundamental, and inherent; to translate it from them to the King in Council, is to annihilate parliament.'[35] Thus it was Chatham rather than Rockingham who stood upon the classical Whig principle of

Parliament's right to tax, and it was Rockingham rather than Chatham who was willing 'to substitute the opinion of the taxed in the place of the judgement of the representative body'.

The importance of Irish affairs in 1773 shrinks into relative insignificance when compared with the drift towards military conflict in America. The repeal of the Townshend duties (save that on tea) did not succeed in re-establishing Anglo-American relations upon a cordial basis. The most that can be said is that, for the most part, the mutual resentment and the growing antagonism with which the mother country and the thirteen colonies viewed each other did not normally express itself in acts of violence. The colonists were apprehensive that the money raised by the duty on tea would go towards the creation of an American Civil List. Furthermore, Americans seem to have believed the diatribes against successive ministries delivered by men like Burke and Wilkes which accused the Court of setting up a despotic system of government.[36] Such themes were taken up by American writers and politicians. In Boston, for example, the propagandist genius of Sam Adams fanned the flames of Bostonian hatred of customs officials. The superficial tranquillity of the years 1770–2, therefore, fails to disguise the gloomy realities of the situation. The American problem had not been settled, the fundamental causes of colonial grievances had not been removed and it is, to say the least, doubtful if it was not already too late for any such reconciliation to be reached.[37]

When the British Government gave what the colonists deemed to be proof positive that it rated the financial interests of the East India Company more highly than the constitutional liberties of the colonists, then the slender ties of loyalty which connected the Americans with the mother country became severely strained. The fateful episode known to history as the Boston Tea Party arose from the Regulating Act of 1773 and the fact that the East India Company in 1773 had on its hands 17 million pounds of tea, worth about £4,000,000.[38] To dispose of some of the surplus, to suppress the illicit trade in Dutch and French tea to America which had sprung up in the last few years and to exercise the sovereignty of the Imperial Parliament, North proposed to Parliament in April 1773 that the East India Company should be permitted a monopoly of the tea trade with America. The scheme was rushed through Parliament within a few weeks and with little opposition. Although North expected that the Americans would drink Company tea because it was cheaper than that which the Americans could obtain from other sources, the Tea Act of 1773 signified to the Americans that Britain, far from moderating her claims over the colonies, was standing firmly by them. The more tea that was sold in America, the more revenue the British Government would obtain; the colonists might well conclude that to obey the Tea Act amounted to admitting the right of the British Parliament to tax Americans for revenue purposes. This was why in 1773 tea became a symbol of British tyranny and why, on 16 December, the men of Boston dumped three shipfuls of it into Boston harbour. Smaller tea-parties took place elsewhere. The rapturous reception which these demonstrations of hostility to British rule received in most (though not quite all) places in America indicated clearly that a large question mark hung over the survival of imperial taxation of the colonists.[39]

Ever since the imposition of the Townshend duties in 1767 the attitude of the Rockingham Whigs towards the American colonists had been curiously circumspect. Although certain individuals, notably old Newcastle and young Richmond, had been on the side of the party's maintaining the support for colonial rights which the first Rockingham ministry had manifested,[40] there were few occasions in the following years when the Rockinghams leapt to the defence of the Americans. As we have seen the Rockinghams did not oppose the Townshend duties and, on occasions, could appear more imperialist than the King.[41] They stood by the Declaratory Act and, like everybody else in Britain, professed shock and anger at riots, disturbances and demonstrations in America.[42] As we have seen, there were pressing political reasons why the Rockinghams had not opposed the Townshend duties. Between 1767 and 1773 the Rockinghams failed to live up to the appellation 'Friends of America' which the Whig historians of the nineteenth century were apt to give them and which, to some extent, the Rockingham Whigs after 1777 were apt to claim.

The Rockinghams were a small political party, struggling to survive, unable to afford the luxury of befriending the Americans, at least until the political drama of the War of Independence presented them with a choice they could not ignore. There were several very good reasons why the Rockinghams did not startle the political world with gestures of liberality towards the colonists in these years. For one thing, the colonists were not being persecuted. America was, on the whole, not an important political issue in Britain in these years. For the Rockinghams to have espoused the colonial cause openly would have weakened them politically and, in particular, it would have destroyed the 'union of the Opposition', one of the most powerful political goals which the Rockinghams wished to achieve. At the same time, the background of mercantile support for the colonists, which had played such a great part in persuading the first Rockingham ministry to repeal the Stamp Act, had gradually evaporated. All this does not imply that the opinions of Rockingham towards America were exactly the same as those of Townshend, Grafton and North. Although he was just as keen as they were to maintain British imperial sovereignty, Rockingham had come to the conclusion in October 1768 that 'merely commercial regulations' rather than internal taxes would be sufficient to register that sovereignty. The idea of making America '*a Revenue Mine*', he considered absurd.[43] Yet Rockingham failed to draw the conclusion that the best and most acceptable method of maintaining sovereignty over the Americans was to abolish *all* the Townshend duties. As he admitted, he failed to urge a more liberal policy towards America, not because he did not believe in it but because of his faint-hearted pessimism that no one would listen.[44]

Nevertheless, it is undeniably true that the Rockinghams did not oppose the Tea Act of 1773. The reasons for their failure to do so are difficult to fathom. It may be plausible to argue that the financial interests of the Burkes and a handful of other Rockinghamites may have inhibited them from opposing the Tea Act[45] but apathy, rather than financial calculation characterised their actions. Like the rest of their fellow-countrymen, they probably under-estimated the effect on America which the regulation of Indian affairs—everyone's preoccupation in 1773—was likely to have. In so far as they considered the problem at all they probably adopted the widely held view that the Americans would gladly drink the cheap Company tea. At the same time, they reacted to the Boston Tea Party as angrily as the ministers did.[46] Nevertheless, Rockingham did not believe in the use of force in America.[47] But how could the Declaratory Act be exercised without the use of force, given the state of America after the Boston Tea Party.

The reaction of the King and his ministers was marked by no such ambiguity. They firmly grasped the nettle proferred by the Bostonians. Not only the right to tax but the right to govern in America was at stake. As George III noted: 'nothing less than a total independence of the British Legislature will satisfy them'.[48] Within a matter of a few days of receiving the news of the Tea Party, the ministers had decided upon a policy of retaliation and coercion as the only means of preserving British rule in the colonies.[49]

The coercive acts passed through Parliament in the spring of 1774 without event and without much opposition. The Boston Port Bill met with no opposition in its principle from the Rockinghams. Dowdeswell and Lord John Cavendish had reservations about it, believing that it was inexpedient and that it might lead to dangerous consequences.[50] The only Rockinghamite violently to denounce the bill was the Duke of Richmond in the Upper House. Of the Bostonians, he said on 11 May: '*they would be in the right to resist, as punished unheard, and, if they did resist, he should wish them success*'.[51] The Massachusetts Bay Regulating bill was rather tardily introduced into the Commons by North in the middle of April.[52] This bill worried the Rockinghams far more than the Boston Port bill. They thought it dangerous and unnecessary to tamper with charters. Dowdeswell accused the ministers of 'struggling to obtain a most ridiculous superiority'.[53] He believed that if this bill passed then none of the chartered colonies could feel safe. Yet the 'friends of America' did not divide the House. Although the bill was debated vigorously on several occasions during its passage through the Commons it was not until 2 May that the Opposition mounted a full scale assault upon the ministry in a packed House. Yet it was on this occasion that the Chathamites, urged on by Chatham himself, declared their opposition to a policy of coercion and spear-headed the opposition to the bill.[54] Dunning attracted all the attention with an excellent speech. As he put it: 'The language was, *Resist and we will cut your throats—acquiesce and we will tax you*'.[55] The Rockinghams rather limply put forward the argument that the Americans should not stand condemned without being heard. Burke, however, attacked the idea that America should be taxed for the purpose of raising revenue. The third coercive act, the Impartial Administration of Justice bill,[56] was likewise more effectively opposed by the Chathamites than by the Rockinghams. The measure of the Opposition, however, is reflected in the division figure on third reading on 6 May when ministers won their bill by 127–24. A similar fate befell the bill in the Lords. Only on third reading on 18 May did the Opposition assert itself. (This was one of the rare occasions when Rockingham spoke in the upper House.) Nevertheless, Ministers were victorious by 43–12.[57] As for the Quartering bill,[58] it passed through the Commons with no opposition at all. Its progress in the Lords was marked by Chatham's return to the political stage. On 28 May he made, as Walpole put it, 'a long feeble harangue' in which he blamed not only the Bostonians but also those who sought to punish them: 'the result of all which he meant to insinuate was that he alone could assert the authority of England and compose the differences in America'.[59] Richmond divided the House and provided the ministry with an encouraging division of 57–16. Thus ministers obtained their coercive acts against pitifully little opposition. Perhaps it was this fact which encouraged them to proceed, late in the session and with few members in town, with the Quebec bill.[60] The implications of this bill for the Americans were serious, and it was tragic that it should have been confused in their minds (although, given the timing, this was inevitable) with the coercive legislation. The Quebec bill threatened to restrict the freedom of frontier colonies to expand westwards and did, in fact, deprive the colonists of control over their relations with the Indians who inhabited the Appalachian wilderness.[61] Unlike the coercive legislation, the Quebec bill was introduced in the Lords where it passed through all its stages between 2 and 17 May, receiving only intermittent and ineffective opposition.[62] Much the same can be said of its progress through the Commons. Although the Opposition protested that the council for Quebec would be nominated, and objected to the allegedly excessive degree of religious toleration being shown towards the Roman Catholic religion and the Roman law of France, its attacks were easily repulsed. On 26 May on third reading the Opposition was defeated by 105–29, and did only marginally better three days later when a motion for the papers upon which the bill was based was lost by 85–46.[63]

On the coercive legislation, then, the Rockingham Whigs presented weak and half-hearted opposition. The reason is not hard to find. They had never been, and never pretended to be, friends to the rights of Americans. They accepted the same set of authoritarian assumptions about the Empire as the ministry and the King. They were just as affronted at the Boston Tea Party as other sections of opinion. They therefore believed just as strongly in the need to punish the Bostonians, their only reservation being the fear that excessive punishment might make the colonists more difficult to govern. The Rockinghams were thus on far firmer ground in opposing the Massachusetts Bay bill than they were on the Boston Port bill. Their fears that the ministry was undermining the chartered rights of the Bay colony were widely shared.[64] It is difficult, however, to credit the Rockinghams with a constructive alternative American policy. They promised to repeal the Tea duty while maintaining the Declaratory Act. But this was not a feasible policy after the Boston Tea Party. Rockingham was deluding himself if he believed that he could put the clock back to 1766. The Americans were no longer willing to observe either the spirit or the letter of the Declaratory Act.[65]

Yet Rockinghamite policy towards America, with all its defects, received its classic exposition and justification during the period when the coercive acts were passing through Parliament. On 19 April Rose Fuller moved for the repeal of the tea duty and the debate was the occasion of Burke's first speech for conciliation. Burke argued that if the British Empire were to survive then the sovereignty of the Imperial Parliament should be universally recognised, although its rights need not be exercised. To this end, it was essential to conciliate the Americans. Burke believed that the repeal of the Tea Duty would effect such a reconciliation and restore trust and harmony to imperial relationships. It is easy to discern the weaknesses of Burke's plan but many of these only became apparent with time. It was not obvious in April 1774 that the repeal of the Tea Duty would not improve imperial relations. Few people in Britain believed that the Declaratory Act could no longer be maintained. In any case, what alternatives were there? That of George III and his ministers was to drive the colonists into rebellion within a year. That of Chatham, to surrender the taxing power, would have abrogated the sovereignty of Parliament.[67] The real weakness of Burke's plan, as of so much of Rockinghamite thinking on America, was that it was not thought out to a detailed and practical conclusion. Burke's plan would stand or fall by the extent to which he could persuade the colonial legislatures to accept conciliation. Burke wished to combine imperial regulation with colonial autonomy. But where would he draw the line? What powers would he allow to remain with the colonial legislatures? Parliament must retain the right to tax but not, apparently, as a revenue-raising instrument. In a crucial passage Burke offers to allow the colonial legislatures such powers which 'are equal to the common ends of their institution'. This was far too ambiguous a formula to appeal to the mass of independent country gentlemen in the Commons, let alone the Americans in the wake of the Boston Tea Party. Perhaps Burke was attempting the impossible in trying to reconcile the vociferous claims of the colonial legislatures with those of the British Parliament. In the last analysis, however, it must be confessed that Burke failed, although nobly, and in the most generous of all causes, that of conciliation, peace and harmony.

Chapter 14

The Rockingham Whigs on the Eve of the American Revolution

On 30 September 1774 the King dissolved Parliament. Although the House of Commons elected in 1768 might have continued to sit for another year there were sound reasons why the ministry chose to go to the country at this time rather than wait until the last possible moment. The Opposition would be —as oppositions almost invariably were—unprepared for a snap election. Furthermore, it would clearly be in the best interests of the ministers to finish with the elections while their coercive policies towards America were fresh in the minds of an approving public. The proposal for a dissolution had the support of most members of the Cabinet and—most important of all—of the King himself. Everything pointed to an election during the parliamentary recess of 1774. But it should not be thought that North was seeking a 'mandate' for his American policies. The function of elections in the political system of the eighteenth century was not to approve or disapprove ministerial policies. In the normal course of events, ministries neither collapsed nor changed their policies as the result of an election. For elections, when they were contested at all, turned upon local issues and their result had little bearing upon national policy. Their timing was a matter of political calculation rather than a question of seeking public approval for legislation either effected or promised. The dissolution of 1774, therefore, took place when it did purely for tactical reasons. It was entirely fortuitous that General Gage's despatches containing the first news of serious and widespread American resistance to the coercive acts were received on the day following the announcement of the dissolution.

After their modest exertions of the previous session the Rockinghams had dispersed to their estates, completely failing to anticipate the American reaction to the coercive legislation.[1] Rockingham was only expressing the opinion of others when he predicted that nothing would happen 'so as to alarm this nation and make the ensuing session a session of great activity and business'.[2] He was numbed at the apathy of public opinion and when the news of the dissolution reached him he was near to despair. 'I confess indeed that I think *all politicks* are now in so low a state & so little likely to revive, that I should feel a hesitation in giving encouragement to an expectation, that we can continue long to drudge on in such unsatisfactory & so unthanked a laborious occupation.'[3] And when to this we add that during October Rockingham was struck with illness, and that Dowdeswell was beginning to surrender to the disease which claimed him a year later, then the conclusion is inescapable that the period in question represents an unfortunate and unhappy one in the history of the Rockingham Whigs.

The Rockingham party at the election of 1774 did not hope to conduct anything more than a holding operation. It did not have the money and the man-power to do so, and it had not made the necessary preparations. The dissolution took Rockingham unawares 'and I am not a little perplexed by it'.[4] He had, moreover, been badly shaken since April when Sir George Savile had declared his intention of retiring from Parliament at the dissolution. Savile was exactly the sort of weighty and respected independent landed gentleman whom the party could ill afford to lose. It required many weeks of persuasion before Savile reluctantly changed his mind.[5] Finally, during Rockingham's illness, Portland deputised for him. But the hero of the 1768 election was unlikely to provide energetic leadership for the Rockingham party. His feud with Lowther over Inglewood Forest was still dragging on, wearing away his patience, wasting away his financial resources and occupying his time.[6]

The Marquis of Rockingham, in spite of his illness, was able to maintain what he had at the election of 1774. At several places his interest was challenged, and he had to fight quite hard to protect it. Savile was once more returned for the county seat in Yorkshire, but at York there was an Opposition. Rockingham's control of York was never seriously in question, but he had of necessity to devote considerable time and trouble to fending off an attack upon the very centre and citadel of Rockinghamite influence. Charles Turner and Lord John Cavendish were safely returned, but Rockingham's energies would have been better engaged at Hull where his interest was much less secure than it was at York.[7] Rockingham could usually count on the nomination of one seat, the other traditionally being ministerialist. William Weddell was retiring and Rockingham wished to replace him with David Hartley. Rockingham and Savile had to use all their influence in the town to enable Hartley to scrape home, by 646 to 581 votes in second place. At Scarborough Rockingham allowed his interest to lapse. His influence had done much to secure the election of F. W. Osbaldeston in 1768. On Osbaldeston's death in 1770 Sir James Pennyman had come in with Rockingham's approval. Now Pennyman switched to Beverley where he won a seat and Rockingham appears to have made no attempt to revive his influence at Scarborough. By 1774 Rockingham enjoyed influence at Hedon through the two sitting Members, Sir Charles Saunders and Beilby Thompson. Savile Finch continued at Malton (where Weddell replaced Burke) while Frederick Montagu's occupation of Higham Ferrers continued without interruption and without incident. Since 1768, on the other hand, Rockingham had been unable to retain the loyalty of Lascelles, who was drifting steadily over to the ministry, and Sir William Meredith. N. Cholmley no longer sat in Parliament. The allegiance of George Dempster, MP for Perth, was strengthened, however, during the years of the 1768 Parliament. The size of Rockingham's group after the election of 1774 was eleven, one more than it had been in 1768.

The Duke of Portland did less well. He could not afford a repetition of the electoral adventures of 1768, although many of his supporters in Cumberland and in Carlisle clamoured for a renewal of the electoral war against Lowther. Portland found it expedient to divide the representation of Cumberland with Lowther, where Henry Fletcher came in, and necessary to remove himself from the contest at Carlisle altogether.[8] Portland faced a further setback in Nottingham. The retirement of Plumptre placed him in great difficulties. Portland tried to bring in his brother, Lord Edward Bentinck, but he was surprisingly pushed into third place.[9] More happily, Portland kept control of Wigan where George Byng and Beaumont Hotham kept their seats. His brother-in-law, Booth Grey, similarly came in unopposed at Leicester. But Thomas Fenwick, whom Portland had helped in 1768 was defeated in the Westmorland County election. In 1768 Portland had brought in no fewer than seven members. Six years later that number had dropped to four.

Amidst these disappointments, Edmund Burke enjoyed a surprising and famous victory. Lord Verney's financial embarrassments weakened his electoral influence and although he kept his own county seat in Buckinghamshire he lost control of the borough of Wendover.[10] Edmund Burke was one of the sitting Members and had to seek election elsewhere. He had been offered support at Westminster on condition that he accepted the radical programme but he was unwilling to endorse the idea of shorter Parliaments.[11] Thereupon he sought refuge in the safe seat which Rockingham was keeping for him at Malton.[12] At this point some merchants of the city of Bristol promised their support for Burke if he should elect to stand there. Burke arrived at Bristol on 4 October. A few days of canvassing were enough to convince him that he stood no chance at all. He left the town on 7 October and arrived at Malton two days later. On his arrival he learned that one of the sitting Members at Bristol, Lord Clare, had declined to continue after one day's polling. Burke's Bristol friends begged him to return and he reached the town on 13 October. Amidst convulsive waves of popular enthusiasm, and after almost a month of electioneering, Edmund Burke became Member for Bristol, one of the greatest personal and political achievements of his life.[13]

Even the Bristol result, undoubtedly the most sensational of the election, turned on local rather than on national or party issues. America was raised as an election issue in only about a dozen constituencies and, even then, usually as part of a radical programme in which parliamentary reform took pride of place.[14] The problem of America appeared less as an issue of principle to most Englishmen in October 1774 than as an administrative and policing action. The sovereignty of the Imperial Parliament had been challenged by the colonists and needed to be reasserted. Furthermore, that body of mercantile opinion which had succeeded in the middle of the 1760s in turning America into a political issue was now on the side of the ministry.[15] And even if it is legitimate to speak of the emergence of great issues in national politics, of radicalism and of imperial relations, the conduct of elections proceeded much as before. Thus the Rockingham Whigs fought the election on traditional lines and in the traditional manner. Opposition lords were left to themselves to protect their own interests. Occasionally, there can be discerned the concert and co-operation between the Rockingham lords which we noticed in 1768. Attempts were made by Rockingham to find seats for friends of the party,[16] and help was occasionally given to candidates by patrons and landlords with interests and influence in a constituency. Informal cooperation existed but on a haphazard and unorganised basis. Had the Rockinghams chosen to exert themselves more strongly than they did, then they might well have met with a greater degree of success. The ministry did not conduct the election particularly efficiently. Lord North left election business to the Secretary to the Treasury, John Robinson, who fell ill in the middle of the election. Furthermore, the Government met with hostility in certain circles. It was unable to find a candidate for the county of Middlesex, and in the City of London the ministerial candidate came bottom of a list of seven.

This was the political background against which the Rockingham Whig party fought the election of 1774. The size of the party had remained approximately stable since the last election in spite of the setbacks which had befallen the Rockingham Whigs. In 1768 there had been 57 members of the party in the Commons. Of these 4 had defected to the Government side[17] and 5 had left Parliament between the two elections.[18] Seven Members entered Parlaiment between 1768 and 1774 and adhered consistently to the Rockingham party.[19] Of the 55 Rockingham Whigs on the eve of the election, however, 15 were not returned.[20] Only 3 new Members either entered Parliament in 1774 or may be grouped with the Rockingham party at the time of the election.[21] The general election of 1774, therefore, reduced the size of the Rockingham party from 55 to 43.[22] Two reasons suggest themselves for this decline. First, the disappearance of the Newcastle connection and the difficulties encountered by Portland account for part of the loss. Second, few new Members were willing to commit themselves to the wastelands of Opposition which the Rockinghams seemed doomed to occupy. This was clearly a serious reverse (although several old Members found seats in 1775 and the size of the party once more began to increase slightly), but it was by no means an annihilation.

The stability of the Rockingham party during the years between the elections was matched by a coherence which was a necessary accompaniment in the emergence of party political activity. There are, for example, five extant division lists relating to the Wilkes issue between January and May 1769.[23] How did followers of Lord Rockingham in the Lower House behave on this issue? Of the fifty-six Rockinghamites then in the Commons only one, Rose Fuller, defied the party and voted with the Government. Table 1 illustrates that of the 56, 37 voted four or five times, roughly two-thirds of the party. Furthermore, on the important amendment to the address on 9 January 1770, 39 of a maximum possible 52 Rockinghamites supported their party. On 25 January 1770, on a motion re-

Table 1   Number of Rockingham Votes

Division	Whig Voters
Five divisions	25
Four divisions	12
Three divisions	4
Two divisions	7
One division	4
None	4

lating to the Middlesex election 40 did so.[24] Again, 38 Rockinghamites followed their party into the division lobby on a
motion opposing the Convention with Spain which ended the
Falkland Islands dispute.[25] Thereafter attendances and party
fervour declined. Nevertheless, on a division on a motion to
bring in a bill to secure the rights of electors on 26 April 1773,
no fewer than 44 Rockinghamites voted against the ministry.[26]
Division figures should always be treated with caution and
handled with respect, but it does seem reasonable to venture
two conclusions. One is that on a suitable issue Rockingham
could rely, even in unfavourable times, upon the support of
three-quarters to four-fifths of his men on a particular issue.
The second is a necessary reminder that the Rockinghams
amounted to only about one-third of the *total opposition vote*. The
size of this vote varied, of course, with the issue and the time
of the session at which a division was forced. Between 1768 and
1774 although it frequently exceeded 120 it rarely exceeded
180; normally it hovered between 120 and 150, of which the
Rockinghams would contribute perhaps 40. These conclusions
are borne out by the 'States' of the House which John Robinson
drew up in March 1772 to inform himself of the likely behaviour
of Members on the Royal Marriages Act. His two lists of likely
opponents of the measure include between 180 and 190 names,
including all but three of those we have identified as Rockinghamites. Similarly, his survey of the Commons in September
1774 lists 132 oppositionists. The number is lower because the
list is incomplete, and a comparison of this list with that of
March 1772 suggests that his complete total might have been
in the region of 170–180.[27] Thus, the Rockinghams had always
to work to secure the support of non-party Members of Parliament who were more inclined to vote in Opposition rather
than with the ministry, but who detested systematic Opposition
and factious behaviour and whose support could never be
relied upon. In short, the Rockingham party was only a
minority element in opposition to the ministry of Lord North,
the bulk of it being made up of independent country gentlemen.

   Although the years from 1768–74 can only be described as
years of failure for the Rockinghams, they were not devoid of
significance and they witnessed important developments inside

L

the party. It would be misleading, for example, to regard its situation in 1774 as *typical* of the fortunes of the Rockingham party in general. It would be fanciful to argue that the Rockingham party was on the verge of disintegration, and that only the American war 'saved' it from extinction. On the contrary, it was not on the verge of disintegration, and its prospects were for some years worsened rather than improved by the War of American Independence. There can be no denying the political failures and personal failings of members of the Rockingham party, the demoralisation of its leaders and its insufficiency of numbers. Ministers could well afford to look with scant respect upon a powerless Opposition. These were bleak years indeed for the Rockinghams when North basked in the confidence of the King and enjoyed overwhelming majorities in both Houses. In the politics of the 1760s, an opposition party could reasonably hope for power when ministries led brief and unstable existences. But the Rockingham Whigs had emerged from the factious politics of that decade as a party, with a stable and identifiable membership and with a particular interpretation of the politics of the reign which singled them out from other groups. After 1770 although they continued to pursue for a while the chimerical ideal of a 'union of the Opposition', they did so with much more independence and confidence than they had in earlier years. The failure of the united Opposition in 1770-1, however, left the Rockinghams isolated and unable to influence the course of political events. Nevertheless, the Rockinghams survived these years. Desertions there were, but they were few. The harsh years of Opposition confirmed the Rockinghams in their belief in the righteousness of their cause and their picture of themselves as martyrs of the constitution struggling against the powerful engines of secret influence. The hopelessness of their cause made it seem all the more just, and the superiority of North made his system of government seem all the more sinister. These were critical, formative years in the psychological development of the Rockingham party. That they were unfavourable years does not make them unimportant.

These were the years which saw the consolidation of the leadership of the Marquis of Rockingham. No one would wish to return to the days when Rockingham was viewed through the eyes of the Whig apologists of the nineteenth century, who, in their turn, derived their view of Rockingham from the contemporary assessments of Burke and Fox. On the other hand, the pendulum has swung against the Whig view of Rockingham to an excessive degree.[28] The criticisms which can be levelled against Rockingham are both numerous and familiar. He was indolent, he lacked political skill, he leaned too heavily upon others and he knew little of government. Moreover few solid legislative achievements stand to *his* credit. On the other hand, Rockingham preserved his party, and enabled it to survive the dark years of Opposition through the exercise of his immense ability to conciliate men. A nonentity could as little have preserved the Rockingham party from opportunism as he could have maintained the loyalty of the Yorkshire gentry for a generation. In spite of frequent illnesses, a much underestimated tendency to despondency, and, perhaps, even a speech defect which may to some degree account for the rarity of his parliamentary speeches,[29] Rockingham kept to his post. It should at least be said for him that his leadership was stronger, the nature of his party and its principles much more decided and its coherence more secure in 1774 than it had been in 1768. In particular, the 'country' element which Rockingham represented had become a particularly potent strain by 1774 and is, perhaps, best illustrated by the large number of Independent Members whose support of the Rockingham party arose largely from their personal regard for Rockingham.[30]

It cannot be stressed too much that the Rockingham Whigs did not treat political issues in isolation as they occurred. They constantly placed them within a coherent, if mythical, view of the politics of the reign of George III which was essentially 'country' in nature. They viewed Government with suspicion rather than envy and regarded what they believed to be unhealthy manifestations of political power with concern rather than jealousy. In this manner they interpreted the actions of successive administrations. The great issues on which the Rockingham Whigs nailed their colours to the mast all related to an alleged court plot whose objective, with the acquiesence of Parliament, was to establish a new and sinister form of despotism in Britain. The Rockingham Whigs saw themselves, therefore, as the defenders of the traditional constitution. It mattered little to them if the misdeeds for which they reproached ministers were not illegal. As Burke declared in the *Thoughts*, the actions of the court cabal attacked the *spirit* of the constitution. The aristocracy, united in party, was the only body in the nation still uncontaminated with the infection of corruption and only through its exertions would the country find its salvation from the schemes of the Court. But the aristocracy must not only defend itself but also make common cause with other victims of the Court's persecution. In this way, the traditional concerns of the aristocracy found room for the emergence of a deeply felt sense of the public interest. It is impossible to grasp the purpose of the involvement of the Rockinghams in the Petitioning Movement of 1769, for example, unless one recalls that not only the petitions but also the overthrow of Grafton were a means to an end. That end was the destruction of the court system. The whole nation, not just the aristocracy, would benefit from its destruction. The nonsense of the Bute myth thus preserved the Rockingham Whigs from a myopic concern with self-interest and brought into the arena of public discussion larger issues. Most of all, the Rockingham Whigs, in their frequently misguided but well meaning and amiable manner, undertook the defence of liberty between the elections of 1768 and 1774. In most of the issues which arose in these years and which impinged upon freedom of speech, freedom of election, the security of property and chartered rights and the defence of the individual, the Rockingham Whig party usually took the popular side. The extent to which they were committed to these noble purposes and the extent to which they succeeded in attaining them may very well be questioned. What is indisputable is the fact that the Rockingham Whig party of 1774 had developed rapidly in the ideological sense since its emergence in the middle of the previous decade. The years between 1768 and 1774 were the formative years for the party of Lord Rockingham.

Chapter 15

Reaction, Conciliation and War 1774–5

In the autumn of 1774 the ministers of George III were pleased with the coercive legislation, exulting in its ready acceptance by Parliament and its general approval in the country. Dartmouth even felt able to make a concessionary gesture towards the colonists from what appeared to him to be a position of overwhelming strength. On 6 July he wrote to General Gage informing him that the Boston Port Act would be withdrawn as soon as the Bostonians had compensated the East India Company for its losses, and when customs dues could once more be collected safely in Boston Harbour.[1] Much, indeed, depended upon Dartmouth, for he alone of the ministers came close to understanding the American problem. To his credit, he rarely indulged in the vicious and vindictive threats against the colonists which were so common in 1774. Although he had supported the coercive acts he had done so in no spirit of hatred. His greatest mistake had been his failure to take the initiative towards a policy of conciliation with the colonies while there remained the possibility that it might have met with some favourable reaction. 'In leaning upon North's resolution, Dartmouth had chosen a very weak reed.'[2] The Bostonians were unlikely to reimburse the East India Company and admit the errors of their ways, and as summer dragged into autumn, the Americans proceeded to pick up the gauntlet which the British Government had so plainly thrown down.

General Gage had arrived in Massachusetts in May 1774 and almost immediately he began to report widespread resistance to the coercive acts. The Boston Port Act came into effect on 1 June. Opposition to it spread like a forest fire but the colonists were united politically as never before.[3] On 5 September the Continental Congress, containing representatives of all colonies except Georgia, met at Philadelphia. By this time, the colonists had unmistakably expressed their resistance to the coercive acts, and their willingness to fight them. In effect, they were repudiating the taxing power of the imperial Parliament, and thus its sovereignty.[4] The First Continental Congress indicated the way feeling in the colonies was going. Although only a small minority of delegates advocated independence, even the vast majority which still hoped for compromise with the mother country rather than rebellion nevertheless joined with the radicals in their determination to resist the coercive acts. The delegates accepted the Navigation Acts (provided that they operated with the consent of the colonists), but proceeded to summarise their grievances in a Petition to the King. The Congress gave rise in October 1774 to the Continental Association which organised resistance to the British in the shape of non-consumption and non-importation agreements.[5] Just as dangerous to the continuation of British rule in America was the dramatic proliferation of militia groups which energetically trained and drilled themselves in the use of arms. By the winter of 1774, then, it was clear to the British Government that the coercive acts had precipitated a crisis of imperial authority which left the sovereignty of the British Parliament little more than a dead letter. If it were to be revived and exercised, then urgent action was required from London.[6]

But in the autumn and winter of 1774–5 the British Government was paralysed with helplessness and indecision. It was easy for Gage to beg for additional troops to restore order but North knew that it would take a year to raise them, if indeed they could be raised. Gage realised that force alone could restore order but that force, once unleashed, would provoke the colonists beyond endurance and drive them to seek in-dependence. Gage, then, was just as reluctant to initiate a military attempt to settle the American question as North was to assume any responsibility for such an attempt.[7] Nevertheless, the King and his ministers had been agreed on the need for a firm line and perhaps a show of strength to restore the colonists to their proper allegiance.[8] When this was not forthcoming ministers were at something of a loss to know what to do next. It was thus to be some time before the policy of coercion was accompanied by its logical counterpoint, that of mili-tary enforcement.[9] But it was not, indeed, until 13 January that the Cabinet agreed, at long last, to reinforce Gage's army.[10]

What was the reaction of the Rockingham Whigs to the failure of the coercive legislation to subdue the Americans and to the ominous drift towards a policy of military enforcement in the winter of 1774–5? Although Rockingham was receiving regular and detailed intelligence from the colonies[11] he did not until a fairly late date come to realise the urgency of the crisis in imperial relations.[12] Rockingham's first priority was to maintain peace for if Britain went to war against her colonies, she would be an easy prey to hostile powers in Europe.[13] But how was war in America to be averted? Rockingham believed that by agitating constitutional issues nothing could be achieved. It was necessary to re-establish trust, 'a conviction on one side, and . . . a confidence on the other, that similar disputes were neither politic nor practicable, and would never be revived again'. Thus the Americans would be brought to acquiesce in the Declaratory Act.[14] The events of 1774 had certainly aroused profound suspicions in America that funda-mental liberties and rights were under assault. But how were these suspicions to be dispelled? Was a change of ministry by itself to effect the miracle? Rockingham was unable to suggest a solution to the imperial problem which would have proved acceptable to the Americans and yet have maintained his party's attachment to the Declaratory Act. It was Burke who instilled something of a sense of urgency into his master and the party. After the pathetic failure of the Opposition's resistance to the Speech from the Throne—registered by a division figure of 264–73 on 5 December 1774[15]—he began to realise the need for strenuous activity. He lamented the absence of public opposition to the coercive policies of the ministry. 'For if no other persons, and no other regular System, are held out to the people at large, as Objects of their confidence in times of distress, they must of Necessity resort to the Ministry.' Burke believed that the party must be active in Parliament. In Dowdeswell's absence, John Cavendish must lead the Opposition in the Commons and Richmond in the Lords. Rockingham should call a party meeting to concert tactics. Thereafter, six or seven leaders should undertake to bring a number of friends to town so that a good attendance could be maintained throughout the session.[16]

Rockingham was not able to respond favourably to Burke's plan for greater vigour. A recent renewal of contacts with Chatham, albeit chilly and distant, may have gone some way towards influencing his decision. Early in the new year Chatham affronted Rockingham when he apprised him of his intention to make a motion in the Lords 'for a sort of reconsideration of that Declaratory Bill and *amend it* or make some alterations in it, which might take out *the sting* (or some words to that purport)'. Chatham's view 'that the *Declaratory Bill* had been the cause of the *revival of all the confusion*' perplexed and angered Rockingham and his friends.[17] The Marquis pointed out that even the Americans had not demanded the repeal of the Declaratory Act, but Chatham thought that this was the spirit of their resolutions. Nevertheless, some leading Rockinghamites such as the Duke of Manchester believed that Chatham should be humoured; if the friends of America allowed personal and political differences to divide them, then they would be powerless to resist the Court.[18] Rockingham felt that Manchester might be right. Although he did not wish to surrender his party's well-established principles on America, he saw no merit in deliberately provoking Chatham. Therefore Rockingham brought his men to town and kept them there during the session, but he refrained from entering into lengthy debates on the American issue.[19] The Marquis thus allowed Chatham to take the initiative in attacking the American policy of the ministers. It was a characteristic

Rockinghamite solution to a problem of political tactics, born of a combination of commonsense and caution, moderation and sloth.

Chatham was thus free to go ahead, and on 20 January 1775 moved a resolution in the Lords for the withdrawal of British troops from Boston. Pleased with the deference shown to him by the Rockinghamites, he resisted the temptation to attack the Declaratory Act, resting his case on the maxim of 'no taxation without representation'. He argued that Parliament ought to be content with the Navigation acts and the regulation of colonial commerce, the colonists remaining free to tax themselves. The debate was noteworthy because the Rockinghams bent over backwards to avoid offending Chatham, speaking and voting in support of him (although Richmond could scarcely bring himself to vote).[20] But their mutual differences remained. Although Chatham trimmed his language somewhat in order to please the Rockinghams, Camden made an extraordinary assertion of the relevance not only of the contract theory but also of natural rights to the American question. He argued that because Britain had violated the contract by abusing her authority, the colonists were, therefore, justified in resisting her sovereignty.[21] The Rockinghams, however, refused to be drawn into a discussion of the Declaratory Act, although Camden had attacked it severely. Indeed, Chatham and Camden were going much too far for contemporary opinion which was convinced that a few subversive elements in America were responsible for the disorders there, and that sound discipline, administered by the British army, would be sufficient to restore law and imperial order. It was no surprise when the motion was lost 68–18.[22] Rockingham's tactic of humouring Chatham by allowing him to take the initiative on America preserved a precarious harmony among the Opposition, but achieved little else.

A similar pattern of events occurred a few days later. On 31 January Chatham informed Rockingham that he intended on the following day to give the Lords 'my poor thoughts . . . for preventing a civil war' in America, but he made it clear that his Conciliation Plan was his own. Nothing had been concerted by the two wings of the Opposition, then, for the

debate in the Lords on 1 February 1775.[23] Chatham's Conciliation Plan did not shirk the major issues. Sovereignty was reposed
in the imperial Parliament—he did not jettison the Declaratory
Act—but the power of taxation was only to be exercised with
the consent of the colonial legislatures. The Crown was to
retain its military prerogatives but no troops were to be
stationed in America. The Philadelphia Congress was to be
recognised as a lawful assembly and was to raise a colonial
revenue. The Admiralty Courts would have their powers
reduced and the coercive acts were to be repealed. There is
much to be said in favour of Chatham's Plan. It removed most
of the grievances of which the Americans complained and it
went far towards establishing the outlines of a new imperial
relationship. But it was not likely to have received an enthusiastic reception by the Americans. They would not have
tolerated British control of the army and they would not have
financed their own submission to the British Parliament. The
Empire, even in Chatham's new scheme of things, remained
too centralised for a people now beginning to demand their
freedom. The Plan, acceptable or not to the Americans,
was summarily dismissed by the Upper House by 61 votes
to 32.[24]

The Rockinghams seem to have had no strong feelings about
the Plan. They voted for it less from any enthusiasm they
felt for it than from their wish to deprive the ministers of the
pleasure of witnessing divisions within the Opposition.
Chatham, at least, had now publicly suggested some sort of
policy for dealing with America. Why did the Rockinghams not
bring forward a Plan of their own? It can be argued that as
long as they continued to defend British sovereignty over
America they ought to have brought forward a policy for
retaining and exercising that sovereignty. Rockingham, in
fact, did not do so because he was preoccupied with the
negative business of staving off disruption in the Opposition.
In any case, he and his friends had reservations about
Chatham's Plan, not only in its rejection of the Declaratory
Act but also because the revenue derived from America would
go to create an independent revenue for *the King*. But to have
made their opinions public and to have outlined a Plan of their

own would have invited dispute with Chatham at a time when opposition unity needed to be maintained against the ministry during the crisis in imperial relations.

With the failure of Chatham's Plan to commend itself to the Lords, the way was clear for ministers to bring forward measures of their own to deal with the deteriorating situation in America. These were varied in their nature and wide-reaching in their implications. By the end of January ministers had already reached two decisions. One was to replace Gage with Amherst.[25] The other was to deal with the uproar in the colonies provoked by the coercive acts. To this end Parliament was persuaded to declare that a state of rebellion existed in Massachusetts.[26] In order to suppress it, North brought forward a bill to restrain the trade of Americans with Britain, and plans were brought before Parliament to increase army and navy personnel.[27] To accompany these measures and to protect themselves from the charge that they were unwilling to seek some accommodation with the Americans, even at this late hour, the ministers agreed upon a Conciliatory Proposition which was presented to the Commons by North on 20 February.[28] The proposal was engagingly simple. Parliament would 'forbear' to levy internal taxes if and when the colonies would individually raise money to pay for the civil and military government. It is important to be clear that the Proposition did not surrender the right to tax; it was waived on grounds of expedience. Furthermore, the money collected was to be spent as Parliament directed, not as the colonies wished. The colonies would only enjoy the revenue accruing from commercial regulations. Although the tactic of maintaining though not exercising a right is reminiscent of Rockinghamite thinking on America, North's Proposition was, in content and in its likely effect, quite different. Parliament would still have exercised the right to tax. The Rockinghams did not, therefore, hesitate to attack the Proposition. Burke put the matter nicely when he claimed that the Americans were contending for the freedom to grant revenue, not the right of collecting it: 'Revenue from a free people must be the consequence of peace, not the condition on which it is to be obtained'.[29] Although North was straining the loyalty of some of the Court's most faithful supporters, the Proposition was accepted by the Commons on 27 February by the massive majority of 274–88.[30] Nevertheless, North must have been living in a world of his own if he believed for one moment that the colonists could have been persuaded to negotiate upon the terms of the Proposition. He must have known from Dartmouth's discussions with Franklin that the Americans would never accept it. On the contrary, it has been suggested that North was trying to divide the colonies because the Proposition applied to them individually and not collectively. What is more feasible, however, is the theory that North hoped to secure an easy passage for the legislation which the ministry was preparing, by enabling himself to claim with some justice that he had held out an olive branch to the colonists.[31] Indeed, he wrote as much to the King, claiming that the Proposition 'will greatly facilitate the passing the Bill now in the House for restraining the Trade of New England'.[32]

The successful passage of government policy through Parliament drew from Burke the first detailed statement of Rockinghamite policy for America since the Boston Tea Party. On 22 March he introduced his Proposals for Conciliation. Rejecting the use of force ('It may subdue for a moment; but it does not remove the necessity of subduing again'),[33] Burke proclaimed the urgent need for conciliation with the colonies and the re-establishment of the Empire upon its traditional principles. In Edmund Burke's imperial vision the relations between the separate parts of the Empire and the central authority remained necessarily undefined, arising as they did from mutual consent and mutual self-interest. In this view of the Empire he found little place for statutory definitions and legal rights. He was prepared to concede a substantial measure of local autonomy to the local branches of the Empire in order to maintain their allegiance, but precisely how much he was prepared to concede depended on local circumstances, on practicalities rather than abstractions. This is not to argue that Burke was pioneering a new concept of Empire. It was never his intention to do so. He wished to restore the old imperial system which had, in his view, worked perfectly well before 1763. Burke wished to repeal the legislation passed since then, and abolish the measures of taxation which had created such disruption in the present reign. Thus he advocated the repeal of the tea duty and of the coercive legislation and the removal or improvement of some of the abuses of which the colonists complained, such as the operation of the Admiralty Courts. But he was less concerned with the *details* of conciliation than with its *purpose*. Burke was never in any doubt that the Americans ought to belong to the British Empire. Common cultural and linguistic traditions bound the colonies to the mother country. Everything ought to be subordinated to the preservation of that connection. It was less important to raise a few thousand pounds than to keep the colonists happy. ('Instead of a standing revenue, you will therefore have a standing quarrel.') Lord North's Conciliatory Propositions would not satisfy the Americans. It was 'neither regular parliamentary taxation, nor Colony grant'. It was taxation without the consent of either Parliament or the colonists. What was needed was a different type of conciliation based upon a proper historical understanding of the nature of the imperial relationship.

All this was perfectly unobjectionable, but Burke did not succeed in finding a formula which would satisfy both Parliament and the colonists. He clung to the Declaratory Act but seemed to be content to waive most practical expressions of the supremacy enshrined within it. At the same time, he did not provide for either a political or an administrative solution to imperial problems. He seems to have assumed that, given a change of heart at Westminster, and, of course, a change of men, deep-rooted political, ideological and administrative problems would mysteriously disappear. Burke's speech, then, was a statesmanlike outline of an ideal world of imperial relationships. It was much less impressive in demonstrating how that world might be established. Burke demonstrated great understanding of the sources of the spirit of liberty in America, but rather less acumen when he came to consider how to deal with it. His recognition that a military solution was not feasible deserves praise when it is recalled that the country had little patience for such ideas. Nevertheless, the division which greeted his speech (270–78) strongly suggests that Burke was unable to convince his contemporaries as readily as he was able to convince some nineteenth century historians of the value of his imperial thought.[34]

It is just possible that Burke and his Rockingham party colleagues might have been encouraged to work out a more detailed and more practicable American policy in 1775 had they enjoyed the support of a popular, mercantile movement of opinion as in 1765–6. It is, in turn, conceivable that at the eleventh hour the Empire in North America might have been saved had such a policy been hammered out, appealing as it would to influential mercantile circles in America. It is, at least, probable, that in 1774–5 there would have been far more popular and parliamentary opposition to the policy of coercion than in fact there was. Burke was painfully aware of the fact that his party lacked mercantile support. As early as January 1775 he was writing: 'If the Merchants had thought fit to interfere last Winter, the distresses of this might certainly have been prevented; conciliatory measures would have taken place; and they would have come with more dignity, and with far better effect, before the Trial of our Strength than after it'.[35] In March of the same year he remarked of the policy of coercion: 'The Merchants have taken steps to oppose these proceedings; but they have not been much regarded; and no small pains are used in all the manufacturing parts of the Kingdom to perswade the people concerned, that the reduction by force of the disobedient Spirit in the Colonies is their sole security for trading in future with America'.[36] Although it would be unwise to minimise the extent of mercantile agitation in 1774–5,[37] there can be no disputing the fact that it was much less widespread than in 1765–6. There is little evidence that the merchants supported the colonists. Even Rockingham found it difficult to raise petitions in Yorkshire.[38] Although they were experiencing some distress on account of the dislocation of trade, there was less hardship than there had been ten years earlier. In 1774–5 the merchants looked to the Government rather than to the Opposition to restore their trade, just as they had done at the time of the Stamp Act. Furthermore, Rockingham remained uninterested in City politics, and thus his party lacked the kind of support which it enjoyed in 1765–6 and, to some extent, in 1768–70. It appears, then, that even if the Rockinghams had bestirred themselves more than they did, they would have met with little success in their endeavour to raise mercantile agitation.[39]

From other points of view, the situation of the Rockingham party early in 1775 was unpromising. On 6 February, William Dowdeswell died at Nice. One of the great pillars of the party was gone. It was no accident that the removal of Dowdeswell from the political scene coincided with Burke's pronouncements upon the American problem. Furthermore, Charles James Fox was just beginning to act with the Rockinghams— he was not yet one of them. But the years of his greatness were at hand, albeit an irresponsible and unpredictable greatness. These changes of personnel among the leaders of the party did not directly affect Rockingham's position. Rockingham had held the party together during the quiet years of the early 1770s. Now, with the quickening of the political temperature, he was beginning to revert once more to the tactic which he had adopted in 1769–71, co-operation with Chatham. Although mutual distrust aggravated differences of policy and principle, Rockingham's tactful handling of Chatham kept open the possibility for future co-operation between them, especially on the American issue. Both Chatham and Burke had outlined their imperial philosophies and there was much common ground between them. It would have been a misfortune if the Opposition allowed its differences entirely to outweigh its common ground. Broadly, speaking, their policies of conciliation were the same. The following statement by Chatham, for example, would have done credit to any Rockingham Whig: 'my whole system for America . . . is to secure to the colonies property and liberty, and to insure to the mother country a due acknowledgement on the part of the colonies, of their subordination to the supreme legislative authority, and superintending power of the parliament of Great Britain'.[40] Although Rockingham was criticised by some of his colleagues[41] and has been criticised by many historians for failing to establish a cordial relationship with Chatham it is difficult to imagine just what Rockingham could have done towards achieving that objective which he had not done in the session of 1775, short of placing his men and his opinions unreservedly at the disposal of Chatham.

Against this background the news that fighting had broken out at Lexington on 19 April came like a bombshell.[42] The revolution now had its martyrs. A grim sense of destiny swept over the colonies as they prepared for war. In order to wage it the second Congress met early in May and assumed the duties of a revolutionary government. The day of the American Revolution had arrived.

Chapter 16

The Problem of Independence 1775–7

The news of Lexington reached England on 26 May, just one day after Parliament had risen for the summer recess. The last few weeks of the parliamentary session had been quiet.[1] It was as if members were exhausted by the events of the last eighteen months, yet languidly anticipating the momentous military drama to come. The outbreak of hostilities in America had long been expected and most Englishmen were prepared for it.[2] A groundswell of patriotic sentiment gathered and during the summer gradually overwhelmed the (frequently under-estimated) pro-American opinion which existed. Of this sentiment the King was the most prominent spokesman. As early as 15 February he had confided in North: 'though a thorough friend to holding out the Olive Branch I have not the smallest doubt that if it does not succeed that when once vigorous measures appear to be the only means left of bringing the Americans to a due Submission to the Mother Country that the Colonies will submit'.[3] As the summer wore on and the British bogged themselves down in fruitless military expeditions, it became clear that only a vigorous war would destroy the rebellion. Even Dartmouth abandoned his hopes either of maintaining peace or even of localising the conflict in the colonies.[4]

The willingness of the British to make war in the colonies

was matched only by their unpreparedness to do so. 'Three separate departments supplied the armed forces and four transported them.'[5] In theory the King was responsible for the army, but George III never succeeded in imparting coherence to the fragmented institutional chaos over which he presided.[6] The army was a collection of local regimental units subject to no regular system of drilling and training. The Commander-in-Chief had no control over military strategy. Instructions to the Commanders went over the head of the Commander-in-Chief from the Secretaries. Interdepartmental rivalry and suspicion were endemic. In particular, the older departments looked with disfavour upon the recently created Secretaryship of State for the Colonies.[7] The unpromising military start made by the British, however, can only partly be ascribed to the institutional weaknesses of the bureaucratic machine. The colonists had seized the initiative and enjoyed the advantages of fighting on familiar territory. It was not just that their morale was superior to that of the luckless British troops who were caught up in the frustrating network of the interdepartmental incompetence of their superiors. A sense of rightousness gripped the Americans who believed that destiny—and time—were on their side. British opinion in the summer of 1775 recognised that imperial authority in the colonies could be exercised only by force. But the troops were not available. Reinforcements could not possibly be sent to America until the following spring. In the meantime, hand-to-mouth expedients succeeded more in enraging the colonies to fever pitch than in ending their rebellion.[8]

As opinion in the colonists hardened against the mother country the harsh military realities of the situation began to dawn on Dartmouth. In September 1775 he had to acknowledge the bitter taste of defeat when he was forced to instruct the new Commander-in-Chief, Howe[9] to evacuate Boston. The policy of conciliation, for which Dartmouth had stood, lay in ruins. The widespread hopes of a speedy military victory had now been cruelly dashed. There was now a war to be won and Dartmouth knew that he was not the man to win it. In November 1775 he took advantage of Grafton's resignation to divest himself of his colonial responsibilities in preference for

the quieter burdens of the Privy Seal.[10] His successor, Lord
George Germain, was an industrious and conscientious
administrator. Moreover, he shared the King's views upon
the conduct of the war and the need for its vigorous prosecution.[11]

It was not long before his presence in the Cabinet began to
make itself felt. For example, in the winter of 1775–6, the
ministry intended to revive the idea of conciliation with the
colonies as a propaganda accompaniment to the vigorous
prosecution of the war which was in store for 1776. Germain
was strongly opposed to conciliation, even as a propaganda
weapon. The Cabinet was contemplating a Conciliation
Commission in the winter of 1775–6 which would have powers
to supersede Governors, suspend assemblies and even raise a
revenue in accordance with the Conciliatory Proposition.
Germain refused to lead such a Commission and his refusal
delayed its appointment until February 1776.[12] Even then the
Cabinet could not agree upon a definition of the Commission's
powers. Everyone agreed that the supremacy of Parliament
must never be surrendered, but how should it be upheld?
North, however, believed that if the Americans could be
persuaded to lay down their arms and to dissolve Congress,
then that should be enough. The Bedfords and the Grenvilles
in the Cabinet sided with Germain in requiring the colonists
to make a declaration of submission. Germain, indeed, threatened to resign unless his view prevailed. North was in a cleft
stick, between Germain at one extreme and Dartmouth at
the other. If either resigned, then North's ministry would be
in grave danger of dissolution. Dartmouth, indeed, was
goaded to the brink of resignation by Germain's demand that
the declaration of submission should precede a treaty with the
Americans. North saved the situation—and perhaps his
ministry—by bringing in the venerable Mansfield to arbitrate.[13]
In the end, the powers of negotiation given to the Commission,
although considerable, were quite insufficient to persuade the
Americans to treat. Although the British made a few concessions, the Conciliation Commission demanded the dissolution
of Congress and of other rebel assemblies as a precondition of a
negotiated settlement. Furthermore, the negotiated settlement

would turn upon American acceptance of North's Conciliatory Proposition. In other words, the Conciliation Commission retained Parliament's right to levy internal taxation. Americans would, of course, never agree to recognise that right.

Meanwhile the Rockingham Whigs, reeling from the shock of the news of the outbreak of hostilities, sought to reconcile themselves to the tragic reality against which they had so frequently warned the country.[14] They were aware of the fact that 'the whole of the continent is enraged', and that the upheavals were not merely the result of the work of a conspiratorial minority.[15] They knew that public opinion in Britain favoured a vigorous prosecution of the war and recognised that 'the good people of England will not much care whether America is lost or not till they feel the Effects in their purses or in their bellies'.[16] But the Rockinghams did care whether America would be lost or not. The last thing they wished to see was the dismemberment of the Empire. On the other hand they worried lest the ragged and ill-equipped American forces be defeated by the superior troops of the mother country. It was not just that they might take a terrible revenge upon the Americans.[17] In Rockingham's mind, the danger was much more serious in that

'It will require indeed a very large Force to conquer the whole continent of America & when it is done, it will require a large Force to be constantly continued there to keep the Continent in subjection: If an arbitrary Military Force is to govern one part of this large Empire, I think, & fear if it succeeds, it will not be long before the whole of this Empire will be brought under a similar Thraldom.'[18]

What Rockingham was hinting at was the fear, universal in opposition circles, that a long war would lead to an inexorable growth in the influence at the disposal of the Crown in the shape of offices, contracts and pensions.[19] Viewing the American War of Independence in the domestic rather than the colonial context, the Rockingham Whigs interpreted the struggle in the colonies as an extension of their own crusade to liberate the British constitution from the trammels of secret influence.

If the Court were to triumph in America, then it would be impossible to allay its progress in Britain.

It is impossible to overstate the pessimism and gloom which settled upon the Rockingham Whigs in the early years of the American War. Rockingham was really alarmed at the danger in which he thought the country stood.

'I confess I begin to believe that the Quintessence of Toryism (wch may synonimously be called the King's Friends system) is both ready and willing if any opportunity offers to reak their vengeance upon us with the assistance of a King of the Brunswick Line, just as they would have been if any of their attempts to reinstate *a Stuart* had succeeded.'[20]

Nevertheless, he thought, there was little point in rousing his party to act, for actions would be wasted as long as public opinion remained vehemently anti-American. Many of his friends shared the Marquis' opinion that only when the military struggles in America led to harmful economic consequences in Britain would the people be ready to listen to the Rockinghams.[21] But Edmund Burke was not prepared simply to wait for things to happen. 'The only deliberation is, whether honest men will make one last Effort to give peace to their Country.'[22] Burke firmly believed that the Rockinghams ought to bestir themselves and attempt to influence opinion, however daunting such an undertaking may appear.

'I do not think that Weeks, or even Months, or years, will bring the Monarch, the Ministers, or the people, to amendment, or alteration of the System. There must be plan and management. All direction of publick humour and opinion must originate in a few . . . I never yet knew an instance of any general Temper in the Nation, that might not have been tolerably well traced to some particular persons.'

Burke argued that Rockingham ought to exert himself because it was in the interests of the country to prevent the ministry from obtaining 'a lease on power' for the duration of the war. He believed that if the meeting of Parliament found the Rockingham party 'in an unprepared State' nothing but disgrace and ruin would attend its proceedings and it ought, then, to secede from Parliament.[23] Burke thus presented the Marquis with two alternatives: vigorous action in the national interest or the humiliation of secession.

Rockingham was almost shamed into action by Burke's expostulations. In September he decided to come to town ten days before the opening of the session in order to organise a manifesto signed by his friends to present to the King. The manifesto would outline the Opposition's position on the American War and, inevitably, condemn the growth of secret influence.[24] This was not enough for Burke. Pieces of paper were no substitute for a constant attendance by the Rockingham party, for active harassment of the ministry and its measures and for a deliberate and sustained attack upon the system of secret influence which had led to the tragic outbreak of hostilities which now endangered the constitution. As always, when he believed great issues to be at stake, Burke tended to exaggerate the size and imminence of the danger, declaring that 'if something is not done before the meeting of Parliament, nothing which can be done afterwards, will avail in the smallest degree'.[25] Rockingham consulted Lord John Cavendish and the Duke of Manchester and, after some heart-searching, decided against proceeding with his plan for a party manifesto. He inclined to the view that the party should not attend Parliament 'on any business or any Measure relative to the proceedings on the American affair'.[26] Burke was disappointed but bowed before the decision of his superiors. 'I am sure I have a most unreserved deference to their judgement in all things', he remarked of the party leaders.[27]

Rockingham, in fact, was reluctant in the uncertain military situation of autumn 1775 to take the responsibility of laying down rigid policy lines on America which might hang round the neck of his party like an albatross. He wished his friends to come to town before the opening of the session so that 'we may know their opinions, and that we may weigh and consult in what manner and mode we should try to express our senti-ments'.[28] Once again, Rockingham wished to lead from behind and to allow no single advisor to impose a policy upon his party. Characteristically, in consulting his friends he adopted a position of compromise between those of his advisors who advocated action and those who would have been content merely with nominal gestures of opposition during the session.[29] Rockingham brought his friends to town, then, and prepared them for opposition, but he laid down no definite policy for the session and contented himself with waiting upon events.

Parliament opened on 26 October 1775. The King's Speech did not mince words. There was a rebellion in America and force was needed to suppress it. Consequently land and sea forces were being increased and Hanoverian mercenaries had already been sent to Gibraltar to relieve the British troops there for duty in America.[30] The Opposition had to choose its ground carefully in view of the widespread support for the British troops in America. Inevitably it reiterated the constant theme that the outbreak of war in America was the consequence of the system of secret influence, but it chose to attack the Speech on the issue of the ministry's introduction of electoral troops into a part of the Empire without the consent of Parliament. After a fourteen-hour debate in which the Opposition speakers, especially Fox and Burke, outshone their opponents, the ministry, nevertheless, remained in a comfortable majority of 278–108; 'and by this account', wrote one of those present, 'I do not think there is any great difference in the list of this year's forces and those of the last'.[31] In the Lords the Opposition did rather better. Rockingham's amendment to the Address attacking the failure of conciliation and deploring the use of force was lost but by the fairly respectable figure of 76–33; the debate also elicited a public declaration of Grafton's opposition to the ministry.[32] Although the ministry's majorities were rock solid they gave little pleasure to the ministers. Furthermore, Lord North was uneasy. He admitted to the Commons on 27 October that he had underestimated the degree of resentment aroused by the introduction of electoral troops into the Empire, and undertook to bring in a bill of indemnity empowering the King to call out the militia in case of a rebellion. In the next few weeks the bill of indemnity passed through its stages quite easily, but they provided the Opposition with frequent opportunities for attacking the allegedly unconstitutional behaviour of the ministry. Indeed, the fact that the ministers themselves believed a bill to be necessary seemed to the Opposition to be a clear admission of the illegality of what they had done.[33]

The Opposition's modest initiative was raised to more statesman like heights by Edmund Burke who, to a packed House of Commons, delivered on 16 November his three and a half hour Conciliation speech. Burke wished to hold out to his fellow countrymen and to the Americans a comprehensive plan of conciliation which would go to the root of the American problem. He desired, moreover, to place on public record a statement of his party's American policy, in order to avoid the imputation that it was acting factiously in refusing to support the ministry's war in America. Burke's speech demanded the repeal of legislation passed since 1766, in particular the coercive acts of 1774.[34] Burke proclaimed the need to explicitly abandon Parliament's right to tax, although sovereignty would continue to repose with the combined powers of King, Lords and Commons. Furthermore, the trade and navigation acts would continue in operation. On the other hand, Burke proposed to recognise Congress and to pronounce a general amnesty upon the Americans as a necessary preliminary to peace negotiations. In the new America Burke envisaged that local assemblies would collect and spend customs duties while the Congress would enjoy legislative authority. All of this anticipated by three years the policy of the North administration, and amounted to the most realistic and promising scheme for conciliation yet devised. What was wrong with Burke's proposals was the underlying motive which prompted them. This was Burke's unfounded assumption that a set of proposals, whatever their terms, would end the fighting. In short, Burke underestimated the Americans' commitment to independence. He failed to understand that they were no longer interested in conciliation.[35]

Burke's Conciliation speech, a statesmanlike attempt to deal comprehensively and sympathetically with the aspirations of the colonists, transcended the bounds of party and, in particular, seemed to open the way to renewed co-operation with Chatham. For the imperial ideas of Chatham and Burke were now very close and there were grounds for expecting that the friends of America might concert their activities rather more cordially than they had in the past. Indeed, Camden positively wished it.[36] There had been little co-operation between them in the ineffectual opposition to the coercive legislation and Chatham had been ill during the spring and again in the summer of 1775. Burke had gone so far as to express his pleasure at the absence from the political scene of a man who had not done America 'a single service'.[37] It was at Shelburne's initiative on the eve of the session that relations between the two wings of the Opposition were resumed.[38] Camden was eager for unity of action and he and Shelburne went some way towards co-operating with Rockingham on the amendment to the Address. In spite of dissensions[39] this was at least a step in the direction of realising the old dream of a united Opposition.[40] At the same time the united Rockinghamite–Chathamite forces were always willing to accept the assistance of prestigious individuals whose support might serve to embarrass North. On this occasion the Duke of Grafton, who had recently resigned from the ministry, was brought into the vortex of opposition politics. On 1 November he supported the Duke of Manchester's motion of censure on the ministers for employing Hanoverian mercenaries without the consent of Parliament.[41] Although this was lost by 53–32, Grafton persevered. Indeed, he was already working behind the scenes with Richmond and the Rockinghams, assisting them with the wording of Richmond's motion in the Lords on 10 November for conciliation.[42] This, too, was lost by 86–33 but the Opposition had at least been active. The pattern of relationships within the Opposition was beginning to assume the character which did not significantly change until 1782.[43]

The revival of co-operation among the constituent elements in the opposition to Lord North's ministry did not, however, effect a single political victory in the 1776 session of Parliament. The enthusiasm of the early weeks of the session was soon exhausted and, after the Christmas recess, never recaptured. The Opposition had stated its policy, put forward proposals for conciliation and come out against the war. Rockingham declared that his party's opposition to war arose from 'our defenceless state at home, the heavy expense the prosecution of a war at so great a distance must cost, the deluge of blood which must of course be spent in such a quarrel, the fear of an attack from our foreign enemies, but above all, the injustice of the cause . . .'.[44] Yet, having put its attitude on public record there was little that the Opposition could do except attack the prosecution of the war. All such attacks, however, could easily appear factious and unpatriotic when British soldiers were laying down their lives in the cause of imperial unity. An Act forbidding trade with the colonists was brought into the Commons on 20 November and the Lords on 12 December. Burke knew that with this bill any final, lingering prospect of conciliation would disappear.[45] But there was nothing the Opposition could do to prevent its passage, save to harangue empty benches in the Commons and tender protests in the Lords.[46] In the new year pessimism and gloom enshrouded the Opposition. 'I look on that people as alienated for ever let the Event of the War be what it may' wrote Burke of the colonists.[47] In retrospect, it is clear that the Rockinghams were living in a state of suspended political animation in 1776, waiting for British troops to be defeated in America. Their motions and speeches in the session of 1776, however, lack conviction because at that time the Rockinghams refused to admit that American independence was either desirable or inevitable. Yet they were, as we have seen, profoundly afraid of the only alternative consequence of the war, a British victory. Yet all the information which the Rockinghams were receiving was leading them to the conclusion not only that the war would be a prolonged and protracted affair but also that there was little chance of the colonists ever again submitting to the yoke of the Declaratory Act.[48] There was not much that the Rockinghams could do, therefore, except to attack the conduct of the war. Fox, on 20 February 1776, moved in the Commons for an enquiry into the failure of the British armies in America. But the more effectively this kind of political tactic was used the more unpatriotic the Opposition appeared. It was not at all surprising that Fox lost his motion by 240–104.[49] Richmond followed it up, nevertheless, moving on 5 March for an Address to the King asking him to send no more troops to America and to sue for peace. Richmond, ably supported by Shelburne, attacked the policy of the ministers and perhaps did something to further the cause of opposition unity but they lost the Address by 100–32.[50] Right up to the end of the session such motions came forward but were invariably defeated. On 22 May, for example, Conway moved for an Address to the King requesting information about the purposes of the war and the terms on which the ministry would be willing to negotiate a peace. Lord John Cavendish seconded and Burke, Fox and some of the Chathamites supported the renegade Rockinghamite. Once again, the verbal brilliance came from the Opposition but the ministerial majority held secure by 171–85.[51]

The factiousness of the Opposition was matched by its unpopularity. The fact that in 1775 two newspapers came out against the American war was little comfort for the Rockinghams who were disappointed at their lack of mercantile support.[52] Burke by this time had swallowed the bitter pill that the merchants were indifferent to the Opposition. 'They consider America as lost, and they look to administration for an indemnity.' They also looked to administration for contracts, remittances, and jobs. In short, Burke realised that some of the merchants might well profit from the war and its attendant needs of freight, provisions, stores, transport and clothing.[53] Richmond, as usual, put his finger on the crux of the problem. 'The merchants and others stirring upon a particular Bill only when it pinches them, will do no good . . . Will they come forth and give general opposition to men they feel are ruining them and the country? til they will, no good can be done.'[54] And of course, they did not. Burke for example, was made painfully aware of their reluctance to do so when his scheme to set up committees of correspondence in the large cities to petition against the measures of the ministry had to be abandoned. This was a telling indication that the Rockinghams did not have anything like that degree of mercantile support which they had enjoyed in 1765–6.

In the session of 1776 they were caught between two stools. It was not the case that they were unprincipled and unpatriotic. They had principles and plans aplenty. The difficulty with the American policy of the Rockinghams was that they stood by the Declaratory Act and continued to advocate conciliation.

They did not realise that to stand by the Declaratory Act made conciliation impossible. They did not understand at this time that the Declaratory Act was a dead-letter and failed to take into account the deteriorating situation in America after 1773 and, thereafter, the outbreak of war. Furthermore, it should always be remembered that George III and Lord North were fighting in America *not* for the rights of the King, but for those of Parliament. It was impossible for the Rockingham Whigs, who had been responsible for the Declaratory Act, to attack the principle of the war in America, and thus they were forced to attack its conduct and its consequences rather than its purposes. The Declaratory Act hung heavily round the necks of the Rockingham Whigs until the defeat of British arms in America forced its abandonment.

The failure of the British to nip the American rebellion in the bud and the continuation of hostilities had led inexorably to the formal proclamation of American Independence.[55] The Declaration of Independence of 4 July 1776 recognised the demise of imperial authority and declared the colonies 'Free and Independent States . . . absolved from all allegiance to the British crown'.[56] At last the Americans had formally repudiated the Declaratory Act and destroyed the foundation of Rockinghamite American policy. Yet a Declaration of Independence of some sort had been widely predicted ever since Lexington, and the newspapers in Britain had been full of rumours of its imminence for months.[57] The Declaration of Independence, moreover, neither surprised nor distressed the Rockinghams. Indeed, on the very day that the Declaration was issued Rockingham was expressing his belief that the British would not be able to conquer America.[58] Nevertheless, the Declaration of Independence placed the Rockinghams in a cleft stick. Edmund Burke was baffled by its consequences. 'I do not know how to wish success to those whose Victory is to separate from us a large and noble part of our Empire. Still less do I wish success to injustice, oppression and absurdity.'[59] Clearly, the Rockingham party had to reconsider its American policy after the Declaration. Fox and Portland urged Rockingham to hold a meeting of the party leaders to discuss the line it was to take on America in the forthcoming session of Parliament.[60] At

Wentworth on 26 August 1776 there gathered Rockingham, Burke, Fox (who was rapidly penetrating the inner circle of the Rockingham party), Lord John Cavendish, Sir George Savile, Frederick Montagu and Governor Johnstone.[61] The meeting, however, was less concerned to establish a new theoretical foundation for the American policy of the Rockingham party than to decide upon the tactics to be adopted by the party in the next session of Parliament. The reason why it did illustrates the fresh dilemma in which the Declaration of Independence had placed the Rockinghams, a dilemma which left them racked with indecision and irresolution for a year and a half, a dilemma which would not be resolved until a clear outcome of the war was forthcoming, and which could most easily be dealt with in the meantime by trying to evade the issues which were at its core. The general feeling of those present was to adopt a policy of secession from Parliament. By doing so they hoped to register their total opposition to the ministry's policy of military repression in America as well as their repudiation of the conduct of the war.[62] At the same time, they would at least be able to delay the evil day when they might have to make a public pronouncement of their attitude towards American independence. The Rockinghams' attitude to independence was ambivalent. They were concerned to maintain the integrity of the Empire, but they nevertheless rejoiced in the defiant stand taken by the Americans against the allegedly tyrannical intentions of the Court. Thus the Rockinghams saw the Declaration of Independence as a projection of the political struggle in the mother country and interpreted it in domestic terms, and not because it might lead to the founding of a nation.[63] They could not bring themselves to express any support for American independence and they assumed that the Americans might yet be won back to their loyalty to the mother country if a fresh system of government in the hands of party men replaced the corrupt system of secret influence. Secession was an attractive policy to the Rockinghams for it gave them the best of both worlds. It allowed them to dissociate themselves completely from the policies of the ministry while enabling them to avoid the vexed question of American independence.

As the date for the meeting of Parliament approached, however, some of the leading men in the party began to have second thoughts. Fox, who was probably more pro-American in his sympathies than any of the other leaders, was dismayed by the news of Howe's occupation of New York. He believed that the Rockinghams should support the Americans with all their strength and all their resources in Parliament. For Fox, to fail to do so would be a culpable dereliction of duty.[64] There were others who believed that the Americans ought not to be deserted in their hour of need by the friends of liberty in Britain. Augustus Keppel strongly advocated the strengthening of the Opposition by close co-operation with Chatham.

> 'I do most sincerely wish some solid junction could be brought about . . . we all think so, and yet have been battling in the way that has never promised the least success for many years together. I think the day is now come that makes it absolutely necessary to try, and ardently, what the whole force of the Opposition joined warmly and honestly can do.'[65]

Faced with conflicting advice, Rockingham chose to leave himself with some little room for manoeuvre. He characteristically decided upon a compromise which contained something to satisfy everybody. He advised his men to come up to town for the meeting of Parliament and in the debate on the Address to declare 'the same sentiments, which we have held from the commencement'. Secession might then follow if events warranted it.[66]

Proceedings on the first day of the session, 31 October 1776, were disastrous for the Opposition. The improvement in the fortunes of British arms in America in the second half of the year left Rockingham's party high and factiously dry. Although Lord John Cavendish moved an amendment to the Address, the Opposition's attack on the ministry was weak and unconvincing.[67] Opposition was made to appear unpatriotic, its criticisms of the war effort as encouragement for the Americans and its talk of conciliation as nonsensically irrelevant to the military necessities of the time. In the two divisions which were taken the Opposition was in the humiliating minorities of 87 against 242, and 83 against 232.[68] On the same day the Marquis of Rockingham moved the same amendment in the Lords. Although Grafton and Shelburne spoke in his support, the amendment was lost by 82–26; of the twenty-six, fourteen signed a protest. The debate was remarkable, however, much less for its (predictable) outcome than for what can only be regarded as the beginning of the Marquis of Rockingham's retreat from the Declaratory Act. He claimed that 'the only sure constitutional taxes which ought to be drawn from the colonies, would be the monopoly of their trade; and the other great advantages drawn from their constitutional dependence and connection with the parent state'. He did not condone American Independence but he laid the blame for the rebellion at the feet of the ministers. All of this left Rockingham's position on America very close to that of Chatham, although he could not bring himself explicitly to disclaim Britain's right to lay internal taxes upon the colonies.[69] Although Shelburne spoke in support of Rockingham, Camden did not and Chatham did not even attend. The prospects of reviving the old dream of a united Opposition seemed to be as distant as they had ever been.

A disunited Opposition could neither defeat the North ministry on its American policy nor persuade it to adopt a more conciliatory line. On 6 November, for example, replying to Lord John Cavendish's motion for the removal of all acts aggrieving the Americans, Alexander Wedderburn laid down the doctrine that there would be no concession to, and no negotiations with the Americans until they surrendered their independence and meekly returned to the imperial fold.[70] In domestic terms, the case for secession strengthened as the session advanced. Furthermore the sudden and dramatic arrival of Benjamin Franklin at Paris in December 1776 darkened the international scene. Franklin's visit presaged a Franco-American alliance and possibly a declaration of war upon England by France. The Rockinghams could not for much longer continue to advocate conciliation when both the British and American Governments were now interested only in a military solution to their differences, when the Americans had already seized their independence and when they were on the point of calling in the assistance of France.[71]

Secession was now all that was left to the Rockingham Whigs. It was to be a brief period of gestation in which fresh ideas were to be conceived slowly, ideas which would lead to the resolution of the contradictions in Rockinghamite thinking on America. Politically the Rockingham Whigs would remain paralysed until they chose *either* to recognise American independence *or* to support the war, *either* to repudiate the Declaratory Act *or* to maintain it. Even in the early weeks of the new year, the Rockinghams continued to advocate conciliation.[72] Their consistent belief in the virtues of a conciliatory policy sprang from their belief that the consequences of British defeat in America—the loss of the colonies— were just as unacceptable as the consequences of British victory.[73] At party meetings on 13 December 1776 and 21 January 1777 the arguments for and against secession were repeated. But Rockingham shivered on the edge of a decision. He could not make up his mind. He reverted to his earlier idea of writing a Remonstrance to the King but, after toying with the idea, he dropped it.[74] It was the influence of Burke which finally tipped the scales and brought Rockingham to declare for a policy of secession. Burke argued that the colonists would, sooner or later, be defeated. The Rockinghams ought to keep their hands clean of any involvement in such a catastrophe. Secession would allow the Rockinghams to make a symbolic, public gesture of their repudiation of Parliament's military solution to the American problem, while enabling them to wait until the people summoned them to repair the terrible damage done to the British constitution and the empire by Lord North and George III. In any case, secession was much preferable to 'A weak, irregular, desultory, peevish opposition'.[75] By the end of January 1777 the Rockingham Whigs had seceded from Parliament.

The secession could have made an impact only if it had been total. But the friends of Chatham, including Camden and even Grafton, did not participate in it. Nor did several Rockingham Whigs, including Saville and Fox. They thoroughly disliked the policy of secession and they remained in their seats. Fox had always disliked the idea of abandoning the Americans and he was keen to keep the banner of liberty flying at home.[76] The Americans were engaged in a struggle to preserve Whig principles and on that account they should be supported. Thus the secession was only partial. It also lacked conviction. To many contemporaries it appeared to be less a gesture arising from principle than a reflection of Rockinghamite weariness, defeat and demoralisation. Furthermore, the secession suited the interests of George III and Lord North perfectly. The King advised his Minister to take advantage of the secession to push contentious legislation quickly through Parliament.[77] This North proceeded to do in February when he brought a bill before the Commons suspending the operation of Habeas Corpus. The friends of Chatham and of Fox, together with Savile and Conway, fought an heroic resistance to the bill but the outcome was never in doubt. Although the Opposition was able to win some slight technical alterations to the bill, the ministers had little difficulty in obtaining parliamentary approval for their measure.[78] Just when a strong attendance by the Rockinghams might have shaken the ministry, or, at least, won further concessions on the Habeas Corpus bill, they were not to be found at their posts. The best that Richmond could say about the secession was that although 'the plan that was adopted has not been steadily pursued' on the whole '*no great harm* has been done'.[79] As the days passed the policy of secession gradually collapsed. On 5 March 1777 Portland told Rockingham of 'the difficulty of putting a stop to the curiosity, and quieting the timidity of our friends' and suggested that the secession be wound up, to be replaced with 'a regular systematic opposition' which would strengthen 'the Whig party'.[80] By the middle of the same month the Duke of Manchester could report that 'the *measure* . . . being no longer *general*, has no weight with the public'.[81] Manchester was right. Many members of the Rockingham party wished to end the secession. They gradually drifted back to town. No more was heard of secession from Parliament.

What brought the Rockingham Whigs to town was, perhaps surprisingly, neither the American War nor the Habeas Corpus bill. It was the King's appeal to Parliament on 9 April

M

to pay off the debts of £600,000 which had accumulated on the Civil List. At once, Rockinghamite suspicions of corruption and secret influence were awakened. On 16 April Lord John Cavendish moved for a committee of enquiry and, strongly supported by Burke and Fox, divided respectably in a full House. In both Houses the cry was the same: if secret influence were ever to be brought under control then the House needed to examine papers of Civil List expenditure.[82] This was an issue on which the Rockinghams could give voice to their hatred of the court system even if they could not prevent the ministry from getting its way. On 18 April, however, they almost did, Lord North winning a division by 137 to 109. His majority was so slim because the country gentlemen disliked the measure and because the ministry was unprepared for a second assault by the Opposition.[83] Nevertheless, after the Civil List issue the session was almost entirely devoid of incident. The Rockinghams had come back to town to end the secession, but having decided to do so they surprisingly refrained from launching an effective attack upon the ministry's conduct of the war. The ending of secession did not give rise to a vigorous Opposition but to rather a languid and lazy one.

The embarrassing straits to which the Rockinghams had been reduced by the secession provoked Burke's *Letter to the Sheriffs of Bristol*. The *Letter*, although published in the middle of May, after the secession had come to an end, was clearly something of an apologia for the conduct of the Rockingham party.[84] Burke insisted that 'all opposition to any measures proposed by ministers, where the name of America appears, is vain and frivolous'. This was so because 'All struggle tended rather to inflame than to abate the distemper of the public counsels. Finding such resistance to be considered as factious by most within doors, and by very many without, I could not conscientiously support what is against my opinion, nor prudently contend with what I know is irristible'. Burke repeated his plea for conciliation, still believing that the Americans might be brought to acquiesce in the Declaratory Act. Nevertheless, the *Letter* marks a further stage in the gradual shift in the American policy of the Rockingham party.

Burke recognised that America could not be brought to heel by force of arms. If the repeal of all the legislation passed since 1763 failed to encourage the Americans to return to their former loyalties then, as a last resort, Burke argued that her independence must be recognised. The only alternative would be a long, damaging and fruitless war of which the British constitution would be the first casualty. The *Letter* is often, and rightly, taken to be an important statement of Burke's rejection of a political philosophy which concerned itself with abstract rights. Historically, it is perhaps more important as a sign that the Declaratory Act was no longer the unshakeable pillar of Rockinghamite American policy.

In parliamentary and political terms, however, the Rockingham Whigs continued to mark time uneasily during the rest of the session. After the Easter recess there was a little flurry of activity in the House of Lords, marked more by its futility than any favourable impression it might have made upon the public mind. On 1 May the Duke of Grafton presented a motion deploring the war, having made strenuous attempts to gain the co-operation of the Rockinghams.[85] The pitiful failure of Grafton's well-meaning attempt to put an end to the war was, however, matched by the theatrical return to Westminster of Chatham who came before the Lords on 30 May to predict a declaration of war by France upon Britain and proclaim the impossibility of a British victory in America. Even Chatham, however, shrank from advocating that the British Government should recognise the independence of the colonies. Like the Rockinghams, he fell back upon the virtues of conciliation, believing at this late stage that it might still be possible to negotiate a settlement with the Americans before Britain became involved in a world-wide struggle against the Bourbon powers. His motion for an Address to the King advocating peace was lost by the overwhelming majority of 99–28.[86] Such was the outcome of Chatham's single parliamentary appearance of the session.

Prospects for a union of the Opposition seemed just as distant as ever.[87] Chatham had been unco-operative and the Rockinghams had been able to summon up absolutely no enthusiasm for his heir-apparent, Lord Shelburne. Burke thoroughly disliked him ('He is suspicious and whimsical').[88] Even Augustus Keppel, the only Rockingham Whig to reach anything like a cordial relationship with him, still felt uneasy in his company.[89] Towards the end of 1776, for example, there were some rumours that Shelburne was to desert the Opposition and take an office in the ministry. There was no substance in these rumours but with an almost neurotic glee the Rockinghams seized on them and found justification in them for their dislike of Shelburne and his principles.[90] There was always much talk of a united Opposition, but in practice few people positively wished to achieve it and the Rockinghams were just as much to blame as anyone for the personal suspicions which wrecked the prospects of opposition unity.

Gloom and pessimism lingered into the summer recess. Continued failure and repeated frustration, the consequences of the dilemma which the Declaration of Independence forced on them were finally beginning to take their toll on the morale of the leaders of the Rockingham party. Edmund Burke was one of the most patient and long-suffering of them but in September he could remark that 'As to public affairs, I attend to them because I must, not because they give me any sort of pleasure'.[91] He was tortured with the constant fear that had plagued him ever since the outbreak of hostilities. If the British won, then liberty would be crushed in the Empire and at home. If the Americans won 'it will be sufficient to keep up the delusion here, and to draw Parliament deeper and deeper into this System of endless hopes and disappointments'.[92] Burke testily began to blame his own party, whose members 'have not that trust and confidence in themselves which their merits authorise', and he adverted to: 'Ill success, ill health, minds too delicate for the rough and toilsome Business of our time, a want of the stimulus of ambition, a degeneracy of the Nation, which they are not lofty enough to despise, nor skillful enough to cure'. He did not exclude himself from their number. As he confessed: 'I do not know how to push others to resolution, whilst I am unresolved myself'.[93] He explained to Fox the reasons for his disillusionment.

'I have ever wished a settled plan of our own, founded in the very essence of the American Business, wholly unconnected with the Events of the war, and framed in such a manner as to keep up our Credit and maintain our System at home, in spite of anything that might happen abroad. I am now convinced by a long and somewhat vexatious experience, that such a plan is absolutely impracticable.'

It was now necessary to live for the moment, to take an occasional chance and to seize a political advantage.[94] At the same time, the Marquis of Rockingham realised that the only thing that could revive the fortunes of his party was the defeat of British armies in America. Yet Rockingham was no traitor. Although he did not positively wish for the defeat of British armies his party would otherwise have little opportunity to do other than repeat the disastrously unsuccessful tactics of the last session. All that Rockingham could suggest was to unite with the Chathamites in opposition and to seek support for a Remonstrance to the King which would protest against the causes of the present calamities.[95] Burke agreed that the party leaders should attempt to counteract the prevailing despondency in the party by appearing to be active. If they did not, then men might start to weaken in their party allegiances and desert to the ministry.[96]

As on previous occasions, however, it was not merely Burke's pleas which swayed the Marquis. It was the general opinion of his friends combined with a slightly improving situation within the Opposition which encouraged him to act with some vigour. Rockingham heard from the Duke of Manchester that Chatham and Shelburne would be likely to attend Parliament regularly in the forthcoming session, and that Camden and Grafton would probably follow their lead. Furthermore, rumours of an impending war with France were becoming so widespread that they could not be ignored.[97] Rockingham now began to sense the likelihood of a serious British military defeat in America.[98] The news that Richmond wanted to be active must also have cheered him. Richmond wanted regular party meetings, the attendance of their friends at Parliament and a committee of enquiry into the conduct of the war.[99] But Portland, who was usually the most pessimistic of men and one of those usually on the side of inaction, recognised that there would be a case for vigorous opposition only in the case of a British defeat in America or a Franco-American alliance.[100] And Savile, who deplored the futility of eve-of-session meetings, recognised that the fate of the Rockingham party rested not upon its own exertions but upon the outcome of the military struggle in America.[101] As usual, Rockingham refused to impose a policy upon his followers. He left it to his friends to decide the strategy for the session at a meeting to be held in London at the start of the session.[102]

Indeed, things were beinning to appear just a little brighter for the Opposition than for some years. Chatham was making more friendly noises than he had for a considerable period. Just before the session he conveyed to Rockingham a copy of a motion he intended to move at the start of the session.[103] On the first day of the session, 18 November 1777, supported by the Rockinghamite peers, Chatham moved for the recall of the British army from America. Yet Chatham argued his case unconvincingly, claiming that this course of action, together with the repeal of all the legislation which the Americans found obnoxious, would not lead to American independence.[104] In the Commons, the Marquis of Granby moved the same motion, and in a lengthy and extravagant debate, in which Burke and Fox did their case and their party no good at all by the violence of their language against Germain, the ministers triumphed by the enormous majority of 243–86.[105] The Opposition was disappointed but not disheartened by these failures. Richmond had been talking for some time about moving for a committee to enquire into the state of the nation, in other words, for a vote of no confidence in the ministry and equivalent to a full scale assault on the ministry. First Chatham, then Rockingham recognised the value of such a proceeding. It would raise the political temperature and attract members to town.[106] A meeting of party leaders on 28 November at Rockingham's London residence approved the plan.[107] As a delighted Edmund Burke put it: 'the friends to Peace never were to all appearances so perfectly united'.[108] Tommy Townshend 'never saw so fair . . . a prospect of union among those in opposition until now'.[109] Even Charles James Fox was much more sanguine than he had been a few months earlier. 'I am clear the opinion of the majority of the House is now with us.' But he thought that it would be months, perhaps even years, before the opinion of Parliament changed: 'unless some unexpectedly favourable events should make people as mad and as sanguine as they were last year'.[110] On 2 December, Richmond's motion for a committee was accepted in the Lords, although Fox's similar motion was lost in the Commons.[111] On the following day the news of the surrender of General Burgoyne's army at Saratoga swept across a disbelieving London.[112]

Chapter 17

The Shadow of Saratoga
1777–8

The British defeat at Saratoga weakened the ministry of Lord North less than it weakened the minister. It gave rise to gloom and despondency but it would be unwise to exaggerate their extent. Country gentlemen might begin to look a little more critically at the administration and its conduct of the war than they had earlier[1] but they did not withdraw their support from it as a consequence of Saratoga. The entry of France into the conflict a few months later, moreover, occasioned a rallying of loyalist support around the ministry in the nation's hour of crisis which left the Opposition isolated in its ostensibly unpatriotic refusal to do other than criticise the King's Government. Much more serious than the reaction of the public to Saratoga was the damage it did to the equanimity and confidence of Lord North. Although George III tried to shrug off the reverse as 'serious but not without remedy',[2] North understood at once that it had placed in question his right to continue to lead the administration. He hoped that 'if a storm should rise upon the late misfortunes, which may be appeased by a change of Minister, no consideration of favour or predilection should make your Majesty persist in your resolution of keeping or excluding any set of men whatsoever'.[3]

North's meaning was clear. Some material change of system was needed. The ministry should be strengthened by an infusion of new blood from somewhere, even from the Opposition. If this were not attempted then he must consider resignation. Indeed, as early as 7 December, William Eden was already begging him not to quit.[4] But Lord North's dissolving confidence cannot have been strengthened when a trickle of men began to desert the ministry.[5] It was only a trickle and too much should not be made of it, but it was enough to worry him.

The Opposition was not slow to take the advantage afforded them by the surrender of Burgoyne's army to attack the hapless minister. On 3 December, within a few hours of the news breaking, Fox was on his feet in the Commons demanding that ministers produce the instructions issued to Howe and Burgoyne. This, after some hesitation, they refused to do. The Opposition's onslaught was informed more by passion and personality than by restraint and self-control. Fox's shafts of withering scorn directed against the hapless Germain were so pitilessly kept up that they even succeeded in bringing the anxious North to his feet. He defended his Secretary of State for America, maintaining that the First Minister must share in the responsibility for Saratoga.[6] The debate marked a quickening of the political pulse. It reached new heights of passion and partisanship and new depths of vilification and abuse which sent shock waves across the ministerial benches. For the first time for many years the Opposition sensed that great events were at hand. Its expectations correspondingly rose and its confidence grew.[7]

Clearly, if the North ministry were beginning to collapse, then the Opposition needed to be not only energetic but united. Although in recent months relations between the Rockinghamite and Chathamite sections of the Opposition had been reasonably friendly,[8] the sequence of events to which Saratoga gave rise chilled their promising cordiality. For Saratoga raised the great question of American independence. Could Britain still retain her rapidly ebbing authority in the colonies? Indeed, was it worth the effort? The Opposition was bitterly divided on these questions. As we have already noticed, the Rockinghams had already begun to abandon the Declaratory Act in the previous session of Parliament and it was their

general opinion that Britain would be unable to retain the
colonies.[9] Saratoga edged them slightly nearer to accepting
the reality of American independence. But when on 5 December
David Hartley moved to end the war and to establish a federal
relationship with an independent America, he was moving too
quickly for the bulk of the Rockingham party. This proposal
predictably encountered hostility from the ministerial benches
but it found no support among the Chathamites, either.[10]
The concept of independence was ambiguous; if they had ever
taken the trouble to examine their attitudes the Rockinghamites and Chathamites might have been able to reconcile
their mutual differences and misunderstandings. The Chathamites' near-hysterical refusal to discuss anything resembling
American independence polarised these differences and tended
to make them harder to reconcile in the future. On the same
day that Hartley made his motion Shelburne was denouncing
the idea of independence in the Lords.[11] Furthermore,
Chatham took such a passionate view of the need to maintain
the connection with the American colonies that he refused not
only to compromise (it would, after all, have required the
continuation of the war to have maintained the connection),
but he would not even discuss the matter. 'I will as soon
subscribe to Transubstantiation as to sovereignty (by right)
in the colonies.'[12] In a bitter and menacing letter to Rockingham, he warned that there ought to be no '*Surrender* of the
Publick into the Hands of an Incapable minority, in such a
terrible crisis'.[13] Rockingham, conciliatory by nature, and as
usual shrinking from unsavoury public wrangles with Chatham,
refrained from fomenting the quarrels and divisions which
would have weakened the Opposition. He chose instead to
concentrate his fire upon the ministers for their inefficient
conduct of the war and their reluctance to make peace.
Although the Rockinghams were rapidly abandoning the
Declaratory Act it would be inaccurate to describe them in
the session of 1777–8 as positive advocates of American independence. Rather, they were advocates of peace.[14] They
were enraged, then, when North, on 10 December, casually
took the wind out of their sails by remarking that after the
Christmas holidays he proposed to bring forward a plan for

treating with the Americans. Nobody knew whether to believe him. Fox and Burke tried to prevent a lengthy adjournment of Parliament over the Christmas holidays while the country was in a crisis but they were unsuccessful.[15]

The Rockinghams did themselves little good by wasting the five week adjournment. As Governor Johnstone remarked, it was illogical of the Opposition to have opposed a lengthy adjournment, and then to have nothing new or constructive to propose when Parliament reassembled.[16] In fact, the tactics adopted by the Rockinghams were negative and unexciting. On the first day, 20 January 1778, Fox went through the conventional opposition routine of demanding the papers relating to the Saratoga campaign. Although ministers opposed Fox's request, North, at least, conceded Parliament's right to see the papers but argued that it would be improper to exercise it on this occasion.[17] Another stratagem used by the Rockinghamites was to attack the raising of troops by private subscription, which had flourished during the recess. This was treading on dangerous ground. Such subscriptions had been a spontaneous demonstration of popular feeling and to attack them made the Rockinghams appear petty and unpatriotic.[18] These manoeuvres not only discredited the Opposition. They did nothing to compose its differences. Chatham absented himself from Parliament, ignoring Rockingham's friendly recommendations to him to attend. The Marquis frankly admitted their differences of view. He restated his own belief that 'America will never again assent to this country having an "actual" power within that Continent', but put it to Chatham that such a difference of opinion ought not to preclude their co-operation in attempting to secure 'an actual Enquiry into the Causes, Mismanagements, etc'.[19] Chatham was burning with resentment at Rockingham's temerity in differing with him on the question of American independence. 'To speak plainly; I confess . . . that *Diversity* of opinions, concerning a *Fundamental* in any *Treaty with America*, and from which I had so fully declared I could not depart, inclines me to think, I had better not stand in the way of others.'[20]

Had the Leaders of Opposition been aware of the difficulties and demoralisation of Lord North, then Rockingham might have adopted a more imaginative and credible strategy and Chatham might have chosen to end his sulking. One problem was the situation of Lord George Germain. Even before Saratoga he was the magnet of a constant stream of complaint and recrimination, especially in military circles. Sir William Howe, for example, wanted to be relieved of his command largely because of his lack of confidence in Germain.[21] Even though the King hinted that it might be desirable to relieve the ministry of the liability which Germain had now become, North was loathe to do anything of the kind. He hated personal conflicts and rivalries and was never happy in trying to resolve them. He was struck with a paralysis of indecision and inaction. He even ignored George III's advice: that he should come before Parliament in January with 'a great outline of measures'.[22] He was totally unprepared for the resumption of parliamentary business, and the Opposition was thus well placed to take advantage of the weaknesses in the ministry. North himself was almost at his last gasp. He well understood the lesson of Saratoga. He told the King that 'it is pretty certain' that never again would Britain be able to levy taxes in America, that his American policy lay in ruins, that he must resign and thus make room for another to pursue a policy of conciliation.[23] George III was thoroughly alarmed. He appealed to North's better nature, to his sense of duty to the monarchy and reminded him of his indispensability and his good-standing with the Commons. For the present, North agreed to stay.[24]

It was as well that he did so for the Opposition was on the point of making its major thrust of the session. On 2 February, after weeks of postponements, both Houses went into committee on the state of the nation. In the Lords Richmond moved that no more troops be sent to America. After a brief and largely uneventful debate Richmond lost his motion by 94–31. Chatham did not appear.[25] In the Commons Fox moved a similar motion. North chose to rely less upon the dispirited ministerial speakers than upon his majority. He called early for the division. In one of the largest Houses of the decade, Fox's motion was lost by 259–165.[26] This was, as Horace

Walpole remarked, 'a surprising minority that much alarmed the Administration',[27] though its size probably had something to do with the abrupt manner in which the ministry terminated the debate, thus appearing reluctant to explain its conduct, past and future. Fox, however, was convinced that 'the opposition is gaining ground'. He thought the day might not be far distant when the ministry would be brought down, especially if the Opposition could agree to recognise American independence.[28] Two days later, the Rockingham Whigs reverted to an issue they had raised earlier. They once more attacked the raising of new levies by subscription. On this issue, even the Chathamite, Dunning, joined them and although the levies were voted by 223–130 the Opposition acquitted itself respectably.[29] On 6 February the momentum of the Opposition's attack was kept up by Burke. In a celebrated speech he attacked the employment in the British service of Indian troops, whose rapacities and cruelties he proceeded to detail in an extravagant and exaggerated manner. Amidst considerable laughter from the ministerial side of the House, the earnest Burke's motion for papers on the use of Indians was lost by 223–135.[30] The initiative remained with the Opposition for just a few days more. On 11 February Fox asked for details of the state of British forces in America. Although he did his case little good by his personal animadversions and by his reckless exaggeration (for example, he stated that 20,000 lives had been lost in America when the actual figure was 1,200), he improved the Opposition vote slightly. His motion was lost by 263–149.[31] Two things can be said about the Opposition's performance in these debates. First, the minority vote was consistently higher than it had been in previous sessions. This was not, however, the consequence of whipping-in by the Rockinghams. This does not represent a sudden growth in the number of Rockingham Whigs. It was the natural effect of military defeat upon which any Opposition with vigour and energy could capitalise. Second, the fact remains that a demoralised and much weakened ministry had beaten off the Opposition's attacks with considerable ease.

It must have been particularly galling for Rockingham, then, that just at the time when his party's much-discussed and long-expected onslaught on the ministry was being repulsed, there blew up a sudden storm of speculation that Chatham was about to be summoned by George III to form a ministry which would proceed to make peace with America. The rumours rose from the expectation that the Lord Chancellor, Lord Bathurst, was about to resign and that Chatham might figure prominently in the consequent ministerial rearrangement. They also owed something to the popular expectation of an impending outbreak of war with France and a widespread opinion that Chatham might be more than willing to inflict new humiliations on his old Bourbon enemy. In reality, although some individuals, and possibly Chatham himself, wanted Chatham back in office,[32] the King did not.[33] Chatham reaffirmed that he would only come forward at the personal behest of the sovereign. Without it, there was no prospect of him taking office.[34] That was not quite the end of the matter. The King had been horrified at the avidity with which many people had seized upon the rumours and reports of imminent ministerial changes. To scotch such expectations once and for all, therefore, he pressed Lord Bathurst to stay in office.[35] It was all a rather ridiculous storm in a tea-cup which did nothing to sweeten relations between Chatham and Rockingham. The Marquis was not only convinced of the unreliability of Chatham but reminded that the Court was constantly seeking opportunities of dividing the Opposition.

North was able to ride out the storms which Saratoga whipped up around his ministry. Nevertheless, his nerve had been badly weakened. The awareness of his own sense of inadequacy to conduct the war with any prospect of success opened his eyes to the advantages of picking up, once again, the threads of a conciliation policy. What became known as the Carlisle Peace Commission had its origins in the early days of December. In the wake of the news of Saratoga, William Eden drafted an outline plan which not only concentrated the country's resources on a naval war but also included provisions for terminating the military conflict on land.[36] During the Christmas recess North worked out proposals for conciliation which he hoped would prove to be acceptable both to America and to Britain. By the end of January, his task was complete.

Indeed, there is enough evidence to suggest that North took advantage of his (undoubtedly sincere) longing for resignation to persuade the King, as a condition of his remaining, to allow a conciliation plan to go forward. George III, who had for some time been warning North against such proposals, especially when it seemed that a Franco-American alliance was about to be signed, now changed his mind and allowed North to proceed. Hoping that his plan would 'greatly hurt Lord Rockingham's party with many factious Persons',[37] North proposed to repeal the tea duty and the Massachusetts Bay Regulating Act and to establish a Commission which would have the power to negotiate with the independent colonies. North acknowledged not only the impossibility of enforcing Parliament's right to tax Americans, but also proposed to repeal the Declaratory Act. This was going far, indeed, but North would not concede the one thing which the Americans now prized above all else, their independence. North's plan might have been just enough to satisfy the Americans in 1775. Now, the prospects for any conciliation proposals which stopped short of conceding independence were bleak. Nevertheless, the fact that North was able to commit the other ministers and the King to these proposals was an achievement of an extraordinary kind and one for which he has rarely received the credit which is his due. Although North ran the very real risk of alienating his own supporters, his conciliatory views prevailed in the Cabinet, where his proposals were formally endorsed on 11 February 1778.[38]

The policy of conciliation now adopted by the ministry was nothing less than North's confession of his own failure to conduct the war successfully. On 19 February, when he introduced his policy to Parliament, the country gentlemen listened incredulously—and the Opposition with cynical disbelief—as North claimed that he had always been an opponent of coercion and that he had never believed that a revenue could be collected from America. On the other hand, the Opposition could do little but support North's proposals for they had been lecturing him for years on the virtues of conciliation. Nevertheless, the Rockinghams found much to quibble at. They did not miss an opportunity of attacking the conduct of the war. Furthermore, they asserted that Parliament and not the ministry should have the right to appoint to the Commission. Fox, however, did not take up this constitutional point very seriously. He could not resist the temptation of confronting the ministers with the widespread rumours of a Franco-American alliance. If these were true, claimed Fox, they made the conciliation policy irrelevant. Ministers had thus to deny rumours which they suspected very strongly to be true.[39] Nevertheless, they had no difficulty with the passage of the conciliation policy through the Commons.[40] On 5 March in the Lords, Richmond, who had been conducting in recent weeks something of a one-man show, furthering the enquiry into the state of the nation by unravelling details of the Government's conduct of the war, made an important speech. In the course of it he declared that Britain should not attempt to retain influence and authority in America even by negotiation. Britain should recognise American independence as a preliminary to negotiating a peace treaty. Predictably, this doctrine was firmly rebutted by Shelburne, who claimed that Britain should retain a superintending power over the colonies.[41] In spite of Richmond's opinions, there were no divisions in the Lords and the conciliation proposals passed both Houses by the middle of March.

Just at this juncture the news was made public that America had signed a military and commercial treaty with the French in the previous month.[42] War between the two countries was now inevitable. On 13 March the British ambassador at Paris was recalled. Although the announcement of the treaty was not unexpected it created a climate of gloom in London. The North Government had not only failed to subdue the American rebellion swiftly but had also failed to localise the conflict. The American rebellion now threatened to become a war in two continents, a war in which success could be as little guaranteed as could the protection of British military interests, and even the security of the British Isles themselves. Opposition leaders held two meetings on 15 March, one for peers and one for the leaders of the Lower House, at which tactics for forthcoming debates were discussed. When Parliament discussed the treaty on 17 March, Fox, in the Commons, was not alone in calling for the resignation of ministers. His claim that the only solution to the American problem was to recognise the independence of the colonies now seemed much less rash and irresponsible than it had done a year earlier. The ministry was too dejected and embarrassed to put up much resistance against the tirades of Fox and Conway. It took sad but safe refuge behind its majority. On this occasion an Opposition amendment to the Address demanding the removal of ministers was rejected by 263–113.[43] The margin was decisive but it is significant that over 100 members were now prepared to vote for the removal of a ministry in the middle of a war. In the Lords, the Duke of Manchester's similar motion was rejected by 100–36.[44] Shelburne did not vote and Chatham did not attend. The issue of the war was tied up and beginning to become entangled with the constitutional issue of the appointment of ministers. On this, as on so much else, the Chathamites and the Rockingham Whigs were at odds.

Lord North's immediate reaction to the news of the Franco-American treaty was to attempt to strengthen the Cabinet by negotiating with some elements in the Opposition. As early as 15 March North had sketched out a plan for the reorganisation of the ministry. Chatham was to be included, at least as a figure-head. ('Honours, and Emoluments, and perhaps of the Cabinet, without any Office.') Thurlow was to replace Bathurst on the Woolsack, while the discredited Germain was to be removed from his office with the compensation of a peerage, his removal enabling Shelburne and Sir John Yorke to become Secretaries. Dunning was to come in as Attorney General and room was to be made for Isaac Barré and Governor Johnstone. Significantly, North put Fox down as a prospective Treasurer of the Navy.[45] North's problem was, of course, to persuade George III to consent to a negotiation to achieve these changes. He argued that unless some such restrengthening of the ministry were forthcoming then the King might fall into the hands of the Opposition and 'Lord Chatham would certainly be more reasonable than Lord Rockingham's party'. The advantages of the plan, North went on, included the maintenance of the dignity of the Crown and its prerogatives, and the confirmation of all office-holders in their places.[46] The King appreciated North's problems but he could not agree with his solution to them. For George III had one almost obsessive preoccupation in 1778: Lord North must remain at the head of the administration. The King, frankly, did not care who served under him, whatever their origins and past conduct, as long as they accepted the need to prosecute the war in America. He thus allowed North to proceed with his negotiation on the understanding that on no account would the King himself negotiate with the Opposition. 'I would rather lose the Crown I now wear than bear the ignominy of possessing it under their shackles.'[47] In other words, the King would accept the assistance of any politicians who came to the aid of the ministry in its time of need, but he was not prepared to make conditions with them. North accepted the King's reservations and the negotiation proceeded.

In fact, it never amounted to more than a polite skirmish. There was never anything approaching a real negotiation. All that occurred was a sounding of attitudes and opinions among a few key figures concerning their willingness to accept office. Briefed by North, Eden saw Fox but found him unprepared to enter office as an isolated individual. Fox, however, was prepared to act with the present ministers, with the exception of Germain, and thought an approach to Shelburne necessary. Fox, then, was content to register his claims to office and to advertise his goodwill to all men. But he also recognised the fact that although he was not yet a central figure among the Rockinghamites, he could not afford to make a move without the security and protection afforded by their party strength.[48] Eden next sounded Shelburne who insisted that 'Lord Chatham must be the dictator'.[49] George III did not like dictators in his Cabinet and his Closet and had no wish to take the soundings any further.[50] North tried to put his foot down by threatening resignation but George III would have no truck with 'a set of men who certainly would make me a slave for the remainder of my days'.[51] North could stamp his feet as much as he liked but the King insisted that 'no consideration in life shall make me stoop to Opposition'.[52] George III reminded North that he had been authorised to negotiate a few acquisitions to the existing ministry, not to replace it.[53] If this were not sufficient to put an end to the discussions, Shelburne told Eden on 18 March that Chatham was uninterested in entering the ministry.[54] There the matter rested for some weeks.

The failure of these 'negotiations' led to a further deterioration of North's confidence and morale. The Woolsack was vacant and needed to be filled. In trying to fill it, George III and North revived a bitter and long-standing rivalry between Thurlow and Wedderburn.[55] George III was anxious to take this opportunity of strengthening the ministry by giving the vacant post to the ambitious Thurlow.[56] What should have been a fairly straightforward appointment was not, in fact, effected until 3 June because bitter rivalries took time to compose. During the March negotiations Wedderburn had been told that in the reconstructed ministry he might expect to receive both the Chief Justiceship of the Common Pleas and a peerage. Now, hearing of the prospective elevation of his great rival, he demanded that North fulfil his 'promise', even though the negotiation had come to nothing. Wedderburn, however, was absolutely indispensable in the Commons. Without him North would have had little support because Germain had been little more than a broken reed since Saratoga. The King persuaded an angry Wedderburn to remain in the Commons until the end of the session, when he might be rewarded with the Chief Justiceship but not the peerage Wedderburn yearned for. Wedderburn was ultimately mollified by being allowed to hold the Attorney Generalship together with the Chief Justiceship. In early June he accepted the Attorney Generalship which Thurlow vacated but without having his other claims satisfied. North's attempt to reconstruct the ministry thus not only failed but backfired. Through the dreary business of the legal promotions the ministry was positively weakened.

While the ministry was suffering these internal strains, the Opposition was preparing itself for further parliamentary assaults. In particular, the Rockinghams were learning to live with the thorny question of American independence. Richmond had declared, on hearing the news of the Franco-American treaty, that 'This Event makes it the more necessary to come out with the Proposition of declaring the Independancy of America. This being done instantly, and publickly, declaring against a War with France notwithstanding this Treaty, is the only means to keep America from joining France as allies'.[57] The Rockinghams had agreed at the party meetings of members of both Houses on 15 March to move a motion in the Lords on 23 March for the withdrawal of all British troops from America. Camden, fearing for the consequences of such a motion on opposition unity, begged Rockingham to postpone the debate and to consult with Chatham.[58] Rockingham appears to have taken no action on this suggestion so that Richmond went ahead with his speech on 23 March and outlined the position of the Rockingham party on American Independence.[59] It says something for the dramatic transformation in British public opinion that Richmond's public pronouncement of the Rockinghamites' agreed conversion to a recognition of American Independence created little more than a ripple of interest. A year earlier, it would have created a sensation. Richmond lost his motion by 56–28 but the significance of the debate lies in the growing confidence of the Rockinghams and their readiness to nail the colours of independence to their mast. Chatham, however, was infuriated and proposed to come to town to answer Richmond before the Lords Committee on the State of the Nation.[60] Richmond was to move an Address to the King on 29 March, but the debate was postponed to 7 April. Chatham decided to avail himself of this opportunity to state his opinions.

Chatham, having abruptly rejected the advances of the Court, now prepared himself for what he sensed might be his last parliamentary occasion. By this time, he was a bitterly disillusioned and pessimistic man.[61] He was adamant in his belief that the Government had pursued a disastrous policy in America and that further calamities lay ahead. Yet he could not console himself with the belief that either the public or even some sections of the Parliamentary Opposition understood the danger in which the country stood. He thus despaired as a recluse at Hayes until Richmond's public championing of American independence stirred him to declare his opinions.

The events of that day have often been described.[62] No doubt Chatham's appearance, in black velvet and wrapped in flannel, supported on crutches, was melodramatic, and intentionally so, but nothing can rob the occasion of its place as one of the great events in parliamentary history. Although the drama and the emotion of the scene cannot be recaptured, the essentials of Chatham's speech can. Richmond spoke to his Address, proclaiming that it was impossible for Britain to subdue the colonies, still more unlikely that she would be able to deal with France as well. For the constitution and economy of Britain to survive, American independence must be recognised. He moved for the withdrawal of troops from America and for the resignation of ministers. Chatham argued against Richmond's address from several points of view. To abandon the colonies would be a confession of national humiliation as well as a preliminary to economic ruin. He refuted Richmond's contention that Britain was militarily incapable of retaining the colonies and, at the same time, waging war successfully upon France. He proclaimed the (very dubious) constitutional idea that the King could not consent to dismembering the Empire. As he concluded, Richmond, with courtesy and dignity, attempted to take up Chatham's argument that the nation could sustain a double war. As Chatham rose to reply to these observations, he collapsed. He lingered for five weeks before his death on 11 May 1778.

The removal of Chatham from the political scene had little immediate political effect. Portland and Burke, indeed, were not sorry to see the last of him.[63] The mantle of the departed statesman fell upon Shelburne, a man who was regarded with equal distrust but less regard by the Rockinghams than Chatham had been.[64] But the divisions in the Opposition continued much as before. Camden, as was his way, did what he could to compose them, recognising that 'the Ministers cannot go on & unless the King can be keeping us divided make a practical bargain with one set, in order to break the other, he must be obliged to widen his bottom'.[65] All that can be said, however, is that the divisions in the Opposition did not become worse in what remained of the session.

Although the long session was now far advanced there

remained enough combustible material to light some small political fires. The most dramatic of these was undoubtedly the mysterious sailing of the French Toulon fleet on 13 April for an undisclosed destination. Fearing for the security of the British Isles, Sandwich was unwilling to allow a British fleet to sail until the destination of the Toulon fleet was known. The British fleet, therefore, did not put to sea until 9 June. Naturally, the Opposition made much of this delay, arguing that it was a further instance of the hopeless incompetence which had consistently marked the conduct of the war and brought such disasters upon the country.[66] The Opposition continued to harass the ministers by probing into their conduct of the war. North and Germain, in particular, were the regular targets for vitriolic tongue-lashings from Fox and Burke. Such an episode took place when the unfortunate Burgoyne returned to face the Commons, and to face a demand for a committee of enquiry into the Saratoga campaign.[67] When to all the Opposition activity of the session 1777–8 arising from the American war is added the emergence of Economical Reform as an issue and a revival of trouble in Ireland,[68] then it is clear that British politics were beginning to discard the the lethargy of earlier years. Important issues of imperial government, military strategy and economic management urgently needed attention. Although it cannot be maintained that the Opposition had brought about this change of fortune, and while its differences over American Independence remained chronic, it nevertheless remains true that the session of 1778 had witnessed political changes of considerable significance. The session had been the most promising and most active for the Rockingham Whigs for many years.

Indeed, such was the state of the ministry, and, in particular, the demoralisation of North, that the King found it necessary once more to agree to soundings with the refreshed and revitalised Opposition. Lord North's morale had been shattered by Saratoga, by the remorseless verbal poundings of Fox and Burke and by the increasing number of issues which were beginning to rain on him. On 6 May he wrote to the King an ominous letter. 'Every hour convinces me more of the necessity your Majesty is under of putting some other person than myself at the Head of your affairs . . . a man of great abilities, who can chuse decisively; one capable of forming wise plans, and of combining and connecting the whole force and operations of government.'[69] North's demoralisation was compounded by the sense of shame which he felt when he reflected that he lacked the courage of his own conviction that he was not fit to govern the country.[70] George III was not prepared to allow Lord North to resign, even if North had had the courage to do so. North was now all that stood between the King and the Opposition, the only barrier between the attempt to preserve and the will to abandon the Empire in America. At the same time, while North longed to retreat from responsibility he was in some curious way attracted by power. His sense of loyalty to the King and, perhaps, his own ambition, were too powerful to allow him to perform the act of political suicide which he was several times in the next few years to threaten. Nevertheless, he did try once more to form a restrengthened ministry. At the end of May it was announced that a new ministry was to be formed in which Lord Weymouth was to have the Treasury and Thurlow the Great Seals, and, a ministry moreover, in which Fox was to be included.[71] The Rockinghams smelled a rat, or, at least, glimpsed a trap. Richmond wondered '*who the persons are* who have weight enough with his Majesty to bring about the plan proposed', and complained at the lack of information concerning 'the number and stations of others, the plan of measures to be pursued, and many other considerations'.[72] Lord John Cavendish was extremely unhappy at the mysterious affair. 'I do not think this a desirable time to our friends to have an offer.'[73] Rockingham found the offer, if it can be called an offer, quite unsatisfactory because it was by no means as extensive as he would have wished to see and it contained no stipulations about changes of policy.[74] The Opposition accepted the prospect of a further period of opposition, and North unhappily agreed to soldier on.[75]

One of the most important effects of the session of 1778 was to polarise politics ever more strongly between North and Rockingham. With Chatham gone, the leadership of the still disunited Opposition now lay unquestionably in Rockingham's hands. On a lengthening list of issues, America, Economic Reform and Ireland, the Rockinghams proclaimed policies and ideas which stood in contradistinction to those of the court. Furthermore, the prospect that a ministry led by Rockingham might take office, absolutely unthinkable a year earlier, was now beginning—and just beginning—to be imaginable. The ministry was more divided, demoralised and unsettled than it had ever been before. Although the situation of Great Britain in 1778 should not be exaggerated—in terms of resources she was able to conduct a long war on several fronts—nevertheless, her diplomatic position looked unpromising and war with France was expected on all sides. George III realised all this. Indeed the key to the domestic political situation for the next three years was the King's steely determination to keep Lord North in office. From every point of view, he was indispensable to George III but he was already beginning to wilt. For the time being, the King was able to supply the deficiencies of North's character and, to some extent, to help to keep him in office. Only the will of George III now stood between Lord North and the prospect of the Opposition, or any part of it, coming into office on terms other than those which the King would have countenanced.

Chapter 18

The War, the Empire and the Rockingham Whigs 1778–9

The context in which the struggle between George III and the Rockingham Whigs was to be resolved was established less by the day-to-day activities of British politicians than by the outcome of the military struggle in the colonies and the naval war in the Atlantic. The strategy adopted by the British Government in the wake of Saratoga was an uncertain combination of conciliation and military retrenchment. The Conciliation Commission never had a chance of success. The Commissioners reached America in June but they were in a weak bargaining position. Secure in the protection of the French alliance, the Americans could afford to take a hard line with the Commission. They were not interested in anything less than a British recognition of American independence. In November 1778 the Commissioners returned home having achieved nothing.[1] Meanwhile, the Government was reconsidering its overall war strategy. At least 30,000 additional troops were needed if the colonies were to be retained. But where were these men to come from? Who was to train, equip and despatch them? These daunting problems occupied the Government in 1778. Unless Washington could be defeated in the next campaign it would be necessary to switch the military effort from the hostile and unwelcoming inland to the more vulnerable coastal towns and ports, where damaging military and naval strikes might wreak havoc upon American commerce. The army would remain in America but would fall back from Philadelphia to New York. In other words, the idea of a naval war was beginning to appeal to the British. British ministers were transferring their attention from a long-term land war in America to the expectation of quick (and cheap) victories against the French in the West Indies, which would bring the new allies scurrying to the conference table. The humiliation of Saratoga would be forgotten amidst glorious victories in the West Indies.[2] The new policy, however, had two weaknesses. In March 1778 when the policy was decided, the navy had less than fifty sea-worthy ships of the line. The thinking behind the new policy might have been sound but the policy could not effectively be implemented until the ships became available. And this led to a second fault in the plan. Precious time was being allowed the Americans to transform their new-found independence into an unshakeable nationhood. During the military stalemate of 1778–81 any lingering prospects of reconquering America disappeared.

With the passing of time, and the continuing failure of the British to effect a decisive improvement in the fortunes of the war, Lord North once more began to wish for the calm waters of retirement but the King, in November 1778, refused to release his minister.[3] North remained loyal to his master, but he had no heart for the political ordeal which now loomed and to which he realised he was unequal. He became more indecisive than ever. During 1779 departmental heads were increasingly left to act upon their own initiative; there resulted a lamentable lack of co-ordination between them. The ministry of North in 1779 was virtually moribund. The most notorious example of his inability to govern was his failure to replace his Secretary of State for the Northern Department, Lord Suffolk, who had become incapacitated in January 1778. North was unwilling either to disturb Suffolk or risk the disruption of the ministry which might follow from attempts to replace him. In spite of the King's entreaties, North could not bring himself to fill the vacant office.[4] In some ways, his reluctance to do so is perfectly understandable given the restlessness and ambition of some of his colleagues. He considered Sandwich for the office, but could not find a candidate for the Admiralty to replace the

First Lord.[5] North next tried to dispose of the office to Hillsborough, but the Bedfords, who had hated Hillsborough for a
decade, were not prepared to see him in a Secretaryship now.[6]
The Bedfords, indeed, had a candidate of their own for the
office. This was young Lord Carlisle, who had headed the
peace commission. North tried to accommodate him with an
offer of the Board of Trade, separated from the American
Department. This offer not only offended Carlisle for its
inadequacy but it infuriated Germain who, naturally, did not
like to see his department truncated in this manner. There were
others who were determined to profit from the uproar which
North's offer to Hillsborough caused. Alexander Wedderburn,
still yearning for his peerage, stirred up a hornet's nest of
intrigue in an effort to gain it. William Eden also tried to prise
a substantial office out of North. It was little wonder that he
wished to retreat from public life. During this period, however,
North was being carefully watched by John Robinson and
Charles Jenkinson who reported his moods and sentiments to
George III. The King was thus well placed to know his
minister's feelings and, when necessary, assist and encourage
him to remain in office.[7] He wrote to North on 25 October 1778
instructing him to prepare a plan 'to effect an Early and Constant attendance during the next Session'.[8] North agreed to do
so though he held out no great hopes for success.[9] Indeed, on
10 November he wrote to the King, asserting 'That the Publick
business can never go on as it ought, while the Principal & most
efficient offices are in the hands of persons who are either
indifferent to, or actually dislike their situation'. North concluded that the country needed 'one directing Minister, who
should plan the whole of the operations of Government'.[10]
But he never believed that he enjoyed the qualifications for
that role. Nevertheless, he was prepared to soldier on for
another session.

The Rockingham Whigs were now waiting for events outside
their control to decide their future. The party was not popular
in the country. Burke remarked that the people 'condemn the
Ministry; but they do not look to the opposition'.[11] Yet this,
together with the fact that the country was at war with France,
and in 1779 was to face an invasion threat, did not deter the

Rockinghams from persisting with their opposition to the ministry and to the Court. The fear of being labelled unpatriotic did not inhibit Fox. With characteristic frankness, he told the Commons on 26 November 1778:

> 'I will take that part which appears to me to be, though bad, the best; I must, consequently, use all my exertions to remove the present ministry by using every means in my power to clog them in this House, to clog them out of this House, and to clog everything they engage in while they continue in office; and I will do so because I consider this to be less ruinous than to submit any longer to their blundering system of politics.'[12]

The Rockinghams, indeed, found in the disasters and humiliations which befell the country in the next few years indisputable confirmation of the truth of the charges they had for years levelled against the court system. They did not think of secession. They believed that in the political system of the nation they now had not merely a useful but a necessary constitutional function to perform. Having for years exposed the evils of the court system, at whatever cost to themselves, it was now their duty to destroy it. With this in mind, Rockingham assembled his men in town for the session of Parliament which began on 27 November 1778.[13]

The parliamentary session of 1778–9 was to be dominated by three issues: the problem of Ireland, the court martial of Admiral Keppel and the prosecution of the war. This latest instalment in the recurring issue of Anglo-Irish relations involved Irish commerce and had arisen from the interruption of Irish trade occasioned by the American war. The British governing class had learned the lesson of America, that Ireland must be conciliated not alienated. Consequently there was general acceptance in Parliament of the need to take measures to assist the recovery of Irish trade.[14] As early as 7 April 1778 the Government introduced proposals into the Commons permitting the direct importation into the colonies from Ireland of all goods except woollens,[15] permitting colonial products to enter Ireland (except Indigo and Tobacco), and abolishing the duties on certain articles passing from Ireland to England.

There was little opposition during committee on 8 and 9 April and, even on second reading, when the interests likely to be adversely affected by the bill had been able to organise themselves, the ministry won the division by 126–77.[16] Further proceedings on the bill occupied the month of May and resulted in the exclusion of certain commodities from its operation (including woollens, glass, cotton manufactures),[17] but the bill received the royal assent on 28 May.

Edmund Burke, in contrast to his factious conduct over the Absentee Tax in 1773, played a prominent and worthy role in attempting to persuade ministers to act generously towards Ireland. In so doing, he severely compromised the security of his parliamentary seat. Burke proceeded, as usual, upon a pragmatic recognition of British interests. If America were lost, then the rest of the Empire must be secured. 'Our late Misfortunes have taught us the danger and mischief of a restrictive, coercive, and partial policy.' Indeed, it would be to the mutual advantage of both countries to adopt a freer trading relationship. 'The prosperity, arising from an enlarged and Liberal System, improves all its objects; and the *participation* of a Trade with flourishing Countries is much better than the *monopoly* of want and penury.'[18] But the merchants of Bristol feared that they would be affected adversely by the bill and demanded that Burke actively oppose it. Burke flatly refused to do so. He declared that he was 'not ready to take up or lay down a great political system for the convenience of the hour'.[19] Adopting an almost functional view of Whig principles, Burke laid down the considerations which ought to inform all political actions, 'promoting the common happiness of all those, who are in any degree subjected to our legislative Authority; and of binding together in one common tie of Civil Interest, and constitutional Freedom, every denomination of Men amongst us'.[20] Burke taught the Rockingham Whigs to learn the lesson of America. In a spirit of conciliation, for example, they supported a bill relaxing the operation of the penal laws against Irish Catholics. Unless religious toleration prevailed, according to Burke, 'Whiggism would certainly be nothing more than the name of a faction'.[21] In Irish affairs in 1778, then, the Rockingham Whigs acted an honourable and not unprincipled part.

The British commercial concessions of 1778, however, were insufficient to protect the Irish from the continuing and worsening economic effects of the American war. In their wake came not only the Volunteer Movement but also a rapid proliferation of non-importation agreements, modelled on American precedents. These expressed Irish anger at the continuing imperial economic restrictions which were widely held to blame for the chronic unemployment and commercial depression which swept Ireland in 1779. The Volunteer Movement, on the other hand, was a natural attempt to provide for civilian defence, ostensibly against the French, but an organised militia such as the Volunteer Movement could just as easily be turned against the British. Furthermore, the emergence of leaders of this embryonic nationalist movement, Grattan and Flood, was an ominous sign for the future of British rule in Ireland. As the economic situation of Ireland worsened in the spring and summer of 1779, Rockingham himself began to have fears for the preservation of public order and the continued attachment of Ireland to the mother country. Unlike Burke, he had vast estates in Ireland, and although he denied that he was motivated by a preoccupation with his rent roll,[23] he was alarmed at reports of popular feeling in and around Wicklow, where he held estates. The ministry refused all requests to consider further economic concessions to the Irish. After consultations with Edmund Burke, Rockingham moved in the Lords on 11 May 1779 for information on the state of Ireland. Supported by Shelburne, Rockingham attacked the ministry's handling of the Irish crisis.[24] Neither of them can have been unaware of the repercussions of their speeches in Ireland.[25] They might, in fact, have had some effect. North's failure to act—in spite of continued pleas from the servants of the paralised ministry in Ireland —infuriated the Irish. In the future they were to look to Rockingham, Shelburne, Fox and Burke to concede further free trade concessions and, ultimately, legislative independence.

The great party issue of the session of 1779 and one which, frankly, occupied the Rockinghams more than the affairs of Ireland, was the court martial of the Rockinghamite Vice-Admiral Keppel. The origins of this dispute go back to the indecisive outcome of the battle of Ushant.[26] Keppel's failure to

engage the French fleet on 23 July 1778 off Ushant undoubtedly deprived Britain of a much-needed naval victory now that
Spanish intervention in the war was merely a matter of time.
On the other hand, the French fleet he encountered was
larger than he had anticipated and, at least, he succeeded in
maintaining the British fleet intact under his command. The
political world, and the newspapers, were divided over the
outcome of the battle.[27] The Opposition, naturally, exulted in
his success.[28] The ministry, however, was more reticent,
although it did nothing at this stage to register its public
disapproval of Keppel's behaviour.[29] Probably the matter
would have ended there had there not appeared in *The Morning
Intelligencer* on 15 October an accusation that Sir Hugh Palliser,
Keppel's second in command, had sought to undermine
Keppel's authority and had acted incompetently. Palliser was a
proud and touchy man, sensitive to any slight upon his competence. Perhaps he over-reacted when he demanded that Keppel
sign a statement not only completely exonerating him but
doing so at the expense of Keppel himself. The Admiral, not
surprisingly in view of Palliser's friendship with Sandwich,
refused to do anything of the kind.[30] Palliser, thereupon,
retaliated by writing a partial defence of his conduct in *The
Morning Post* of 5 November 1778, an action which found few
defenders apart from King George III.[31] A first-rate public
scandal involving the honour and integrity of a hero of the
Opposition on the one hand, and a friend of the Court on the
other, ensured that much more would be heard of the Ushant
engagement in the 1778–9 session of Parliament.[32]

When Parliament reassembled for the new session on 28
November the Earl of Bristol in the Lords, speaking for the
Opposition, demanded an enquiry into the battle of Ushant.
Sandwich defended Palliser, denying that an enquiry was
necessary, and thereby imputed blame to Keppel. His speech
marked the formal, public attachment of the ministry to
Palliser's cause.[33] Battle was now joined. In the Commons on
the same day both Keppel and Palliser spoke, the former with
caution and moderation, the latter, asserting that he did not
fear an enquiry.[34] But on 9 December Keppel, not Palliser, was
told to prepare his defence for court martial proceedings. Two

days later an astonished House of Commons heard that Keppel, not Palliser, was to be made the scapegoat for Ushant.[35] The whole affair, with its flavouring of persecution, was tailor-made to touch the tender susceptibilities of the Rockinghams. The integrity of Keppel and of the Whig aristocracy was at stake in this latest sinister move of the Court. In short, nothing could have been better calculated to revive Rockinghamite suspicions of secret influence and its insidious spread into all quarters of national life.

Early in 1779 at Portsmouth Vice-Admiral Keppel was court martialled. Proceedings there monopolised the attention of the public for the five weeks of their duration. It was not only an important political and naval affair but also a significant social occasion. Keppel basked in some heady self-congratulation, encouraged no doubt by the steady stream of Rockinghamites who made the pilgrimage from town to enjoy the case and applaud their hero. Palliser was unable to substantiate any of the charges which were made against Keppel.[36] Furthermore, Palliser was able to produce only a few witnesses in his favour. Keppel, on the other hand, read a defence to the Court which was a master-piece of controlled bitterness and scarcely concealed integrity and self-righteousness. (This was not surprising because none other than Edmund Burke had played a large part in its composition.)[37] Beside the majesterial cadences of Burke, Palliser's complaints and charges looked petty and spiteful. Amidst general rejoicing Keppel was discharged on 11 February 1779.[38] Illuminations, riots and bonfires spread with the news through the country. The city of London voted Keppel its freedom and this was followed by a stream of congratulatory messages from towns, counties, mercantile bodies and gilds. To judicial acquittal and popular rejoicing was now added parliamentary exoneration. On 12 February 1779 the Commons formally thanked Keppel for his 'courage, conduct and ability' and the Lords followed suit four days later.[39] Upon the crests of this wave of public sympathy the Rockingham Whigs sought to take parliamentary advantage of the Keppel trial.

The acquittal of Keppel left Palliser open to charges of negligence. Keppel refused to press them, but Palliser was honour bound to demand a trial. The King, realising that Palliser might become a political liability, followed Weymouth's advice: that Palliser in the present circumstances should be dismissed to avoid a hue and cry in the Commons.[40] Charles Fox, however, would not be denied. On 19 February in the Commons he moved for the removal of Palliser. The timing was unfortunate for, on that very morning, unknown to Fox, Palliser had submitted his resignation and his court martial had been decided upon.[41] The ministry stood its ground and on its dignity, refusing to discuss the subject while a court martial was pending. In some embarrassment and confusion, Fox had to withdraw his ill-timed motion.[42] If, with their defence of Keppel, the Rockingham Whigs had found a more popular subject than for some years, then they seemed determined to throw away that advantage. Fortunately, they saw that it was wiser to leave the unfortunate Palliser alone for the time being and to attack the big guns in the ministry, especially the First Lord of the Admiralty. On 23 February Fox moved for papers respecting the Brest fleet.[43] This was only a preliminary to a formal assault upon Sandwich's naval strategy throughout the campaign of 1778. On 3 March Fox censured him for sending out Keppel with a fleet of inadequate size to engage the French. Ministers tooks this as an issue of confidence. Although they emerged victorious from the division they were decisively mauled in debate. North, Germain and Sandwich wilted under the blast from the Opposition benches. The division figure of 204–170 was startling. Although the low ministerial figure reflected poor organisation rather than loss of support, the Opposition vote was an ominous portent to North.[44] Fox should have moved in for the kill, but he waited too long, and when he attacked he did so on too many fronts at once. On 8 March he over-reached by attacking all at the same time the ministry's domestic, American, European and Naval policies. North defended his ministry with no little vigour, a fact that was reflected in the division figure, 246–174.[45] The Opposition showed that with proper organisation and on the right issue it could hold 170 men in town for a wide-ranging and comprehensive attack upon the ministry.[46] But it could not do so indefinitely. On 15 March the Commons

N

debated Dunning's motion on the power of the Admiralty Board to order a court martial. This would have been an excellent opportunity on which to attack the Government a month earlier, but interest in the Keppel–Palliser affair was by now fast ebbing. The Opposition was defeated by 228–135.[47] The ministry was able to beat off the first real challenge it had had to face in years with considerable ease once it organised itself. The session was advancing and Members were leaving town. Moreover, the news of the war was favourable. The capture of St Lucia and the securing of St Vincent left the West Indies safe for the British fleet. Furthermore, the Opposition campaign seemed to be something of a two-man show, staged to display the debating genius of Charles James Fox and to publicise the integrity of Keppel. For the rest of the session the Opposition's campaign was almost entirely in the hands of these two men, who recited the same arguments and went over the same ground time after time. (Burke took surprisingly little part in these debates for reasons that have never been much discussed. He may have shared in the widespread feeling that Keppel was using the Opposition to protect himself.) To many independent Members, moreover, the Keppel case smacked of personal rancour and private malice. In the eighteenth century the independent Members disliked bringing the services into disrepute and, having made their opinions of the Keppel incident clear to the ministry and the King, they were not prepared to be made the playthings of party politics. Although they might criticise Sandwich they were not prepared to join the Opposition in its series of bitterly personal attacks upon the First Lord which occupied much of what remained of the session.[48] Such personal rancour seemed irrelevant to the danger in which the country stood of a combined French-Spanish invasion. In spite of their vigour and their persistence, Fox and Keppel lost much of the support which, earlier in the session, they had enjoyed.

Throughout the session, the inevitable accompaniment to the Keppel trial was the Opposition's constant attack upon the American policy of the Government. By the time the session opened on 26 November 1778 the Rockinghams' policy, voiced principally now by Fox, was well-established. It proceeded from the assumption that the British could not subdue the Americans. Their attempt to do so had drawn the French into the war in an attempt to take advantage of her colonial embarrassments and Spain might yet follow her example. Tactically it would be wise for the British Government to recognise American independence and to proceed to lay the foundations of a sound commercial relationship with her, leaving Britain free to pursue the war upon her real enemies, the Bourbons. The Rockinghams by now rejected the possibility that some formula weakening the right of Parliament to tax the colonies might be the answer to the American problem. The Rockinghams argued that the country's resources should not be wasted in a fruitless war in the colonies, but ought to be harnessed in a national war against the Bourbon powers. Most Englishmen, even George III, agreed tht it was desirable to concentrate resources against the Bourbons, but as yet very few believed that it was necessary to abandon the Empire in America, perhaps to the French, in order to do so. Fox, therefore, had constantly to discriminate between the two wars. In his speech in the debate on the Address on 26 November 1778, he was at pains to emphasise that the war against France was a legitimate struggle against the traditional enemy of the country, its interests, its colonies and its constitution. The war against America was a war against Englishmen, a bottomless pit into which the North Government seemed bent on pouring British men and money. It was therefore not worth prosecuting. Fox avoided discussion of the vexed question of the rights of Parliament. He never argued that Parliament had no right to prosecute the war against the colonies, only that to prosecute such a war was inexpedient. The Declaratory Act had stated that Parliament's right to tax the colonies existed 'in all cases whatsoever'. Because the Declaratory Act left no loopholes, Fox had to ignore it. But he did not and could not afford to evade the argument of ministers that it was not for Parliament to tell the King what kind of war he might and might not pursue. He responded by asserting that the Rockingham party had no wish to take away any part of the King's executive prerogatives, but it maintained that it was part of Parliament's constitutional duty to refuse to support either a policy of which it disapproved or a set of men in which it had no confidence.

As the session proceeded, the Opposition sought to demonstrate the validity of these arguments with reference to current events and particular instances. At the beginning of the session, for example, the Rockinghams threw up their hands in horror at the behaviour of the Conciliation Commissioners in America. On their arrival in America they had issued a manifesto to the Americans, threatening them with devastation and destruction if they persisted in their alliance with the French. The Chathamites found this as distasteful as Rockingham found it repugnant. Both wings of the Opposition brought their friends to town for the beginning of the session.[49] They decided to attack the ministry on the constitutional point that the waging of war was part of the royal prerogative; therefore the advice tended by the ministers to the Commissioners was unconstitutional, infringing, as it seemed to do, the royal prerogative. In the Lords the amendment to the Address was lost by 67–35, in the Commons by 226–107.[50] It was just after the opening of the session, however, that the Rockinghams became absorbed in the Keppel affair. They failed, therefore, to launch a sustained attack upon the constitutional aspects of the ministry's American policy.[51] It was not, indeed, until after the Easter recess that the Opposition mounted a lively and well-supported onslaught upon the ministry's American policy. The Opposition settled down to some serious business and on 29 March secured the appointment of a Committee of Enquiry into the Conduct of the War. The Committee sat from 22 April to 30 June 1779. On 29 April in the Committee Opposition motions to consider the conduct of Cornwallis were defeated by 180–155 and 181–158.[52] Unwisely, the King and North treated their close shave rather too lightly, believing that Opposition had shot its bolt for the session.[53] The could not have been more mistaken. Opposition members were so jubilant after the division on 29 April that, after a meeting of party leaders on 1 May at Savile's London residence,[54] they kept up the pressure by bringing forward a motion for a parliamentary examination of Cornwallis. North, sensing that the feeling of the House was against him, did not oppose it.[55] While this was proceeding, and the Committee was

rumbling towards an inconclusive end on 30 June, the Opposition occasionally brought forward motions to test opinion in
the House. Sir William Meredith, however, did not divide the
House on 11 June when he moved for peace with America.[56] A
few days later the Opposition's motion resisting the prorogation
of Parliament until the Committee of the Whole on the
Conduct of the War had concluded its deliberations was
defeated by 142–70.[57] On the last day of the session Lord
John Cavendish's motion advising the ministers to concentrate
the nation's resources on the war against the Bourbons was lost
by 156–80.[58] The session of 1778–9, like its predecessor, found
the Rockingham Whigs active and, within the bounds of
what an opposition party could reasonably hope to achieve,
tolerably successful. They had tested the ministry's nerve and
run it close in Parliament on more than one occasion. They had
enjoyed a good deal of public sympathy over Keppel's court
martial and had made their opinions and influence felt on
matters relating to Ireland and the conduct of the war.

The significant advance in the political weight of the Opposition and the corresponding weakening in the cohesion of the
ministry was recognised during the session. In January 1779
negotiations to take some leading members of the Opposition
into the ministry were revived. Fox was involved in them at the
outset for on 24 January 1779 he wrote to Rockingham about
the desirability of taking office should the occasion arise. He
asserted that it would be preferable to serve the country in
office than by persisting in a 'fruitless opposition'. He wanted
to know Rockingham's terms and conditions for office and
asked him if he would have 'anything to do with any Ministry,
that is *not entirely* of your own framing'. Furthermore, he wanted
to know what Rockingham's reaction would be if a coalition
between part of the ministry and part of the Opposition could
be negotiated.[59] In a letter to Burke, written on the same day,
Fox revealed his ambitions a little more clearly than he had
to Rockingham. With disarming frankness, he told Burke that
the Rockinghams would never be able to form a ministry
exclusively from their own number, and complained about
their apparent distrust of the King and their determination to
force him to employ them.[60] Fox believed that it was idle to

preserve the party's principles and virtue in a powerless Opposition. He believed that it was far better to take practical steps to reduce royal influence than to do nothing about it. If the Rockinghams would not take office when a reasonable opportunity to do so occurred, they should not complain if others did. In effect, Fox was warning the Rockinghams lest they present unreasonable terms in a future negotiation. Richmond, to whom Fox may have written a similar letter, certainly interpreted Fox's attitude as such a threat. He told Fox that in any negotiation 'we must know precisely, either what change of measures is proposed by others, or the detail of that share of Government which is offered, to enable us to carry on our plans. . . . Without one of these it is merely an offer of places without power, under a bargain to screen those whom we have been so long condemning'. As to Fox's scarcely concealed threat of taking office with some Rockinghamites, Richmond merely remarked that in that event 'I hope and trust we shall not be dismayed, but still shall persevere in resisting what we think wrong, and in preventing some mischief, it we cannot do much positive good'.[61]

Although Fox's actions may be dismissed as mere political ambition he had, nevertheless, raised interesting and, for the future, significant questions. It was taken for granted, with the passing of Chatham, that in a new administration formed from opposition elements the Rockingham Whigs would obviously be the dominant element. But how dominant were they to be? To what extent would there be a clean sweep of the old ministers? What terms were they to insist upon as a condition of coming into office? To what extent did the Rockinghams realise that if George III refused to take them as a party ministry, then they would have to work with other groups, especially that led by Shelburne? How would Shelburne regard such a prospect and how should he be treated? Richmond's answer, however consistent with orthodox Rockinghamite theory it may have been, did not adequately deal with these questions. Fox was sharp enough to perceive that the country would view with great distaste the picture of George III bowing his head to party government. He appreciated that without royal confidence a ministry could not long stand. Since the soundings of the previous year, Fox had manifestly grown impatient of the political self-righteousness of the Rockingham party. What set Fox apart from the Rockinghamites was his rejection of their preoccupation with political principles which condemned the party to years of futile opposition. This is not to say that Fox was unprincipled. He was pragmatic enough to see that the court system could only be changed by a change of men. Such a change could take place as well by negotiation as by the unlikely prospect of the parliamentary overthrow of the North administration.

In the event, the 'negotiations' came to nothing. North, ever anxious to seek escape from the responsibilities of office, wished to bring in Grafton, Camden and Fox, a coalition to be made palatable to the King by keeping the Treasury in the hands of men loyal to the Crown, like Weymouth or Gower. The King allowed the talks to proceed.[62] Weymouth saw Grafton on 2 February, but he saw little prospect for coalition and nothing came of the soundings.[63] Like several other such soundings in these years, these 'negotiations' created much interest in the Opposition, whose leading members had to define their terms and conditions. Because the negotiations of these years never became serious discussions for a change of ministry, this process of definition was not taken as far as it might have been. The consequences of this fact were to leave the Rockinghams unprepared for power, even when the North ministry fell three years later.

Notwithstanding the importance of the activities of the Opposition in the session of 1779, there can be no doubt that the most sensational event of the year was the threatened invasion of Great Britain in the summer. The Spanish had entered the war in 1779 anxious to recapture Gibraltar and, perhaps, Minorca, Jamaica and Florida (her losses in the Seven Years War). To this end she pressed upon the French the desirability of striking quickly at the heart of the British Empire. The combined fleets of France and Spain assembled 30,000 troops in sixty ships of the line in the Channel in June. The country faced a dangerous crisis when, incredibly, the cumbersome Bourbon fleets slipped inside the British Channel fleet. Everything now seemed to rest upon the redoubtable

Commander in Chief of the Army, Sir Jeffrey Amherst,[64] and the far more questionable state of the British home defences. Amherst kept his head while all around him were losing their nerve. He refused to be panicked by the North Cabinet into changing his troop dispositions whenever a panic seized them, as it did every few days. Nevertheless, it was as well that the country's home defences were not tested.[65] In the second half of August the Channel fleet took advantage of a change in the wind to enter Portsmouth for necessary revictualling. At about the same time the Bourbon fleets, stricken with illness among their crews, decided to withdraw.

By this time political differences on the war gave rise to partisanship on almost every conceivable matter. The Rockinghams were even able to find something to object to in the middle of the invasion scare itself. It was significant that some of the county meetings, assembled to raise volunteer regiments by subscription, expressed distinctly anti-ministerial sentiments.[66] Rockingham, however, believed that the raising of the militia in this way was illegal because the Lords had recently thrown out a bill which would have permitted the militia to be doubled in size.[67] Burke went to rather ridiculous extremes in upholding his master's views. Although he had never liked the subscriptions he was not content to dismiss them as 'calculated to cheat the people of their money' but went so far as to detect something sinister in the volunteer regiments which, he claimed, might be used to establish the secret influence of the Court on a military basis.[68]

The recess passed, then, with the Rockinghams feeling themselves out of sympathy with the widespread mood of patriotic fervour. In fact, the stronger the tide of patriotic fervour ran, the more deeply the Rockinghams nourished their hatreds. In this they were assisted by a voice from the past. General Burgoyne became formally attached to the Opposition during May 1778, just a few days after his return to England. He was stung with the refusals both of the King to allow him an audience and of the ministry to allow an enquiry into his conduct. Refusing an order to return to America on grounds of bad health, which were patently false, he proceeded to speak and vote with the Opposition, believing, after Saratoga, that military victory in America was impossible. In May 1779 there at last began the enquiry into his conduct which he had always wanted. He was much distressed at the uncertain nature of its conclusions. His relations with the ministry deteriorated further during the summer of 1779 until at the end of September he resigned his office. He now began to disclose to Rockingham private correspondence between himself and Germain, attempting to ingratiate himself with the Marquis and his party by playing upon their suspicions of incompetence and corruption in the conduct of the war. Rockingham, usually a good judge of character, was thoroughly taken in by the treacherous Burgoyne. In particular, Rockingham began to credit George III with a more direct and obtrusive participation in the court system than he had hitherto done.[69]

At the same time, and the coincidence is interesting, Burke was reaching a high point of indignation about the ruin into which the court system was leading the country. It was perhaps in October that he drew up some articles of impeachment against the ministers, the principles of which he wished to insert into an amendment to the Address in the new session. Grafton persuaded Rockingham to abandon this idea.[70] While Burke's hatred of the court system reached a new peak, he was naturally worried by the revival of gossip about negotiations with the Court and by the dilatoriness of his leader. He urged Rockingham to form his own plan, conformable to his previous statements. 'There is a cry among all your Lordship's friends, that something ought to be done.'[71] A sense of anticipation began to rise within Burke, almost as though he knew that great events were at hand. Rockingham concurred with his sentiments. He was quite unwilling to entertain any thoughts of further negotiations because he believed that the ministry was on the point of disintegration.[72] In the autumn and winter of 1779 the confidence of Burke and Rockingham began to infect the Opposition. One of its symptoms was the establishment of greater trust and cordiality between the Rockingham Whigs and the Chathamites than had existed for a decade. Shelburne announced in the Lords on 1 December 1779 that

'He had united with those with whom he had the honour to act for several years; their principles were the same; their future role of conduct was to be correspondent; whatever different opinions they might have held they no longer interefered with their general plan; they were confidentially and fully united in the great leading principle, of new men and new measures; if the salvation of the country was to be effected, it was only by those means; or if the country was to be saved from the ruin which threatened us on every side, it was only by a change of system.'[73]

Furthermore now that the Opposition was stronger and more united than for many years, the ministry of Lord North was almost on the point of disintegration.

The ministerial crisis had begun in March 1779 when Suffolk had died. North's suggestion that Hillsborough replace him met with the hostility of Wedderburn who threatened to resign. North let the matter drift for the sake of his peace of mind. He refused to risk his ministry for the sake of a Secretary. The paralysis within the ministry hardened because North's stomach for the political fight had gone. The ministry was kept in existence only by the will of the King. At his behest, Jenkinson and Robinson reported North's opinions and dispositions to the King, and kept the business of government moving with some semblance of energy. At the same time the experience and, in the circumstances, the indispensability of Sandwich and Germain, gave the ministry at least the appearance of continuity which was enough to conceal the fact that the first Minister was now merely a cipher. The King summed up the situation of Lord North when he wrote to Germain that 'although he is not entirely to my mind, and there are many things about him I wish were changed, I don't know who would do so well, and I have a great regard for him and a very good opinion of him'.[74] After the invasion crisis North's indecision froze into paralysis. Robinson was in despair. 'Nothing done, or attempting to be done, no attention to the necessary arrangements at home, none to Ireland, nothing to India, and very little I fear to foreign affairs, a Cabinet totally disjointed.'[75] Although Robinson and Jenkinson and, especially,

Sandwich, showed a little spirit, it was George III who kept the ministry together.[76] But even the King must have been worried at the prospects for the demoralised Government in the forthcoming session. In October, with Jenkinson's help, he sketched out contingency plans in case he had to treat with the Opposition as a last resort. North, indeed, was still groaning that 'nothing but a change of men can save the country'.[77]

The Bedfords had the same idea. They believed that they could force North's withdrawal and carry on the Government themselves.[78] In October, Gower, and in November, Weymouth resigned, hoping to bring the ministry down with them. George III was not to be bullied in this manner but his determination to retain his freedom of action meant that he would have to negotiate with the Opposition. This he did not mind doing, although 'it must be coalition with my administration, not the yielding the reins of Government to Opposition! I must be sure that Measures should not be changed'.[79] But Thurlow, the indispensable link between the King and the Bedfords, was sceptical of the likely success of the plan and thus no soundings were made.[80] It remained to fill the vacancies. This the King managed to achieve without changing the character of the ministry. Bathurst succeeded Gower and Hillsborough succeeded Weymouth. When the new session opened on 25 November 1779 the ministry had only just been able to survive. But by any standards it was quite unfitted to deal with one of the most sudden and surprising upheavals in politics and opinion in modern British history which now followed.

Part Five

CLIMAX

1780–2

Chapter 19

The Rockingham Whigs
and the Reform Movement
1779–80

If Lord North had known that the parliamentary session he was about to face at the end of 1779 was to be the most strenuous and tumultuous of any of the reign of George III until that time, then he would almost certainly have resigned. North's torment was already considerable enough. What made it so painful was the fact that there appeared to be no period to it. Both at sea and on land everything pointed to a long and bitter war. Since Saratoga it had been one of the primary strategic assumptions of the ministry that the war must be won at sea. Although the Bourbon powers had now given up the idea of invading England, their fleets enjoyed perfect freedom to roam the channel, and even controlled the West Indian waters. In America, South Carolina and Georgia were secure. In May 1779 Cornwallis had taken Charleston and moved into North Carolina but he had failed to press home his advantage. The constant British expectation that the colonies might individually be brought back to their allegiance was disappearing in the indecisive and fruitless campaigns. On all fronts the ministry was fighting a war which threatened to drag on indefinitely and inconclusively. News of further disturbances in Ireland filled North's cup of woe. In the last days of the recess he felt unable to face another long parliamentary session and he proceeded to go through his by now customary routine of begging to resign. He was chronically suspicious of the Bedfords, lamenting that 'everyone was leaving him, and were plotting to desert him and disgrace him, and overturn the King's government'.[1] He was hurt at the hostility which Thurlow manifested towards him.[2] But in spite of these facts and his further protestations that he was unable to take decisions, the King abruptly ordered him to stay at his post.[3] As on other occasions since 1766 George III's distaste for ministerial changes inclined him to cling to a minister whom he ought to have released from his responsibilities. For in politics, and certainly in war, nothing succeeds like success. North had already demonstrated his incapacity as War Minister. If George III wished to succeed in his objectives of destroying American independence and defeating the Bourbon powers, then he ought to have allowed him to resign. North's continued pleas to resign had, however, one consequence. 'I begin almost to doubt whether He does not mean to retire' wrote an alarmed Jenkinson to the King on 30 November.[4] Therefore, the King agreed to his Minister's demand that certain members of Opposition be sounded. The King, in fact, may have seen some advantages in North's suggestion for he was now beginning to worry at the bad news coming out of Ireland.[5] Yet the King permitted soundings to be made only on the condition that the integrity of the Empire be respected, the war carried on and *'no blame be laid on any* past measures'.[6]

The negotiations demanded by North proceeded in early December. The King saw Thurlow on 3 December and asked him to sound the Opposition. Thereupon Thurlow interviewed Camden but found him uninterested in office either for himself or his friends. The Rockinghams being excluded by the conditions of the negotiation, there was nothing left for Thurlow but to approach Shelburne.[7] Shelburne had no particular wish to help salvage the fortunes of the North ministry. To negotiate seriously with North would arouse the distrust of the Rockinghams and sour the cordial relationships which had existed between them during the last year. On the other hand, it would be unwise to return a direct negative to Thurlow's enquiries. Shelburne, therefore, chose a middle way, insisting that he was against American independence and in favour of further negotiations, suggesting at the same time, that the King ought to make a more specific offer rather than the generalities proffered by Thurlow.[8] The King was by no means discouraged by Shelburne's reply. On 11 December 1779 he permitted Thurlow to tell him that North's position need not stand in the way of some accommodation between himself and Shelburne.[9] This was still insufficient to satisfy Shelburne who ended the negotiation.[10] As a consequence the King was furious with the Opposition. 'Nothing less will satisfy them than a total change of Measures and Men; to obtain their Support I must deliver up my Person, my Principles, and my Dominions into their hands.'[11] Perhaps it was fortunate for the King that Lord North was recovering his spirits and his confidence. The latest eruption of popular disturbance in Ireland had galvanised him into action, and if his Irish policy was little more than an attempt to buy peace with further commercial concessions, it was better than nothing.[12]

These discussions, however insignificant in content, were not devoid of importance. They had succeeded in their first objective of giving North time to overcome his panic. Furthermore, the soundings of December 1779 mark the very faint beginnings of a *rapprochement* between the King and Shelburne. They also found Rockingham reflecting upon the situation of his own party. He assumed that the war could not be won, that the ministry, though corrupt and unsuccessful, was not becoming noticeably less popular and that the longer these conditions prevailed, the greater the injury which would be done to the liberties and constitution of the country. Rockingham mused: 'Perhaps a total change of *men* and *measures*, & *system* in the Governmt: [*sic*] of this country might have effect on the councils of some foreign countries . . . who might think that it was no longer a Court system to combat, but that the whole nation wd; unite & make the utmost efforts'.[13] Rockingham's long term objectives were clear: the overthrow of the North ministry and of the system of secret influence, peace with America and war on the Bourbons. For the present, however, he had to be content with making plans for the eagerly-awaited session of Parliament. Although he hoped that his friends would not take factious advantage of the difficulties

of the ministry over Ireland, he nevertheless gave his approval
to popular agitation in Ireland, because he believed that any
slower advance would not have been half as fruitful. Rockingham was determined to be on hand when Irish affairs were
discussed in Parliament and, mainly for that purpose, chose to
come to town a week before the opening of the session.[14] His
friends followed suit. They were in good humour, knowing
something of the uncertainty of North's position and its likely
effects upon the ministerial vote. Even the ministerialists
expected the Opposition to be formidable.[14] In that quarter,
the delicious feeling was spreading that the years of futile and
hopeless opposition might at last be at an end.[15]

The parliamentary session which opened on 25 November
1779 was to be dominated by the campaign for economical
reform. Attempts to reduce the influence of the Crown and
the ministry in Parliament were by no means new. They had
been an integral part of the old country and Tory platforms
of the late seventeenth and early eighteenth century; they
arose from the fear that if the executive encroached upon the
legislative organs of the state nothing could resist the corruption
of politicians by office and pensions, a corruption which would
spread rapidly through the body politic like a cancer. The
objective of the country party, however, was not to make
Parliament more efficient or more representative. It was to
restore the checks and balances in the constitution and the
proper separation between the executive and the legislature.
To this end, many suggestions were made towards the end of
the seventeenth century. Demands for the exclusion from
Parliament of office-holders, pensioners and contractors were
a powerful and popular political force at the turn of the
century.[16] Such demands, however, were natural at a time
when the size and scope of the bureaucracy were rapidly
increasing. In a similar way, the alleged reassertion of royal
power after 1760 was regarded with wide-spread suspicion.
Although modern research has shown that the influence of the
Crown was, in fact, diminishing after 1760, the Rockinghams
were by no means alone in asserting that it had systematically
increased.[17] Although, in strictly factual terms, it is true that
'the reformers stirred up a great deal of fuss about nothing',[18]

many contemporaries believed that the power and independence of Parliament were declining. It seemed to follow that this must be accompanied by an increase in the power of the executive branch of Government. The ministerial instability of the 1760s and the disasters of the second half of the 1770s, however, indicated that Government had not been *strengthened*. However mistakenly, the Rockingham party adopted this diagnosis of the political ills of the nation. To cure them, they advocated the re-establishment of the proper relationship between the executive and the legislature. This had always been implicit in their protests against Lord Bute and secret influence. Rockingham noted in a memorandum: 'Unhappily for the King & unhappily for this Country, the Idea & expectation of the extent of the Influence of the Crown was soon tried & succeeded almost in the very outset of His Majesty's Reign'.[19] Therefore the Rockingham party consistently sought to reduce the influence of the Crown.

It was perhaps no accident that proposals to attain this end first issued from the ex-Tory Dowdeswell. As early as 17 February 1768 he brought forward a motion to disfranchise revenue officers.[20] The bill was thrown out but it remained a symbol of Rockinghamite principles.[21] Two years later, on 12 February 1770, Dowdeswell moved a similar motion. The debate was significant in that it taught the Rockinghams that attacks on executive influence struck a chord with the independent country gentleman. Dowdeswell lost his motion by 263–188, a more than respectable minority figure.[22] The years after 1768 witnessed other types of pre-occupation with the influence of the Crown. As early as 1769 the Rockinghams had demanded an enquiry into Civil List expenditure when North asked Parliament to pay debts on the Civil List. The Rockinghams achieved nothing except to place on record their adherence to the principle of parliamentary scrutiny of royal expenditure.[23] This they reasserted a year later when the Opposition supported George Grenville's motion demanding the production of the Civil List accounts for 1769.[24] In April 1770 Dowdeswell stated quite clearly the theory of accountability. 'It was the duty parliament owed to its constituents, to desire some reassurances of that nature; that there was reason to believe the annual expence Vastly exceeded . . . it was the duty of parliament whenever the public money was apparently squandered to bad purposes, to make enquiry how it had been so squandered.'[25] Furthermore, given radical enthusiasm for Wilkes and Liberty, the rights of electors and, on a much more limited scale, for parliamentary reform the Rockinghams were forced to explain how they would deal with corruption. In supporting the petitioning movement, Dowdeswell said that the petitions 'call loudly for the exertion of public virtue, to strike at the roots of that corruption, by which the State is reduced to the most deplorable conditions both at home and abroad'.[26]

As we saw earlier, Edmund Burke in the *Thoughts* had much to say about corruption and its cure and his discussion is instructive of certain important elements in Rockinghamite theory. Burke not only rejected parliamentary reform but also the traditional nostrum of a *Place Bill*. The fact that he did so suggests that the Rockingham Whigs had inherited the ideas of the Pelhams. For, Burke did not wish completely to separate the legislature from the executive. It was necessary to maintain *some* connection between them. As Burke put it:

> 'It is not easy to foresee, what the effect would be of disconnecting with Parliament, the greatest part of those who hold civil employments, and of such mighty and important bodies as the military and naval establishments. It were better, perhaps, that they should have a corrupt interest in the forms of the constitution, than that they should have none at all.'

What Burke wished to remove was *secret* influence. 'I would not shut out that sort of influence which is open and visible, which is connected with the dignity and service of the State, when it is not in my power to prevent the influence of contracts, of subscriptions, of direct bribery, and those innumerable methods of clandestine corruption, which are abundantly in the hands of the Court.' But Burke certainly wished to retain offices, which might be filled by the men of the Rockingham party. Burke and his party colleagues were clearly anxious lest the corrupt influence of the Crown discredit the legitimate influence of the executive, and thus give rise to a clamour against it which might not be easily resisted.

In this manner, every financial novelty became the subject of immediate concern. Lord North's innocent Lottery Bill of 1771 was seen by Dowdeswell as 'an iniquitous project to bribe the servants of the public to betray their trust', and a means by which the Crown might attack the independence of Parliament.[27] In the same spirit the Rockingham Whigs opposed North's Regulating Act of 1773. As early as April 1772 Rockingham suspected that 'The Lucrative Offices, and Appointments relating to the E.I. Companys Affairs, will virtually fall into the Patronage of the Crown (to add) to the ways and means of corruption'.[28] This was why the Rockinghams were so keen to defend the chartered independence of the East India Company. If the patronage of the Company fell into the hands of the Court, then the court-dominated executive would ride roughshod over the constitutional rights of Parliament. In the same way, the outbreak of war in America was attributed by the Opposition not to political or diplomatic blunders but 'the indiscriminate support ministers received, to whatever measures they thought proper to propose, though ever so destructive . . .'.[29] This indiscriminate support existed because 'the influence and allurements of the Crown are so great and may be so exercised by his ministers—that even the sense of Parliament itself may be occasionally affected by them'.[30] And the system fed upon itself. If corruption had led to the war, then the war led to further corruption. It is not surprising, then, that the Rockinghams wanted peace. In the dark years of the 1770s the Rockinghams continued their crusade against the influence of the Crown but they needed a new Bute to explain the survival of the weak North ministry. Burke thought he had 'great reason to suspect that Jenkinson governs everything' and that 'To follow Jenkinson, will be to discover My Lord Bute, and My Lord Mansfield, and another person as considerable as either of them'.[31] Such a belief was not confined to the Rockingham Whigs. Even Wraxall commented upon the widespread rumours that 'As Lord Bute gradually retired into the shade of private Life, and became insensibly forgotten, Mr Jenkinson proportionably came forward in his own person, and on his own proper Merits'.[32]

Suspicion of the King in the minds of the Rockingham Whigs went back at least as far as the ministry of 1765–6 and George III's persistent refusal to discipline recalcitrant office-holders. Although they conformed to the traditional practice of criticising the King's ministers rather than the person of the monarch himself, there can be little doubt that they suspected George III himself of involvement in the system of secret influence. In 1777 Parliament was asked to pay debts of £600,000 on the Civil List. Scrupulous though King George III's handling of Civil List, Secret Service and Privy Purse money was,[33] the Rockinghams sniffed corruption and demanded the publication of secret service and pension fund accounts. It was not their intention to make Household expenditure more efficient, but rather to reduce the King's freedom of action in the constitution. In other words, the Rockingham Whigs were using one of the perennial deficits in the Civil List for political purposes. The debates of 1777, however, recognised the right of Parliament to investigate the Civil List. Even the ministers did not deny that. What separated the Government and the Rockinghams, then, was not a difference of principle over the right, but a question of expediency over how far Parliament ought to exercise its right.[34]

After Saratoga the impulse towards economic reform began to quicken.[35] On 2 March 1778 Thomas Gilbert protested against exorbitant expenditure and demanded a committee of enquiry to investigate abuses. On 9 March he moved to impose a tax of 25 per cent on placemen and pensioners and his motion was lost by the narrowest of margins, 147–141.[36] Perhaps it would have passed had not some Rockingham Whigs, including Fox, Burke and even Savile, voted *against* Gilbert's motion. That they did so should not occasion surprise. As Burke had stated in 1770, they were opposed only to *secret* influence. They had no wish to tax the innocent office-holder. Gilbert's motion was too sweeping for them for it affected the innocent as well as the guilty. There were other ways of dealing with the influence of the Crown. Even without the opposition of the Rockinghams, however, the ministry saw the danger signs and therefore agreed to Isaac Barré's motion for a Committee to Enquire into public expenditure.[37] It was not long before the Rockinghams joined in the assault on the ministry. There was much talk floating around about the unwarranted profits which contractors were making out of the war and Sir Philip Jennings Clerke decided to take advantage of it. His motion to bring in a bill excluding Contractors from the Commons was carried by 71–50 on 13 April 1778. On 1 May the bill passed its second reading by 72–61, but was lost by a hair's breadth on third reading, 113–109.[38] The moral was clear and the opportunity too good not to be repeated. In February 1779 Sir Philip Jennings Clerke reintroduced his bill and the same thing happened. Leave was given to bring in the bill by 158–43[39] and it passed its first two readings but the House refused to commit it.[40] Long before the Petitioning Movement of Christopher Wyvill, then, the Rockinghams had demonstrated their attachment to the country party remedies for curing the ills of the State. From these it was a natural progression to the adoption of a policy of economic reform.

The Yorkshire Movement clearly reflected the traditional political beliefs of the independents and freeholders of the counties. It had come into existence as a movement of opinion protesting against the allegedly incompetent and corrupt management of the war and demanding a reduction of the high taxes and wastefulness of the financial expenditure which supported it. But the Yorkshire Movement also owed much to two sources, the Middlesex reformers and the Rockingham Whigs. The Middlesex by-election of 1779 had revived metropolitan radicalism and given currency to the idea of the formation of an association of county committees.[41] This idea had arisen from the calling of two Middlesex county meetings, the second of which, on 22 November, provided for monthly county meetings while Parliament was sitting. But the issue went deeper than a question of the rights of electors and talk of an enquiry into the disorders in the country was heard. At a third meeting on 20 December Jebb addressed a freeholders' meeting on the virtues of an association of county committees. The idea of defending the rights of freeholders through a network of county committees, then, owed much to Middlesex.

But the Yorkshire movement was also influenced by the Rock-ingham Whigs.[42] Some of the moralistic aspects of the move-ment reflected old Rockinghamite platitudes. Wyvill's concern for honesty and virtue in politics, for the restoration of national harmony, for economy in government, for an end to corruption and extravagance and for the reduction of royal influence—his concern in all these things reflected the country party element in Rockinghamite ideology. Where Wyvill differed from Rockingham, essentially, was in his conviction that the influence of the aristocracy was just as great a threat to the country as that of the Crown. Wyvill's programme, first announced in a circular on 29 November, embraced the protection of the rights of freeholders, the reduction of influence in all its aspects and manifestations, and an increase in the number of county members. Wyvill proposed that a county meeting should be called to collect the sentiments of the York-shire freeholders and gentry, and prepare a petition to the Commons demanding economy and a reduction in the Civil List. By 8 December Wyvill had received over 200 encourag-ing replies to his initial circular.[43] He decided to go ahead with his plan for a county meeting to launch his petition, an endeavour in which his success would require the support of Rockingham.

Rockingham gave that support, much though he disliked Wyvill's wish to change the composition of Parliament.[44] Until Rockingham's agents actively encouraged Wyvill to proceed, the county was 'very tardy and lethargic'.[45] Rocking-ham saw no reason to resist a movement in his home county, most of whose objectives he sympathised with, as did many of his Yorkshire supporters.[46] Indeed, only by lending his support to the movement might the Marquis have been able to control and perhaps to direct its activities. Nevertheless, he was not prepared to tolerate 'opinions *doubtful in their effect*' among the objectives of the movement although he had no objection to economic reform petitions from Yorkshire and other counties. In short, Rockingham saw the Petitioning Movement as a useful adjunct to the parliamentary activities of his party which were already under way.[47] It is just a little unfair, therefore, to state that the Rockinghams, 'Eager to catch at the slightest measure of popular support, from the beginning of December ... were taking note of the preliminary hints from Yorkshire'.[48] The Rockinghams had already begun to formulate an economic reform programme and they would have exploited the issue in the next session of Parliament if the Yorkshire movement had never been heard of. No doubt, the expectation of enjoying popular support stimulated them to exploit the issue further, but it was not the only motivation. Burke had been preparing his plans of economic reform for weeks before Wyvill's activities had broken the surface of politics.[49] And if he had not, other counties would still have gone ahead. The fact is too frequently overlooked that Middlesex was to have a county meeting on 7 January 1780 which, in its turn, might have come to supply the impetus for the movement which the Yorkshire county meeting ultimately did supply.[50] In any case, the Petitioning Movement in the country had scarcely begun to move when the Rockinghams brought economic reform to Parliament.

On 7 December 1779 Richmond in the Lords moved for reform of the Civil List. Rockingham laid down the intellectual framework within which his party's sponsorship of economic reform operated.

'I declared that a *great reduction* of offices (sinecures, etc., etc.) which were now held by Persons in Parliament—must be made. I stated that very *early* after his Majesty's accession —the word was given out—that the power and influence of the Crown was sufficient to support any *men as ministers*, that Party was immediately, as it were, enlisted and arranged under that head ... of the Kings Friends—that that system had continued—that it was the grand support of the bad men and bad measures, and that without it, it would have been impossible for the country to have been so ruined and exhausted as it has been.'[51]

Although the Chathamites lined up behind the Rockingham Whigs, Richmond's motion was lost by 77–36. Shelburne continued the campaign in the Lords, moving on 15 December for a scrutiny of the Army extraordinaries. This was little more than a symbolic gesture, although Shelburne attempted to support his case by reference to specific instances of corruption, and his motion was easily defeated.[52] In the Commons, on the same day, Burke gave notice of his plan for economic reform, basing its need upon the proposition 'that the whole of our grievances are owing to the fatal and overgrown influence of the crown'. He promised that his plan would serve as the basis of economy and would reduce influence. He promised to save £200,000 a year and to eliminate fifty placemen.[53] The Rockinghams thus made public their commitment to economic reform and expressed their willingness to work with the county movement.

At first the leaders of the county movement was not very happy at the prospect of working with party politicians. It was not until 19 December that Rockingham received word that they would be welcome at the county meeting.[54] Anticipating that the party would attempt to influence proceedings, the movement's organisers skilfully sought to outmanoeuvre Rockingham. Although he made clear his sentiments upon reform and the conduct of the county meeting, Wyvill was able to do much as he wished. He insisted that the Rockinghams should have no veto upon the agenda and chairman of the meeting, and affirmed that petitions should be directed to the Commons alone, and not the Lords.[55] Furthermore, Wyvill envisaged something rather more substantial than the committees of correspondence which Burke had in mind; he was thinking in terms of a national association.[56]

Six hundred gentlemen and a few peers assembled at York for the long awaited county meeting on 30 December. These included Rockingham, the Dukes of Devonshire and Rutland, all the younger Cavendishes and all the MPs for constituencies within the county. It was a respectable rather than a popular gathering. The tone was very much set by Wyvill who stressed the independence of the meeting from party influence. He summarised the misfortunes of the country and declared that economic reform was the cure for them. He produced a petition to the Commons which summarised the philosophy of the movement. Deploring the economic effects of the war upon the country, it went on to complain at exorbitant salaries, unmerited pensions and other manifestations of the growing influence of the Crown. The petition demanded economy, redress of grievances and an enquiry into public expenditure. The petition was carried with only one dissentient, as might have been predicted. More important, however, was the carrying of a resolution late in the afternoon when many people had gone home. This provided for the establishment of a committee 'for effectually promoting the objects of the petition and to support that laudable reform, and such other measures as may conduce to restore the Freedom of Parliament'. This crucial last clause left the door open for parliamentary reform. And although nothing was formally decided at York about relations with other county committees there can be no doubt that Wyvill intended to promote the establishment of similar committees elsewhere. It is with this in mind that the meeting's decision to exclude peers and MPs from the Yorkshire County Committee should be interpreted. Wyvill had laid down the objectives of the Petitioning Movement and intended to secure their implementation by keeping control of the movement in his own hands. In view of these facts, it is a little surprising that Rockingham and Burke were so pleased with the outcome of the Yorkshire county meeting. They had a few reservations. Burke was disappointed that Wyvill's petition had been voted rather than one prepared by the Rockinghamites but 'I think they have done *extremely* well'.[57] Rockingham, too, though a little disappointed that the petition was to be addressed only to the Commons, was glad that the assembly had been in favour of peace with America. 'I very *well like* what has been done', he told his wife. To Burke he wrote that he was not displeased by the exclusion from the committee of peers and MPs. 'I should have scarce made an alteration.'[58] Rockingham does not seem to have been aware of the number of points on which he had allowed the Yorkshire gentlemen and freeholders to have their way. For the present, however, he was prepared to accept the secondary role in the Petitioning Movement which the county meeting had allocated to him.[59]

The exclusion of Rockingham's friends from the committee had serious consequences.[60] On 21 January 1780 the Yorkshire committee went to the lengths which Rockingham had been dreading. A plan of Association was prepared which would be put to a county meeting on 28 March. The plan went much further than the petition. It aimed at shortening the duration of Parliament and obtaining a 'more equal representation of the people'. The committee also decided that no member of the association should vote for a candidate at the next general election who refused to sign a declaration supporting parliamentary as well as economic reform.[61] Rockingham was much distressed at this. He was not only opposed to parliamentary reform. He adhered to Burke's theory of the independence of the Member of Parliament and he deplored the binding nature of tests; in particular he believed it ridiculous to call for a test when there were so many different kinds of parliamentary reform. Rockingham remained convinced that the root of the troubles that the country was in stemmed not from its electoral system but 'arise from the *corruption of men when chosen into Parliament*'.[62] By the end of January 1780, Rockingham was a good deal less happy with the progress of the Petitioning Movement than he had been a month earlier.

During the early months of 1780 the fortunes of the Rockingham Whig Party were inextricably interlinked with those of the Petitioning Movement and thus waxed and waned with them. In the spring a movement of economic reform opinion swept the country like a forest fire. (Perhaps it is more accurate to say that the underlying inclinations of many sections of the British political nation towards the elimination of corruption were being tapped at the right time and with the right methods.) In January sixteen county meetings took place, in February and March nine more. In this period, too, some of the great cities, London, Westminster, York, Nottingham, Reading, Gloucester and Newcastle also petitioned.[63] The movement found such widespread support not only because of its ideological appeal to the nation but because, in organisational terms, it was a considerable advance upon that of 1769. In 1780, the petitions aired a specific grievance or set of grievances. They were submitted to Parliament and action was expected to be taken. In 1769, on the other hand, the petitions had been directed to the King and had merely demanded a general election. The organisational techniques employed in 1780 were certainly far more sophisticated than anything the earlier movement had thrown up. The committees of correspondence of each petitioning county and town provided permanence and were an agency of the first importance in promoting the dissemination of information which was so essential to the success or failure of the movement. Although Yorkshire was not typical in that its organisation was considerably more sophisticated than existed elsewhere, the activities of its committee give some idea of its effectiveness. The committee met weekly to exchange addresses with other committees, thus acting as the lynch-pin of the whole movement. Within Yorkshire it organised and co-ordinated an army of helpers and canvassers and directed the flow of lecturers and propaganda, whose success was evidenced by the fact that over 10,000 signatures to the Yorkshire petition were collected by the end of January.[64]

The Yorkshire meeting of 30 December 1779 was the signal for other parts of the country to petition. Hampshire followed suit on 3 January 1780 while Middlesex, meeting on 7 January, as might have been expected, went further than Yorkshire in resolving to participate in a national association of county committees.[65] In general, the Rockingham Whigs figured prominently in the petitioning counties.[66] This is not surprising. Rockingham and Burke had always envisaged that they would, and by doing so, help to restrain the Movement from running to extremes. In most places the Rockinghams were able to co-operate with the local gentry and freeholders in organising petitions which confined themselves to the subject of economic reform. Meetings, such as that at Westminster on 2 February 1780, showed that the Rockingham Whigs were just as prepared to co-operate with radicals. Although Fox was the chairman of the committee at Westminster, and although leading Rockinghamites like Portland and the Cavendishes were on the committee, they rubbed shoulders with radicals like Wilkes and Sawbridge. Given the background of political excitement and Fox's inability to control himself, it was not surprising that Fox and some of his friends loudly proclaimed their adherence to the idea of Association and their commitment to parliamentary reform. It is, however, too easy to dismiss Fox's rabble rousing as a lovable example of uncontrolled populism. Fox was, in fact, studiously vague on the subject of an association. Although he outlined what was to be the foundation of his political thought—that the Commons ought to be responsive to the popular will—he related this belief to the Rockinghamite theory that the independence of the Commons had to be re-established if the secret influence of the Crown were to be resisted. Thus Fox's strongest argument in favour of an association of petitioning counties was that it was the best method of combating corruption. In other words, Fox was out to restore the constitution of the country, not to change it.

Nevertheless, as the weeks went by, the Petitioning Movement seemed to be dominated by an increasingly radical impulse. Buoyed up by promising returns from the counties, Wyvill organised a meeting of deputies of the corresponding counties in London for 11 March 1780. What emerged from the subsequent series of meetings was a Plan of Association much more radical than anything which Rockingham could ever have countenanced. The plan included tests for parliamentary candidates, 100 additional county members and annual Parliaments.[67] The Plan was to be the subject of a Yorkshire county meeting on 28 March and Rockingham was determined to make his voice heard before it met. Rockingham went as far as he could to reconcile himself to the increasingly radical objectives of the Petitioning Movement. He accepted in full its economical reform ideas and he proclaimed himself no enemy to Parliaments shorter than seven years. But he was firmly opposed to other types of parliamentary reform, especially the abolition of rotten boroughs.[68] In spite of the fact that a full and fair hearing was given to the views of the Marquis, the York meeting of 25 March accepted Wyvill's Plan. The only concession to the Marquis was the redefinition of 'shorter Parliaments' which now became triennial rather than annual.[69]

This was a watershed in the relations between the Rockingham Whigs and the Petitioning Movement. The Movement could no longer expect the automatic support of the Rockingham Whigs and the Rockingham Whigs could not rely upon the support of the Movement at the general election which was expected later in 1780. Rockingham was much distressed at the outcome of the meeting of 28 March.[70] He was, indeed, in an unenviable and difficult situation. His party had been divided by the Movement and his friends seemed to insist upon publicising their divisions, and this at a time when maximum unity was required if a severe defeat were to be inflicted upon the ministry. The emergence of parliamentary reform as a major political issue, furthermore, weakened relations between Rockingham and the Chathamites.[71] The parliamentary activities of the Opposition were soured by bitter divisions between Shelburne and Rockingham, disputes in which Richmond had to be the conciliator to preserve sufficient harmony to maintain a working relationship within the Opposition.[72] Rockingham was profoundly suspicious of the new kind of mass politics which threatened the political world of the landed family and the aristocratically owned borough, of propertied power and influence. Shelburne, much less bound up within the eighteenth century electoral world than Rockingham, was able to preserve a more flexible and open mind upon the question of reform. It was circumstance which separated the two men. Rockingham should not be misunderstood. He held strong liberal sympathies, and, for a man of his class and generation, many reformist ideals. He was not stiff-necked and he was not disinclined to compromise. The success of Wyvill and his friends in beating off the Rockinghamite bid for control of the movement, and the quickening of the reformist impulse which led its leaders to embrace a Plan of Association with its attack on the rotten boroughs, ended Rockingham's brief flirtation with parliamentary reform. Shelburne was much more radical in his views than Rockingham. Although he was no more successful than Rockingham in influencing the activities of his county committee,[73] the heir to Chatham had long been committed to parliamentary reform. Without a party whose unity he might have to take into consideration, Shelburne could afford to indulge his restless and enquiring spirit in schemes of parliamentary reform. For the time being, however, attention was switched to Parliament and a tenuous unity was maintained for a while.

The famous parliamentary drama of the session began on 8 February 1780 when Sir George Savile presented the Yorkshire petition to the Commons. He stressed the independent origin of the petition, claiming that it was not a party measure and that it had no connection with Edmund Burke's much anticipated plan of economical reform.[74] This was merely the *hors d'oeuvre* of what followed three days later when Burke presented his plan. He was at his best on this occasion, in control both of himself and of his material. His speech was a masterpiece of logic and rhetoric. He had the ear of a sympathetic House and he did not do his case the violence of overstating it. He thus refrained from offending the country gentlemen. The fundamental premise from which his proposals followed relentlessly was that offices which did not serve the public should be abolished. His intention was to reduce influence by minimising waste and extravagance. Thus the feudal anachronisms of separate administrations for Lancaster, Chester, Wales and Cornwall were to be ended. The royal Household was not to be spared. Useless offices were to be swept away here, too. Furthermore, the third secretaryship was to be abolished. Burke did not wish to waste time. He understood that approval had been given to the principle of his reforms when the House agreed to give him leave to bring in his bills without a division.[75] His tactical plan was to press on as quickly as possible before the impetus lent to his plan by the support of public opinion ran out. Burke was perhaps too optimistic. In hoping to reduce the influence of the Crown Burke wished to streamline and to centralise the State by abolishing jurisdictions which had hitherto been separate. To this end he proposed to limit the amount of money spent on pensions but not to abolish them. He proposed to cut out some hereditary offices but shrank from eliminating such offices entirely. This was not enough to satisfy the men of Yorkshire and the Middlesex radicals because it was never Burke's purpose either to make the Commons more democratic or the executive more efficient. It was surely significant that on 14 February, when Burke introduced bills for the sale of crown lands and for the separate establishments of Wales and the duchies, Isaac Barré moved for a committee to examine public accounts.[76] It was even more significant that on the the following day, Sir George Savile, after consultations with Wyvill the night before, moved for a list of places to be furnished (which was accepted) and a list of pensions (which was not because of the sudden and unaccountable illness of the Speaker). On 21 February Savile repeated his motion but precious time had allowed North to muster his forces and he was able to carry an amendment limiting the list to those payable at the Exchequer.[77]

Nevertheless Burke pressed on. His Establishment Bill received its first reading on 23 February 1780.[78] North prepared himself for a war of attrition in committee where Burke's bill, or at least the most contentious of its clauses, could be eliminated or abolished. He was worried at the uproar which he expected to follow his heavy budget, to be introduced on 6 March. Fearing that its consequences might 'force the Government to give way to opposition & their measures'[79] he dug in his heels and fought. On 8 March North saved the Third Secretaryship by seven votes, 208–201.[80] The battle for economic reform, and for North's ministry was now on. On 13 March the Opposition succeeded in carrying a clause abolishing the Board of Trade by 207–199.[81] The crucial moment, in retrospect, seems to have come on 20 March when the regulation of the Household and Civil List was under discussion. The Independents baulked at the thought of bringing the Civil list, and especially the Household, under parliamentary scrutiny. The division figure of 211–158 rejecting Burke's proposal represented the widespread desire of the Independents to allow the King an untrammelled disposition of Civil List monies, once they had been voted. Yet for Burke and the Rockinghams, this was the root and branch of corruption. Burke believed that unless he could carry the parts of his bill relating to the Household and the Civil List, the rest of the bill would be ineffective; 'there is not the smallest Chance for doing any Service whatsoever for the publick'.[82]

Dunning's famous resolution, then, came after the fate of the economic reform legislation had been settled and when the Opposition needed to obtain recognition of the fundamental

o

principles underlying its economic reform programme. The Easter recess—from 24 March to 5 April—might have delivered the ministry from any further embarrassment during the session had not Fox moved for a call of the House on 6 April 1780, when a committee was to consider all the forty petitions which by now had been received. Neither Fox nor Dunning informed the ministry of what they intended. The stage was set for one of the most famous events in the history of Parliament. On 6 April Dunning rose to complain of the part taken by the Commons. In response to the expressed opinions of over 100,000 people the House had merely accepted one clause of Burke's bill. Dunning abstracted two basic propositions from the petitions and subjected them to the test of parliamentary approval. These were:

> 'that the influence of the crown has increased, is increasing and ought to be diminished.
>
> That it is competent to this House to examine into, and to correct, abuses in the expenditure of the civil list revenues, as well as in every other branch of the public revenue, whenever it shall appear expendient to the wisdom of this House to do so.'

The second was much more substantial than the first, essentially a catchy slogan rather than a statement with meaningful and practical implications. The Opposition won a great victory when the first resolution carried by 233–215. The second passed without a division. But nothing was done either to follow these up or to make them effective. It was, then, a glorious day for the Opposition but one for which Dunning, rather than the Rockingham Whigs, should take the credit, as Rockingham himself confessed, for his industry in bringing members to town and for his excellent speaking.[83] The passage of Dunning's resolution marked, however, a further symbolic extension of the claims of the House of Commons. It was the Lower House rather than the King which was responsible for the unbalancing of the eighteenth century's much vaunted balance of the constitution. The principle that the personal and political expenditure of the monarch came under parliamentary surveillance had been stated. Fox understood this to be the import of the events of 6 April[84] and, to judge by the avowedly anti-monarchical tone of many of that day's speeches, this was indeed the case.[85]

The day of Dunning's resolution was the zenith of the great Opposition economic reform campaign. Although North's immediate reaction was once more to think of resignation the King made him forget his self-pity and this he soon did.[86] During the rest of the session he showed his ability to delay, to wait patiently and allow the Opposition to exhaust itself. After 6 April opposition slowly began to decline. On 10 April Dunning obtained the approval of the House for a resolution providing for the payment of MPs in an attempt to safeguard their independence, but he was defeated when he attempted to disqualify thirteen placemen. 'Things begin to wear a better appearance', wrote George III reassuringly to Lord North.[87] Even more ominously three days later the Opposition lost Crewe's bill excluding revenue officers from voting at elections.[88] The following day, the Speaker fell ill and business was delayed for a week until his recovery.[89] On 24 April Dunning went much too far for the liking of independent Members when he demanded that Parliament should not be dissolved until the petitions were acted upon. This was a thinly disguised attack upon the royal prerogative of dissolving Parliament, and the division figures show that several members were frightened by it. Dunning lost his resolution by 242–203.[90] After the debate Fox 'advised Dunning to make no more motions'.[91] Dunning, who had done so much to raise the Opposition so high, was, in part, responsible for its fall. While Burke's bill died in committee, Dunning's resolutions gathered dust. They could not change the cruel fact that 'The People in opposition though numerous, were not strong enough to carry anything & . . . not quite united amongst themselves; their new allies in general came to them unwillingly, & though they voted with them, for fear of their Elections, were allways glad to leave them'.[92] Lord North spoke truly when he remarked that those who might sincerely have voted for Dunning's resolutions of 6 April might think twice when they saw the 'improper lengths it was meant to extend the effects and consequences of these resolutions'.[93] On 11 May Camden wrote sadly: 'Our popular exertions are dying away, & the country returning to its old state of lukewarm indifference, the Minority in the House of Commons dwindle away every day, & the Opposition is at variance with itself'.[94] With elections looming and with the sick feeling that they had run the ministry so close but had been unable to shake it the Opposition withdrew the field of parliamentary battle.

The Opposition had revealed the limitations upon the parliamentary support which the Rockinghams might expect to command. It now proceeded to publicise its internal dissensions. Shelburne seems to have behaved with some moderation, on the whole, and at least tried to keep Rockingham's confidence by assuring him that he did not wish the reform movement to go to extremes.[95] But the subject of parliamentary reform, which Rockingham and Burke found so distressing and to which Rockingham ascribed the failure of the Opposition during the session,[96] provided opportunities for the expression of conflicting opinions. On 8 May Alderman Sawbridge brought in his annual motion for the reform of Parliament. Burke took this opportunity of expressing his (and Rockingham's) opposition to more frequent Parliaments, reiterating the familiar arguments that more frequent elections would lead to more frequent bribery, more frequent violence and more frequent intimidation. Fox spiritedly defended Sawbridge, laying down his doctrine that the influence of the Crown could best be checked by that of the people. It must have been small consolation to Rockingham, as he reflected upon the divisions in his party, that Sawbridge's motion was thrown out by 182–91.[97] It must have grieved him even more when Richmond decided to rebut Burke's opinions in the House of Lords.[98] On 3 June the Duke of Richmond threw down the gauntlet to the conservatives within the Rockingham party. He moved a resolution for annual Parliaments and universal suffrage, a combination of proposals which went even further than most radicals would have thought desirable. His plan was based upon that of the Westminster Association, which also envisaged equal electoral districts and the registration of eighteen year olds. To Richmond, as to Fox, drastic parliamentary reform was necessary to curb the influence of the Crown. Yet Richmond was far more radical. For Richmond denounced *all* manner of influence, including the rotten boroughs.[99] Rockingham kept his patience but he must now have been extremely worried by the opinions of two of his most talented men, Fox and Richmond. For both of them, especially Richmond, were coming close to rejecting the basic dictum of the Rockingham Whig party, that the influence of the Crown was at the root of the evils facing the nation. Richmond was rapidly growing disillusioned with the Rockingham party, with Opposition and with politics. The events of 1780 were the turning point in his relationship with the Rockinghams. The issue of parliamentary reform had wrenched him away from his old loyalty to the party and had placed him in an uneasy situation somewhat outside the party's boundaries.[100] Shelburne was also becoming increasingly irritated with the timidity and conservatism of the Rockinghams and went into something like a temporary political retirement towards the end of the session. Richmond and Shelburne were clearly drifting into each others arms. Lady Rockingham shrewdly sized up the situation: 'Satisfy my mind Dear Duke of Richmond . . . don't let me see such a man as Ld Shelburne (who every soul thinks of alike) seem to be encroaching upon your Mind and beguiling it into all his labarinths'.[101] Dissensions within the Rockingham party and growing suspicion of Shelburne were among the most solid legacies of the session of 1780.

At exactly this point the Gordon riots intervened both to quicken these tendencies and to swell the loyalist reaction in the country against radicals and reform. On 2 June Lord George Gordon[102] presented to the Commons the petition of the Protestant Association, formed in London in February 1779 to protest against Savile's Catholic Relief Act of the previous year. This sparked off a series of anti-catholic riots which paralysed the capital for a week during which London was at the mercy of the mob. Parliament itself was threatened for a while, ironically while Richmond's motion was under debate.[103] The authorities were terrified by this manifestation of mob violence and panicked. Few men in the capital had any sympathy for the rioters. Most observers saw the Gordon riots as a terrifying consequence of a premeditated plot, and they were determined to scotch any possibilities of its recurrence. The Rockinghams reacted by blaming everything upon the ministers. 'Had Ministers taken any precautions beforehand or exerted themselves at first, all this mischief might have been prevented or stopp'd.'[104] The Rockinghams, however, were not united in their reaction to the Gordon riots. At one extreme the Duke of Manchester supported the idea of repealing the relief Act, an idea which Richmond deplored.[105] Edmund Burke showed something of his real stature at this time. He displayed much courage in walking the streets of London during the riots, trying to calm the people, and maintaining his support for the Relief Act.[106] But more serious than these differences was the effect that the riots had upon the Rockingham party's relations with Shelburne.

The reform movement of 1779–80 had only temporarily brought the two sections of the Opposition to act together. With its apparent failure, their differences once more manifested themselves. Rockingham accused Shelburne of having done much to foment the Gordon riots by his sympathetic attitude towards the Protestant Association.[107] It is true that Shelburne had always disliked the Catholic relief act of 1778 but on the question of the suppression of the riots he was much more liberal than the Rockinghams and even opposed the use of troops, advocating lenient treatment of convicted rioters.[108] It was not simply a question of the Rockinghams' 'conservatism' contrasting with Shelburne's 'liberalism'. Burke had more real sympathy for the Catholics of England and Ireland than Shelburne ever had, and much as he deplored the riots, Burke stood out against the punitive retribution of ignorant men.[109] Shelburne, however, was once more out of step, once more acting what appeared to the Rockinghams to be a sinister part. At the end of the session, then, the victorious Opposition of the spring had become a gloomy, demoralised and divided band.[110]

The ministry had now come through its trial by ordeal. North's nerve had proved to be much stronger than anyone could have predicted when the session opened. Nevertheless, this was a good time for him to seek an accession of strength.

The Opposition's crusade had failed and the Rockinghams and Shelburne were at odds. The time was ripe for the weary but victorious North to attempt to profit from its fratricidal differences. There was nothing surprising in such an endeavour. Talk of such a coalition had been almost continuous since the soundings of the previous year. Many ministerialists shared a naive conviction that the Rockingham Whigs were motivated purely by self interest and that they could thus be easily bought with office.[111] George III, furthermore, never opposed negotiations with the Opposition providing that the existing ministry were strengthened and not replaced.[112] What precipitated the discussions of the summer of 1780 was the impact of the Gordon riots. The Rockinghams were reminded of their community of interest with the ministry in preserving social and political order. Rockingham and Portland even attended the Privy Council on 7 June to press for the full penalties of the law against the rioters. Two further circumstances facilitated these negotiations. On 15 June there had come the news of the British capture of Charlestown. At the same time, a dissolution of Parliament was expected daily. For the first time in months the political initiative lay with the ministers. There followed an exchange of view between the ministry and the Rockingham Whigs on the conditions upon which a coalition might be negotiated. On 28 June Lord North held a conversation with Frederick Montagu and professed his desire to form 'a strong and efficient Government'. This sounding forced Rockingham to define his own conditions for office. These were extensive. He demanded changes of policy. These included a policy of peace and the recognition of American Independence, the passing of Crewe's and Clerke's bills as well as the major parts of Burke's bill. As for men, Rockingham named Richmond and Fox as Secretaries, Keppel as First Lord of the Admiralty and although nothing specific was mentioned about the army and the Treasury, he implied that there must be changes. These demands would have amounted to a new administration pursuing new policies. On 30 June North laid these terms before the King and although no detailed reaction was forthcoming until 7 July the King's opinions were given to North and Thurlow on 3 July. He was quite unprepared to change his policies. He was willing to make a gesture of conciliation to the Rockinghams by allowing a few of their number to take minor offices but he was not prepared to go further. Portland, Manchester, Townshend, and Burke would be welcome in his employ, and Fox 'if any lucrative, not ministerial office can be pointed out for him' . . . but not Richmond and not Rockingham. There was clearly no prospect for an agreement and on 7 July when Rockingham received Montagu's version of the King's terms, he considered the negotiations to be at an end. There was no point in persevering with them. George III was not interested in a coalition on the Rockinghams' terms, and the Rockingham Whigs were not willing to bargain away their consistency and their political principles.[113]

In retrospect, it is necessary to censure at least certain parts of Rockingham's conduct in these negotiations. Although it is incontestably the case that he acted consistently with his party's principles and that he behaved with scrupulous courtesy towards all individuals involved in the negotiations, he neglected Shelburne. Although it is true that Shelburne considered himself to be separated from the Marquis by this time, and that he was never included in the proposed arrangements, nevertheless Rockingham was playing a dangerous game in omitting even to send to his principal colleague in Opposition some intimation of what had happened. In view of the failure of the overtures, it was surely in Rockingham's own interest to have done so. Relations between the two wings of the Opposition were already bad enough without awakening Shelburne's sensitive suspicions. It is not argued that Rockingham acted a false part. He was not purposely going behind Shelburne's back because the negotiations never concerned Shelburne. But in ignoring him, Rockingham was storing up future trouble for himself.[114] Furthermore, Rockingham may be criticised from another point of view. Although he and his friends undoubtedly assumed that he would take the Treasury, the King did not. It was never made clear to him that this was a condition. The Marquis' tendency to excessive moderation was damaging at this time because it led the King to believe that Rockingham might be persuaded to waive his own claims to office in a future arrangement and to allow his followers to serve with and thus strengthen the present ministry. For the present, these were details. Within two years, they were to be political considerations of enormous weight.

The unsuccessful negotiation cleared the way for the dissolution of Parliament. The lively and dramatic session had ended in parliamentary failure and tactical defeat for the Rockinghams but the session was of crucial significance in the development of the Rockingham Whig party. The future of the party rested upon its ability to overthrow North and storm the Closet. The closer the Rockinghams edged towards their objective in the years after Saratoga the greater the gulf separating them from the Court seemed to be. In short, a constitutional crisis was looming between the party pretensions of the Rockingham ministry and the political and constitutional ideas of George III. The negotiations of 1780 left the Rockinghams still more suspicious of the Court than hitherto. The Marquis was left in no doubt that the King would never agree to his terms. As he wrote to John Lee: 'there seems to be a *decisive disinclination* to almost every idea on which (I think) a government either in regard to *measures* or *persons* can be formed'.[115] At the same time the session had widened the rifts between the Rockingham party and Shelburne and opened distressing fissures within the Rockingham party itself. Although the Marquis' authority was never questioned[116] his leadership was lax and easy-going, allowing almost unfettered freedom to Fox and to Richmond to expound their reformist ideas. But just when the seeds of party disunity were beginning to grow, the exigencies of a general election rescued the Rockinghams from their internal conflicts and once more led them to attempt to consolidate, and perhaps to extend, their place in the country.

Chapter 20

The Victory of the Opposition 1780–2

The failure of the negotiations of June–July 1780 left the ministers with no reason for delaying a dissolution of Parliament. There were a host of accompanying considerations which persuaded them that an early election would be in their interests. No end to the war was in sight. Notwithstanding the victory at Charlestown and the rather optimistic rumours concerning the collapse of the rebels' cause to which it had given rise, the British navy remained stretched to the limit. Ireland was in an inflammatory situation. The parliamentary session of 1780 had been almost as difficult for the Government in Dublin as it had been in Westminster. The Volunteer Association, backed up by a vociferous public opinion, assisted the Irish Opposition, led by Grattan and Flood, to run the Government very close on motions to cede legislative independence to the Irish in March and April. The situation in Ireland gradually deteriorated until, by the summer, ministers faced the ominous fact that the Mutiny Act was unenforceable. If this were not enough, relations between Britain on the one hand and both Holland and Russia on the other had rapidly worsened during the year.[1] The imminent prospect of a wider war persuaded the ministers to clear the decks by holding the general election, due within a year, in the late summer of 1780. The King was keen to go ahead with the elections. Any doubts that remained must have been banished by the electoral arithmetic of John Robinson. His figures, in fact, showed that an election would result in a House *less* favourable to the ministry than the present one. His assessment of the present House was

'pro' 290   'hopeful' 19   'doubtful' 16   'con' 233.

His first calculation of the effects of an early election were

'pro' 252   'hopeful' 47   'doubtful' 70   'con' 189.

This was clearly an unsatisfactory result. But it was when he looked a little more closely (and less accurately) at the large number of 'doubtfuls' that he was able to produce the figures which Lord North and the King wanted. He stole over forty of the seventy doubtfuls, so that in his overall conclusion he predicted a result of 343–215.[2]

Rockingham was angry at the news of the dissolution, probably because he was unprepared for electoral battle in Yorkshire where he could expect an uphill fight against the Associators.[3] At York, for example, the Associators looked as though they might prove troublesome to the two sitting members, Lord John Cavendish and Charles Turner, and at one time the success of Lord John seemed to be in doubt. Rockingham, however, provided an excellent demonstration of the political tactics which he knew best and at which he excelled. As he described them:

'I think I have done some good by conversing with many of our leading citizens & friends at York, & have shewn them the necessity and propriety of trusting to the experience and proof they have had of men's principles, rather than to trust to the accidental circumstances of any persons who may be ready to adopt any speculative proposition merely to gain favour at the moment.'[4]

He stood out against the Associators. Wyvill had perforce to offer a compromise to the Rockinghams. If they agreed to the proposal for an additional 100 county members then he would not oppose Rockinghamite candidates at York. Rockingham sternly rejected these terms.[5] By doing so he did not jeopardize the chances of his candidates at York and both were returned. The position of his candidates in the county was rather different. The Marquis supported Sir George Savile and Henry Duncombe, an ardent Associator, against the ministerialist Lascelles. Although the return of Savile and Duncombe was never in doubt, Rockingham had to work *with* the Association because of their mutual desire to defeat a supporter of the Government. Yet Savile continued to express his support for triennial elections and 100 additional county members. Rockingham swallowed his annoyance, continued to proclaim his public support for Savile and patiently soldiered on. After over £12,000 had been subscribed to a fund for Savile and Duncombe, Lascelles was forced to withdraw.[6] Rockingham had further cause for elation in Yorkshire. The Dundas family which controlled the borough of Richmond had transferred its loyalty to the Rockingham Whigs in 1780 after a decade of attachment to the ministry. This brought into the Rockingham fold not only Sir Lawrence Dundas and his son Thomas, who sat for Richmond, but also Charles Dundas who came in at Orkney and Shetland at the 1780 election.[7] Rockingham was also fortunate because Sir Thomas Frankland's seat at Thirsk fell into his lap and he was able to nominate the two members, Beilby Thompson and Sir Thomas Gascoigne, who were returned there without opposition. William Weddell remained at Malton but his colleague, Savile Finch, had to make room for Edmund Burke. Other Yorkshire friends and connections of the Marquis included Lady Rockingham's relative, Sir John Ramsden, who came in for one of Edward Eliot's seats, Grampound.[8] Although Sir James Pennyman continued his occupation of Beverly he was to support Shelburne in 1782. Elsewhere in Yorkshire, Rockingham's men did less well. The Marquis had to abandon Hedon, and the two seats there.[9] An even greater reverse was undoubtedly the defeat of David Hartley at Hull. Hartley was a friend of Savile and was thus likely to have enjoyed the support of the Associators but, partly because of his pro-American views, he was not popular in Hull.[10] Frederick Montagu continued his quiet occupation of Higham Ferrers. Rockingham was the beneficiary of the dissolution of the old Albemarle connection, its two surviving members, the Keppel brothers, bestowing upon Rockingham for the moment their complete loyalty.[11] Lord Verney continued his long possession of one of the Buckinghamshire county seats and George Dempster, his loyalty to Rockingham hardening with the years, once more came in at Perth. The size of Rockingham's connection stood at seventeen after the election of 1780, an increase of six since the last general election.[12]

The great Cavendish connection was the next largest group within the confederation of connections known as the Rockingham Whig party. In 1774 it included Lords Frederick and George Cavendish, Richard Cavendish and Sir Anthony Abdy.[13] Although Lords Frederick and George went out in 1780, a new Lord George (Augustus Henry) had come in in 1775. Richard Cavendish switched from Lancaster to Derbyshire in 1780. Abdy had left Parliament in 1775. Of the original four, then, only one remained. To Richard Cavendish and Lord George Augustus Henry, however, can be added three Walpoles. A marriage connection brought within the Cavendish fold Horatio Walpole at Wigan in 1780 (partly on Portland's interest). Thomas Walpole followed his friend Grafton into Opposition in 1775, as did his brother Richard. Sir G. W. Vanneck was their brother-in-law and may be grouped with them although his connection with Rockingham was much less strong. This is not all. The marriage of the fifth Duke of Devonshire into the Spencer family secured the attachment of Lord Althorp, H. Minchin, W. C. Sloper and W. Tollemache. Finally, what Professor Christie has termed 'friends and associates' of the Cavendishes include the two MPs for Lancaster, A. Rawlinson and W. Braddyll, and Dudley Long. Very largely through extending family connections, then, the tiny Cavendish connection had grown from four in 1774 to thirteen in 1780.

The Portland connection had fallen to four in 1774. Its members had been Henry Fletcher for Cumberland, G. Byng and B. Hotham for Wigan, and B. Grey for Leicestershire. Of these only Hotham, who went out in 1775, was not returned in 1780. Lord Edward Bentinck, who went out in 1774, came back a year later for Nottinghamshire. Henry Bridgeman, MP for Wenlock, supported the Rockingham party in its opposition to the American War, and he was rewarded for his loyalty when Portland helped to bring in his son for Wigan in 1780. Portland's independent friends include J. Bullock, R. H. Coxe, T. Lucas and John Scudamore. Unlike the Cavendish group, the size of this connection grew more through political conviction (over the American war) than through marriage. It increased from four in 1774 to ten in 1780.

In 1774 there had been nothing resembling a Foxite group or connection. By 1780 one had sprung into life because of the magnetism of Fox's personality, the recklessness of his social (and perhaps his political) life and his public stand on the American war and reform. Most of these members had not been long in Parliament. Fox had entered the House in 1768, his two early friends E. and A. Foley in 1768, and 1774, respectively. But all the other members of Fox's group committed themselves to the Opposition after 1774. In 1775 H. Pigot, J. Crewe, R. Fitzpatrick and Lord Upper Ossory did so. In the following year, T. W. Coke followed suit. In the three following years three members followed their example: E. Winnington, J. Burgoyne, and T. Grenville in 1777, 1778 and 1779, respectively. At the 1780 election a flush of new members attached themselves to Fox. These were R. B. Sheridan, E. Coke, Lord Maitland, St A. St John, John Townshend and Edward Monckton. Most of these men were radical by temperament, their connection with Fox personal in nature and their attachment secured by conviction rather than by patronage. A new political generation was emerging which had not been bred in the Rockinghamite struggles of the 1760s and knew nothing of Lord Bute and little of Lord Chatham. These seventeen members were a powerful and talented addition to the Rockingham party, whose opinions and activities did much to freshen its tardy proceedings and to liberalise its traditional aristocratic ideas.

In addition to all these members there were an additional seventeen independent members of the Rockingham party. These were: William A'Court, T. Anson, Sir E. Astley, William Baker, C. Barrow, R. Benyon, Sir T. Bunbury, Sir W. Clayton, R. Gregory, J. Hanbury, H. Harbord, W. H. Hartley, Sir R.

Hotham, Lord Ludlow, W. Plumer, J. Shaw Stewart and T. Skipwith. Finally there were nine members belonging to smaller patronage groupings but which attached themselves to the Rockinghamite opposition. These were the three members of the Duke of Bolton's connection, Sir P. J. Clerke, Thomas Stanley, and Sir Charles Davers. Thomas Lister brought in J. Lee and J. Parker while Charles Anderson-Pelham brought in F. E. Anderson and John Harrison.

The size of the Rockingham party was thus eighty-three after the election of 1780. Who were these men, what were their origins and how did the party compare with its situation six years earlier?

Between 1774 and 1780 the heavy hands of Wentworth-Woodhouse, Welbeck and Chatsworth still hung heavy over the party. To one or other of these great houses a large number of independent Members attached themselves. Furthermore, the size of the party had grown to such an extent that it could no longer be described as a connection or a faction. The party was a confederation, not merely of clans or connections, but also of radicals and independents. The Rockingham party was thus a far more complex political entity than it had been in 1774. It was also a much larger one. It had grown in size from 56 to 83, an increase of approximately 50 per cent. Several explanations for this improvement immediately suggest themselves. A large number of men had grouped themselves around Charles Fox, a new and startlingly attractive influence in the party.[14] Further, the family connections, especially the Cavendishes, had extended their ramifications through the political world. Even in the age of the American Revolution, marriage played an important part in determining the political allegiance of many members who were already in Parliament. Nevertheless, the American war and the growth of radical movements increasingly acted as a wedge between politicians, creating a polarity of attitudes which made the old ideal of independency a much less feasible political philosophy than it had been a generation earlier. The American war did not 'create' or 'save' the Rockingham Whig party. Although no fewer than 42 of the 83 members of the party had attached themselves to the party since the election of 1774, 34 had done so *before* 1768. From one point of view, then, the old Rockingham party of the 1760s was now joined in the late 1770s by a large number of new adherents.

Nevertheless, we should not forget that the Rockingham Whigs were not the only party in opposition and that parties existed also within the ministry. In fact, there were parties of different types. There were the parties of office (such as those of Sandwich and North), the parties based upon electoral in-fluence (such as those of Lowther and Grafton), the family connections (such as those of Gower and Rutland) and the party of talent and principle (that of Shelburne, which did not claim to be a party at all). Party was thus capable of different manifestations. The Rockingham party included parties of several types within its fold. The essential unifying factor, however, was the personal loyalty of its members to the Marquis of Rockingham. Nevertheless, it required more than this to keep such a widely based party together. It required the loyalty generated by the great families which in turn was transmitted to Rockingham. It also required a solid structural backbone of electoral influence and patronage. The Rocking-ham Whig party was thus unique not only in its size but because it was a combination of different types of parties and included independents as well. Parliament was not yet divided into two parties but party was growing within the House of Commons. By 1780 the Rockingham Whigs had expressed their own political philosophy and stated their own policies for putting the nation to rights. Party was, therefore, already a refuge to which the nation might look in time of national crisis. Party was not yet permanent in the British political system but it was already necessary. If Lord North were to fall there would be no alternative but to allow the Rockinghams to come into office, to make peace with America and to pass their economic reform legislation. It would, in contemporary terms, amount to a constitutional revolution.

We should also remember that political issues were far more likely to influence a Member of Parliament than to influence those who voted for him. Professor Christie has pointed to 'the clear, abrupt division which sundered two groups of parties in Parliament',[15] but this sharp division was rarely reflected in the constituencies. Furthermore the Rockinghams were only involved in a few contests where issues mattered. In this category would fall, perhaps, the non-contested election of Savile in Yorkshire, the undoubted political nature of the contest of Admiral Keppel in Surrey and that of Fox in Westminster. It is perhaps no coincidence that the Associations were active in all these places. Yet we should not leap to conclusions. In Essex, Devonshire and Gloucestershire the Association took no part in the election and elsewhere radical candidates were returned without the aid of Associations and Committees (Newcastle, Plymouth and Worcester, for example). Yet in other places which witnessed a fairly clear cut conflict between Government and Opposition candidates, the larger boroughs such as Norwich, Liverpool, London, Southwark and Bristol, national issues were inextricably interwoven with local factors. It was from one of these constituencies that there came the most disappointing result of all for the Rockinghams.

Burke had been in Bristol for about a fortnight when the dissolution was announced. The partial canvass which he had already completed revealed that he was in a vulnerable position. And although he allowed his name to go forward he had little hope of success. On 9 September he had to withdraw after further canvassing had failed to improve his prospects. The reasons for his defeat are not difficult to find. His support for Catholic relief had stirred the muddy waters of Bristol prejudice and his willingness to extend Free Trade to the Irish positively infuriated large sections of the powerful Bristol mercantile community. Although Edmund Burke had been an exceptionally able member, and one who attended to the interests of his constituents[16] in so far as his principles allowed him to do so, he had not visited Bristol between 1776 and 1780. He thus never succeeded in endearing himself personally to his constituents. In any event, his defeat was not really a surprise. In terms of the history of Bristol, the election result of 1774 had been an aberration. It was normally impossible for two Whigs to be elected. As the second of these, Burke had little chance of being elected in 1780 even if he had never made his provocative and controversial pronouncements on religion and trade.[17] Burke thereupon sought a safe refuge, and Rockingham found him one at Malton. To move from one of the important trading cities of the nation to his patron's pocket borough was a great humiliation for Burke. Partly for this reason, the year 1780 has usually been regarded as a watershed in his career. There was, indeed, much to depress Burke not only about his own career but also the state of his party. For Burke thoroughly deplored the dangerous and divisive topic of parliamentary reform with which several of the leaders of his party had begun to flirt in 1780. That these included men of the stamp of Richmond, Fox and even Savile distressed Burke. He did not believe that parliamentary reform was popular in the country, still less that it had been necessary to agitate the question. To have done so only divided his party to the advantage of the Court.[18] For years Burke had been expounding the need for the public voice to support the Rockingham party. Now that the public voice had been heard he was disappointed to find that some sections of it were unwilling to follow the Rockingham party on reform. Just at the moment when he believed the public to be awakening, just when it might have been possible to educate it into the principles of the Rockingham party it was surely folly for some of the party's leaders to canvass parliamentary reform. This together with the failure of his titanic efforts to achieve economical reform left him sceptical of the possibility of achieving any success in the future. Burke had become disillusioned with his party and doubtful of its ability to achieve the tasks he had set for it years before.[19]

Nevertheless, the 1780 election was a setback for the ministry rather than for the Opposition. The outcome of the election as judged by Robinson gave the ministry a paper majority of only 26 compared with the 128 he had led the King and the ministers to expect.[20] North could rely upon the unswerving loyalty of the 140 members of the Court and administration group and that of 80 supporters from the factions. But this total of 220 was about 60 votes short of a parliamentary majority. The extra votes which the ministry needed would have to come from the independents. The security of his ministry now rested on a knife edge. If two circumstances coincided then North would be brought down. If the independents deserted him, and if the Opposition brought all its strength to town, then he would be in very great difficulties. Although this did not seem likely to occur in September 1780, nevertheless, we should remember that the policies of the ministry and of the Opposition could not be reconciled. If the ministry's policies failed, then there would be no alternative but for the King to turn to Rockingham and to Shelburne. Yet we should not anticipate the events of 1782. The Rockingham Whigs numbered something over 80 and they could rely in normal circumstances on the support of slightly over a further 30 votes from other opposition groups.[21] Everything depended upon the independents and these men would not lightly turn against the King's minister. Only a national disaster might induce them to do so.

Although the election was more than satisfactory for the Rockinghams, the Marquis himself, suffering from the revival of an old stomach complaint, from over-work, from the shattering disappointment of the Bristol result and from the lack of success which had attended the activities of his party in the last session, relaxed his activities after the election with the result that his party was unprepared for the new session. 'I am much worn down in mind, health, and spirits: I much fear this country is utterly undone, I cannot form a comfortable idea on which to ground the possibility of its recovery.'[22] All he could think of was a revival of the economical reform campaign which had served the Opposition well in the past twelve months. Further than that, Rockingham could not see. To make matters worse, Shelburne refused to come to town, burning with resentment at Rockingham's hostility to parliamentary reform while Rockingham blamed Shelburne for causing the discussions which had sapped the vigour of Opposition.[23].

The new Parliament assembled for the first time on 31 October 1780 for a short pre-Christmas session to pass essential supplies. The critical test of strength between Government and Opposition came over the ministry's choice of a new Speaker to replace Sir Fletcher Norton, whose attachment to economical reform in the last session had given offence to the King. North proposed to replace Norton with Frederick Montagu, a loyal Rockingham Whig, and a man whose integrity and honesty

were absolutely unquestioned. He was, furthermore, a relative
of North, a lawyer of some repute and, from all points of view,
likely to make an effective Speaker. Nevertheless, Montagu
was worried at the reaction of his friends to his taking office
in a system which he had for years denounced. After much soul
searching Montagu declined.[24] North was forced to find an
alternative Speaker but he could do no better than nominate
the mediocre Charles Wolfran Cornwall, a placeman at the
Treasury Board. He had little to commend him for the post
and was, furthermore, related to the new scourge of the
Rockingham Whigs, Charles Jenkinson. Their opposition to
his appointment was as inevitable as it was predictable. Even
though Cornwall was such a weak candidate for the Speakership his appointment was carried on 31 October by 203–134.[25]
A week later the Opposition amendment to the Address was
defeated by 212–130.[26] The Address congratulated the King
upon military successes in America, and, indeed, the news
from America appeared to lend support to this view. It was
significant that none of the independents supported the
Opposition speakers. This was the Indian summer of North's
ministry, when many still believed that the colonies could be
conquered and when the despatches from America lent some
support for this optimistic view. Thus, however narrow their
theoretical majority might be, the ministers could rest assured
by early November 1780 that the excitement of the previous
session was not going to be repeated. As early as 7 November
1780 Grafton wrote to Shelburne, lamenting that 'In the
political line, as little seems to be expected from the present as
from the last House'.[27] As the memorable year drew to a close,
Lord North's ministry seemed to be more secure than it had
been for some years. The Irish Parliament had been prorogued
in September and would not meet again for eighteen months.
In America the situation in Carolina and the Virginias was
giving rise to continued high optimism. Only the European
situation gave cause for concern.[28] The Christmas recess was
quiet and uneventful. Little correspondence among the
Opposition leaders survives for these weeks. Little was probably
written.

The weakness of the Opposition was apparent immediately

Parliament reassembled on 24 January 1781. The Army Extraordinaries provoked a long debate, at the end of which North obtained the £3,000,000 he had requested by the extraordinary figures of 180–57. As the King shrewdly observed, 'if care is taken that nothing improper is by surprise brought in on the House . . . Lord North will find this one of the least troublesome Sessions He has been engaged in'.[29] On the following day, the Opposition fared only slightly better when it attempted to make political capital out of the diplomatic crisis which was beginning to threaten the ministry. Its attack on North's handling of the Dutch problem was rejected by 180–101.[30] The Rockinghams had been staking everything, however, upon reviving the issue of economic reform. They delayed the call of the House twice in an attempt to procure a large attendance of their friends to support their major attack of the session against the ministers. The test case was to be the reintroduction of Burke's bill. On 15 February 1781, to the astonishment of the Opposition, the ministry did not oppose its introduction. The reasons for North's tactics lie deep in the lists of Members prepared by Robinson. These showed that of the 463 Members then in attendance Robinson thought he could rely only upon 223 as against 214 to the Opposition; and although he described 23 as 'hopeful' an alarming '40' he consigned to the 'doubtful' category.[31] This was too close for comfort. On the issue of economic reform, always dangerous for any government, the huge majorities which the ministry enjoyed on the Speakership, the Address and issues of foreign policy, threatened to melt away. North refused a stand-up fight and neatly side-stepped the Opposition's thrust. But battle, if deferred, could not be avoided. Gradually North brought himself to face the climax of the session. It came on 26 February on the second reading of Burke's bill when the ministers won by the decisive if not altogether comfortable majority of 233–190.[32] Robinson's list had proved to be too generous to the Opposition. On its best issue the Opposition could not muster 200 votes. If it were to have any hope at all of running the ministry close it would need a further 30–40 votes at least. During the rest of the 1781 session it was unable to find them and the ministry was safe.

If it was safe, it was not particularly happy. On 8 March Sir Philip Jennings Clerke, one of the economic reform heroes, demanded an enquiry into the circumstances surrounding the £12,000,000 loan which North had negotiated for the forthcoming year.[33] The enquiry was refused and therefore George Byng on 12 March moved for papers relating to the loan.[34] The reluctance of ministers to make public their transactions relating to the loan raised a good many Rockinghamite eyebrows. As Hartley put it: 'The only view of the minister in forming a loan is the premium . . . for making a good bargain. Why so? Because the undertakers of the loan being the ministers' favourites and having no monied connexions it is given to them at an exorbitant rate on account of their *inability* in the negotation of money matters'.[35] The Rockinghams, led by Savile, moved for an enquiry into the loan on 26 March but were defeated by 209–163[36]

The Opposition had palpably failed in its attempt to defeat the ministry on economic reform. It was not merely that the Opposition had suffered a numerical defeat. The precise conjunction of circumstances which had stimulated the great crusade of 1780 did not exist a year later. For one thing, the international situation was, in general, brighter. Furthermore, the ministry was in better shape and had the general election behind it. Ireland was, on the whole, quiet. Perhaps most important of all, there no longer existed the feeling among the Rockinghams that they were involved in a crusade supported by public opinion. Indeed, the Yorkshire movement itself was falling on hard times. At the second assembly of deputies held in March 1781, disputes and dissensions broke out even amongst a sparsely attended gathering. The sorry state of relations between the Associations and the Rockingham Whigs was made evident by the reluctance of Rockingham to sponsor even the moderate petition which the assembly drew up, and, furthermore, by their unenthusiastic support of the petition when Dunning presented it to the Commons on 8 May, when it was rejected by 212–135.[37] To some extent, it would be true to say that the Rockingham Whigs were growing indifferent to the movement in the country. Richmond, moreover, had no interest whatsoever in making futile gestures when the Opposition was divided among Rockingham and Shelburne. They were now hoping for political salvation with every despatch from America.

Towards the end of the session the Rockingham Whigs shifted their attention from the issue of economic reform to the conduct of the war. At first, this strategem failed to evoke any kind of response from the independents. Nevertheless, the Rockinghams persevered with it for the time being for the very good reason that in the last two to three months the despatches from America had begun to evaporate the heady optimism of the winter. Although the attendances were small the Opposition's harassment of the ministry had a certain nuisance value. On 30 May 1781 W. H. Hartley moved for peace with America. His motion attracted 72 votes against the ministry's 106.[38] On 12 June Charles James Fox took up the same theme. His powerful speech summarised the general unease which was accumulating in England over the uncertain situation of the army in America. He attacked the assumption which had for so long underpinned British strategy: that the loyalists constituted a large proportion of the colonial population and that they were awaiting 'liberation' by the British armies. He ridiculed the campaign in the Carolinas, where success had been consolidated by retreat. It was just a little ominous for North that a handful of independents and former ministerialists supported Fox, even though his motion was lost by 172–99.[39] The debate was something of a moral victory for Fox. By the end of the session ministers had been reminded that although the storm of economic reform was dying down a different hurricane might still blow up. Yet North had survived both the general election and the parliamentary session with little difficulty. Although his situation still bristled with problems there was no immediate threat to his position. Everything would depend on the outcome of the war.

The war in America was now approaching its climax. The Rockinghams, and especially Burke, felt in their bones that the current campaign was likely to prove decisive one way or the other.[40] He found the long period of uncertainty somewhat unnerving: 'A strange game of Bopeeps has been long playing, and that is all we have for our millions'.[41] To some extent

Burke was right. Indeed, the victories of the previous year had not been consolidated. After the victory at Charlestown Cornwallis had entered North Carolina and then in May 1781, breaching his instructions, Virginia, where he established a base at Yorktown. There followed a terrible series of blunders and delays in which the navy failed to provide supplies and reinforcements. When the French fleet isolated him by cutting his lines with New York, Cornwallis was doomed. A combined Franco-American force under Washington extracted his surrender at Yorktown. The surrender of the last British army in America heralded the reality of American independence.[42] There were no more troops available in England to send to America. Most serious of all, there was no prospect of reconquering America without endangering other parts of the Empire. In the summer of 1781 West Florida and Tobago had been lost, Minorca had been invaded, and Bourbon fleets had the freedom of British waters. The security of the British Isles might have again been threatened had the American war continued. Finally, opinion in Britain rapidly swung against the American war after Yorktown. The British had suffered a resounding moral as well as a military victory.[43]

The news of Yorktown reached London on 25 November, two days before the new session was to begin. The Opposition was caught off guard and was totally unprepared to take the ministry by surprise. Rockingham and Shelburne remained at odds.[44] Rockingham, moreover, had not wanted to organise his friends until news of the outcome of the Yorktown campaign became known because he saw little point in persisting with hopeless opposition against an apparently invincible ministerial majority.[45] Although the news of Yorktown lowered the spirits of supporters of the Government, its majority was not threatened. The Address did not mention America and the Opposition seized upon this as an ominous indication that even now the Government still persisted with the idea of conquering America. The Address was voted 218–129.[46] Yet ministers were uneasy, still reeling from the shock of Yorktown and facing the daunting prospect of rethinking their American policy. Sir Walter Rawlinson, for example, a friend of Sandwich, a loyal ministerialist since he had entered the House in 1774 and occupying the Admiralty borough of Queenborough blanched when he read the Address and found no reference to America. This he took as a veiled commitment to continue with the war. Sir Walter now offered either to vacate his seat or to refrain from attending Parliament when America was being discussed. Like most people, he was convinced that the war must end.[47]

The Rockingham Whigs were slow to exploit the marvellous opportunity which Yorktown gave them. Their unreadiness to profit from the misfortunes of the ministry was indirectly to have serious consequences. The amendment to the Address, for example, was not moved by a Rockinghamite but by Dunning. Furthermore, the first significant attack from the Opposition upon the strategic aspect of the war came not from a Rockingham Whig but from their old enemy, Sir James Lowther. On 12 December he interrupted the Committee of Supply with a motion to end the war in America; he was defeated by only 220–179. Not only was this an important breakthrough in numerical terms, the Opposition having gained fifty votes since the beginning of the session. As the Minister himself admitted, operations in America in future could not be on anything like the same scale as in the past. His frankness was a direct condemnation of the failure of his own policies.[48] In fact, only Germain of the Cabinet was in favour of further military efforts in America after Yorktown; yet even he confessed to the King of 'the general dislike to the American War among the real friends of the Government'.[49] George III still wished North to continue but he was angered by North's realisation that the war could not go on and that independence must follow.[50] As Christmas approached the ministers well understood the implications of Yorktown but they could not afford to express their views for obvious political and diplomatic reasons. On the other hand, the Opposition was not able fully to profit from ministerial misfortunes because of its own divisions. On the issue of independence, Barré and Dunning voiced the familiar Shelburnite objections to complete American independence while Fox and Burgoyne argued that British recognition of independence was an essential preliminary to full scale war upon the Bourbon powers. Although both wings of the Opposition now agreed that not only men but measures ought to be changed, there was nothing like complete agreement between them as to the measures to be pursued in a future ministry, and still less over the disposal of places. Furthermore, although the Opposition might have been convinced that a change of policy must mean a change of ministry, the independents had not yet reached a similar conclusion.[51]

During the Christmas recess the divisions within the ministry intensified. The old hostility between Germain and Sandwich fed, as it always had, upon rivalry was now heightened by military and naval failure. Sandwich appeared to be doomed after Yorktown. While he was First Lord of the Admiralty, and in spite of his unquestioned energy, drive and conscientiousness, Britain had lost control of the seas. His reputation sank further when on 12 and 13 December there occurred yet another of those indecisive naval battles off Ushant. It was Sandwich who had to bear the brunt of the criticism for it. On the other hand, the conduct of the army in America had been scarcely distinguished. Lord George Germain, therefore, was just as much a liability to the ministry as Sandwich was. Among those who believed that the administration could not possibly bear the burden of retaining both men was Henry Dundas[52] who, with his friend, Richard Rigby, influenced the votes of a crucial dozen members and who had for some time been unhappy with Germain. Dundas pressed for Germain's resignation, arguing that if the ministry were to survive then new policies were needed, and America ought to be abandoned. Germain, in effect would be the scapegoat for the failure of the old policies. In January 1782, therefore, North rid himself of Germain, anxious to retain not only Dundas' votes but also his support in the House of Commons. In effect, however, Germain's dismissal did not have the effect that Dundas wished. It was not Germain who was the stumbling block to a change of policy. It was George III. Neither the King nor North thought that Germain's dismissal would lead to a change of policy. Germain had been sacked to preserve the ministry's majority not to change its policies. Indeed, Germain had been removed so that Sandwich might stay. And Sandwich was bound to attract like a magnet the storm of criticism that burst around the Admiralty in the wake of Yorktown.

The Opposition looked on with interest and with pleasure. It was clear that the ministry had been panicked into dismissing Germain. If Sandwich could be driven from office then surely the ministry must fall. The Opposition had long hated Sandwich, especially since the Keppel affair. To attack him now would be an almost perfect strategem. It would not raise the divisive issue of independence and it would appeal to the independents. On 24 January Fox moved for an enquiry into the administration of the navy. Ministers were reluctant to assume the unrewarding burden of defending Sandwich and feared to oppose Fox's motion outright. They decided to postpone the committee until 7 February. This gave ministers time to pull themselves together and to make some sense of the mountain of materials which Sandwich had been collecting in his own defence since the beginning of the session. On 7 February the first nail was knocked into the coffin of Lord North's ministry. After Fox's brilliant and scathing condemnation of Sandwich, his charge of 'gross mismanagement' was repulsed by the narrow majority of 205–183, a startlingly close division. Inevitably the issue was raised once again by the Opposition. On 20 February 1782 Fox moved a motion of censure against Sandwich in the Commons. In a full and excited House the ministry won the day by 236–217. On this occasion the rats began to desert the sinking ministry. Six former supporters voted against the ministry and a further 16 abstained. Of the 22 only 6 came from the Court and administration group. The other 16 came from the independents and the small parties supporting the ministry.

The Government, divided and demoralised, was clinging to power by the narrowest of margins. All that remained between the ministry and its overthrow was the fact that the principle of the war had not yet been repudiated by the House of Commons. In an all-out attempt to persuade the House to repudiate it the Opposition brought forward the venerable Conway on 22 February to lead their attack upon the principle of the war. He moved to end all attempts to subdue the Americans by force. His motion was defeated by a single vote, by 194–193. The temptation to repeat the performance was too great to resist. After a debate in which the whole question of the confidence of Parliament in the ministry was at stake Conway carried a similar motion by 234–215. North realised that the swing of opinion against him in the House during the previous few weeks meant that whatever the King might say, his ministry could no longer survive.[53]

What Rockingham and his friends had been dreaming of for years was at last taking place. In that crucial division on 27 February 1782, 40 supporters of the ministry failed to support it. Half of them abstained and half of them voted for Conway's motion. Most of these were independents. Lord North was reaping the poor harvest of the election result of 1780. Only ten county members supported Lord North while no fewer than fifty-six voted with the Opposition. Even the staunchest Government supporters, the Gower faction, for example, were refusing to support it now. It was the end for North. He told the King that he could not go on.[54] If the King needed convincing further than the Opposition was prepared to convince him. On 8 March Lord John Cavendish introduced a list of resolutions whose import was avowedly to remove the confidence of the House from the ministry. Although the ministers won the divison by 226–216 they could not continue to govern. The 8 March division was a slight setback to the Opposition, for eleven ministerialists returned to the fold on this occasion. Yet this was less a revival of confidence in the ministry than an eleventh hour pang of conscience on the part of some of the independents, who were not accustomed to forcing the hand of the Crown in the matter of removing and appointing ministers. The moral was clear. The Opposition had to strengthen its appeal to the independents. One way of doing this was to persuade a respected independent to lead its attack on the ministry. Thus on 15 March Sir John Rous, a county member for Suffolk, moved a motion of no confidence in the ministry on account of its conduct of the war. Even those who had supported the war could not deny the fact that it had been lost; and many of them passed judgement upon those who had lost it. Further, some of the independents who might have been reluctant to dictate to the King who his ministers ought to be had their consciences eased by the prevailing talk about the formation of a coalition acceptable to the King. Although the ministry won the division by 236–227 it was a pyrrhic victory. More important than numbers was the undeniable fact that ministers had by now lost the will to govern. Opposition prepared to administer the *coup de grâce* to Lord North. A motion was put down for 20 March demanding the removal of the ministers. As some Government supporters drifted quietly away from town North knew it was the end. On 20 March North at least showed the courage to face the House in person to announce the termination of his twelve-year-old ministry.[55] Defeat in war had led inexorably to political change at home, of that there was no doubt. But in the confused situation of politics in March 1782 it was by no means clear that if Lord North had been defeated then the Rockingham Whigs had necessarily won. To destroy the political system of George III which had existed with remarkably few changes since 1767 was one thing. What to build in its place, and how to build it, were the problems facing Opposition politicians after the collapse of the North ministry.

Chapter 21

The Rockingham–Shelburne Ministry (1782)

The fall of North had been the outcome of a national military disaster. It had not been a party victory and to claim that the Rockingham Whigs had alone been responsible for it is seriously misleading. North had been defeated by a temporary alliance of all the Opposition parties after Yorktown. The Rockinghams could not have prevented men like Lowther, Conway and, of course, the Shelburne Whigs from taking a full share in the collapse of the ministry, even if they had wanted to. In this way it was their victory almost as much as it was the Rockinghams'. To some extent, then, it seemed logical that George III should allow these men a position in the new ministry of some importance. Because the unique problems of the Rockingham–Shelburne ministry arose from the manner of its formation we must focus our attention upon the circumstances and motivations of George III, Rockingham and Shelburne.

After the division of 27 February 1782 when Conway's motion to end the war was carried by 234–215 the Court was forced to recognise that the North administration was doomed. It did not follow that the King had to bend the knee to the Rockinghams. North advised him on 28 February that 'it may be feasible to divide the Opposition, and to take in only a part'.[1] George III, however, did not want any part of the

Opposition on any terms and for some time he struggled to find some alternative to them. He sent Thurlow to sound Gower and Weymouth to discover if the three of them could not patch some sort of government together which might maintain what was left in America and negotiate peace treaties with the other powers.[2] These soundings came to nothing. Even the King's closest political advisers recognised that a new arrangement must include at least part of the Opposition.

The decisive turning point in the King's attitude seems to have been the debate and division on 8 March. After the debate Lord North advised him that the Rockinghams could not be ignored. Trying to sugar the bitter pill for the King's consumption, he remarked that the Rockinghams might not be unreasonable and that they might not demand the resignation of Thurlow.[3] George III was a very worried man. 'I certainly must maturely deliberate before I can return any answer.'[4] This was one of the most painful moments in the life of George III. It was hard enough for him to face the prospect of American independence without having at the same time to cope with distasteful political upheavals. The negotiation of the summer of 1780 had made clear the terms upon which Rockingham would take office and he had not changed his mind since then. The King must also have been aware that the united Opposition had been co-operating with much success and some cordiality in recent weeks.[5] He could expect little sympathy from the Opposition, which was likely to demand the strictest terms.[6] George III did not wish to become a prisoner of the Opposition. If he could divide it then he might be able to retain at least some freedom of action.

On 10 March he sent for the ever faithful Thurlow.[7] No precise details of the audience survive, but Thurlow did record some 'Hints', presumably to assist him in the undertaking of forming a new ministry, with which the King charged him.[8] Thurlow aspired to bring in Members of 'all parties and sects'. He recognised that the King's deepest wish, to strengthen the present ministry, was quite out of the question. 'There must be quite a new system of men and it is wholly impossible to accede to the present.' This could only mean the removal of North and

Sandwich and approaches to the Rockinghams and to the Shelburnites. The King need not be a prisoner of a new ministry, especially if room were found for Grafton, Camden and Temple. Armed with these preparations Thurlow set about his task. On 11 March he spoke with Rockingham in the House of Lords for ninety minutes. He made it clear that he had the authorisation of the King to discuss with him the formation of a new ministry 'upon a broad bottom and publick views'. The King would require some assurances from Rockingham but Thurlow did not state what these were. Instead he arranged a further meeting with Rockingham for 13 March.[9]

Because of the Chancellor's indisposition the meeting had to be postponed until 14 March. In the meantime, the King reminded Thurlow that 'my language went to a broad bottom, not the delivering myself up to a Party'.[10] At the same time, Richmond advised the Marquis, now that his great hour had come, to 'keep back and be very coy'.[11] Rockingham did nothing of the kind. With commendable frankness he laid down his conditions for coming into office. A scribbled, undated memorandum in Rockingham's hand almost certainly related to this conversation with Thurlow. 'America—Independency—No Veto Establishment Bill—great parts of Excise & Custom House Officers re-Bill Contractors—Bill [*sic*] Peace—general if possible and Oeconomy—in every Branch.'[12] In policy, then, there was to be a massive reversal of that pursued by North. As to men, the Marquis refused to have men 'who had been considered as *obnoxious ministers*'. Furthermore he demanded the resignation of those who belonged to 'a sort of secret system, from which may be attributed all the evils of the reign'.[13] In other words, Rockingham was refusing to negotiate on the 'broad bottom' lines hinted at by Thurlow. Furthermore, Rockingham insisted upon the Treasury for himself.[14]

These were stiff conditions, indeed. They were reinforced by the fact that Rockingham was not just speaking for himself. His actions were approved at a meeting of party leaders held that same night.[15] It is no surprise that they were, for Rockingham was merely acting consistently with the previously expressed statements and policies of his party. Yet the terms were as stiff as anything George III had encountered in politics since the days of George Grenville. In effect, Rockingham was asking him to withhold his power of veto over policy and to put into abeyance the prerogative of appointing ministers. George III was not prepared to comply with Rockingham's demands. He preferred to go to any lengths to avoid becoming the slave of a party. Through Thurlow the King returned an answer to the Rockinghams which appeared to agree to their policy demands although it contained the escape clause that such matters were best finalised after an arrangement had been negotiated. Nothing was said about offices.[16] Indeed, the King had not the slightest intention of agreeing to sweeping office changes if they could possibly be avoided. Rockingham at once became suspicious and told Thurlow: 'I must confess that I do not think it an adviseable measure, first to attempt to form a ministry by arrangement of office, and for the persons who take office afterwards to meet in order to decide upon what principles or measures they are to act'.[17] There could be no compromise between Rockingham and George III. When Thurlow and Rockingham met again on 18 March they failed to reach any agreement.[18] What is more, Rockingham was noticeably more intransigent than he had been before. When Thurlow asked Rockingham if he had any further conditions, Rockingham replied 'saying he would not bind himself that at no time and upon no occasion a circumstance might not arise that might demand some alteration'.[19]

On the same day that the negotiations with Rockingham collapsed, George III made overtures to Shelburne. North believed that it might be possible to put together a ministry which would include Shelburne, Thurlow, Gower, Weymouth, Grafton, Rutland, Temple, Camden and Lowther.[20] Such a ministry had much to commend it. It would satisfy the widespread feeling that changes both of ministry and of policy were necessary. It would bring in most sections of the Opposition without throwing the King into the arms of the Rockingham Whigs. At the same time, it would lack unity and would not be sufficiently strong to impose strict conditions upon the King. Shelburne, moreover, was much less inclined than Rockingham to hurry into rash steps to grant the colonies their indepen-

P

dence. Although he had come gradually to the view that
political subordination could no longer be exercised, he had
stressed as recently as 4 February 1782 that he would never
consent to acknowledge American independence. 'He was
known to differ from his most intimate friends and respectable
connexions on the subject'.[21] Furthermore, time was short.
On 15 March the ministry survived by only nine votes and on
20 March North resigned. Shelburne was now the object of
the King's attention. The fall of North and the intransigence
of Rockingham combined to drive him into Shelburne's arms.
On the day that North resigned, Shelburne and Thurlow met.
Rigby wrote to Lady Spencer: 'The Chancellor has seen Lord
Shelburne who without mentioning any Measures whatsoever,
declined holding any discourse with any Person but the King
himself'.[22] On 21 March Shelburne had an interview with the
King in which he refused to take the lead in the sort of ministry
George III was contemplating. Although the King made
explicit his preference for Shelburne over Rockingham,[23] a
fairly clear implication of his prospective support for him in a
Rockingham–Shelburne ministry, Shelburne was in too weak a
position even to think of coming into office without the
Rockinghams. There is no reason to ascribe treachery to him
at this stage. He had few followers and needed the protection
of the Rockinghams if he were not to become a creature of the
Court. He thus advised Thurlow to send for Rockingham.
However, he also hinted that if the King had

> 'an invincible aversion to this measure, rather than see his
> health impaired, or that he should risk any desperate
> measure, I certainly would not run away from any oppor-
> tunity of serving his Majesty or the public, providing the
> objection went no further than . . . the overt act stated of
> sending to Lord Rockingham in the first instance.'[24]

This implied declaration of Shelburne's intent to assist the
beleaguered monarch was all that the King needed to seize the
initiative. On 23 March the King told Shelburne that he
would negotiate with Rockingham but only if Shelburne acted
as his intermediary.[25] This was of crucial importance. The
King, by acting through Shelburne, might be able to confuse

the issues and cloud the confrontation between himself and Rockingham.

The pattern for the Rockingham–Shelburne ministry was now being formed. The King was slowly realising that if he were forced to take Rockingham—and in view of Shelburne's reluctance to serve without him, he probably would, then at least he might be able to secure better terms from the politicians than had appeared remotely possible when Thurlow had spoken to Rockingham earlier in the month. If Shelburne did prove friendly it might be possible to retain Thurlow in office. George III was beginning to think that he might not lack allies against the Rockinghams. On 24 March Shelburne, now taking over the role of negotiator which Thurlow had filled until then, conveyed to Rockingham the King's offer of the leadership of a ministry to include Camden, Grafton and, of course, Shelburne. Rockingham did not like it and insisted that 'a cabinet should be formed as is suitable to the execution of the very Important Measures which Lord Rockingham had the honour of submitting to His Majesty, through the Lord Chancellor'. Furthermore, he refused to take part in a ministry unless he could discuss the arrangement with the King in person.[26] So far, Rockingham had neatly blocked the King's manoeuvrings and had stood his ground. That he had done so is best attested by the King's anger at Rockingham's riposte. He told North on 25 March: 'I have not much reason to expect my confidence will be gained by the high demands, if not beat down before laid before me, of the great party'.[27] Nevertheless, Rockingham was becoming angry at Shelburne's game. He was assuming airs of superiority and hinting at his intimacy with the King in a manner which much offended Rockingham. As early as 22 March Shelburne told Rockingham, according to Lady Spencer, 'that he had seen the King, that he had been so happy as to convince His Majesty of the fairness of his conduct, that he hoped he had done no harm to the General Cause but that it was very awkward and unpleasant to him not to be at liberty to say more'.[28] Rockingham was both envious of Shelburne's dramatic rise to influence in the Closet and distressed at the unhappy disputes in the Opposition at its hour of triumph. In a fit of anger he refused to take part.[29] It required a meeting of his friends and three hours of persuasion on 25 March before Rockingham changed his mind.[30] In doing so, he made two disastrous errors. He dropped his demand for a personal discussion with the King. Further, he insisted 'on carrying into execution such an arrangement as may be satisfactory to the public eye and may give strength and cement to the principle on which this administration is to be formed'.[31] But what exactly did this mean? In terms of policy, Rockingham's demands were well known and Shelburne had persuaded the King to agree to them.[32] But what of offices? Apart from generalisations about obtaining the Treasury and the efficient offices, Rockingham had never been particularly explicit about them. Now, Rockingham agreed to serve *before* the distribution of offices had been settled. The King and Shelburne might hope, with some reason, that if they satisfied Rockingham on policy then he might not unfairly be expected to tolerate the presence within the ministry of politicians from outside his own party. On the night of 25 March and on the afternoon of the following day Rockingham and Shelburne deliberated over the disposal of offices.

The King and Shelburne drove a hard bargain. As expected, Rockingham took the Treasury and Shelburne and Fox the two Secretaryships. Lord John Cavendish became Chancellor of the Exchequer. Only one other Rockingham Whig (excluding Richmond) obtained a cabinet place. This was Keppel who went to the Admiralty. Grafton became Lord Privy Seal and Conway became Commander-in-Chief. The Duke oj Richmond, who cannot be regarded as a Rockinghamite by this time, took the Ordnance. As for the Woolsack, the Rockinghams had assumed that either the venerable Camden or the brilliant Dunning would replace the sour Thurlow—the Rockingham Whigs were weak in legal talent and had no candidate of their own. Rockingham and his friends were astonished, then, to be presented with a double *fait accompli*. The King's friend, Thurlow, was to remain as Lord Chancellor while Dunning, the hero of 1780, was compensated with a peerage (he became Lord Ashburnham) and a cabinet place as Chancellor of the Duchy of Lancaster. As a symbolic gesture of their dissatisfaction with this arbitrary method of distributing offices, the Rockinghams pressed for a peerage for Fletcher Norton. That Rockingham was reduced to seeking peerages for nonentities like Norton shows the depths to which the great administration had sunk almost before it had been launched. In the end the Rockinghams obtained the peerage for Norton, but they succeeded only in driving Shelburne and the King even more firmly into each other's arms. In the final outcome, Rockingham's reluctance and inability to force the King on the matter of cabinet appointments left his party occupying only a minority of cabinet offices.[33] He should, perhaps, have listened to Burke, who had advised Rockingham to insist upon an interview with the King 'because it frequently happens that in conversations through the intervention of third persons, however honourable, very essential mistakes may be made; & in such circumstances your Majesties orders may be misconceived by me, or my humble opinions imperfectly conveyed to your Majesty'.[34] The Marquis' failure to follow Burke's advice was to have disastrous consequences for his party.

That Rockingham was outmanoeuvred by George III and Shelburne is obvious. That it was intentional is readily confirmed since Shelburne wrote to the King on the night of 25 March, confident that he had managed 'to keep things within the bounds prescribed by Your Majesty'.[35] Although it is the case, as Dr Cannon convincingly argues, that 'Shelburne was to be built up as a counterpoise to the Rockinghams'[36] it remains true that to some extent Rockingham facilitated the workings of the plot against him by agreeing to a disposal of offices over which he had no right of veto, and which left his party in a minority in the Cabinet. It was good political tactics for George III to refuse to see Rockingham in person for it kept the Marquis at arms length and weakened further his fragile relationship with Shelburne. The King wished to use Shelburne as a counterweight to Rockingham in the ministry. Shelburne's conception of the new ministry as a broad bottom administration was far removed from the Rockinghams' aspirations towards party government. Shelburne made no attempt to press men and policies upon the King and

George III can hardly be blamed for preferring him to Rockingham.

The King proceeded to lavish his support upon Shelburne. He promised him not only that he should be 'fully consulted on the Plan of the new administration', but also that he should enjoy an equal share of the patronage with Rockingham.[37] In so far as he followed the wishes of the Commons and made no attempt to delay the granting of independence to America, George III acted scrupulously and constitutionally in March 1782. It was well within the bounds of his prerogative to prefer one set of men to another. He was thus prepared to set aside his opinions on matters of policy so long as he was able to exercise final authority over appointments. Shelburne's behaviour is more open to question. His sudden concern for the monarchy astonished the political world. It was, of course, a scarcely concealed disguise for the pursuit of his own ambition. Furthermore, his treatment of Rockingham was neither honest nor open. Nevertheless, Shelburne did his country a valuable political service in 1782. He prevented a constitutional crisis. It was he who acted as the bridgehead between the King and the Rockinghams. By breaking the *impasse* which existed between them, he steered the country away from a breakdown of government, made possible the negotiation of American independence, and the passage of considerable amounts of reforming legislation.

Although there was a general understanding that Shelburne was to be Rockingham's equal in the distribution of patronage, there remained considerable ambiguity over the practical workings of appointment to minor offices.[38] Because the King feared Rockingham, he accused the Marquis of 'wanting to get all Patronage into his hands, to the exclusion of Ld Shelburne'.[39] Shelburne wished to have something from the King in writing.[40] The King was glad to oblige. Not wishing to 'yield to the importunities of Lord Rockingham, which would reduce him to a Secretary of State, acting under the former, instead of a colleague' the King wrote to Shelburne:

'He was assured that he should not only be fully consulted on the plan of the new administration, and that the changes proposed should be communicated to the king by him, but that after the Administration should be formed, all ecclesiastical and civil preferments should be jointly recommended by the Marquis of Rockingham and him, which seemed the more natural, as the Administration was proposed to continue on the plan it was formed, a broad basis, and that persons who like the above two noblemen had accepted offices only from a view of being serviceable to their country at a perilous time could have no other wish but to recommend the best and ablest men on all occasions, and consequently must rejoice at being obliged to consult together, as the means most conducible of having such vacancies filled up to the advantage of the state.'[41]

George III thus chose to interpret the 'constitutional revolution' of March 1782 not as a victory for party but as the replacement of the North ministry by a broad bottom ministry in which Shelburne and Rockingham were to be co-equal partners.

A perfect example of the manner in which even trifling disputes between Rockingham and Shelburne could shake the very foundations of the ministry involved the office of Steward of the Household. The problem arose after Carlisle's dismissal from the office of Vice-Treasurer of Ireland. Carlisle was a member of the Gower faction, and Rockingham wished to compensate him in some way to avert the wrath of the Gowers. He proposed to give Carlisle the Stewardship of the Household if the incumbent, the Duke of Manchester, would take the Chamberlain's staff. Shelburne, for his part, was anxious to accommodate the Marlborough family. Marlborough's brother, Lord Charles Spencer, was to be deprived by Burke's Establishment bill of his post of Treasurer of the Chamber. He, too, required compensation and the Stewardship of the Household would have suited him admirably. A vicious patronage struggle ensued in which Rockingham became so angry that, according to his rival, he demanded that 'everything must go through him, as (it) did through Lord North, or where that Precedent is not sufficient, through himself when last in Office'.[42] Shelburne and the King were not prepared to concede Rockingham's claim that 'everything must go through

him', for it seemed to them to be an assertion of party government. Rockingham was arguing that everything should go
through the First Lord to avoid the imputation that the
ministry was a government by departments in which the King
rather than a party held sway. Shelburne, on the other hand,
assured the King that: 'I conceive the natural course of business
to be, first for the Department to submit any business to Your
Majesty, and to be consider'd afterwards by the Cabinet under
Your Majesty's Reference'.[43]

George III agreed with him:

> 'Certainly it is quite new for business to be laid before the
> Cabinet and consequently advice offered by the Ministers
> to the Crown unask'd; the Minister of the Department used
> always to ask the permission of the King to lay such a point
> before the Cabinet, as he cldnt [*sic*] chuse to venture to take
> the direction of the Crown upon him without such sanction;
> then the Advice came with propriety'.[44]

In the end George III refused to appoint Carlisle until some
arrangement satisfactory to Marlborough had been made. He
and Shelburne had made their point. The King, in particular,
was pleased to have this opportunity of reasserting the royal
right to adjudicate in disputes between his ministers. In the
end Carlisle was appointed to the Stewardship on 11 May but
it had been a pyrrhic victory for Rockingham.[45] Because he had
had to fight so hard to win the battle over this appointment
he saw that his authority was limited and that it could be
exercised only with royal approval. His anger and frustration
at this state of affairs found expression in rising fears that
Shelburne had become a tool of the system of secret influence.
These suspicions found apparent confirmation when Shelburne
began to gather a small group of men around him, in particular
the circle of Henry Dundas, which included none other than
Charles Jenkinson.

The Rockingham Whigs might have been forgiven for
wishing in the prevailing circumstances to hurry through an
ambitious programme of economic reform legislation. Believing
that the ministry was being attacked by the sinister forces of
secret influence it appeared to be an urgent necessity to

retaliate by legislative means. These suspicions were confirmed when the ministers discovered a debt on the Civil List of £290,000. The prospects for such legislation were, in fact, quite good. With the exception of Thurlow, the Cabinet was agreed on the principle expressed in Dunning's resolution. The King had withdrawn his veto on economic reform and the Northites were expected to attend Parliament irregularly. But because there was nothing standing in the way of economic reform it was much less exciting. Parliament had been recessed on 27 March until 8 April. On the latter date leave was given to bring in the ministry's economic reform legislation, Crewe's and Clerke's bills and Burke's Establishment bill.

Crewe's act to disfranchise revenue officials had been around in one guise or another for many years as a manifestation of the Rockinghams' commitment to economic reform. Two things should be said about Crewe's act. It was not an attempt to defend the rights of electors. It had the avowedly political objectives of destroying corruption and of overthrowing an allegedly powerful court system. In this context it was an attempt to *restrict* the rights of electors. Furthermore, the act failed to do what it set out to do. It was clearly the work of a political party which was more concerned with ideological purity than with administrative practicality. The act did not work well because it had been badly drafted. There were too many loopholes in it. It was based upon inadequate information. Revenue officers were believed to form a large part of the electorate in about seventy seats, thus affecting the return of 140 Members.[46] But this was a great exaggeration. Modern research has shown that the impact of the votes of revenue officers might be felt in only about one tenth of this number of constituencies.[47] Clerke's Act was rather more simple and direct in its operations. It removed from the Commons the 15–20 government contractors who usually sat there. Yet even this tiny group had never been a united block supporting the North ministry. Furthermore, the bill did not extend to other groups, such as shareholders and officials of the great trading companies, who also might have close and frequent relations with the Government. Little was achieved by either of these acts, in the short or in the long term. Indeed, they advertised the weaknesses of the ministry. In particular, in the debates on the Contractors' bill in the Lords, Thurlow spoke out against it and the ministry and Shelburne appeared to acquiesce in the Lord Chancellor's remarks.[48]

The core of the great economic reform programme was Burke's Establishment bill. The King took the line that as long as Crewe's and Clerke's bills passed, there was no need for statutory regulation of the Household, affirming that it 'could now be settled by interior regulations' which the Cabinet might approve. George III encouraged Shelburne and Thurlow to concert their activities in delaying the bill.[49] It took all of Fox's energies to persuade a cabinet meeting on 12 April that the Establishment bill should go through in its original form. 'I told them I was determined to bring the matter to a crisis. As I am, and I think a few days will convince them that they must yield entirely. If they do not, we must go to war again . . . I am sure I am ready.'[50] It was not, however, until a further cabinet on 15 April that the matter was finally settled.[51] But many doubts remained in the minds of individuals. Camden, Grafton and Conway hesitated to impose Household Reform upon a reluctant King. Nevertheless the King agreed to the bill on 24 April.[52] On 2 May it was presented to the House of Commons.[53] The passage of economic reform through Parliament was routine except for the fact that Thurlow and Shelburne spoke against the Contractors' bill in the Lords, a serious and embarrassing indication that the King disliked the measure and was assenting to it only with great reluctance.[54]

In this way, much of the glory and exultation of the economic reform victory was lost, as the bills passed through apathetic Houses with the stony approval of George III, the sullen resentment of Thurlow and the elusive snipings of Shelburne. Furthermore, the measure was noticed to be much less radical than the Establishment bill of 1780. Burke admitted that he now expected to save only one third of the sum (£200,000) which he had thought it possible to save then.[55] Nevertheless, his economic reform proposals removed 134 offices in the Household and the ministry, twenty-two of them tenable with a seat in the Commons. The Board of Trade and the third Secretaryship were abolished. Other departments affected were the Board of Green Cloth, the Lords of Police in Scotland, the Board of Works, the Great Wardrobe, the Jewel Office, and the Paymaster of Pensions. Burke also divided the Civil List budget payments into eight classes, each with its official responsible for the budget, whose accounts were to be presented to the Treasury. Burke was able to effect few savings in pensions, although he reduced the total amount to £90,000 per annum. But his 1782 plan did not include some of the more dramatic of the 1780 proposals, the abolition of the separate jurisdictions of Wales, Lancaster, and Cornwall. Although the Rockinghams were probably preparing further legislation,[56] they had neither the time nor the information which would have enabled them to carry out detailed measures of economic reform. Their achievement was limited but contemporaries regarded it as a substantial innovation. Furthermore, the King's hostility towards economic reform suggests that he hated the principle of it. To his chagrin parliamentary control of the Civil List had been not only asserted in theory but established in practice, while several useful correctives of traditional abuses were implemented. In the wider perspective, however, these reforms did little to tilt the balance of the constitution towards the Commons. In fact, they may have done the opposite. Wraxhall noticed at the time that economic reform led inevitably to an increase in the importance of honours and peerages which now acquired greater weight as political weapons.[57]

Some of the immediate economic reform objectives of the Rockingham Whigs were achieved, then, but after years of expectancy to disappointingly little effect. An alternative method of destroying secret influence was parliamentary reform. A cabinet which included Fox, Richmond and Shelburne might have been expected to make a serious attempt to place the British representative system upon a more equal basis. One reason why it did not was the attitude of the King. It was perhaps this which led to Shelburne's sudden disenchantment with the idea. As late as January 1782 he had been busy working out a plan which would have added more county Members, shortened the duration of Parliaments and eliminated rotten boroughs.[58] Richmond was rather more consistent. He always claimed that it had been a condition of his joining the ministry that Rockingham should agree to the establishment of a Commons committee to investigate plans for parliamentary reform.[59] He became increasingly restless at the failure of the ministry to do anything to fulfil this promise. Indeed, the furthest that Rockingham would go was to admit a scheme of parliamentary reform, 'If we could amongst us settle some Plan that should unite the opinions of the public'.[60] There was little prospect of that. The ministry was already irreparably divided on the subject and could never have reached agreement. Consequently on 30 April Richmond met with Wyvill and the Younger Pitt.[61] They agreed to proceed to test the opinion of the Commons on the subject. Pitt moved on 7 May 1782 for a Committee of the House to consider the state of the representation. He was defeated by 161–141, a division on which Rockingham's party was split down the middle and on which Rockingham's own sentiments coincided with those of North. Together they conspired unwittingly to frustrate the greatest prospect of success that parliamentary reform enjoyed in the seventy years before the Reform Bill of 1832.[62] The consequences for the Rockingham party were unfortunate. Its divisions on the subject did not heal. Richmond was extremely angry at Rockingham's attitude and edged closer to Shelburne.[63] Fox was extremely disappointed and tended to lose interest in reform, allowing the mantle of the 'man of the people' to slip from his shoulders and to be worn by William Pitt.[64]

With the exception of the problem of peace-making, perhaps the most pressing single issue facing the ministry was that of Ireland. The immediate background was the growing anticipation in Ireland, after the defeat of Cornwallis at Yorktown, that further concessions might be extracted from the British. This was the demand raised by the Volunteers at a great meeting at Dungannon on 15 February 1782. The Irish, furthermore, can only have been encouraged by Shelburne's irresponsible speech in the Lords on 11 April, which seemed to hold out to the Irish the hope of legislative independence.[65] The new Lord Lieutenant was the Duke of Portland, who recognised at once that there were only two alternatives open to the British: to maintain their authority by force of arms or to concede the Irish demands. 'Unless large Concessions are made *there will be an end of all Government* & there is not any man of sense in or out of Parliament nor an Englishman nor Irishman who has paid any attention to the present circumstances in this Country who does not deprecate delay as well as resistance.'[66] Portland's solution could not possibly have pleased the King who did not look kindly upon the prospect of signing away another part of the Empire. Although Shelburne was the minister in whose department Irish problems fell, he was reluctant to take a prominent part in their solution. Such advice as he did give contradicted his public statement and opposed concessions.[67] Fox's opinion was quite different. He was closely in touch with Grattan and a close friend of Fitzpatrick, Portland's Irish Secretary. Although he was at first equivocal, closer examination of the topic persuaded him that Portland's suggestion should be followed; a thorough-going constitutional settlement ceding Ireland her just demands was necessary if there were to be a lasting solution to the Irish problem.[68] While the discussion raged in London Portland was persuading Grattan to have the Irish Parliament adjourned from 4 to 27 May. Shelburne deplored unnecessary delay in case Portland be driven to make even greater concessions than were necessary. But he did little to aid matters by making legislative independence—the only possible solution—appear unpleasant and undesirable to George III.[69] There was little that could be done, however, to resist the powerful movements demanding Irish legislative independence. At a cabinet meeting on 15 May the decision was made and two days later Parliament passed a resolution providing for it, repealing an act of 1720 which confirmed Poynings Law.[70] This had the desired effect of satisfying opinion in Ireland. On 27 May the Irish Commons voted £100,000 for the navy.

There was one further dimension to the Irish problem. Party was just beginning to be a factor to be reckoned with in Irish politics. The Irish Opposition had for some years enjoyed a rudimentary coherence. Now it began to establish links with the Rockinghams. At the beginning of the ministry Rockingham had contacts with the leaders of the Irish Opposition and it appeared that the co-operation and assistance of these men might be bought at the expense of some offices.[71] Fox had already written to Charlemont, asking: 'In short why should not the Whigs (I mean in principle, not in name) unite in every part of the Empire, to establish their principles so firmly that no further faction will be able to destroy them'.[72] Had Rockingham had any hesitation about allying with the Irish Opposition, its talk of an Absentee Tax would have removed it.[73] On 11 May Portland wrote a long and worried letter to Rockingham: 'respecting my powers of forming an Administration and whether it is necessary to take the King's pleasure upon the alterations I shall have to propose in the law and revenue departments where a very considerable change must be made to carry on the Government with any credit or safety'. He felt unable to meet the Irish Parliament when it reassembled on 27 May 'unless I can produce them a new system of men as well as of measures'.[74] This he was able to achieve, but, inevitably, it provoked bitter hostility among those displaced.[75] Nevertheless, there can be no escaping the conclusion that on Irish affairs, the ministry, led and persuaded by the Rockinghams, achieved a fairly satisfactory solution to the Irish problem by adopting the only sensible policy which would have maintained both peace and British rule in Ireland.

The culmination of the tensions which crippled the Rockingham–Shelburne ministry came with the problem of making peace with America. Fox was the foreign secretary and thus had responsibility for peace negotiations with the European powers. Shelburne, as colonial secretary, had responsibility for the negotiation of peace with America. Shelburne was unwilling to write off the chance of maintaining some sort of relationship with the Americans. He had no intention of accepting Fox's view that American independence ought instantly to be recognised as a preliminary to treating with the European powers. This wide, but not impassable, divergence of opinion was, however, sharpened by the rivalry and suspicions which existed between Fox and Shelburne. The creation of a new system of Secretaryships in 1782, with the establishment of a Home Secretaryship (Shelburne) and a

Foreign Secretaryship (Fox), would have created problems in any event. As the negotiations with America were in Shelburne's hands while those with the European powers were in Fox's hands, thus the personal, political and bureaucratic difficulties which the ministry faced conspired to worsen a situation which already bristled with problems. On the great question of peace, as on other issues, the Rockinghams believed that Shelburne was plotting against them. Briefly, Shelburne chose one Richard Oswald[76] to negotiate in Paris with Benjamin Franklin. Meanwhile, Fox had appointed Tom Grenville[77] to open negotiations with the French. Although the details are complex, the crux of the matter was that the King threw his weight behind Shelburne, with the result that Oswald's negotiations appeared more 'official' than those of Grenville. He had some justification for doing so. On 23 April the Cabinet did not authorise unconditional independence as Fox wished. Fox seems to have ignored this decision. His only justification for doing so is that he found the Bourbon terms so high that the only way of breaking up the solid block of powers arraigned against Britain would be to detach the Americans by offering her independence. This may have been good tactics, but it was not according to the letter of the cabinet minute.[78] When the King threw his weight behind Shelburne,[79] Fox and the Rockinghams were furious. They worked busily to persuade the Cabinet to amend its American policy in the direction of Fox's opinions. Victory seemed to be theirs when the Cabinet agreed on 23 May to instruct Grenville to propose independence unconditionally.[80] Shelburne refused to accept this decision and he clearly falsified the Cabinet's deliberations in his reports to both the King and Oswald.[81] When Fox heard of Shelburne's trickery he exploded with rage and demanded that the Cabinet reaffirm its decision. But at successive Cabinets on 26 and 30 June Fox found himself in a minority. As he walked out of the former meeting he threatened to resign.[82] As he stormed out of the second meeting, according to Grafton, 'he declared with much regret that his part was taken to quit his office'.[83] Clearly, the peace negotiations were paralysed and the ministry was on the brink of dissolution.

On 1 July, in the middle of this great political crisis, the

Marquis of Rockingham died. He had been ill in early May and had been unable to attend to business for a week. He then recovered and although frail, was able to participate fully in the business of the ministry until 23 June, when his health once again began to cause concern. On 28 June his death was predicted, but on the following day he recovered slightly. At noon on the first day of July he fell victim to 'a momentary struggle, a convulsive fit'.[84] His friends and political associates were stricken with regret and disappointment. Henry Duncombe wrote: 'It was with infinite Concern I learnt the Death of that invaluable Man, & of . . . that Honest Statesman. . . . The confusion consequent upon his Loss & the Disunion in these Councils, which he alone knew how to reconcile & cement, plainly speaks the Degree and Depth of our Misfortune'.[85] The very real grief and distress of the Marquis' friends is the most eloquent testimony of the regard and respect in which he was held. Not even his political enemies ever queried his disinterestedness and his honesty. His ability in presiding over the formation, the survival, the lean years, and finally the victory of the Whig party which bore his name was such that he stamped the authority of his personality upon its future. His successor, the Duke of Portland, was a man very much in Rockingham's mould. No one would claim great abilities or spectacular achievements for Rockingham. Yet he was able to attract men and to bring them to reconcile their views in the interests of the party. No other politician attracted the cluster of brilliant talents which surrounded him. Savile, Dowdeswell, Burke and Fox and many others were prepared to endure political privations in the interests of their leader. It is no accident that the removal of Rockingham from the centre of power gave rise to a renewed political crisis and plunged his party into one of the greatest controversies of its history.

The Rockinghams settled on a new leader with little difficulty. On the day after Rockingham's death, a meeting at Fox's decided to offer the leadership to the Duke of Portland, the Lord Lieutenant of Ireland. If Fox is excluded from consideration, the only other possible candidate for the unenviable position was Richmond. Although much more

talented than Portland, his reforming views made him unacceptable to many in the party. More serious, his growing
attachment to Shelburne put him out of consideration.

To dispose of the leadership to an amiable nobleman whom
Charles James Fox could manipulate was an easy matter.
More problematic was the attitude to be adopted by the party
towards Shelburne. On 28 June Shelburne was already plotting
to succeed Rockingham. Anticipating his death, he was
planning a ministry led by himself which would include Pitt
and Jenkinson but not, he hoped, Fox.[86] Fox himself had some
slight pretensions to consider himself the successor to Rockingham but he was never a serious contender.[87] A few hours after
Rockingham's death the King wrote to Shelburne offering
him the Treasury and the ambitious Shelburne gladly accepted.
The friends of Rockingham had been caught unprepared. Fox
was furious. He would serve only under Portland and told the
King as much on 3 July.[88] On the following day, amidst
considerable confusion, he resigned. Richmond was unable to
persuade him to stay, even though he seems to have won some
concessions from Shelburne on American Independence.[89]
Fox gave several reasons for his resignation. He asserted that
the Cabinet ought to have chosen the successor to Rockingham and that because it was the Rockinghams and not
Shelburne who had a majority in it, Portland should have
succeeded Rockingham.[90] Fox's doctrine was a curious
innovation. It was a strongly established convention of the
constitution that the King had the right to choose his First
Minister. Even if the Cabinet had been consulted, it is very
likely that a majority of its members would have opted for
Shelburne rather than Portland. Upon whom could Fox have
relied, other than Cavendish and, just possibly, Keppel?
Even if Fox's curious constitutional doctrine were legitimate it
might not have placed Portland at the Treasury. Furthermore,
Fox claimed that he had to resign because the conditions upon
which the Rockingham–Shelburne ministry had been negotiated had been violated by Shelburne.[91] But had they? The
only conditions to which the King had agreed were matters
of policy. He had bent over backwards to avoid pledging his
word to the party theories of the Rockinghams. Fox used a

further argument. He stated that the Rockingham Whigs had a parliamentary majority and that therefore their leader ought automatically to be the First Lord of the Treasury. But it was not at all obvious that the Rockinghams did have a majority in the Commons, still less in the Lords. The House of Commons had an undoubted right to withdraw its support from ministers, as it had done in the early months of 1782. But it was not accepted constitutional doctrine that the Lower House ought to dictate to the King who his ministers were to be. On the contrary, both the Cabinet and the Commons ought to support the minister of the King's choice. Shelburne was the King's free choice and believed that the other ministers ought to rally round and serve under him. As Dr Derry has nicely put it: 'While Fox suspected a plot on the King's part to impose Shelburne on the cabinet, George III discerned a conspiracy of disappointed men seeking to hound his chosen minister to destruction by denying to their sovereign his legitimate right of choosing his own servants'.[92]

In these circumstances, when there were few good reasons for resigning from office, it is not surprising that few men followed Fox's example. Many observers thought that Fox should not have retired until a measure of importance was brought forward by Shelburne upon which he might have resigned.[93] Richmond believed 'that the party had better give him (Shelburne) a tryal, as the likelyest method of keeping the party together on a respectable footing'.[94] Nevertheless, at a meeting at Fitzwilliam's house on 6 July, attended by about forty Rockinghamites, Richmond was unable to prevent some resignations. Fox and Cavendish, of course, had already chosen that course of action. The crucial decision was that of Richmond. If he had resigned then several other cabinet members might have followed him but he did not. Even Keppel stayed, out of loyalty to the naval service. Portland and Fitzpatrick ultimately came home from Ireland and resigned their offices. Sheridan and Burke went out, and John Lee gave up the post of Solicitor General. Three of the four Treasury Lords and two of the Admiralty Lords came out. A dozen resignations, however, were insufficient to shake the ministry of Shelburne. Fox had made the first of those disastrous gambles with which his political career is studded, and he lost. As Burke sadly asked: had Rockingham died so that Shelburne could become the master of the Closet? To resign was a hopeless gesture of defeat.[95]

In the Commons debate on 9 July, the epilogue to the dramatic crisis following Rockingham's death, Fox dropped all pretence and struck directly at the court system which had elevated Shelburne to the Treasury.[96] He claimed that with Shelburne in office party government and collective responsibility were impossible. Fox saw, underpinning personal and political differences, a fundamental constitutional disagreement between Shelburne, the representative of the system of secret influence and the Rockingham Whigs. The supremacy of Shelburne indicated a return to departmental government in which the King wielded great power and a rejection of party government. Supporters of Shelburne claimed in the debate, with considerable justification, that he had violated none of the conditions and principles upon which the Rockingham–Shelburne ministry had been established. Although Fox claimed that he had violated an agreement that the ministry would be a party ministry, there had never been, except perhaps in the optimistic minds of Rockingham, Fox and Burke, such an understanding. George III had managed to avoid agreeing to one.

Shelburne stood on the side of tradition and established custom. Men were not used to party government. It could not, for example, survive the death of its leader in office. Although the crisis which followed Rockingham's death was unhappy and unfortunate for the Rockingham party, it did at least focus the searchlight of public attention upon the conflicting principles which were at stake. Shelburne declared that in July 1782 the Rockinghams were aiming at the tyranny of party.[97] The struggle between George III and Fox was far more than a struggle for place and personnel. Fox, in his own wayward manner, was continuing the Rockinghamite crusade for the establishment of party government. At the same time, it was developing in ways that Rockingham might not have approved. Although Rockingham had his grudges, the personal hatred Fox engendered with George III was new. Fox's curious assertion that the Cabinet had the right to appoint the First Lord of the Treasury was a novel, unrepeated and unacceptable extension of Rockinghamite ideas. He was unfair in misrepresenting Shelburne's sincerely held Chathamite principles as a sinister desire to set up the standard of autocratic government. Yet the conflict between Fox and Shelburne, and after him, Pitt was essentially a conflict between party and non-party government. Fox argued that whatever measures of reform might be at issue it was necessary to ensure 'that the immediate power which governs you is not only capable from talents, but proper from integrity and firmness'. There was an abiding need for vigilance against the executive. 'All the misfortunes which have befallen this country, have originated principally in the want of due and general attention to this principle. The system has been to divide men against men, to separate the force of each of them, and to subvert the foundations of reciprocal confidence.'[98] The language of the 1760s was thus echoed in the 1780s. The most important thematic element in British politics in the reign of George III was the conflict between the ideas of the Rockingham Whigs and those of Chatham and George III. By 1782 party had attained a status, an acceptability and a pivotal position in politics which in 1760 would have appeared unthinkable. The Rockingham Whig party borrowed much from its Pelhamite parentage and its country ancestors but it bequeathed traditions and principles which established the content of opposition politics after 1783.

CONCLUSION

Chapter 22

Conclusion

After the high hopes of the spring of 1782 the autumn brought disenchantment and despair to the Rockingham Whigs. They had come into office full of vigour and good intentions. Within a few weeks they had launched policies on a large number of issues. To their credit, they did not abandon in Government the programmes for which they had campaigned in Opposition. The implementation of a reform programme and the pacification of America and Europe were soon under way. The ministry did much and promised more. But the crippling disputes between the Rockinghams and Shelburne bedevilled the present stability and future success of the ministry. The death of Rockingham permitted George III to reassert his power of appointing ministers. The Rockinghams were in disarray and unprepared for such a crisis.

The history of the Rockingham–Shelburne ministry and the appointment of Shelburne to the Treasury reinforced Rockinghamite fears of the continuing operations of a sinister court cabal. Events gave them a fresh currency, a new relevance, and enabled the Portland Whigs to draw from a mythological well an endless stream of conviction that the plan of the present reign to destroy the aristocracy was being as avidly pursued in the 1780s as it had allegedly been twenty years earlier. Moreover, the crisis of the next two years hardened political attitudes still further and blew up a storm of political hysteria. Both Fox and George III went to extremes. Fox has often been blamed for assuming a reversionary interest in the heir to the throne in the autumn of 1782 and there is no doubt that the connection did him much harm. At the same time, it was a traditional Opposition ploy to use the heir to the throne as a weapon in the political battle. It must have been particularly tempting for Fox to do so when he was incensed at what he took to be the King and Shelburne's underhand tactics during the last few months. As in 1766, the Rockingham Whigs believed that the principles and activities of the court system and the Chathamites were conspiring against them. The resulting hatred of Shelburne and the King was the emotional foundation of the Fox–North coalition. The coalition may have been unholy but it has its roots far back in the history of the Rockingham Whig party. Indeed, the actions of both sides in these critical years were the logical outcome of attitudes taken up and principles expounded earlier in the reign of George III. Those who supported the King believed that the independence of the monarchy was at issue while those who supported Fox believed that the independence of Parliament was at stake. During the constitutional crisis of 1782–4, therefore, the battle between the principles of the Court and of Chatham, on the one hand, and those of Rockingham and Burke, on the other, was played out. That the King and the son of Chatham emerged victorious in 1784 demonstrated that the appeal to party was much less powerful than the mighty currents of loyalty to the monarch and the cry 'Measures not Men'. The Court's victory in 1784 did not, however, put an end to the war. The friends of Fox and Portland continued to proclaim party principles and consistently rested their criticisms of the ministry of the Younger Pitt upon the allegedly unconstitutional manner in which he had come into office in December 1783.

After 1782 the old Rockingham party was under new management but it could never divest itself of those influences which had shaped its character in its formative years. In the early 1760s the British political system could not possibly have survived the stresses imposed upon it by the greatest war which the country had ever fought. The solidarity of the Whigs weakened while the Tories lost such coherence as they still maintained with the passing of the Jacobite bogey and the ending of their proscription in 1760. During the political turmoil of the early years of the reign of George III the Rockingham party emerged. It represented the marriage of the Pelhamite traditions of aristrocratic solidarity in party to the country party's ideals of purity and economy. The immediate catalyst was the role of Lord Bute in politics. The reaction was dramatic. The speed with which the Duke of Newcastle became the Leader of the Opposition in 1762 was matched only by the speed with which so many of his friends deserted him. Furthermore, early suspicions of Bute were aroused not merely by events but by the conspiratorial mentality of the eighteenth century which could transform a few well meaning gestures of loyalism into a dangerous conspiracy to overthrow the constitution. Personal factors also counted for much. The virtual absence of leadership left by Newcastle in 1764–5 allowed Cumberland and then Rockingham to influence the development of the Rockingham party in their own ways. However, the most decisive stage in the emergence of the Rockingham party was undoubtedly the period from the beginning of the ministry of 1765 to the Edgecumbe affair. Their experience in office left the Rockinghams in no doubt of the reality of the threat to the established political practices of the country posed by the 'double cabinet' system. The circumstances of the coming to power of the Chatham administration convinced them that Bute and Chatham were in league. Even more important, the Edgecumbe affair deprived Rockingham of both his 'Court' and his 'Chathamite' wings. By the end of 1766 the nature of the Rockingham party had clearly emerged, its attitudes were fairly well defined and its enmities manifest.

As we have seen, at this time the party owed as much to Newcastle as it did to Rockingham. But within a few years it had acquired a structure, an identity and a philosophy which, taken together, make the Rockingham party the 1770s a different political creature to the Newcastle connection of the early 1760s. The Rockingham Whigs, realising that the old party distinctions were dead, consciously sought to establish new ones. In order to do so, they kept themselves clear of the corrupting influences of the Court. Occasionally, they even termed the Court and its followers 'Tory' while reserving to themselves a belief that they were the heirs of the Whig tradition and the custodians of Revolution principles. In the eighteenth century, moreover, the country party had normally been an anti-party group. The Rockingham Whigs, however, had imbibed enough Pelhamite precepts to recognise the advantages of acting in party. Indeed, they not only defended the role of connections in politics and maintained that Opposition was legitimate. They defended and glorified party. Although the Rockingham party proclaimed that its purpose was to take over and purify the government of the country, the party leaders sometimes seemed happy to remain in Opposition. Indeed, Fox's innocent yet perfectly understandable wish to rush into office was greeted with aloof bewilderment by Rockingham, Richmond and Burke. The Rockingham Whigs were essentially a country party of Opposition.

The Rockingham party was unique in its time. It was larger than other parties and was to have a much longer life. It was not a faction and it was not a personal connection. It was not a family group and it was not even a confederation of families. The Rockingham party embraced parties of different types and included a large proportion of independents. It was dedicated to specific public purposes and not merely to immediate self-interest. Although the Rockinghams could certainly behave factiously on occasion, their ability to do so should not encourage a retreat into a meaningless cynicism about the motives of men. The history of the Rockingham party is far more than a struggle of the 'outs' who wanted to be 'in'. They naturally wished to obtain place and enjoy power but it should be remembered that they wished to do so for particular purposes. It may be argued, however, that the conservatism of the Rockingham Whigs illustrates their self-interest. For example, it could be maintained that in their economic reform campaign the Rockinghams' wished to preserve the structure of offices and patronage of the Government, shorn of the worst abuses, to enjoy for themselves. This, of course, was what

Burke would have been ready to accept. He argued for a change of men rather than a reform of institutions. At the same time, the Rockingham Whigs probably reflected prevailing sentiment in the country. Radical parliamentary reform did not yet have the mass appeal which it was later to have.

The place of the Rockinghams in the history of party in Britain is significant. In view of the eighteenth century's lack of enthusiasm for party, the ability of the Rockinghams to establish a party, to survive the lean years and to return to office is, in the context of the times, remarkable. The Rockinghams had faults and weaknesses in plenty. They were at times indolent and on some issues they were divided. But then, so were all oppositions and most administrations of the century. The setbacks of the 1770s undoubtedly, and very naturally, gave rise to pessimism and demoralisation but to speak of the party's 'decline and near disintegration' exaggerates the extent of the party's misfortunes.[1] Furthermore, the party served a useful constitutional function. Its preoccupation with Bute and secret influence may have been misguided but it served at least to draw attention to the crucial question of the appointment of ministers, the activities of the executive and its relationship to the King. Although its anxieties *were* exaggerated there was *some* foundation for them. Bute *did* occupy a position in the early months of the Grenville ministry which was of very doubtful constitutional propriety indeed. Furthermore, the revival of the connection between the King and Bute in 1766 suggests that the Rockinghams were justified in directing attention towards the situation of the *quondam* favourite.[2] The Rockinghams built their suspicions of Bute into an edifice of corruption and despotism. To destroy it they advocated constitutional principles which were not spurious. The lengths to which they were prepared to go should not be underestimated. By the end of the 1770s they had acquired a distinct dislike of George III. They had dropped all pretence of liberating a King 'in toils'. They were perfectly prepared to thrust their way into office and force him to adopt a set of policies and a system of government unpalatable to him. In 1782 they almost succeeded in effecting a constitutional revolution.

In the longer term, the Rockingham Whig party is the crucial link between the politics of mid-Hanoverian England and the great Whig and Tory parties of the nineteenth century. Continuity can be demonstrated in the party history of England from the Pelhamite connection of the reign of George II to the Rockingham Whigs and the Portland/Foxite party of the 1780s, and thereafter to the Whig party of Grey and the age of reform.[3] In so far as this can be shown to be the case, the present author advances a 'Whig' interpretation of the party history of the later eighteenth century. There is an underlying and clearly discernible process of development in Whig history from the mid-eighteenth century onwards. That process became irreversible in the 1780s with the solid, organisational developments which Dr Ginter has unearthed, and which continued into the next century.[4] The institutional-isation of party consolidated the rise of party.

Yet party could only be organised when party existed, when men had become accustomed to working together in a common cause and over a long period of time. At the human level, no one was more indispensable than the Marquis of Rockingham in enabling his men to work together. Edmund Burke may be pardoned the fulsome praise of his master which he lovingly wrote for the inscription on Rockingham's mausoleum at Wentworth.

'A man worthy to be held in remembrance, because he did not live for himself. His abilities, industry, and influence, were employed without interruption to the last hour of his life to give stability to the liberties of his country, security to its landed property, increase to its commerce, independence to its public councils, and concord to its empire. These were his ends. For the attainment of these ends, his policy consisted in sincerity, fidelity, directness and constancy. . . . In opposition he respected the principles of Government; in Administration, he provided for the liberties of the people. He employed his moments of power in realising everything which he had proposed in a popular situation—the disting-uishing mark of his public conduct. . . .

'He far exceeded all other statesmen in the art of drawing

together, without the seduction of self-interest, the concurrence and co-operation of various dispositions and abilities
of men, whom he assimilated to his character and associated
in his labours. For it was his aim through life to convert
party connection, and personal friendship (which others
had rendered subservient only to temporary views and the
purposes of ambition), into a lasting depository of his
principles, that their energy should not depend upon his
life, nor fluctuate with the intrigues of a Court, or with the
capricious fashions amongst the people; but that by securing
a succession in support of his maxims, the British Constitution might be preserved, according to its true genius, on
ancient foundations, and institutions of tried utility.'

Appendix

The Membership of the Party of the Duke of Newcastle 1762–4

Surviving division lists, used with care, and checked against the biography of the Members enable an estimate to be reached for the membership of Newcastle's party in these crucial, early years. In particular, they allow the historian to reconstruct the gradually increasing number of Members who after December 1762 began to show their allegiance to Newcastle.

1 DECEMBER 1762

There are two lists of the minority in the Newcastle Papers. One (B.M. Add. MSS 33000, ff. 193–4) gives 63 names. Another 5 may be added from Lord John Cavendish's list drawn up from memory (ibid., 32945, ff. 239–41). Sixty-eight names of the minority of 74 can therefore be retrieved. The fact that the 'Young Friends' were supported by only 37 Pelhamites is so important that I give the list in detail. Of the 68 members known to have voted in the minority, 31 were *not* Pelhamites. They comprised:

Six Tories: W. Blackett, W. Bootle, T. Cholmondeley, Sir T. Grosvenor, Sir W. Knatchbull, T. Staunton.

Five acted with Newcastle at a later date: T. Anson, W. Dowdeswell, Lord Galway, G. Hunt, G. Jennings.

The remaining twenty: A. Champion, Lord Clive, T. Coventry, P. Fonnereau, T. Fonnereau, Z. Fonnereau, J. Henniker, Edward Lascelles, Edwin Lascelles, J. Major, Sir J. Mawbey, Lord North, T. Pitt, Sir J. Rushout, N. Ryder, Lord Palmerston, Sir F. Vincent, J. Walsh, J. Wilkes, Sir T. Whichcot.

THE 37 SUPPORTERS OF NEWCASTLE

W. A'Court
Sir W. Ashburnham
J. Buller
J. Butler
Lord G. Cavendish
Lord J. Cavendish
N. Calvert
N Cholmley
C Fitzroy
Sir A. Gilmour
Sir J. Gibbons
Lord Grey
F. Honeywood

H. B. Legge
Sir G. Methan
H. Meynell
Lord Middleton
J. Murray
J. Norris
T. Pelham
J. Plumptre
Sir F. Poole
H. Powell
J. Robinson
T. Robinson
Sir G. Savile

C. F. Scudamore
F. W. Sharpe
'Spanish' Charles
  Townshend
T. Townshend Jnr
G. V. Vernon
Lord Villiers
T. Walpole
J. West
J. White
W. Willy
W. Woodley

Three Pelhamites (Lord Gage, John Shelley and T. Townshend Snr) were shut out of the division and they have not been included here.

9 AND 10 DECEMBER 1762

The sources for the following estimates of membership of Newcastle's following are the lists in the Newcastle Papers (B M. Add. MSS 32946, ff. 273–6; 33000, ff. 232–5; 33002, ff. 476–8; 33035, ff. 50–41 and J. Almon, *History of the Late Minority*, pp. 85–88).

I consider that the following 32 members should be added to the 37 discovered from the minority of 1 December.

Lord Ancram
A. Archer
Sir G. Armytage
Sir W. Baker
Sir J. Barrington
B. Burton
J. Calvert
W. Coke
J. Dodd
J. Fitzwilliam
B. Fisher

B. Forester
Lord Gage
J. Hervey
J. Hewett
Sir J. Mellish
Lord F. Cavendish
R. Cavendish
T. L. Dummer
T. Noel
Col. G. Onslow
G. Onslow

J. Offley
J. Scawen
J. Sergison
Sir E. Simpson
J. Shelley
J. Thomlinson
T. Townshend Snr
A. Wilkinson
W. Whitmore
Lord Winterton

MARCH 1763: THE DUKE OF NEWCASTLE'S LISTS OF 'SURE FRIENDS OF MY OWN IN THE HOUSE OF COMMONS'

This list provides six names who do not appear above.

J. Bentinck   (a newcomer to Parliament)
Sir H. Bridgeman   (had voted *for* the peace)
R. Burton   (had not voted in December)
Sir M. Fetherstonehaugh (had not voted in December)

J. Page   (might have voted in December)
W. Plumer   (Newcastle wrote R. Plummer but there was no
                               member of that name. He must mean the new
                               member for Lewes)

By the end of the session of 1763, therefore, 75 Members can with some
confidence be said to belong to Newcastle's party.

THE DIVISION OF 15 NOVEMBER 1763

The lists of the minority which provide an additional 17 members of
Newcastle's party can be found in the Newcastle Papers (B M. Add.
MSS 32952, ff. 403–5; 32953, ff. 25–7), Sir J. Fortescue, op. cit., I, pp. 54–8
and L. B. Namier, *Additions and Corrections*, p. 19. The 17 members are:

G. Brudenell	W. Fitzherbert	H. Walpole
P. Burrell	C. Hanbury	R. Walsingham
Sir K. Clayton	Sir W. Meredith	T. Tracy
Sir G. Colebrooke	A. Nesbitt	Sir G. Warren
H. Curwen	H. Penton	T. Watson
S. Finch	Lord H. Powlett	

By this time Lord Ancram and Sir F. Poole were no longer in Parliament.
Newcastle's following in the Lower House amounted, therefore, to 90
members.

THE GENERAL WARRANTS DIVISIONS OF FEBRUARY 1764

In January 1764 Frazer Honeywood died, reducing the number of New
castle's following to 89. These divisions together with the lists of membership of Wildman's club reveal that a further 20 members were supporting
Newcastle at this time. By the end of the session the party's strength was 109.
   The division lists on General Warrants are as follows:

6 February, B.M. Add. MSS 32958, ff. 370–3, 405–7.
14 February, ibid., 32953, ff. 269–70.
17 February, ibid., 32956, ff. 68–71, 118–21, 186–9. There are also lists
   of this division in the Newdigate MSS 2548–56 and in J. Almon, *History
   of the Late Minority*, pp. 279–82.

The 20 names are:

Sir A. Abdy	T. Fitzmaurice	Sir C. Saunders
G. Adams	Rose Fuller	G. Tufnell
T. Anson	Richard Fuller	Sir E. Walpole
A. A'Court Ashe	G. Hunt	Sir G. Yonge
Sir P. Brett	G. Jennings	C. Yorke
J. Bullock	H. M. Praed	J. Yorke
H. S. Conway	J. Scudamore	

MAY 1764: THE DUKE OF NEWCASTLE'S LIST OF 'SURE FRIENDS'

In May Newcastle estimated the size of his own following at 175. He includes the 109 names above together with 66 others. These 66 can be grouped as follows:

Friends of Pitt (8):

I. Barre	J. Grenville	W. Pitt
J. Calcraft	Sir J. Grifin Grifin	L. Sulivan
G. Cooke	J. Pitt	

Independents—those marked * were Tories—(28):

B. Bathurst*	J. Hewett	D. Rolle*
Sir W. Beauchamp- Proctor	R. Hunt* Sir R. Ladbroke	Sir J. Rushout J. Rushout
P. Bertie*	P. Legh*	H. Sturt*
H. C. Boulton	Sir R. Long*	J. Tempest*
N. Cholmley	R. Milles	Sir C. Treise*
T. Coventry	Sir R. Mostyn*	J. Tuckfield*
Sir E. Dering*	Sir T. Palmer	C. Tudway
S. Egerton	J. P. Pryse	Sir F. Vincent
Sir H. Harbord	Sir M. W. Ridley	

Distant Friends of Newcastle (13):

M. Barne	P. Honywood	E. Popham
D. Campbell	J. H. Medleycott	R. Stevens
Sir W. Codrington	W. Monckton	C. Forester
P. Denis	J. Morgan	
Sir G. Heathcote	T. Morgan	

The remaining 17 on Newcastle's list were fairly obscure men with no identifiable political alignment. Newcastle, in short, was not listing his 'Sure Friends' at all. He was listing those who had supported him on General Warrants and those he expected to support him in the next session. In one sense, Newcastle was right. There were about 175 men in the Commons who would vote with him on the right issue. But 66 of them were in too distant a relationship to Newcastle and his friends, figure rarely, if at all, in their correspondence and appear to have no real contact with his connection and its life. I estimate that Newcastle had about 109 followers in the Commons at the end of the 1764 session.

THE HOUSE OF LORDS

There is in the Newcastle Papers a list of peers who voted against the Cider Tax. They are 41 in number but eleven of them appear to have no

Q

discernible connection with Newcastle and his friends. These eleven are in italics (*see* B.M. Add. MSS 32948, ff. 155–8):

Dukes	Earls	Viscounts	Bishops
Bolton	Ashburnham	*Folkestone*	Chichester
Devonshire	Bessborough	Spencer	Ely
Grafton	Cornwallis	Torrington	*Hereford*
Newcastle	Dartmouth		Litchfield
Portland	*Fauconberg*	**Barons**	Lincoln
	Ferrers	Abergaveny	Norwich
Marquis	Hardwicke	Archer	Oxford
Rockingham	*Oxford*	*Foley*	St Asaph
	Plymouth	Fortescue	Worcester
	Suffolk	Grantham	
	Temple	*Grosvenor*	
		Lyttleton	
		Monson	
		Sondes	
		Walpole	
		Ward	
		de Broke	

To the 30 Newcastle peers listed above may be added:

The Duke of Cumberland	The Earl of Albermarle
The Earl of Lincoln	The Earl of Jersey
The Earl of Winchelsea	The Earl of Bristol
The Earl of Scarborough	The Earl of Bristol
	Baron Edgecumbe

To the 30 Newcastle peers who voted against the Cider tax, then, there can be added nine who did not, making a total of 39 Newcastle peers in the Upper House. See also ch. 2 n. 57 for a similar calculation.

Bibliography

The following list of sources indicates only those materials which have been of the greatest assistance in the preparation of this book.

MANUSCRIPT SOURCES

I. BRITISH MUSEUM

Almon Papers	Add. MSS 20735
Auckland Papers	Add. MSS 34412, 34414–15, 34442
Bathurst Papers	Loan Collections 57/1–3
Dashwood Papers	Egerton MSS 2136
Egmont Papers	Add. MSS 47012
Fox Papers	Add. MSS 47559, 47580, 47582
Grenville Papers	Add. MSS 42084
Hardwicke Papers	Add. MSS 35361–2, 35375, 35420–1, 35424, 35430, 35609, 35638, 35881
Holland House Papers	Add. MSS 51324, 51338, 51379, 51382–7, 51389, 51405–6, 51408, 51415, 51421, 51423, 51424, 51425, 51430–6, 51447
Liverpool Papers	Add. MSS 38204–5, 38209, 38212, 38307
Martin Papers	Add. MSS 41354–5
Newcastle Papers	Add. MSS 32915, 31917–20, 32927, 32929, 32931, 32939, 32941–56, 32958–64, 32960–7, 32970–8, 32980–2, 32987–91
Northington Letter Book	Add. MSS 38716
Thurlow Transcripts	Egerton MSS 2232
Wilkes Papers	Add. MSS 30868–70

2. PUBLIC RECORD OFFICE

30/8. Chatham Papers
S.P. (Dom) 44/117, 142
T.S. 11/920/3213
W.O. 34/114, 116

3. SHEFFIELD PUBLIC LIBRARY

Wentworth Woodhouse MSS

Rockingham Papers

In addition to the basic R1 series, chronologically arranged, the following bundles contained valuable material. R2, R3, R9, R10, R14, R15, R22,

R23, R25, R35, R42, R48, R49, R53, R81, R97, R125, R136, R137, R140, R144, R146, R149, R151, R155, R161, R168

Burke Papers

Bk 3, Bk 4a, Bk 6, Bk 9, Bk 11–14, Bk 23, Bk 25, Bk 27, Bk 29

Fitzwilliam Papers

F7, F48–9, F63b, F125d, F128
H1–10, H24–31

4. OTHER LOCAL RECORD OFFICES

Berkshire Record Office	Braybrooke Papers
	Hartley Papers
Essex Record Office	Braybrooke Papers
Hertfordshire Record Office	Baker Papers
Leeds Public Library	Ramsden Papers
Middlesex Record Office	MRC/Com
	Old Bailey Proceedings, 1768
Northamptonshire Record Office	Fitzwilliam Papers
Nottingham University Library	Portland MSS
Staffordshire Record Office	Dartmouth Papers
East Suffolk Record Office (Ipswich)	Albemarle Papers
	Barrington Papers
West Suffolk Record Office (Bury St Edmunds)	Grafton Papers
Warwickshire Record Office	Newdigate Papers
Yorkshire (North Riding) Record Office	Zetland Papers
William M. Clements Library	Dowdeswell Papers

5. PRIVATE COLLECTIONS

Althorp MSS	Althorp, Northampton
Devonshire MSS	Chatsworth, Bakewell, Derbyshire
Glynn MSS	By courtesy of the Glynn Family
Longleat MSS	Longleat, Wiltshire
Woburn MSS	Bedford Estate Office

PRINTED PRIMARY SOURCES

CORRESPONDENCE, MEMOIRS, ETC.

Albemarle, Lord, *Memoirs of the Marquis of Rockingham* (2 Vols, 1852)
Almon, J., *A Collection of Papers Relative to the Dispute between Great Britain and America* (1777)

Almon, J., *The Correspondence of John Wilkes* (5 Vols, 1805)

Almon, J., *Anecdotes of the Life of William Pitt* (7th edn, 1810)

Almon, J., *The Parliamentary Register, 1774–80* (17 Vols, 1775–80)

Anson, W. (Ed.), *Autobiography of the 3rd Duke of Grafton* (1898)

Barrington, S., *Political Life of Lord Barrington* (1814)

Bateson, M. (Ed.), *The Duke of Newcastle's Narrative of Changes in the Ministry, 1765–7* (1898)

Belsham, W., *Memoirs of the Reign of George III* (1795)

Burke, Edmund, *Correspondence*, Vol. I, to 1768, Ed. T. W. Copeland (1958); Vol. 2, 1768–74, Ed. L. Sutherland (1960); Vol. 3, 1774–8, Ed. G. Guttridge (1961); Vol. 4, 1778–82, Ed. J. Woods (1963); Vol. 5, 1782–9, Ed. H. Furber (1965)

Campbell, Lord J., *Lives of the Lord Chancellors* (8 Vols, 1845–69)

Cavendish, Sir H., *Debates of the House of Commons, 1768–74* (Ed. J. Wright, 2 Vols, 1841–3)

Chatham, Lord, *Correspondence* (Eds W. S. Taylor and J. H. Pringle, 4 Vols, 1838–40)

Cobbett, W., *The Parliamentary History of England,*

Doddington, Bubb, *Political Journal of George, Bubb Doddington* (Eds J. Carswell and L. Dralle, Oxford, 1965)

Elliot, G. F. S., *The Border Elliots* (1897)

Ferguson, J. (Ed.), *Letters of George Dempster and Sir Adam Ferguson, 1756–1813* (1934)

Fitzmaurice, Lord, *Life of William, Earl of Shelburne* (2 Vols, 1912)

Fonblanque, E. B., de, *Life and Correspondence of John Burgoyne* (2 Vols, 1876)

Fox, C. J., *Memorials and Correspondence* (Ed. Lord John Russell, 4 Vols, 1853–7)

Fox, H., *Letters to Henry Fox* (Ed. Earl of Ilchester, 1915)

George III, *Correspondence*, 1760–83 (Ed. Sir J. Fortescue, 6 Vols, 1928)

George IV, *Correspondence of George, Prince of Wales* (Ed. A. Aspinall, Vol. i, 1964)

Grafton, *The Autobiography of the Third Duke of Grafton* (Ed. Sir W. Anson, 1898)

Grenville, G., *The Grenville Papers* (Ed. W. T. Smith, 4 Vols, 1852–3)

Grenville, G., Additional Grenville Papers, 1763–5 (Ed. J. Tomlinson, Manchester, 1962)

Harris, G., *Life of Hardwicke* (3 Vols, 1847)

Jesse, J. H., *Memoirs of the Life and Reign of George III* (2nd edn, 3 Vols, 1887)

Jucker, N., *The Jenkinson Papers, 1760–6* (1949)

Lennox, *Life and Letters of Lady Sarah Lennox, 1745–1826* (Eds, Countess of Ilchester and Lord Stavordale, 1901)

Newman, A., *Leicester House Politics, 1750–60* (Camden Miscellany, 4th Series, VII)
Nicholls, J., *Recollections and Reflections of Public Affairs during the Reign of George III* (1822, 2 Vols)

Ormond, G. W. T., *The Armiston Memoirs* (Edinburgh, 1887)

Russell Lord, J., *The Bedford Correspondence* (3 Vols, 1843–6)

Sandwich, *Sandwich Papers* (Eds G. R. Barnes and J. H. Owen, 3 Vols, 1933)
Sandwich, *The Fourth Earl of Sandwich: his Diplomatic Correspondence 1763–5* (Ed. F. Spencer, Manchester, 1961)
Sedgwick, R. R., *Letters of George III to Lord Bute* (1939)

Thomas, P. D. G., *The Parliamentary Diaries of Nathaniel Ryder* (Camden Miscellany, VII, 1969)

Wade, J., *Letters of Junius* (2 Vols, 1850)
Walpole, H., *Correspondence* (Eds W. S. Lewis and R. S. Brown, Yale, 1941)
Walpole, H., *Memoirs of the Reign of George III* (Ed. G. Barker, 4 Vols, 1894)
Walpole, H., *Last Journals 1771–83* (2 Vols, 1859)
Wraxall, N., *Historical Memoirs of my Own Time* (Ed. R. Askham, 1904)
Wyvill, C., *Political Papers respecting Parliamentary Reform* (6 Vols, 1794)

Yorke, P. C., *Life and Correspondence of Hardwicke* (3 Vols, Cambridge, 1913)

HISTORICAL MANUSCRIPTS COMMISSION

Abergavenny MSS
Carlisle MSS
Dartmouth MSS (Vols 1–3)
Denbigh MSS
Foljambe MSS
Lothian MSS
Rutland MSS (Vols 2 and 3)
Stopford–Sackville MSS
Townshend MSS
Various Collections (Vols 6 and 8)

PERIODICALS, PAMPHLETS AND NEWSPAPERS

Almon, J., *The History of the Late Minority* (1765)
An Analysis of the Thoughts on the Causes of the Present Discontents, and of the Observations on the Same (1770)

The Annual Register (1758–83)
Considerations on the Present Dangerous Crisis (1763)
Cooper, G., *The Merits of the New Administration Truly Stated* (1765)
The Gentleman's Magazine
Lloyd, C., *A Critical Review of the New Administration* (1765)
The Remembrancer
A Short History of the Administration during the Summer Recess (1779)
The Speech of the Rt Hon Charles James Fox to the Electors of Westminster, 17 July 1782
A View of the Several Changes made in the Administration of Government since the Accession of his Present Majesty (1767)
A Vindication of the Earl of Shelburne (1782)
A Word at Parting to the Earl of Shelburne (1782)

SECONDARY SOURCES

PUBLISHED BOOKS

Allen, L., *History of Portsmouth* (1817)
Alvord, C. W., *The Mississippi Valley in British Politics* (1911)
Armytage, F., *The Free Port System in the British West Indies* (1953)

Bailyn, B., *Ideological Origins of the American Revolution* (Cambridge, Massachusetts, 1967)
Baker, N., *Government and Contractors* (1971)
Bargar, B., *Lord Dartmouth and the American Revolution* (University of South Carolina Press, 1965)
Basye, A. H., *The Lords Commissioners of Trade and Plantations, 1748–82* (New Haven, 1925)
Binney, J. E. D., *British Public Finance and Administration 1774–92* (1958)
Black, E. C., *The Association* (Harvard, 1963)
Bonsall, B., *Sir James Lowther and Cumberland and Westmorland Elections 1754–75* (Manchester, 1960)
Bourguet, A., *Le Duc de Choiseul et l'Alliance Espagnole* (Paris, 1906)
Brooke, J., *The Chatham Administration, 1766–8* (1956)
Brooke, J., *George III* (1972)
Brown, J. W., *Empire or Independence* (Louisiana, 1941)
Browning, O., *Political Memoranda of Francis, 5th Duke of Leeds* (1884)
Butterfield, H., *George III and the Historians* (1957)
Butterfield, H., *George III, Lord North and the People* (1948)

Cannon, J., *The Fox–North Coalition, 1782–4* (Cambridge, 1969)
de Castro, J. P., *The Gordon Riots* (Oxford, 1926)
Christie, I. R., *The End of North's Ministry 1780–2* (1958)
Christie, I. R., *Wilkes, Wyvill and Reform* (1962)

488 *The Rise of Party in England*

Christie, I. R., *Crisis of Empire* (1966)
Christie, I. R., *Myth and Reality in Late Eighteenth Century British Politics* (1970)
Coleridge, E. M., *Life of T. Coutts* (2 Vols, 1919)
Cone, C. B., *Burke and the Nature of Politics, The Age of the American Revolution* (University of Kentucky Press, 1957)
Coupland, R., *The Quebec Act* (1925)
Craig, M. J., *The Volunteer Earl*

Derry, J., *Charles James Fox* (1972)
Dickerson, O. M., *The Navigation Acts and the American Revolution* (1951)
Donoughue, B., *British Politics and the American Revolution, 1773-5*

Ehrman, J., *The Younger Pitt* (1969)

Feiling, K., *The Second Tory Party* (1938)
Foord, A. S., *His Majesty's Opposition, 1714-1832* (1964)

Geddes, A., *Portsmouth during the French Wars* (1970)
Ginter, D., *Whig Organization in the General Election of 1790* (University of California Press, 1967)
Gipson, L. H., *The Coming of the Revolution* (New York, 1954)
Goebel, J., *The Struggle for the Falkland Islands* (Yale, 1927)
Gore, Brown R., *Chancellor Thurlow* (1953)
Gunn, J., *Factions No More* (1971)
Guttridge, G. H., *English Whiggism and the American Revolution* (University of California Press, 1965)
Guttridge, G. H., *The Early Career of Lord Rockingham, 1730-65* (University of California Publications in History, 1952)

Hardy, F., *Life of Charlemont* (1810)
Harlow, V. T., *Founding of the Second British Empire* (2 Vols, 1962, 1964)
Henly, Lord R., *Memoirs of Northington* (1831)
Hinkhouse, B. J., *The Preliminaries of the American Revolution as seen in the British Press, 1763-75* (New York, 1926)
Holmes, G., *British Politics in the Reign of Anne* (1967)
Holmes, G., *Britain after the Glorious Revolution* (1969)
Holmes, G., & Speck, W., *The Divided Society: Party Conflict in England 1694-1714*
Horn, D. B., *Great Britain and Europe in the Eighteenth Century* (1967)

Ilchester, Lord, *Life of Fox* (2 Vols, 1920)

Jarrett, D., *The Begetters of Revolution: English Involvement with France, 1759-89* (1973)
Johnston, E. M., *Great Britain and Ireland, 1760-1800* (1963)
Judd, G. P., *Members of Parliament, 1734-1832* (1955)

Kammen, M. G., *Rope of Sand* (1968)
Kemp, B., *King and Commons* (1957)
Kemp, B., *Sir F. Dashwood: an Eighteenth Century Independent* (1967)

Labaree, B. W., *The Boston Tea Party* (Oxford, 1966)
Langford, P., *The First Rockingham Ministry, 1765–6* (Oxford, 1973)
Lutnick, S., *The American Revolution and the British Press* (University of Missouri Press, 1967)

Mackesy, P., *The War for America* (1964)
Macalpine, I., & Hunter, R., *George III and the Mad Business* (1969)
Madariaga, de I., *Russia and the Armed Neutrality of 1780* (1967)
Maier, P., *From Resistance to Revolution* (New York, 1972)
Martelli, G., *Life of Sandwich* (1967)
Mansfield, H., *Statesmanship and Party Government* (Chicago, 1965)
Mitchell, L., *Charles James Fox and the Disintegration of the Whig Party, 1782–94* (Oxford, 1971)
Morgan, E. S., & Morgan, H., *The Stamp Act Crisis* (Chapel, 1953)

Namier, L. B., *England in the Age of the American Revolution* (2nd edn, 1966)
Namier, L. B., *Structure of Politics at the Accession of George III* (2nd edn, 1957)
Namier, L. B., *Crossroads of Power* (1962)
Namier, L. B., & Brooke, J., *The House of Commons, 1754–90* (3 Vols, 1964)
Namier, L. B., & Brooke, J., *Charles Townshend* (1964)
Natan, A. (Ed.), *Silver Renaissance*
Nobbe, G., *The North Briton* (Columbia University Press, 1939)
Norris, J., *Shelburne and Reform* (1963)

O'Connell, M. R., *Irish Politics and Social Conflict in the Age of the American Revolution* (University of Pennsylvania Press, 1965)
O'Gorman, F., *The Whig Party and the French Revolution* (1967)
O'Gorman, F., *Edmund Burke: his Political Philosophy* (1973)
Olson, A. G., *The Radical Duke: the Career and Correspondence of the Third Duke of Richmond* (Oxford, 1961)
Oswald, J., *Memorials of J. Oswald* (Edinburgh, 1825)

Pares, R., *George III and the Politicians* (Oxford, 1953)
Perry, T. W., *Public Opinion, Propaganda and Politics in Eighteenth Century England* (1967)
Phillips, N. G., *Yorkshire and National Politics, 1783–4* (Christchurch, 1961)

Ramsey, J. F., *Anglo-French Relations, 1763–70* (University of California Press, 1939)
Rashed, Z., *The Peace of Paris* (1951)
Rea, R., *The English Press in Politics, 1760–74* (Lincoln, Nebraska, 1967)
Ritcheson, C. R., *British Politics and the American Revolution* (University of Oklahoma Press, 1964)

Robbins, C., *The Eighteenth Century Commonwealthman* (1959)
Rude, G., *Wilkes and Liberty* (1962)
Ruville, von A., *William Pitt* (3 Vols, 1907)

Sedgwick, R. R., *The House of Commons, 1715–54* (2 Vols, 1970)
Sosin, J., *Agents and Merchants* (University of Nebraska Press, 1965)
Sosin, J., *Whitehall and the Wilderness* (University of Nebraska Press, 1961)
Speck, W., *Tory and Whig: The Struggle in the Constituencies, 1701–16* (1970)
Spector, M. M., *The American Department of the British Government, 1768–82* (New York, 1940)
Stinchcombe, W., *The American Revolution and the French Alliance* (Syracuse University Press, 1961)
Sutherland, L., *The East India Company in British Politics* (Oxford, 1952)

Thompson, E., *The Making of the English Working Class* (1968)
Thomson, M. A., *The Secretaries of State, 1681–1782* (1932)
Turberville, A. S., *The House of Lords in the Eighteenth Century* (1927)

Valentine, A., *Lord George Germain* (1964)
Valentine, A., *Lord North* (2 Vols, 1967)

Walcott, R., 'English Party Politics, 1688–1714' in *Essays in Modern English History in Honour of W. C. Abbott* (Cambridge, Massachusetts, 1954)
Walcott, R., *English Politics in the Early Eighteenth Century* (Oxford, 1956)
Wector, D., *Edmund Burke and his Kinsmen* (Boulder, Colorado, 1938)
Werkmeister, L., *The London Daily Press, 1772–92* (1963)
Wickwire, F. B., *British Subministers and Colonial America, 1763–83* (Princeton University Press, 1966)
Wiggin, L. M., *The Faction of Cousins: a Political Account of the Grenvilles* (Yale University Press, 1958)
Williams, B., *William Pitt* (2 Vols, 1913)
Williams, B., *Cartaret and Newcastle* (1943)
Winstanley, D., *Personal and Party Government* (1910)
Winstanley, D., *Lord Chatham and the Whig Opposition* (1912)

ARTICLES

Adair, D., 'The Stamp Act in Contemporary English Cartoons', *William and Mary Quarterly*, 3rd Series, **X** (1953)
Adams, R. G., 'A View of Cornwallis' Surrender at Yorktown', *American Historical Review*, **XXXVII** (1931–2)
Alstyne, R. van, 'Thomas Walpole's Letters to the Duke of Grafton on American Affairs', *Huntington Library Quarterly*, **XXX** (1966–7)
Alstyne, R. van, 'Europe the Rockingham Whigs and the War for American Independence', *Huntington Library Quarterly*, **XXV** (1961)

Aylmer, G., 'Place Bills and the Separation of Powers: the Seventeenth Century Origins of the Non-Political Civil Service', *Transactions of the Royal Historical Society* (1965)

Basye, A. H., 'The Secretary of State for the Colonies, 1768–82', *American Historical Review*, **XXVIII** (1922)

Beckett, J. C., 'Anglo-Irish Constitutional Relations in the late eighteenth century', *Irish Historical Studies*, **XIV** (1964–5)

Brewer, J., 'Party and the Double Cabinet: Two Facets of Burke's Thoughts', *Historical Journal*, **XIV** (1971)

Brewer, J., 'The Misfortunes of Lord Bute', *Historical Journal*, **XVI** (1973)

Brewer, J., 'The Faces of Lord Bute: A Visual Contribution to Anglo-American Political Ideology', *Perspectives in American History*, **VI** (1972)

Bunce, J. E., 'Rockingham, Shelburne and the Politics of Reform, 1779–1808, in *Studies in Modern History*, Ed. G. L. Vincitorio (New York, 1968)

Chaffin, R. J., 'The Townshend Acts of 1767', *William and Mary Quarterly*, 3rd Series xxvii (1970)

Christelow, A., 'French Interests in the Spanish Empire during the ministry of the Duc de Choiseul, 1759–61', *Hispanic American Review*, **XXI** (1941)

Christie, I. R., 'Was There a New Toryism in the Earlier Part of George III's reign', *Journal of British Studies*, **V** (1965–6)

Christie, I. R., 'The Wilkites and the General Election of 1774', *Guildhall Miscellany*, **II**, iv (1962)

Christie, I. R., 'The Marquis of Rockingham and Lord North's Offer of a Coalition', June–July 1780, *English Historical Review*, **LXIX** (1954)

Christie, I. R., 'The Yorkshire Association: A Study in Political Organisation', *Historical Journal*, **III** (1960)

Christie, I. R., 'Economical Reform and the Influence of the Crown, 1780', *Historical Journal*, **XII** (1956)

Collyer, C., 'The Rockinghams and Yorkshire Politics, 1742–61', *Publications of the Thoresby Society*, **XLI**

Collyer, C., 'The Rockingham Connection and Country Opinion in the Early Years of George III', *Publications of the Thoresby Society* (1954)

Evans, E. G., 'Planter Indebtedness and the Coming of the Revolution in Virginia', *William and Mary Quarterly*, 3rd Series, **XIX** (1962)

Fryer, W. R., 'King George III: his Political Character and Conduct, 1760–84', *Renaissance and Modern Studies*, **VI** (1962)

Ginter, D., 'The Financing of the Whig Party Organization, 1783–93', *American Historical Review*, **LXXI** (1966)

Greene, J. P., & Jellison, R. M., 'The Currency Act of 1764 in Imperial-Colonial Relations', *William and Mary Quarterly*, 3rd Series, **XVIII**

Guttridge, G. H., 'The Whig Opposition in England during the American Revolution', *Journal of Modern History*, **VI** (1934)

Haas, J., 'The Pursuit of Political Success in Eighteenth Century England', Sandwich, 1740–71, *Bulletin of the Institute of Historical Research*, **XLIII** (1970)

Hodge, H., 'The Repeal of the Stamp Act', *Political Science Quarterly*, **XIX** (1904)

Hull, C., & Temperley, H. V., 'Debates on the Declaratory Act and the Repeal of the Stamp Act', *American Historical Review*, **XVII** (1911–12)

Humphrey, A. L., 'Lord Shelburne and East India Company Politics, 1766–9', *English Historical Review*, **XLIX** (1934)

Humphries, R., & Scott, S., 'Lord Northington and the Laws of Canada', *Canadian Historical Review*, **XIV** (1933)

Imlach, B., 'Earl Temple and the Ministry of 1765', *English Historical Review*, **XXX** (1915)

Jarrett, D., 'The Regency Crisis of 1765', *English Historical Review*, **LXXXV** (1970)

Keir, D. L., 'Economical Reform, 1779–87', *Law Quarterly Review*, **L** (1934)

Kemp, B., 'Crewe's Act, 1782', *English Historical Review*, **LXVIII** (1953)

Langford, P., 'William Pitt and Public Opinion, 1757', *English Historical Review*, **LXXXVIII** (1973)

Langford, P., 'The Rockingham Whigs and America, 1767–73', in *Statesmen, Scholars and Merchants*, Eds A. Whiteman, P. Dickson and J. S. Bromley (Oxford, 1973)

Laprade, W. T., 'The Stamp Act in British Politics', *American Historical Review*, **XXXV** (1930)

Large, D., 'The Decline of the Party of the Crown and the Rise of Parties in the House of Lords', *English Historical Review*, **LXXVIII** (1963)

McCurry, A. J., 'The North Government and the Outbreak of the American Revolution', *Huntington Library Quarterly*, 3rd Series, **XXXIV** (1970–1)

Mahoney, T. H. D., 'Edmund Burke and the American Revolution: The Repeal of the Stamp Act', in *Edmund Burke, The Enlightenment and the Modern World* (Detroit, 1967)

Middleton, R., 'William Pitt, Anson and the Admiralty, 1756–61', *History*, **LV** (1970)

Morgan, E., 'Colonial Ideas of Parliamentary Power', *William and Mary Quarterly*, 3rd Series, **V**

Morgan, E., 'The Postponement of the Stamp Act', *William and Mary Quarterly*, 3rd Series, **VII**

Newman, A., 'Leicester House Politics, 1748–51', *English Historical Review*, **LXXVI** (1961)

O'Connor, T. M., 'The Embargo on the Export of Irish Provisions', *Irish Historical Studies*, **II**

O'Gorman, F., 'Party and Burke: The Rockingham Whigs', *Government and Opposition*, **III** (1968)

O'Gorman, F., 'Edmund Burke and the Idea of Party', *Studies in Burke and his Time*, **XI** (1969–70)

Olson, A. G., 'The Duke of Richmond's Memorandum, 1–7 July 1766', *English Historical Review*, **LXXV** (1960)

Phillips, N. C., 'Edmund Burke and the County Movement, 1780', *English Historical Review*, **LXXVI**

Reitan, E. A., 'The Civil List in Eighteenth Century Politics: Parliamentary Supremacy versus the Independence of the Crown', *Historical Journal*, **IX** (1966)

Ritcheson, C. R., 'The Elder Pitt and an American Department', *American Historical Review*, **LVII** (1952)

Robbins, C., 'Discordant Parties: A Study of the Acceptance of Party by Englishmen', *Political Science Quarterly*, **LXXIII** (1955)

Rude, G., 'The Gordon Riots: A Study of the Rioters and their Victims', *Transactions of the Royal Historical Society* (1956)

Savelle, M., 'The Emergence of an American Attitude towards External Affairs 1750–75', *American Historical Review*, **LII** (1947)

Sedgwick, R. R., 'William Pitt and Lord Bute', *History Today*, **VI**, No. 10 (1956)

Sedgwick, R. R., 'Letters from William Pitt to Lord Bute, 1755–58' in *Essays Presented to Sir Lewis Namier*, Eds A. J. P. Taylor and R. Pares (1956)

Snyder, H. L., 'Party Configuration in the Early Eighteenth Century House of Commons', *Bulletin of the Institute of Historical Research*, **XLV** (1972)

Sutherland, L., 'Edmund Burke and the First Rockingham Ministry', *English Historical Review*, **XLVII** (1932)

Sutherland, L., & Woods, J., 'The East India Speculations of William Burke', *Proceedings of the Leeds Philosophical and Literary Society*, **XI** (1966)

Thomas, P. D. G., 'The Beginning of Parliamentary Reporting in Newspapers', *English Historical Review*, **LXXIV** (1959)

Thomas, P. D. G., 'John Wilkes and the Freedom of the Press', *Bulletin of the Institute of Historical Research*, **XXXIII** (1960)

Thomas, P. D. G., Charles Townshend and American Taxation, 1767', *English Historical Review*, **LXXXIII** (1968)

Tyler, J. E., 'Lord North and the Speakership, 1780', *Parliamentary Affairs*, **VIII** (1955)

Tyler, J. E., 'A Letter from the Marquis of Rockingham . . . on the Irish Absentee Tax, 1773', *Irish Historical Studies*, **VIII** (1952–3)

Underdown, P., 'Edmund Burke, the Commissary of his Bristol Constituents', *English Historical Review*, **LXIX** (1954)

Watson, D., 'The Rockingham Whigs and the Townshend Duties', *English Historical Review*, **LXXXIV** (1969)
Watson, D., 'William Baker's Account of the Debate on the Repeal of the Stamp Act', *William and Mary Quarterly*, 3rd Series, **XXVI** (1969)
Watson, D., 'The Rise of the Opposition at Wildman's Club', *Bulletin of the Institute of Historical Research*, **XLIV** (1971)
Willcox, W. B., 'Rhode Island in British Strategy, 1780–1', *Journal of Modern History*, **XVII**

UNPUBLISHED THESES

Davies, J. A., '*An Enquiry into Faction among British Naval Officers during the American War of Independence* (Liverpool, M.A., 1964)
Hamer, M., *From the Grafton Administration to the ministry of North, 1768–72* (Cambridge, Ph.D., 1970)
Hardy, A., *The Duke of Newcastle and his Young Friends in Opposition, 1762–5* (Manchester, M.A., 1956)
Ogden, D., *The Whig Tradition and Opposition Politics, 1760–83* (Manchester, M.A., 1972)
Smith, B. R., *The Committee of the Whole to Consider the American Papers, 1766* (Sheffield, M.A., 1957)
Sturgess, G., *The Rockingham Whigs, 1768–74* (Manchester, M.A., 1970)
Wall, D., *The Second Rockingham Ministry* (Sheffield, M.A., 1957)
Watson, D. H., *Barlow Trecothick and other Associates of Rockingham during the Stamp Act Crisis* (Sheffield, M.A., 1958)
Watson, D. H., *The Duke of Newcastle, the Marquis of Rockingham and Mercantile Interests in London and the Provinces, 1761–8* (Sheffield, Ph.D., 19)

References to pp. 13–15

INTRODUCTION

[1] I. R. Christie, *Myth and Reality in Late Eighteenth Century British Politics* (1970), p. 9.

[2] J. H. Plumb, *The Growth of Political Stability in England, 1675–1725* (1967), p. xiii.

[3] 'For the very word "structure", suggesting as it does a static system, is oddly inappropriate when applied to so dynamic a political world as that of Britain after the Glorious Revolution. After 1688, and even more after 1694, the whole country was shaken and torn by the furious tempest of party' (G. Holmes (Ed.), *Britain after the Glorious Revolution* (1969), p. 14). That an organised Whig party existed in the 1780s cannot be doubted. For its development see J. Cannon, *The Fox–North Coalition, 1782–4* (Cambridge, 1969); Frank O'Gorman, *The Whig Party and the French Revolution* (1967); D. E. Ginter, 'The Financing of the Whig Party Organisation, 1783–93', *American Historical Review*, **LXXI** (1966), pp. 421–40; *Whig Organisation in the General Election of 1790* (California, 1969).

[4] This defies precise definition. It is enough to notice here that the terms expressed political attitudes of a very general kind such as support or suspicion of political absolutism and administrative centralisation. The 'country' was thus *not* an alternative Government in embryonic form nor were these concepts causally related to the emergence of parties. They represent another film or perhaps another level of political consciousness.

[5] *See* R. Walcott, 'English Party Politics, 1688–1714', in *Essays in Modern English History in Honour of W. C. Abbott* (Cambridge, Massachusetts, 1941); *English Politics in the Early Eighteenth Century* (Oxford, 1956).

[6] The chief statements of the modern view are G. Holmes, *British Politics in the Reign of Anne* (1967); J. Plumb, op. cit.; G. Holmes (Ed.), *Britain after the Glorious Revolution*, op. cit.; G. Holmes and W. Speck (Eds), *The Divided Society: Party Conflict in England, 1694–1716* (1967); W. Speck, *Tory and Whig: The Struggle in the Constituencies, 1701–15* (1970). At the time of writing the latest contribution to the revision of the party history of these decades (H. L. Snyder, 'Party Configuration in the Early Eighteenth Century House of Commons', *Bulletin of the Institute of Historical Research*, **XLV**, 1972), concludes, after reviewing 'direct contemporary evidence for the party preference of virtually every Member who sat between 1698 and 1722', that almost all Members 'had been almost completely submerged in the now dominant division of Whigs and Tories' (pp. 39, 40). The author is able to calculate the reliability of contemporary lists of Members at 90 per cent and more. 'The close correlation of all these figures fully supports the argument . . . that party affiliations were easily identified and commonly known' (ibid., p. 50).

[7] The sage remarks of Dr Cannon (*The Fox–North Coalition*, pp. 241–2) are essential reading for those who imagine that parties cannot be regarded as 'real' until a two party system with a mass electorate emerged in the nineteenth century.

[8] J. Plumb, op. cit., p. 134.

[9] R. Sedgwick (Ed.), *The House of Commons, 1715–54* (2 Vols, 1970), Vol. I, pp. 62–7.

[10] It is difficult to assess precisely how many Tories embraced Jacobitism, although the latter creed was far more widespread than has traditionally been allowed. What is clear is that although many of the Tories would lift their glass to 'the king over the water' very few would lift a finger in 1745. Mr Sedgwick's statement ('the available evidence leaves no doubt that up to 1745 the Tories were a predominantly Jacobite party, engaged in attempts to restore the Stuarts by a rising with foreign assistance', op. cit., p. x) seems curiously exaggerated.

[11] Ibid., pp. 38–42. As early as 1716 there had been forty of them (ibid., p. 25).

[12] 'Connection' is a much-used term but one whose usefulness has yet to be demonstrated. Its definition is inexact. Connections exhibited a wide variety of characteristics. Some were small, some large. Some lasted for a day, some for a generation. Most, but not all, were based on a family grouping. Many families, however, were frequently divided amongst themselves. See, for example, Lewis M. Wiggin, *The Faction of Cousins: a Political Account of the Grenvilles, 1733–63* (Yale University Press, 1958).

[13] G. Holmes, *Politics in the Reign of Anne*, pp. 47–8.

[14] As S. Foord, *His Majesty's Opposition, 1714–1832* (Oxford, 1964).

[15] C. Robbins, 'Discordant Parties: A Study of the Acceptance of Party by Englishmen', *Political Science Quarterly*, **LXXIII** (1955).

[16] J. Cannon, op. cit., p. x, n. 3.

[17] Sir L. Namier & J. Brooke, *The House of Commons*, 1754–90 (3 Vols, 1964), Vol. I, pp. 198–9.

[18] L. B. Namier, *England in the Age of the American Revolution* (2nd edn, 1966), pp. 51, 53. Mr Brooke goes so far as to deny that there was any continuity between the parties of Rockingham and Fox (*The Chatham Administration, 1766–8* (1956), p. 219).

[19] It is worth noting here that Burke identified the Rockingham Whigs not only with the aristocratic Whiggery of the Pelhams but also with the Junto of Anne's reign. The Rockinghams, in fact, reconciled the Pelhamite legacy of Whig solidarity and aristocratic dominance in politics with the 'Revolution Principles' which the Junto had paraded at the Sacheverell trial: limited monarchy, parliamentary power, hereditary right and the Protestant succession. In other words, without divesting themselves of their Pelhamite antecedents, the Rockinghams attached themselves to the older Whig–Country tradition of the reign of Anne. There was nothing anomalous, then, in the emergence of a distinctly 'country' element in the history of the Rockingham Whigs.

CHAPTER 1

[1] Sir Thomas Robinson's only claim to high office was his friendship with Newcastle. He had extensive diplomatic experience but his inability to control the Commons provoked ridicule, discrediting in advance a weak administration which was shortly to have a war in three continents upon its hands.

[2] 'No ministry ever found Parliament so easy to manage' (A. S. Foord, op. cit., p. 296). The political settlement of June 1757 represented the greatest victory in the eighteenth century of the ideal of 'Broadbottom'. Almost all politicians united behind the throne. Their motives were undoubtedly weariness with factious opposition and the needs of the war-time crisis. The magetism and leadership of Pitt were not yet a factor and only became apparent later. Pitt's reputation with the public, moreover, had hardly begun to establish itself; see P. Langford, 'William Pitt and public opinion, 1757', *English Historical Review*, **LXXXVIII** (1973). Dr Langford draws attention to the significant rallying around Pitt of old Tories whose 'support for the Devonshire–Pitt Administration was one of the more remarkable features of the period' (ibid., p. 67). This represented a revival of 'country' politics with Pitt's 'sweeping promises of reform, the declared intention to abandon the so-called "Hanoverian" policy, and the ambitious plans for the re-establishment of British naval and military credit' (ibid., p. 68). Pitt's coalition with Newcastle in 1757, therefore, would not have endeared itself—or Pitt—to those who had hitherto supported him.

[3] R. R. Sedgwick, *Letters of George III to Lord Bute* (1939), pp. xxii–iii; J. Brooke, *George III* (1972), pp. 27–8, 32, 46. He was Commander-in-Chief of the army until 1757 when he resigned his command after a less than distinguished role in the continental war.

[4] For the latest and most authoritative refutation of the legends that Bute was the Princess' lover, see J. Brooke, *George III*, pp. 48–9.

[5] Lord Fitzmaurice, *Life of William, Earl of Shelburne* (2 Vols, 1912), Vol. I, p. 33, 1737–1805; MP Chipping Wycombe 1760–1 when he succeeded to the Irish earldom on the death of his father. First Lord of Trade, April–September 1763; Secretary of State for the Southern Department, 1766–8; Home Secretary, March–July 1782; First Lord of the Treasury, July 1782–April 1783.

[6] Another—just possibly—was Horace Walpole. There is a moment in the *Memoirs* when he confesses his uncertainty of the truth of the charges he had been making against Bute (*Memoirs of the Reign of George III* (Ed. G. Barker, 4 Vols, 1894), Vol. IV, pp. 88–90).

[7] For the following, see L. B. Namier, *England in the Age*, pp. 97–109; R. R. Sedgwick, op. cit., pp. xlv–xlix; R. R. Sedgwick, 'William Pitt and Lord Bute', *History Today*, **VI**, No. 10 (1956); R. R. Sedgwick, 'Letters from William Pitt to Lord Bute, 1755–8', in *Essays Presented to Sir Lewis Namier*, Eds R. Pares and A. J. P. Taylor (1956).

[8] According to Mr Brooke (*George III*, p. 51) Bute's appointment as Groom of the Stole implied that he would 'have the reversion of first minister in the next reign' but this was the opinion of Leicester House and not that of the coalition.

[9] See Brooke, op. cit., pp. 35–7, 56–7, 65; Sedgwick, op. cit., pp. iiv–viii; Namier, op. cit., pp. 83–93. There are still some loose ends which it would be interesting to tie up. To what extent, for example, were the King and Bute affected by the marked renaissance of 'Patriot King' ideas in and especially after 1760? As Professor Butterfield commented some years ago: 'The men in the neighbourhood of Bute certainly seem to have imagined themselves to be collaborating in a new system, a comprehensive change of policy' (*George III and the Historians* (1957), p. 225). See, for example, *The Political Journal of George, Bubb Doddington*, Eds J. Carswell and L. A. Dralle (Oxford, 1965), pp. 401–2, 407. It would seem incredible that Bute, and perhaps even the King, could have remained unaffected by the upsurge of anti-aristocratic prejudice which his accession evoked.

[10] It goes without saying that the fact that the future King entertained no designs on the constitution at the time of his accession does not of itself allow us to assume that the King was always to act in the future with strict constitutional propriety.

[11] The Prince to Lord Bute, 19 December 1758, Sedgwick, op. cit., pp. 20–1. Mr Brooke has underlined Bute's personal responsibility for instilling into his pupil 'calumnies on those responsible for the conduct of the most successful war in British history' (op. cit., pp. 63–4).

[12] The Prince to Lord Bute, 4 May 1760, Sedgwick (op. cit., pp. 44–6).

[13] This is printed in A. Newman, 'Leicester House Politics, 1748–51', *English Historical Review*, **LXXVI** (1961), pp. 577–89 and is summarised in A. S. Foord, op. cit., pp. 271–9. Briefly, the Great Outline is a day-by-day guide to the actions of the new King in the early days of his reign. As the natural heir to the traditions of Prince Frederick's Court, Bute might perhaps have been expected to have worked out a clearer plan for the accession than he did. In October 1760 the King and Bute had failed to prepare lists of their supporters and were totally unprepared for a general election. As Dr Newman demonstrates, however, there is some resemblance between the objectives of Bute and Prince George and those of Prince Frederick (which themselves owe much to the plans for the accession of George II in 1727). These similarities include the conciliation of the Tory gentry, the breaking of party distinctions and the cleansing of government.

[14] To some extent he succeeded. See the discussion of his part in the peace negotiations in 1762 in I. R. Christie, *Myth and Reality*, pp. 94–7.

[15] This is *not* to contend that George III followed a 'Tory' policy. But his action manifested a determination to exercise the prerogative of appointment by the King, i.e. to attempt to have a say in *who makes policy*.

[16] The failure of George II's correspondence to survive and the neglect which he has suffered at the hands of historians have all too frequently led posterity to view his reign through the eyes of George III. George III's intention to effect political changes was motivated more by bitter, per-

sonal resentments than by an accurate assessment of the fortunes of the monarchy under his predecessor. It is true that George II was not a strong King. He was never a free agent. His fear of Tories left him with much less room for manoeuvre than George III was to enjoy in the 1760s and his power was threatened by the Prince of Wales of the day in 1737–42, 1747–51 and 1755–6. Although he had sometimes to take ministers into his service against his will so did George III on many occasions. His powers have been grotesquely underestimated. It was not just that he was interested in military affairs, as is often conceded. He took a wide and conscientious interest in all political matters. His interest in appointments, ecclesiastical as well as secular, showed no sign of diminution in the 1750s. So far is it from the truth to assert that he was a prisoner of the Whigs that it is almost impossible to insist strongly enough that even on policy matters his ideas could be of great influence. His concern for Hanover became one of the guidelines of British foreign policy in the 1740s and 1750s. Perhaps to an extent that compares more than favourably with his successor, George II demanded that he be kept constantly informed and consulted on all matters. It is certainly the case that he had his differences with his ministers and that he sometimes had to suffer embarrassing rebuffs. On the other hand, he found the Pelhams the most reliable and practicable source of support for his Government. For the most part, they respected his trust, showed themselves willing to respect his prerogatives and had an interest in maintaining them entire. George III, in short, greatly underestimated his grandfather's position. J. B. Owen, 'George II Reconsidered' in *Statesmen, Scholars and Merchants*', Eds. A. Whiteman, J. Bromley and P. G. M. Dickson (Oxford 1973).

[17] Pitt's strategy, however, was much less novel than most historians have assumed and his domination and command of the war effort less complete. 'Government was by department and this was a principle which Pitt, unlike Newcastle, firmly, and sensibly observed' (R. Middleton, 'Pitt, Anson and the Admiralty 1756–61', *History*, **LV** (June, 1970), p. 199).

[18] There is a detailed account of this important interview in L. B. Namier, *England in the Age*, pp. 120–1.

[19] *Leicester House Politics, 1750–60, from the Papers of John, 2nd Earl of Egmont*, Ed. A. Newman, *Camden Miscellany*, 4th Series (1969), Vol. VII, p. 215.

[20] George III to Lord Bute, mid-November 1760, Sedgwick, op. cit., pp. 48–50.

[21] This seems to have rankled with him. He complained to Newcastle: 'Nobody knew anything; nobody knew to whom to apply, etc.' (24 January 1761, B.M. Add. MSS 32918, ff. 45–6, Newcastle Papers).

[22] A general election had to be held within six months of the demise of a monarch and Newcastle was the only politician with the experience to manage the elections. Equally important, perhaps, was the fact that the Duke's City connections were likely to be needed to obtain a loan for 1761.

[23] By February Newcastle believed that Bute did not wish to have any personal contact with him (Newcastle to Hardwicke, 2 February 1761, B.M. Add. MSS 35420, ff. 174–5, Hardwicke Papers).

[24] *Leicester House Politics*, p. 215.

[25] Newcastle, in particular, was ready to believe the worst. He expected that even though he would have the management of the election his friends would suffer and the Court would secure the return of 50 of its friends. (Hardwicke to Newcastle, 3 February 1761, B.M. Add. MSS 35420, f. 228, Hardwicke Papers.)

[26] J. Nicholls, *Recollections and Reflections* (1822, 2 vols), Vol. I, pp. 8–9.

[27] 'Secret Memorandum', 21 January 1761, B.M. Add. MSS 32917, ff. 461–4, Newcastle Papers.

[28] 'Substance of what pass'd in my Conversation with Lord Bute This Day' (10 March 1761, ibid., 32920, ff. 64–71, Newcastle Papers). Newcastle claimed that Devonshire and Hardwicke agreed with his view of 'bringing my Lord Bute into a ministerial office, and To make Him, who did Every Thing, Responsible with the other ministers' (Newcastle to Mansfield, 18 March 1761, B.M. Add. MSS 32920, ff. 295–6, Newcastle Papers). For Bute's reluctance to take office, see *The Political Journal of George Bubb Doddington*, pp. 402–3, 411, 418.

[29] Even Horace Walpole, who regarded Bute's appointment as 'injudicious' and 'preposterous', does not say that it was unconstitutional. (*Memoirs*, Vol. I, pp. 43–4.) There has been some support for the view that Bute's appointment was 'natural' in that his political 'weight' deserved some recognition. Support for this view cannot be found in Bute's political talents and there is only a little support for it in his two fortuitous inheritances: the death of his father-in-law which left his wife a fortune of over £1 million and the death of his uncle, the Duke of Argyll, the most powerful of the Scottish peers, whose influence passed to Bute. There seems no escape from the conclusion that Bute owed his advancement solely to his relationship with the King.

[30] A situation which led Pitt to threaten resignation. (Memorandum of a Meeting at the Cockpit, 12 February 1761, B.M. Add. MSS 32918, ff. 467–70, Newcastle Papers.) *'Mr Pitt would depend upon Nobody; But would go directly to the King, and make His Representation or tell His Opinion, To His Majesty, without passing Thro' any other Channel.'* (Memo of a Meeting at Newcastle House with C(ount) V(iry), 26 February 1761, ibid., 32920, ff. 285–9.)

[31] 'Substance of what pass'd in my Conversation with Lord Bute This Day' (10 March 1761, loc. cit.: Hardwicke to Newcastle, 13 March 1761, B.M. Add. MSS 32920, f. 158, Newcastle Papers).

[32] J. Brewer, 'The Misfortunes of Lord Bute: A Case Study in Eighteenth Century Political Argument and Opinion', *Historical Journal*, **XVI** (1973). Although Bute claimed that he was 'not very solicitous about the world's opinion' he confessed to Sir Francis Dashwood that 'I have already been hardly dealt with' (*n.d.* May 1761, B.M. Egerton, MSS 2136, ff. 20–1, Dashwood MSS). The presentation of this question by Sir Lewis Namier (*England in the Age*, p. 161) was perhaps slightly misleading. He stated that there were only two 'logical' attitudes to take towards the appointment of Bute: either to allow the King the unrestricted exercise of the prerogative

or to deny the Crown any influence in the House of Commons. It is not clear that one is necessarily faced with such stark alternatives.

[33] In 1763, for example, even the conservatively minded Hardwicke, told George III that a King of England 'would sometimes find it necessary to bend and ply a little; that it was not to be understood as being forced; but only submitting to the stronger reason, for the sake of himself and his government' as monarchs since William III had done. (P. C. Yorke, *Life and Correspondence of Hardwicke* (Cambridge, 1913, 3 Vols)) Vol. III, p. 515 (hereafter referred to as Hardwicke).

[34] For verification of Maudit's influence, see Z. Rashed, *The Peace of Paris* (1951), pp. 68–9.

[35] B. Williams, *William Pitt* (2 Vols, 1913), Vol. ii, p. 74.

[36] On the Franco-Spanish alliance, the work of A. Bourguet, *Le Duc de Choiseul et l'Alliance Espagnole* (Paris, 1906) is still of considerable value. It should be supplemented with A. Christelow, 'French Interests in the Spanish Empire during the ministry of the Duc de Choiseul, 1759–61', *Hispanic American Review*, **XXI** (1951), pp. 513–37.

[37] As the King did not hesitate to inform him. (Newcastle to Bedford, 13 September 1761, *The Bedford Correspondence*, Ed. Lord John Russell (3 Vols, 1842–6), Vol. iii, p. 44.)

[38] See the letters of the King to Bute of 19 and *circa* 27 September 1761, Sedgwick, op. cit., pp. 63–4. Bute was full of jealousy and envy of Pitt. (Bute to Doddington, 8 October 1761, *Doddington*, pp. 425–6.)

[39] See the letters of Newcastle to Hardwicke of 21, 23 and 26 September for the substance upon which these rumours were based, printed in *Memoirs of the Marquis of Rockingham*, Ed. Lord Albemarle (2 Vols, 1852), Vol. i, pp. 37–44.

[40] The letters are printed in *Correspondence of William Pitt, Earl of Chatham* (4 Vols, 1838–42), Eds W. S. Taylor and J. H. Pringle, Vol. ii, pp. 151–2. Pitt was careful to take his leave of the King in the most ceremonious manner. 'Great Civility passed on both sides.' (Henry Fox to Welbore Ellis, 10 October 1761, B.M. Add. MSS 51387, ff. 98–9, Holland House MSS.) The court press, however, immediately began to attack Pitt (J. Brewer, op. cit., p. 13).

[41] Newcastle to Devonshire, 9 October 1761, *Hardwicke*, Vol. III, p. 29. The squabble is dealt with in detail by L. B. Namier, *England in the Age*, pp. 294–302.

[42] On this subject see the important unpublished PhD thesis by D. A. Watson, *The Duke of Newcastle, the Marquis of Rockingham and the Mercantile Interests in London and the Provinces, 1761–8* (Sheffield, 1968), pp. 77–80, 83–4, 99, 102.

[43] The King to Bute, 18 November 1761, Sedgwick, op. cit., pp. 69–70, q. Namier, op. cit., p. 298. (The King was reporting a conversation with Devonshire.) By early January 1762 the Court was beginning to hope that on the issue of the continental war Newcastle might resign (L. B. Namier, op. cit., pp. 308–9).

[44] Newcastle to Devonshire, 15 October 1761, B.M. Add. MSS 32929, f. 190, Newcastle Papers, *q*. Namier, op. cit., p. 305.

[45] D. Watson, op. cit., pp. 108–12.

[46] The Fourth Duke of Devonshire, 1720–64, First Lord of the Treasury in the Devonshire–Pitt ministry of 1756–7 and one of Newcastle's closest and most respected friends. He was Lord Chamberlain and a member of the Cabinet in the Pitt–Newcastle coalition.

[47] The resignation of Newcastle is dealt with at great length by L. B. Namier, *England in the Age*, pp. 302–26. The diplomatic background which illuminates so much of the personal conflict of these months can be found in A. von Ruville, *William Pitt* (3 Vols, 1907), Vol. iii, pp. 41–59.

[48] 'The world expects a total rupture between Lord Bute and the late King's servants', Horace Walpole to George Montagu, 29 April 1762 (*Correspondence of Horace Walpole*, Ed. W. S. Lewis and R. S. Brown, Jnr, Yale, 1941, Vol. X, pp. 25–7).

[49] Newcastle to Bedford, 15 May 1762, *The Bedford Correspondence*, Vol. iii, p. 80. That this was not the real motive for his resignation is convincingly demonstrated by Namier, op. cit., pp. 316–18.

[50] Newcastle to Sir Joseph Yorke, 14 May 1762, *Hardwicke*, Vol. III, pp. 355–8.

[51] For George III's jubilation at having rid himself of Newcastle, see his letter to Bute of 4 June 1762, Sedgwick, op. cit., p. 113.

[52] Hardwicke to Newcastle, 7 December 1762, B.M. Add. MSS 32945, ff. 339–40, Newcastle Papers.

[53] Newcastle to Rockingham, 14 May 1762, ibid., 32938, ff. 262–4; Newcastle to Hardwicke, 21 May 1762, ibid., 35421, f. 263, Hardwicke Papers, *q*. Namier, op. cit., p. 325. Newcastle's chronic indecision and his consequent reliance upon his friends may be ascribed not only to his constant fear of taking responsibility but also to a shrewd, if slightly ridiculous, fear of impeachment. He, no doubt, recalled clearly the frequent attempts made by the Opposition of the time to impeach Sir Robert Walpole.

[54] The King to Bute, 19 May 1762, Sedgwick, op. cit., pp. 107–8; Newcastle to Rockingham, 14 May 1762, Wentworth Woodhouse MSS, Rockingham Papers, RI–240A. Sheffield Public Library. Newcastle wrote to Rockingham before he made his statement to the King: 'But I shall take Care, That His Majesty shall know, when I resign, That I am at Liberty To act, as I shall think proper, upon Every Occasion, That may happen. I say this, Because My Lord Bute insisted with My Lord M[ansfield] That *I* would not oppose. That must depend upon Their Conduct, and the Opinion of my Friends. . . .'

[55] D. Watson, op. cit., pp. 134–7. For the press war between the Court and the Newcastle Whigs, which began in the early summer of 1762 see J. Brewer, op. cit., pp. 12–15.

[56] Since the disputes of the 1750s, however, the King and Cumberland had reached a fairly amicable understanding, largely on the King's initiative who, on his accession, had announced his desire 'to introduce a new

custom into his family, that of living well with all his family'. (Horace
Walpole to Sir Horace Mann, 1 November 1760, *Walpole Correspondence*,
Vol. XXI, 448–51.) Henry Fox, at least, believed that Cumberland was
more keen on Opposition than Newcastle was. (*The Life and Letters of Lady
Sarah Lennox, 1745–1826*, Ed. The Countess of Ilchester and Lord Stavordale
(1901), pp. 64–5.)

[57] The appointment of Grenville and the advancement of Bute were
parts of a cabinet rearrangement in which Halifax became First Lord of
the Admiralty, Lord Barrington replaced Grenville and Sir Francis Dashwood succeeded Barrington as Chancellor of the Exchequer. Charles
Wyndham, the 2nd Earl of Egremont (1710–63) was Secretary of State
for the Southern Department, October 1761–August 1763.

[58] L. B. Namier, op. cit., pp. 342–3.

[59] Newcastle to Devonshire, 20 August 1762, B.M. Add. MSS 32941,
f. 321, Newcastle Papers. He told the King on 3 September that 'he fear'd
the giving up St Lucia would be attack'd, yet confess'd candidly enough,
that our state of finances requir'd peace'. George III to Lord Bute,
3 September 1762, Sedgwick, op. cit., pp. 130–1. Newcastle's attitude to the
cession of St Lucia—the only substantial difference from the terms of
which he had approved in office—was ambivalent. Characteristically, he
relied upon the advice of his friends. Rockingham opposed the cession but
Devonshire and Hardwicke thought it insufficiently important to warrant
opposition to the peace terms.

[60] Newcastle to Hardwicke, 7 October 1762, B.M. Add. MSS 32943,
ff. 90–2, Newcastle Papers. Newcastle told Charles Yorke that Cumberland's opinion was that there ought to be a new plan with Newcastle at the
Treasury 'leaving Lord Bute . . . as Groom of the Stole'. Charles Yorke
to Hardwicke, 1 September 1762, B.M. Add. MSS 35353, f. 287, Hardwicke
Papers. Cumberland and Devonshire were hoping by the end of July to
persuade Bute to retire. Cumberland to Devonshire, 28 July 1762, Devonshire MSS.

[61] L. B. Namier, op. cit., pp. 287–9. There could be a distant, and a
very distant, connection between Newcastle's behaviour and the fact that
it was at this time that Bute's name became universally traduced. *The
North Briton* of 24 July 1762 remarked 'how fashionable the word *favourite*
is grown, how common in every mouth, what a remarkable stress is laid
upon it; and with what marks of discontent it is generally accompanied'.
Furthermore, pro-Bute propaganda accused Newcastle of stirring up a
dangerous opposition. See, for example, the anonymous *Considerations on the
Present Dangerous Crisis* (1763), pp. 27–8.

[62] For details of the peace negotiations, see Z. Rashed, op. cit., pp. 165–87.
The Cabinet disagreements are dealt with in L. B. Namier, op. cit., pp. 349–51.
John, Fourth Duke of Bedford (1710–71), Secretary of State for the
Southern Department, 1748–51, Lord Lieutenant of Ireland, 1756–61,
Lord Privy Seal, 1761–3, Lord President of the Council, 1763–5.

[63] Henry Fox had been in Parliament since 1735 and had been Secretary
of State for the Southern Department 1756–7. A politician whose places,

achievements and reputation all failed to match up to his great talents, Fox was perhaps the only man of his era who could stand up to Pitt in debate. He was leader of the Duke of Cumberland's connection until October 1762. His cynicism, materialism and his exploitation of the Paymastership of the Forces (1757–68) are notorious. In the opinion of Mr Brooke, Bute's employment of Fox was 'the turning point in the King's friendship with Bute' (*George III*, p. 95). For Bute's sentiments, see L. B. Namier, *op. cit.*, pp. 350–1.

[64] Henry Fox undoubtedly expected Newcastle to go into Opposition (*Life and Letters of Lady Sarah Lennox*, pp. 64–5). See Bute to the Duke of Rutland, 13 October 1762, *H.M.C. Denbigh*, pp. 291–2. Bute to Fox, *n.d.* late November 1762, B.M. Add. MSS 51379, Holland House MSS.

[65] Cumberland interpreted this as a warning shot not only across his own but across Newcastle's bows. Cumberland to Devonshire, 24 October 1762, Devonshire MSS. In early November the King had decided that 'votes against the government at a time like this ought to be made an example of' (George III to Lord Bute, Sedgwick, op. cit., pp. 154–5).

[66] L. B. Namier, op. cit., pp. 361–3.

[67] Ibid., pp. 363–5.

[68] Cumberland to Devonshire, 29 July 1762, Devonshire MSS.

[69] There was some justification for this. Devonshire had spent most of the summer and autumn at Chatsworth, Buxton or Bath. Nevertheless, this seems to have been an excuse. 'I differed so entirely in opinion with Ld Bute that I was ready to wait on him as Lord Chamberlain but I could not serve him in a Ministerial Capacity' (Devonshire to Newcastle, *n.d.* late November 1762, Devonshire MSS). Rockingham assumed that Kinnoul would resign because 'he can not act with those, who put the Government upon Measures that are contrary to those which supported the King's family at the Head of the Constitution' (Rockingham to Devonshire, *n.d.* November 1762, Devonshire MSS).

[70] For his criticisms of the peace see his letter to Newcastle of 20 September 1762, the contents of which are reproduced in Newcastle to Rockingham, 20 September 1762, Wentworth Woodhouse MSS R.I–302. But see also, Devonshire to Rockingham, 2 August 1762, ibid., RI–271. There were rumours in the summer that the Court intended to rid itself of Devonshire's services. See the letters of Charles Price to the Duke of Portland, 31 July and 19 August 1762, Portland MSS, University of Nottingham Library.

[71] The letters of Egremont to Devonshire of 29 September and 20 October, demanding his presence are curt and preremptory (Devonshire MSS).

[72] Mr Brooke comments (*George III*, p. 98) that 'Few things in King George III's long life show him in so poor a light' as striking Devonshire's name off the list of councillors. The Devonshires had never voted against the Hanoverians and dismissal from the privy council was a rare and humiliating punishment. 'The only excuse for the King's petulance is that he was young, impatient, and frightened' (ibid.).

[73] Newcastle, not surprisingly, regarded the dismissal of Devonshire as

a direct consequence of Fox's alliance with the Court. 'The Minister of Power, without Ministerial Office, or Responsibility.' (Newcastle to Rockingham, 23 October 1762, B.M. Add. MSS 32943, ff. 395–6; 28 October 1762, ibid., 32944, ff. 112–13, Newcastle Papers.) Newcastle was increasingly obsessed with the fear 'That no Violences would be omitted which could tend to & establish, The Sole Power of the Minister' (Newcastle to Hardwicke, 1 November 1762, ibid., ff. 185–7).

[74] 'War seems to be declared at home with the utmost virulence. I am the mark for the party watch word, but the whole is in reality aimed at the King himself whose liberty is now to be decided on, liberty that his poorest subject enjoys of choosing his own menial servants.' (Bute to Sir James Lowther, 17 November 1762, N. Jucker (Ed.), *The Jenkinson Papers, 1760–6* (1949), pp. 86–7.) The Devonshire affair had sinister undertones which worried Newcastle. 'It was to be a Measure of Power to frighten Every Body thro' Your Grace', he told the martyred Devonshire (Newcastle to Devonshire, 15 November 1762, Devonshire MSS).

[75] L. B. Namier, op. cit., p. 387. Temple estimated the Opposition at about 150. Lord Temple to John Wilkes, 25 November 1762, W. T. Smith (Ed.), *The Grenville Papers* (4 Vols, 1852–3), Vol. ii, pp. 5–7.

CHAPTER 2

[1] Hardwicke to Charles Yorke, 9 September 1762, *Hardwicke*, Vol. III, pp. 415–17.

[2] Charles Yorke was Solicitor-General from 1756–61, Attorney-General from 1762–3. Seeking, after the family tradition, the Woolsack, he refused to answer Newcastle's call for him to resign after the dismissal of Devonshire. He was MP for Reigate, 1747–68 and for Cambridge University from 1768 until his tragic death in 1770.

[3] Charles Yorke to Newcastle, 13 September 1762, *Hardwicke*, Vol. III, pp. 418–23. Newcastle echoed this view: 'Nothing can be done without Mr Pitt' (Newcastle to Devonshire, 16 November 1762, Devonshire MSS).

[4] Pitt expressed his hostility to Bute at a preliminary meeting on 5 November. 'Conversation between Mr Pitt and Mr Nuthall, 5 November 1762; as related to Mr Walpole' (B.M. Add. MSS 32944, f. 277, Newcastle Papers). For the meeting on 17 November there is a detailed report in Newcastle's letter to Devonshire, 20 November 1762, ibid., 32945, ff. 83–92 q. L. B. Namier, op. cit., pp. 388–9. A few days later Pitt was down with the gout and the friends of Newcastle were not even sure if he would attend the debates on the peace (Hardwicke to Newcastle, 27 November 1762, ibid., f. 168). Rumours that Pitt might even *support* the peace alarmed some circles in the City so strongly that *The North Briton*, No. 24, was almost entirely devoted to refuting them. (G. Nobbe, *The North Briton*, (Columbia University Press, 1939), pp. 114–17.)

[5] Hardwicke to Newcastle, 9 October 1762, *Hardwicke*, Vol. III, p. 420.

[6] Newcastle to Hardwicke, 3 October 1762, B.M. Add. MSS 32942, f. 428, Newcastle Papers.

[7] Newcastle to Devonshire, 16 November 1762, Devonshire MSS.

[8] Newcastle to Cumberland, 19 October 1762, B.M. Add. MSS 32943, f. 311, Newcastle Papers.

[9] Newcastle to Hardwicke, 29 November 1762, ibid., 32945, ff. 196–8.

[10] Devonshire to Newcastle, 1 November 1762, ibid., 32944, ff. 317–18.

[11] Newcastle to Devonshire, 23 November 1762, *Hardwicke*, Vol. III, p. 435.

[12] Hardwicke to Charles Yorke, 9 September 1762, loc. cit.; Hardwicke to Newcastle, 27 November 1762, *Hardwicke*, Vol. III, pp. 435–7.

[13] George Onslow to Newcastle, 27 November 1762, B.M. Add. MSS 32945, ff. 200–1, Newcastle Papers partly q. L. B. Namier, op. cit., p. 391–2. On 27 November Newcastle had already written, in some desperation, to Hardwicke, 'The D. of Grafton, and our warm friends, press extremely the bringing on *some point*, immediately, or, we shall lose all our friends'. See also D. Watson, 'The Rise of the Opposition at Wildmans Club', *Bulletin of the Institute of Historical Research*, **XLIV** (1971) which includes an account of the emergence of the 'Young Friends'. My account and interpretation differ slightly in points of detail and emphasis from those of Dr Watson.

[14] George Onslow to Newcastle, 30 November 1762, ibid., ff. 227–30 q. L. B. Namier, p. 392.

[15] The Duke of Grafton, the future Prime Minister, succeeded his father in 1757 when he was only twenty-two years old. He had hitherto made no impression on politics, although he had been in the Commons from 1756–7, had been a Lord of the Bedchamber to Prince George, 1756–7 and Lord Lieutenant of Suffolk, 1757–63. Those who attended the dinner are listed by Namier, *op. cit.*, p. 392, together with their ages. They are as follows: Grafton (27), Lord George Cavendish (35), Lord John Cavendish (30), Lord Middleton (32), Tommy Townshend Junior (29), Spanish Charles Townshend (34), Lord Villiers (27), George Onslow (31), Richard Hopkins (33). All were Members of Parliament except Grafton and Hopkins. Three others can only be regarded as 'Young Friends' but did not attend the dinner: Thomas Pelham (34), Thomas Walpole (35), and, in spite of his fifty-seven years, William Baker. For biographical information on these members see Sir L. Namier and J. Brooke, *The House of Commons, 1754–90*.

[16] Onslow, Villiers and Townshend were office-holders who had not thought it appropriate to resign over the *Devonshire* affair.

[17] Pitt was sent to but he refused to co-operate with the Newcastle Whigs in Parliament (L. B. Namier, op. cit., 393–4).

[18] As late as 7 December Newcastle was ignorant of Pitt's intentions and uncertain of tactics for the Lords and Commons ('Memorandum, 7 December', B.M. Add. MSS 33000, f. 219, Newcastle Papers).

[19] For the debate see Horace Walpole, *Memoirs*, Vol. i, pp. 222–3,

Newdigate Diary, B. 2542, Warwickshire County Record Office; Sir W. Anson, *Autobiography of the Third Duke of Grafton* (1898), p. 24. The account in *The Parliamentary History* is extremely scanty and gives only Pitt's speech in detail. There is, however, a list of the minority (**XV**, pp. 1257–72). For the division, *see* the Appendix.

[20] For the basis upon which these calculations have been made, *see* the Appendix. Biographical information about these members may be found in L. B. Namier and J. Brooke, op. cit. The remarks of L. M. Wiggin, *The Faction of Cousins*, p. 280, that 'the small minority was composed of the followers of Pitt and Cumberland as well as scattered Tories' is farcically superficial.

[21] To Sir Horace Mann, 20 December 1762, *Correspondence of Horace Walpole*, **XXII**, pp. 109–11.

[22] L. B. Namier, *England in the Age*, pp. 417–18.

[23] Kinnoul to Newcastle, 26 December 1762, B.M. Add. MSS 32945, ff. 376–87, Newcastle Papers, *q.* Namier, op. cit., p. 417.

[24] Devonshire to Rockingham, 26 December 1762, RI–339. Wentworth Woodhouse MS.

[25] Devonshire to Newcastle, 29 December 1762, B.M. Add. MSS 32945, ff. 424–5, Newcastle Papers.

[26] Grafton's opinion was that 'many persons will join us when there appears to be some measures concerted and agreed upon. . . . If we only attack at intervals we allow time for those who must be disgusted to be reconciled to their old party, whereas when they have in their own pique joined with us, their retreat again can no longer be so easy' (Grafton to Newcastle, 1 January 1763, ibid., 32946, f. 25). The contrary opinion, that of Hardwicke, was not quite so different as it at first appears. 'To be calling out for, and hunting after points every week, which may not be very considerable in themselves and wherein few persons may think themselves concern'd, will only serve, to lessen and weaken the Minority and expose our friends instead of serving them.' On the other hand, Hardwicke believed that a systematic Opposition was feasible in the coming session because 'several opportunities and offerings must necessarily be given, of which proper advantage may be made . . .' (Hardwicke to Newcastle, 1 January 1763, ibid., ff. 2–3). It was the question of initiative, then, rather than a difference of opinion on the legitimacy of Opposition which separated Grafton from Hardwicke. The timing, not the legitimacy, of Opposition was in question.

[27] L. B. Namier, op. cit., pp. 404–5. Fox to Bute, late November 1762, Lord Ilchester, *Life of Fox* (1920, 2 Vols), Vol. ii, pp. 214–15.

[28] Among these were Henry Bridgeman, Lord Villiers, Thomas Pelham, Lord Gage, George Onslow, Tommy Townshend Junior, and Charles Fitzroy.

[29] See the letters of Rockingham to Devonshire of 30 December 1762 and 5 January 1763, Devonshire MSS. Further details can be found in letters from certain Yorkshire friends of Rockingham to the Marquis, especially Sir George Armytage, 2 January 1763, RI–348 Stephen Croft, 2 January

1763, RI–347 Wentworth Woodhouse MSS. There is some evidence that Rockingham even attempted to prevent his supporters from resigning. See the letters to Rockingham of N. Gream, 4 January 1763, RI–350, T. Place, 6 January 1763, RI–353 and J. Lister, 22 March 1763, RI–368d.

[30] See the details for Sussex in B.M. Add. MSS 32946, ff. 179–81, 323–4. Newcastle Papers.

[31] Other extracts from this important letter from Newcastle to Devonshire, 23 December 1762, are quoted in L. B. Namier, op. cit., p. 405. The original is in the Devonshire MSS.

[32] Namier's reference to this episode (ibid., p. 415) suggests that Newcastle's behaviour was mildly ridiculous. It was, however, most effective. To a very large extent he succeeded. *See below*, Chapter 5.

[33] For an account of the formation of the club see D. Watson, op. cit., p. 57.

[34] For Newcastle's disapproval of the club see his letter to Devonshire, 23 December 1762, B.M. Add. MSS 32945, f. 341, Newcastle Papers, *q.* L. B. Namier, op. cit., p. 417 and D. Watson, op. cit., p. 57. Devonshire disliked the club because 'When once an opposition is formed, it may be very proper, but 'till that is settled, it would only have the appearance of faction . . .'. (Devonshire to Newcastle, 26 January 1763, B.M. Add. MSS 32945, f. 373, Newcastle Papers.)

[35] L. B. Namier, op. cit., pp. 416–18; A. S. Foord, op. cit., p. 311.

[36] Namier took a cynical view of the relations between Newcastle and the 'Young Friends'. He was suspicious of any connection between them and warned against 'mistaking the survival of a name for an inheritance of personality and for a continuity of ideas' (op. cit., pp. 417–18). But there was *no* conflict of ideas and there *was* an inheritance of personality. Nomenclature is surely unimportant.

[37] This point was first suggested by Dr Watson in his thesis (pp. 211–12) and is repeated in his article (op. cit., p. 58). The problem is surely resolved by the wording of Legge's letter to Devonshire of 2 February 1764 (Devonshire MSS), 'It gives me infinite pleasure to hear how very ill. . . . Administration take our new Establishment in Albemarle Street'.

[38] For the 'progress' of the club established in December 1762 see Dr Watson's article, pp. 58ff.

[39] Newcastle to Devonshire, 12 December 1762, B.M. Add. MSS 32945, ff. 280–1, Newcastle Papers.

[40] Charles Townshend had been in Parliament since 1747 and after holding a series of minor offices he became Secretary at War in March 1761 until December 1762. He returned to office briefly as First Lord of Trade, February–April 1763.

[41] Newcastle to Devonshire, 23 December 1762, Devonshire MSS.

[42] This was, nevertheless, a powerful factor because the erosion of Newcastle's hitherto powerful position in the City and the general acquiescence with which the peace had been greeted there had seriously weakened his influence and self confidence. (D. Watson, *The Duke of Newcastle*, pp. 161–2.)

[43] Grafton to Newcastle, 1 January 1763, B.M. Add. MSS 32946, f. 25, Newcastle Papers.

[44] Newcastle to Hardwicke, 31 January 1763, ibid., f. 264.

[45] Newcastle to Devonshire, 20 November 1762, ibid., 32945, ff. 83–92.

[46] Charles Pratt, later Lord Camden, was in the Commons between 1757 and 1762 but he made a greater mark upon the legal than the political profession. He was Attorney-General 1757–62 and Chief Justice of Common Pleas, 1762–6.

[47] Lord Jersey to Newcastle, 21 December 1762, B.M. Add. MSS 32945, f. 341, Newcastle Papers.

[48] Tommy Townshend Junior to Newcastle, 25 December 1762, ibid., ff. 326–8.

[49] Newcastle to Devonshire, 31 January 1763, ibid., 32946, ff. 266–8.

[50] Pitt to Devonshire, 5 February 1763, Devonshire MSS. According to one correspondent, Pitt had come round to accept the prospect of Newcastle taking office again. (Rose Fuller to Newcastle, 5 February 1763, B.M. Add. MSS 32946, ff. 329–30, Newcastle Papers.)

[51] Devonshire to Newcastle, 17 February 1763, ibid., 32947, f. 21.

[52] For the debate see Newdigate MSS, B2543; Rigby to Bedford, 10 March 1763, *Bedford Correspondence*, Vol. iii, pp. 218–20, Rockingham to Newcastle, 4 March 1763, B.M. Add. MSS 32947, f. 180. Newcastle Papers.

[53] Rigby to Bedford, 10 March 1763, loc. cit.; Temple to Newcastle, 9 March 1763, B.M. Add. MSS 32947, f. 216. J. Almon, in *The History of the Late Minority* (1965), pp. 91–2 claims that this dinner marked the birth of the coalition in opposition of Pitt and Newcastle. He lists those present as the Dukes of Devonshire, Bolton, and Portland, the Marquis of Rockingham, Lords Temple, Cornwallis, Albemarle, Ashburnham, Hardwicke, Bessborough, Spencer, Sondes, Grantham, Villiers and Messrs. Pitt, James Grenville and Sir George Savile.

[54] Newcastle immediately began to draw up lists of 'Sure Friends of My Own in the House of Commons' (B.M. Add. MSS 32948, ff. 138–9, 140–1, Newcastle Papers). The latter is dated 16 April. An examination of these lists dispels any possibility that Newcastle's connection was melting away. See Appendix.

[55] MP for Worcestershire, 1761–75. Something of a self-made expert on finance and a future leading adviser to Rockingham. He was not yet attached to Newcastle's party.

[56] The document is an enclosure in Newcastle to Devonshire, 28 January 1763, Devonshire MSS.

[57] Newcastle to Hardwicke, 26 March 1763, B.M. Add. MSS 32947, ff. 319–20; Newcastle to Albemarle, 27 March 1763, ibid., ff. 329–30. These divisions in the Lords enable some estimate to be made of Newcastle's following there. A list in the Newcastle Papers (B.M. Add. MSS 32947, f. 337) gives 40 names of peers who opposed the Cider Tax to which can be added 3 more from a list in *The Annual Register*, 1763, p. 119. Of these 43, exactly a dozen had no connection with Newcastle. To the remaining

31, however, it is possible to add a further 9 peers supporting Newcastle who did not vote against the Cider Tax. His following in the upper House, therefore, may be estimated at about 40. See also pp. 481–2.

[58] Dr Watson has argued in his thesis (p. 181) that Newcastle's lack of enthusiasm for the issue stemmed from the fact that his City interests were not at stake.

[59] Hardwicke to Newcastle, 1 July 1763, B.M. Add. MSS 32949, ff. 252, Newcastle Papers.

[60] Legge to Newcastle, 17 March 1763, ibid., 32947, ff. 240–1; Hardwicke to Newcastle, 18 March 1763, ibid., ff. 244–5.

[61] B. Kemp, *Sir Francis Dashwood* (1967), p. 57.

[62] George III to Bute, 28 March 1763, Sedgwick, op. cit., p. 206; Fox to Bute, 29 March 1763, Bute MSS.

[63] See the two letters of George III to Bute in the second half of November 1762, Sedgwick, op. cit., pp. 165–7 and ibid., **lxi–ii.** Bute wrote to Fox on 28 November 1762: 'they teaze me, they hurt my delicacy, they render me impatient'. (B.M. Add. MSS 51379, ff. 120–1, Holland House MSS; Ilchester, op. cit., 11, p. 167.)

[64] Bute to Bedford, 16 February 1763, *Bedford Correspondence*, Vol. III, pp. 204–5.

[65] Fox to Bute, 11 March 1763, and 24 March 1763, B.M. Add. MSS 51379, ff. 148–53, 154–7, Holland House MSS. Fox, like Bute, had no stomach for the political battles to come. On the verge of reaching the pinnacle of power, his personal courage failed him. After decades of opportunism in politics, his nerve was still unequal to his ambition.

[66] George III to Bute, second half of November 1763, Sedgwick, op. cit., pp. 166–7; 5 March 1763, pp. 197–8. Fitzmaurice, op. cit., Vol. I, p. 149.

[67] Bute to Grenville, 1 April 1763, *The Grenville Papers*, Vol. II, pp. 40–1; Grenville to Bute, 25 March 1763, ibid., pp. 33–40; George III to Lord Bute, 17 March 1763, Sedgwick, op. cit., pp. 203–4.

[68] *See*, for example, George III to Bute, 4 April 1763, ibid., pp. 209–10. Halifax and Egremont remained as Secretaries. Although the Duke of Bedford refused to come in he advised his friends to stay in office. Shelburne became President of the Board of Trade. Fox and Dashwood obtained peerages and became Lord Holland and Lord Despencer, respectively.

[69] George III to Lord Bute, Sedgwick, op. cit., pp. 214–15. Bute wrote that Grenville was 'the only man in the House of Commons in whom he could confide so great a trust'. (To Bedford, 2 April 1763, *Bedford Correspondence*, Vol. III, p. 224.)

[70] Bedford to Bute, 7 April 1763, *Bedford Correspondence*, Vol. III, pp. 227–30.

[71] I. R. Christie, *Myth and Reality*, pp. 50–3.

[72] *Life and Letters of Lady Sarah Lenox*, pp. 76–7.

[73] Newcastle to Devonshire, 23 July 1762, B.M. Add. MSS 32941, ff. 36–9, Newcastle Papers.

[74] Rockingham to Newcastle, 15 May 1762, ibid., 32938, ff. 287–90.

[75] Newcastle to Hardwicke, 19 December 1762, ibid., 32945, f. 313. *See also Hardwicke*, Vol. III, pp. 439–42.

[76] Pitt to Walpole, 19 November 1762, *Hardwicke*, Vol. III, p. 431. See n. 4 supra.

[77] Newcastle to Hardwicke, 1 November 1762, B.M. Add. MSS 32944, ff. 185–7, Newcastle Papers. Henry Fox commented that hostility to the peace was nothing more nor less than hostility to the personality of Bute (Ilchester, op. cit., Vol. II, 185).

[78] Almon in *The History of the Late Minority* (1766) (p. 65) does not assert that the Massacre was 'unconstitutional'. His only comment in this vein is that it was unprecedented for men to be dismissed from the revenue boards 'which ought to be sacred during good behaviour'. Hardwicke, too, believed that the dismissals 'cannot be called a breach of the Constitution . . . tho' undoubtedly the carrying it to so many persons out of the House is an extension beyond example in former times'. (Hardwicke to Newcastle, December 1762, B.M. Add. MSS 32946, f. 4, Newcastle Papers.)

[79] Devonshire to Newcastle, 17 February 1763, B.M. Add. MSS 32947, f. 21, Newcastle Papers.

[80] *See*, for example, the extensive quotations from *The North Briton* in G. Nobbe, op. cit., pp. 101–20, 141–59, 172–83. For a general discussion of Bute's unpopularity, see J. Brewer, op. cit., pp. 3–19.

[81] J. Almon, *History of the Late Minority*, p. 77.

[82] Devonshire to Newcastle, 9 April 1763, B.M. Add. MSS 32948, f. 84, Newcastle Papers. As early as 2 July 1762 Devonshire had written to Newcastle thinking it 'not impossible that Ld Bute may desire to quit a responsible Employment & take a place about the King's person, in that case how cou'd he be trusted' (ibid., 32938, ff. 227–30). For expectations of an early end to the Grenville ministry, see George Onslow to Newcastle, 8 April 1763, James West to Newcastle, 8 April 1763, ibid., 32948, ff. 64, 65.

[83] This is the conclusion of J. Brewer (op. cit., pp. 37–8). While I think Dr Brewer's argument is acceptable I feel that it would be strengthened by relating it to the political attitudes held by the old Whigs *before* 1760.

[84] The old corps well understood the need for solidarity in office. Hardwicke wrote to Newcastle on 1 June 1757 (*Hardwicke*, Vol. II, pp. 397–8). 'I would not have you come in upon no plan at all, for that will be without any strength at all . . . 'twill all be a rope of sand without consistency and without strength. . . .' Of the First Lord of the Treasury, Hardwicke wrote to Newcastle on 3 January 1755 (ibid., pp. 225–6) 'there must be some principal person to receive applications, to hear the wants and the wishes and the requests of mankind . . . that it was impossible for the King to be troubled with all this himself . . . that ministers bore all the blame and resentment of disappointed persons, and they could never carry on his affairs without having some weight in the disposition of favours.' For the 'Whig Tradition' and its adaptability to the politics of opposition, see A. S. Foord, *His Majesty's Opposition*, pp. 312–15.

CHAPTER 3

[1] J. Almon, *The Correspondence of John Wilkes* (1805, 5 vols), Vol. I, pp. 91–3. For a detailed discussion of the circumstances of the publication of No. 45 *see* G. Nobbe, op. cit., pp. 202–8. The date of publication was 23 April.

[2] For the most authoritative discussion of General Warrants, *see* Mark A. Thomson, *The Secretaries of State, 1681–1782* (1932), p. 112ff. Forty-nine persons were seized with Wilkes (ibid., p. 118). For details of the seizure, *see* G. Nobbe, op. cit., pp. 214–20. Charles Yorke, the Attorney General, and Fletcher Norton, the Solicitor General deposited opinions that No. 45 *was* a seditious libel *not* protected by privilege and that privilege did not extend to breach of the peace, treason and felony. Number 45 clearly did not come under the last two categories (although they toyed with treason for a time) and it was thus necessary to show that No. 45 tended to a breach of the peace. No wonder Lord Hardwicke warned his son against putting his opinion into writing! (Lord Hardwicke to Charles Yorke, 30 April 1763, B.M. Add. MSS 35353, ff. 316–17, Hardwicke Papers.)

[3] Although the ministry was to be attacked for its high-handed and authoritarian methods and the scant respect which it paid to the liberties of the subject in the Wilkes case, we should keep its actions in perspective. Far from threatening the liberties of Englishmen the ministry of Grenville bungled the affair to an astonishing extent. Ministers were asking for trouble, whatever the provocation they had suffered, in using a General Warrant against a popular figure like Wilkes for their action was certain to provoke a well-publicised and protracted legal scandal. Wilkes himself was already a public hero in the eyes of the London mob. His arrest was greeted with angry disorder, his release with joyful rioting. The press immediately seized on the incident as an attack upon the Englishman's birth-right of free speech. Ministers, indeed, had made a rod for their own backs the day they agreed to issue a General Warrant against John Wilkes. A further complication was that Wilkes was a Member of Parliament. Ministers plunged into the legal quagmire of precedent and custom from which they were to find it exceedingly difficult to extract themselves before Parliament took up, as it was almost bound to do, the case in the next session. The Government, in short, had provoked a first rate public outcry.

Two further considerations brought the Wilkes issue directly into the vortex of opposition politics, Wilkes' relationship with Temple and the political aspect of the judiciary. As member for Aylesbury Wilkes was well known in Temple's county of Buckinghamshire. Indeed, he had been the sheriff of the county in 1754–5 and at the time of his arrest he was a colonel in the county militia. But Wilkes political career had not prospered— Wilkes was a popular, not a parliamentary, orator—and after Temple's resignation in October 1761 he appeared to have little prospect of advancement. He was prepared, therefore, to take to journalism. For his part, Temple was anxious to indulge his own restless and meddling spirit in the

Grub Street sensationalism of the London press of the day. He became Wilkes' patron and subsidised his acrimonious attacks upon Bute in *The North Briton*. When the ministry attacked Wilkes, therefore, they thus threw down the gauntlet to Temple and the friend and brother-in-law of Pitt did not flinch from taking up the challenge. He decided to apply for a writ of Habeas Corpus. The normal course of action would have been to apply to the Chief Justice in the King's Bench, Lord Mansfield, an old Whig but as a friend of Charles Yorke unlikely to prove well disposed towards Wilkes. Temple, therefore, applied to the Court of Common Pleas whose Chief-Justice, Sir Charles Pratt, was a friend of Pitt and Temple. On 6 May Pratt dismissed the charge that libel could lead to a breach of the peace. By implication, the actions of ministers stood condemned by Pratt's decision. Condemned or not, they were determined to take their revenge on Temple and this they did by depriving him of his Lieutenancy of Buckinghamshire. In this way the Wilkes affair became a first rate political as well as legal scandal.

[4] 'Newcastle was particularly addicted to the use of general warrants for the arrest of persons and issued more than any other Secretary' (Thomson, op. cit., p. 116 and n. 4). Hardwicke, however, was even more concerned for Newcastle's consistency than Newcastle was (Hardwicke to Newcastle, 1 May 1763, B.M. Add. MSS 32948, ff. 199–200, Newcastle Papers). 'All I mean is that we should not too hastily make *Cause commun* with Mr Wilkes'. Newcastle was fully aware of the embarrassments surrounding his position. (Newcastle to Devonshire, 2 May 1763, ibid., ff. 203–4.) For his comments about parliamentary privilege see his letter to White, 27 May 1763, ibid., ff. 291–3.

[5] George Onslow refused to accompany Temple on his famous visit to Wilkes in the Tower without Newcastle's approval. George Onslow to Newcastle, 2 May 1763, ibid., f. 205. Grafton accompanied Temple but refused to stand bail for Wilkes lest such an action be regarded as 'the shadow of an offence' against the person of the King. (Grafton to Temple, 3 May 1763, *Grenville Correspondence*, Vol. II, pp. 53–5.)

[6] Cumberland to Newcastle, 31 October 1763, B.M. Add. MSS 32952, ff. 141–2, Newcastle Papers, Devonshire to Newcastle 20 August 1763, ibid., 32950, ff. 182–3. How Devonshire must have shuddered when he read Onslow's letter of 29 June (Devonshire MSS) in which Onslow reports that Wilkes 'desires to be understood as being devoted to the Service of the Opposition, in any Plan of Writing that may be thought right', and that he 'intends to begin his Weekly entertainment of us, about a Fortnight before the Parliament begins'.

[7] Hardwicke to Charles Yorke, 18 April 1763, ibid., 35353, f. 312, Hardwicke Papers.

[8] 'I desire you will take a note out of this letter, & then burn it; for I have nothing to do in this matter'. (30 April 1763, G. Harris, *Life of Hardwicke* (3 Vols, 1847), Vol. III, p. 342.)

[9] Hardwicke to Newcastle, 1 May 1763, loc. cit.

[10] Newcastle's dream was a Pitt–Devonshire ministry which would allow

R

him considerable influence. Yet he was not prepared to sacrifice his friendship with Cumberland and Devonshire for Pitt's sake, although he regarded
the situation of the 'Young Friends' as a negotiable matter. (Hardwicke
to Devonshire, 19 August 1763, Devonshire MSS.)

[11] Newcastle to Hardwicke, 10 April 1763, B.M. Add. MSS 32948,
ff. 1–2, Newcastle Papers; Newcastle to Devonshire, 21 May 1763, Devonshire MSS. In early June Pitt's view was that 'Wilkes was entitled to
privilege. He doubted very much whether the *North Briton*, No. 45, is a
libel, & whether the holding it to be so would not in a high degree infringe
ye liberty of ye press, as to censuring ye transactions or advice of ministers'.
(Hardwicke to Newcastle, 8 June 1763, G. Harris, op. cit., Vol. III,
pp. 357–60.)

[12] Charles Yorke to Newcastle, 14 June 1763, ibid., 32949, ff. 124–7,
Hardwicke, Vol. III, pp. 506–8. Yorke was only the latest of a steady
stream of visitors to Hayes in the summer.

[13] Newcastle to Devonshire, 11 August 1763, ibid., 32950, ff. 65–8,
Hardwicke, Vol. III, pp. 516–19.

[14] Minutes by the Duke of Newcastle, 11, 20 and 24 September 1763,
Devonshire MSS, Copy.

[15] Minute by the Duke of Newcastle, 3 October 1763, ibid.

[16] The situation was very difficult for Newcastle as he must increasingly
have realised as he tried to reconcile the two irreconcileables. Charles
Yorke naturally kept his distance from Newcastle as he realised that if
Pitt came into office he would make Pratt a peer and bring him into the
Cabinet (*Hardwicke*, Vol. III, p. 537). When Pitt and Yorke met on
12 October in an attempt to settle their differences they fell into an angry
series of exchanges. Pitt blamed Newcastle for the failure of the meeting.
(Pitt to Newcastle, 12 October 1763, B.M. Add. MSS 32951, ff. 413–14,
Newcastle Papers.)

[17] His brother, John, also resigned his post as a Commissioner of Trade
at the same time 'for the sake of those friends, with whom I shall ever wish
to act'. (John Yorke to Rockingham, 9 November 1763, R.146–14, Wentworth Woodhouse MSS.)

[18] Draft of a letter from Rockingham of 31 October 1763, probably to
Newcastle, ibid., RI–389; *Hardwicke*, Vol. III, p. 545.

[19] Newcastle to Devonshire, 2 November 1763, B.M. Add. MSS 32952,
ff. 184–5, *Hardwicke*, Vol. III, pp. 546–7, reporting Pitt's comments to
Cumberland on 31 October.

[20] Newcastle to Cumberland, 2 November 1763, ibid., f. 216, *Hardwicke*,
Vol. III, p. 546.

[21] Bute to Bedford, 2 April 1763, *Bedford Correspondence*, Vol. III, p. 224.

[22] *Grenville Papers*, Vol. I, pp. 452–3.

[23] J. Brooke, *George III*, p. 103.

[24] For confirmation of Bute's frequent contacts with the King, *see Grenville
Papers*, Vol. III, p. 220.

[25] The Newcastle Whigs had been watching Bute very carefully indeed.
As early as 9 June Newcastle thought Bute 'displeased with the present

administration, and wished to know whether the Opposition would come in'. (Newcastle to Hardwicke, 9 June 1763, B.M. Add. MSS 32949, ff. 70–1, Newcastle Papers; *Hardwicke*, Vol. III, pp. 503–4.) Hardwicke's own account of the overture can be found in his letter to Lord Royston, 5 August 1763, ibid., pp. 512–16. The Newcastle Whigs had, in fact, been expecting some such approach from the Court but they regarded this as an attempt by Bute to divide and rule them. (Devonshire to Newcastle, 2 August 1763, Devonshire MSS; Newcastle to Devonshire, 25 August 1763, ibid.) Newcastle's opinion of Bute remained the same. 'Lord Bute is the Sole Minister. . . . Nobody else does any Thing of Consequence. . . . His Influence is full as great as ever & will continue so . . . His Weak, disjointed, divided Administration will try to divide us in the recess.' (Newcastle to Devonshire, 19 August 1763, Devonshire MSS.)

[26] G. F. S. Elliot, *The Border Elliots* (1897), p. 378; Fitzmaurice, op. cit., Vol. I, pp. 207–8.

[27] Bute, partly voluntarily but also partly at Grenville's insistence, left town early in September for Luton Hoo. At the same time, Shelburne, who acted with Bute throughout these negotiations, lost his office as First Lord of Trade.

[28] Egmont replaced Sandwich at the Admiralty, while Sandwich became Secretary of State for the Northern Department, Halifax moving to the Southern Department; Hillsborough replaced Shelburne at the Board of Trade. Bedford entered the ministry as Lord President. Bedford, Sandwich and Egmont kissed hands on 9 September.

[29] Devonshire to Rockingham, 30 August 1763, RI–382, Wentworth Woodhouse MSS. Rockingham received a similar letter from Pitt but was much more suspicious of his motives than Devonshire. (Rockingham to Sir George Savile, 29 August 1763, *H.M.S. Foljambe*, p. 144.)

[30] 20 August 1763, Devonshire MSS.

[31] Pitt to Newcastle, 12 September 1763, B.M. Add. MSS 32951, ff. 7–8, Newcastle Papers, also *q.* in D. Jarrett, *The Begetters of Revolution: England's Involvement with France, 1758–89* (1973), p. 59.

[32] For these disputes see *Grenville Correspondence*, Vol. II, pp. 206–14. For Grenville's need of patronage to build up a party *see* J. Haas, 'The Pursuit of Political Success in Eighteenth Century England: Sandwich, 1740–71', *Bulletin of the Institute of Historical Research*, **XLIII** (1970), pp. 72–3.

[33] N. Jucker, op. cit., p. 216; J. Tomlinson (Ed.), *Additional Grenville Papers, 1763–5* (Manchester 1962), p. 47ff.

[34] Sandwich told Dashwood that the ministry wanted the evidence against Wilkes marshalled by the opening of the session, especially proof that he had admitted to the editorship of *The North Briton*. (1 November 1763, B.M. Egerton MSS 2136, ff. 85–6, Dashwood MSS. *See also* J. Nobbe, op. cit., pp. 239–43.)

[35] Grenville to George III, 14 November 1763, Sir J. Fortescue (Ed.), *Correspondence of George III* (6 Vols, 1927–8), Vol. I, p. 63.

[36] 'Minutes of the Opinions of members of the Duke of Newcastle's Party, to be represented by the Duke to Mr Pitt', 11 and 20 September

1763, B.M. Add. MSS 35428, f. 64, Hardwicke Papers; 'Duke of Newcastle's memoirs of a Conversation with Mr Pitt on 27 September 1763, ibid., 32951, ff. 192–205, Newcastle Papers.

[37] Newcastle to Devonshire, 19 December 1763, B.M. Add. MSS 32954, ff. 54–61, Newcastle Papers.

[38] Newcastle to Devonshire, 20 July 1763, ibid., 32949, ff. 379–83; Devonshire to Newcastle, 2 August 1763, ibid., 32950, ff. 8–15.

[39] Rockingham to Devonshire, 14 November 1763, ibid., 35430, ff. 7–8, Hardwicke MSS.

[40] D. Jarrett, op. cit., p. 49.

[41] Newcastle to Devonshire, 14 October 1763, Devonshire MSS.

[42] Horace Walpole, *Memoirs of the Reign of George III*, Vol. I, pp. 247–8.

[43] The debate is given in Newdigate MSS B. 2543. The account in *The Parliamentary History* (**XV**, pp. 1354–64) is inadequate. The division list reveals seventeen Members who can be regarded as Pelhamites who had not supported the connection in the previous session. *See* the Appendix.

[44] There are details of the debate on 23 November in *Fortescue*, Vol. I, pp. 61–2 but *see also* L. B. Namier, *Additions and Corrections* (Manchester, 1939), p. 2 and Appendix 2; H. Walpole, *Memoirs*, Vol. I, pp. 324–9; H. Walpole to Sir Horace Mann, 12 December 1763, *Correspondence of Horace Walpole*, Vol. XXVII, pp. 186–91.

[45] A von Ruville, *William Pitt*, Vol. III, pp. 129–31.

[46] There are details of the debate in *Fortescue*, Vol. I, pp. 62–3. There is a list of the minority peers in Add. MSS 32953, f. 109. The list is as follows: The *Dukes* of Bolton, Cumberland, Devonshire, Grafton, Newcastle, Portland; the *Marquis* of Rockingham; the *Earls* of Albemarle, Ashburnham, Bessborough, Bristol, Cornwallis, Dartmouth, Fauconberg, Jersey, Lincoln, Scarborough, Shelburne, Stratford, Temple; *Viscounts* Folkstone, Torrington; *Barons* Abergavenny, Dacre, Edgecumbe, Fortescue, Grantham, Monson, Onslow, Sandys, Sondes, Walpole; the *Bishops* of Chichester, Lichfield and St Asaph. A protest was signed by the following seventeen: Bessborough, Devonshire, Portland, Grantham, Scarborough, Ashburnham, Abergavenny, Walpole, Temple, Bolton, Bristol, Grafton, Cornwallis, Folkstone, Dacre, Fortescue and the bishop of Lichfield. Only four names appear here who did not vote against the Cider Tax. They are Lords Shelburne and Strafford and Viscounts Onslow and Sandys. None of them were particularly close to Newcastle or his party. The Newcastle peers in the Lords continued to number about forty. 'We have Weight, but not Numbers; & what is still worse, a great superiority of Debaters against us', wrote Newcastle to Pitt on 13 December 1763 (Copy, Devonshire MSS).

[47] Charles Townshend, writing to Rockingham about Pitt's speech on 16 November stressed that he 'spoke very little to the address, & seem'd to have sought an occasion of throwing out His sentiments on union, proscription and the destruction of parties.' (16 November 1763, R146–27, Wentworth Woodhouse MSS.)

[48] Dr Watson ('Rise of the Opposition at Wildmans') concludes that

even the young men who may have wanted a club 'took no definite steps for some time, perhaps because of Newcastle's opposition. They probably met together informally at dinners but there is no evidence that any more specific action was taken' (p. 61. See also p. 63). 'Failure of the opposition to co-ordinate its actions before parliament met may thus have been the event which sparked off the actual formation of the club'.

[49] Ibid., pp. 64–5; Legge to Newcastle, 30 January 1764, B.M. Add. MSS 32955, ff. 314–15, Newcastle Papers; J. Almon, *History of the Late Minority*, p. 297.

[50] J. Almon, op. cit., pp. 297–300; *Grafton Autobiography*, p. 25, Thomas Wildman to Newcastle, 25 January 1764, B.M. Add. MSS 32955, f. 301, Newcastle Papers.

[51] The importance of this activity on this occasion should not be underestimated. See Lord John Cavendish to Newcastle, 10 February 1764, B.M. Add. MSS 32955, f. 421, Newcastle Papers. Newcastle to Lord John Cavendish, 11 February 1764, ibid., ff. 434–5.

[52] The list in J. Almon, op. cit., 298–300 is the same as that in the Newcastle Papers, B.M. Add. MSS 33035, f. 90, except that the latter adds Sir Matthew Fetherstonehaugh. Also see D. Watson, op. cit., pp. 65–6.

[53] Lord Corke and Baron Ravensworth.

[54] Dr Watson ('Rise of the Opposition at Wildmans Club', p. 68) comments that eighty-eight of the ninety-eight MPs voted in the minority on 17/18 February.

[55] Ibid., pp. 68–9; J. Almon, *History of the Late Minority*, pp. 310–11, exaggerates, however, when he claims that at the end of the session of 1764 the club had almost ceased to exist.

[56] See the report by George Onslow to Newcastle, 6 February 1764, B.M. Add. MSS 32955, f. 366, Newcastle Papers. The motion was on a procedural point relating to the production of the warrant by which Wilkes had been apprehended. There are two identical lists of the minority in the Newcastle Papers, B.M. Add. MSS 32955, ff. 370–3, 405–7.

[57] Newcastle to Lord John Cavendish, 11 February 1764, loc. cit.

[58] A similar one was drawn up by Pitt and conveyed to the meeting; the only difference was that Pitt's motion restricted the declaration of illegality to MPs.

[59] Grenville to the King, 15 February 1764, *Grenville Correspondence*, Vol. II, pp. 261–4. There is a list of the minority in the Newcastle Papers, 32955, ff. 269–70. Newcastle believed that sickness prevented some of his friends from attending. (Newcastle to Legge, 16 February 1764, ibid., 32956, f. 7.)

[60] For accounts of the debate, *see* H. Walpole, *Memoirs*, Vol. I, pp. 368–70; J. West to Newcastle, 17 February 1764, B.M. Add. MSS 32955, f. 419; George Onslow to Newcastle, 17 February 1764, ibid., 32956, f. 19, Newcastle Papers.

[61] He was greatly embittered at the fact that 40–50 Members voted with the Opposition who had not done so before. (Grenville to Lord Northumberland, 26 February 1764, Tomlinson, op. cit., pp. 93–6.)

[62] Grenville to Lord Northumberland, 10 March 1764, ibid., pp. 100–1.

[63] See A. Hardy, op. cit., p. 191, n. 1. Few contemporaries believed, however, that there would be a change of ministry, e.g. Lord Barrington to the Earl of Buckinghamshire, 26 February 1764, H.M.C. Lothian, pp. 248–9.

[64] D. Watson, op. cit., p. 68.

[65] Newcastle to John White, 19 June 1764, B.M. Add. MSS 32960, ff. 17–19, Newcastle Papers.

[66] The size of Newcastle's party had been enlarged by about twenty in the course of the session as a whole and now stood at 109. (See the estimates in the Appendix.)

[67] This was a charge commonly made by opponents of the Newcastle party, e.g. 'they who enlist under the banner of party, and discriminate themselves by the odious distinctions of *Whig* or *Tory*, never mean honestly' (*Considerations on the Present Dangerous Crisis*), 1763, p. 27). Pamphlets of this kind blamed the Opposition for forming a party *before* Bute had had a chance to show his talents (pp. 27–8).

[68] J. Brooke, *George III*, p. 103. See the letters of George III to Lord Bute of c. 4 and late April 1763, Sedgwick, op. cit., pp. 209–10, 233. For Jenkinsons' narrative of relations between Bute and Grenville, see N. Jucker, op. cit., pp. 393–400.

[69] See, *inter alia*, Bute to Shelburne, 4 September 1763, Fitzmaurice, op. cit., Vol. I, pp. 207–8. It is noteworthy that Bute had approached Pitt even *before* the death of Egremont (*Grenville Correspondence*, Vol. II, pp. 90–1, 93–4). Bute also approached Bedford, through Shelburne, for the King. (Fitzmaurice, op. cit., pp. 200–3; Ilchester, op. cit., Vol. II, pp. 268–9.) See above pp. 74–5 and n. 25–7.

[70] Grenville to Egremont, 4 August 1763, *Grenville Correspondence*, Vol. II, pp. 85–8, 202–4.

[71] Ibid., pp. 101, 208–10.

[72] Richard Pares' suggestion to this effect (*George III and the Politicians*, Oxford, 1953, p. 105 and n. 5) has been largely ignored but it seems to be borne out by the evidence (see 24 above).

[73] For these disputes see *Grenville Correspondence*, Vol. II, pp. 507, 518, 522–3, 535.

[74] Examples of references to Bute are so numerous that it would be both pedantic and misleading to set them out. Newcastle summed up a common opinion in July 1763 (to Devonshire, 13 July 1763, Devonshire MSS) when he declared that 'Lord Bute is, & wishes to be, as Much the Minister, & Man of Power as ever' while the cabinet was 'an Insignificant Set of Men, Divided amongst themselves'.

[75] At Christmas 1763 several such dismissals had taken place, including those of Shelburne, Calcraft and A'Court but Grenville had at that time managed to dissuade the King from dismissing Conway (George III to Grenville, 16 and 25 November 1763, *Grenville Correspondence*, Vol. II, pp. 162, 166). As soon, however, as the King heard of Conway's vote he decided to dismiss him (George III to Grenville, 18 February 1764, ibid.,

p. 267; Grenville to Lord Hartford, 18 April 1764, ibid., pp. 296–9). There can be no doubt that Grenville agreed with the King. He had warned Conway of the distinction 'between a *conscientious vote* upon a *particular measure* and a regular *system* of opposition' but Conway persisted in aligning himself with Newcastle (ibid., pp. 325–7). Grenville vigorously defended the principle of dismissing those in systematic opposition in his letters to Thomas Pitt of 15 May and 19 June 1764 (ibid., pp. 320–4; 353–60).

[76] Charles Townshend to Newcastle, 29 April 1764, B.M. Add. MSS 32958, f. 250, Newcastle Papers; Newcastle to Albemarle, 17 October 1764, ibid., 32962, ff. 340–1.

[77] Newcastle to T. Townshend, 30 April 1764, ibid., f. 307. J. Almon to Lord Temple, 12 November 1764, *Grenville Correspondence*, Vol. II, pp. 457–60.

[78] Newcastle always turned to men of his own generation rather than to the young men of Wildmans. As he put it: 'a *Huzza* at *Wildmans* once a week, will not do alone'. (Newcastle to Legge, 20 July 1764, ibid., 32963, f. 51.)

[79] Lord Hardwicke to Charles Yorke, 11 April 1764, ibid., 35361, ff. 95–6, Hardwicke Papers.

[80] 7 May 1764, ibid., 32958, ff. 327–8, Newcastle Papers.

[81] Newcastle to John White, 19 July 1764, Devonshire MSS (Copy).

[82] Pitt to Newcastle, 19 October 1764, B.M. Add. MSS 32962, ff. 347–50, Newcastle Papers, printed, with errors, in *Chatham Correspondence*, Vol. II, pp. 296–8.

[83] Rockingham to Newcastle, 23 November 1764, B.M. Add. MSS 32964, ff. 93–6, Newcastle Papers.

[84] Albemarle to Newcastle, 24 October 1764, ibid., 32963, ff. 19–20.

[85] Newcastle to Yorke, 20 November 1764, ibid., 32964, ff. 42–3.

[86] Namier and J. Brooke, *Charles Townshend* (1964), p. 128. For Townshend's soundings of ministers see M. Morton to Grenville, 15 October 1764, *Grenville Correspondence*, Vol. II, pp. 448–9; Charles Jenkinson to Grenville, 20 November 1764, ibid., Vol. II, pp. 465–6.

[87] Newcastle wrote to Rockingham shortly before Devonshire's death: 'I think Every Thing depends upon the Duke of Devonshire's Health' (*n.d.* September–October 1764, Ramsden MSS, Leeds City Library). Charles Townshend wrote to Temple on 4 October 1764 that the death of Devonshire would 'entirely change the dispositions of many individuals, and much vary, if not reverse, the general and former order of things' (*Grenville Correspondence*, Vol. II, pp. 441–2).

[88] Newcastle to Rockingham, 14 November 1764, B.M. Add. MSS 32964, ff. 37–8, Newcastle Papers.

[89] D. Watson, op. cit., pp. 72–4.

[90] George Onslow to Newcastle, 21 December 1764, B.M. Add. MSS 32964, f. 347, Newcastle Papers.

[91] The debate is given in H. Walpole, *Memoirs*, Vol. II, pp. 51–62; J. Almon, *The History of the Late Minority*, ff. 305; Newdigate MSS 82545.

[92] On 6 February, the adjournment was defeated by 245–49, an example

of the huge majorities which supported Grenville's American policy. It was significant that among the most ardent advocates of the Stamp Act were Charles Yorke and Charles Townshend. According to Horace Walpole (*Memoirs*, Vol. II, p. 68) the Stamp Act was 'little understood here at that time . . .'. The report of the debate in *Camden Miscellany*, 4th Series, Vol. VII by Ryder (pp. 253–61) is the best account available.

[93] George Onslow to Newcastle, 1 April 1765, B.M. Add. MSS 32966, ff. 136, Newcastle Papers.

[94] Cavendish had also been to Hayes to see Pitt in March, ibid., 32966, f. 39, Newcastle to Rockingham, 26 March 1765, *Albemarle*, Vol. I, pp. 181–2.

[95] Horace Walpole to Sir Horace Mann, 11 February 1765, *Correspondence of Horace Walpole*, Vol. XXIII, pp. 283–5.

CHAPTER 4

[1] D. Jarrett, 'The Regency Crisis of 1765', *English Historical Review*, **LXXX** (1970).

[2] I feel that Mr Jarrett overestimates the extent of Cumberland's leadership of the Whigs *before* the Regency Crisis. While he was, of course, their nominal leader and he was to negotiate them into office in 1765, he had been ill during the winter of 1764–5 and thus had had little to do with politics. I can find few traces of his exerting strong political influence. For example, his view that it would be unwise to raise the issue of General Warrants and establish a systematic opposition was largely ignored, even by Newcastle who was aiming at 'a national opposition' (Newcastle to Rockingham, 1 January 1765, Ramsden MSS).

[3] J. Brooke, *George III*, p. 111. Hardwicke put it rather differently in writing to Newcastle of the King's desire 'to keep all the branches of the Royal Family in suspense and expectation: to disgust none and to gratify none' (B.M. Add. MSS 32966, f. 215, Newcastle Papers).

[4] On 4 April the Easter recess had begun thus allowing the isolated King to manoeuvre his tricky path among the politicians while few of them were in town At their meeting on 7 April Cumberland objected to the haste with which the King wished to rush the Regency bill through Parliament. This deterred the King from mentioning to his uncle his plan of ridding himself of Grenville. This he had to intimate to him later through Northington, that with 'Such an Administration, nothing great could be done; that they lived from Day to Day'. See 'The Duke of Cumberland's Account' in *Albemarle*, op. cit., Vol. I, pp. 185–203, of which there is a MS copy in the Wentworth Woodhouse MSS R. 2. (It should be noted that the chronology is a week late throughout.)

[5] The King's treatment of Grenville at this time was appalling. I thoroughly agree with Mr Jarrett that the minister, on the other hand, 'behaved with perfect rectitude' (op. cit., p. 296). Cumberland rather

than Grenville was advising the King and, in fact, he treated him as autocratically as George Grenville ever did. Although he failed to dissuade the King from postponing the Regency Bill until the next session he bullied him into inserting the names of the princes of the blood into the bill. In its original form the King had reserved to himself the nomination not only of the Regent but also of five other members of the Regency Council. On 26 April George III instructed his ministers to amend the bill accordingly (*Grenville Papers*, Vol. III, p. 131).

⁶ Although Cumberland saw Newcastle on 15 April to inform him of the King's desire to change his ministry. (Mary Bateson (Ed.), *A Narrative of Changes in the Ministry, 1765–7* (1898), p. 3.)

⁷ For Newcastle's aversion to the idea of an unnamed Regent see his Memorandum of 30 April 1765 (B.M. Add. MSS 32966, ff. 281–4, Newcastle Papers).

⁸ H. Walpole, *Memoirs*, Vol. ii, pp. 118–16; B.M. Add. MSS 35881, ff. 251–6, Charles Yorke's Parliamentary Papers. Those who divided in the minority were Temple, Grafton, Shelburne, Fortescue, Bolton, Thanet, Ferrers, Torrington and Cornwallis. Horace Walpole wrote (*Memoirs*, Vol. ii, p. 108) 'I found the young men warm against the bill, and full of the idea that it was solely calculated to re-establish the empire of the Princess and the Favourite'. Newcastle's opposition to the bill was inhibited not only by his wish to avoid embarrassing Cumberland, who was now well in the King's confidence, but also because he had been responsible to a large extent for the Regency Bill of 1751.

⁹ H. Walpole, op. cit., Vol. ii, pp. 116–20.

¹⁰ For an explanation and discussion of the bill's progress through Parliament see D. Jarrett, op. cit., pp. 299–304. See also *Fortescue*, Vol. I, pp. 78–91 and Namier, *Additions and Corrections*, pp. 24–5.

¹¹ Albemarle to Newcastle, 8 May 1765, B.M. Add. MSS 32966, f. 351, Newcastle Papers. For the meeting of the 'Young Friends' on 8 May at Savile's, see George Onslow to Newcastle, 9 May 1765, ibid., f. 345. There is a report of the debate in Grenville to George III, 9 May 1765, *Grenville Correspondence*, Vol. III, pp. 25–34. The argument against naming the Regent was that to do so would provoke a reversionary interest. In the debate on 9 May Lord North claimed that to name the Regent would encourage faction and he thought it enough that 'This Bill secures a Protestant Regent of the House of Brunswick, resident in England'.

¹² Albemarle, op. cit., Vol. i, pp. 191–2.

¹³ *Grafton Autobiography*, pp. 42–3.

¹⁴ 'Butal–Ducal' was the name given to the King's plan of allying Bute and Cumberland by Temple, and is stressed by Mr Jarrett as the mainspring of the King's actions in the Regency Crisis. Mr Jarrett explains Pitt's inclusion in the arrangements because the King wanted a stable administration and one which would unite the best men of all parties (op. cit., p. 304). It would appear that both Cumberland and Newcastle instinctively felt that Pitt must be included in any arrangement which included Newcastle's party (Bateson, p. 3). Grafton would not take part in any arrangement in

which Pitt was not included (Albemarle, Vol. I, pp. 193–4, *Grafton Autobiography*, pp. 41–4).

[15] Pitt stated these conditions to Albemarle, Cumberland's friend, when the latter went to see him at Hayes on 14 May (Albemarle, op. cit., Vol. I, p. 193). Temple's conditions were very similar (ibid., p. 195). Pitt re-stated the terms when Albemarle and Cumberland visited Hayes again on 19 May (ibid., pp. 201–3).

[16] Ibid., pp. 306–9: since the Act of Settlement it had been illegal to quarter troops in London and their use on occasions such as this together with the need to quarter them around the city limits was always unpopular. That the King restored the honour of Captain General on Cumberland, withdrawn after Klosterseven, must have given Pitt even further food for thought.

[17] Lord Frederick Cavendish to Lord Rockingham, 21 May 1765, RI–449, Wentworth Woodhouse MSS.

[18] Ibid., Bateson, p. 13; for Pitt's suspicions of a Bute–Cumberland plot, see Fitzmaurice, op. cit., Vol. I, pp. 228–9. Pitt would not have Northumberland at the Treasury although he would accept him in some other office (N. Jucker, op. cit., p. 370; *Grenville Papers*, Vol. III, p. 226). See also the letters of Lord Charles Fitzroy to Grafton, 25 and 29 May, *Grafton Autobiography*, pp. 51, 79.

[19] *Grenville Papers*, Vol. III, pp. 173–5; Bateson, p. 16. The 'Young Friends' were infuriated at Cumberland's part in confirming Grenville in office. (George Onslow to Newcastle, 24 and 25 May 1765, B.M. Add. MSS 32966, ff. 467, 473, Newcastle Papers.)

[20] *Grenville Correspondence*, Vol. III, p. 41, Fortescue, op. cit., Vol. I, pp. 113–15 and L. B. Namier, *Additions and Corrections*, p. 30. Bateson, pp. 17–18. Almost at once the King and Grenville began to quarrel over patronage, e.g. Sandwich to Bedford, 29 May 1765, *Bedford Correspondence*, Vol. III, pp. 284–5, original in Woburn MSS LI, f. 146; N. Jucker, op. cit., pp. 371–3. Horace Walpole could not resist comparing George III in shackles to Grenville with George II in shackles to Pelhams, 'and all done without the help of the Whigs' (Horace Walpole to George Montagu, *Correspondence of Horace Walpole*, **X** (1941), pp. 152–5).

[21] On the day he accepted Grenville back, the King signed the instrument of Regency, appointing the Queen, who had obtained her majority on 21 May, as Regent (D. Jarrett, op. cit., p. 316).

[22] Grenville forbade the King to hold any political contacts with Cumberland, an instruction which George III ostentatiously ignored (*Grenville Correspondence*, Vol. III, p. 183).

[23] J. Almon, *History of the Late Minority*, p. 322, confirmed by Cumberland's account in Albemarle, Vol. I, p. 194.

[24] The lists can be found in B.M. Add. MSS 32958, f. 399, 32966, ff. 395–407, 436–7, 33000, f. 381, Newcastle Papers.

[25] Newcastle to Rockingham, 17 May 1765, ibid., 32966, f. 422; Fortescue, I, pp. 113–15.

[26] 'For His Royal Highness's Consideration', 21 May 1765, ibid., ff. 436–7.

[27] David Hartley to Sir George Savile, 6 June 1765, D/E.Hy/047, Hartley MSS. Berkshire Record Office.

[28] Bateson, pp. 15–16; George III to Cumberland, 12 June 1765, Fortescue, Vol. I, pp. 118–19.

[29] Ibid.

[30] Brooke, op. cit., pp. 116–20.

[31] Fortescue, Vol. I, p. 102–3, L. B. Namier, *Additions and Corrections*, p. 28; Bateson, p. 15–16, *Grafton Autobiography*, p. 47; Albemarle, Vol. I, p. 207. The account in Bateson illustrates Newcastle's thinking perfectly. He was opposed to the inclusion of Egmont in the arrangement not because Egmont was a friend of the King but because it might offend Pitt.

[32] *Grafton Autobiography*, p. 47; *Grenville Papers*, Vol. III, p. 176; Horace Walpole, *Memoirs*, Vol. II, pp. 122–3; R. Phillimore, *Memoirs of Lord Lyttleton* (2 Vols, 1845), Vol. II, p. 678.

[33] Bateson, p. 15.

[34] Bedford to the Duke of Marlborough, 13 June 1765, *Bedford Correspondence*, Vol. III, pp. 286–8. That Bedford's attack upon Bute was premeditated cannot be doubted. (*See* his *Minutes of Matters to be Mentioned to the King on Wednesday*, 12 June 1765; ibid., pp. 288–90.) George III was left in no doubt of Bedford's hatred of the favourite (George III to Northington, 12 June 1765, Fortescue, Vol. I, pp. 116–17).

[35] *See* the letters of the King and Cumberland of 13 June, Fortescue, Vol. I, pp. 119–20. Grafton's opinion, on the following day, was that Pitt would be willing to discuss arrangements with the King (Horace Walpole, *Memoirs*, Vol. II, pp. 132–3).

[36] At an audience granted to Cumberland on 16 June (N. Jucker, op. cit., p. 375).

[37] Fortescue, Vol. I, pp. 123–5; L. B. Namier, *Additions and Corrections*, pp. 31–2.

[38] B.M. Add. MSS 35428, f. 72, Hardwicke Papers.

[39] Fortescue, Vol. I, pp. 123–5; L. B. Namier, *Additions and Corrections*, pp. 31–2; Bateson, p. 23; *Grafton Autobiography*, p. 85. In spite of the general optimism which prevailed after this interview the King asked Cumberland to sound Rockingham and others not only on the question of alliance with Pitt but also 'what they have to propose if Mr Pitt should decline office without it' (20 June 1765, Fortescue, Vol. I, p. 120). He was, furthermore, very worried indeed about the revival of the Prussian alliance. He described its effects as 'the ramming Austria deeper with France and kindling a new War by unnecessary alliances . . . things I can neither answer to my God nor to my conscience.' Fortescue, Vol. I, p. 125. The *Grafton Autobiography* (p. 85) suggests that the King's reservations were not against Pitt's system 'but the precipitate mode of doing it, against the opinion of the ministers thro' whose hands the negotiation with the foreign courts must pass'.

[40] Pitt saw the King after Temple's interview (*Grenville Papers*, Vol. III, p. 201) and later that night the King wrote to Pitt summoning him to an

audience the next day. The messenger called at Temple's house in Pall Mall by mistake on the way to Hayes (ibid., p. 64). It was at this audience that Pitt declined to continue with the negotiation (Bateson, p. 24).

⁴¹ Bateson, p. 24; *Grenville Correspondence*, Vol. II, pp. 200–1.

⁴² *Grenville Papers*, Vol. III, pp. 197–8.

⁴³ *Grafton Autobiography*, p. 30. See also Pitt's anxious letter to Temple after the second interview, 22 June 1765, *Grenville Papers*, Vol. III, pp. 200–1.

⁴⁴ Grenville to Bedford, 25 June 1765, *Bedford Correspondence*, Vol. III, pp. 298–9; Northington to Temple, 2 July 1765, *Grenville Correspondence*, Vol. III, p. 64; J. Almon, *History of the Late Minority*, p. 328.

⁴⁵ *Grafton Autobiography*, pp. 53–4; Cumberland to Albemarle, 26 June 1765, Albemarle, Vol. I, pp. 213–14; Pitt to Lord Lyttleton, 1 July 1765, *Chatham Correspondence*, Vol. II, pp. 315–16.

⁴⁶ Bateson, p. 24. Why Pitt advised the King to persevere with Grenville is a baffling question (N. Jucker, op. cit., p. 377).

⁴⁷ D. Watson, op. cit., pp. 75–6. Sandwich was convinced that if Cumberland was 'desperate enough to form an administration without Pitt and Temple . . . it will not be a long-lived one'. (Sandwich to Bedford, 26 June 1765, *Bedford Correspondence*, Vol. III, pp. 302–3.) It is well worth noting that Pitt and the King parted on cordial terms, a fact of great importance during the next twelve months. (See Fortescue, Vol. I, p. 121, for their letters of 25 June.)

⁴⁸ *See*, for example, Grenville to Lord Hillsborough, 26 June 1765, Tomlinson, op. cit., pp. 285–7; Grenville to Bedford, 25 June 1765, *Bedford Correspondence*, Vol. III, pp. 298–9.

⁴⁹ Cumberland to Albemarle, 26 June 1765, Albemarle, Vol. I, pp. 213–14; Bateson, p. 25; The editor is incorrect in assuming that Grenville knew nothing about these soundings until 2 July. He mentioned them in his letter to Lord Powis on 28 June 1765 (Tomlinson, op. cit., pp. 287–8).

⁵⁰ *Grafton Autobiography*, p. 86; Temple's absolute refusal to take office had become definite when he returned to Stowe (*Grenville Papers*, Vol. III, p. 204). Cumberland had come to town from Windsor on the previous day. He saw Grafton, Newcastle and possibly Rockingham on 28 June and was impressed by their willingness to take office, as was the King. (Albemarle to Newcastle, 29 June 1765, B.M. Add. MSS 32967, ff. 155, Newcastle Papers.)

⁵¹ Cumberland to Albemarle, 26 June 1765, Albemarle, op. cit., Vol. I, pp. 213–14; Bateson, p. 25.

⁵² Newcastle to Ashburnham, 27 June 1765, B.M. Add. MSS 32967, ff. 142–3, Newcastle Papers.

⁵³ Ibid.

⁵⁴ The twelve who voted for taking office were Newcastle, Rockingham, Portland, Grantham, the three Cavendish lords, Bessborough, Walsingham, Conway, Albemarle and Fitzroy. Had Grafton been present it is probable that he would have voted with these twelve. Those who voted against were Ashburnham, Tommy Walpole and, interestingly enough, four

'Young Friends', George Onslow, 'Spanish' Charles Townshend, Tommy Townshend and Lord Villiers. Details of this important meeting can be found in Bateson, p. 26; *Grafton Autobiography*, p. 54; Albemarle, op. cit., pp. 218–20. There are also several accounts in B.M. Add. MSS 33003 and Copies. For a discussion of the measures agreed upon at the meeting *see* Chapter 5.

[55] Newcastle to Portland, 1 July 1765, B.M. Add. MSS 32967, f. 186, Newcastle Papers.

CHAPTER 5

[1] Fortescue, Vol. I, pp. 136–8, L. B. Namier, *Additions and Corrections*, pp. 32–3. In this list Charles Townshend appears as one of the Secretaries of State and Conway as Chancellor of the Exchequer. It appears, too, that Rockingham still hoped to bring in Shelburne at the Board of Trade.

[2] The standard work on this subject is G. H. Guttridge, *The Early Career of Lord Rockingham, 1730–65* (University of California, Publications in History, Vol. XLIV, 1952). Guttridge covers the ground adequately but does not relate Rockingham's career to the party history of the 1760s. Richard Pares reflected the bewilderment of most historians at Rockingham's dramatic rise to power when he discussed the collective resignations at the end of 1762 and commented, 'I cannot think of anything else that Rockingham had done' (*King George III and the Politicians*, p. 96, n. 2). It is, to say the least, doubtful, if Rockingham's resignation in 1762 gave him a title to the Treasury in 1765, the confidence of the King and the support of his party. It is likewise idle to fall back on the explanation that Rockingham was an 'aristocrat' and thus 'naturally' succeeded to Newcastle's position of authority and leadership. There were other 'aristocrats' in the party. The problem is to explain why Rockingham rather than anyone else was thought to be equipped for the Treasury in 1765.

[3] On the death of his father in December 1750 (when Charles was twenty years of age) the rentals of the family estates in Ireland, Yorkshire and Northamptonshire amounted to over £20,000. His marriage to Mary Bright, heiress to the fortunes of the Ramsden family in Yorkshire, brought him an extra £5,000 a year and a capital sum of over £50,000. Furthermore Rockingham's father had made Wentworth Woodhouse, the family seat in Yorkshire, one of the great aristocratic palaces of England. In short, the vast wealth of the family enabled Rockingham to intervene in politics with generosity and liberality.

[4] When Rockingham attained his majority in 1751 he succeeded to the offices which his father's loyalty to Walpole and the Pelhams had accumulated. The young Marquis found it impossible to avoid local politics because he became Lord Lieutenant of both the West Riding and the City of York and *Custos Rotulorum* of the North and West Ridings of the County and also of the City of York. His family connections inevitably brought him into the complex network of the Whig establishment. One of his

uncles was William Murray, later the distinguished judge, Lord Mansfield, and one of Newcastle's closest friends. It was, in fact, Murray who brought Rockingham into the circle of Newcastle and who acted as his closest advisor.

⁵ Rockingham badly misjudged the position. To have disturbed the peace of the county and to claim to nominate even one member was, for one of his years (he was then twenty-three), a demand of great temerity which the independently minded Yorkshire gentry would not tolerate. Furthermore, he was attempting to exert his influence against two ministerial candidates—something his father had never done. Rockingham was aware that he was splitting the Whig interest in the county and he was chastised for it by Murray. (*See* W. Murray to Rockingham, 4 August 1753, RI–33, Wentworth Woodhouse MSS. *See also* Rockingham's letter to Savile of 18 July and to an unknown recipient of 16 July, ibid., RI–28.) Rockingham was angry at the outcome of his venture. He secured from Lord Holdernesse a promise that Savile should have the next vacancy for the county, an empty and valueless promise which Holdernesse might not have been able to honour. (Murray to Rockingham, 24 July 1753, ibid., RI–30. *See also* the draft of a letter about the County election in the Rockingham papers, *n.d.* probably August 1753.) 'Some cowardly counsellors intimidated me, and we have let slip such an opportunity of showing my interest to the utmost advantage that could have been wished' (RI–27, Wentworth Woodhouse MSS).

⁶ Murray strongly advised Rockingham to try for only one seat. Murray to Rockingham, 24 November, early December and 15 December, 1753, RI–43,–51–53, Wentworth Woodhouse MSS.

⁷ Rockingham to Savile, 11 December 1758, RI–131, Wentworth Woodhouse MSS; Guttridge, op. cit., p. 20.

⁸ Rockingham to the Rev. George Leigh, 13 January 1761, RI–184, Wentworth Woodhouse MSS; Guttridge, op. cit., p. 21.

⁹ Newcastle to Rockingham, 21 January 1761, B.M. Add. MSS 32917, f. 465, Newcastle Papers, *q.* Guttridge, op. cit., p. 22.

¹⁰ C. Collyer, 'The Rockingham Connection and Country Opinion in the early years of George III', *Publications of the Thoresby Society*, Vol. VII (1954), pp. 251–73 and n. 5.

¹¹ Ibid., p. 254.

¹² Murray had always been the driving force behind the naturally indolent young lord. (Murray to Rockingham, 17 August 1753, RI–38, Wentworth Woodhouse MSS. *See also* Murray to Rockingham, 17 September, 1751, RI–6, Wentworth Woodhouse MSS.)

¹³ Murray to Rockingham, 22 October and 1 November 1753, RI–43,–46. Wentworth Woodhouse MSS. Yet at this time, as at most stages of his political career, Rockingham kept himself well informed of parliamentary business. *See*, for example, George Quarme to Rockingham, 1 June 1754, RI–57; Baron Sondes to Rockingham, 7 February 1757, RI–86, Wentworth Woodhouse MSS.

¹⁴ *See*, for example, the actions of the Secretary at War, Lord Barrington,

in 1756 in placing troops at Rockingham's disposal for the re-establishment of order at Sheffield where riots against the high price of corn threatened the peace of the town. Although the troops were not needed, Barrington had placed them at Rockingham's disposal for use at his own discretion so that 'you may have the whole credit' (31 August 1756, RI–79, Wentworth Woodhouse MSS; Guttridge, op. cit., p. 18).

[15] Murray to Rockingham, 4 August 1753, RI–33, Wentworth Woodhouse MSS. Newcastle rejoiced in Rockingham's success at York City. Murray to Rockingham, 6 and 15 December 1753, RI–52, –53. Furthermore, at the Hull election of 1757 Rockingham was supported by ministerial influence. (Newcastle to Rockingham, 25 and 29 June 1757, RI–90, –94, Rockingham to Newcastle, 27 June 1757, RI–91, Wentworth Woodhouse MSS.)

[16] Newcastle to Rockingham, 25 June 1757, RI–90; Lord Dupplin to Rockingham, two letters of 28 June 1757, RI–92, –93; Lord Dupplin to Rockingham, 1 October 1757, RI–106; the Duke of Devonshire to Rockingham, 15 October 1757, RI–110 (Wentworth Woodhouse MSS).

[17] For George II's fondness for Rockingham, see the letters of Murray to Rockingham of 1 and 4 October 1756, RI–82, –83. See also Sir George Savile to Rockingham, 24 October 1756, RI–84, Wentworth Woodhouse MSS.

[18] Newcastle to Temple, 28 September 1758, *Chatham Correspondence*, Vol. i, p. 359; Pitt to Newcastle, 27 September 1759, ibid., Vol. i, p. 434. Kinnoul to Rockingham, 16 November 1759, RI–156 and Newcastle to Rockingham, 31 January 1760, RI–161, Wentworth Woodhouse MSS.

[19] Guttridge, op. cit., p. 24. There is a lengthy *Memorandum* about the Bedchamber dispute in the Devonshire MSS in the form of a diary from 21 to 28 August 1761.

[20] B.M. Add. MSS 32927, ff. 392–3, Newcastle Papers.

[21] Rockingham to Colonel Forrester, Draft, 29 October 1761, RI–204, Wentworth Woodhouse MSS.

[22] Newcastle to Rockingham, 14 May 1762, RI–239, Wentworth Woodhouse MSS.

[23] Newcastle to Rockingham, 17 August 1762, RI–278, Wentworth Woodhouse MSS.

[24] Rockingham to Cumberland, 3 November 1762, RI–323, Wentworth Woodhouse MSS. Printed Albemarle, op. cit., Vol. I, pp. 142–3.

[25] Ibid; Rockingham to Granby, c. 5 November 1762, ibid., RI–321b.

[26] Collyer, op. cit., pp. 258–9.

[27] Ibid., p. 259. See also above p. 55.

[28] Devonshire wished to concert with Rockingham the resignation of their Lieutenancies to secure the maximum effect. (Devonshire to Rockingham, 26 December 1762, RI–339, Wentworth Woodhouse MSS.)

[29] Newcastle to Rockingham, 31 January 1763, ibid., RI–362.

[30] Devonshire to Rockingham, 30 August 1763, ibid., RI–382.

[31] Tomlinson, op. cit., pp. 31–8 passim.

[32] Guttridge, op. cit., pp. 34–6; Rockingham to Devonshire, 31 October 1763, RI–389, Wentworth Woodhouse MSS. Newcastle to Devonshire, 2 November 1763, B.M. Add. MSS 32952, ff. 204–13, Newcastle Papers; Rockingham to Charles Yorke, 14 November 1763, ibid., 35430, ff. 7–8, Hardwicke Papers.

[33] Newcastle to Rockingham, 8 September 1764, RI–433, Wentworth Woodhouse MSS.

[34] His health, and that of the Duchess was steadily deteriorating. 'I am quite weary of our great parties', he wrote on 18 February 1765 (B.M. Add. MSS 33077, f. 120, Newcastle Papers). He was deeply aware of his own political inadequacies and realised full well that neither Pitt nor the King liked him. His former mercantile and financial links with the City had, by this time, completely eroded (D. Watson, *The Duke of Newcastle*, pp. 276–80).

[35] In fact, the Yorkes had little ground for complaint with Grenville and they probably had no intention or desire of bringing him down. (See, e.g. Hardwicke to Charles Yorke, 26 May 1765, B.M. Add. MSS 35361, f. 152, Hardwicke Papers.)

[36] 'My friends very justly reproved me for idling my time away in the country during a great part of the session', admitted Grafton in his *Autobiography* (op. cit., p. 31).

[37] The earliest I have seen is that of Lord Edgecumbe to Rockingham of 11 July (RI–460, Wentworth Woodhouse MSS). Rockingham did not always manage appointments even to his own satisfaction. He was distressed, for example, when the Marquis of Lorne refused to allow his loyalty to Bedford to be shaken by his appointment to the Command of the Royal Regiment (Lorne to Bedford, 6 September 1765, LII, f. 134, Woburn MSS).

[38] Cumberland to Rockingham, 23 August 1765, R2–21, Wentworth Woodhouse MSS.

[39] Rockingham appears to have granted only eighteen new pensions after August 1765 at a total cost of £3,100 p.a. In the same year (1765–6) there was a saving of over £9,000 due to death, resignation and discontinuation (R. 15–5, Pensions Book, Wentworth Woodhouse MSS).

[40] Newcastle had terrible torments about removing the incumbent Privy Seal, the Duke of Marlborough, and he might not have taken office at all had not Marlborough resigned voluntarily. We should not jump to the conclusion that Newcastle's loyalty to the King was unreserved or unlimited. It took all Cumberland's skill to dissuade Newcastle from trying to elicit from the King a promise never again to consult Bute. (B.M. Add. MSS 32968, f. 142, Newcastle Papers.) Furthermore, as he wrote to Lord Ashburnham on 27 June 1765, he would only be prepared to serve the King 'upon a supposition that His Majesty enables them to do it by agreeing to their public measures, and to the removal of such persons as shall be necessary to convince the world that my Lord Bute has not the power to protect his friends' (ibid., 32967, f. 142).

[41] In early July Newcastle was happily composing and endlessly amending

long lists of removals and reinstatements. (Fortescue, Vol. I, pp. 129–32, 136–8, 153–5, L. B. Namier, op. cit., pp. 33–4.)

[42] Lord George Sackville to General Irwin, 29 July 1765, *H.M.C. Stopford-Sackville*, Vol. I, pp. 100–2.

[43] *Grenville Papers*, Vol. III, p. 201.

[44] Even from the middle of June. (See Newcastle to Rockingham, 19 June 1765, B.M. Add. MSS 32967, f. 70, Newcastle Papers.)

[45] Nevertheless the Duchess of Grafton went out of her way to become friendly with Lady Rockingham (The Duchess of Grafton to Lady Rockingham, *n.d.* 1765, Ramsden MSS).

[46] *Grafton Autobiography*, p. 54.

[47] Grafton to Pitt, 21 August 1765, ibid., p. 57. Also printed *Chatham Correspondence*, Vol. II, p. 320.

[48] Rockingham went to see him on 4 July but found him reluctant to accept, allegedly on account of the King's coldness towards him, since he had accepted the Pay Office on 24 May. Charles Townshend to Lord Townshend, 4 July 1765, *Grenville Papers*, Vol. III, pp. 67–8.

[49] The King saw Lord Townshend on 7 and 9 July and Charles on 10 July (ibid., Vol. III, pp. 207, 209, 211, 217). During and after these soundings Charles retained the Pay Office and Lord Townshend his post at the Ordnance. (George III to Egmont, 9 July 1765, Fortescue, Vol. I, p. 148.)

[50] Charles Yorke to Hardwicke, 3 July 1765, B.M. Add. MSS 35428, ff. 75–80, Hardwicke Papers; 4 July 1765, ibid., f. 96, printed G. Harris, op. cit., Vol. III, p. 449; 22 August 1765, ibid., 35361, f. 214.

[51] *Grenville Papers*, Vol. III, p. 219.

[52] Charles Yorke to Lord Hardwicke, 3 July 1765, loc. cit.; George III saw clearly that Charles Yorke did not share the suspicion of Bute which Newcastle and others felt and deduced that Yorke would be a useful addition to the ministry. On 9 August he interviewed him and finally persuaded him to except (George III to Egmont, 7 and 8 July 1765, Fortescue, Vol. I, pp. 139, 145, 147).

[53] Whose view it was that 'every man in office or out of it may vote with his opinion' (Dowdeswell to Sir Edward Winnington, 17 September 1765, Dowdeswell MSS). Dowdeswell was only offered the post when both Conway and Charles Townshend had turned it down. His acceptance was to be of the greatest importance in the history of the Rockingham party, but of course, no one anticipated the fact at the time.

[54] *George III and the Historians* (1957), p. 265.

[55] 'Measures', 27 June 1765, B.M. Add. MSS 32967, f. 178, Newcastle Papers.

[56] Ibid., Memorandum, 32967, ff. 332–3.

[57] But it is not clear how seriously Rockingham wanted Shelburne, because the same office was then being offered to Lord Dartmouth. Most probably Rockingham correctly anticipated Shelburne's refusal.

[58] *Grafton Autobiography*, pp. 55–9.

[59] Bateson, pp. 36, 40.

[60] Newcastle to Albemarle, 4 July 1765, B.M. Add. MSS 32967, ff. 220, Newcastle Papers.

[61] Rockingham scarcely ever bothered to reply to Newcastle's missives. (Newcastle to Onslow, 7 October 1765, ibid., 32970, f. 209.)

[62] R–14, passim, Wentworth Woodhouse MSS. Of course, of the twenty, some were dead and others no longer politically active. The rest had made their peace with the Court. Horace Walpole rather nastily put it that 'The Duke of Newcastle is busy in restoring clerks and tide-waiters, in offering everybody everything . . .' (Horace Walpole to Sir Horace Mann, 12 August 1765, *Correspondence of Horace Walpole*, Vol. XXII, pp. 322–6). Lord Chesterfield commented that the number of removals was unusual. (Lord Chesterfield to his son, 15 July 1765, *Chatham Correspondence*, Vol. II, p. 315 NI). According to George Grenville: 'a very general removal is talked of in consequence of these changes already made, either by resignations or dismission' (George Grenville to Hans Stanley, 12 July 1765, D'Oyly MSS).

[63] Newcastle to Rockingham, 23 September 1765, B.M. Add. MSS 32970, f. 16, Newcastle Papers.

[64] These lists are to be found in Fortescue, Vol. I, pp. 129–32, 136–8, 142–4, 153–5. They should be used with L. B. Namier's *Additions and Corrections*, pp. 35–6.

[65] 28 October 1765, B.M. Add. MSS 32971, f. 177, Newcastle Papers.

[66] Newcastle to Albemarle, 30 October 1765, ibid., f. 201.

[67] Newcastle to Rockingham, 4 November 1765, ibid., f. 248.

[68] 9 November 1765, ibid., f. 317.

[69] Ibid., 32972, f. 333.

[70] The King to Egmont, 8 July 1765, Fortescue, Vol. I, p. 146.

[71] 10 January 1766, Sedgwick, op. cit., p. 242.

[72] *Grenville Papers*, Vol. III, p. 217.

[73] Memorandum, November–December 1765, Fortescue, Vol. I, p. 173.

[74] Memorandum, November–December 1765, ibid., p. 166. On 6 July Cumberland told the leaders of the new ministry of the King's 'strongest assurances that my Lord Bute should not be suffered to interfere in the least degree in any publick business whatever; or that, if those friends who might remain in office, did not vote with, and by speaking, support the present Administration, His Majesty promised to remove them the next day' (Bateson, pp. 30–1).

[75] Bateson, p. 2.

[76] R. 14–2, Wentworth Woodhouse MSS.

[77] 'Measures', 1 July 1765, B.M. Add. MSS 32967, f. 178, Newcastle Papers.

[78] Grenville to Bedford, 7 July 1765, Tomlinson, op. cit., p. 294. Sandwich even believed the dismissal of Despencer to be nothing less than an elaborate move on Bute's part to give a false public impression of his loss of influence. Sandwich to Bedford, 10 July 1765, *Bedford Correspondence*, Vol. III, p.308.

[79] The King was in turn infuriated with the ministers for their frequent attacks upon Bute. See his letter to Bute of 10 January 1766 (loc. cit.).

[80] Memoranda, R. 83, 2, 3, Wentworth Woodhouse MSS.

[81] *Memoirs*, Vol. I, p. 223.

[82] Newcastle to Albemarle, 20 July 1765, B.M. Add. MSS 32968, f. 90, Newcastle Papers.

[83] R. 156–1, Wentworth Woodhouse MSS.

[84] Ibid., R. 156–4.

[85] *See*, for example, Col. Ligonier to Stanley Porten, 1 November 1765, Ripley Court MSS: Richard Rigby to Bedford, 3 November 1765, LII, f. 178, Woburn MSS.

[86] Lord North refused an offer of the Vice-Treasurership of Ireland, an alarming and significant rebuff for the ministry from a former dependant of Newcastle. (See Newcastle to Dartmouth, 15 November 1765, *H.M.C. Dartmouth*, Vol. III, pp. 179–80; Lord North to Newcastle, B.M. Add. MSS 32971, f. 390, Newcastle Papers.)

[87] The King wrote to Bute on 10 January 1766 (loc. cit.) 'the Ministers from the hour of the Duke of C's death wanted to approach Mr Pitt'.

[88] Pitt to Cooke, 7 December 1765, *Chatham Correspondence*, Vol. II, p. 342.

[89] As late as July Rockingham probably assumed that Pitt would not be needed in the ministry. A few enigmatic phrases in one of his memoranda read: 'The disposition of the Law Offices—seem prudent—on the supposition of Mr Pitt &c not taking part—now—or expected hereafter' (R. 14–2, Wentworth Woodhouse MSS).

[90] Ibid., R. 14–9.

[91] R. 156–5, Wentworth Woodhouse MSS.

[92] Pitt to Lady Rockingham, *n.d.* Monday, November 1765, ibid., R. 156–1, Enclosure. The Minute was issued in response to petitions of merchants and manufacturers of Bristol, Manchester, Liverpool, Lancaster and Halifax. (See John Roberts to Rockingham, 29 November 1765, R. 35h, Wentworth Woodhouse MSS.)

[93] Rockingham to Lady Rockingham, 28 November 1765, R. 156–6, Wentworth Woodhouse MSS.

CHAPTER 6

[1] In October 1763 the Grenville Ministry decided to implement the Molasses Act which laid down that all molasses, rum and sugar imported into the American colonies should carry a duty of 6d per gallon. After considerable lobbying between the mercantile interests and the West Indian planters the rate was set at 3d. This was by no means prohibitive but the revenue raised was to go to defray the cost of defence incurred in the colonies. This decision was incorporated in the Sugar Act of 1764. The Act regulated imports of sugar, wine and coffee by fixing duties payable on them. These modest impositions, however, were balanced by the offer of bounties for the colonial production of indigo, hemp and flax. (*See* J. Sosin, *Agents and Merchants*, University of Nebraska Press, 1965, pp. 38–41 and references there given.) A more detailed and authoritative

account of the origins and passage of the Sugar Act can be found in F. B. Wickwire, *British Subministers and Colonial America, 1763–83* (Princeton University Press, 1966, pp. 110–22). The Currency Act of 1764 had its origin in Charles Townshend's work on the Molasses act. (*See* C. R. Ritcheson, *British Politics and the American Revolution*, University of Oklahoma Press, 1954, pp. 18–19.) For its place in the history of the American Revolution see J. P. Greene and R. M. Jellison, 'The Currency Act of 1764 in Imperial–Colonial Relations, 1764–76', in *William and Mary Quarterly*, 3rd Series, **XVIII**.

[2] P. D. G. Thomas (Ed.), 'The Parliamentary Diaries of Nathaniel Ryder, 1764–7', *Camden Miscellany*, 4th Series, VII, p. 236, 9 March 1764.

[3] The extension of stamp duties to America had been occasionally mooted in the eighteenth century, most recently during the Pitt–Newcastle coalition in 1757. The revival of the idea in 1763 was a natural occurrence in the climate of opinion in Britain which considered it obligatory to impose internal taxation upon the Americans with the objective of raising a revenue to defray the costs of colonial defence (Professor E. Morgan argues in a fascinating paper that it is an historiographical myth that the colonists accepted the validity of external taxation, such as the levying of customs dues, while rejecting that of internal taxation. Morgan finds that the colonists had *never* admitted the right of Parliament to exact the former ('Colonial Ideas of Parliamentary Power'. *William and Mary Quarterly*, 3rd Series, **V**).) In December 1762–January 1763 the idea of a tax on stamps arose at the suggestion of Henry McCulloch, an experienced colonial administrator. He worked out a plan in some detail which was then taken over by the Treasury clerks. Grenville, it should be noted, had little to do with the details of the act. Only in December 1763 did he give his assent to the draft which had by then been painstakingly drawn up. The Stamp Act was thus ready and could have been incorporated in the 1764 budget. Grenville delayed its enactment for one year ostensibly to allow the colonists to produce an alternative scheme of their own choosing. Dr Watson has argued that Grenville's major consideration was his expectation of a hostile reaction in Parliament to the Stamp Act. (D. Watson, op. cit., pp. 252–3; E. S. Morgan, 'The Postponement of the Stamp Act', *William and Mary Quarterly*, 3rd series, **VII**.) Professor Wickwire has usefully reminded us that Grenville did not, in fact, tell the separate colonies what their quota might be and it was, to say the least, difficult for them to suggest how an unknown sum might be collected (op. cit., p. 193). The only alternatives to the Stamp Act would appear to be:

1. That the colonists represented in a Congress should themselves *request* a tax. This would have respected both the rights of the imperial Parliament and of the colonial assemblies.
2. To represent the Americans in the imperial Parliament.
3. To establish a Colonial Fund to which the particular colonies would contribute.
4. To establish a system of requisitions and quotas.

The second of these was unacceptable to the British, although it was discussed at the time. (*See* one such plan in *English Historical Review*, **XXII**). The fourth might have been a possibility had it not already been used (and, so the English would say, abused by the colonists) during the Seven Years War. The first and the third would have been unacceptable to the colonists.

⁴ *Ryder Diaries*, pp. 258–9, 6 February 1765.

⁵ A flood of protest against the Stamp Act began to rise in May. The Virginia Assembly, led by the young Patrick Henry, threw down the gauntlet to the British Government. The Virginia Resolves proclaimed not only the principle of consent to taxation but the right of the colonists to resist the Stamp Act. In August rioting broke out on a large scale, starting in Boston. This was not indiscriminate mob violence. Those who led the Opposition to the Stamp Act were articulate men, journalists, lawyers, merchants and printers. 'Sons of Liberty' clubs, organising resistance, proliferated throughout the colonies. The unity of continental resistance to the Stamp Act was expressed in the Stamp Act Congress which met in New York in October. Although the Congress, representing nine State Assemblies, adopted a moderate tone this served to attract a wide spectrum of support behind the resistance to the Act. Finally, the sudden emergence of non-importation and non-consumption agreements threatened to dislocate Anglo-American trade. Even a large army could not have forced the Americans to comply with the Stamp Act and if such an attempt had been made it is quite possible that the American Revolution would have been precipitated by ten years.

⁶ A Treasury Board of 2 September had already confirmed that 'all acts of the British Legislature extend and are in force in every part of His Majesty's dominions'. There are copies of these minutes in the Wentworth Woodhouse MSS, R–28.

⁷ P. Langford, *The First Rockingham Administration, 1765–6* (Oxford 1973, pp. 81–3). Given the state of British public opinion, however, it is difficult to see what else they could have done. (*See* also J. Almon, *A Collection of Papers Relative to the Dispute between Great Britain and America, 1777*, pp. 38–42.)

⁸ In this context there is invaluable material in the Wentworth Woodhouse MSS: R. 23 and R. 25 consist of letters from Stamp distributors describing their difficulties, R. 22 consists of a set of precis of Governors' reports. Perusing reports such as these one is led to wonder if the Stamp Act could have been enforced even if the Americans had been favourable to it. There was a great deal of inefficiency and confusion. Some parts of the colonies were short of the vellum parchments, properly stamped and marked with the relevant level of duties.

⁹ P. Langford, op. cit., pp. 117–18.

¹⁰ Newcastle had already taken pains to establish links with the mercantile community in September 1765 (D. Watson, op. cit., pp. 302–4) Trecothick was the indispensable link between the ministry and the merchants. His work had been minutely investigated by the indefatigable Dr Watson. (*Barlow Trecothick and Other Associates of Lord Rockingham during*

the Stamp Act Crisis, 1756-6, unpublished M.A. thesis, 1964, Sheffield. *See also* M. G. Kammen, *A Rope of Sand* (Cornell University Press, 1968), pp. 118-21.)

[11] L. Sutherland, 'Edmund Burke and the First Rockingham Ministry', *English Historical Review,* **XLVII** (1932), pp. 50, 59-60.

[12] The petitions can be found in the Wentworth Woodhouse MSS, R. 56, 57, 58, 59, 60. For the growing crescendo of protest in the press, see F. Hinkhouse, *The Preliminaries of the American Revolution and the British Press* (Columbia, 1926), pp. 60-8.

[13] Newcastle has the honour of being perhaps the first of the ministers to contemplate repeal. ('Items for the Duke of Cumberland', 13 October 1765, B.M. Add. MSS 32970, f. 312, Newcastle Papers.) Charles Yorke had been Attorney General when the Stamp Act passed, although he had had considerable reservations about its advisability. Nevertheless, he felt a good deal of hostility towards the disorderly colonists.

[14] Rockingham to Trecothick, *n.d.* R. 81-181, Wentworth Woodhouse MSS; D. Watson, *The Duke of Newcastle,* pp. 313-14.

[15] Rockingham to Viscount Irwin, 25 October 1765, *H.M.C. Various,* **X** (Wood MSS), p. 183.

[16] 'Points for Consideration with My Lord Rockingham', 28 October 1765, B.M. Add. MSS 32971, f. 173, Newcastle Papers.

[17] Sandwich to Bedford, 10 July 1765, *Bedford Correspondence,* Vol. III, p. 310.

[18] Rockingham to George III, 16 December 1765, Fortescue, Vol. I, p. 199. Rockingham lists the peers (sixty in number) who attended the reading of the speech and also eighteen 'Remarkable Absentees' (ibid., pp. 208-11). Rockingham's earlier, and silly, intention had been to say *nothing* of America in the King's speech. It was only the timely communication of the rebellion at New York on 1 November 1765 which changed his mind. (Rockingham to Newcastle, 12 December 1765, B.M. Add. MSS 32972, f. 214, Newcastle Papers.)

[19] 'The D. of Bedford gave a great dinner on the day before the House meets in order to concert measures for an attack which he intends to make on the Ministry in the House of Lords. G. Grenville says that he is not to assist at this Council, & that he does not mean to say any thing in the H. of Commons unless he is attacked himself.' (Charles Townshend to David Hartley, 10 December 1765, D/EHy/f. 83, Hartley MSS.) Newcastle was extremely worried about the 'violent motions' which he expected the Bedfords to bring forward and warned Rockingham to be ready for them. ('Mems for Lord Rockingham', 10 December 1765, B.M. Add. MSS 32972, f. 190, Newcastle Papers.)

[20] Grenville had, in fact, been ready to divide on the Address ever since the end of November because of rumours that the Stamp Act might be repealed. (Grenville to Bedford, 28 November 1765, *Bedford Correspondence,* Vol. III, pp. 323-4.) For a report of the debate and a list of speakers *see* Conway to George III, 17 December 1765, Fortescue, Vol. I, pp. 201-2; *see also* L. B. Namier's *Additions and Corrections,* pp. 41-2. There is a brief

account of the debate in Horace Walpole, *Memoirs*, Vol. II, pp. 235–6 but it adds little to the above.

[21] For accounts of the debate see Rockingham to George III, 17 December 1765, Fortescue, Vol. I, pp. 203–4; Horace Walpole, *Memoirs*, Vol. II, pp. 236–7. The attack on the ministry in the Lords was the more serious and had been the longer in contemplation. There is a list of the ninety-seven peers present in R. 53–19 in the Wentworth Woodhouse MSS.

[22] For accounts of the debate see Conway to the King, 18 December 1765 and Rockingham's letter to George III of the same date, Fortescue, Vol. I, pp. 204–5; L. B. Namier, op. cit., p. 42.

[23] On 20 December Grenville lost a division 77–35 on a procedural point concerning the date of the reassembly of the House of Commons.

[24] Details of these meetings may be found in Rockingham's letters to Newcastle of 31 December 1765 and 2 January 1766 (B.M. Add. MSS 32972, f. 384; 32973, ff. 11–13, Newcastle Papers.)

[25] R. 65–6, Wentworth Woodhouse MSS.

[26] B.M. Add. MSS 32972, f. 333, Newcastle Papers.

[27] Ibid., 32973, ff. 11–13.

[28] There is very little in the surviving letters which Pitt wrote in December to suggest that he was *gradually* coming to accept a new imperial theory. *See* Pitt to Shelburne, *n.d.* December 1765, Pitt to Shelburne, *Chatham Correspondence*, Vol. II, pp. 359–61, 361–63. As Dr Langford points out (op. cit., p. 142) Shelburne in his speech to the Lords on 17 December had clearly spelled out the theory of parliamentary supremacy.

[29] The debate is reported, *inter alia*, in *Chatham Correspondence*, Vol. II, 364N–72N; Horace Walpole, *Memoirs*, Vol. II, pp. 260–70; Burke to Charles O'Hara, 18 January 1766, *Burke Correspondence*, Vol. I, pp. 231–3; Fortescue, Vol. I, pp. 244–6; 'Mr West's Paper', 14 January 1766, B.M. Add. MSS 32973, ff. 133–5, Newcastle Papers. The debate in the Lords on the same day is reported in letters from Grafton and Rockingham to George III of the same date, Fortescue, Vol. I, pp. 226–7.

[30] Lord George Sackville to General Irwin, 17 January 1766, *H.M.C. Stopford-Sackville*, Vol. I, pp. 103–5.

[31] Rockingham to Charles Yorke, 20 January 1766, B.M. Add. MSS 35430, f. 31, Hardwicke Papers *q.* L. B. Namier and J. Brooke, *Charles Townshend*, pp. 139–40.

[32] Charles Yorke to Rockingham, 25 January 1766, RI–560, Wentworth Woodhouse MSS, Albemarle, Vol. I, pp. 287–8; for George III's considerable reservations about repeal see below p. 163 ff.

[33] R. 49–8, 9, Wentworth Woodhouse MSS. It may be over-simplistic but it is just possible that the Rockinghams passed the Declaratory Act because they believed in it. That a Declaratory act might have facilitated repeal may have been a secondary consideration.

[34] D. Watson, op. cit., pp. 361–3, 376–7. I cannot go all the way with Dr Watson when he claims that for Rockingham 'The merchants now represented his only hope of survival'.

[35] Newcastle alluded to a meeting of the leading ministers on 21 January,

predicting that 'you are all like to differ widely among yourselves'. (Newcastle to Rockingham, 20 January 1766, B.M. Add. MSS 32973, f. 202, Newcastle Papers.)

[36] Dyson had been Secretary to the Treasury under Bute and Grenville and a Lord of Trade since April 1764. His opposition to the repeal of the Stamp Act led Rockingham to demand his dismissal and his case became something of a *cause célèbre* in Rockinghamite mythology. Jenkinson was more closely attached to the person of Bute than Dyson was. He was Bute's private secretary in 1762-3 and became a Secretary to the Treasury under Grenville. When Grenville fell he lost his office and was to oppose repeal. Jenkinson was the archetypal bureaucrat and King's Friend. Sir Fletcher Norton was a Buteite who succeeded Charles Yorke as Attorney General in December 1763. He emerged as a force to be reckoned with during the debates on General Warrants in February 1764 when he was one of the few defenders of General Warrants to emerge from the debates with any distinction.

[37] For this debate, see Horace Walpole's *Memoirs*, Vol. II, pp. 270-3; Conway to George III, 28 January 1766, Fortescue, Vol. I, pp. 246-7. It was on this occasion that Burke made his maiden speech.

[38] MP for Ayr, a supporter of Bute and Grenville, a distinguished lawyer and at the beginning of a long and successful political career in 1765-6.

[39] Horace Walpole, *Memoirs*, Vol. II, pp. 276-7; Conway to George III, 1 February 1766, Fortescue, Vol. I, pp. 249-50, L. B. Namier, *Additions and Corrections*, p. 50. The letter from Onslow to Pitt in *Chatham Correspondence*, Vol. II, p. 378 is wrongly dated 14 February. It refers to this debate and was probably written on 31 January 1766.

[40] Conway listed the following ministerialists who voted against the Government on the issue: J. Oswald, Sir G. Elliott, J. Dyson, Lord George Sackville, Lord R. Bertie, Lord R. Manners, Col. Hotham, Col. Burgoyne, T. Molyneaux, Sir G. Pocock, C. Price, Col. R. Brudenall, W. Ellis, H. Stanley, Lord A. Gordon, Lord Strange, M. B. Campbell. He also noted that Charles Townshend, W. G. Hamilton and R. Wood did not vote. Fortescue, Vol. I, pp. 249-50. The King, in fact, did not know that ministers intended to take such an active part on this occasion. George III to Conway, 1 February 1766, ibid., pp. 221-2. George Onslow wrote to Newcastle on the day of the debate (B.M. Add. MSS 32973, f. 321, Newcastle Papers): 'Our majority was but small, but 'tis wonderful it should be at all. We were deserted by all, I wish we may always desert' us' [*sic*].

[41] The original resolutions were enclosed by Rockingham in his letter to Newcastle of 23 January 1766 (B.M. Add. MSS 32973, ff. 244-5, Newcastle Papers). For Newcastle's opinion see his reply of 24 January (ibid., ff. 246-7). For Charles Yorke's differences with Newcastle see the latter's letter to Rockingham of 25 January (ibid., f. 275). It should not be supposed that Newcastle's liberality towards the colonists was based upon anything other than a sharp appreciation of British self-interest, profitable trade, the conciliation of the colonists and the protection of the American trade of British merchants. See his letter to the Archbishop of Canterbury, 2 February

1766 (ibid., ff. 342–4). For Rockingham's insistence that Charles Yorke be consulted see his letters of 19 (misdated 17) and 20 January (B.M. Add. MSS 35430, ff. 31–2, 33, Hardwicke Papers).

[42] For this debate see *Ryder Debates*, pp. 261–76, Newdigate MSS B2546; Horace Walpole, *Memoirs*, Vol. II, pp. 277–82; Lord George Sackville to General Irwin, 10 February 1766, *H.M.C. Stopford-Sackville*, Vol. I, pp. 106–8. The best account of the debate, however, is in 'Debates on the Declaratory Act and the Repeal of the Stamp Act, 1766' (*American Historical Review*, **XVII**, 1911–12).

[43] For reports of this debate see Newdigate MSS B2546/15; *Ryder Debates*, pp. 276–82; Horace Walpole, *Memoirs*, Vol. II, pp. 283–4. There are also accounts written during the debate itself by James West to Newcastle (5 February 1766, B.M. Add. MSS 32973, ff. 361–2, 6 February 1766, f. 363, Newcastle Papers). The House had assembled on 4 February but nothing of note had occurred.

[44] Sir Grey Cooper wrote to Rockingham after Pitt's speech that Pitt 'could not be more explicit in his goodwill to Administration and his resolution to support them thro' this great measure' (RI–573, Wentworth Woodhouse MSS). George Onslow scribbled a note to Rockingham during the debate (B.M. Add. MSS 32973, f. 359, Newcastle Papers). 'Pitt has decisively declared in favour of the Ministry—that it was happy for this country that they were about the King's person, happier if their principles were rivetted in his heart'.

[45] Pitt described himself during the debate in the following terms, 'He has no connexion with those who attack in flank or in front, or a flying squadron who attack the rear. He places confidence in those of the Ministry whom he knows think their principal rights and the measures they propose in this House a proper mixture of authority and dignity' (*Ryder Debates*, p. 281).

[46] For reports of this debate, see Newdigate MSS B2546/18; Ryder Debates, pp. 289–91; Horace Walpole, *Memoirs*, Vol. II, pp. 284–7.

[47] *Ryder Debates*, p. 284. 'I have scarce ever seen a majority better pleased or more elated, nor a minority apparently more dejected. Every one of your friends seems to think, this is the very moment to form a strong, complete Whig Administration. You have beat Ld Bute, the D. of Bedford, the Cocoa Tree and Lord Temple united.' (James West to Newcastle, 7 February 1766, B.M. Add. MSS 32973, f. 377, Newcastle Papers.) For the King's astonishment at the size of the majority see Rockingham to Newcastle, 8 February 1766, ibid., ff. 383–4. There is a list in the Newcastle Papers (B.M. Add. MSS 32974, f. 25) sent by Sir Alexander Gilmour to Newcastle on 18 February of the 17 Scottish members who supported the Government, the 8 who were absent and the 20 who opposed.

[48] See the letters of Rockingham and Grafton to George III of 3 and 4 February 1766, Fortescue, Vol. I, pp. 253, 254.

[49] For the debate of 4 February see the letters of Rockingham and Grafton to George III. (Fortescue, Vol. I, pp. 255, 256; Bateson, p. 47.)

[50] The debate is reported in Rockingham's letter to George III of

6 February, Fortescue, Vol. I, p. 251. *See also*, Lord George Sackville to General Irwin, 10 February 1766, *H.M.C. Stopford–Sackville*, pp. 106–8.

[51] Rockingham to George III, 6 February 1766, ibid., p. 261.

[52] Bateson, pp. 47–8.

[53] See the following tables:

Table 2(A)   Those Peers voting *with* the Government on 4 February*

ARCHBISHOPS:	Canterbury	York		
BISHOPS:	Bath & Wells	*Lichfield*	*London*	St Davids
	Chichester	Landaff	Norwich	Worcester
	Exeter	Lincoln	Rochester	
DUKES:	*Argyll*	Dorset	Manchester	Portland
	Bolton	Grafton	Newcastle	
LORDS:	*Abercorn*	Delamere	Harrington	*Northington*
	Albemarle	*Denbigh*	Holderness	Peterborough
	Ashburnham	Digby	Ilchester	Pomfret
	Berkeley	Edgecumbe	Litchfield	Sandys
	Bessborough	*Eglinton*	Marchmont	Scarborough
	Boston	Egmont	*Marsh*	Spencer
	Cardigan	Falmouth	Masham	Talbot
	Cathcart	Grantham	Monson	Tankerville
	Cholmondeley	Harcourt	Montagu	Townshend
	Dartmouth	Hardwicke	Morton	Winchelsea

* Of these 60 names, the 9 names *italicised* voted AGAINST the Government on 6 February. Lord Morton was absent.

The list has been compiled from the following MSS in the Wentworth Woodhouse MSS:

List of those present on 4 February, 127 names, R. 53–5.

List of those for and against the ministry, 4 February, R. 53–26.

List of those for the Government on 4 February, R. 53–17.

List of those present on 6 February, 118 names (really 117 because Lord Denbigh is given twice), R. 53–6.

Table 2(B)   Those Peers voting *against* the Government on 4 February†

BISHOPS:	Bangor	Carlisle	Chester	Durham	Gloucester
DUKES:	Ancaster	Bedford		Bridgewater	Marlborough
	Beaufort	Beaulieu			
LORDS:	Bolingbroke	Eglinton	Legh	Shaftesbury	
	Botetourt	Essex	Lovdon	Suffolk	
	Bruce?	Exeter	Lyttleton	Temple	
	Buckinghamshire	Ferrers	Macclesfield	Trevor	
	Bute	Gower	Mansfield	Willoughby	
	Cadogan	Guildford	Sandwich	Waldgrave	
	Coventry	Halifax	Scarsdale	Weymouth	
	Despencer?	Hyde			

† There is no complete list in the Rockingham papers but using the lists it is possible to discover forty-three who opposed the ministry.

⁵⁴ The committee continued to sit until April and among its recommendations was the measure which later became the Free Ports Bill. The membership and activities of this committee are clearly of the greatest importance in the history of the Rockingham ministry. The evidence is in R. 27, Wentworth Woodhouse MSS, and is printed in B. R. Smith, *The Committee of the Whole to consider American Papers* (unpublished M.A. thesis, Sheffield, 1956); D. Watson, op. cit., pp. 367–88. For the activity of the Committee see R. 42 Wentworth Woodhouse MSS.

⁵⁵ There are few accounts of this debate. The most comprehensive is published by D. Watson, 'William Baker's Account of the Debate on the Repeal of the Stamp Act', *William and Mary Quarterly*, 3rd series, **XXVI** (1969). There are fragments in Horace Walpole's *Memoirs*, Vol. II, pp. 295–8 and in the letters of Conway and Rockingham to George III on 22 February 1766, Fortescue, Vol. I, pp. 273–5. More detailed accounts can be found in James West's three letters to Newcastle of the date of the debate. (B.M. Add. MSS 32974, ff. 45–6, 47, 49, Newcastle Papers.)

⁵⁶ There is a list of the minority in R. 54–11. Wentworth Woodhouse MSS. Rockingham noted, with characteristic foreboding, that the fifteen Scottish Members who voted with the ministry were outnumbered by the twenty-four voting against it.

⁵⁷ 'William Baker's Account', p. 262.

⁵⁸ B.M. Add. MSS 32974, ff. 68–9, Newcastle Papers. Also *see* p. 163 ff.

⁵⁹ For reports of the debate *see* Newdigate MSS B2541/3; Onslow to Newcastle, 24 February 1766, B.M. Add. MSS 32974, ff. 77–9, Newcastle Papers; *Ryder Debates*, pp. 310–14; Conway to George III, 25 February 1766, Fortescue, Vol. I, p. 276; Horace Walpole, *Memoirs*, Vol. II, 299–301; G. Onslow to William Pitt, 25 February 1766, *Chatham Correspondence*, Vol. II, pp. 394–6. The persistent appearance of Dyson and Norton in these debates left many with the impression that Bute's friends were against repeal, e.g. *Chatham Correspondence*, Vol. II, p. 396N.

⁶⁰ *Ryder Debates*, p. 316; Onslow to Newcastle, 26 February 1766, B.M. Add. MSS 32974, f. 91, Newcastle Papers; Newcastle to the Earl of Hopetoun, 27 February 1766, ibid., f. 101.

⁶¹ *Ryder Debates*, pp. 316–20; Horace Walpole, *Memoirs*, Vol. II, pp. 302–7; Newdigate MSS 2546/2; Onslow to Newcastle, 4 March 1766, B.M. Add. MSS 32974, ff. 134–5, Newcastle Papers.

⁶² Newcastle to Rockingham, 23 February 1766, ibid., f. 69; James West to Newcastle, 7 March 1766, ibid., f. 153.

⁶³ R. 53–20, Wentworth Woodhouse MSS. This was more realistic than an earlier 'state' (ibid., 30) which listed 84 for, 47 against, and 45 doubtful. But even this was better than an earlier, ludicrous estimate giving 135 for, 26 against and 20 doubtful. There is a document in the Wentworth Woodhouse MSS (R. 53–25) listing those present and their attitude to repeal. Seventy are recorded as favourable, 55 against and 11 doubtful. This is undoubtedly a classification of another list of those present (R. 53–8) which gives the same 136 names.

[64] Lord Hardwicke to Charles Yorke, 8 March 1766, Albemarle, Vol. I, pp. 313–14.

[65] *American Historical Review*, **XVII** (1911–12), pp. 576–86. There is an incomplete list of the voting in the Wentworth Woodhouse MSS (R. 53–20). There are brief accounts of the debate in the letters of Grafton and Rockingham to George III, 12 March 1766, Fortescue, Vol. I, pp. 280–2. Those who signed the protest are listed in Fortescue, Vol. I, p. 283 but see L. B. Namier, *Additions and Corrections*, p. 54.

[66] Hinkhouse, op. cit., pp. 75–9, for the joyous newspaper reaction.

[67] Burke to Charles O'Hara, 14 March 1766, *Burke Correspondence*, Vol. I, pp. 239–41. As early as 14 February Newcastle was writing to Rose Fuller about 'some other regulations, which, I hear, are now depending and seem to be very proper' (B.M. Add. MSS 32974, f. 440, Newcastle Papers).

[68] L. Sutherland, op. cit., p. 66.

[69] From Bristol, Lancaster, Liverpool, London and Manchester. (See D. Watson, *The Duke of Newcastle*, pp. 416–46.)

[70] The Committee to examine the American Papers was busily engaged throughout March and April in interviewing well-rehearsed candidates. It is possible that fear of opposition delayed the bringing forward of the measures. See the letters of George Onslow to Newcastle and John West to Newcastle, of 30 April 1766 (B.M. Add. MSS 32975, ff. 56, 58, Newcastle Papers).

[71] There are grounds for believing that these measures were limited in their effect and that they failed to live up to the expectations placed in them. (See P. Langford, op. cit., pp. 196–8.)

CHAPTER 7

[1] Even Lord Holland believed that Bute was in regular communication with the King late in 1765. (Lord Holland to Bute, 9 November 1765, B.M. Add. MSS 51379, f. 175, Holland House Papers.) For the contacts between the King and Bute, *see* J. Brooke, *George III*, pp. 127–8.

[2] Bute, of course, looked on with amused contempt as he saw his enemies committing political suicide. (Lord Bute to J. Oswald, n.d., *Memorials of J. Oswald* (Edinburgh, 1825), pp. 418–19).

[3] George III to Lord Bute, 10 January 1766, Sedgwick, op. cit., p. 241.

[4] See pp. 124–5, 134–5.

[5] Bateson, p. 39. Newcastle gave the King the benefit of the same opinion. (Newcastle to Grafton, 6 November 1765, B.M. Add. MSS 32971, f. 289, Newcastle Papers.) It was probably Newcastle who urged the Cabinet to approach Pitt. It approved a negotiation with Pitt in principle but in effect deferred the matter until Pitt should come to town. 'Business this evening at the Duke of Grafton's' (13 November 1765, ibid., f. 368).

[6] See above pp. 134–5.

[7] Shelburne to Pitt, 21 December 1765, *Chatham Correspondence*, Vol. II,

pp. 353–8; Fitzmaurice, Vol. I, pp. 252–4; Albemarle, Vol. I, pp. 236–7; Rockingham might have known of the meeting held by Bute and Northumberland on 10 December to organise the 'King's Friends'. The King wisely refused to have anything to do with the meeting. (George III to Bute, 10 January 1766, loc. cit.)

[8] Pitt to Shelburne, *post*-21 December 1765, *Chatham Correspondence*, Vol. II, pp. 358–61; Pitt to Thomas Nuthall, 9 January 1766, ibid., pp. 361–3.

[9] *Grafton Autobiography*, p. 62; George III to Lord Bute, 10 January 1766, loc. cit.; Rockingham, Grafton and Conway took the decision to approach Pitt without informing Newcastle. (Rockingham to Newcastle, 2 January 1766, B.M. Add. MSS 32973, ff. 11–13, Newcastle Papers.)

[10] After the reconciliation of Temple and Grenville in May 1765 it was most unlikely that Temple would serve with Pitt without bringing in Grenville or, at least, some of his friends. Temple, for his part, was most unlikely to wish to attach himself closely to men who wanted to undo his brother's policy on America. Temple went to see Pitt at Bath towards the end of the old year but the two men reached no understanding (Albemarle, Vol. I, p. 260).

[11] George III to Northington, 8 January 1766, Fortescue, Vol. I, pp. 212–14; *Grafton Autobiography*, p. 63.

[12] Newcastle was, nevertheless, anxious lest resignations by Grafton and Conway destroy the ministry. (Newcastle to Rockingham, 8 (misdated 9) January 1766, Albemarle, Vol. I, pp 264–5.) Newcastle's willingness to step down was undoubtedly sincere. 'Minute of what I propose to say to the King' (B.M. Add. MSS 32973, f. 127, Newcastle Papers).

[13] For the coincidence of the King's and Rockingham's opinions see George III to Rockingham, 8 January 1766, Albemarle, Vol. I, p. 266; George III to Rockingham, 10 January 1766, Fortescue, Vol. I, p. 218; Albemarle, Vol. I, p. 267.

[14] George III to Northington, 8 January 1766, loc. cit.

[15] Rockingham to George III, 10 January 1766, Fortescue, Vol. I, p. 218.

[16] George III to Northington, 11 January 1766, Fortescue, Vol. I, p. 219; *Grafton Autobiography*, p. 63.

[17] Rockingham to George III, 15 January 1766, Albemarle, Vol. I, p. 270.

[18] Fortescue, Vol. I, p. 237. From the wording of a letter from Rockingham to the King (16 January 1766, ibid., p. 235) it seems that Grafton saw Pitt alone. The wording of the King's Memorandum including a report of the interview with Pitt made to him by Rockingham and Grafton suggests that both were present (ibid., Vol. I, pp. 237–9). Other accounts may be found in *Grafton Autobiography* (p. 67) and a longer one given to Newcastle by Rockingham noted by the former in B.M. Add. MSS 32973, ff. 194–6, Newcastle Papers.

[19] Pitt did not think he would accept and confessed that he had seen little of Temple recently. He left it to the present ministry to sound Temple but made it clear that if Temple demanded the inclusion of Grenville or his friends then he (Pitt) would not take part. (Fortescue, Vol. I, pp. 237–9).

[20] The King's undated letter to Rockingham (Albemarle, Vol. I,

pp. 271–2) is, in fact, a letter of 21 January instructing Rockingham in great detail how to break off the negotiation with Pitt. It is also printed in Fortescue (Vol. I, pp. 243–4), and is clearly a reply to Rockingham's earlier letter of 21 January (ibid., pp. 239–40). Grafton could not understand why the business was 'dropt after having had so favourable an appearance' (*Grafton Autobiography*, p. 68). I think that there is just enough evidence to indicate that the King wished to keep open his options with respect to Pitt, and that he did not wish to give the impression of breaking off the negotiation with excessive finality. Mr Brooke, however, suggests that the King completely failed to understand Pitt. 'Unfortunately the King was a plain man, not apt to look beyond the obvious meaning of words. He failed to take the hint. All that he understood was that Pitt wished to dissolve the Rockingham ministry' (*George III*, p. 128). Contemporaries were quick to spot the unusual nature of Pitt's behaviour. *See, inter alia, Life and Letters of Lady Sarah Lennox*, pp. 186–7; Lord George Sackville to General Irwin, 17 January 1766, *H.M.C. Stopford-Sackville*, Vol. I, pp. 104–5; 'Mr Pitt's conduct has occasioned great confusion'. (Horace Walpole to Sir Horace Mann, 9 February 1766, *Correspondence of Horace Walpole*, Vol. VI, p. 395; Charles Hotham to the Earl of Huntingdon, 21 January 1766, *H.M.C. Hastings*, Vol. III, p. 147.)

[21] The King to Northington, 9 January 1766 (Fortescue, Vol. I, p. 216). The last part of this letter suggests very strongly that the King was aware of the need to avoid incautious action.

[22] Lord Egmont to George III, 16 January 1766 (Fortescue, Vol. I, pp. 233–4); 'List of a New Ministry', 16 January 1766 (Misplaced and misdated in Fortescue, I, p. 350). The discussions began on 15 January when ministers seemed to be losing their nerve after Pitt's speech of the 14 January. (See the letters of George III to Egmont, 15 and 16 January 1766, ibid., pp. 232, 233–4.)

[23] Rockingham to Charles Yorke, 25 January 1766 (B.M. Add. MSS 35430, ff. 37–8, Hardwicke Papers, printed in Albemarle, Vol. I, p. 288).

[24] Albemarle, Vol. I, p. 292.

[25] Bateson, pp. 30–1. See above p. 124.

[26] As Conway put it in a letter to the King on 1 February (Fortescue, Vol. I, p. 249) there could have been no 'conscientious distinctions' on a trivial matter such as an election petition and thus ministers correctly interpreted what was happening as a symbol of a threatened, organised opposition to the ministry from within the citadels of Whitehall and Westminster.

[27] Newcastle to Rockingham, 31 January 1766 (B.M. Add. MSS 32973, f. 319, Newcastle Papers).

[28] The King had written to Bute on 10 January (loc. cit.) that it was not only permissible but a positive duty for the friends of Bute who differed from the ministry to vote against it! That ministers badly needed reassurance can be gauged from the King's remarks in his letter to Northington, 3 February 1766 (Fortescue, Vol. I, p. 252, Bateson, p. 49).

[29] The King 'freely' gave Rockingham permission to state that he was

for repeal if enforcement was out of the question. (See George III's Memorandum, Fortescue, Vol. I, p. 269 and see L. B. Namier, *Additions and Corrections*, pp. 50–2.)

30 It was impossible because the repeal bill was a supply bill which could not be amended in the Upper House. Furthermore, by this time it would have been regarded as constitutionally questionable for a supply bill to be rejected in the Lords.

31 Fortescue, Vol. I, p. 269.

32 For the embarrassment which Strange's comments brought upon Rockingham, see John Offley to Rockingham, 11 February 1766, RI–576, Wentworth Woodhouse MSS; Albemarle, Vol. I, pp. 300–1; *Grenville Papers*, Vol. III, p. 364. It is interesting that Pitt advised George Onslow 'to put the best construction on all the King's words and actions towards us'. (Onslow to Pitt, 12 February 1766, B.M. Add. MSS 32973, f. 423, Newcastle Papers.) 'The report of a great person having this day told Lord Strange, his opinion was against the repeal does infinite damage in the City.' (James West to Newcastle, 11 February 1766, ibid., f. 411.)

33 Newcastle to the Archbishop of Canterbury, 15 February 1766, ibid., 32974, ff. 5–7: '*Lord Rockingham was allowed, on Friday last, to say that the King was for the Repeal;*—added in His Majesty's own hand, *there having nothing passed in that conversation,* but what related, to the *repeal or enforcement.* Thus it now stands; His Majesty seemingly in good humour with us all' (Bateson, p. 52; Fortescue, Vol. I, pp. 266, 268–9 and L. B. Namier, *Additions and Corrections*, p. 52). The originals of the three papers printed in Albemarle (Vol. I, pp. 301–2) can be found in R. 161, Wentworth Woodhouse MSS.

34 Lord Denbigh (1719–1800), a Lord of the Bedchamber.

35 The inference is that the incident occurred on the day before repeal came before the Commons (21 February, RI–161–5, Wentworth Woodhouse MSS).

36 Ibid., R–161–2. In Rockingham's hand.

37 The original undated memoranda are in the Wentworth Woodhouse MSS, R. 161.

38 Ibid., R. 161–3.

39 I. R. Christie, *The Crisis of Empire* (1966), p. 64. *See* also the same writer's comments (*Myth and Reality*, p. 99, n. 1). 'The explanation is most probably that the King may not have been careful with his phrasing in his talk with Strange or that Strange was not careful, or still more likely that those politicians who were opposed to repeal only heard those parts of Strange's remarks which they wanted to hear.'

40 Some Rockinghamites were at the time careful to stress that the King had *not* set out to weaken the ministry and that it still enjoyed his confidence. (*See, inter alia,* Lord Frederick Cavendish to Lord Bathurst, 23 February 1766, B.M. Bathurst Loan, 57/1, f. 260–1.) Another way of looking at the occurrence was that of Horace Walpole. (To Sir Horace Mann, 1 March 1766, *Correspondence of Horace Walpole*, Vol. VI, p. 401.) 'The ministers instead of tossing their places into the middle of the Closet, as I should

have done, had the courage and the virtue to stand firm, and save both Europe and America from destruction.'

[41] When he heard the rumours of the King's lukewarm attachment to repeal the Duke of Bedford, horrified by the policy of repeal, penned a minute which the Duke of York passed to the King: 'that shou'd his Majesty be enclin'd to pursue the *modification* instead of the *total repeal of the Stamp Act* . . . the D. of Bedford will be happy to receive his Majesty's commands for his attending him and offering his assistance in the most dutiful manner on the *present important occasion* through such channel and at such time as shall be convenient to his Majesty.' The minute is printed in Fortescue, Vol. I, p. 272 (although it is attributed to the King) and in *Bedford Correspondence*, Vol. III, p. 329. The original is in the Woburn MSS, LIII, f. 52.

[42] The King to the Duke of York, 18 February 1766, Fortescue, Vol. I, p. 273.

[43] James West to Newcastle, 23 April 1766, B.M. Add. MSS 32975, f. 11, Newcastle Papers.

[44] James West to Newcastle, 24 April 1766, ibid., f. 15.

[45] James West to Newcastle, 25 April 1766, ibid., f. 25. There is also a lengthy account of this debate in Sir Grey Cooper's letter to Rockingham of 26 April (Albemarle, Vol. I, pp. 325–9).

[46] Edmund Burke to Charles O'Hara, 11 March 1766, *Burke Correspondence*, Vol. I, pp. 244–5. The Marquis of Rockingham believed that the repeal would be violently opposed in the Lords. See his letter to William Weddell, 14 March 1766 (the second half of which is in Lady Rockingham's hand) Ramsden MSS. In fact there were no divisions in either House. That the repeal was a popular measure is reflected to some extent in the fact that over a dozen petitions in favour of repeal were received.

[47] For the debate see Newdigate MSS B2546/8. Dowdeswell's performance on this occasion was 'more spirited and alive than ever I knew him'. (George Onslow to Newcastle, 18 April 1766, B.M. Add. MSS 32974, ff. 425–6, Newcastle Papers.)

[48] There was a very poor attendance in the Committee on the Window Tax because, it was alleged, members did not wish to be tainted with the odium of having supported it. (James West to Newcastle, 28 April 1766, ibid., 32975, f. 35.) A motion to throw the tax out on the report stage was lost by 176–136. (See James West to Newcastle, 29 April 1766, ibid., f. 52, Newdigate MSS, B2546/21).

[49] Michael Roberts, *Splendid Isolation, 1763–80* (University of Reading, 1970), pp. 20–2.

[50] D. Jarrett, op. cit., pp. 83–4.

[51] Horace Walpole, *Memoirs*, Vol. II, p. 315; L. B. Namier and J. Brooke, *The House of Commons, 1754–90*, Vol. III, p. 298. Pitt's statement should not astonish the modern reader. He disliked Bute but he had never shared Rockingham's antipathies towards him.

[52] Newcastle's Memorandum, 18 April 1766, B.M. Add. MSS 32973, ff. 417–23, Newcastle Papers.

[53] In late February, Rockingham approached Shelburne. He had been

persuaded that Conway and Grafton might break ranks if some approach to Pitt were not made. Rockingham talked of changes in the ministry which would exclude the friends of Bute and Bedford. (Shelburne to Pitt, 24 February 1766, *Chatham Correspondence*, Vol. III, pp. 7–11.) Pitt thought little of this plan and took the opportunity to reaffirm his reluctance to come into office by 'court cabal or ministerial connexion' (Pitt to Shelburne, 24 February 1766, ibid., pp. 11–12).

[54] See P. Langford, op. cit., p. 231.

[55] Richard Rigby to the Duke of Bedford, 24 April 1766, *Bedford Correspondence*, Vol. III, p. 333; Bateson, p. 59; Albemarle, Vol. I, p. 324.

[56] Pitt said on 29 April that 'if he had anything to do, he should be against all distinctions of parties, or connections, that he would take the best and ablest men from them all' (Bateson, p. 58). Conway was by this time already apprehensive about Pitt. He wrote to Grafton on 20 April 1766: 'I must own Mr Pitt's behaviour appears to have more passion and levity in it than I cou'd have believed, and yet I shou'd be much for sounding him, that we may appear consistent' (*Grafton Autobiography*, p. 87). Yet Conway wrote to Rockingham on the following day that he thought Pitt's behaviour made any connection between them impossible (RI–359, Wentworth Woodhouse MSS).

[57] Bateson, pp. 50–3.

[58] Ibid., p. 53.

[59] *Grafton Autobiography*, pp. 71–2; George III to Northington, 28 April 1756, Fortescue, Vol. I, p. 295.

[60] Grafton summarised his reasons: 'The weakness of the cabinet as now exposed, the great bodies of Men not included, many of ability, with a large share of those of Property' as well as the ministry's lack of 'the only man who stands sufficiently above the rest' (*Grafton Autobiography*, pp. 71–2). Grafton might have added that he was sick of bearing the burden of defending the ministry in a difficult House of Lords while his senior partner, Rockingham, scarcely ever spoke or attended.

[61] Bateson, p. 57; *Grafton Autobiography*, p. 74.

[62] There was a meeting at Northington's on 1 May but nothing came of it (Bateson, p. 63; Fortescue, pp. 301, 303–6). Of the ministers, Egmont and Northington were in favour of reconciliation with Bute, as indeed Richmond, Grafton's successor, was to be. (*See* A. G. Olson, 'The Duke of Richmond's Memorandum, 1–7 July 1766', *English Historical Review*, **LXXV**, 1960.) The argument which these men used to support a reconciliation with the Buteites was that such a move was 'the only means of dissolving that union of Ld Bute's friends which will be very uneasy to every Administration while it lasts'. (James White to Newcastle, 10 May 1766, B.M. Add. MSS 32975, f. 152, Newcastle Papers.) Newcastle and Rockingham thought the ministry strong enough to continue without support from that quarter and although they recognised the need for a strengthening of the ministry believed that the Bedford Whigs were the most likely group to approach with any hope of success.

S

[63] Egmont to George III, 1 May 1766, Fortescue, Vol. I, pp. 297–8; 2 May 1766, ibid., pp. 299–301; Bateson, pp. 61–2.

[64] The desperation of George III should not be underestimated. His health was beginning to worsen and his desire to establish a stable ministry now outweighed every other objective in his mind. (See his moving letter to Bute of 3 May 1766, Sedgwick, op. cit., p. 248. See also the letters of Egmont to George III, 4 and 18 May 1766, Fortescue, Vol. I, pp. 303–6, 308–9.)

[65] Egmont to George III, 4 May 1766, Fortescue, Vol. I, pp. 303–6.

[66] Conway and Egmont were to be the Secretaries, Hillsborough was to go to the Admiralty and Lord North was to become a Lord of Trade. The King forbade Egmont to take a responsible position. (Albemarle, Vol. I, p. 338; Newcastle to Rockingham, 2 May 1766, B.M. Add. MSS 32975, ff. 72–4, Newcastle Papers). On the intended reshuffle see also Rockingham to Newcastle, 14 May 1766 (ibid., ff. 178–80) and Namier and Brooke, *Charles Townshend* (pp. 142–4). For North's refusal see North to Rockingham, 24 May 1766 (Albemarle, Vol. I, p. 345, and Bateson, p. 69). Newcastle, of course, was in his element during the speculative cabinet building which went on in early May. There is no hint in his letters and lists of a desire to remain in office against the King's wishes. Indeed, the last thing he wanted was 'a too hasty resolution of leaving the King's service without giving time to His Majesty to form an Administration'. (Newcastle to Rockingham, 2 May 1766, loc. cit.) His ideal ministry would have included Charles Townshend as a third Secretary but with a peerage (Newcastle thought him too unreliable to lead the Commons). Newcastle disliked the idea of Egmont as a Secretary: 'no one man can have time, to do the duty of Secretary of State and attend the King every day, and give that attention to the settlement and government of our Colonies, which in their present situation they will require'. (Newcastle to Conway, 7 May 1766, ibid., f. 104.)

[67] The proposal of Yorke must have come from Newcastle because Rockingham declared that he had not considered him for a Secretaryship. (Rockingham to Newcastle, 16 May 1766, ibid., ff. 195–6.) Although Hardwicke rejected the offer, he entered the inner Cabinet at this time.

[68] The King also disliked the apparent nepotism of the ministry. Conway was Richmond's father-in-law, Conway's brother, Lord Hertford, was Lord Lieutenant of Ireland and notorious for his nepotism there. (George III to Lord Egmont, 16 May 1766, Fortescue, Vol. I, p. 307; Egmont to George III, 18 May 1766, ibid., pp. 308–9.) Richmond had been earlier attached to Grenville (something which can hardly have endeared him to the King), but he had become attached to Rockingham and Cumberland in 1765. (Richmond to Albemarle, 4 July 1765, Albemarle MSS, LI/I/13 (9).)

[69] Egmont to George III, 4 May 1766, Fortescue, Vol. I, pp. 303–6.

[70] This they decided at a cabinet at Northington's on 26 May. (Bateson, p. 69; Rockingham to George III, 27 May 1766, Fortescue, Vol. I, p. 345, Namier, *Additions and Corrections*, p. 57.) As early as 17 April Newcastle

had written that 'The establishment of the King's brothers will meet with great difficulties in Parliament. Mr Pitt and Lord Strange against it'. (Mems for Lord Rockingham, B.M. Add. MSS 32973, f. 397, Newcastle Papers.) Rockingham unsuccessfully tried to persuade the King's brothers to persuade the King to postpone the matter. (Rockingham to Newcastle, 29 May 1766, ibid., 32975, f. 289.) There is a useful account of the affair in Lord George Sackville's letter to General Irwin, 10 June 1766 (*H.M.C. Stopford Sackville*, Vol. I, pp. 111–12).

[71] Newcastle to Rockingham, 29 May 1766, B.M. Add. MSS 32975, f. 291, Newcastle Papers.

[72] For the King's anger against the ministry, and Rockingham in particular, see his letter to Bute, 3 May 1766. (Sedgwick, op. cit., p. 249; George III to Egmont, 28 May 1766, Fortescue, Vol. I, p. 347, Namier, *Additions and Corrections*, p. 57.) Northington advised the King to stand firm and pledged his own support for him. (Northington to George III, 28 May 1766, Fortescue, Vol. I, pp. 345–6.)

[73] There is a list of speakers in the Wentworth Woodhouse MSS, R. 49–29.

[74] Rockingham to George III, 5 June 1766, Fortescue, Vol. I, p. 355. There is a detailed account of the interview between Rockingham and Dyson in a letter of Dyson to Sir Gilbert Elliot, 23 August 1766 (Minto MSS *q*. Namier and Brooke, *House of Commons, 1754–90*, Vol. II, p. 372).

[75] Northington to George III, 5 June 1766, Fortescue, Vol. I, p. 356; George III to Rockingham, 5 June 1766, ibid., p. 355.

[76] Northington had already hinted to the King that after the end of the session 'I must humbly receive Your permission to treat in my own way, such Cabinet Councils'. (Northington to George III, 29 May 1766, Fortescue, Vol. I, pp. 347–8; Bateson, p. 78.) The King's account of his discussion with Northington on 6 July is summarised in Rockingham's letters to Newcastle, 6 July 1766 (B.M. Add. MSS 32976, ff. 19–21, Newcastle Papers). See also Richmond to Newcastle, 7 July 1766 (ibid., f. 31). At least three important offices were vacant; these were the Vice-Treasurership of Ireland, the Treasurership of the Navy and the post of ambassador to Spain.

[77] The King's letter to Bute of 12 July 1766 (Sedgwick, op. cit., pp. 250–4) is clear evidence that Bute was never involved in the 1766 negotiations with Pitt.

[78] About 1757 appeared *An Account of the European Settlements in America* in which Edmund Burke played some part in compiling the material and William Burke some part in writing. In this and in Edmund's *Essay Towards an Abridgement of English History* (1757) as also in his *Fragments of a Tract Relative to the Laws against Popery in Ireland* (*c.* 1761–2) he displayed his instinctive humanitarian sympathies and his desire for reform within a stable, propertied social order.

[79] Hamilton sat in the Commons for several constituencies from 1754–90, was a Lord of Trade, 1756–61 and Chief Secretary to the Lord Lieutenant of Ireland, 1761–4. 'Single Speech' Hamilton never, in fact, spoke in the Commons. He was never attached to the Rockinghams.

[80] It was only later that Burke began to express a personal veneration for the Marquis which was not in evidence in 1765–6. For example, in his Speech on American Taxation, 1774, he said: 'I did see in that noble person such sound principles, such an enlargement of mind, such clear and sagacious sense, and such unshaken fortitude, as have bound me, as well as others, much better than me, by an invictable attachment to him from that time forward.'

[81] Burke had already had some connection with the Opposition to George Grenville's administration. He may have done some writing for it in 1764–5 and probably attended Wildmans club on one or two occasions. (C. Cone, *Burke and the Nature of Politics* (University of Kentucky Press, 2 vols, 1957, 1964), Vol. I, p. 61. See also Lucy Sutherland, 'Edmund Burke and the First Rockingham Ministry', loc. cit., pp. 55–6.)

[82] Burke was in favour of taking in not only the Butes but even the Tories! (Burke to Charles O'Hara, 4 July 1765, *Burke Correspondence*, Vol. I, p. 207; *The Annual Register*, **VII**, pp. 30–3.)

[83] Burke to O'Hara, 31 December 1765, ibid., p. 229; Burke to Richard Burke Senior, *ante*-4 January 1766, *Burke Correspondence*, p. 230; Bateson, p. 121.

[84] *Grafton Autobiography*, p. 108; The wording of Burke's letter to Charles O'Hara (19 August 1766, *Burke Correspondence*, Vol. I, p. 264), where he complains that he had 'had no civility from any of the new people' tends to contradict the view later propagated by Burke that he had never seriously considered the prospect of serving under Chatham. (To Markham, 9 November 1771, ibid., Vol. II, pp. 269–70.)

[85] The first expressions of these ideas are to be found in his admittedly propagandist *Short Account of a Late Short Administration* (1766).

[86] George III to Lord Bute, 12 July 1766, loc. cit.

[87] Ibid.

[88] In fact a handful of Grenvillites did return to office including Robert Nugent, Hans Stanley, Charles Jenkinson and Lord Hillsborough.

[89] Loc. cit.

[90] George III to Northington, 6 July 1766, Fortescue, Vol. I, p. 367; Northington to Pitt, 7 July 1766, *Chatham Correspondence*, Vol. II, pp. 434–5; George III to Pitt, 7 July 1766, ibid., p. 436; Fortescue, Vol. I, p. 368. Pitt to George III, 8 July 1766, ibid., p. 368 and *Chatham Correspondence*, Vol. II, p. 438; Pitt to Northington, 8 July 1766, ibid., p. 437.

[91] Northington to George III, 11 July 1766, Fortescue, Vol. I, p. 371; Bateson, p. 82.

[92] The King kept a memorandum of this important discussion. It is printed but misdated and misplaced in Fortescue, Vol. I, pp. 175–7; *Grafton Autobiography*, p. 90; Bateson, p. 82.

[93] See the discussion in H. Butterfield, *George III and the Historians* (pp. 283–93). Professor Butterfield claimed that Brooke (*The Chatham Administration 1766–8* 1956), underestimated the King's 'desire to exploit the implications of the original idea' of the ministry, to destroy faction by

extracting the best men from each group. Butterfield is right to remind us of the *intentions* of George III but he does not show that the 'superintending idea' continued to be important after July 1766. Yet he is right to remind us (p. 289) that the King was prepared to break with Bute in his desire to destroy party, even Bute's. But the historian should remember that what statesmen *do* is more important than what they *say*. It is true that in the mind of George III the Chatham administration was supposed to be *sui generis* but Pitt himself saw that it was not feasible to destroy party at that time, a point Butterfield misses.

⁹⁴ Pitt wrote to Shelburne on 13 July asserting 'As yet, all stands till Lord Temple comes to town, and his answer to accept or decline the Treasury be final' (*Chatham Correspondence*, Vol. III, pp. 12–13). On the same day Pitt offered Conway a Secretaryship but the prospect of Temple's inclusion deterred Conway from accepting because of be a very great differences over America (Bateson, pp. 82–4). It was to their fact of the greatest importance in the next two years that Conway, the lynch-pin which kept the Chatham administration in existence, only took office because Temple refused. (Northington to Temple, 13 July 1766, *Grenville Papers*, Vol. III, pp. 263.) Northington told Pitt of his message the following day (*Chatham Correspondence*, Vol. II, pp. 440–1), but remarked to the King that Temple's reply was not as warm as Pitt's and 'much more guarded'. (14 July 1766, Fortescue, Vol. I, p. 372.)

⁹⁵ George III to Pitt, 15 July 1766, *Chatham Correspondence*, Vol. II, p. 443, Fortescue, pp. 375–6. The King probably meant that Temple was leaning to Grenville rather than to the Rockinghams. George III's private memorandum suggests strongly that the King thought it unlikely that Temple would accept. (Fortescue, Vol. I, p. 376.)

⁹⁶ Pitt to his wife, 17 July 1766, *Chatham Correspondence*, Vol. II, p. 448.

⁹⁷ Temple to Grenville, 18 July 1766, *Grenville Papers*, Vol. III, p. 267. See also Temple to Lady Chatham, 27 July 1766, *Chatham Correspondence*, Vol. II, pp. 467–70. Grenville wrote to the Earl of Buckinghamshire, 20 July 1766 (*H.M.C. Lothian*, pp. 263–4): 'The modest proposal made to Lord Temple by Mr Pitt, whom he saw but once during the three days he was in town, was that he should stand as a capital cypher in the most responsible office in the kingdom unsupported by any of his friends, whilst [*sic*] Mr Pitt . . . was to guide, nominate and form the whole'. Furthermore, Temple 'might have had some office for the present and have a Cabinet office on some future vacancy, but not now'.

⁹⁸ According to Grenville's letter to Whately (20 July 1766, *Grenville Papers*, Vol. III, pp. 273–7). Temple was extremely dissatisfied with the absence of new policy measures in contemplation, resentful of Pitt's privileged position in the ministry and doubtful if Pitt really wanted him.

⁹⁹ See also Temple's remark 'Thus ends this political farce of my journey to town, as it was always intended'. (Temple to Grenville, 18 July 1766, loc. cit.)

¹⁰⁰ Northington to George III, 15 July 1766, Fortescue, Vol. I, p. 376.

¹⁰¹ The King might well have guessed that he could have Pitt without

Temple. (John Calcraft to Pitt, 15 July 1766, *Chatham Correspondence*, Vol. II, p. 445.)

[102] Temple's refusal also led to Pitt abandoning the idea of creating a separate department for American affairs. (See C. R. Ritcheson, 'The Elder Pitt and an American Department', *American Historical Review*, **LVII,** 1952.)

[103] Bateson, pp. 90–1. For Conway's satisfaction at Grafton's appointment see his letter to Pitt of 21 July 1766 (*Chatham Correspondence*, Vol. II, pp. 453–5). For Pitt's attitude to Grafton see *Grafton Autobiography* (pp. 90–1). What endeared Pitt to Grafton was his loyalty. Pitt wrote to Nuthall 'I am, indeed, most proud of the honour the Duke of Grafton has done me. The testimony is genuine, not the result of cabal; and dignity and spirit of character meeting with high rank, add every flattering circumstance to the favourable suffrage with which his Grace has been pleased to distinguish his humble servant.' (1 June 1766, *Chatham Correspondence*, Vol. II, p. 423.)

[104] Namier and Brooke, *Charles Townshend*, pp. 148–9; Grafton to Pitt, 25 July 1766, *Chatham Correspondence*, Vol. II, pp. 459–61, part printed in Namier and Brooke, pp. 151–2. Townshend's dissatisfaction at only receiving the Exchequer was well known. (See Lord Harcourt to Charles Jenkinson, 26 August 1766, Jucker, op. cit., pp. 425–6.)

[105] Rockingham to Newcastle, 21 July 1766, B.M. Add. MSS 32976, ff. 199–200, Newcastle Papers; Pitt to Thomas Walpole, 18 July 1766, Lullings MSS. Rockingham was most disappointed that Conway took the Northern department because the Southern 'includes a Great Patronage & would have been of use to our Friends—if it had been in a real Friends hands'. (Rockingham to Newcastle, 26 July 1766, B.M. Add. MSS 32976, ff. 253–4, Newcastle Papers.)

[106] Horace Walpole to George Montagu, 10 July 1766, *Correspondence of Horace Walpole*, Vol. X, pp. 221–2.

[107] Camden to Grafton, 24 July 1766, *Grafton Autobiography*, pp. 94–5. Camden also worried about Pitt's health and its consequences 'for the nation can not be dallied with any longer'. George III knew of Pitt's ill health from the outset (see Fortescue, Vol. I, p. 376).

[108] *Grafton Autobiography*, p. 97.

[109] Horace Walpole was doubtful of the ministry's success from a very early stage. 'You see the new colour of the times: the style will be exalted, but it will be far from meeting with universal submission. The House of Grenville is not patient: the great families that will be displaced are by no means pleased. The dictator, I think, will not find his new magistracy pass on so smoothly as his former. . . .' (Horace Walpole to Sir Horace Mann, 23 July 1766, *Correspondence of Horace Walpole*, Vol. XXII, p. 440.)

[110] Rockingham to Newcastle, 6 July 1766, B.M. Add. MSS 32976, ff. 19–21, Newcastle Papers.

[111] Richmond to Newcastle, 6 July 1766, ibid., f. 25.

[112] Newcastle to Rockingham, 7 July 1766, ibid., f. 29.

[113] Hardwicke to Rockingham, 11 July 1766, RI–643, Wentworth Woodhouse MSS, part printed Albemarle, Vol. I, pp. 363–4.

[114] Richmond picked up some such gossip (Albemarle, Vol. I, p. 368) and this appears to have convinced Newcastle. (Newcastle to White, 11 July 1766, B.M. Add. MSS 32976, f. 70, Newcastle Papers.)

[115] Newcastle to Rockingham, 12 July 1766, ibid., ff. 111–12. Burke believed that Bute and Chatham were in league almost from the first. (Burke to Charles O'Hara, 29 July 1766, *Burke Correspondence*, Vol. I, pp. 261–4.)

[116] Newcastle to White, 11 July, B.M. Add. MSS 32976, ff. 69–70, Newcastle Papers.

[117] Newcastle to White, 20 July 1766, ibid., f. 179.

[118] Rockingham to Newcastle, 18 July 1766, ibid., ff. 161–2; 26 July, ibid., ff. 253–4. Rockingham, of course, had no right whatsoever to be consulted over the arrangements. It is true that Bute had advised the King when he resigned in 1763 but this had not been the case with Newcastle in 1762 or with Grenville in 1765. There was no convention that bound a monarch to seek the advice of the outgoing First Lord.

[119] There are accounts of this incident in Rockingham to Newcastle, 28 July 1766 (B.M. Add. MSS 32976, f. 309, Newcastle Papers). In his letter to Conway on 27 or 28 July (and not 25 as Albemarle gives; Vol. II, p. 5) Rockingham explains his warmth: 'which may be attributed to the strong persuasion that I am in, that Mr Pitt's intentions and conduct are and will be the most hostile to our friends'. (See also, Charles Lloyd to Grenville, 28 July 1766, *Grenville Papers*, Vol. III, pp. 282–4.)

[120] Newcastle to Rockingham, 12 July 1766 (B.M. Add. MSS 32976, ff. 111–12, Newcastle Papers). Newcastle, and perhaps others, was also worried that any signs of factious opposition might meet with a Massacre such as had happened in 1762–3. (See Newcastle to Rockingham, 12 July, B.M. Add. MSS 32976, ff. 111–12, Newcastle Papers, partly *q.* J. Brooke, *The Chatham Administration* (1956), p. 20.)

[121] Camden to Grafton, 13 July 1766, Grafton MSS. Indeed, Pitt did not remove many. Lord Breadalbane gave up the Privy Seal of Scotland to Stuart Mackenzie. Lord George Sackville and the elderly Pelhamite, Lord Grantham, both lost their offices. Those who resigned were Charles and James Yorke and Lords Hardwicke, Dartmouth, and Cavendish, and William Dowdeswell. Great pressure was put upon Dowdeswell to take either the Paymastership or the Board of Trade but he refused, believing that the ministry would only be of short duration. (See the letters of Conway and Grafton to Dowdeswell, 16 and 25 July, Dowdeswell MSS.) But it should not be thought that Dowdeswell refused out of loyalty to Rockingham but at pique over losing the Exchequer. (See his letter to his wife, 30 July 1766, Sir Henry Cavendish's *Debates of the House of Commons during the Thirteenth Parliament of Great Britain* (2 Vols, 1841), Vol. I, pp. 579–80.) For Rockingham's relief at his men being allowed to remain in office see his letter to Newcastle, 17 July 1766 (B.M. Add. MSS 32976, ff. 161–2, Newcastle Papers).

CHAPTER 8

[1] Albemarle to Rockingham, 29 August 1766, RI–682 Wentworth Woodhouse MSS, Albemarle, Vol. II, p. 13.

[2] Rockingham to Newcastle, 29 August 1766, B.M. Add. MSS 32976, ff. 488–9, Newcastle Papers.

[3] J. Brewer, 'The Misfortunes of Lord Bute', p. 17.

[4] Newcastle to Rockingham, 9 November 1766, RI–702 and enclosure, Wentworth Woodhouse MSS.

[5] Rockingham attended a meeting of peers at Grafton's home. See Grafton to George III, 11 November 1766, Fortescue, Vol. I, pp. 411–12 for a full list. Newcastle is not included in it.

[6] Burke to O'Hara, 19 August 1766, *Burke Correspondence*, Vol. I, p. 265. Grafton remarked that 'his mistrust of the friends of the Duke of Newcastle was greater than could be conceived' (*Grafton Autobiography*, p. 103).

[7] The earldom was Grafton's own idea. Chatham would not have been so solicitous. Grafton's important letter to Pitt of 9 October has been seriously truncated by the editors of the *Chatham Correspondence* (Vol. III, p. 100). This important passage has been omitted. 'I hope I have not gone too far in my letter to Ld Monson: I understand that to him there was not to be an offer of exchange from the place to an Earldom, but that I was to acquaint him that for the King's service it was necessary that his Place should be opened, that to prove it arose from no disregard, *I had reason to think* a rise in the Peerage would be granted if desired by his Lordship. To this effect I wrote and am uneasy from an apprehension in your note least I have gone too far by so doing.' Chatham Papers.

[8] Grafton himself was uneasy at the language. (See his letter to Monson, 9 October 1766, B.M. Add. MSS 32977, f. 198, Newcastle Papers.)

[9] Rockingham to Scarborough, 20 November 1766, RI–709, Wentworth Woodhouse MSS, Albemarle, Vol. II, pp. 19–24.

[10] *Grafton Autobiography*, pp. 99–102, Jucker, op. cit., p. 429; *Grenville Papers*, Vol. III, pp. 302–10, 377–8.

[11] J. Brooke, *The Chatham Administration*, pp. 38–42.

[12] Conway to Chatham, 22 November 1766, *Chatham Correspondence*, Vol. III, pp. 126–7; Grenville to Temple, 21 November 1766, *Grenville Papers*, Vol. III, pp. 344; *Grafton Autobiography*, p. 103; Rockingham to Newcastle, 18 November 1766, B.M. Add. MSS 32977, f. 416, Newcastle Papers.

[13] See, for example, Hardwicke to Rockingham, 20 November 1766, RI–710, Wentworth Woodhouse MSS.

[14] The meeting of 19 November is fully reported in J. Brooke, op. cit., pp. 55–6. (See also Rockingham to Scarborough, 20 November 1766, RI–709, Wentworth Woodhouse MSS, Albemarle, Vol. II, pp. 19–23.) The views of Newcastle were pessimistic and gloomy. He disapproved of the plan and did not think that many of their friends would leave their offices over the Edgecumbe affair. Even if they did, Newcastle doubted if Conway

would join them. Even if he did, Newcastle thought that the ministry would be strengthened by the Bedfords, Grenvilles and Buteites and not by the Rockinghams. (See Newcastle's 'Short Narrative', B.M. Add. MSS 32978, f. 18, Newcastle Papers.)

[15] Portland to Newcastle, 21 November 1766, ibid., 32978, ff. 11–12.

[16] Rockingham to Charles Yorke, 27 November 1766, Albemarle, Vol. II, pp. 25–6. Charles Yorke was almost as unhappy in opposition as he had been in office. He would have served in the Chatham ministry only if Northington had remained on the Woolsack. The King offered him Common Pleas but without a peerage. This was far from adequate to satisfy Yorke. (Charles Yorke to Lord Hardwicke, 29 July 1766, B.M. Add. MSS 32976, f. 323, Newcastle Papers.) During the autumn of 1766 Yorke was inactive in Opposition and it was only with the East India Company issue of the session of 1767 that Yorke returned to political life.

[17] *See* Chapter 9.

[18] *The Chatham Administration*, pp. 61–2.

[19] Burke to O'Hara, 27 November 1766, *Burke Correspondence*, Vol. I, pp. 280–1; Horace Walpole to Grafton, 25 November 1766, Grafton MSS; Conway to Portland, 26 November 1766, Portland MSS. Onslow to Newcastle, 26 November 1766, B.M. Add. MSS 32978, f. 86, Newcastle Papers.

[20] D. Watson, *The Duke of Newcastle*, p. 467.

[21] 'All the Rockingham party, and most of the Bute party, voted with the majority' (*Grenville Papers*, Vol. III, p. 395). *See also* Conway's letter to the King, 5 December 1766 (Fortescue, Vol. I, p. 422), 'Ld Rockingham's friends in the majority.'

[22] Grafton was fully aware of the dangers of precisely this way of proceeding and was as gracious towards the Bedfords as the situation would allow him to be. (Grafton to Bedford, 17 December 1766, Woburn MSS LIV, f. 180.)

[23] The King to Chatham, 2 December 1766, Fortescue, Vol. I, p. 420 and *Chatham Correspondence*, Vol. III, p. 137. See also the King's letter to Chatham of 28 November 1766 where George III is confident 'that my administration follow strenuously my example in opposing factious bands, in whatever quarters they appear though willing to receive able and good men, let their private friendships be where they will' (Fortescue, Vol. I, pp. 417–18 and *Chatham Correspondence*, Vol. III, p. 134).

[24] Bedford to the Duke of Marlborough, 29 November 1766, *Bedford Correspondence*, Vol. III, pp. 355–6.

[25] J. Brooke, op. cit., p. 83.

[26] Rockingham thought that 'making Mr Grenville *Minister*, would be the most inconsistent Act for us, that could be thought of, & that of Course we—who were determined to Act consistently, would never join in such a Plan. That our Credit had rose with the Publick by opposing Mr G. [*sic*] measures—when he was *Minister*—& that we had confirmed our Credit—by reversing his Measures when we were in administration.'

(Rockingham to Dowdeswell, 8 January 1767, RI–743, Wentworth Wood-house MSS, printed Albemarle, Vol. II, p. 32.)

[27] 'If you seek their connection and desire their assistance *in general*, will it not shew an anxiety of acquiring power at any rate? Will it not make them rise in their demands? Will it not authorise them to prescribe the terms? And in case of failure will it not give your enemies a pretence, and the impartial world some ground to suppose that that uprightness and disinterestedness to which you owe your great credit had been warped by an eagerness after power and emoluments.' (Portland to Newcastle, 17 December 1766, B.M. Add. MSS 32978, f. 478, *q*. J. Brooke, op. cit., p. 86.)

[28] Lord Bessborough to Newcastle, 12 December 1766, ibid., f. 282.

[29] Newcastle to Portland, 14 December 1766, Portland MSS. *See also* Rockingham to Portland 4 December 1766 (ibid.). 'Every day, more and more—Ld Chatham's Union & dependence on Ld Bute will appear & I should hope will occasion Some of our Friends now in Office to re-consider The Propriety of their remaining.'

[30] 'Is not the present Court System built on the ruins of his, and where would you lay the foundation of his, but on the ruins of theirs. All these considerations satisfye me, that their turn never can be the next, whilst any party, of not more strength, and more practicability, may be found; and it may, very easily. I look therefore upon our Cause, viewed on the side of power, to be, for some years at least, quite desperate; from the difficulty, not to say impossibility, of its coaliting with any body in or out of possession.' (Burke to O'Hara, 15 January 1767, *Burke Correspondence*, Vol. I, pp. 290–2.)

[31] Lord to Lady Rockingham, 18 April 1767, R. 144–1, Wentworth Woodhouse MSS.

[32] Lord George Sackville to General Irwin, 9 December 1766 (*H.M.C. Stopford-Sackville*, Vol. I, pp. 114–17). There is also an interesting account of the debate in George Grenville's letter to the Earl of Buckinghamshire, 22 November 1766 (*H.M.C. Lothian*, pp. 272–4).

[33] Ibid.

[34] Chatham to Charles Townshend, 2 January 1767, *Chatham Corre-spondence*, Vol. III, pp. 153–4.

[35] For Townshend's holdings of Indian stock see L. B. Namier and J. Brooke, *Charles Townshend*, pp. 161–2.

[36] 8 March 1767, B.M. Add. MSS 32980, f. 228, Newcastle Papers. Chatham was so angry at Townshend's behaviour that he left for Bath where he remained for several months. His unsuccessful attempt to replace Townshend with Lord North is described in *Grafton Autobiography* (p. 123) and *Grenville Papers* (Vol. IV, pp. 213–14).

[37] *Ryder Debates*, p. 334.

[38] Burke to Charles O'Hara, 30 and 31 March 1767, *Burke Correspondence*, Vol. I, pp. 302–4. This was by no means the first expression of this attitude among the Rockingham Whigs (see, for example, Newcastle to Rockingham, 9 December 1766, B.M. Add. MSS 32978, f. 241, Newcastle Papers). But

the Rockinghams were preoccupied with the Edgecumbe affair and its consequences until and after the end of 1766. It was the passing of time and the constant publicity given to Indian affairs, and especially the alleged abuses in the Indian system of government, which opened the eyes of the Rockinghamites to the political dangers of Indian patronage.

³⁹ *Ryder Debates*, pp. 338–40.

⁴⁰ For the Dividends bill see the account in J. Brooke, op. cit., pp. 132–4. *See* also L. B. Namier and J. Brooke, op. cit., pp. 169–72. The increase in the dividend was the work of the party in the Company led by Laurence Sulivan ('the Opposition') who had close contacts wtih the Rockinghams, George Dempster, Lord Verney and William Burke. The increase represented a defeat for the ministerial interest there led by Shelburne. (See A. L. Humphrey, 'Lord Shelburne and East India Company Politics, 1766–9', *English Historical Review*, **XLIX**, 1934.) The Rockinghams 'often planned their parliamentary activities in collaboration with the Sulivan party'. (L. Sutherland, *The East India Company in Eighteenth Century Politics* (Oxford, 1952), p. 155.) For the (limited) extent of the investment of the Rockingham Whigs *see* L. S. Sutherland and J. Woods, 'The East India Speculations of William Burke,' *Proceedings of the Leeds Philosophical and Literary Society*, **XI**, Pt. VII (1966).

⁴¹ Newcastle to Mansfield, 28 May 1767, B.M. Add. MSS 32982, ff. 248–9, Newcastle Papers; Rockingham to Newcastle, 11 June 1767, ibid., ff. 301–2. There is a draft of a Protest against the Dividends Bill in the Wentworth Woodhouse MSS, RI–802.

⁴² *See* Whately to Grenville, 20 October 1766, *Grenville Papers*, Vol. III, pp. 331–6 for a somewhat unenthusiastic airing of the idea.

⁴³ Burke was against the scheme and left the meeting (*Burke Correspondence,* Vol. I, p. 296, n. 1). Charles Yorke thoroughly disliked the factiousness of the plan and would not even attend the meeting. (Charles Yorke to Lord Hardwicke, 11 February 1766, B.M. Add. MSS 35362, ff. 63–4, Hardwicke Papers, *q.* Brooke, op. cit., p. 105.) The eminent Savile was loftily against the proposal, too. (*See* his letter to Rockingham, January 1767 (probably *post* 11 February) RI–747, Wentworth Woodhouse MSS.)

⁴⁴ Rockingham to Newcastle, 21 February 1767, B.M. Add. MSS 32980, ff. 188–9, Newcastle Papers, *q.* Brooke, op. cit., p. 106.

⁴⁵ Ibid., Newcastle to Portland, 22 February 1767, Portland MSS. Had the Rockinghams not moved for a reduction, George Grenville certainly would.

⁴⁶ There are few detailed accounts of this debate. That of Horace Walpole is the longest (*Memoirs*, Vol. II, pp. 421–4) but there are also accounts in *Ryder Debates* (pp. 332–3) and Newdigate MSS (B. 2547). The letters of Lord Belayse to Lord Fauconberg of 28 February and 2 March (Fauconberg MSS) provide additional detail.

⁴⁷ Burke to O'Hara, 28 February 1767, *Burke Correspondence*, Vol. I, pp. 296–7; *see also* the rather similar comment of Grafton in his report to Chatham of 28 February, *Chatham Correspondence*, Vol. III, p. 224. 'The

Bedfords, Grenvilles, Rockinghams, and Newcastles united with most others, who had county or popular elections.'

[48] Burke to O'Hara, 28 February 1767, loc. cit.

[49] Horace Walpole to Sir Horace Mann, 2 March 1767, *Correspondence of Horace Walpole*, Vol. XXII, p. 489; 8 March 1767, ibid., p. 494.

[50] The Mutiny Act of 1765 was now found to be scarcely less odious than the Stamp Act had been a year earlier. The act required the colonists to provide certain supplies for troops, especially food, salt and bedding. The act was tantamount to a concealed form of taxation in the view of the colonial radicals, violating their precepts of 'No Taxation without representation'. This running sore was exacerbated by resolutions which accompanied the repeal, largely ignored by Parliament, but soon found to be distasteful to the colonists. These required those who had suffered loss or damage to property in the Stamp Act agitation to be compensated, an obligation which Conway laid upon the colonial assemblies in June 1766. This revival of bitter memories together with its implications of further financial demands was an irritant to the colonists.

[51] Robert J. Chaffin, 'The Townshend Acts of 1767', *William and Mary Quarterly*, 3rd series, xxvii, p. 90, n. 3.

[52] Shelburne was not noticeably 'liberal' in his ideas. It is worth citing a few lines of his letter to Chatham of 16 February 1767, omitted from the badly mauled version in the *Chatham Correspondence* (Vol. II, p. 206). Of the Quartering Act he wrote: 'I see no way of enforcement, excepting giving the Governor Power, in case the Assemblys refuse to provide the Troops as was the first intention of the Act, then to billet, *on Private Houses as was the practice during the War*'. For an extended discussion of the extent to which Shelburne was willing to go to enforce the Quartering Act, *see* Chaffin (op. cit., pp. 103–4).

[53] In June 1766 the New York assembly refused to obey the Mutiny Act. This was perhaps to have been expected. New York was the headquarters of the British Army in America and the enforcement of the act there would undoubtedly have been a heavy burden upon the citizens. But when Georgia and South Carolina followed the example of New York it was clear that an explosive situation was developing. Although the colonial assemblies in the end decided to comply with the law they did so grudgingly and inadequately, much to the annoyance of British public opinion. That opinion was even more sorely tested when in December 1766 the Massachusetts assembly voted an indemnity for offences committed during the agitation against the Stamp Act. Even worse, in January 1767 250 New York merchants petitioned parliament against those bulwarks of the imperial system, the Navigation acts. Those who had prophesied that the repeal of the Stamp Act would, far from pacifying the colonists, only induce them to take more drastic measures, had been proved right.

[54] The best account of this crucial exchange is in the Newdigate MSS, B. 2548/3. Townshend 'pledged himself that something should be done this Session towards creating a revenue to bear the burden . . . that he did not mean a revenue adequate but pledged that he would do everything

to form a revenue in time to bear the whole'. The only implication which can be placed upon Townshend's remarks is that, sooner or later, the colonists would be required to pay the whole cost of imperial defence which amounted to over £750,000. George Grenville commented in his letter to the Earl of Buckinghamshire on 27 January 1767 that Townshend 'held a very strong language that America ought to pay that expense, and disclaim'd in very strong terms almost every word of Lord Chatham's language on this subject, treating his Lordship's distinction between *Internal and External* Taxes with the same contempt that I did, and calling it *absurd, nonsensical* and ridiculous to the highest degree . . .' (*H.M.C. Lothian*, p. 275). This letter requires that Brooke's argument that no one present caught the significance of Townshend's remark be modified (see *The Chatham Administration*, p. 94).

[55] The most recent and most authoritative such interpretation is that of P. D. G. Thomas, 'Charles Townshend and American Taxation', *English Historical Review*, **LXXXIII** (1968).

[56] Chaffin, op. cit., pp. 91–7. The author argues, I think convincingly, that the actions of Grafton and Townshend since the beginning of the Chatham ministry require a revision of traditional interpretations of the Chatham ministry's policy towards America. The following should be stressed:

(*a*) Starting in September Grafton began to collect information not only on the raising of quitrents but the whole question of colonial finance, presumably as a first step towards devising new measures of taxation.

(*b*) About the same time, a tightening up in the enforcement of the Navigation acts was set on foot.

(*c*) Shelburne did not criticise these manifestations of a 'harsh' American policy and, indeed, expressed much interest in it. He even agreed with the idea of raising of a revenue to fund the Civil List in each colony. Clearly, Shelburne's authoritarian belief in the military enforcement of the Declaratory Act antedates his expression of his belief in his letter to Chatham of 1 February 1767 (*Chatham Correspondence*, Vol. III, pp. 182–8). Furthermore, it should be noted, Chatham's defence of the Americans during the repeal debates, was conditional upon their continuing obedience to Great Britain.

[57] *Ryder Debates*, pp. 330–1; Conway to George III, 18 February 1767, Fortescue, Vol. I, p. 453.

[58] It was not until 26 April, however, that the ministry reached a final decision, accepting Townshend's Civil List proposals while rejecting the (equally illiberal) suggestions of Shelburne for 'a military governorship and billeting in private houses' and Conway's 'local extraordinary port duty' on New York (R. J. Chaffin, op. cit., pp. 104–5). Included in the Townshend plan, however, were provisions to tighten up customs checks and to suspend the legislative functions of the New York assembly until it complied with the Quartering Act (see F. Wickwire, op. cit., pp. 125–30). Chaffin's ingenious account suggests that Grafton began at this point to obstruct Townshend's plan for America—especially his wish to punish New York and reform the customs by establishing a Board of Commissioners.

Having come so far, but not wishing to proceed without ministerial approval, Townshend hesitated until on 8 May his 'champagne' speech attacked his colleagues and 'seemed to recommend the Rockinghamites for ministers with himself at their head' (ibid., p. 114). Townshend professed his wish to see 'a long and permanent administration of people of rank, ability and integrity and experience, particularly of those who had been formerly in office'. (James West to Newcastle, 8 May 1767, B.M. Add. MSS 32981, f. 323, Newcastle Papers.) Thus he was able to brush aside the protests of Grafton.

[59] Dowdeswell even proposed extending the Mutiny Act enabling the civil authorities to billet on private homes (*Grafton Autobiography*, pp. 176–7). The Rockinghams *did* have a constitutional ground for attacking the ministry's proposals for dealing with New York in that the suspension of the colony's constitution (which was what the disabling the Governor to assent to the assembly's resolutions amounted to) was illegal. (See Rockingham to Charles Yorke, 3 May 1767, B.M. Add. MSS 35430, ff. 73–4, Hardwicke Papers.) Nevertheless, they were less concerned with New York than with tirades against the influence of the Crown (*Grafton Autobiography*, pp. 176–8; *Ryder Debates*, pp. 342–7).

[60] There is a good deal to be said for this interpretation by Chaffin (op. cit., pp. 119–21). Townshend's plans for America *were* relatively moderate but I think Chaffin exaggerates when he asserts that 'the clique's proposals were more drastic than Townshend's proposals' (p. 121). The real criticism to be levelled against the Rockinghams was that they lacked a coherent plan for America. They were more interested in pleasing Townshend or Grenville than in providing a constructive alternative to the American policies of either.

[61] See Newcastle to Rockingham, 28 February 1767, B.M. Add. MSS 32980, f. 187, Newcastle Papers.

[62] See the thoughtful paper by D. Watson, 'The Rockingham Whigs and the Townshend Duties', *English Historical Review*, **LXXXIV** (1969), pp. 561–5.

[63] Newcastle, in particular, was closely in touch with Bedford, especially during the political crisis of May 1767. See, for example, his letters to Bedford of 23 and 29 May 1767 (Woburn MSS, LV, ff. 96, 104).

[64] As many contemporaries noticed: 'The different partys composing the Opposition are not likely to agree any further than in demolishing the present Minister, so that whether we shall soon see any plan of credit or stability established is beyond my understanding' (Lord George Sackville to General Irwin, 7 April 1767, *H.M.C. Stopford-Sackville*, Vol. I, p. 121). On 10 April in the Lords, for example, the combined forces of the Rockingham and Bedford Whigs might have run the ministry close on a question to set aside an act of the Massachusetts legislature granting amnesty for the culprits as well as compensation for the victims of the Stamp Act agitation. The ministry won 63–36 but Newcastle and nine others went away before the division. Rockingham and several friends voted *for* the ministry and against Bedford. (Newcastle to Princess Amelia, 11 April 1767; Newcastle

to Sir William Baker, B.M. Add. MSS 32981, ff. 125, 138, Newcastle Papers.) This is commentary enough upon the extent to which a union of the Opposition was realised.

⁶⁵ *Grenville Papers*, Vol. IV, pp. 220–1.

⁶⁶ Ibid., p. 215.

⁶⁷ See Rockingham's letters to his wife on 31 March and 3 April 1767 (R. 156–7, 10, Wentworth Woodhouse MSS). See also Newcastle to Albemarle, 27 and 29 March 1767 (B.M. Add. MSS 32980, ff. 359–9, 424, Newcastle Papers).

⁶⁸ For the details of what follows see J. Brooke, op. cit., pp. 142–7.

⁶⁹ Rockingham was ill during May and many of his duties were assumed by Richmond who was astoundingly assiduous at this juncture. See Richmond to Lady Rockingham, *n.d.* June 1767, Ramsden MSS.

⁷⁰ Indeed, since December 1766 but he finally decided to resign in May 1767, *Grafton Autobiography*, pp. 141–2, 176–8. The King was aware of his determination by late May. (George III to Chatham, 30 May 1767, Fortescue, Vol. I, pp. 480–1.) Had Conway resigned, Grafton certainly would have done, a factor which weighed heavily with the King. (See George III to Lord Hertford, 17 July 1767, Fortescue, Vol. I, pp. 499–500.) The session dragged on, it must have seemed endlessly for Grafton until the end of June as the House of Lords debated the Dividends bill.

⁷¹ For the King's growing impatience with Chatham see their exchanges of 13, 15, 17, 20 and 25 June 1767 (Fortescue, Vol. I, pp. 488–94); *see also* L. B. Namier, *Additions and Corrections* (pp. 78–9).

⁷² *Grafton Autobiography*, pp. 136–9.

⁷³ Fortescue, Vol. I, p. 495. Northington's paper of 28 May concerning the state of the ministry is probably an earlier version of that sent to the King (*Grafton Autobiography*, pp. 174–5). Grafton has never been given such modest credit as he deserves for fighting an heroic struggle in the defence of the monarchy during these weeks. During June he bestirred himself and beat off with little difficulty the Opposition's attacks in the Lords (winning divisions on 17 and 25 June on the East India dividends bill by 73–52 and 59–44, respectively). He must have seen the need for negotiations more clearly than anyone else. Unsuited to political responsibility he had suffered from Chatham's neglect more than anyone, found Conway determined to resign, Northington contemplating the same course of action, Charles Townshend threatening it unless the ministry were restructured and Camden and Shelburne cold and unfriendly to him. On the last day of the session (2 July) Grafton, in collusion with Northington, drafted a carefully worded letter to the King. They refused to bear the responsibility of creating a temporary ministry which would last only until the return of Chatham. In other words, they were saying to the King that Chatham ought to take the responsibility of strengthening the ministry himself, or else retreat from office. This could have been a *cri de coeur* from Grafton or a clever method of forcing the King to give his approval to the urgently needed negotiations. Furthermore, once the

King had decided to allow the negotiations to proceed Grafton lost no time in opening the discussions.

[74] Conway, furthermore, gave Rockingham to understand that Chatham would resign in the near future (Bateson, op. cit., p. 108). For the July negotiations I have relied heavily upon the account by J. Brooke (op. cit., pp. 162–217). On occasion I venture to differ from his great authority, however, in some matters touching the Rockinghams. On Rockingham's belief that the Treasury was to be vacant see J. Brooke, pp. 176–8. Grafton was always able to avoid being specific about the projected ministry by using the argument that he could not discuss particular offices until Rockingham presented him with a plan and this, of course, was what the Rockinghams found it difficult to achieve, in view of their need to maintain cordial relations with the Bedfords.

[75] Newcastle to Rockingham, 11 September 1767, RI–858, Wentworth Woodhouse MSS.

[76] Rockingham confided in Hardwicke his fear that 'we shall not be sufficiently strong to check the power we had reason to be attentive to' (2 July 1767, RI–876, Wentworth Woodhouse MSS, partly printed Albemarle, Vol. II, pp. 50–4).

[77] The Dowdeswell Memorandum is extensively discussed in J. Brooke, op. cit., pp. 213–16. I find less surprising than Mr Brooke the traditional elements in the Memorandum such as the acknowledgements that government is the King's and attach more significance to Dowdeswell's acceptance of a developing Rockinghamite framework of ideas.

[78] Rockingham lectured the King on this point on 22 July, a natural reflection of his abiding resentment at the mutiny of some office holders in 1766. (Rockingham to Hardwicke, 26 July, loc. cit.)

[79] Rockingham to Dowdeswell, 9 September 1767, RI–857, Wentworth Woodhouse MSS. There is a very similar letter to Portland in the Portland MSS of 15 September (printed Albemarle, Vol. II, pp. 57–9 misdated 17 September).

[80] Rockingham to Dowdeswell, 20 October 1767, Dowdeswell MSS. This line of proceeding is strikingly similar to that professed by Newcastle in his unfamiliar opposition late in 1762. The Duke professed 'Those Measures, upon which I have ever *acted*; & . . . The same System both at Home & Abroad, which I have been brought up in, & from which Nothing can divert me'. (Newcastle to Stone, 15 October 1762, B.M. Add. MSS 32943, ff. 224–31, Newcastle Papers.)

[81] Rockingham to Hardwicke, 26 July 1767, loc. cit. It is worth remarking here that the Dowdeswell Memorandum continues the depersonalisation of the Bute Myth and the transition from the myth of Lord Bute to that of Secret Influence. According to the Memorandum, when Rockingham obtains the King's ear, George III will be told that public misfortunes 'must be imputed not to the influence of particular persons but to the prevalence of a political principle which says that the power of the Crown arises out of the Weakness of the administration'.

⁸² Burke to Rockingham, 1 August 1767, *Burke Correspondence*, Vol. I, pp. 316–18. It will be apparent that Burke occupied a lowly place in Rockingham's counsels at this time. (Dowdeswell and not he wrote the Memorandum!) Burke, in fact, speaks of his own 'humble Situation' in a letter to John Hely Hutchinson on 3 August (ibid., pp. 318–20).

⁸³ Rockingham to Dowdeswell, 9 September 1767, RI–857, Wentworth Woodhouse MSS. Newcastle, however, kept up his contacts with the Bedfords and tried to impress them with the Rockinghams' good intentions. (See Newcastle to Bedford, 2 October 1767, Woburn MSS LVI, f. 92.) These had little effect upon the Bedfords and, in particular, did not remove their conviction that in their dealings with the Rockinghams they had always been 'tractable and reasonable', and that it was up to the Rockinghams to make some proposals and to take the initiative in securing their mutual co-operation. (Rigby to Bedford, 12 October 1767, ibid., f. 124.)

⁸⁴ Rockingham simply was not sure of the Bedfords. Albemarle visited Woburn on 3 October where he found Bedford 'not pressing for any direct declarations or entering into arrangements'. (Rockingham to Dowdeswell, 9 November 1767, RI–869, Wentworth Woodhouse MSS.) Rockingham might well have taken this as a rebuff, especially in view of Bedford's avowed intention of seeing Grenville before Parliament met. My interpretation here is slightly but significantly different to that of Mr Brooke (op. cit., pp. 316–17). At the same time, Rockingham was angry with Grafton. The death of Charles Townshend in September had not led to an offer of the vacant Exchequer to the Rockinghams but to Lord North, who accepted it.

⁸⁵ For Rockingham's increasingly hostile attitude to Conway see his letter to Dowdeswell of 9 November, loc. cit.

⁸⁶ Why did Grenville do it? According to Bedford, he was insulted by a remark made by Rockingham at Newmarket, that he would never co-operate with Grenville in anything. (B.M. Add. MSS 32931, ff. 289–92, Newcastle Papers; *Grenville Papers*, Vol. IV, pp. 234–5.) Burke gives an interesting account of the debate in his letter to Charles O'Hara, 27 November 1767 (*Burke Correspondence*, Vol. I, pp. 335–7). Newcastle made a last ditch attempt to repair the damage by going to see Bedford on 26 November, but it was now too late and nothing came of the interview. (Newcastle to Hardwicke, 26 November 1767, B.M. Add. MSS 32987, f. 123, Newcastle Papers.)

⁸⁷ Camden rudely refused to attend the reading of the Speech. (Camden to Grafton, 23 November 1767, Grafton MSS; see also *Grafton Autobiography*, p. 172.)

⁸⁸ The division of Shelburne's Secretaryship might have provoked him to resign, something which George III would gladly have welcomed. (Lord Despencer to Grafton, 14 November 1767, B.M. Egerton MSS 2136, ff. 107, 108, Dashwood MSS.) Grafton, however, intentionally or not, handled Shelburne with such skill and diplomatic finesse that the latter's resignation was not forthcoming. (See Shelburne's own account in

Fitzmaurice, Vol. I, pp. 327–9; Shelburne to Lady Chatham, 13 December 1767, *Chatham Correspondence*, Vol. III, pp. 292–8.) Conway was to keep his Secretaryship until the new year so that it would not look as though he were turned out (*Grenville Papers*, Vol. IV, p. 206). This was not all. Marlborough was promised a Garter and Thomas Brand a peerage. Lord Charles Spencer took an Admiralty post and Henry Thynne a Household appointment. (Horace Walpole, *Memoirs*, Vol. III, p. 100; Onslow to Newcastle, 21 December 1767, B.M. Add. MSS 32987, f. 384, Newcastle Papers.)

[89] *Grafton Autobiography*, p. 183.

[90] Ibid; Grafton to George III, 22 December 1767, Fortescue, Vol. I, pp. 511–12. Several observers commented upon Grafton's dexterity and the fact that he had successfully managed the negotiations alone. (A. Forrester to R. A. Neville, 22 December 1767, Braybrooke Papers, D/DBy. C.3/3; Lord George Sackville to General Irwin, 25 December 1767, *H.M.C. Stopford-Sackville*, Vol. I, p. 125; T. Whately to G. Grenville, 1 January 1768, *Grenville Papers*, Vol. IV, pp. 241–2.)

[91] Rockingham to Richmond, 14 December 1767, R. 9–8 (Copy in Lady Rockingham's hand), Wentworth Woodhouse MSS.

[92] Newcastle to Rockingham, 21 December 1767, RI–919, ibid.

[93] Suspicion of Bute's abiding influence was surprisingly widespread and affected even Junius (see *Grenville Papers*, Vol. IV, p. 239). Lord George Sackville commented in his letter to General Irwin of 25 December (loc. cit.) that unless Grafton takes Bute into account 'his arrangement will not be very permanent'.

[94] The Bedfords, of course, had of necessity to oppose the Dividends bill as they had done in the previous session. To have changed their course so blatantly and so soon after coming into office would have undermined their reputation. Grafton was anxious to minimise his difficulties with the bill in the Lords and himself sent out attendance notes. (Grafton to Despencer, 28 January 1768, B.M. Egerton MSS 2136, f. 115, Dashwood MSS.)

[95] Portland estimated the number of tenants involved at between 300 and 400. (Portland to Charles Yorke, 17 February 1768, B.M. Add. MSS 35638, f. 228, Hardwicke Papers.)

[96] Rockingham to Albemarle, 23 February 1768, H.A. 67. 461/203, Albemarle MSS.

[97] Ibid.; *The Parliamentary History*, **XVI**, pp. 410–11. For the preparations for the debate see Rockingham to Charles Yorke, 21 January 1768 (B.M. Add. MSS 35430, ff. 101–4, Hardwicke Papers), and Rockingham to Portland, 20 January 1768 (Portland MSS).

[98] Grafton to Chatham, 21 January 1768, *Chatham Correspondence*, Vol. III, pp. 311–13. There is a similar letter from Camden on 22 January (ibid., pp. 314–16).

[99] George III to Chatham, 23 January 1768, ibid., p. 318.

CHAPTER 9

[1] *The Chatham Administration*, p. 282.

[2] See the Appendix.

[3] Sir E. Simpson (May 1764), J. Hervey (July 1764), H. B. Legge (August 1764) and W. Willy, in May 1765.

[4] Lord H. Powlett (July 1765), Lord Middleton (August 1765), A. Wilkinson (September 1765), T. L. Dummer (October 1765), C. Hanbury (December 1765), T. Watson (December 1765), Sir G. Metham (March 1766) and W. Woodley (July 1766).

[5] C. Barrow (close to Dowdeswell), Edmund Burke (Rockingham's Secretary), Dowdeswell himself (who was not quite of the Rockingham party before he became Chancellor of the Exchequer in July 1765), T. Connolly (through his connection with Richmond), Augustus and William Keppel and Sir S. Cornish (close to Sir Charles Saunders, attached through Cumberland's influence). The Rockingham ministry was almost certainly the time and occasion for the following to become attached to the party. Sir W. Codrington, G. Dempster, H. Harbord, Lord G. Lennox, F. Montagu, Lord Verney and W. Weddell.

[6] Those who left Parliament were J. Butler and T. Sergison (December 1766), J. Thomlinson (February 1767), B. Fisher had already detached himself from the Rockinghams before he left Parliament in May 1767. The six new supporters were Lord Edward Bentinck (December 1766), F. W. Osbaldeston (November 1766), James West Junior (June 1767), William Baker had become 'active' early in the life of the Chatham ministry. It is almost impossible to place a precise date upon Aubrey Beauclerk's adherence to the Rockinghams. Lord Downe's attachment dates from the spring of 1767.

[7] The eighteen are as follows: A. Archer, A. A'Court, Sir K. Clayton, J. Dodd, B. Forester, Richard Fuller, Sir John Mellish, A. Nesbitt, T. Noel, J. Page, H. Powell, R. Praed, J. Scudamore, T. Tracy, G. Tufnell, G. V. Vernon, Sir E. Walpole, W. Whitmore.

[8]
Sir W. Ashburnham*	T. Fitzmaurice	J. Roberts*
Sir J. Barrington*	C. Fitzroy	T. Robinson
Sir P. Brett	J. Fitzwilliam	C. F. Scudamore*
Sir H. Bridgeman	Rose Fuller	F. W. Sharpe
G. B. Brudenell*	Lord Gage*	J. Shelley*
J. Buller*	Sir J. Gibbons	(Spanish)
J. Bullock	Sir A. Gilmour*	Charles Townshend*
P. Burrell	G. Hunt	T. Townshend Jnr*
B. Burton	G. Jennings	T. Townshend Snr*
R. Burton	H. Meynell	Lord Villiers*
J. Calvert	G. Onslow*	H. Walpole
N. Calvert	Col. G. Onslow*	T. Walpole
H. S. Conway*	T. Pelham*	Sir G. Warren
W. Fitzherbert*	H. Penton	Sir G. Yonge

* Office-holders.

[9] *The Chatham Administration*, p. 243.

[10] Sir A. Abdy
W. A'Court
G. Adams
T. Anson
A. Archer
Sir G. Armytage
G. Aufrere
Sir W. Baker
A. Beauclerk
J. Bentinck
Lord E. Bentinck
Sir B. Bridges
E. Burke
W. Burke
B. Burton
Lord F. Cavendish
Lord G. Cavendish
Lord J. Cavendish
R. Cavendish
N. Cholmly
Sir W. Codrington
W. Coke
T. Connoly
H. Curwen
G. Dempster
W. Dowdeswell

Sir M. Fetherstone-
haugh
S. Finch
B. Forester
C. Forester
R. Fuller
Lord Grey
C. Hanbury
H. Harbord
Sir G. Heathcote
J. Hewett
P. Honywood
A. Keppel
Gen. Keppel
L. Lawrence
Lord G. Lennox
J. Luther
Sir W. Meredith
Lord Mexborough
R. Milles
G. Monson
F. Montague
C. Morgan
J. Morgan
T. Morgan
Sir R. Mostyn

J. Murray
T. Noel
J. Norris
F. W. Osbaldeston
J. Page
R. Pennant
H. Penton
W. Plumer
J. Plumptre
Sir C. Saunders
Sir G. Savile
J. Scawen
T. Tracy
G. Tuffnell
Lord Verney
G. Vernon
R. Walsingham
W. Weddell
J. West
J. White
J. Whitehead
W. Whitmore
Lord Winterton
C. Yorke
J. Yorke

[11] H. Crabb Boulton
J. Bullock
Sir K. Clayton
W. Clayton
Sir S. Cornish
T. Dummer

G. Hunt
Sir R. Ladbroke
R. Lloyd
T. Medlicot
J. Nesbitt

J. Offley
J. Scudamore
Sir W. Stanhope
H. Thrale
P. O. Wyndham

[12] W. Aislabie*
I. Barré
Sir W. Beauchamp
N. Calvert
Sir G. Colebrooke*
* Office-holder.

P. Dennis
W. Ellis
G. Jennings*
J. Mellish*
J. Offley

Lord Pigot
T. Pownall
R. Stevens*
F. Vane*

[13] C. Barrow*
E. Bouverie*
T. Cholmondeley
* Office-holders.

Sir E. Dering*
S. Egerton*
S. Eyre

P. Rashleigh
J. Tuckfield

[14] T. Coventry   I. Rebow   Sir F. Norton   A. Wedderburn
[15] Sir F. Basset   J. Dodd

[16] *Members of the Rockingham Party on the Eve of the Election of 1768:**

Sir A. Abdy	C		S. Finch	R
W. A'Court			Lord Grey	P
G. Adams			*H. Harbord*	
T. Anson			J. Hewett	
Sir G. Armytage	R		*A. Keppel*	A
Sir W. Baker	N		*W. Keppel*	A
C. Barrow			*Lord G. Lennox*	Rich
A. Beauclerk			Sir W. Meredith	R
Lord E. Bentinck	P		*F. Montagu*	R
J. Bentinck	P		J. Murray	
E. Burke	V		J. Norris	N
W. Burke	V		J. Offley	N
Lord F. Cavendish	C		*F. W. Osbaldeston*	R
Lord G. Cavendish	C		W. Plumer	
Lord J. Cavendish	C		J. Plumptre	
R. Cavendish	C		Sir C. Saunders	A
N. Cholmley	R		Sir G. Savile	R
Sir W. Codrington			J. Scawen	
W. Coke			*Lord Verney*	V
Sir G. Colebrook			R. Walsingham	C
T. Connoly	Rich		*W. Weddell*	R
Sir S. Cornish	A		J. West	N
H. Curwen	P		*J. West Jnr*	N
G. Dempster	R		J. White	N
W. Dowdeswell			Lord Winterton	N
Lord Downe	R		C. Yorke	Y
Sir M. Fetherstonehaugh			J. Yorke	Y

R = Rockingham   P = Portland   Rich = Richmond
N = Newcastle   A = Albemarle   Y = Yorke
C = Cavendish   V = Verney

* New members since 1764 appear in italics.
My estimate is slightly higher than that of J. Brooke, op. cit., pp. 275–91.
I place Lord Winterton and Robert Walsingham into the Newcastle and
Cavendish groups, respectively, and I add the Independents W. A'Court,
G. Adams and T. Anson.

[17] *The First Rockingham Ministry*, p. 275.

[18] There are traces of Rockingham's intervention in support of his
friends in Huntingdonshire, Liverpool and Perth Burghs. (W. Elliston to
Rockingham, December 1767, RI–895, Wentworth Woodhouse MSS; the
Duke of Manchester to Rockingham, December 1767, RI–898, ibid.; Sir
William Meredith to Rockingham, 21 November 1767, 22 November 1767,
RI–876, 879, ibid.; George Dempster to Rockingham, 7 January 1768,
RI–927.)

[19] I choose, fairly arbitrarily, to include from this time onwards, Charles
Turner, MP for York, as a Rockingham Whig, although his status is
admittedly ambiguous. He was a Whig of independent standing who had

refused to join the Rockingham Club of York and thus to run as a Rocking-hamite candidate enjoying subsidies from the Marquis. Turner believed that the Rockingham Club was unconstitutional because a peer stood at its head attempting to influence the return of Members of Parliament. Shortly after this election, however, Turner was acting as a Rockinghamite, accepting Rockingham's leadership of the Whig cause in the county and in the country. (See Rockingham to Turner, 21 February 1768 and *n.d.*, Draft, RI–983, Wentworth Woodhouse MSS; Lady Rockingham to Portland, 22 March 1768, R–158–123, ibid.)

[20] For details of the Lewes election, see J. Brooke, op. cit., pp. 344–7. Newcastle's party included J. Offley, J. Norris, J. West, T. Hay, W. Baker. This total of five represents a drop of two.

[21] Hartley to Portland, 14 March 1768; Lieutenant David Maitland to Portland, 1 April 1766, 7 September 1766, 2 October 1767, Portland MSS.

[22] There is a detailed factual summary of these events in B. Bonsall, *Sir James Lowther and Cumberland and Westmorland Elections, 1754–75* (Manchester University Press, 1960).

[23] Further, some London merchants approached Portland to urge him to oppose the interests of the unpopular Duke of Northumberland. Probably because he did not wish to over-extend his resources by an incursion into unfamiliar territory, Portland declined. (John Bindlay to Portland, 21 July and 20 August, 1765, Portland MSS.) At the 1768 Election Portland gave assistance outside his own boroughs. For *Coventry* see the letters of W. Robertson to Portland, 22, 28 and 30 November 1767, Portland MSS. For *Leicester* see G. Meredith to Portland, 22 June 1767, 28 July 1767, 3 August 1767, 10 September 1767, Portland MSS; George Grey to Portland, 30 July 1767, 7 April 1768, ibid. I estimate Portland's following at seven after the election. Fenwick's support had not yet revealed itself while Booth Grey cannot accurately be regarded as a Rockingham Whig in spite of Portland's assistance.

[24] Richmond to Lady Rockingham, 27 March 1768, Ramsden MSS.

[25] I think it is straining the evidence much too far to claim that there existed a relationship between the Rockingham Whigs and mercantile opinion. Dr Watson points out that twenty-three Lancaster merchants signed a letter in support of Lord John Cavendish but what is surely more important is that the majority of Lancaster merchants did not follow suit, Cavendish having to seek Rockingham's support and assistance to come in at York (D. Watson, op. cit., p. 539). It is, naturally, true that some Rockinghamites were merchants or had some mercantile connections, such as Sir William Meredith, but such men usually brought themselves in to Parliament and did not owe their seats to Rockinghamite intervention. In short, the Rockinghams had been unable to maintain that support of the mercantile community which they had enjoyed in 1765–6, although some individual members of the Rockingham party had their separate connections with trade and industry. (Charles Barrow, Sir William Codrington, Sir George Colebrooke, George Dempster and Henry Fletcher.)

[26] The nine who were not returned: G. Adams, Sir G. Armytage, Sir

W. Baker, J. Bentinck, R. Cavendish, W. Coke, J. West Jnr, J. White, Lord Winterton. The twelve new Members were: Sir E. Astley, W. Baker, G. Byng, Sir W. Clayton, R. H. Coxe, H. Fletcher, T. Hay, B. Hotham, Lord Ludlow, G. Musgrave, B. Thompson, and Charles Turner.

[27] Burke to O'Hara, 9 June 1768, *Burke Correspondence*, Vol. I, p. 353.

[28] Rockingham to Albemarle, 17 May 1768, Albemarle MSS.

[29] Savile to Hartley, 4 April 1768, D./EHy F. 83, Hartley MSS.

[30] For a discussion of these ideas, see A. S. Foord, op, cit., pp. 310–15.

[31] Mr Jarrett has reminded us against ascribing purely personal and political causes for this political instability. He relates it to the impact upon British society of 'the effects of the most cataclysmic war the country had ever fought' (*The Begetters of Revolution*, pp. 43–4).

[32] For the extent of belief in Bute's influence, see J. Brewer, op. cit., pp. 3–11.

[33] That the Rockingham Whigs, like everybody else, exaggerated the seriousness of Bute's influence does not allow us to conclude that there was no danger at all to the constitution in the 1760s. As we have seen, Bute was a powerful influence with the King, both before *and after* his resignation in April 1763. At the very least, it should be recognised that the uproar occasioned by Bute's alleged position in the politics of the time prevented the continuation of his friendship with the King and may thus have done something to protect the constitution.

[34] J. Brooke, *The Chatham Administration*, p. 220.

[35] *His Majesty's Opposition*, pp. 338ff.

CHAPTER 10

[1] Sir Edward Hawke was First Lord of the Admiralty from 1766 to 1771 and MP for Plymouth 1747–76. He was responsible for the great naval victory at Quiberon in 1759. A great sailor, Hawke never made a comparable reputation in politics.

[2] For rumours of general uncertainty see Rev. Parry to Lord Bathurst, n.d., May 1768, B.M. Loan 57/1 f. 81. Bathurst MSS; R. J. Phillimore, *Memorials and Correspondence of Lord Lyttleton*, ii, p. 749. For a report that Gower was to succeed Grafton, see Whately to Grenville, 4 June 1768, *Grenville Papers*, Vol. IV, p. 301.

[3] Rockingham to Dowdeswell, 11 August 1768, RI-1083, Wentworth Woodhouse MSS.

[4] *H.M.C. Stopford–Sackville*, Vol. I, p. 127. Grafton's attempt to force upon Shelburne the appointment of an Envoy Extraordinary at Naples was widely believed to presage Shelburne's resignation. (See the letters of Rigby to Bedford, 6 June 1768, 4 July 1768, Woburn MSS, LVII, ff. 70, 86.)

[5] For the general opinion among ministers see Barrington to Gage, 1 August 1768, H.A. 174/107, f. 87. Barrington Papers. For the attitude of

the press to America which was likewise hostile, see Hinkhouse (op. cit., pp. 141–2).

[6] Rockingham to Newcastle, 11 August 1768, B.M. Add. MSS 32990, ff. 405–7, Newcastle Papers; Burke to O'Hara, 1 September 1768, *Burke Correspondence*, Vol. II, pp. 13–15. See also the opposition press reaction against the dismissal of the deserving Amherst and the promotion of the destitute and sinister Botetort (J. Wade (Ed.), *The Letters of Junius* (2 vols, 1850), Vol. II, pp. 206–36).

[7] Rockingham to Newcastle, 13 June 1768, B.M. Add. MSS 32990, ff. 206–7, Newcastle Papers.

[8] Newcastle to Bessborough, 16 May 1768, ibid., f. 75. Rockingham's determination continued in spite of a friendly meeting between Burke and Whately. (T. Whately to Grenville, 4 June 1768, *Grenville Papers*, Vol. IV, pp. 299–305.)

[9] Dowdeswell to Rockingham, 14 August 1768, Dowdeswell Papers, partly q., J. Brooke, op. cit., pp. 369–73. It should not be overlooked that at this time Grenville was also re-examining his American ideas, it must be confessed, without changing his conclusions. See his letters to William Knox of 27 June, 15 and 28 July, 11 and 19 September and 9 October, Knox MSS, *H.M.C. Various*, Vol. VI, pp. 95–102.

[10] R 63–18, *n.d.*, Wentworth Woodhouse MSS; Rockingham to Joseph Harrison, 19 May 1769, RI–1186, ibid., printed Albemarle, Vol. II, pp. 78–81. Newcastle was strongly of the opinion that the ministry intended to use force to make the Americans submit. (Newcastle to Rockingham, 12 September 1768, B.M. Add. MSS 32991a, ff. 94–5, Newcastle Papers, 15 September, 1768, ibid., f. 101.) Portland agreed, and thought that the policy of ministers 'was extending the influence of the Crown by putting additional means of corruption into its hands'. (Portland to Newcastle, 8 October 1768, ibid., f. 211.)

[11] George III to Grafton, 15 and 22 September 1768, 5 October 1768, Fortescue, Vol. II, pp. 42–3, 46–7, 49–50; Weymouth to Grafton, 6 September 1768, Grafton MSS.

[12] George III to Chatham, 14 October 1768, Fortescue, Vol. II, p. 57; *Chatham Correspondence*, Vol. III, p. 343.

[13] Rigby wrote to Bedford on 13 October (Woburn MSS, LVII, f. 206) that Chatham told Camden that the reasons for his resignation were 'the bad state of his health and the little prospect he thinks he has of being able to return to business. He intreated the Chancellor not to think of quitting the King's Service and declaimed his strongest wishes for the support of the present ministry'.

[14] Rigby wrote to Bedford on 1 November (ibid., f. 212) that Bristol had Chatham's approval for accepting the appointment.

[15] At once Sandwich began to pursue Grafton in search of greater patronage. See the copy of his letter to Grafton of 24 October 1768, ibid., f. 194.

[16] *Cavendish Debates*, Vol. I, pp. 30–46; *Parliamentary History*, **XVI,**

pp. 466–74. There is also an account of the debate in Rigby's letter to
Bedford of 9 November 1768, Woburn MSS, LVII, f. 224.

[17] *Cavendish Debates*, Vol. I, pp. 52–61.

[18] Lord Suffolk to Portland, 17 November 1768, Portland MSS.

[19] *Chatham Correspondence*, Vol. III, p. 349 nI.

[20] Grenville to Lord Suffolk, 25 November 1768, *Grenville Correspondence*,
Vol. IV, pp. 398–9.

[21] Yet Rockingham did not as yet take the prospect too seriously. 'To
us indeed who are mighty indifferent about any of these Gentry these
events only afford matter of Entertainment'. (Lord to Lady Rockingham,
28 November 1768, R. 156–17, Wentworth Woodhouse MSS.)

[22] See Burke to Richard Burke Jnr., 14 January 1766, *Burke Correspondence*,
Vol. I, pp. 230–1.

[23] Wilkes returned to England in February and promptly wrote a letter
to George III begging his pardon. No reply was forthcoming. (J. Almon,
The Correspondence of . . . John Wilkes (5 Vols, 1805), Vol. iii, pp. 263–4.)

[24] His failure is puzzling. He was already something of a popular hero
and it does not quite meet the case to suggest that his poor performance
was a result of his late arrival on the scene. He appeared equally late at
Middlesex. Professor Christie (*Wilkes, Wyvill and Reform* (1961), p. 28)
suggests that Chatham's nominal leadership of the ministry may have
weakened Wilkes' chances. His other suggestion, that William Beckford,
a powerful and influential figure in the City was opposed to Wilkes, is
much more feasible.

[25] Since the canvass was so short, it is unlikely if Professor Christie's
explanation of this result ('excellent organisation of canvassing and the
transporting of voters', op. cit., p. 28) can be regarded as more than a
partial explanation. The most impressive aspect of the election was the
groundswell of popular feeling for Wilkes which inhibited Opposition and
which lent a carnival-like inevitability to his success.

[26] There is no doubt that ministers were under strong pressure from the
King to take action against Wilkes. The King wrote to North on 25 April
that 'the expulsion of Mr Wilkes appears to be very essential and must be
effected' (Fortescue, Vol. II, p. 21). The matter was already being discussed
as early as 3 April (*Grafton Autobiography*, p. 199). Many government
supporters wanted immediate action against Wilkes, including Barrington,
Sir Gilbert Elliot, Dyson and the Bedfords. (See the letters of J. West to
Newcastle, 14 and 16 May 1768, B.M. Add. MSS 32990, ff. 57, 63, Newcastle Papers.) Grafton and Camden were not happy at the idea of expelling
Wilkes from Parliament, but they were not able to suggest an alternative
method of dealing with him. (Rockingham to Newcastle, 12 April 1768,
ibid., 32989, ff. 321–3; Newcastle to Rockingham, 13 April 1768, ibid.,
ff. 329–30; *Grafton Autobiography*, pp. 199–201.) Gower, Weymouth, North
and Conway were strongly in favour of expulsion (George III to Grafton,
2 May 1768, Grafton MSS). Grafton was careful, however, to avoid
raising the Wilkes case in the short session of 1768.

[27] Sir John Fielding to Robert Wood, 28 March 1768, S.P. (Dom)

44/142, p. 103, cited G. Rude, *Wilkes and Liberty* (1962), p. 43. Sir John Fielding to Robert Wood, 5 April 1768, S.P. (Dom) 37/6.80/16, p. 233, et seq.

²⁸ Wilkite supporters distributed handbills—40,000 according to one account—begging people not 'to disturb the peace or molest any person . . .' (Rude, op. cit. p. 42).

²⁹ *The Annual Register*, 1769, p. 60.

³⁰ What precipitated the incident was the arrival of civilian reinforcements of the troops, something a London crowd would never tolerate. 'There was no firing till there were a great many people coming from London Bridge who were say'd to be soldiers and sailors together—that they had many of them sticks and had just turned into St George's Fields when the soldiers began to fire' (Evidence of Peter Goules, T.S. II. 920/3213). The management of 'law and order' by the Government should not be judged by this incident. The task of maintaining order fell on Weymouth, the Secretary of State and Barrington, Secretary at War. They worked harmoniously together. Barrington, in particular ensured, that the troops used were properly instructed. See 'Measures to be Taken by the Secretary of State with regard to the riots' (*n.d.*, Longleat MSS; Weymouth to Northumberland, 29 March 1768, P.R.O. S.P. (Dom) 44/142, f. 12). Although the King's attitude towards the rioters was characteristically stern it is doubtful if his opinions did more than confirm the attitudes of his ministers. (George III to Barrington, 28 March 1768, H.A. 174–11. Barrington MSS; George III to Weymouth, 29 March 1768, Longleat MSS 38 f. 1.q. J. H. Jesse, *Memoirs of the Life and Reign of George III* (2nd ed, 3 Vols, 1887), Vol. I, p. 426.)

³¹ Rude underestimates the significance of this aspect of the crowd's mentality. A bookseller, Mr Derbyshire, said, 'Mr Gillam told me he had orders from the ministry to fire upon the people, and that there must be some men killed, and that it was better to kill five and twenty today than to have an hundred to kill tomorrow' (Old Bailey Proceedings, 1768, 227, et seq).

³² It would be unwise to claim that this new force had any sort of ideological foundation. Ideas rarely went beyond the 'Wilkes and Liberty' level although there were some slogans directed against the ministry, Scotsmen in general and Bute in particular. Particular trades related the affair to their own interests. Thus the Coalheavers marched and shouted 'Wilkes and Liberty and coalheavers for ever'. There were a few reminiscences of No. 45, General Warrants and so on together with the expected smattering of resentment against the rich and privileged but scarcely enough to warrant E. P. Thompson's curious description of the Wilkite crowd as 'a transitional mob, on its way to becoming a self-conscious radical crowd (*The Making of the English Working Class*, 1968, p. 75).

³³ Burke to O'Hara, 11 April 1768, *Burke Correspondence*, Vol. I, p. 349; Richmond to Newcastle, 3 April 1768, B.M. Add. MSS 32989, f. 294, Newcastle Papers; Newcastle to Richmond, 4 April 1768, ibid., f. 299.

³⁴ Burke to O'Hara, 9 June 1768, *Burke Correspondence*, Vol. I, pp. 352–3.

³⁵ Rockingham to Newcastle, 1 May 1768, B.M. Add. MSS 32990, ff. 1–4, Newcastle Papers; 17 May 1768, RI–1058B Wentworth Woodhouse MSS.

³⁶ Wilkes also put his hands on and published a letter from Weymouth to his troops about riot prevention, but presented it in such a way that it appeared that the St George's Field Massacre had been long premeditated. (St James' Chronicle, 8 December 1768; B.M. Add. MSS 30883, f. 69; Wilkes MSS.) There can be no doubt at all that Wilkes was looking for trouble. He rejected peace feelers from the ministry in November (J. Almon, op. cit., Vol. III, pp. 293–5).

³⁷ The decision to expel was finally taken in the Cabinet in late January. There were powerful elements in the Cabinet which were not disposed to take strong measures against Wilkes. Camden was much distressed at the prospect of taking measures against him (P.R.O. 30/8/62, ff. 149–50; G. F. S. Elliot, *The Border Elliots*, pp. 407–8). Although Granby and Hawke were not the most influential of Cabinet Ministers they shared Camden's view (Lord Hertford to George III, 25 January 1769, Fortescue, Vol. II, p. 73; H. Walpole, *Memoirs*, Vol. III, p. 175). Conway's doubts were perhaps the most important of all. He had fastidiously refrained from being drawn during the debates in November 1768 on a petition submitted by Wilkes, outlining his grievances. (H. Walpole, *Memoirs*, Vol. III, p. 183; Harris to Hardwicke, 17 December 1768, B.M. Add. MSS. 35608, f. 309.) In such a situation, the attitude of the King was crucial. While Grafton was wavering, uncertain of his line, the King's stern attitude towards Wilkes helped to indicate where Grafton's duty might lie. The expulsion of Wilkes was 'a measure Whereon almost my crown depends' (George III to Lord Hertford, 27 January 1769, Fortescue, Vol. II, p. 75).

³⁸ An attempt had been made on 23 January to allow Wilkes the immunity granted by parliamentary privilege against imprisonment for seditious libel but it had been lost by 165–71. (Lord North to George III, misdated November 1768, Fortescue, Vol. II, p. 61. Lists of Speakers are appended, pp. 61–2. For the debate on 3/4 February 1769, see North's report to George III, ibid., pp. 79–80.)

³⁹ 10 February 1769, *Cavendish Debates*, Vol. I, pp. 226–7. Wilkes was returned again for Middlesex, this time without opposition, on 16 February only to be expelled from the Commons the following day. Then the Court produced Henry Lawes Luttrell, a poor candidate, who was already in Parliament! (He sat for the Cornish borough of Bossiney.) He had few metropolitan connections and the Court could hardly have made a worse choice. The third election was the famous victory won by Wilkes by 1143 votes to 296 on 13/14 April 1769. On 15 April the House declared Luttrell elected by 197–143. North reported the debate to George III in a letter of 16 April and listed the speakers. (Fortescue, Vol. II, pp. 89–90.) For George III's very real glee see his reply to North of the same date, ibid., p. 90. He was, however, already worried at the likely effects of the seating of Luttrell upon public opinion (George III to Rochford, 16 April 1769, Fortescue, Vol. II, p. 309).

[40] As was demonstrated on 8 March when Burke's motion for an enquiry into the St George's Fields Massacre was defeated by 245–39, 'the finishing stroke to the opposition this session', reported Rigby to Bedford (9 March 1769, LVIII, f. 8, Woburn MSS).

[41] *Wilkes and Liberty*, p. 106.

[42] Grafton himself was fairly active, intervening in several counties against the petitioners and encouraging his colleagues to stand firm against them. Grafton's marriage into the Bedford family during the summer stabilised his situation both personally and politically.

[43] For the preparation of the petition, see Rude, op. cit., pp. 71–2. The drafting of the petition owed more to Burke than to Dowdeswell, although it was Dowdeswell who suggested that 'one of our friends' present it. The initiative certainly came from the Middlesex Petitioners and not from the Rockinghams but the identity of the man responsible remains a mystery. Professor Rude is, of course, right in believing that James Adair had an important connecting role but there is no evidence that it was he who made the first move (R. 87–1–2, Wentworth Woodhouse MSS; *Wilkes and Liberty*, pp. 200–2).

[44] Lord John Cavendish warned the Commons: 'If we despise and set at naught the opinions of the people, and act upon our own feelings, the power of the House of Commons is gone, and with it all the advantages of our complicated state of government' (*Cavendish Debates*, Vol. I, p. 414). For other accounts of this important debate, see Lord Temple to Lady Chatham, 9 May 1769 (*Chatham Correspondence*, Vol. III, pp. 357–9) and Burke to Lord Charlemont, 9 May 1768 (*Burke Correspondence*, Vol. II, p. 23). There is an analysis of the minority in J. Brooke, *The Chatham Administration* (pp. 351–2), which concludes that new Members were slightly more likely to support the Opposition than the old Members were.

[45] See, for example, Burke to Rockingham, 23 September 1770, *Burke Correspondence*, Vol. II, pp. 159–62.

[46] Richmond to Rockingham, 10 March 1769, RI–1169, Wentworth Woodhouse MSS, printed in A. Olson, *The Radical Duke* (Oxford, 1961), pp. 129–31; Richmond to Rockingham, 7 May 1769, RI–1183, Wentworth Woodhouse MSS.

[47] Rockingham to J. Harrison, 19 May 1769, RI–1186, ibid. George Grenville did not share these views. See, for example, George Grenville to the Earl of Buckinghamshire, 16 August 1769 (*H.M.C. Lothian*, pp. 287–8).

[48] 9 May was the last day of the session. There is a list of those present and the toasts drunk in *The Chatham Correspondence* (Vol. III, pp. 359n–60n).

[49] Temple to Lady Chatham, 10 May 1769 (*Chatham Correspondence*, Vol. III, pp. 359–61). It was Sir George Savile's view that if enough petitions could be raised, then they would have to be complied with. (Savile to John Hewett, 2 September 1769, *H.M.C. Foljambe*, pp. 146–8.)

[50] Burke to Rockingham, 9 July 1769, *Burke Correspondence*, Vol. II, pp. 43–6; Thomas Whately to Grenville, 7 September 1769, *Grenville Papers*, Vol. IV, pp. 440–52. Grenville, however, was almost as suspicious of the Rockinghams as Burke was of the Grenvilles. (Grenville to Whately,

14 September 1769, ibid., pp. 452–3; Burke to O'Hara, 31 May 1769, *Burke Correspondence*, Vol. II, pp. 26–7.)

[51] Burke to Rockingham, 15 October 1769, *Burke Correspondence*, Vol. II, pp. 87–9.

[52] Portland to Rockingham, 3 December 1769, RI–1250, Wentworth Woodhouse MSS, printed with many inaccuracies in Albemarle, Vol. II, p. 143.

[53] Fitzwilliam to Rockingham, 1 December 1769, ibid., RI–1248 and Albemarle, p. 142.

[54] Rockingham to Burke, 15 October 1769, *Burke Correspondence*, Vol. II, pp. 98–95.

[55] Rockingham to Dowdeswell, 20 October 1769. RI–1238, Wentworth Woodhouse MSS.

[56] Rockingham to Burke, 29 June 1769, *Burke Correspondence*, Vol. II, pp. 35–40.

[57] G. Rude, *Wilkes and Liberty*, pp. 109–10. The petition is printed in *The Annual Register, 1769*, pp. 201–2.

[58] G. Rude, op. cit., pp. 112–13. The account in G. Guttridge (*English Whiggism and the American Revolution* (1966), pp. 38–9) of the Bristol petition suggests that Rude underestimates the extent of Rockinghamite feeling in Bristol.

[59] An initial meeting on 16 June appointed a committee on which the Rockinghamites had a majority. This committee drafted a petition which a county meeting of 2,000 freeholders on 26 July approved in preference to a radical petition; the petition was ultimately signed by 1494 freeholders and presented to the King on 24 August.

[60] G. Rude, op. cit., pp. 113–15. Guttridge seems to paraphrase Dowdeswell's own complaints to Burke about the slowness of the petitions to take effect (10 August 1769, *Burke Correspondence*, Vol. II, pp. 53–4) as the fault of 'people of rank and fortune'. The real reason is perhaps more complex for what kind of radical tradition did Worcestershire have? As Dowdeswell remarked in September (To Burke, 5 September 1769, ibid., pp. 69–71) the 'injudicious list of grievances, which filled the first petitions, still more disinclined the sober part of the people to signing petitions'. Yet Dowdeswell was himself partly to blame for the weakness of the movement in Worcestershire. He did not even speak in support of the Worcester petition on 9 August at a great meeting in the Worcester guildhall. (Charles Cocks to Lord Hardwicke, 17 September 1769, B.M. Add. MSS 35609, ff. 43–4, Hardwicke Papers.)

[61] It is important to realise certain facts pertaining to the petitions. Those which petitioned the King to dissolve Parliament must have alienated many men who might have disapproved of the seating of Luttrell. Another election coming just a year after the last would not be welcomed in many circles (although it might have been something of an inducement to freeholders). Fear of expense and popular disorder would have carried the day. Second, in Horace Walpole's words: 'Was prerogative the champion to resort to in defence of injured freedom' (*Memoirs*, Vol. III, pp. 254–5).

It is worth noting that the Rockingham Whigs in 1769 were appealing *to the monarch* to defend the country *against Parliament*. In any case, would a general election have made much difference to the composition of Parliament? And even if Grafton were frightened from office, would a menacing Opposition be likely to commend itself to the King?

[62] The incomplete account in E. C. Black, *The Association* (Harvard, 1963, p. 119) has been superseded by that of Rude (op. cit., pp. 117–18). For the intervention of Burke and the Rockinghams in Buckinghamshire see *Burke Correspondence* (Vol. II, p. 48 et seq.).

[63] Rockingham to Burke, 29 June 1769, ibid., p. 38. Yet Rockingham had said in July (To Crofts, 11 July 1769, RI–1209, Wentworth Woodhouse MSS). 'I almost foresee that the time is probably not far distant when the still aggravating conduct of this administration, drove on by the Bute system &c joyn'd to other great national distresses, may occasion the necessity, not only of this countys meeting and petitioning but indeed of all.'

[64] Abdy to Rockingham, 21 June 1769, RI–1200, Wentworth Woodhouse MSS. For verification of Abdy's influence see Rockingham to Dowdeswell, 19 September 1769, RI–1230. Albemarle, Vol. II, pp. 104–6.

[65] See, *inter alia*, Burke to Rockingham, 2 and 30 July 1769, *Burke Correspondence*, Vol. II, pp. 41, 51–2.

[66] Dowdeswell to Rockingham, 5 August and 5 September 1769, Dowdeswell MSS.

[67] For Rockingham's decision see his letter to Dowdeswell of 19 September 1769, loc. cit. For his reluctance to dictate to Yorkshiremen see his letter to Burke of 13 September, *Burke Correspondence*, Vol. II, pp. 61–5 and *see also* Rockingham to Crofts, 20 September 1769, RI–1231, Wentworth Woodhouse MSS. Rockingham although worried lest the Yorkshire gentry take up such a scheme as a Place Bill was prepared to call a county meeting if they desired one. (Rockingham to Portland, 15 July 1769, Portland MSS.)

[68] Rockingham's organisation was centred on York. Two of his agents, Dring and Croft did much of the routine work, distributing copies of the petition, publicising it and deploying an army of sub-agents. In some places the petition was canvassed from house to house. (See R. 10, Wentworth Woodhouse MSS.)

[69] This in spite of Dowdeswell's fears that an old statute forbade petitioning in the county. It required Alexander Wedderburn's assurances that the Bill of Rights overrode the statute in question before Dowdeswell would proceed with any vigour. (Dowdeswell to Rockingham, 11 and 20 October, RI–1235, 1238, Wentworth Woodhouse MSS.)

[70] G. Rude, op. cit., p. 124.

[71] Ibid., p. 125.

[72] Ibid., pp. 125–6.

[73] As Rude points out (ibid., p. 126 & n.) Devon and Herefordshire were among those counties which did *not* demand a dissolution of Parliament.

[74] Ibid., pp. 127–8.

[75] G. Rude, op. cit., pp. 128–9.

[76] Ibid., pp. 129–32.

[77] The four counties without Rockinghamite influences were Cornwall, Devon, Wiltshire and Kent. The boroughs with Rockinghamite influence were: Berwick (marginally), Exeter, Hereford, Liverpool, Newcastle and Worcester. Those boroughs without Rockinghamite influence were Bristol, Coventry, London, Morpeth, Southwark and Westminster. The counter-Petitioning Movement has been neglected. In at least four counties (Essex, Kent, Surrey and Shropshire) addresses were voted which approved of the expulsion of Wilkes; likewise in five boroughs (Cambridge, Bristol, Coventry, Liverpool and Oxford). In several places it was found to be impossible to launch petitions. (In Essex, Hertfordshire, Norfolk, Nottinghamshire, and Lincolnshire. That Lancashire and Cumberland could not be raised is surprising in view of Rockinghamite influence there.)

[78] See the letters of Sir William Meredith, Sir Matthew Fetherstonehaugh and Sir William Meredith of 10 July, 5 August and 20 October 1769, respectively; Portland MSS; Portland to Rockingham, 16 July 1769, RI–1211, Wentworth Woodhouse MSS.

[79] Rockingham to Albemarle, 2 October 1769, RI/V/5 (9), Albemarle MSS.

[80] Grafton to Camden, 29 August 1769, *Grafton Autobiography*, pp. 238–40. The poverty of Grafton's political resource was illustrated by a fantastic attempt to recall the aged, irascible and inebriated Northington to politics. (Northington to Grafton, 10 December 1769, Grafton MSS.)

[81] The grounds for their resignation consisted of their rejection of the ministry's handling of the Wilkes case and an attachment to Chatham which not only continued to this time but which strengthened as Chatham renewed his personal contacts with them later in the year. (Camden to Grafton, 1 September 1769, *Grafton Autobiography*, pp. 240–1; Rigby to Bedford, 9 November 1769, Woburn MSS, LVIII, f. 154. For Chatham's relations with the two men see Calcraft to Chatham, 26 May 1769 (P.R.O. 30/8/25, f. 27, Chatham Papers: Chatham to Temple, 8 November 1769, *Grenville Papers*, Vol. IV, pp. 478–9; Lord G. Germain to Mr Hamilton, B.M. Add. MSS 39779, ff. 20–21, Autograph Letters; Temple to Lady Chatham, 21 November 1769, P.R.O. 30/8/25, ff. 174–5; Calcraft to Chatham, 25 November 1769, *Chatham Correspondence*, Vol. III, pp. 363–5).

[82] The most lengthy and best documented account of Yorke's death remains that of D. A. Winstanley, *Personal and Party Government* (Cambridge, 1910), pp. 296–315. It should be supplemented with the material in the Wentworth Woodhouse MSS, especially the letters of Hardwicke to Rockingham of 15, 15, 17, 19, 19 and 21 January, RI–1265–70.

[83] Dowdeswell to Rockingham, 20 September 1769, Dowdeswell MSS.

[84] Rockingham to Albemarle, 22 October 1769, RI/V/5b Albemarle MSS.

[85] Rockingham to Portland, 5 December 1769, Portland MSS.

[86] Although Rockingham took the trouble to compile lists of supporters (R. 10–19, Wentworth Woodhouse MSS) Burke and Dowdeswell were beside themselves at the Marquis' leisurely progress to London. (Dowdes-

well to Rockingham, 16 December 1769, Dowdeswell MSS; Burke to Rockingham, 18 December 1769, *Burke Correspondence*, Vol. II, pp. 121–3.) For complaints of Rockingham's lack of urgency see J. Yorke to Hardwicke, 5 January 1770 (B.M. Add. MSS 35373, Hardwicke Papers). Nevertheless, no fewer than 80 Opposition Members turned up at the Thatched House tavern on the eve of the session and about 180 at the Cockpit. (Chatham to Calcraft, 8 January 1770, *Chatham Correspondence*, Vol. III, p. 398.)

[87] *The Parliamentary History*, XVI, pp. 668–728. In the Lords on the same day the government peers trounced the Opposition in debate. On this day Camden in the Lords and Granby in the Commons opposed the ministry of which they held cabinet office. It was the signal for their curiously long-delayed resignations. They were accompanied by a handful of other office-holders, including three Lords of the Bedchamber.

[88] The influence of Junius has likewise been much exaggerated. During the critical period from mid-December to mid-January not a single Junius letter was published. The most recent one had been on 14 December.

[89] George III to Lord North, 23 January 1770, Fortescue, Vol. II, p. 126. North's willingness to accept was known on 27 January. See the King's letter to Grafton of that date (Grafton MSS).

[90] Newdigate MSS B2021; J. Calcraft to Chatham, 26 January 1770, P.R.O. 30/8/25, ff. 33–4; *The Parliamentary History*, **XVI**, pp. 785–99. Dowdeswell's motion was to the effect that on election matters the ministers ought to observe the law and custom of the land. This was, superficially, an unexceptionable assertion but it was directed against the activities of the Grafton ministry over the Wilkes case and likely to impress the Independents.

[91] *The Border Elliots*, pp. 406–7. Although the fall of Grafton had long been anticipated it came as something of a surprise in January 1770. (Robert Thompson to E. Weston, 30 January 1770, *H.M.C. Weston Underwood*, p. 420; Lady Chatham to Calcraft, 30 January 1770, *Chatham Correspondence*, Vol. III, pp. 413–14.) The appointment of North had a salutory effect. At once men began to rally to him and supporters of the ministry began to feel a little more optimistic (*The Border Elliots*, pp. 406–7).

[92] *The Parliamentary History*, **XVI**, pp. 800–07.

[93] *Chatham Correspondence*, Vol. III, pp. 414–15.

[94] E. Langton to Lord Hardwicke, 2 February 1770, B.M. Add. MSS 35609, f. 144, Hardwicke Papers; *The Border Elliots*, pp. 407–8. Horace Walpole, *Memoirs*, Vol. IV, pp. 87–8.

[95] J. Harris to Lord Hardwicke, B.M. Add. MSS 35609, ff. 149–50, Hardwicke Papers. For prior contacts and co-operation see Rockingham to Chatham, 17 and 18 February 1770, *Chatham Correspondence*, Vol. III, pp. 415–23.

[96] Although the number of petitions raised in 1769 (about 30) compares badly with the number of petitions and addresses raised in the early weeks of 1784 (about 200) the total number of signatories was about the same. (J. Cannon, *The Fox–North Coalition*, Cambridge, 1969, pp. 185–8.)

CHAPTER 11

[1] For fuller exposition of this approach see the present author's *Edmund Burke: His Political Philosophy* (1973).

[2] In November 1766 Conway approached Burke with implied offers of office. Burke entertained the idea of accepting, provided that: 'in accepting it, and in holding it, I must be understood to belong not to the Administration but to those who were out; and that therefore if ever they should set up a standard . . . I must be revocable into their party and join it'. (Burke to O'Hara, *post*-2 November 1766, *Burke Correspondence*, Vol. I, p. 279.) A few months later, a correspondent suggested to Burke that he might take office. This time, there was no hesitation at all in Burke's reaction: 'Good God! how do you think it possible, that I should take on with such an administration, in the conduct of such measures, as the present . . . surely the least particle of pride and spirit would never suffer one to engage under a person who is incapable of forming any rational plan'... (Chatham). (Burke to O'Hara, 30 and 31 March 1767, ibid., pp. 302–3.)

[3] This brief account is noteworthy for Burke's comment that the ministry was removed at Chatham's instigation. He is much kinder to Bute: 'With the Earl of Bute they had no personal connexion, no correspondence of councils. They neither courted him nor persecuted him'. Burke could not resist, however, some reference to the revolt of the placemen. 'In the prosecution of their measures, they were traversed by an opposition of a new and singular character; an opposition of placemen and pensioners.'

[4] Dixon Wector, *Edmund Burke and his Kinsmen* (Boulder, Colorado, 1938).

[5] Burke to O'Hara, 23 December 1766, *Burke Correspondence*, Vol. I, pp. 284–5.

[6] Burke to Rockingham, 1 August 1767, ibid., pp. 316–18.

[7] Burke, of course, had himself shared some of these reservations. See his letter to Rockingham of 2 July 1769 (ibid., Vol. II, pp. 40–2).

[8] Rockingham to Dowdeswell, 19 September 1769, Albemarle, Vol. II, p. 106.

[9] Whately to Burke, 30 August 1769, *Burke Correspondence*, Vol. II, p. 59.

[10] Burke to O'Hara, 28 August 1769, ibid., p. 57.

[11] Burke to Dr W. Markham, *post*-9 November 1771, ibid., p. 259. On this point, it is worth commenting that William Dowdeswell prepared the following motions: Repeal of the Stamp Act, 1766, Land Tax reduction, 1767, 'Expulsion does not create Incapacitation', April 1770, Falkland Islands, November 1770 and February 1771. To what extent have the widespread exaggerations of Burke's role in the Rockingham party arisen from the fact that Dowdeswell has been a far less fashionable figure and that far less of his private correspondence has survived? It is astonishing that there exists not one biography of this talented and charming figure who for over a decade stood at the centre of the Rockingham party and who, had he lived longer, must surely have played a prominent role upon the national political stage. He, rather than Burke, stood close to Rocking-

T

ham between 1766 and 1774, if any one man did. Dowdeswell had helped to bring down Bute over the Cider Tax, had been one of the heroes of the General Warrants debates of 1764 and had held senior office in the ministry of 1765–6. Burke could claim none of these advantages. (Nor could he claim Dowdeswell's independence. As MP for Worcestershire Dowdeswell did not owe his seat to a Whig patron.) How natural, then, that the older, weightier, more experienced Dowdeswell should have enjoyed a greater influence in the Rockingham party than Burke.

[12] During Rockingham's illness in 1771 Richmond assumed the leadership of the party. He wrote a significant note to the Marquis: 'The want of you to keep people together, particularly the House of Commons Gentlemen is too apparent. There are many of them who will upon most occasions vote with us, but want to be spoke to, and have the matter explained to them beforehand. This is a part I cannot supply, for I do not know half of them, and the thing that influences them is the personal regard they have for you' (16 February 1771, RI–1363, Wentworth Woodhouse MSS).

[13] As Burke admitted to Rockingham in a letter of 1 August 1767, *Burke Correspondence*, Vol. I, pp. 316–18: 'the world greatly mistook you, if they imagined, that you would come in otherwise than in Corps; and that after you had thought your own bottom too narrow, you would condescend to build your administration on a foundation still narrower'.

[14] Burke quickly picked up the Rockinghamite catch-phrases, about making a virtue of necessity in Opposition and being in Opposition on account of disinterestedness. (Burke to O'Hara, 2 December and 23 December 1766, *Burke Correspondence*, Vol. I, pp. 283–4, 284–7.)

[15] J. Gunn, *Factions no More* (1971), pp. 12–15.

[16] *Statesmanship and Party Government* (Chicago, 1965), c.V.

[17] G. H. Guttridge, *English Whiggism and the American Revolution* (University of California Press, 1965), p. 10.

[18] 'His System is got into firmer and abler hands.' Burke to Rockingham, 29 December 1770, *Burke Correspondence*, Vol. II, pp. 174–6. Rockingham assumed that real power did not lie with Grafton in 1768–70 but elsewhere. (Rockingham to J. Harrison, 19 May 1769, RI–1186, Wentworth Woodhouse MSS.) Portland thought the present system was based upon the principles of Prince Frederick's Court. (Portland to Rockingham, 3 December 1769, Albemarle, Vol. II, pp. 145–7.) On 22 January 1770, Rockingham pronounced to the House of Lords that the disorders of the kingdom stemmed from no accidental cause but 'had grown up by degrees from the Moment of His Majesty's accession to the Throne', as a plot to elevate prerogative to dwarf the powers of ministers (*The Parliamentary History*, **XVI**, pp. 741–5).

[19] Portland objected strongly to Bute being let off so lightly: 'for surely at the time you are declaring war and irreconcileable enmity to the whole party of *Kingsmen*, it must appear very strange to show any tenderness to their Chief'. (Portland to Rockingham, 3 December 1769, Albemarle, Vol. II, pp. 145–7.) Horace Walpole was unhappy at the inclusion of 'a

vague idea' in the place of the personality of Bute (*Memoirs*, Vol. IV, p. 89).

[20] Not even his party colleagues nor those who reviewed the *Thoughts* commented upon the stress laid by Burke upon party. (J. Brewer, 'Party and the Double Cabinet: Two Facets of Burke's Thoughts', *Historical Journal*, **XIV**, 3 (1971), pp. 486–7, 493–4.)

[21] The pamphlet is first talked of in the summer of 1769 when Burke's intention to write a justification for the party received the enthusiastic assent of Rockingham. He wrote to Burke on 29 June: 'I am exceedingly glad you have begun to look over the Papers of the last 9 years—that indeed would be a most useful work and would do more good in giving right ideas to the publick—than all the proceedings have done hitherto of late' (*Burke Correspondence*, Vol. II, pp. 35–40).

[22] Dr Brewer argues that Burke's main concern was to argue the case not for party but for the united Opposition (op. cit., pp. 484–5; 488). In view of Burke and the Rockinghams' attitude towards the union of the Opposition (discussed in the last chapter) I cannot accept this conclusion. Burke, I feel, was most concerned to argue the claims of the Rockinghams to predominance in the united Opposition and in a future ministry.

[23] The idea to circulate the drafts was almost certainly Rockingham's. (See Rockingham to Burke, 4 November 1769, *Burke Correspondence*, Vol. II, p. 104; Burke to Rockingham, *post*-6 November 1769, ibid., pp. 108–9.) The circulation of such drafts was a normal proceeding among the Rockingham Whigs (J. Brewer, op. cit., pp. 483–4).

[24] 'I think it would take universally, and tend to form & unite a party upon real & well-founded principles which would in the end prevail and re-establish order and Government in this country.' (Rockingham to Burke, 15 October 1769, *Burke Correspondence*, Vol. II, p. 92.)

[25] Burke commented: 'This project, I have heard, was first conceived by some persons in the court of Frederick Prince of Wales'.

[26] I have discussed this point in my articles: 'Edmund Burke and the Idea of Party', *Studies in Burke and his Times*, **XI**, No. 2 (1969–70), particularly pp. 1430–1; 'Party and Burke: The Rockingham Whigs', *Government and Opposition*, **III**, No. 1 (1968), pp. 95–6.

[27] This is not to deny that Burke believed that the Rockingham Party ought to seek office by every legal means at its disposal. But the most important offices must go to members of the Rockingham party and not to men 'who contradict the very fundamental principles upon which every fair connexion must stand'.

[28] Richmond to Rockingham, 12 February 1771, RI–1358, Wentworth Woodhouse MSS, *q.* A. Olson, op. cit., pp. 131–45. See also R. Pares, op. cit., p. 77, N2. Chatham's comment that the pamphlet had done harm is in his letter to Rockingham, 15 November 1770 (Albemarle, Vol. II, pp. 193–4). It is not easy to see what harm it did do. However, Burke pronounced his party's rejection of parliamentary reform just when Chatham was being converted to it and when Shelburne was beginning

to expose himself to the utilitarian ideas of Price and Priestley (J. Norris, op. cit., pp. 84–6).

²⁹ The only other known pamphlet response to the *Thoughts* was an anonymous *An Analysis of the Thoughts on the Cause of the present Discontents, and of the Observations on the same* (1770).

³⁰ It should scarcely need to be added that Burke's theory of party was largely unoriginal. To depict him as a lonely, far sighted, prophet of party is nonsensical. The ideas of Opposition and party conflict had already become far more acceptable than they had been fifty years earlier and it is an absurd, though still widely held view among historians, that in the 1760s, and even later, parties were thought to be illegitimate and even treasonable. (See J. Gunn, op. cit., pp. 20–1, 27–8; A. S. Foord, op. cit., *passim.*)

CHAPTER 12

¹ Simon Fraser to Lord Townshend, 13 February 1770, *H.M.C. Townshend*, p. 407.

² Horace Walpole to Sir Horace Mann, 27 February 1770, *Correspondence of Horace Walpole*, Vol. XXV, p. 200; Rockingham to Portland, 17 March 1770, Portland MSS. North turned the knife in the Opposition's wound when he took advantage of the indignation aroused by a petition presented to the King from the City by Bedford on 15 March. The petition (or 'Address, Remonstrance, & Petition') rudely demanded a dissolution. Sir Thomas Clavering (MP for various constituencies, but for Durham country, 1768–90) wished to embarrass the Opposition by moving for copies of the petition and a resolution condemning it. Clavering was an influential County Member who had supported the Opposition until 31 January 1770. His turning against the Opposition and the massive majority which his resolution enjoyed (284–127) was a damaging blow to the Opposition (*Cavendish Debates*, Vol. I, pp. 535–45).

³ RI–1293A.

⁴ This was, no doubt, partly why George III reposed so much confidence in North as opposed to Grenville in 1763–5. North never pretended that it was he who was responsible for the distribution of patronage. He usually made it clear to the beneficiary concerned that the honour came from the King, which, indeed, it did. See, for example, North to Bathurst, *n.d.* 1770, B.M. Bathurst Loan, I.f. 572.

⁵ The decision to repeal the duties had been taken when the Grafton cabinet had decided by 5–4 to remove them, excepting that on tea (1 May 1769). If Hawke had been present, the Cabinet would have been equally divided. Yet there can be no escaping the conclusion that the hard-liners in the Cabinet, led by Hillsborough, were influencing George III more and more. There is no doubt that he would strongly have opposed abolishing the tea duty. (Hillsborough to George III, 15 February 1769, Fortescue, Vol. II, pp. 81–2, *Grafton Autobiography*, p. 374.)

[6] The debate is given in *The Parliamentary History*, **XVI,** pp. 852–74; *Cavendish Debates*, Vol. I, pp. 483–500; Lord Belasyse to Lord Fauconberg, 6 March 1770, Fauconberg Papers. Lord North listed the speakers in an enclosure to the King of 5 March 1770 (Fortescue, Vol. II, p. 132). The retention of the tea duty was a symbolic demonstration of imperial authority which severely weakened any lingering attachment to the mother country still felt by many Americans. It certainly seems to have had a critical effect upon the thought of Benjamin Franklin (L. H. Gipson, *The Coming of the Revolution*, New York, 1954, pp. 198–9).

[7] The debate of 9 May is given in *Cavendish Debates*, Vol. II, pp. 14–24; Dowdeswell to Chatham, 10 May 1770, *Chatham Correspondence*, Vol. III, pp. 450–5. For North's list of speakers see the list in his enclosure to the King of 9 May, Fortescue, Vol. II, p. 146; G. Guttridge, op. cit., pp. 69–70.

[8] In February 1769 Parliament had been informed that debts on the Civil List amounted to £300,000. Dowdeswell's motion for details of court expenditure was defeated on 28 February 1769 by 164–89 (*The Parliamentary History*, **XVI**, pp. 598–601). On 2 March Rockingham spoke in the Lords demanding papers relating to the Civil List. (Richmond to Rockingham, 10 March 1769, RI–1169, Wentworth Woodhouse MSS, *q.* in full by A. Olson, op. cit., pp. 129–31 and, in part by Albemarle, Vol. II, pp. 91–2.)

[9] *Cavendish Debates*, Vol. I, pp. 479–83.

[10] In his speech Chatham absolved the King from all responsibility, heaping all his abuse upon Grafton for his secret transactions. Chatham apparently chose to forget that Grafton had for many months been his own *locum*. *Chatham Correspondence*, Vol. III, pp. 423n–426n.

[11] Dowdeswell claimed that in 1769 alone the deficit had been no less than £140,000 (2 April 1770, *The Parliamentary History*, **XVI**, p. 925). This estimate was in line with much Rockinghamite thinking at this time. Rockingham, for example, was calculating that the average annual costs of the royal family in the first eight years of the present reign was £149,322 8s 3d, compared with £106,866 18s 11d in the last eight years of the reign of George II (R. 15, R. 28, Wentworth Woodhouse MSS).

[12] As will be argued later, the economical reform campaign of 1779–80 has its origin in motions of this type which became fairly frequent after 1768, and which have been unfortunately neglected by historians. See Chapter 19.

[13] This happened even on minor matters. On 17 February 1770, Rockingham sent Chatham details of a proposed motion on the navy (*Chatham Correspondence*, Vol. III, pp. 415–18). Although Rockingham understood that Chatham's health prevented him speedily determining what line to take, many opposition lords, meeting on the evening of 18 February, were clearly weary of delay (Temple to Lady Chatham, 18 February 1770, P.R.O. 30/8/62, f. 194, Chatham Papers).

[14] Rockingham to Chatham, 27 April 1770, *Chatham Correspondence*, Vol. III, pp. 445–7; Chatham to Rockingham, 27 April 1770, RI–1295, Wentworth Woodhouse MSS, Albemarle, Vol. II, pp. 174–5.

¹⁵ '. . . the Peers are not invested with their powers and privileges for their sole benefit, but that they possess them as trusts, which they are to use for the general good.' (The Duke of Richmond on 30 April 1770, *The Parliamentary History*, **XVII**, pp. 214–16. See also Richmond to Portland, 26 April 1771, Portland Papers.)

¹⁶ Chatham to Rockingham, 10 May 1770, RI–1297, Wentworth Woodhouse MSS; Albemarle, Vol. II, pp. 180–2.

¹⁷ Rockingham to Chatham, 11 May 1770, RI–1298, Wentworth Woodhouse MSS, Albemarle, Vol. II, p. 182; Chatham to Rockingham, 12 May 1770, RI–1299, ibid., p. 183–4; Rockingham to Chatham, 12 May 1770, RI–1300, ibid., p. 184; Chatham to Rockingham, 14 May 1770, RI–1301, ibid., p. 185.

¹⁸ *The Parliamentary History*, **XVI**, pp. 747–55, 22 January 1770.

¹⁹ Professor Christie (*Wilkes Wyvill and Reform* (1962), p. 51) attributes Chatham's stress on increased county representation to his desire to please the Rockinghamites. But there is no evidence for this. On the other hand, there is considerable evidence to suggest that Temple persuaded Chatham to drop the proposal to shorten Parliaments. (J. Norris, op. cit., p. 79; Temple to Chatham, 18 April 1771, *Chatham Correspondence*, Vol. IV, pp. 154–5; Chatham to Shelburne, 22 April 1771, ibid., pp. 156–8.)

²⁰ Rockingham once told Chatham that union in Opposition did not imply that his friends should do as Chatham wished on every occasion. (Rockingham to Chatham, 11 May 1770, *Chatham Correspondence*, Vol. III, pp. 455–6).

²¹ *Grafton Autobiography*, p. 241.

²² Lord Barrington to Lord Albemarle, 12 October 1770, RI/V/8, Albemarle MSS.

²³ Burke's reaction was to contemplate the feasibility of the secession of his party from Parliament. (Burke to O'Hara, 21 May 1770, *Burke Correspondence*, Vol. II, pp. 137–40.)

²⁴ Chatham to Shelburne, 29 September 1770, *Chatham Correspondence*, Vol. IV, pp. 471–2.

²⁵ Rockingham to Burke, 5 and 26 September 1770, *Burke Correspondence*, Vol. II, pp. 151–4, 162–3.

²⁶ The lack of Rockingham's influence in the City was demonstrated when a member of the Bill of Rights society was returned to Parliament unopposed at a by-election. Barlow Trecothick was elected to complete Beckford's term as Mayor in June, but he and the Rockinghams could only stand by helplessly as Wilkites, Bill of Rights men and Chathamites wrestled for power in the City. Rockingham ignored Burke's advice to carry the party fight into the City. (Burke to Rockingham, 23 September 1770, *Burke Correspondence*, Vol. II, pp. 159–62.)

²⁷ Richmond had never tamely followed Rockingham's views. In 1766 he had been in favour of an approach to the Bute party. In 1767 he had disapproved of Rockingham's intransigence towards other groups. In 1769 he had taken no part in the Petitioning Movement and since then had shown his attachment to the party only in sending Rockingham his proxy

on two occasions. (Richmond to Rockingham, 10 March 1769, RI–1169, Wentworth Woodhouse MSS, *q.* A. Olson, pp. 129–31.)

[28] Richmond to Rockingham, 18 April 1770, Albemarle, Vol. II, pp. 177–9, RI–1293A, Wentworth Woodhouse MSS; *The Parliamentary History*, **XVI**, pp. 1010–14.

[29] Richmond to Rockingham, 21 January 1771, RI–1350. Wentworth Woodhouse MSS.

[30] Richmond to Rockingham, 16 February 1771, R. 158–45–1, *q.* A. Olson, pp. 146–7.

[31] Burke wrote to Rockingham on 16 February 1771 (*Burke Correspondence*, Vol. II, pp. 196–200): 'Indeed *the D. of Richmond is very attentive to any method of keeping us together, and of connecting us with the high and mighty allies.* Every day after a debate in the house of Peers he has a *dinner* for those who dine; and he frequently sees *that great being who never dines;* and sooths and manages him, as far as I can judge, in a very firm and very conciliatory manner.'

[32] In January Lord Suffolk became Secretary of State for the Northern Department while Wedderburn became Solicitor General (Thurlow became Attorney General). The other Grenvillites either supported the ministry immediately (like Thomas Whately) or (like Lord Clive) took a little longer to do so.

[33] Rockingham to Dowdeswell, 12 January 1771, RI–1347, Wentworth Woodhouse MSS.

[34] Richmond to Rockingham, 21 January 1771, RI–1350, Wentworth Woodhouse MSS.

[35] Burke to Rockingham, 29 December 1770, *Burke Correspondence*, Vol. II, pp. 174–6. *See also* his rather more mordant comments in his letter to O'Hara (31 December 1770, ibid., pp. 177–9). 'As to us, it is not easy to conceive into what a total indifference we are sunk, and in this twilight condition, neither peace nor war, we desire no glimmering of light, have neither hope nor fear; neither wish peace nor apprehend war; but go on just as we are bid; just as if all that was transacted belonged totally to another people; and that we had no kind of interest in it.'

[36] Towards the end of the year Chatham reiterated his detestation of Rockinghamite principles, declaring that unless the Rockinghams succumbed to his will he would 'separate from so unorthodox a congregation' (Chatham to Calcraft, 28 November 1770, *Chatham Correspondence*, Vol. IV, pp. 31–2). Rockingham made it clear to Chatham not only that a union of the Opposition was vital if the constitution of the country were to be preserved, but also that its acceptance depended upon the voluntary decision of his followers (Rockingham to Chatham, 15 November 1770, RI–1328, Wentworth Woodhouse MSS).

[37] The standard works on the Falkland Islands crisis are J. Goebel, *The Struggle for the Falkland Islands* (Yale, 1927); J. F. Ramsey, *Anglo-French Relations, 1763–70* (University of California Press, 1939), pp. 206–29. In January 1766 England had occupied one of the Falkland Islands, Port

Egmont, in spite of Spanish claims to sovereignty over them. A minor incident in the winter of 1769 triggered off Spanish retaliation, which took the form of occupation of the island. Lord Weymouth, the Secretary of State for the Southern Department, demanded an apology and the restoration of the island. The Spaniards, in their turn, demanded that her sovereignty be recognised. The incident scarcely warranted a diplomatic incident, let alone a full scale war but there was a good deal of talk about a war in England and, more important, some realisation that the country was hopelessly unprepared to fight one (e.g. the letters of Barrington, the Secretary at War, to Lord Albemarle, 12 October and 20 December 1770 (RI/V/8, Albemarle MSS) show the extrme straits to which the army was reduced in its attempts to fill its regimental quotas. 'We are trying to enlist Irishmen & Foreigners in order to make our augmentation the more speedily. . . . We take any able bodied men for the infantry.') At the same time, half of the fleet was unseaworthy and the repair yards in a scarcely operable condition. (Sandwich to North, 10 September 1772, *Sandwich Papers*, Vol. I, p. 24. See also N. Tracy, 'The Royal Navy as an Instrument of British Foreign Relations between the Peace of Paris and the War of the American Revolution', University of Southampton, unpublished Ph.D. Thesis, 1972.)

[38] *The Parliamentary History*, **XVI**, pp. 1081–1119.

[39] Ibid., pp. 1191–1224; *Cavendish Debates*, Vol. II, pp. 57–88. A week later a motion requesting details of the dispositions of the Spanish fleet obtained only 43 votes (ibid., pp. 177–84).

[40] George III shared North's anxiety to prevent war and, thus assured of support in the Closet, North was able to force the bellicose Weymouth from office on 16 December 1770 without danger to his own position from the Bedfords and to replace him with Rochford. Peace with Spain was now possible and negotiations towards it steadily proceeded.

[41] Chatham, of course, was quite prepared to take on Spain, and France, too, if necessary. (See his letters to Calcraft, 29 December 1770 and to Barrè on 22 January 1771, *Chatham Correspondence*, Vol. IV, pp. 64–5, 73–4). On the eve of the debate on 25 January 1771 Chatham ostentatiously threw in his lot with the Rockinghams by sending Calcraft to attend a meeting at Richmond's at which tactics for the debate were discussed (Chatham to Barre, 24 January 1771, ibid., pp. 84–5). Richmond was naturally extremely anxious to consult Chatham (Richmond to Rockingham 22 and 23 January 1771, RI58–46, Wentworth Woodhouse MSS).

[42] Rockingham to Burke, 30 January 1771, Burke Correspondence, II, pp. 188–9, *Cavendish Debates*, Vol. II, pp. 218–26.

[43] *Cavendish Debates*, Vol. II, pp. 231–43. If Rockingham had been in town he would probably not have allowed such a strategy to have been adopted. It was his firm conviction that the peace ought in no circumstances to be attacked (Rockingham to Burke, 3 February 1771), Burke Correspondence, II, 190–2.

[44] *Cavendish Debates*, Vol. II, pp. 272–306 (there is a list of the minority in J. Almon, Vol. IX, pp. 142–4). The Rockinghams made strenuous

efforts to bring their friends to town. Richmond held meetings and dinners every day between 5 and 13 February. (Richmond to Rockingham, 12 February 1771, RI–1358, *q.* A. Olson, op. cit., pp. 131–45.)

[45] It would be foolish to credit the Rockinghams with a coherent foreign policy whose value might have mitigated the factiousness of their attack on North during the Falkland Islands crisis. They continued to assume, as Newcastle had assumed, that the next war would be fought in central Europe and that the Bourbon powers' hostility arose from their fear of British power in Europe. The Rockingham Whigs were no more successful than other political groups or individuals in discerning that the great problem of British diplomacy, the threat of isolation, was already overtaking the country. Not realising this they were unable to propose any remedies for it, if, indeed, remedies there were.

[46] P. D. G. Thomas, 'John Wilkes and the Freedom of the Press', *Bulletin of the Institute of Historical Research*, **XXXIII** (1960).

[47] Burke to Rockingham, 23 September 1770, *Burke Correspondence*, Vol. II, pp. 159–62.

[48] Rockingham to Burke, 15 December 1770, ibid., pp. 170–2.

[49] Yet Camden was unhappy with Chatham's proposals and thought them unlikely to prove acceptable. (Camden to Chatham, 11 November 1770, P.R.O.30/8/25, ff. 129–30, Chatham Papers; Chatham to Calcraft, 28 November 1770, *Chatham Correspondence*, Vol. II, pp. 31–2.)

[50] *Cavendish Debates*, Vol. II, pp. 121–47; *The Parliamentary History*, **XVI**, pp. 1211–1301.

[51] *The Parliamentary History*, **XVI**, pp. 1312–22.

[52] *Memoirs*, Vol. IV, p. 148.

[53] Rockingham to Burke, 15 December 1770, *Burke Correspondence*, Vol. II, pp. 169–72. Rockingham to Dowdeswell, 11 February 1771, *Cavendish Debates*, Vol. II, p. 354, *q.* I. R. Christie, *Myth and Reality*, p. 202 n. 1, RI–1357, Wentworth Woodhouse MSS.

[54] Dowdeswell to Rockingham, 8 February 1771, RI–1356, Wentworth Woodhouse MSS. 'Neither Burke nor I can see the least possibility of further concessions without giving up our principles.'

[55] Rockingham to Dowdeswell, 11 February 1771, RI–1357, ibid.

[56] Rockingham to Burke, 14 February 1771, *Burke Correspondence*, Vol. II, pp. 192–6.

[57] Chatham wrote to his friends in late February: 'Mr Dowdeswell peremptorily, will move his bill concerning Juries in the course of next week; when the friends of the constitution will, it is hoped, strenuously resist this compound of connection, tyranny, and absurdity—not to say collusion'. Chatham to Barrè, 21 February 1771, *Chatham Correspondence*, Vol. IV, p. 100. This was Chatham's reaction to a desperate, eleventh hour plea by Richmond not to obstruct. 'We differ only in the means' he wrote on 20 February, ibid., pp. 97–9. Dowdeswell had long been critical of Richmond's conciliatory attitude to Chatham because Chatham's terms for a 'compromise' amounted to nothing less than an admission by Dowdeswell that he drop his bill and agree that Camden should move in

the Lords a bill based upon Chatham's ideas. This high-handedness was enough to bring Rockingham to agree with Dowdeswell and to encourage him to proceed with his own bill. (Rockingham to Dowdeswell, 11 February 1771, RI–1357, Wentworth Woodhouse MSS; Albemarle, Vol. I, pp. 200–3.)

[58] Lord North to the King, 7 March 1771, enclosing a list of speakers (Fortescue, Vol. II, pp. 226–7). For the King's satisfaction see his letter to North of 8 March 1771, ibid., p. 227. The debate is given in *The Parliamentary History*, **XVII**, pp. 43–4; *Cavendish Debates*, Vol. II, pp. 352–77. For Barrè's amusement see his letter to Chatham of 8 March 1771, *Chatham Correspondence*, Vol. IV, pp. 109–14. For Calcraft's muted joy at the division see his letter to Chatham, 8 March 1771, *q.* D. Winstanley, *Lord Chatham and the Whig Opposition* (Cambridge, 1912), p. 432.

[59] This was the cousin of Newcastle's nephew and, like George Onslow, he had been a supporter of the Chatham administration. On this subject see P. D. G. Thomas, 'The Beginning of Parliamentary Reporting in Newspapers, 1768–74', *English Historical Review*, **LXXIV** (1959), and the same author's 'John Wilkes and the Freedom of the Press', *Bulletin of the Institute of Historical Research*, **XXXIII** (1960).

[60] This was the famous occasion when the House was divided twenty-three times in one night. (*Cavendish Debates*, Vol. II, pp. 256–60.)

[61] The Lord Mayor (Brass Crosby), Wilkes and Richard Oliver discharged the arrested men, and thus it proved impossible for the House to have its resolutions enforced. Brass Crosby was MP for Honiton (1768–74) and Richard Oliver was MP for London (1770–80). Oliver was committed to the Tower on 19 March, on which date there were three divisions, 272–90, 214–97, 170–38. (Lord North to George III, 19 March 1771, Fortescue, Vol. II, p. 234.) For Crosby's committment on 27 March there was a division of 202–39 (ibid., p. 244), and there is a list of the minority in J. Almon, op. cit. (Vol. IX, p. 56).

[62] For the effects of these transactions see A. Aspinall, 'The Reporting and Publishing of the House of Commons Debates, 1771–1834', in *Essays to Sir Lewis Namier*, Eds. R. Pares and A. J. P. Taylor (1956). Although the Speaker retained the right to expel reporters if asked to do so by members it was not frequently exercised. It was not, in fact, until 1853, however, that journalists began to enjoy the *right* of attendance.

[63] Rockingham to Dowdeswell, 28 March 1771, Albemarle, Vol. II, pp. 207–8. For a list of those who accompanied Rockingham see ibid., p. 209.

[64] Chatham to Barrè, 21 March 1771, *Chatham Correspondence*, Vol. IV, pp. 119–20.

[65] Already before the printers case, Chatham had quarrelled with the Wilkites over press-warrants (J. Norris, *Shelburne and Reform*, p. 76).

[66] Chatham to Rockingham, 25 April 1771, *Chatham Correspondence*, Vol. IV, pp. 165–6; Rockingham to Chatham, 26 April 1771, ibid., pp. 166–70. For the debate, see ibid., pp. 171n–175n.

[67] Burke to Rockingham, 29 December 1770, *Burke Correspondence*, Vol. II, pp. 174–6.

[68] Rockingham to Burke, 14 February 1771, ibid., pp. 192–6.

[69] Richmond to Rockingham, 12 February 1771, loc. cit. Chatham's view of such statements as this, as of Burke's *Thoughts* was, of course, unfavourable. He wrote to Shelburne on 10 January 1772 to remark that 'the narrow genius of old corps' connection has weakened Whiggism, and rendered national union on revolution principles impossible; and what but such an union can have any chance to withstand the present corruption' (*Chatham Correspondence*, Vol. IV, pp. 186–7).

[70] Walpole has a story (*Memoirs*, Vol. IV, pp. 326–7) that Grafton wished to remain outside the Cabinet because he would not wish to act a subordinate part inside it. The real reason, however, for his refusing to be in the Cabinet was 'that He ever thought the confidential Cabinet too numerous', according to George III. (See his letter to North, 11 June 1771, Fortescue, Vol. II, p. 255.) It is at about this time that the relationship between George III and Lord North became warmer and more cordial. In June 1771 the King promised him a garter. (George III to North, 9 June 1771, ibid., p. 252.)

[71] A typical example is his willingness to bestow a residentiaryship of St Paul's upon the bishop of Lincoln, a close friend of Hardwicke. (Lord North to Lord Hardwicke, 1 July 1771, B.M. Add. MSS. 35424, f. 24, Hardwicke MSS.)

[72] Dowdeswell was already suspicious of Germain's intentions as early as February 1771. (See his letter to Rockingham of 16 February 1771, Dowdeswell MSS.) Meredith did not actually accept a post in the Government until 1774.

[73] Rockingham to Burke, 14 February 1771, loc. cit.

[74] Burke to Rockingham, 29 December 1770, *Burke Correspondence*, Vol. II, p. 174–6.

[75] Ibid.

[76] Richmond to Rockingham, 15 March 1772, RI–1397, Wentworth Woodhouse MSS.

[77] The Duke of Manchester to Rockingham, 10 December 1771, RI–1388, ibid., printed Albemarle, Vol. II, pp. 210–11; Rockingham to Dowdeswell, 19 December 1771, loc. cit.; Burke to Rockingham, 29 December 1771, *Burke Correspondence*, Vol. II, pp. 174–6.

[78] Rockingham's final decision was in favour of attending: 'tho' perhaps we may have Nothing to do, yet our being inactive may probably have much less Consequence'. (Rockingham to Portland, 2 January 1772, Portland MSS.)

[79] George III to Lord North, 26 February 1772, Fortescue, Vol. II, p. 325.

[80] There is a detailed account of the debates in Horace Walpole's, *Last Journals* (2 Vols, 1859), Vol. I, pp. 24–74, *passim*, *The Parliamentary History*, **XVII**, pp. 396–424; 446–7.

[81] But *not* the Rockingham Whigs and *not* permanently. In fact, Fox returned to office in December 1772 until February 1774 as a Lord of the Treasury.

[82] George III to Lord North, 12 March 1772, Fortescue, Vol. II, p. 328.

[83] See Burke's later remarks in his letter to O'Hara of 18 November 1772 (*Burke Correspondence*, Vol. II, pp. 286–8; Horace Walpole, *Last Journals*, Vol. I, p. 45). The amendments would, in one way or another, have drastically curtailed the independent authority over members of the royal family which the King was seeking.

[84] The petition had been denied a hearing in the Commons by 217–71 on 6 February. There is a list of the minority in Almon (Vol. IX, pp. 332–3). There is an interesting account of the debate in Horace Walpole, *Last Journals* (Vol. I, pp. 9–13): 'Many of our friends are divided in opinion' on the subject, wrote Rockingham to Burke on 7 February 1772 (Ramsden MSS).

[85] Richmond to Rockingham, 26 April 1772, Albemarle, Vol. II, pp. 224–5, A. Olson, op. cit., pp. 150–2, RI–1403 Wentworth Woodhouse MSS.

[86] Burke had come out against his party on this occasion. Burke to the Countess of Huntingdon, 6 February 1772, *Burke Correspondence*, Vol. II, pp. 298–9. Burke's fundamental attitude on this issue was that those who enjoyed the benefits of establishment ought to subscribe to it: 'it was thought unreasonable, that the publick should contribute to the Maintenance of a Clergy without knowing any thing of their doctrine'. (To John Cruger, 30 June 1772, ibid., pp. 308–10.)

[87] 3 April 1772, *The Parliamentary History*, **XVII**, pp. 435–7.

[88] 26 April 1772, RI–1403, Wentworth Woodhouse MSS, printed Albemarle, Vol. II, p. 224. There are a few strands of evidence connecting the Rockingham Whigs with the Dissenters in the 1760s. On 1 July 1765, Newcastle suggested 'That the King's Minister should send for. . . . The most Eminent Dissenting Ministers, in, and about, London; & acquaint Them, That it is His Majesty's Intention To give His Royal Protection to The Protestant Dissenters. . . . This would greatly secure the Dissenters in the Countrey, who take Their Part, from the behaviour of the Dissenters, in, & about, London, Their Correspondents'. (Memorandum, B.M. Add. MSS 32967, ff. 177–80, Newcastle Papers: there is a copy in the Wentworth Woodhouse MSS RI.) Furthermore, Dr Watson argues that 'the most likely reason why Rockingham took no measures to set up an episcopate in America after the repeal of the Stamp Act was the fear of annoying the dissenters both at home and in the colonies' (*The Duke of Newcastle*, p. 64).

[89] Rockingham wrote in 1773: 'The relief they ask is in my mind highly reasonable and it is one of those matters, on which our friends in general like to shew themselves, as some test of the principals [*sic*] on which they avow to act'. (Rockingham to Burke, 9 February 1773, *Burke Correspondence*, Vol. II, pp. 423–4.)

[90] 'The Rockingham party is more insignificant than ever'. (Rev. W. Mason to F. F. Foljambe, 9 May 1772, *H.M.C. Foljambe*, Vol. I, p. 148.)

[91] Burke to Dowdeswell, 27 October 1772, *Burke Correspondence*, Vol. II, pp. 349–53. Rockingham also hoped that 'a Suspension of our attendance . . . would much alarm the Ministry—would force Several Parts of opposition

into more Attention towards us, & would also apprize the Publick of the danger they are in'. (To Dowdeswell, 30 October 1772, RI–1409, Wentworth Woodhouse MSS.)

[92] Burke to Rockingham, 29 October 1772, *Burke Correspondence*, Vol. II, pp. 353–7.

[93] Dowdeswell to Burke, 8 November 1772, ibid., pp. 366–7.

[94] Richmond to Burke, 15 November 1772, ibid., pp. 370–1; Richmond to Rockingham, 2 November 1772, RI–1411, Wentworth Woodhouse MSS.

[95] Rockingham to Burke, 24, 27 and 28 October 1772, *Burke Correspondence*, Vol. II, pp. 342–47. Rockingham to Dowdeswell, 30 October 1772, RI–1409, Wentworth Woodhouse MSS.

[96] Rockingham to Dowdeswell, 17 November 1772, RI–1412 A & B, ibid.

[97] Savile took the line that there was no issue of sufficient magnitude available which would render a secession warrantable. Savile to Rockingham, *n.d.* October 1772, RI–1410, ibid.

[98] Burke to Rockingham, 11 November 1772, *Burke Correspondence*, Vol. II, pp. 368–9.

[99] Burke to Rockingham, 19 November 1772, ibid., p. 378; Rockingham to Burke, 20 November 1772, ibid., p. 380.

CHAPTER 13

[1] The great Bengal famine in 1769 caused a steep decline in Company finances which was felt for some years afterwards. In 1771 the dividend was raised to $12\frac{1}{2}$ per cent and continued at that controversially high rate a year later. (This was in spite of the currency and credit crisis which swept Europe in 1772.) When the Company renewed the dividend in September 1772, the Government felt constrained to take action. Indeed, Indian affairs had been raised with increasing frequency in Parliament during the last few years. In spite of the superhuman activities of Warren Hastings to reform the Government and administration of Bengal, time was against him. Charges of corruption and maladministration were rife. On 16 April 1772 a committee of enquiry was appointed in the Commons, led by John Burgoyne. The establishment of this committee was opposed by the Rockinghams. (*The Parliamentary History*, **XVII**, pp. 461–63.) They also opposed its report, which laid much of the blame upon Lord Clive for the misgovernment of India. It may have been no coincidence that at this time Rockingham was trying to persuade Clive to support his party.

[2] George III to Lord North, 5 April 1773, Fortescue, Vol. II, p. 470. For a detailed account of the passage of the Regulating Act see L. S. Sutherland, *The East India Company in Eighteenth Century Politics*, Chapter 11.

[3] Rockingham to Portland, 20 November 1772, Portland MSS.

[4] The Marquis was seriously worried at the situation of his party and 'never felt more distress on any matters relating to politicks, than I do at

this present moment, on the Confused state in which Our Friends are, & must be at the meeting of Parlt'. (Rockingham to Dowdeswell, 17 November 1772, RI–1412, Wentworth Woodhouse MSS.) It was no doubt this consideration which led him to abandon the idea of secession. (Rockingham to Burke, 20 November 1772, loc. cit.)

⁵ Burke to Rockingham, 23 November 1772, *Burke Correspondence*, Vol. II, pp. 382–6. Rockingham firmly believed 'that *We* ought not to join in *Compelling* the Company *even* to do what would be right and prudent for them. (To Dowdeswell, 17 November 1772, R.78–13, Wentworth Woodhouse MSS.)

⁶ Rockingham to Charles Turner, 7 April 1772, RI–1402, ibid.

⁷ Richmond to Rockingham, 10 September 1773, R.158–63, ibid.

⁸ Rockingham to Dowdeswell, 30 November 1772, RI–1415, Wentworth Woodhouse MSS.

⁹ Burke to Rockingham, 23 November 1772, *Burke Correspondence*, Vol. II, pp. 382–6. J. Woods and L. Sutherland, 'The East India Speculations of William Burke', loc. cit., for the limited financial motivations of the Burkes in Indian affairs.

¹⁰ Dowdeswell to Burke, 3 November 1772, ibid., pp. 360–1.

¹¹ Burke to Dowdeswell, 27 October 1772, ibid., p. 351.

¹² The deleterious effects of the Rockinghamites' ineptitude on the Indian question were painfully apparent. Burke commented: 'My great uneasiness is about our own Corps, which appears to me in great danger of dissolution. Nothing can prevent it, in my opinion, but the speedy and careful application of Your Lordships own peculiar, persuasive and conciliatory manner, in talking over publick Business and leading them into a proper line of Conduct.' (Burke to Rockingham, 7 and 10 January 1773, *Burke Correspondence*, Vol. II, pp. 403–11.)

¹³ Rockingham to Portland, 8 January 1773, Portland MSS.

¹⁴ Chatham to Shelburne, 24 May 1773, *Chatham Correspondence*, Vol. IV, pp. 264–5.

¹⁵ Burke thought such a line of action 'is impolitic, is unwise, and entirely repugnant to the letter as well as the spirit of the laws, the liberties, and the constitution of this country' (*The Parliamentary History*, **XVII**, pp. 833–37).

¹⁶ Other demands were not conceded, including a bill to give security of tenure for Irish judges.

¹⁷ E. M. Johnston, *Great Britain and Ireland*, 1760–1800 (1763) Appendix E. See also Rockingham's Account Books, A.866. Wentworth Woodhouse MSS. V. T. Harlow (*The Second British Empire* (2 Vols, 1952–64), Vol. I, p. 517, n. 29) maintains that the absentee landlords took £1,000,000 per annum in rents. Rockingham estimated the figure at £368,500 (R3–166, Wentworth Woodhouse MSS).

¹⁸ Rockingham never denied that self-interest motivated him in 1773, but argued 'that I shall not willingly be guilty of any Negligence in a manner, wherein the Private Interests of so many are affected, & who while they are acting in their own defence, have also the Satisfaction of knowing & feeling, that the Interest, Good Policy & Freedom of the

Empire would suffer if the principles of the proposed Partial Land Tax on Absentees was adopted & carried into Execution'. (Rockingham's Second Circular Letter, R3–45, ibid.) He told Sir William Mayne that the belief that 'the warmth I profess agt this project . . . may be supposed to be in part occasioned by the consideration of my own interest' was unfounded. 'I trust I am not so biassed, & when I argue with myself, I think this measure of government so contrary to every principle on which I have acted . . .'. (J. E. Tyler, 'A Letter from the Marquis of Rockingham to Sir William Mayne on the proposed absentee Tax of 1773', *Irish Historical Studies*, Vol. VIII (1952–3), p. 367.) Burke claimed that self interest 'is not the sole nor the principal motive' of Rockingham's actions. (Burke to Sir Charles Bingham, 30 October 1773, *Burke Correspondence*, Vol. II, pp. 474–81.)

[19] Tyler, op. cit.; Rockingham to Richmond, *n.d.* 1773, R3–47, R1–1460, Wentworth Woodhouse MSS.

[20] Burke to Sir Charles Bingham, 30 October 1773, loc. cit. He had to admit, however: 'There is a superficial appearance of Equity in this Tax, which cannot fail to capitivate almost all those who are not led by some immediate interest to an attentive examination of its intrinsick merits'. (Burke to Rockingham, 29 September 1773, *Burke Correspondence*, Vol. II, pp. 464–71.) Burke's hostility to the Absentee Tax should be treated with the greatest reserve. Earlier in his life Burke had advocated just such a tax but this he now found it convenient to forget. Burke knew better than most how much harm the absentee landlords did to Ireland. About ten years earlier, in his *Tracts on the Popery Laws* he had campaigned against the privileges and inequalities in Irish society.

[21] Richmond to Rockingham, 31 October 1773, RI–1460A. Wentworth Woodhouse MSS, printed A. Olson, op. cit., pp. 156–9 and, in a form which can only be described as a travesty, by Albemarle, Vol. II, pp. 230–1.

[22] Rockingham to Burke, 20 September 1773, *Burke Correspondence*, Vol. II, pp. 458–9. See also Rockingham to Bessborough, Copy, 21 September 1773, RI–1446. Wentworth Woodhouse MSS printed Albemarle, Vol. II, pp. 228–9. Rockingham always sought to deny the imputation of faction. He wrote to Lord Upper Ossory on 13 October 1773 (R. 149–4, ibid.). 'In this concern I shall wish to act, so as to avoid any imputation of making this matter a mere Engine of Opposition. The Concerns of so many are Interested in very different political general ideas that I think the only Rule of Conduct should be what is equally right for all.'

[23] Rockingham to Bessborough, 21 September 1773, loc. cit.

[24] The replies to the circular (in R.3, Wentworth Woodhouse MSS) include letters from many landowners not normally associated with the Marquis. These included Lord Hertford, Lord Hillsborough, Lord Weymouth and the Duke of Chandos. There is a list of 42 peers and 46 others who were absentee landlords in the Wentworth Woodhouse MSS (R3–162). What must have pleased Rockingham almost as much as this was the very cordial reception which his circular received by members

of his own party who had little stake in Ireland, e.g. Sir Thomas Dundas wrote to Rockingham on 7 November (Zetland MSS) remarking that although his direct concern in Ireland was small yet 'I am very glad to see that the Opposition to this unprecedented and unjust measure, is to be taken up in the manner your Lordship mentions . . .'.

[25] The remonstrance was largely composed by Burke.

[26] George III to North, 19 October 1773, Fortescue, Vol. III, p. 16.

[27] Rockingham to Lord Upper Ossory, 13 October 1773, R.149–4, Wentworth Woodhouse MSS.

[28] George III to Lord North, 14 November 1773, Fortescue, Vol. III, p. 32.

[29] R3–152, Wentworth Woodhouse MSS.

[30] It should not be thought that a regular Opposition existed in Ireland, still less that it was the creature of the absentee landlords. For one thing, there were absentees of both the government and opposition groups. For another, the political influence of the absentee landlords was 'intermittent and uncertain', in Johnston's phrase (op. cit., p. 268).

[31] C. B. Cone, op. cit., p. 249.

[32] All the Rockinghams obtained from these soundings was a request from Wilkes to resume their payments to him. (John Wilkes to Chase Price, 6 November 1773, RI–1463(*a*) Wentworth Woodhouse MSS; Chase Price to Rockingham, 16 November 1773, RI–1463(*b*), ibid.) Rockingham was using Serjeant Glyn to spread Rockinghamite propaganda against the Absentee Tax in the City. (See his letters of 25 and 26 October to Glyn, Glyn MSS.)

[33] *The Annual Register* for 1773 described the Rockinghams rather sadly as 'the remains of the old Whig and revolution interest' (p. 62).

[34] Chatham to Shelburne, 24 October 1773, *Chatham Correspondence*, Vol. IV, pp. 299–302.

[35] Chatham to Shelburne, 4 November 1773, ibid., pp. 305–9.

[36] Wilkes, of course, had always been a symbolic figure to the Americans. For the picture of himself which he deliberately chose to paint for the sake of the Americans, see his letters to the Sons of Liberty in Boston (B.M. Add. MSS 30870, Wilkes Papers).

[37] Men hostile to British rule were already in positions of considerable influence in many colonial legislatures. In other words, the crisis did not ebb during 1770–2. It was merely awaiting a further incident or set of incidents before it revived.

[38] No problem need have arisen if Lord Dartmouth, an ex-Rockinghamite who became secretary of State for the Colonies in 1772, had followed Benjamin Franklin's sensible proposals, to repeal the Tea duty, allow the Company to export the tea to America and thus undercut the smuggled tea. This plan would have conciliated the colonists and assisted the recovery of the East India Company.

[39] Of course, the Boston Tea Party was greeted with enthusiasm throughout the colonies, but especially on the eastern seaboard. There is an excellent modern account of these events by B. W. Labaree (*The Boston Tea Party*, O.U.P. 1966).

⁴⁰ Newcastle to Rockingham, 12 September 1768, RI–1096, Wentworth Woodhouse MSS; Richmond to Rockingham, 12 December 1768, ibid., RI–1129.

⁴¹ See above pp. 203–4, 233–4; there are some examples of this aspect of Rockinghamite thinking (and some unnecessarily severe strictures upon the Rockinghams) in the essay by P. Langford ('The Rockingham Whigs and America, 1767–73' in *Statesmen, Scholars and Merchants* (O.U.P. 1973), Eds A. Whiteman, J. S. Bromley, and P. G. M. Dickson).

⁴² e.g. Rockingham to Burke, 30 January 1774, *Burke Correspondence*, Vol. II, pp. 515–16.

⁴³ Rockingham to Joseph Harrison, 2 October 1768, RI–1100, Wentworth Woodhouse MSS, Albemarle, Vol. II, pp. 78–80. For the decline of mercantile support for the colonists see p. 334.

⁴⁴ Rockingham to Joseph Harrison, 19 May 1769, RI–1186, Wentworth Woodhouse MSS.

⁴⁵ This is suggested by B. Donoughue, *British Politics and the American Revolution* (1964), p. 24.

⁴⁶ Lord John Cavendish to Rockingham, 29 January 1774, RI–1479. Even Chatham was shocked and angered. (Chatham to Shelburne, 20 March 1774, *Chatham Correspondence*, Vol. IV, p. 336.)

⁴⁷ Rockingham to Burke, 30 January 1774, loc. cit. The main reason the Rockinghams disliked the idea of settling the American problem by force was that they believed it would presage either military success, in which case the constitution would be at the mercy of the army, or a lengthy military struggle, which itself would throw up a large number of additional offices and sinecures. (Dowdeswell to Rockingham, 14 August 1768, Dowdeswell MSS.)

⁴⁸ Memorandum by the King on American affairs (Fortescue, Vol. III, pp. 47–8, dated 1773? but almost certainly 1774).

⁴⁹ Parliament, it is important to note, had reassembled on 13 January 1774. On 29 January, only two days after the news of the Tea Party reached England, the Cabinet decided that 'effectual steps be taken to secure the Dependence of the Colonies on the Mother Country' (B. Donoughue, op. cit., p. 34). For the care with which ministers worked out their coercive policy, see ibid., pp. 35–52.

⁵⁰ Ibid., pp. 76–86. The bill closed the harbour at Boston until compensation was paid to the East India Company and removed the Customs House centre to Salem (*The Parliamentary History*, **XVII**, 1163–1189).

⁵¹ H. Walpole, *Last Journals*, Vol. I, p. 364. That Richmond was very much on his own is evident when we consider that even Barré condemned the Tea Party.

⁵² The bill provided for the substitution of the elective council by one nominated by the Crown and for the appointment of the local law officers by the Governor of the colony. For the debates, see *The Parliamentary History* (**XVII**, pp. 1192–9, 1277–89, 1300–16).

⁵³ Ibid., pp. 1198–9.

⁵⁴ The bill passed its third reading by 239–64. The debate is discussed in some detail by B. Donoughue (op. cit., pp. 95–9).

⁵⁵ H. Walpole, *Last Journals*, Vol. I, p. 359.

⁵⁶ The act gave the Governor the power to transfer a prisoner to another colony for trial if he considered that it was impossible to obtain an impartial jury. This was, of course, a move to protect officials who might be charged with attempting to enforce the coercive acts. (*The Parliamentary History*, **XVII**, pp. 1199–1210, 1274–7, 1289–97, 1316–21, 1350–1.)

⁵⁷ Richmond to Rockingham, 18 May 1774, RI–1490, Wentworth Woodhouse, MSS. B. Donoughue, op. cit., pp. 100–1.

⁵⁸ This act extended earlier Quartering acts to permit Quartering in private homes. It is astonishing, in view of the unpopularity of quartering, that this act was not confined in its effects to Massachusetts.

⁵⁹ *The Parliamentary History*, **XVII**, pp. 1353–7, 28 May 1774; *Last Journals*, Vol. I, p. 369.

⁶⁰ The Quebec Act was quite separate from the coercive acts and had quite different antecedents, stemming from the need to order civil government both in Canada and the west. The settlement of boundaries and jurisdictions caused great offence to the Americans because the jurisdiction of the Quebec Governor was extended south and westwards along the St Lawrence, down through the Great Lakes and connecting up with the Mississippi. (See Donoughue, op. cit., pp. 105–26.) Donoughue argues (pp. 110, 126) that the Rockinghams had agreed in June 1766 with most of the provisions of this act. Their opposition on this occasion is consequently depicted as factious as well as impotent. Yet (*a*) no evidence is produced to support this statement (*b*) what the Rockinghams were considering in 1766 were purely legal matters of a technical nature (F. B. Wickwire, op. cit., pp. 148–9) (*c*) the small attendances of which Donoughue speaks (op. cit., pp. 125–6) were common to the Government as well as the Opposition side of the House and were, in any case, inevitable given the fact that the bill was only introduced into Parliament after Easter, in a session in which a dissolution was continuously being expected.

⁶¹ It thus appeared to the colonists that the ministry, not content with attacking their pockets, their liberties, their charters and their constitutions, was now discriminating against them and in favour of the Roman Catholic French-speaking Canadians.

⁶² H. Walpole, *Last Journals*, pp. 365–6.

⁶³ *The Parliamentary History*, **XVII**, pp. 1357–99.

⁶⁴ There were, however, some in the Rockingham party who were less happy than Rockingham was to oppose the Massachusetts Bay Bill because they believed that many of the colonial charters urgently needed reform. (The Duke of Manchester to Rockingham, 20 April 1774, RI–1486 Wentworth Woodhouse MSS. Albemarle, Vol. II, pp. 242–3.)

⁶⁵ R.49–1, Wentworth Woodhouse MSS. Jottings for a speech on the Boston Ports Bill.

⁶⁶ Fuller's motion was lost by 187–49. *The Parliamentary History*, **XVII**,

pp. 1210–74; Lord North to George III, 19 April 1774, Fortescue, Vol. III, pp. 95–6.

⁶⁷ Chatham's dream of a federal empire in which the local assemblies enjoyed sovereign power over a wide area of activities, stripped of its rhetoric, could hardly have existed in practice. He never defined the role of the Imperial Parliament, its relationship to the local legislatures, the location of authority over military and naval matters and the circumstances in which a component might or might not secede or be allowed to secede.

CHAPTER 14

¹ Burke to Rockingham, 18, 25 September 1774, *Burke Correspondence*, Vol. III, pp. 28–36.

² Rockingham to Burke, 13 September 1774, ibid., pp. 22–6.

³ Rockingham to Portland, 1 October 1774, Portland MSS.

⁴ Ibid. He had expected no dissolution before the second half of November.

⁵ Rockingham to Savile, May 1774, Ramsden MSS; Rockingham to Savile, *n.d.*, ibid., Rockingham to Savile, 9 August 1774, RI–1497, Wentworth Woodhouse MSS; Lady Rockingham to Savile, 10 August 1774, RI–1499; Lady Rockingham to Lord Rockingham, August 1774, RI–1500, ibid.; Savile to Portland, 2 October 1774, Portland MSS.

⁶ In the summer of 1773 Lord Weymouth made an unsuccessful attempt to reconcile Portland and Lowther.

⁷ Rockingham to Lord John Cavendish, 5 and 6 October 1774 (wrongly dated 1768, RI–1511, Wentworth Woodhouse MSS); Burke complained to Rockingham of Cavendish's inattention to his duties (5 January 1775, *Burke Correspondence*, Vol. III, p. 89). Cavendish tried to throw some of the blame for their difficulties at York upon Charles Turner. (Cavendish to Rockingham, 5 October 1774, RI–1512, Wentworth Woodhouse MSS, partly *q* B. Donoughue, op. cit., p. 190.) The result was Turner, 828, Cavendish, 807, M. B. Hawke, 647.

⁸ B. Bonsall, op. cit., pp. 122–40; Charles Howard to Lord Carlisle, 7 October 1774, *H.M.C. Carlisle*, p. 280.

⁹ Portland to Rockingham, 8 October 1774, RI–1514, Wentworth Woodhouse MSS; Rockingham to Sir Charles Sedley, 8 October 1774, RI–1515, ibid.; Sedley to Rockingham, 9 October 1774, RI–1517, ibid.; Rockingham to Portland, 9 October 1774, Portland MSS. Bentinck, however, came in for the county in 1775.

¹⁰ The Rockingham lords would not help Verney. Richmond even supported Temple against him. Burke's acid response to such behaviour ought, once and for all, to dispose of the lingering view that he was invariably obsequious to the Whig lords. (Richmond to Burke, 26 September 1774, *Burke Correspondence*, Vol. III, p. 37; Burke to Richmond, *post*-26 September 1774, ibid., pp. 38–40.)

¹¹ C. B. Cone, op. cit., p. 266 for details.

¹² Rockingham to Burke, 2 October 1774, *Burke Correspondence*, Vol. III,

p. 49. The Marquis had been driven to distraction by Edmund Burke's insistence that he would continue in Parliament only if his cousin, William, were also a Member but there was little prospect of finding a seat for him in 1774: 'this situation of Burke is a great additional perplexity'. (Rockingham to Portland, 1 October 1774, Portland MSS.)

[13] See the documentation in B. Donoughue, op. cit., pp. 192–3; L. B. Namier and J. Brooke, *The House of Commons*, Vol. I, pp. 285–6; C. B. Cone, op. cit., pp. 267–75. The offer to Burke had been in contemplation since the summer, and Burke knew of it. (Burke to Wilson, 1 July 1774, *Burke Correspondence*, Vol. III, pp. 3–4). Henry Cruger, MP for Bristol, visited Edmund at Beaconsfield in July but their discussion scarcely touched on electoral matters. It was, however, another group in the city of Bristol headed by Richard Champion, a Quaker manufacturer, which made the final offer to Burke in October. The final result was Cruger, 3565, Burke, 2707, Brickdale, 2456, Lord Clare, 283. That the Bristol radicals were a little suspicious of Burke is reflected in the fact that 20 per cent of those who voted for Cruger gave their second votes to Brickdale.

[14] Portsmouth is a good example of a borough which was shortly to debate national issues with some vigour, and where in 1774 there appeared to be the materials for a campaign in which national issues might play a part. Portsmouth was a government borough but the corporation revolted against ministerial control and put a candidate of its own, a Dissenter, who came within three votes of ousting the ministerial candidate. But even this exciting election was not fought out on national or imperial issues but on the rights of out-voters. (*The Hampshire Chronicle*, 26 September 1774; Lake Allen, *History of Portsmouth* (1817, p. 108; A. Geddes, *Portsmouth during the French Wars, 1700–1800* (1970), p. 15.)

[15] Since 1765–6 the merchants had to a large extent diversified their trade. Very few of them were by 1774 wholly dependent upon the American market. It is not without significance that although there were a dozen or so petitions against the coercive acts, the Rockinghams never thought of organising a campaign of mercantile protest against them.

[16] For example, William Baker requested help from Rockingham (14 September 1774, RI–1505, Wentworth Woodhouse MSS) but received a negative response. It was one of Rockingham's mistakes not to have encouraged Baker (who did not find a seat until 1777) for he was an important London merchant and might have assisted Rockingham to establish an interest in the City.

[17] The two Yorkes, Charles and John, Sir William Meredith and Rose Fuller.

[18] T. Anson (1770), Sir S. Cornish (1790), F. W. Osbaldeston (1770), J. West (d. 1772) and Sir M. Fetherstonehaugh.

[19] G. Adams (1770), Lord R. Cavendish (1773), W. Coke (1772), Sir T. Frankland (1768/9), J. Hanbury (1768/9), Sir J. Pennyman (1770), T. Skipwith (1769).

[20] Of the original 48 the 15 who went out were: W. Baker, A. Beauclerk, Lord E. Bentinck, W. Burke, N. Cholmley, H. Curwen, Lord Downe,

Richard Fuller, J. Hewett, G. Musgrave, J. Murray, J. Norris, J. Offley, J. Plumptre, W. Weddell. The 33 who were returned again were: Sir A. Abdy, W. A'Court, Sir E. Astley, Sir C. Barrow, E. Burke, G. Byng, Lords F. G. and J. Cavendish, Sir R. Clayton, Sir W. Codrington, T. Connolly, R. H. Coxe, G. Dempster, W. Dowdeswell, S. Finch, H. Fletcher, T. Hay, H. Harbord, B. Hotham, A. Keppel, W. Keppel, Lord G. Lennox, Lord Ludlow, F. Montagu, W. Plumer, Sir C. Saunders, Sir G. Savile, J. Scawen, B. Thompson, C. Turner, Lord Verney and R. Walsingham.

[21] D. Hartley, Governor Johnstone and Lord Lumley.

[22] Dr Donoughue has an estimate of the Rockingham Whig Party (*British Politics and the American Revolution*, Appendix One) which is, superficially, approximately the same as my own. His list of thirty-eight contains, however, Charles James Fox and the Foley group. It is true that Fox was already being regarded as a member of *opposition* but he was not for some time yet to be a member of the Rockingham Whig party. Furthermore, Dr Donoughue's list of Independents, 'not regular members' of an opposition group contain the following names which seem to me to belong indisputably in the Rockingham camp: Sir E. Astley, W. Coke, R. H. Coxe, Sir T. Frankland, J. Hanbury, T. Hay, Sir J. Pennyman and C. Turner.

[23] Their locations are given in Namier and Brooke, op. cit., Vol. I, pp. 528–9). The five divisions are those of 27 January (278–131), 2 February (239–136), 3 February (219–137), 15 April (197–143) and 8 May (221–152).

[24] The locations of the division lists are given in Namier and Brooke, op. cit. (Vol. I, p. 529).

[25] The location of the division list is given in Namier and Brooke, op. cit. (Vol. I, p. 529). The division figure was 224–180.

[26] In a division of 201–151. For the division list see Namier and Brooke, op. cit. (p. 530).

[27] Ibid., pp. 529–31. Mr Donoughue bases his hostile assessment of the Rockinghams upon a single division list. It is difficult to agree with him that a division as late as 6 May 1774 with an Opposition vote as low as twenty-four is 'an interesting and useful piece of evidence' (op. cit., p. 136). Division lists are of only limited use and a single list is of very little value. To conclude that this list shows that the Rockinghams 'found it difficult to convince and to muster their regular supporters to vote against the Government's American policies' (ibid., p. 141), is unwarranted. Furthermore, it presupposes that the Rockinghams *were* adamantly opposed to the Coercive acts.

[28] See, for example, the attitude of A. Olson (*The Radical Duke*) who speaks of the party's 'decline and near disintegration' and who places much of the blame upon the indolence of Rockingham and his failure to hold party meetings on the eve of the sessions of 1773, 1776, 1777 and 1778 (pp. 33–4). A hostile and provocative assessment of Rockingham is provided by Mr Brooke (*The Chatham Administration*, pp. 24–6).

[29] Some contemporaries and some historians have found amusing the failure of Rockingham to speak frequently in the House of Lords. Although

it is not clear if he suffered from a speech defect, Rockingham was almost physically incapable of speaking in public. He was affected by a nervous disorder which manifested itself in severe palpitations, trembling and other types of physical discomfort. (See, for example, the Duchess of Grafton to Viscountess Irwin, *H.M.C. Lindley Wood*, p. 184.) When he was able to overcome this handicap, Rockingham could speak tolerably well, to judge from the favourable comments which greeted his rare speeches. Furthermore, Rockingham certainly *intended* to speak more frequently than he did. There are many drafts and sketches of speeches which he never made in the Wentworth Woodhouse MSS.

³⁰ These included W. A'Court, G. Adams, Sir E. Astley, C. Barrow, Sir R. Clayton, Sir W. Codrington, W. Coke, R. H. Coxe, G. Dempster, W. Dowdeswell, J. Hanbury, H. Harbord, T. Hay, Lord Ludlow, Lord Lumley, Sir J. Pennyman and R. Walsingham.

CHAPTER 15

¹ B. Donoughue, op. cit., p. 16.

² B. Bargar; *Lord Dartmouth and the American Revolution* (University of South Carolina Press, 1965), p. 145.

³ It is now generally conceded that in terms of psychology and ideology the Americans were *already* united, having earlier in the century absorbed the political language and ideological concepts of British opposition groups. These they now proceeded to utilise against the claims of the British Parliament. The classic statement of this view is B. Bailyn, *The Ideological Origins of the American Revolution* (Cambridge, Massachusetts, 1967). What must not be overlooked, however, is the extent to which Americans were influenced by anti-ministerial attitudes in Britain in 1774 itself. Americans avariciously digested news from Britain, especially parliamentary speeches and opposition pamphlets. For contacts between the Opposition in America and Opposition circles in Britain (see P. Maier, *From Resistance to Revolution* (New York, 1972) *passim*).

⁴ For Americans' growing suspicion of the King's involvement in the American policy of his ministers and their gradual rejection of his authority (see ibid., pp. 237–41).

⁵ The unity of American resistance to the coercive legislation should not, however, be exaggerated. Sectional and geographical differences tended to restrict the amount of sympathy upon which the Bostonians could rely. Perhaps the most important legislative act tending to unite Americans was the Quebec Act. Furthermore, the very idea of a Congress was attractive to very many Americans who thought that the radicals of Boston and Virginia might best be held in check by that means.

⁶ The Earl of Dunmore, writing to Dartmouth from Williamsburg on 24 December 1774 (*H.M.C. Dartmouth*, Vol. II, p. 243), illustrates the extent to which imperial authority had sunk. 'The Associations first in part entered into by the Colony and adopted by the Continental Congress are

now enforcing throughout the country with great vigour. A committee is chosen in every county to carry the Association of the Congress into execution. They inspect the trade and correspondence of any merchant, watch the conduct of any inhabitant, may send for, catechize, and stigmatize him if he does not appear to follow the laws of their Congress. Every city besides is arming an independent Company to protect their Committees and to be employed against Government should occasion require. . . . The power of Government . . . is intirely disregarded if not wholly overturned. Not a Justice of the Peace acts except as a Committee-man.'

[7] Gage once wrote with disarming honesty about his own position: 'I have endeavoured to be a mediator, if I could establish a foundation to work upon. . . . I should hope that decency and moderation here would create the same disposition at home'. (Gage to Peyton Randolph, 20 October 1774, *H.M.C. Dartmouth*, Vol. II, pp. 231–2.)

[8] The King wrote to North as early as 11 September 1774 to affirm that 'the dye is now cast, the Colonies must either submit or triumph' (Fortescue, Vol. III, pp. 130–1). For the ministry's policy in 1774–5 see Alann J. McCurry, 'The North Government and the Outbreak of the American Revolution', *Huntington Library Quarterly*, 3rd Series, **34** (1970–1), pp. 141–6.

[9] A couple of ships of war were sent to Boston in October but apart from this, and a few other ineffective gestures, nothing else was ventured by the end of 1774 (A. McCurry, op. cit., pp. 142–3). It is extraordinary that nothing was done at this time to strengthen the navy. Although the reputation of Sandwich has been somewhat rescued by modern scholars (he had, for example, tried with some success to resist North's cheeseparing economies since 1772), he seemingly acquiesced in the estimates for 1775. Astonishingly, these provided for 4,000 *fewer* sailors than in the previous year. He was also content with an army of 17,500. Furthermore, it was not until 1 December 1774 that ministers actually asked the law officers to determine that Massachusetts was legally in a state of rebellion. (Thurlow and Wedderburn pronounced in the affirmative on 13 December).

[10] B. Donoughue, op. cit., pp. 219–30. There was only one alternative to a policy of military enforcement and that was a policy of political conciliation. Indeed, to some slight extent the confusion and uncertainty surrounding British policy towards America in 1774–5 may be accounted for by the consideration given to conciliation by the ministers. The Opposition, furthermore, was for several years to advocate a conciliatory policy. But how practical was it and to what extent did North and Dartmouth make a sincere attempt to achieve it? In late November 1774 Benjamin Franklin was unofficially approached and he drew up a list of the concessions which he considered the Congress was most likely to demand. These amounted to the abandonment of the coercive legislation, the admission by Britain of the principle of consent in all future economic and commercial links between Britain and the colonists, and the control of salaries of royal officials by the assemblies. The only concession to the British offered by Franklin lay in his recognition that the colonists ought

to provide partial compensation for the tea lost by the East India Company. In effect, Franklin was demanding not only the renunciation of the taxing power by the British Parliament, but also the repudiation of the Declaratory Act, the weakening to vanishing point of British military power in America and the commercial reorganisation of the Empire. The King, the Cabinet and Parliament would never accept such proposals and Dartmouth knew it. There is a detailed discussion in B. D. Bargar, *Lord Dartmouth and the American Revolution* (pp. 134-7). It is clear from Bargar's account that rather more progress was made in these discussions than is conventionally allowed. Briefly, Franklin offered to pay for the tea thrown into Boston harbour, and Dartmouth offered to repeal the tea act. Moreover, Dartmouth assented to Franklin's request that acts affecting colonial manufactures should be investigated, and that revenues from acts of imperial regulation should go to the colonists. Franklin sought to overcome the enormous problem surrounding the imperial taxing power by only activating it in wartime when requisitions would operate, which would bar a direct relationship to the English Land Tax. Dartmouth was willing to review the coercive legislation but drew the line at allowing the colonial legislature to review the laws of trade and to refuse the quartering of troops. Finally, Dartmouth was *not* willing to compromise over the Quebec act. Nevertheless, he was able to persuade his colleagues in January that the policy of military enforcement of the coercive acts ought to be accompanied by a last attempt at peace negotiations, and that these ought to proceed from the principle that the colonists should raise their own revenue to finance both civil and military expenditure. It is by no means clear how sincerely these conciliation proposals were intended by the Cabinet. Even Dartmouth must have known, after his discussions with Franklin, that these proposals would be completely unacceptable to the Americans. Probably the Cabinet agreed to go through the motions of a policy of conciliation in order to defend itself from adverse comment at home, rather than to attempt to make one final, realistic attempt to come to grips with the American problem. Indeed, conciliation was far from the minds of several members of the Cabinet—and of the King. The restoration of imperial rule and the pacification of Massachusetts were their paramount concerns.

[11] In particular, Rockingham did not lack information of the rapidly deteriorating British position and the readiness of the colonists to resist by force if necessary (e.g. Rev. T. Coombe to Rockingham, 5 November 1774, RI–1532, Wentworth Woodhouse MSS).

[12] In September, at least, he did not believe that America would be the crucial issue of the next session. (Burke to Rockingham 18, 25 September 1774, *Burke Correspondence*, Vol. III, pp. 28–36.)

[13] Rockingham to Mansfield, 1 November 1774, RI–1525, Wentworth Woodhouse MSS, printed Albemarle, Vol. II, pp. 257–9.

[14] Rockingham to George Dempster, 13 September 1774, RI–1504, Wentworth Woodhouse MSS, printed Albemarle, Vol. II, pp. 252–7.

[15] *The Parliamentary History*, **XVIII**, pp. 45–6. Burke may have been encouraged by the fact that in spite of the weaknesses of opposition the

ministry had agreed, having earlier refused, to make available to the House of Commons papers relating to America (ibid., pp. 59–60).

[16] Burke to Rockingham, 5 January 1775, *Burke Correspondence*, Vol. III, pp. 88–90.

[17] Rockingham to Burke, 7, 8 January 1775, *Burke Correspondence*, Vol. III, pp. 90–3.

[18] Manchester to Rockingham, 18 January 1775, RI–1539, Wentworth Woodhouse MSS, printed Albermarle, Vol. II, pp. 265–7.

[19] Richmond to Rockingham, 28 January 1775, RI–1540, ibid., pp. 268–9.

[20] 'The Duke of Richmond told me that for two hours he could scarcely resolve to vote for the motion' (*Last Journals of Horace Walpole*, Vol. II, p. 447).

[21] *The Parliamentary History*, **XVIII**, pp. 164–5.

[22] Although the Rockinghams had been anticipating something from Chatham they did not know what to expect. 'More would have been in the Minority if Lord Chatham had thought proper to give notice of his motion to the proper people.' (Burke to the Citizens of Bristol, 20 January 1775, *Burke Correspondence*, Vol. III, pp. 101–3.) All that Chatham confided to Shelburne was an intimation of 'an address to send immediate orders for removing the forces from Boston' (19 January 1775, *Chatham Correspondence*, Vol. IV, pp. 374–5).

[23] RI–1543 Wentworth Woodhouse MSS. After receiving Chatham's abrupt note, Rockingham wrote to Portland in some mystification: 'His letter is in *words* civil, but it is very strange conduct, and not such as ought to be' (31 January 1775, Portland MSS). Rockingham also wrote to Shelburne but found that nobleman none the wiser concerning Chatham's plans. (Rockingham to Shelburne, 31 January 1775, RI–1545, Wentworth Woodhouse MSS; Shelburne to Rockingham, 1 February 1775, ibid., RI–1546.) At the very last minute, Richmond tried unsuccessfully to act as an intermediary between the two sections of the opposition. (Richmond to Chatham, 1 February 1775, *Chatham Correspondence*, Vol. IV, pp. 391–3.)

[24] Dartmouth was very unsteady in his conduct. He stated in the debate that he would be willing to allow the bill to lie on the table. Sandwich was vehement in his opposition to anything which might undermine yet further what was left of imperial authority in America. His speech and the temper of the debate brought Dartmouth into line and he voted in the majority. (*The Parliamentary History*, **XVIII**, pp. 198–203; B. Bargar, op. cit., pp. 131–3.) Franklin had been in touch with Chatham while he was preparing the bill but his influence upon it was inconsiderable. One reason why there was little consultation with the Rockinghams may have been the fact that Chatham hurried his bill into the Lords on 1 February, knowing that the ministry intended to make an important statement of policy on the following day.

[25] Gage had made himself unpopular in ministerial circles by his liberal attitude towards the colonists and his eagerness to see negotiations between the Massachusetts deputies and the ministry while the coercive acts were

suspended. Furthermore, because Gage was Governor of the Bay Colony as well as Commander in Chief it was thought that he might not be sufficiently mobile to deal with disturbances up and down the continent. Gage retained his position because Amherst refused the ministerial offers.

[26] It had no alternative after the latest stream of reports from America and by a new opinion of the law officers (B. Donoughue, op. cit., pp. 239–40). On 6 February the Opposition divided the House on an Address to the King which asserted that urgent measures were needed to deal with the rebellion in the colonies. The division figure was 288–105 (*The Parliamentary History*, **XVIII**, pp. 233–65). The Address was debated in the Lords on the following day and passed after a lengthy debate by 104–29. The Opposition entered a protest against the Address on the grounds that it amounted to a declaration of war and contained nothing of a conciliatory nature (*The Parliamentary History*, **XVIII**, pp. 265–96. There is a division list in Portland's hand in the Wentworth Woodhouse MSS RI–1551. H. Walpole, *Last Journals*, Vol. I, pp. 457–8).

[27] For the passage of this bill, see A. McCurry, op. cit. (pp. 150–2).

[28] For the origins of North's Proposal see B. Donoughue, op. cit., p. 246; J. Sosin, *Agents and Merchants*, pp. 213–14; W. Brown, *Empire or Independence* (Louisiana, 1941), pp. 35–47; B. D. Bargar, op. cit., pp. 138–40.

[29] For the debate, see *The Parliamentary History*, **XVIII**, pp. 320–37.

[30] The ministerial press was also stridently opposed to North over the Proposition. (S. Lutnick, *The American Revolution and the British Press* (University of Missouri Press, 1967), pp. 50–1.)

[31] The Congress rejected the Proposition in July as 'unsatisfactory because it imports only a suspension of the mode, not a renunciation of the pretended right to tax us'.

[32] The real feelings of ministers can best be gauged by their speeches on this bill. In the main debate, on the report stage on 6 March, ministerialists were quite clear that they regarded the bill as a punishment for the resistance of the colonists to the Tea act and the coercive legislation. Conciliation was not mentioned. Of course, the Opposition seized on this fact. Charles James Fox (who had resigned his Lordship of the Treasury in February 1774 and begun to support the Opposition consistently by the end of the 1774 session), criticised ministers for using taxation as a form of punishment and predicted that this bill would simply alienate the Americans further. Nevertheless, the division figure of 215–61 indicated the prevailing sentiment. (*The Parliamentary History*, **XVIII**, pp. 379–92, 411–12. H. Walpole, *Last Journals*, Vol. I, pp. 468–71.) The debates on the bill in the Lords were remarkable chiefly for the weakness and lack of preparation on the part of the Opposition. Rockingham was able neither to bring his own men to town nor to concert strategy and attendance with Chatham. On 15 March the bill was committed by the enormous majority of 104–29 and passed its third reading the following day by 73–21 (*The Parliamentary History*, **XVIII**, pp. 421–58). Richmond even refused to come to town. 'I am growing daily less capable of being useful' he wrote to Rockingham and lamented that 'we are ever much hurried when we are most fatigued &

less able to do business' (12 March 1775, RI–1559, Wentworth Woodhouse MSS). An additional bill, to apply to the colonies of New Jersey, Pennsylvania, South Carolina, Virginia and Maryland passed through Parliament in March and April with scarcely any opposition.

³³ *The Parliamentary History*, **XVIII**, pp. 478–538. The quality of the three-hour speech was immediately recognised by friends and foes alike. (Rockingham to Burke, 22 March 1775, *Burke Correspondence*, Vol. III, p. 139.)

³⁴ It is interesting to compare the conciliation plans of Burke, Chatham and North. Burke and Chatham shared much common ground, including their belief in the need for peace and their retreat from taxing the Americans. Even North agreed, to a large extent, that the colonists should tax themselves. Chatham and Burke differed from North mainly in their rejection of the coercive legislation. On the other hand, it was North and Chatham rather than Burke who saw, correctly, that whatever Burke might say about rights, the American problem turned on the issue of sovereignty. Nevertheless, Chatham and Burke took up very similar positions, advocating conciliation and the ending of all attempts to tax the colonists. Chatham argued from the principle of representation, Burke from expediency, but their conclusions were much the same. It seems extraordinary, in retrospect, that Chatham and the Rockinghams were unable to work more closely together after 1775.

³⁵ Burke to Richard Champion, 10 January 1775, *Burke Correspondence*, Vol. III, pp. 94–7.

³⁶ Burke to the Committee of Correspondence of the New York General Assembly, 14 March 1775, ibid., pp. 133–6.

³⁷ Dr Donoughue (op. cit., p. 238) draws attention to petitions from merchants in London, two from Bristol, one from Glasgow, Norwich, Dudley, Liverpool, Manchester and Wolverhampton demanding conciliation which were either ignored or lost in committee. C. R. Ritcheson commented that the petitions were 'moderate in tone and few in number, these missives evidenced no very profound revulsion against American measures' (op. cit., p. 181.) Leeds and Nottingham, and probably other places, presented petitions in favour of ministerial policy (J. Sosin, *Agents and Merchants*, pp. 218–20).

³⁸ John Smith to Rockingham, 6 February 1775, RI–1550. Wentworth Woodhouse MSS, for the loyalist spirit in Leeds. Rockingham would not accept the fact that the loyalists were more than a small minority. (Rockingham to P. Milnes (in Lady Rockingham's hand), 15 February 1775, RI–1553, ibid.)

³⁹ As Burke readily acknowledged. (Burke to Rockingham, 23 August 1775, *Burke Correspondence*, Vol. III, pp. 189–95.)

⁴⁰ Chatham to General Tarleton, *n.d.* 1775, *Chatham Correspondence*, Vol. IV, p. 407.

⁴¹ Richmond to Rockingham, 17 February 1775, RI–1554, Wentworth Woodhouse MSS.

⁴² In February Dartmouth had instructed Gage to take the initiative

against the Bostonians, especially by depriving them of their arms. The Lexington engagement was a natural consequence of this instruction.

CHAPTER 16

[1] Burke, although tired and ill, had presented a Remonstrance from the New York General Assembly which claimed exclusive rights of internal taxation for the colonies. On 15 May North dismissed the Remonstrance because it violated the Declaratory Act and it was thrown out by 186–67. (Burke to the Committee of Correspondence of the New York Assembly (for which he was a paid agent), 7 June 1775, *Burke Correspondence*, Vol. III, pp. 164–7.)

[2] F. J. Hinkhouse, op. cit., pp. 183–6.

[3] Fortescue, Vol. III, p. 175. Although it is often assumed that the King's views merely reflected British opinion towards America, there was considerable sympathy for the Americans in Britain in the summer of 1775 (Hinkhouse, op. cit., pp. 185–97). The King's views, however, were unhappily inflexible. 'That Parliament did not have the *full taxing* power over the colonies,' he wrote in July, 'I will ever vehemently oppose' (George III to Lord North, 9 July 1775, Fortescue, Vol. III, pp. 233–4). He protested his devotion to the preservation of imperial integrity, but the narrowness of his vision and the rigidity of his views left his ministry set fair upon a path which led to its destruction. By his own admission, the American war was 'the most serious in which any Country was ever engaged'. (George III to Lord North, 11 July, 1779, ibid., Vol. IV, pp. 350–1.) When North was beginning to question whether the war was really worth all the efforts being expended upon it, the King claimed that if America obtained her independence then 'the West Indies must follow them. Ireland would soon follow . . . then this Island would be reduced to itself, and would soon be a poor island indeed' (ibid.). It is not suggested that the King alone was responsible either for the war or for the loss of the colonies. But it can at least be said that he failed to exercise any kind of effective supervision of the war effort, that he persisted in a military solution of the American problem when it had clearly become irrelevant and that he clung to the impotent and discredited North administration because he feared the political upheaval which its replacement might entail.

[4] The Congress sent its so-called 'Olive Branch' to London on 8 July. This requested the King to redress American grievances. Although the Olive Branch did not represent the opinion of all members of the Congress, its summary rejection by the King caused great offence in America. (See B. Bargar, op. cit., pp. 151–6.)

[5] P. Mackesy, *The War for America* (1964), p. 12.

[6] For an account of the King's activities with respect to the war (see J. Brooke, *George III*, pp. 179–83).

[7] A separate department for the colonies had come about with the

accession of the Bedfords. Hillsborough was the first Secretary, Dartmouth the second. For an account of the office (see A. H. Basye, 'The Secretary of State for the Colonies, 1768-82', *American Historical Review*, **XXVIII** (1922), pp. 13-23).

[8] The Proclamation of Rebellion issued on 23 August 1775 put the formal seal upon the outbreak of hostilities. Such a Proclamation had been mooted as early as December 1774 and was revived in the summer of 1774 at the instigation of the King and Suffolk. A draft was prepared (possibly without North's approval) by Suffolk and Eden and submitted by Robinson to North. (See the correspondence in *H.M.C. Abergavenny*, pp. 10-11.)

[9] William Howe, MP for Nottingham 1758-80. He was one of the three Major-generals sent to America in 1775. He became Commander-in-Chief on Gage's recall.

[10] Grafton, the Lord Privy Seal, had become disillusioned with the coercive policy and, according to some reports, was persuaded by Fox to voice his objections to it. This he did in Parliament at the beginning of the session and he consequently resigned in November 1775. Dartmouth put forward his own name for the vacant office, ignoring both Lord Weymouth's prior claims and the King's suggestion that he become Groom of the Stole with a seat in the Cabinet (George III to Lord North, 6 November 1775, Fortescue, Vol. III, p. 277). A scheme to place Dartmouth in one of the other Secretaryships floundered because neither Rochford nor Suffolk would agree to be moved (and in effect to be demoted) (North to the King, 8 November 1775, ibid., p. 282). In the end the *impasse* was resolved when Weymouth was persuaded to take the Southern Secretaryship, an office he had held from 1768 to 1770. (Rochford was prevailed upon to resign.) Dartmouth's pride was satisfied with the Privy Seal. The King, of course, was furious with Dartmouth. 'It is too much when all things seemed well settled to have them disturbed by the absurdity of one individual.' (George III to Lord North, 9 November 1775, ibid., pp. 282-3.) North had believed that 'unless some method is found out of preventing the dissatisfaction of Lord Weymouth & Lord Dartmouth, the Ministry will be dissolved'. (Lord North to George III, 7 November 1775, ibid., p. 278.) What North had in mind, no doubt, was the prospect that without Dartmouth in the Cabinet he would become a prisoner of Suffolk and the Bedfords. Nevertheless, those members of the Cabinet who were worried lest North's easy-going ways and love of compromise might endanger the progress of the war, had already begun to renew their contacts with Germain some time earlier. Suffolk and Eden had been in touch with Germain during the summer. (Suffolk to Eden, 20 June 1775, B.M. Add. MSS 34412, f. 339, Auckland Papers; Eden to North, 13 September 1775, ibid., 36490, ff. 6-7.)

[11] In some ways, however, the appointment of Germain backfired upon those who had promoted it. Weymouth and Suffolk soon discovered that they had brought into the Cabinet a man who was unwilling to remain a docile, junior partner to them, as first Hillsborough and then Darmouth had done. (There are details of the feud between the Secretaries in M. M.

Spector, *The American Department of the British Government, 1768–82* (New York, 1940) Chapter 5.)

[12] Eden to Germain, 3 & 21 October 1775, *H.M.C. Stopford–Sackville*, Vol. II, pp. 10–12.

[13] Mansfield's decision was accepted: that the colonies should be invited to make proposals for negotiation. Those which did not, would be recognised to be at war with Britain.

[14] The Rockingham's intelligence service was almost as good as that enjoyed by ministers. See, for example, The Duke of Manchester to Rockingham, 30 May 1775 (R63–14, Wentworth Woodhouse MSS).

[15] Rockingham to Burke, 23 June 1775, *Burke Correspondence*, Vol. III, pp. 172–3.

[16] Richmond to Burke, 16 June 1775, ibid., pp. 170–1.

[17] Burke to Richard Champion, 19 July 1775, ibid., pp. 179–80.

[18] Rockingham to the Duke of Manchester, 28 June 1775. (Copy in Lady Rockingham's hand), RI–1569, Wentworth Woodhouse MSS. 'The American war more than any other event seemed to provide final confirmation of the plot to subvert the British constitution and men's political liberties. Here was the example *par excellence* of the plan to increase prerogative, expand corruption and the powers of the Crown, and enslave the subject. Although Bute's immediate role in the government's activity in the 1770s was thought to be negligible, the responsibility for the attack on the colonists' liberties was inexorably traced back to his establishment many years before of the dual system of government.' (J. Brewer; The Faces of Lord Bute: A Visual Contribution to Anglo-American Political Ideology', *Perspectives in American History*, Vol. VI, 1972.)

[20] Rockingham to the Duke of Manchester, loc. cit.

[21] Ibid.; Rockingham to Burke, 11 September 1775, R1–1600, Wentworth Woodhouse MSS. Richmond, characteristically, took an unusual and a deeply humane stance. '. . . it is the artisan, the Labourer and manufacturer and Merchant who will feel' the effects of the war. (Richmond to Burke, 16 June 1775, loc. cit.)

[22] Burke to Rockingham, 4 August 1775, *Burke Correspondence*, Vol. III, pp. 182–4.

[23] Burke to Rockingham, 22, 23 August 1775, ibid., pp. 190–4.

[24] The object of the manifesto was to convince *the King* that the disasters of the colonial relationship had arisen from the system of secret influence. (Rockingham to Burke, 11 September 1775, ibid., pp. 203–6.)

[25] Burke to Rockingham, 14 September 1775, ibid., p. 211.

[26] Rockingham to Lord John Cavendish (in Lady Rockingham's hand), 18 September 1775, R158–84, Wentworth Woodhouse MSS, Rockingham to Burke, 24 September 1775. Ibid., RI–1602.

[27] Burke to Rockingham, 1 October 1775, *Burke Correspondence*, Vol. III, pp. 222–5.

[28] Rockingham to John Scudamore, 16 October 1775, RI–1610, Wentworth Woodhouse MSS. At this time, Rockingham attempted to define the new meaning of party names: 'the Warmth & Eagerness

with which most glaringly, the old Tory Party adopt & join in forwarding there Views are matters . . . (which) should not be totally unattended to by Persons, who would not content themselves with being nominal Whigs, nor would suffer Combinations to arise again, nor would wish to see the strongest Union cemented among Men who would rejoice to Eradicate every Whig Principle out of the Dominions of his Majesty.' (Rockingham to Sir John Griffin Griffin, 22 October 1775, D/DBy.C9/17 Braybrooke MSS. Essex Record Office.) It is worth remarking that, such labels were very common in pamphlets and the press (see, for examples, S. Lutnick, op. cit., p. viii).

[29] Burke to Portland, 5 October 1775, *Burke Correspondence*, Vol. III, p. 226.

[30] Horace Walpole commented that the speech contained 'three or four gross falsehoods': the first, that the Americans designed to establish an independent empire . . . second, that Foreign Powers had offered us assistance . . . the third was, pleading the conciliatory plan of last winter as indication of disposition to peace. . . . But the most striking part was the King's notification of a design of sending Commissioners to treat with any provinces that should with to return to their duty'. Walpole concludes that the Americans would never treat with the present ministry (*Last Journals* Vol. I, p. 510).

[31] A. Storer to Lord Carlisle, 27 October 1775, *H.M.C. Carlisle*, pp. 298–9.

[32] *The Parliamentary History*, **XVIII**, pp. 708–29.

[33] Ibid., pp. 1002–05, 1027–8; H. Walpole, *Last Journals*, Vol. I, pp. 518, 521.

[34] But not, it was noticed, the Quebec Act, whose retention would certainly have inflamed the colonists against the mother country as strongly as ever.

[35] *The Parliamentary History*, **XVIII**, pp. 963–92, Burke gave his speech careful preparation over a two-week period. In opposition circles it was much anticipated and Rockingham canvassed for a good attendance. (Rockingham to Sir John Griffin Griffin, 9 November 1775, D/DBy.C9/18. Braybrooke MSS; Rockingham to Burke, 7 November 1775, *Burke Correspondence*, Vol. III, pp. 235–36.)

[36] Camden even approved Burke's Conciliation proposals in advance of the speech (Rockingham to Burke, 7 November 1775, loc. cit.). He wanted 'to show ourselves at the beginning of the session'. (Camden to Rockingham, 30 October 1775, RI–1620, Wentworth Woodhouse MSS.)

[37] Burke to C. O'Hara, 17 August 1775, *Burke Correspondence*, Vol. III, pp. 185–8. According to Horace Walpole (*Last Journals*, Vol. I, pp. 494–5) in June 1775 Chatham had refused to admit Rockingham's claims to the Treasury in a future joint ministry.

[38] J. Priestley to Sir G. Savile, 28 October 1775, *H.M.C. Savile-Foljambe*, p. 146; Savile to Priestley, 29 October 1775, ibid.; Shelburne to Rockingham, 25 October 1775, RI–1614, Wentworth Woodhouse MSS.

[39] Camden disapproved of using Lords Protests as a political weapon too frequently (see his letters to Rockingham of 28 and 29 October 1775,

RI–1616 (*a*) and (*b*), ibid. However, when Shelburne prepared a protest of his own he persuaded Richmond to sign it and Richmond then persuaded Rockingham to do so (see the letters of Richmond to Rockingham, 29 and 31 October, 17 and 1 November 1775, RI–1618, 1621 and 1623, ibid.). In fact, Rockingham had already drafted a protest of his own a copy of which he sent to Camden. Attempts were then made, notably by Richmond and Lord John Cavendish to merge the two.

[40] Camden to Grafton, 4 January 1776, *Grafton Autobiography*, pp. 279–80.

[41] *The Parliamentary History*, **XVIII**, pp. 798–815.

[42] Fox to Grafton, 4 and 12 November 1775, *Grafton Autobiography*, pp. 276–7; Rockingham to Shelburne, 31 October and 3 November 1775, Lansdowne MSS; Rockingham to Camden, 3 November 1775, Copy, RI–1624, Wentworth Woodhouse MSS, printed Albemarle, Vol. II, pp. 287–8; Camden to Rockingham, 4 November 1775, ibid., RI–1625, printed Albemarle, Vol. II, pp. 288–9; Camden to Grafton, 4 November 1775, Grafton MSS.

[43] Contacts between Rockingham, Grafton and Shelburne remained cordial in the weeks after the Christmas holidays. They exchanged information and opinions quite regularly, e.g. Grafton to Shelburne, 22 February 1776, Lansdowne MSS; Grafton to Rockingham, 22 February 1776, R.166–12, Wentworth Woodhouse MSS; *Grafton Autobiography*, pp. 280–1.

[44] *The Parliamentary History*, **XVIII**, p. 1268.

[45] Burke to R. Champion, 15 December 1775, *Burke Correspondence*, Vol. III, pp. 238–9.

[46] *The Parliamentary History*, **XVIII**, p. 1088. A protest was entered signed by seven peers. For Richmond's pessimism and his disillusion with the opposition see his important letter to Rockingham, 11 December 1775 (RI–1637 Wentworth Woodhouse MSS, printed A. Olson, op. cit., pp. 168–70 and Albemarle, Vol. II, p. 290).

[47] Burke to O'Hara, 7 January 1776, *Burke Correspondence*, Vol. III, pp. 243–7.

[48] Burke to R. Champion, 19 March 1776, ibid., pp. 253–5; Richard Champion Rockingham, 16 and 28 December 1775, RI–1639, 1647 Wentworth Woodhouse MSS; Sir John Wentworth to Rockingham, 4 December 1775, RI–1634b ibid.

[49] H. Walpole, *Last Journals*, Vol. II, pp. 21–2, *The Parliamentary History*, **XVIII**, pp. 1143–56.

[50] H. Walpole, *Last Journals*, Vol. II, pp. 24–5; *The Parliamentary History*, **XVIII**, pp. 1188–1227 Richmond's thinking on America is, like all aspects of the man, quite fascinating. Already in June 1775 he had reconciled himself to the loss of the American colonies (Richmond to Burke, 16 June 1775, *Burke Correspondence*, Vol. III, p. 170).

[51] H. Walpole, *Last Journals*, Vol. II, pp. 43–7. Parliament was prorogued on 24 May.

[52] In late 1775 *The Gazetteer* began to attack the ministry and by the middle of the following year Woodfall's *Morning Chronicle* began to follow

suit. (S. Lutnick, *The American Revolution and the British Press*, 1775–83 (Missouri, 1967), pp. 60–3.)

[53] Burke to Rockingham, 14 September 1775, *Burke Correspondence*, Vol. III, pp. 206–11. On the contractors, see N. Baker, *Government and Contractors* (1971).

[54] Richmond to Rockingham, 11 December 1775, loc. cit.

[55] The campaign of 1776 had not gone according to Germain's plan. Although Howe succeeded in escaping from Boston and in reaching New York, up in the north, Carleton had been thrown back to Quebec. It was not until September that New York was taken, that troop reinforcements and supplies arrived. It was a slow and weary year of frustration for the British who had planned on a quick campaign.

[56] For the emergence of an American consciousness see M. Savelle, 'The Appearance of an American Attitude towards External Affairs, 1750–75', *American Historical Review*, **LII**.

[57] Horace Walpole scarcely mentions it, *Last Journals*, Vol. II, pp. 62–5. For the anticipation in the press see the interesting discussion in S. Lutnick, op. cit., pp. 74–87. 'By May 1776, all of London was speculating upon the possibility of such a declaration' (ibid., p. 75). 'The Opposition press, which had heretofore recognized much justice in the claims of America, was not embarrassed by the Declaration' (ibid., p. 76).

[58] Rockingham to Richard Champion, 4 July 1776, RI–1668, Wentworth Woodhouse MSS. The Opposition press took the same line (S. Lutnick, op. cit., pp. 77–9). Charles Fox had predicted in a letter to Lord Upper Ossory as early as 24 June 1776 that the Americans would 'finally succeed'. (Lord John Russell (Ed.), *Memorials and Correspondence of Charles James Fox* (4 vols, 1853–7), Vol. I, p. 143.)

[59] Burke to Richard Shackleton, 11 August 1776, *Burke Correspondence*, Vol. III, pp. 286–7.

[60] Fox to Burke, 17 August 1776, ibid., pp. 290–1; Portland to Rockingham, 19 August 1776, RI–1676, Wentworth Woodhouse MSS.

[61] He had been a Governor of West Florida from 1763–7. Initially connected to Bute and Lowther, he drifted into Opposition around 1770. The outbreak of the American war confirmed his political position. He was friendly with Burke and tried to reconcile the Rockingham and Lowther groups.

[62] Portland to Rockingham, 19 August 1776, loc. cit.; Keppel to Rockingham, 14 September 1776, RI–1680, Wentworth Woodhouse MSS; Charles James Fox to Rockingham, 13 October 1776, RI–1686, printed *Fox's Memorials*, Vol. I, p. 145.

[63] This point is fully discussed in R. W. Van Alstyne, 'Europe, the Rockingham Whigs and the War for American Independence' (*Huntington Library Quarterly*, **XXV** (1961), pp. 1–5).

[64] Fox to Rockingham, 13 October 1776, loc. cit.

[65] Keppel to Rockingham, 14 September 1776, R2–96, Wentworth Woodhouse MSS. Chatham, however, was still unwell and such occasional revivals of strength as he could muster did not lead him to involve himself

U

in politics. (See T. Townshend to David Hartley, 13 October 1776, D/EHy.F.84. Hartley MSS.)

[66] Fox to Burke, 13 October 1776, *Burke Correspondence*, Vol. III, p. 294.

[67] It took all of Rockingham's arts of persuasion to induce the Marquis of Granby to support the Opposition. He refused to move an amendment to the Address but agreed to second it. (See Rockingham's letters to Granby of 30 and 31 October 1776, *H.M.C. Rutland*, Vol. VII, p. 7.)

[68] Burke to Richard Champion, 2 November 1776, *Burke Correspondence*, Vol. III, pp. 298–300; *The Parliamentary History*, **XVIII**, pp. 1397–1431.

[69] *The Parliamentary History*, **XVIII**, pp. 1369–70; H. Walpole, *Last Journals*, Vol. II, pp. 81–2.

[70] J. Almon, *The Parliamentary Register* (17 vols, 1775–80), Vol. VI, pp. 56–8.

[71] Rockingham to an unidentified recipient, early December 1776, RI–1695 *a* & *b* (Drafts) Wentworth Woodhouse MSS; The Duke of Manchester to Rockingham, 18 December 1776, RI–1696, ibid.; Rockingham to Lord Stormont, December 1776 (Copy in Lady Rockingham's hand), RI–1699, ibid.

[72] Rockingham to Burke, 6 and 7 January 1777, *Burke Correspondence*, Vol. III, pp. 315–17.

[73] G. H. Guttridge ('The Whig Opposition in England during the American Revolution', *Journal of Modern History*, **VI** (1934), pp. 1–13) rightly stresses the fact that the King and Lord North stood on the Whig principle of Parliament's right to tax, a principle which the Rockingham Whigs could not very well attack. Their reluctance to do so was an essential prerequisite for the secession for the Rockinghams believed that having placed their principles on record they could legally do no more. In particular, they were unable to convince the King of the folly of the policy of his ministers, surrounded as he was by creatures who kept him ignorant of the realities of the situation in America.

[74] Burke did in fact write one but it was never used! (Address to the King, January 1777, *Works of the Right Honourable Edmund Burke* (Bohn British Classics 1889), Vol. V, pp. 461–72).

[75] Burke to Rockingham, 6 January 1777, *Burke Correspondence*, Vol. III, pp. 318–25. How personal Burke's concept of party was. He regarded the secession almost as a personal act by Rockingham '. . . with regard to the *party*, and the *principles*, for whose sake the party exists, all hope of their preservation, or recovery, depends upon your preserving your reputation'.

[76] Fox to Rockingham, 13 October 1776, *Fox's Memorials*, Vol. I, pp. 145–7; *Grafton Autobiography*, pp. 289–90.

[77] George III to Lord North, 15 November 1776, Fortescue, Vol. III, p. 402.

[78] The debate in the Commons on 6 February is given in *The Parliamentary History* (**XIX**, pp. 3–20), that in the Lords on 20 February (ibid., pp. 51–2). (See also H. Walpole, *Last Journals*, Vol. II, pp. 95–6.)

[79] Richmond to Rockingham, 19 February 1777, RI–1712, Wentworth Woodhouse MSS, printed Albemarle, Vol. II, pp. 308–9.

80 Portland to Rockingham, 5 March 1777, RI–1717, Wentworth Woodhouse MSS.

81 The Duke of Manchester to Rockingham, 15 March 1777, RI–1720, ibid.

82 *The Parliamentary History*, **XIX**, pp. 103–42, 160–87; H. Walpole, *Last Journals*, Vol. II, pp. 110–11. Lord John Cavendish apologised 'on the secession of himself and his friends on the plea of despair of doing any good . . .'.

83 E. Reitan, 'The Civil List in Eighteenth Century Politics', *Historical Journal*, 1966.

84 The secession had aroused considerable opposition in Burke's Bristol constituency and to some extent the *Letter* was Burke's attempt to defend himself at his home base. Burke was answered by the Earl of Abingdon, an eccentric if intelligent champion of popular, American and republican rights. His pamphlet, *Thoughts on the Letter of Edmund Burke Esq. to the Sheriffs of Bristol* attacked the Rockinghamite secession violently, asserting that constructive work could still have been done by the party in the detailed amendment of bills and in exercising vigilance over the executive.

85 See the three letters of Grafton to Rockingham on 28 and 29 April and 1 May 1777, RI–1721*a* & *b*, 1722, 1723, Wentworth Woodhouse MSS.

86 *The Parliamentary History*, **XIX**, pp. 317–20. Camden had given Rockingham five days notice of the motion. (Camden to Rockingham, 25 May 1777, Ramsden MSS.) There was thus little time for any positive co-operation on this issue. (Rockingham to Chatham, 29 May 1777, RI–1725, Wentworth Woodhouse MSS.) Burke urged Rockingham to impress upon Chatham the need to assert that conciliation should be undertaken by Parliament and not by the executive. (Burke to Rockingham, c30 May 1777, *Burke Correspondence*, Vol. III, pp. 342–3.)

87 T. Townshend to David Hartley, 18 November 1776, D/EHy.F.83. Hartley MSS. George Johnstone had written to the Marquis of Granby on 29 November 1776, that there had been 'a perfect reconciliation and union'. (*H.M.C. Rutland*, Vol. III, p. 7).

88 Burke to Garrett Nagle, 2 August 1776, *Burke Correspondence*, Vol. III, pp. 283–5.

89 A. Keppel to Rockingham, 5 January 1777, RI–1651, Wentworth Woodhouse MSS.

90 Perry Wentworth to Rockingham, 10 and 26 December 1776, RI–1694, RI–1698, ibid.

91 Burke to Garrett Nagle, 3 September 1777, *Burke Correspondence*, Vol. III, pp. 370–2.

92 Burke to R. Champion, 25 September 1777, ibid., pp. 376–7.

93 Burke to William Baker, 12 October 1777, ibid., pp. 388–9.

94 Burke to Fox, 8 September 1777, ibid., pp. 380–8.

95 Rockingham to Burke, 26 October 1777, ibid., pp. 392–3.

96 Burke to Rockingham, 5 November 1777, ibid., pp. 399–400.

97 The Duke of Manchester to Rockingham, 2 October 1777, R2–24–1, Wentworth Woodhouse MSS.

[98] Rockingham to Portland, 5 November 1777, Copy in Lady Rockingham's hand, RI–1740, ibid.

[99] Richmond to Rockingham, 2 November 1777, RI–1739, partly printed Albemarle, Vol. II, pp. 315–19. (See also his letter to Rockingham of 19 August 1777, RI–1731, Wentworth Woodhouse MSS, partly printed Albemarle, Vol. II, pp. 310–11.)

[100] Portland to Rockingham, 6 November 1777, RI–1741, ibid.

[101] Savile to Rockingham, 15 November 1777, RI–1742, ibid., partly printed Albemarle, Vol. II, pp. 321–4.

[102] Rockingham to Granby, 6 November 1777, *H.M.C. Rutland*, Vol. III, p. 10; Rockingham to Portland, 5 November 1777, loc. cit.

[103] Chatham to Rockingham, 18 November 1777, R151–6, Wentworth Woodhouse MSS; Rockingham to Chatham, 19 November 1777, *Chatham Correspondence*, Vol. IV, pp. 450–4. The first hint of his intervention is in Camden to Grafton, 29 October 1777 (*Grafton Autobiography*, p. 293).

[104] H. Walpole, *Last Journals*, Vol. II, pp. 163–4. Chatham lost his motion by 97–28 (*The Parliamentary History*, **XIX**, pp. 354–80).

[105] H. Walpole, *Last Journals*, Vol. II, pp. 164–6; *The Parliamentary History*, **XIX**, pp. 513–32, 381–402; *Fox's Memorials*, Vol. I, pp. 157–8.

[106] Chatham wrote to Rockingham on 27 November (R151–11, Wentworth Woodhouse MSS) urging action if the public were to be impressed '*All must unite* at present, or All must be lost'. He also agreed to second Richmond's motion for a state of the nation. (See also Chatham to Rockingham, 28 November 1777, R151–13, Wentworth Woodhouse MSS.)

[107] Rockingham to Granby, 28 November 1777, *H.M.C. Rutland*, Vol. III, p. 10; Camden to Rockingham, 28 November and 3 December 1777, RI–1744, 1746, Wentworth Woodhouse MSS.

[108] Burke to R. Champion, 1 December 1777, *Burke Correspondence*, Vol. III, pp. 405–6.

[109] T. Townshend to Granby, 28 November 1777, *H.M.C. Rutland*, pp. 10–11.

[110] Fox to Upper Ossory, 29 November 1777, *Fox's Memorials*, Vol. I, pp. 159–60.

[111] *The Parliamentary History*, **XIX**, pp. 472–85.

[112] Germain's strategy for the 1777 campaign was to defeat the Americans by a dual movement of the British armies. That from Canada should swoop south to Albany while the New York army should drive up northwards to join it. Yet Burgoyne and Germain believed that Howe could take Philadelphia and that he might still have time to reach Albany to join the Canadian army. Howe reached Pennsylvania at the end of August, having set out with the news from Burgoyne that his army had reached Ticonderoga too late to obtain his desired military objectives. There was no longer any prospect of Howe linking up with Burgoyne. Burgoyne was now alone on his fateful march to New York. At Saratoga his army surrendered on 13 October 1777.

CHAPTER 17

[1] After Saratoga it was clear that Britain was faced with a long and arduous struggle in America which would need larger supplies of men and resources than had hitherto been envisaged. Saratoga was an invitation to any hostile foreign power—and that meant the Bourbons—to intervene on the side of the colonists. The arrogant optimism in British military circles in 1775–7 reflected the universal British belief that the rebellion was collapsing. Saratoga signalled the loss of the Hudson area, from which an offensive campaign was to have been mounted. Yet, it would be a gross exaggeration to suggest that Britain faced defeat in America after Saratoga. She faced a long and uphill struggle but with her resources and her economy intact.

[2] George III to North, 4 December 1777, Fortescue, Vol. III, p. 503.

[3] North to George III, 4 December 1777, ibid., pp. 503–4.

[4] William Eden to North, 7 December 1777, B.M. Add. MSS 34414, f. 395, Auckland Papers.

[5] Lord Barrington gave notice that he wished to apply for the Chiltern Hundreds (Shute Barrington, *Political Life of Lord Barrington* (1814), pp. 181–2). On 2 December Sir William Meredith resigned his post in the Household.

[6] Shelburne to Chatham, 4 December 1777, *Chatham Correspondence*, Vol. IV, pp. 465–8; H. Walpole, *Last Journals*, Vol. II, pp. 170–1.

[7] Burke had a feeling that great events were at hand. 'I shall go to the Country. I shall endeavour, by other thoughts and other occupations to quiet that anxiety which possesses me, from an opinion, possibly an opinion very wild and erroneous, that this is, perhaps that this is [*sic*] the most critical moment for the publick, for the party, and for all those noble Objects to which your Lordship has devoted your Life, that ever did happen' (Burke to Rockingham, 16 December 1777, *Burke Correspondence*, Vol. III, pp. 416–18).

[8] See, for example, the letters to Granby from Rockingham, Tommy Townshend and G. Johnstone of 28, 28 and 29 November, respectively, (*H.M.C. Rutland*, Vol. III, pp. 10–12). Rockingham visited Shelburne on 4 December 1777 (Shelburne to Chatham, 4 December 1777, loc. cit.). Rockingham also wrote to Chatham on the same day (ibid., pp. 470–1). It is probable that the undated letter in the Wentworth Woodhouse MSS (R151–22) is a reply. 'I consider the present *impression* to be favourable to every good and wise purpose of the true friends to the publick. I shou'd think a *moment* should not be lost to call for the *instructions* of the *combined Labrynth* of imbecility, cruelty, and horror of Burgoyne's instructions.'

[9] Richmond on 2 and Burke on 3 December claimed that reconquest of America was now impossible. Richmond declared on 11 December that negotiations for peace with America would be useless unless a recognition of American independence was conceded at the outset (*The Parliamentary History*, **XIX**, p. 608).

[10] *The Parliamentary History*, **XIX**, pp. 549–60.

[11] See ibid., pp. 486–502 for the debate on Chatham's motion for the instructions to Burgoyne. It was lost by 40–19.

[12] Fitzmaurice, Vol. II, pp. 9–10.

[13] 9 December 1777, RI–151–14–1, Wentworth Woodhouse MSS.

[14] For Rockingham's passionate desire for peace see *inter alia*, his letter to Lord Effingham, 25 December 1777 (Copy in Lady Rockingham's hand), RI–1748, Wentworth Woodhouse MSS).

[15] H. Walpole, *Last Journals*, Vol. II, p. 173.

[16] Johnstone to Rockingham, 21 January 1778, RI–1760, Wentworth Woodhouse MSS.

[17] On 27 January, however, the ministers granted the substance of Fox's demands. *The Parliamentary History*, **XIX**, pp. 644–7.

[18] Ibid., pp. 617–44, 22 January 1778.

[19] Rockingham to Chatham, 26 January 1778 (Copy in Lady Rockingham's hand), R151–16, Wentworth Woodhouse MSS. It is printed with some errors in *Chatham Correspondences* (Vol. IV, pp. 489–91).

[20] Chatham to Rockingham, 26 January 1778, R151–10, Wentworth Woodhouse MSS, printed in *Chatham Correspondence*, Vol. IV, p. 492.

[21] Germain to George III, 1 December 1777, Fortescue, Vol. III, pp. 500–1.

[22] George III to Lord North, 13 January 1778, ibid., Vol. IV, pp. 14–15; 17 January 1778, ibid., pp. 17–18.

[23] North to George III, 30 January 1778 (misdated 29 January), ibid., pp. 26–9.

[24] George III to North, 31 January 1778, ibid., pp. 30–1.

[25] *The Parliamentary History*, **XIX**, pp. 650–2. Chatham ignored Rockingham's desperate pleas for his attendance. See his letters to Rockingham of 27 January 1778, loc. cit.

[26] Ibid.; George III to North, 2 February 1778, Fortescue, Vol. IV, p. 34, Fox to Fitzpatrick, 3 February 1778, *Fox's Memorials*, Vol. I, pp. 166–71.

[27] *Last Journals*, Vol. II, p. 188.

[28] Fox to Fitzpatrick, 3 February 1778, loc. cit.

[29] *The Parliamentary History*, **XIX**, pp. 685–9.

[30] Ibid., pp. 694–706.

[31] Ibid., pp. 719–21. On the same day Lord Effingham moved a similar motion in the Lords. When Gower hinted that the necessary parts of the instructions might be given, Effingham withdrew his motion (H. Walpole, *Last Journals*, Vol. II, p. 198).

[32] E. M. Coleridge, *Life of Thomas Coutts* (1919, 2 Vols), Vol. I, p. 97; A. von Ruville, op. cit., Vol. III, pp. 332–5.

[33] North to George III, 16 February 1778, Fortescue, Vol. IV, p. 38; George III to Lord North, 17 February 1778, ibid., pp. 38–9.

[34] Lady Chatham to Thomas Coutts, 22 January 1778, *Chatham Correspondence*, Vol. IV, pp. 485–6; E. M. Coleridge, op. cit., pp. 98–101.

[35] Gower to Bathurst, 18 February 1778, *H.M.C. Bathurst*, p. 17.

[36] Eden to North, 7 December 1777, B.M. Add. MSS 34414, ff. 395–8, Auckland Papers. There is an interesting discussion of this letter in C. R. Ritcheson, *British Politics in the Age of the American Revolution* (pp. 258–9). The most comprehensive discussion of the Conciliation proposals can be found in W. A. Brown, op. cit. (pp. 205–302).

[37] Lord North to George III, 30 January 1778, Fortescue, Vol. IV, pp. 26–9.

[38] By 9 February the King was hurrying North to present his proposals to Parliament, so frightened was he of the disposition of the French. (George III to North, 9 February 1778, ibid., p. 36; Germain to General Irwin, 3 February 1778, *H.M.C. Stopford–Sackville*, Vol. I, p. 139.) Germain's opinions, however, were more liberal than those of North. Germain advocated the repeal of all the acts of the British Parliament passed since 1763. (George III to Lord North, February 1778, Vol. IV, p. 35.) North was, of course, risking the alienation of his known following. John Robinson doubted whether the ministry could carry the repeal of the Declaratory Act (Robinson to Jenkinson, 11 January 1778, B.M. Add. MSS 38209, f. 240, Liverpool Papers).

[39] *The Parliamentary History*, **XIX**, pp. 762–79.

[40] It took the form of two bills. The first enabled the King to appoint Commissioners to treat with the Americans. The second declared Parliament's intention not to exercise the right of taxation.

[41] *The Parliamentary History*, **XIX**, pp. 842–55.

[42] Such a treaty had been rumoured since before the Declaration of Independence (Lutnick, op. cit., pp. 132–7). In January 1778 rumours were at fever pitch and were shared by the Opposition (Granby to Rockingham, 5 January 1778, RI–1758, Wentworth Woodhouse MSS; Augustus Keppel to Rockingham, 7 January 1778, ibid., RI–1759). Lord North, in fact, had glumly predicted such a treaty in August 1777 (North to George III, 22 August 1777, Fortescue, Vol. III, p. 470). Immediately upon the receipt of the news of Saratoga, the ministers sent an envoy to Paris to negotiate with the American Commissioners, of whom Benjamin Franklin was the leader. The French were already negotiating with the Commissioners. Although the ministry offered the Americans as many concessions as they believed might be acceptable to British public opinion, they did not offer independence. With the failure of these discussions the Franco-American treaty was inevitable.

[43] *The Parliamentary History*, **XIX**, pp. 922–50; H. Walpole, *Last Journals*, Vol. II, pp. 229–31.

[44] *The Parliamentary History*, **XIX**, pp. 915–21.

[45] These proposals seem to have been worked out by Suffolk, Eden and Wedderburn. (There is a copy of them in B.M. Add. MSS 34415, f. 1. Auckland Papers.) North's wish to change his ministry may have originated in January. Then, Robinson saw Governor Johnstone who 'thought Lord George Germain and Lord Sandwich must go out', wrote Robinson to North 'that it was in your Lordship's power to make a broad bottom by a considerable coalition . . . that he thought he could bring Charles Fox in,

and that the Duke of Grafton and all his friends would come in, with Lord Camden and the Grenvilles; and he rather thought also the Shelburnes might' (31 January 1778, Abergavenny MSS).

[46] Lord North to George III, 15 March 1778, ibid., pp. 56–7.

[47] George III to Lord North, 15 March 1778, ibid., pp. 57–8.

[48] *Fox's Memorials*, Vol. I, pp. 180–1.

[49] Fitzmaurice, Vol. II, p. 17.

[50] George III to North, 16 March 1778, Fortescue, Vol. IV, pp. 59–60.

[51] George III to North, 16 March 1778, ibid., p. 61.

[52] George III to North, 17 March 1778, ibid., p. 65.

[53] George III to Lord North, 17 March 1778, ibid., p. 65. The King wrote to Barrington: 'He did not think a general sweep could answer any good purpose, but produce a contrary effect, especially as Lord Chatham's health was so precarious, the ill consequences of which had been experienced in the year 1768' (Shute Barrington, op. cit., pp. 197–8).

[54] *Fox's Memorials*, Vol. I, pp. 186–7; Fitzmaurice, Vol. II, p. 18. North was still telling the King on 19 March that Chatham ought to be First Lord of the Treasury (Fortescue, Vol. IV, p. 68).

[55] In October 1777, on the announcement of the intended resignation of the Chief Baron of the Exchequer, North offered the office to Thurlow. The Attorney-General had his eye on the Woolsack and had no wish to bury himself within the fastness of the Exchequer. (North to Thurlow, 30 October 1777, B.M. Egerton MSS 2232, f. 11; North to Eden, 4 November 1777, B.M. Add. MSS 34414, ff. 309–10, Auckland Papers.) North thereupon offered the post to Wedderburn who proceeded to squeeze every advantage that he could from his bargaining position. He was so essential to North's survival in the Commons—at least, North, who probably exaggerated Wedderburn's indispensability, thought so—that he was able to extract from North, through Eden's mediation, a promise of the Common Pleas and, significantly, a peerage, whenever Thurlow received one (North to Wedderburn, 14 November 1777, *H.M.C. Abergavenny*, p. 19.) Yet for North to offer over-generous terms to Wedderburn risked offending not only Thurlow but also the King. (North to Eden, 4 November 1777, loc. cit.; George III to North, 29 October 1777, Fortescue, Vol. III, p. 486. This letter should be preceded by that from North to the King, misdated 29 December by Fortescue and consequently misplaced, ibid., p. 528.) In view of the King's predilection for Thurlow, North was in some danger of being unable to fulfil the promises he had made to Wedderburn (George III to North, 28 October 1777, ibid., p. 485).

[56] George III to Lord North, 2 April 1778, ibid., Vol. IV, pp. 93–4.

[57] Richmond to Rockingham, 15 March 1778, RI–1770, Wentworth Woodhouse MSS, printed A. Olson, op. cit., pp. 172–3 and Albemarle, Vol. II, pp. 347–8.

[58] Camden to Rockingham, 21 March 1778, RI–1771, Wentworth Woodhouse MSS.

[59] *The Parliamentary History*, **XIX**, pp. 959–62.

[60] According to Horace Walpole, on 30 March: 'General Conway was

with Lord Shelburne and the Duke of Grafton, and laboured to unite them, and persuade the whole Opposition to union; but Lord Shelburne declared Lord Chatham would hear of nothing but the dependence of America' (*Last Journals*, Vol. II, pp. 247–8).

[61] A. von Ruville, op. cit., pp. 340–3 and Appendix ii; *The Parliamentary History*, **XIX**, 1012–28. The most detailed account of Chatham's opinions in his last months, in addition to his speech on 7 April, is Camden's letter to Robert Stewart, 29 March 1778 (Camden MSS).

[63] Portland refused to attend his funeral on 9 June and even regarded his death as 'a fortunate event' (Portland to Rockingham, 9 June 1778, RI–1782, Wentworth Woodhouse MSS, partly printed Albemarle, Vol. II, pp. 356–7). Burke's sarcastic descriptions of Chatham's convulsions are no more edifying. (Burke to R. Champion, 11 April 1778, *Burke Correspondence*, Vol. III, p. 427.) On 13 May, on the contrary, Lord John Cavendish had 'moved to address the King to settle a permanent fortune on the Earldom of Chatham, which was agreed to' (H. Walpole, *Last Journals*, Vol. II, p. 268).

[64] Burke to R. Champion, 11 April 1778, loc. cit.

[65] Lord Camden to Fanny Stewart, 3 June 1778, Camden MSS.

[66] *The Parliamentary History*, **XIX**, pp. 1134, 1162–6, 1174.

[67] This was on 26 May when Burgoyne's openness impressed the Commons. The motion for a Committee was lost by 144–96 (ibid., pp. 1176–99).

[68] See below, pp. 380–2, 406–7.

[69] Lord North to George III, 6 May 1778, Fortescue, Vol. IV, pp. 131–2.

[70] Lord North to George III, 7 May 1778, ibid., pp. 133–5.

[71] Portland to Rockingham, 29 May 1778, RI–1778, Wentworth Woodhouse MSS, printed Albemarle, Vol. II, p. 353

[72] Richmond to Rockingham, 31 May 1778, RI–1779, Wentworth Woodhouse MSS, part printed Albemarle, Vol. II, pp. 354–5.

[73] Lord John Cavendish to Rockingham, 1 June 1778, RI–1780, Wentworth Woodhouse MSS, part printed Albemarle, Vol. II, pp. 355–6.

[74] Rockingham to A. Keppel (Copy in Lady Rockingham's hand), 23 June 1778, R154–4, Wentworth Woodhouse MSS.

[75] George III to North, 2 June 1778, Fortescue, Vol. IV, pp. 162–3; North to George III, 2 June 1778, ibid., pp. 163–6.

CHAPTER 18

[1] The Commission had left England on 16 April 1778 but, in the absence of an accompanying military drive of much vigour, it was placed in an unenviable position. Congress refused to negotiate unless the Commission recognised American independence. For the work of the Commission see W. Brown, op. cit., pp. 244–99. ('Not for one moment did it have a chance of succeeding', ibid., p. 292.) See also C. R. Ritcheson, *British Politics and the American Revolution*, pp. 263–83; S. Lutnick, op. cit., pp. 121–31. For the attitude of Americans to their new and not altogether uncomfortable

bedmates see W. C. Stinchcombe, *The American Revolution and the French Alliance* (1969, Syracuse University Press).

[2] There were plausible economic arguments to support such a strategy. Imports to Britain from the islands, for example, were worth three times as much as those from the East India Company. George III adopted a realistic view of the war. He backed the plan adopted in the wake of Saratoga. As he put it, 'providing Nova Scotia, the Floridas and Canada with troops, and should that not leave enough for New York which may in the end be the case we must abandon that place, then we must content ourselves with distressing the Rebels, and not think of any other conduct till the end of the French war which if successful will oblige the Rebels to submit to more reasonable (terms) than can at this hour be obtained'. (George III to Lord North, 12 August 1778, Fortescue, Vol. IV, pp. 186–7.)

[3] Lord North to George III, 10 November 1778, ibid., pp. 214–17; George III to Lord North, 14 November 1778, ibid., pp. 220–1.

[4] George III to Lord North, 28 December 1778, 10 January 1779, ibid., pp. 239, 258.

[5] George III to Lord North, 29 January 1779, ibid., p. 263; Lord North to George III, 5 February 1779, ibid., p. 267; George III to Lord Weymouth, 6 February 1779, ibid., p. 267; Lord North to George III, 8 February 1779, ibid., pp. 268–9; George III to Lord North, 1 March 1779, ibid., pp. 293–4.

[6] George III to Lord North, 6 April 1779, ibid., p. 325.

[7] It was Jenkinson who informed the King of Wedderburn's scheming and Eden's behaviour. (21 February 1779, ibid., pp. 285–6; 28 April 1779, ibid., pp. 329–30.) Sometimes there is no other way to describe Jenkinson's activities than that of royal spy. (Jenkinson to George III, 4 May 1779, ibid., pp. 334–5; 12 June 1779, ibid., pp. 354–5.) It was on Jenkinson's advice that the King attempted to bring Wedderburn to heel. (Jenkinson to George III, 15 May 1779, ibid., p. 342; George III to Lord North, 17 May 1779, ibid., p. 343; Robinson to George III, 4 July 1779, ibid., p. 387,) North's hint in July that he would like to be relieved of his responsibilities met with a fierce rejoinder from the King: 'no man has a right to talk of leaving me at this Hour' (George III to Lord North, 2 July 1779, ibid., p. 384). See also the series of letters between George III and Lord North of 15 and 16 June 1779 (ibid., pp. 355–8 and p. 382 where North's letter is undated and misplaced.)

[8] George III to Lord North, 25 October 1778, ibid., p. 210.

[9] Lord North to George III, 25 October 1778, ibid., pp. 210–11.

[10] Lord North to George III, 10 November 1778, ibid., pp. 214–17.

[11] Burke to R. Champion, 9 October 1778, *Burke Correspondence*, Vol. IV, pp. 24–6.

[12] *The Parliamentary History*, **XIX**, pp. 1323.

[13] Fox to Rockingham, 18 November 1778, RI–1792, Wentworth Woodhouse MSS.

[14] M. R. O'Connell, *Irish Politics and Social Conflict in the Age of the American*

Revolution (University of Pennsylvania Press, 1965), pp. 25–36. For the distressed state of Irish trade see *H.M.C. Lothian*, pp. 305–10, 317–20.

[15] For the (limited) effect of the embargo on the export of Irish provisions see T. M. O'Connor, 'The Embargo on the Export of Irish Provisions' (*Irish Historical Studies*, Vol. II, pp. 3–11).

[16] *The Parliamentary History*, **XIX**, pp. 1112–14; 1115–24.

[17] Ibid., pp. 1124–6.

[18] Burke to Samuel Span, 9 April 1778, *Burke Correspondence*, Vol. III, p. 426.

[19] Samuel Span to Burke and John Cruger, 13 April 1778, ibid., p. 429; Burke to Samuel Span, 23 April 1778, ibid., pp. 431–6. See also Burke to Harford, Cowles & Co., 2 May 1778, ibid., pp. 440–4. Even worse, Burke refused even to go to his constituency during the Easter recess, pleading the need for rest after 'the most laborious Session I remember since 1768' (Burke to John Noble, 24 April 1778, ibid., pp. 437–9).

[20] Ibid.

[21] Burke to an unidentified recipient, *circa*-3 June 1778, ibid., pp. 454–6. For the Catholic Relief Act see O'Connell, op. cit., pp. 108–28.

[22] O'Connell, op. cit., pp. 37–167.

[23] Rockingham to William Denham, 26 May 1779, Copy, 1830*a*, Wentworth Woodhouse MSS.

[24] *The Parliamentary History*, **XX**, pp. 635–57; *H.M.C. Knox*, pp. 261–2.

[25] H. Butterfield, *George III, Lord North and the People, 1779–80* (p. 1948), pp. 89–96. On 2 June Shelburne moved a similar motion, supported by Richmond. As on 11 May the motion passed but nothing was done (*The Parliamentary History*, Vol. XX, pp. 663–75).

[26] Vice-Admiral Keppel had been chosen commander of the home fleet, a post for which he resumed active duty in the spring of 1777. It was a curious choice. He was only half-way down the list of Vice-Admirals; his Rockinghamite connections, his refusal to serve in American waters and his lack of enthusiasm for the American war were well known. Furthermore, he had quarrelled with Sandwich in 1775. He had, however, an excellent naval record. In the Seven Years war he had been outstandingly successful at Quiberon and had taken Havannah, in 1762.

[27] S. Lutnick, op. cit., 140–1.

[28] 'You have saved us twice in one summer' wrote Burke to Keppel with unpardonable exaggeration. *Post*-1 August 1778, *Burke Correspondence*, Vol. IV, pp. 13–14.

[29] Keppel gave them little chance to do so. He acted throughout with great caution, reinforced with the conviction that he had not infringed any part of his orders. His own version of events is given in a letter to Philip Stephens, 20 June 1778. (H.A. 67; 1057/2. Albemarle MSS, Ipswich and West Suffolk Record Office. See also Keppel to Sandwich, 21 June 1778, G. R. Barnes and J. H. Owen, *Sandwich Papers* (3 Vols, 1933), Vol. II, p. 98). Perhaps Keppel sensed that something might happen. He wrote to Rockingham on 13 July 1778 to assure him that the Brest fleet had thirty-

two ships of the line to his own twenty-four (RI–1785, Wentworth Wood-house MSS).

[30] Originally, Palliser had defended Keppel to Sandwich. (See his letters to Sandwich of 20 June and 6 July 1778, *Sandwich Papers*, Vol. II, pp. 97, 110.)

[31] T. Keppel, *Life of Keppel* (1843, 2 vols), Vol. II, pp. 77–8. Walsingham to Sandwich, 11 November 1778, *Sandwich Papers*, Vol. II, p. 209; George III to Lord Sandwich, 5 November 1778, ibid., pp. 207–8; J. A. Davies, *An Enquiry into Faction among British Naval Officers during the American War of Independence* (Unpublished M.A. Thesis, Liverpool, 1964), p. 86 for a discussion of its authorship.

[32] Richmond to Keppel, 15 November 1778, *Life of Keppel*, Vol. II, p. 84.

[33] Ibid., p. 85.

[34] *The Parliamentary History*, **XIX**, pp. 1381–5.

[35] Ibid., **XX**, pp. 53–7; even before the debate John Lee had seen the charges and the attempt to exonerate Keppel swung into action. John Dunning, the friend of Shelburne, was persuaded to help and, within twenty-four hours, had made up his mind to carry on a struggle against the Admiralty decision to court martial Keppel even *after* it was over. (Dunning to Rockingham, 12 December 1778, RI–1799, Wentworth Woodhouse MSS.) Keppell was already a martyr. Rockingham wrote to Sir John Grifin Grifin on 14 December of the debate of the 11 December 1778 (D/DBy C9/27, Braybrooke MSS), 'I am sure you would have felt infinite satisfaction both in *seeing* & in *hearing* Ad. Keppel. What a Scene of Iniquity is opening. I think it *will be persisted in*, & *drove on* to the Utmost'.

[36] Palliser failed to show that Keppel had failed to make adequate preparation for the engagement, that he had been guilty of incompetence in exposing Palliser's ship to enemy fire, that Keppel had not ordered a second attack, that Keppel had retreated and that Keppel had not pursued the retreating enemy.

[37] It is clear from the Burke Papers (Bk. 13) that Burke drafted and then corrected and merged drafts made by Dunning and Erskine. Burke had always treated Keppel with the greatest respect, and was gripped with a sudden fear that the Admiral might suffer the same fate as Admiral Byng. It is the fact of Burke's authorship (however partial) which explains why contemporaries and historians were so impressed with Keppel's defence.

[38] When it became known that Palliser had not been in a proper position to judge the entire engagement, and that the log books of some of the captains supporting Palliser had been altered in ambiguous circumstances, the acquittal of Keppel was simply a matter of time. (Letter Book of Congratulations on Acquittal, H.A. 67, 461/252, Albemarle MSS.)

[39] Ibid.; *The Parliamentary History*, **XX**, pp. 130–1, 133. The euphoria even embraced crusty old Lord Abingdon who told Rockingham that the acquittal was a victory 'more glorious to Mr Keppel than the defeat of the French fleet' (12 February 1779, RI–1814, Wentworth Woodhouse MSS, printed in *Life of Keppel*, Vol. II, p. 189). Thereafter Abingdon was

closely attached to Rockingham. (See I. R. Christie, *The End of North's Ministry, 1780-2* (1958) for an analysis of Abingdon's little connection.)

[40] Weymouth to George III, 13 February 1779, Fortescue, Vol. IV, p. 277. The King at once passed on this advice to North (13 February 1779, ibid., pp. 277-8).

[41] The trial dragged on between 12 April and 5 May but the public was by this time weary of the affair and hardly noticed his acquittal.

[42] *The Parliamentary History*, **XX**, pp. 144-8.

[43] Ibid., pp. 152-5.

[44] Ibid., pp. 174-204. North's reaction was a frank admission to the King that he had not taken sufficient care with attendance (4 March 1779, Fortescue, Vol. IV, pp. 294-7). The King did not panic. He rallied North to action and restated his determination never to surrender to the Opposition. (See the King's letters to North of 4 and 5 March 1779, ibid., pp. 297, 299.)

[45] *The Parliamentary History*, **XX**, pp. 204-38. North's report to the King of 8 March is in Fortescue, Vol. IV, pp. 300-1. There is also a list in a memorandum by Sandwich (ibid., p. 304) of Members who did not attend on 3 March but who were expected to attend on 8 March.

[46] See Rockingham to Granby, 5 March 1779, Rutland MSS (summarised in *H.M.C. Rutland*, p. 17) for Rockingham's energy at this time and his conviction that he could keep the 170 Members in town. Camden, however, remarked 'I rely little upon that. It is with difficulty they are collected & then . . . are dispersed again as suddenly as the American Militia, for it is impossible to keep an army of volunteers together longer than is necessary for one or two actions'. (To Robert Stewart, 11 March 1779, Camden MSS.)

[47] *The Parliamentary History*, **XX**, pp. 282-304. North's report of the debate to George III, 16 March 1779 is misplaced in Fortescue, Vol. IV, pp. 279-80.

[48] The King had been willing to get rid of Sandwich in December on the grounds that 'nothing can so effectively remove the hatred and faction' in the navy but now that he believed that Sandwich might be a useful instrument with which to humiliate the Opposition he did not have 'the smallest doubt of the Propriety of keeping Lord Sandwich in his present Employment, and even saying that at this hour no person is so well qualified for holding it'. (Letters of George III to Lord North, 28 December 1778, 6 April 1779, ibid., pp. 239, 325 (misplaced).) As late as 13 May Fox moved for the proceedings at Palliser's court martial to be laid before the House. His motion was rejected by 157-58. (Lord North to George III, 13 May 1779, ibid., pp. 340-1; *The Parliamentary History*, **XX**, pp. 623-35.) Although the Opposition had not seriously weakened the ministry on the Keppel affair Rockingham reflected with some contentment that only nineteen county members had supported the ministry on issues arising from the court martial as against forty-five who had supported the Opposition (R-138-4. Wentworth Woodhouse MSS).

[49] Rockingham to Thurlow, 28 November 1778, R-140-23, ibid.;

Rockingham to Sir John Grifin Grifin, 1 December 1778, D/DBy.C9/25 Braybrooke MSS; Camden to Rockingham, 2 December 1778, RI–1796, Wentworth Woodhouse MSS.

[50] *The Parliamentary History*, **XIX**, pp. 1279–1319, 1321–76. In the Lords Rockingham acquitted himself admirably in one of his rare speeches.

[51] Shelburne made it clear, on 7 December, that he 'still retained his opinion, that America severed from Great Britain, the mother country, could not exist as an independent state; its splendor and glories would be no more, and she would be but a power of the second order in Europe' (ibid., **XX**, pp. 1–43). Shelburne was speaking in reply to Richmond's motion relative to the manifesto issued by the Commissioners. The motion was lost by 71–33. Thereafter, the Keppel affair monopolised the attention of the Opposition to such an extent that Grafton could write to Shelburne as late as 15 April 1779 that the Rockinghams had not yet decided 'whether they approve or not any motion on the American business this session' (Lansdowne MSS).

[52] Lord Howe (MP Dartmouth 1757–82 and naval Commander-in-Chief in America, February 1776–July 1778) and his brother William Howe (MP Nottingham, 1758–80, Commander-in-Chief, America, 1775–8) had both become disillusioned with the ministry. The first had been a member of the Conciliation Commission, the second had quarrelled with Germain both before but especially after Saratoga and wished to resign. The Howe brothers returned to England in the autumn of 1778 and gradually fell in with Opposition. (Lord Howe supported Keppel against Palliser.) Their intimate knowledge of America and their resentment against the ministry were of considerable use to the Rockingham Whigs during the Committee of the Whole.

[53] Lord North to George III, 30 April 1779, Fortescue, Vol. IV, pp. 330–2; George III to Lord North, 30 April 1779, ibid., pp. 332–3.

[54] Rockingham was not involved in these activities. Burke wrote him a sharp letter on 30 April (*Burke Correspondence*, Vol. IV, pp. 65–6), 'I think we ought to have your Lordships Sentiments in some way or other. We were strong last Night, but rather by adventitious and accidental Votes than our Own original and natural powers.'

[55] *The Parliamentary History*, **XX**, pp. 746–8, 3 May 1779.

[56] Ibid., pp. 836–54. Lord North to George III, 12 June 1779, Fortescue, Vol. IV, pp. 353–4 and Enclosure, pp. 351–2 (misplaced and misdated). There had already been a brief discussion in the Commons on 2 June when ministers insisted that peace did not lie in their hands. It was up to the Americans to treat. (G. Dempster to Rockingham, 3 June 1779, R–140–1, Wentworth Woodhouse MSS.)

[57] 15 June 1789, *The Parliamentary History*, **XX**, pp. 854–76; Lord North to George III, 15 June 1779, Fortescue, Vol. IV, pp. 357–8; Rockingham to Burke, 13 June 1779, *Burke Correspondence*, Vol. IV, pp. 88–9.

[58] Lord North to George III, 18 June 1779, Fortescue, Vol. IV, pp. 359–60.

59 RI–1810, Wentworth Woodhouse MSS; printed in *Fox's Memorials*, Vol. I, pp. 206–10, Albemarle, Vol. II, pp. 371–4.

60 *Burke Correspondence*, Vol. IV, pp. 39–41.

61 Richmond to Fox, 7 February 1779, *Fox's Memorials*, Vol. I, pp. 213–23.

62 See the letters of George III to North on 1 February 1779, Fortescue, Vol. IV, pp. 264–5.

63 George III to Lord Weymouth, 1 February 1779, ibid., p. 265; Lord Weymouth to George III, 2 February 1779, ibid., p. 266. The previous letter is, in fact, a reply to this letter. It is misplaced.

64 Amherst had replaced Burgoyne as Commander-in-Chief early in 1778.

65 At Amherst's disposal were 21,000 regular cavalry and infantry with a reserve of 30,000 militia. His decision to concentrate his troops on the most dangerous and vulnerable areas, the coasts of Kent and Sussex, while holding back a striking force for the defence of the capital was sensible. He threw out a battalion to Rye and a cavalry regiment to Chichester to allay the progress of the enemy if he landed. The naval bases of Plymouth, Portsmouth and Chatham had garrisons but west of Plymouth there was nothing to defend the country except one militia regiment. The militia in 1779 still had serious weaknesses. Even at Warley, supplies, even of firearms, were low (W.O. 34/116, f. 37; 34/230, f. 121). The parochial pride of regiments rendered them difficult to organise and to move and rioting was endemic (W.O. 34/114, f. 115 for a riot of the Iniskilling dragoons). The weaknesses of the militia were partly made good by the efforts of the Volunteer Associations which raised subscriptions to raise and equip men for militia service. These associations were usually based on county units, organised at county meetings and modelled on the example of the Middlesex Volunteer Association. Within a month of its formation in July 1779 the Middlesex Association had raised over £20,000 (Middlesex County Record Office, M.R./L./Com. Ia.Ib.2c).

66 There are details of that at Hertfordshire in W. Baker's letter to Burke of 4 August 1779, *Burke Correspondence*, Vol. IV, pp. 108–10 and at Hampshire in that of W. Baker to the Duke of Portland, 30 October 1779, Portland MSS. In Nottinghamshire, however, sentiment was distinctly pro-ministerial (Portland to Burke, 29 July and 8 August 1779, Portland MSS).

67 Rockingham to Burke, 7 August 1779, *Burke Correspondence*, Vol. IV, pp. 110–12.

68 Burke to Rockingham, 8 August 1779, ibid., pp. 112–14.

69 Burgoyne contacted Burke and visited him before he wrote to Rockingham. Burke to Burgoyne, 1 September 1779, ibid., pp. 127–8; Burgoyne to Rockingham, 12 October 1779, R152–2, Wentworth Woodhouse MSS; Rockingham to Burgoyne, 31 October 1779, R–152–6, ibid.

70 Bk. 6, Wentworth Woodhouse MSS; Grafton to Rockingham, 24 November 1779, R–163–5, ibid., Burke to Portland, 16 October 1779, *Burke Correspondence*, Vol. IV, pp. 150–5.

71 Burke to Rockingham, 17 October 1779, ibid., pp. 155–9. But Camden was as pessimistic as ever. He advocated 'a firm and temperate Opposition

in short speeches, a few debates without rancour'. Camden to Grafton, 16 September 1779, *Grafton Autobiography*, pp. 308–9.

[72] Rockingham to Burke, 3 November 1779, *Burke Correspondence*, Vol. IV, pp. 159–64.

[73] *The Parliamentary History*, **XX**, p. 1165.

[74] *H.M.C.* Knox, p. 267.

[75] Robinson to Jenkinson, early August 1779, B.M. Add. MSS 38212, ff. 57–8, Liverpool Papers. Even Robinson 'complains of his want of support in the Cabinet, tho' he acknowledges that Ld North is the original cause of the bad situation of everything'. (Lord Sandwich to George III, 16 August 1779, Fortescue, Vol. IV, pp. 409–10.)

[76] See, for example, Lord Sandwich's letters to George III of 13 and 14 September 1779, ibid., pp. 434–6; George III to Lord North, 27 September 1779, ibid., pp. 450–1.

[77] Lord North to George III, 18 October 1779, Fortescue, Vol. IV, pp. 464–5.

[78] Jenkinson suspected that when Gower, Weymouth, Thurlow and Rigby dined together on 17 November it was 'to drive Lord North out of your Majesty's Service' (19 November 1779, Fortescue, Vol. IV, pp. 489–90)

[79] George III to Jenkinson, 7 November 1779, Fortescue, Vol. IV, pp. 477–8. Gower had told North in person that he disliked his method of doing business and that nothing but a coalition with some parts of the Opposition could retrieve the fortunes of the ministry. (Lord North to George III, *n.d.* Fortescue, Vol. IV, pp. 442–4—from internal evidence the letter can be dated 28–29 October 1779.)

[80] Jenkinson reported to George III on 7 November that Thurlow wanted North, Sandwich and Germain to go and to be replaced by Grafton, Shelburne and Camden (ibid., pp. 475–7). For Thurlow's contempt for North (he would not even negotiate for him) see Jenkinson's letter of 8 November to the King (ibid., pp. 478–9).

CHAPTER 19

[1] Jenkinson to Robinson, 30 November 1779, B.M. Add. MSS 38212, ff. 248–53, Liverpool Papers. 'The President of the Council has been but once at the Board in the course of the summer recess. The Secretary for the Southern Department has dropped all connection with the Minister. The Chancellor has declared, that without a change, the Empire must be ruined, and all the House of Bedford hold the same language.' (*A Short History of the Administration during the summer recess* (1779), p. 74.)

[2] North to George III, 30 November 1779, Fortescue, Vol. IV, pp. 500–2. For Thurlow's hostility, see Jenkinson to George III, 8 November 1779 (ibid., pp. 478–9).

[3] George III to Lord North, 30 November 1779, ibid., pp. 502–3.

[4] Ibid., pp. 503–4.

[5] George III to Lord North, 1 December 1779, ibid., p. 506.

[6] December 1779, ibid., pp. 507–8. Thurlow had already demonstrated his willingness to treat with Grafton, Camden and Shelburne but 'there was no treating with the Rockinghams for various reasons' (Thurlow to George III, 8 November 1779, ibid., pp. 478–9).

[7] 9 December 1779, ibid., pp. 513–14.

[8] George III to Thurlow, 16 December 1779, ibid., pp. 520–23.

[9] George III to Thurlow, 11 December 1779, ibid., pp. 517.

[10] George III to Thurlow, 16 December 1779, loc. cit.

[11] Ibid.

[12] For months the Lord Lieutenant of Ireland had been begging the ministry to take some decisions. North did not look at the Irish papers before rioting at Dublin on 15 November forced him to do so. North hurriedly conceded to the Irish the right to trade with all nations, including other parts of the empire, on the same basis as the English. (H. Butterfield, *George III, Lord North and the People*, pp. 85 ff.) The size and suddenness of the concessions astonished the Irish, to say nothing of the Rockingham Whigs. (Burke to John Powell, 9 December 1779, *Burke Correspondence*, Vol. IV, pp. 171–2; Burke to M. Miller, 9 December 1779, ibid., p. 173.) The cabinet minutes of 5 and 8 December 1779 are in Fortescue, Vol. IV, pp. 509, 511–13. There had already been unanimity in the Irish Parliament on these concessions. (Lord Frederick Cavendish to Lady Spencer, 18 and 19 October 1779, Althorp MSS. For the debate in the Commons on 13 December 1779, see *The Parliamentary History*, **XX**, pp. 1272–84.)

[13] Rockingham to Keppel, 3 November 1779, RI–1864, Wentworth Woodhouse MSS. There still lingered the notion that the Americans would be ready to treat with the Rockinghams (*A Short History of the Administration*, p. 76).

[14] Rockingham to Savile, 8 November 1779, *H.M.C. Savile–Foljambe*, pp. 152–3; Rockingham to Keppel, 3 November 1779, loc. cit.

[15] Lord Frederick Cavendish to Lady Spencer, 22 November 1779, Althorp MSS, William Weddel to his wife, 28 November 1779, Ramsden MSS.

[16] J. Plumb, *The Growth of Political Stability*, pp. 140–5; G. Aylmer, 'Place Bills and the Separation of Powers: the Seventeenth Century Origins of the 'non-political' Civil Service', *Transactions of the Royal Historical Society* (1965); D. L. Keir, 'Economical Reform, 1779–87, *Law Quarterly Review*, 50 (1934).

[17] I. R. Christie, 'Economical Reform and the Influence of the Crown', *Historical Journal*, **XII** (1956). Professor Christie calculates that the number of placemen in the Commons declined from 250 to 200 and the number of seats at the disposal of the Crown from 30 to 24 between 1760 and 1780.

[18] Ibid., pp. 153–4.

[19] Ramsden MSS. The cancer, Rockingham made clear in one of his rare speeches, had begun when George III came to the throne when the maxim was adopted 'That the royal prerogative alone was sufficient to support government to whatever hands the administration should be committed' (*The Parliamentary History*, **XVI**, p. 742). Richmond had

reaffirmed in 1773 that the 'System of Government which had prevail'd almost constantly during this Reign, the grand Principle of which, is to make the King govern by his own Power & the weight of His Influence, instead of the old system of governing by that Party or Set of men who had most personal Influence in the Country'. (Richmond to Rockingham, 10 September 1773, RI–1443, Wentworth Woodhouse MSS, A. Olson, op cit., pp. 154–6.

[20] Although Rockingham had already written to Charles Yorke on 17 January 1768 suggesting that some restraint on customs and excise officers voting in elections was needed to prevent 'the further Extension of the already overgrown Influence of the Crown' (B.M. Add. MSS 35430, ff. 95–8, Hardwicke Papers).

[21] J. West to Newcastle, 17 February 1768, ibid., 32988, f. 355, Newcastle Papers; H. Walpole, *Memoirs*, Vol. III, pp. 112–13.

[22] *The Parliamentary History*, **XVI**, pp. 834–40.

[23] February 1769, ibid., pp. 598–602.

[24] Ibid., pp. 843–9.

[25] Ibid., pp. 924–7. Burke spoke in 1770 to the effect that: 'Public money has been shamefully squandered, and no account given of millions that have been misapplied to the purposes of venality and corruption' (ibid., p. 722).

[26] Ibid., p. 680, 9 January 1770.

[27] 2 April 1771, ibid., **XVII**, pp. 165–6.

[28] Rockingham to Charles Turner, 7 April 1772, RI–1402, Wentworth Woodhouse MSS; Rockingham to Burke, 24 October 1772, *Burke Correspondence*, Vol. II, pp. 342–43.

[29] *The Parliamentary History*, **XVIII**, p. 1378. The Duke of Richmond on 31 October 1776.

[30] Rockingham to Burke, 11 September 1775, *Burke Correspondence*, Vol. II, pp. 204–5.

[31] Burke to Rockingham, 5 January 1777, ibid., Vol. III, pp. 89–90.

[32] N. Wraxall, *Historical Memoirs of My Own Time* (1904), p. 329.

[33] See the masterly survey of George III's finances in J. Brooke, *George III*, pp. 201–16.

[34] E. Reitan, '*The Civil List in Eighteenth Century British Politics*: Parliamentary Supremacy versus the Independence of the Crown', *Historical Journal*, **IX**; *The Parliamentary History*, **XIX**, pp. 104, 120, 133–6, 155–6.

[35] That it had never died is best attested by Richmond's letter to Rockingham of 2 November 1777 Albemarle, Vol. II, pp. 315–19, A. Olson, op. cit., p. 50).' I would also very much wish you to consider of some Plan which you would execute if in Power for reducing the Influence of the Crown within proper Bounds. . . .'

[36] *The Parliamentary History*, **XIX**, pp. 873–4, 875.

[37] Ibid., pp. 972–80.

[38] Ibid., pp. 1089–91, 1094–5. All of this does not bear out Professor Christie's contention that the ministry defeated the bill with ease (*Wilkes, Wyvill and Reform*, pp. 68–9).

[39] *The Parliamentary History*, **XX**, pp. 124–6.

[40] By 165–124. *Commons Journals*, **XXXVII**, p. 219.

[41] The by-election took place because of the death of Sergeant Glynn and was a struggle between George Byng, the radical candidate and G. F. Tufnell, indirectly the ministerial candidate. In the end, neither was returned and a compromise candidate was returned without a contest.

[42] H. Butterfield, op. cit., pp. 189–91. Professor Christie makes the interesting point (*Wilkes, Wyvill and Reform*, p. 70) that the Middlesex movement had largely run out of steam when the leadership of the radical movement was transferred to Yorkshire.

[43] For the circular, of late November 1779, see C. Wyvill, *Political Papers respecting Parliamentary Reform* (1794, 6 Vols), Vol. III, pp. 115–17.

[44] Rockingham to S. Croft, 12 December 1779, RI–1869, Wentworth Woodhouse MSS.

[45] S. Croft to Rockingham, 28 November 1779, R–136–17, ibid.

[46] P. Milnes to Rockingham, 8 December 1779, RI–1867, ibid.

[47] Croft on 13 December sent a questionnaire to Rockingham (R–136–3, ibid.) to which Rockingham supplied answers written by Burke. These were that the objects of a county meeting should be to enquire into the origins of the present crisis, to prepare a plan of reform for the permanent establishment of economy in Government and for reducing royal influence in Parliament, to draw up a petition to present to Parliament to be signed throughout the country and to establish a Committee of Association to correspond with other petitioning bodies. Rockingham wrote much the same to Croft (12 December 1779, loc. cit.), but he added 'I much wish—speculative propositions might be avoided—*short Parliaments* or *more County Members*—or *diffusing the right of voting to every individual*—are at best crude propositions'.

[48] I. R. Christie, op. cit., p. 75.

[49] Burke's plans were being circulated among the leadership of the Rockingham party before 27 November, when the Yorkshire gentry began to stir. The first letter Rockingham appears to have received informing him of such activities was that from Croft on 28 November, loc. cit.

[50] In Middlesex the Rockinghams had been active since the middle of November and thus, once again, they cannot be accused of jumping on to a Yorkshire band-wagon. To some extent, the fact that the Middlesex County meeting on 7 January closely followed the example of Yorkshire can be attributed to this. As Burke wrote to Rockingham of the Middlesex meeting: 'It was well, very well' (7 January 1780, *Burke Correspondence*, Vol. IV, pp. 188–9).

[51] *The Parliamentary History*, **XX**, pp. 1255–67; Rockingham had been canvassing his friends for some time to attend Parliament. He had even canvassed Temple for that lord's proxy. (Temple to Rockingham, 6 December 1779, RI–1866, Wentworth Woodhouse MSS.) Furthermore, he had been maintaining contacts with Grafton for some weeks. (Camden to Grafton, 17 October 1779, Grafton MSS; Grafton to Rockingham, 24 November 1779, R163–7, ibid.).

[52] *The Parliamentary History*, **XX**, pp. 1285-92. According to Rutland, there would have been a better attendance had notes been sent out. 'Though our numbers were small, yet appearances were strongly in our favour.' (The Duke to the Duchess of Rutland, 8 December 1779, *H.M.C. Rutland*, Vol. III, pp. 22-3.) Rutland named Lords Paget, Say and Sele and Townshend as new Opposition voters. The Common Council of the City of London voted an Address of Thanks to Richmond and Shelburne. (*The London Chronicle*, **28**, December 1779).

[53] *The Parliamentary History*, **XX**, pp. 1293-1300. Shelburne had been worried in case Burke had it in mind to propose something of which Shelburne could not approve. Burke reassured him on this point (14 December 1779, *Burke Correspondence*, Vol. IV, pp. 174-5).

[54] S. Croft to Rockingham, 10, 16, and 19 December 1779, R136-2, 4, 5a. Wentworth Woodhouse MSS.

[55] Rockingham thought much of this point. He wished to avoid appearing to countenance any reduction in the power of the House of Lords because Shelburne would be offended if he did so. (Rockingham to Lady Rockingham, 2 January 1780, R140-10, ibid.)

[56] See the discussion in E. C. Black, *The Association*, pp. 42-5. There are drafts of a set of seven resolutions for the meeting in the Wentworth Woodhouse MSS. (R137/3, R 138/1, 13-15).

[57] Burke to Lady Rockingham, 2 January 1780, *Burke Correspondence*, Vol. IV, pp. 177-8. John Lee had drafted a petition which followed Rockinghamite thinking but Wyvill rejected it. (J. Lee to Rockingham, 13 December 1779, R137-4, Wentworth Woodhouse MSS; Crofts to Rockingham, 19, 26 and 28 December 1779, R136-5a, 6, 7, ibid.)

[58] Rockingham to Lady Rockingham, 2 January 1780, R140-45-1, ibid.; Rockingham to Burke, 1 January 1780, *Burke Correspondence*, Vol. IV, pp. 176-7.

[59] J. E. Bunce, 'Rockingham, Shelburne and the Politics of Reform, 1779-80', in *Studies in Modern History* (Ed. G. L. Vincitorio (New York, 1968), pp. 160-1, 163-4). It is possible that Burke's statement of the Rockinghamite position (see above p. 410) was intended to influence the proceedings at the county meeting. Bunce notes that although the Rockinghams had little influence over the meeting of 30 December 1779 nevertheless they were credited with such influence, and thus blamed for stirring up popular feeling in court circles.

[60] Rockingham calculated that 32 Members of the committee were favourable to him, 12 were probably reliable and only 18 were not reliable (R-138-17, Wentworth Woodhouse MSS). Only 15 Members, however, attended a committee meeting on 14 January. Because there was a rule that 21 should be a quorum the meeting was postponed to 21 January.

[61] C. Wyvill, *Political Papers*, Vol. I, pp. 67-8.

[62] Rockingham to P. Milnes, 28 February 1780, RI-1881, partly printed in Albemarle, Vol. II, pp. 395-400. Rockingham had expressed his disapproval of tests from the very beginning and Wyvill and his friends can

have been in no doubt of his opinions. (Rockingham to S. Croft, 12 December 1779, RI–1869.)

[63] In Nottingham and Gloucester radicals organised rival meetings, so hostile were they to the gentry's domination of the movement. In Cambridgeshire the Opposition Dukes of Manchester and Rutland used local radicalism to attack the ministerialist Hardwicke family. Furthermore, local Rockinghamites, unpopular though their adherence to a policy of peace with America and the recognition of American independence was, found it to their advantage to confine local discussions to economical reform. (Harbord Harbord to David Hartley, 20 January 1780, D./Eh/y.F.88, Hartley MSS.)

[64] For some details of the Yorkshire Association, see I. R. Christie, 'The Yorkshire Association 1780–4: A Study in Political Organisation', *Historical Journal*, **III** (1960), pp. 144–61. No research has been done for other Associations. Comparative treatment of the Associations would be a most useful supplementary aid to our understanding of the events of 1780.

[65] For events at Middlesex see *The Remembrancer*, IX (1780), pp. 105–19, *passim*.

[66] It has been estimated that of 27 county meetings, 12 were inspired by the Rockinghams. In a further 11 Rockinghamites figured to some extent. Only in 4 were there no traces of Rockinghamite involvement. (N. C. Phillips, 'Edmund Burke and the County Movement', *English Historical Review*, **LXXVI**, pp. 254–78.)

[67] The Plan was the outcome of private talks between Wyvill and other deputies in February (C. Wyvill, *Political Papers*, Vol. I, pp. 111–15). Only twelve counties and four cities bothered to send deputies to the meeting.

[68] See the similar letters of 23 March 1780 which Rockingham wrote to S. Croft and H. Zouch (RI–1882, 1883 Wentworth Woodhouse MSS; the latter is printed in Albemarle, Vol. pp. 402–6). Just a little later Burke wrote his famous letter to Joseph Harford which contains one of his most complete rejections of parliamentary reform. 'It would be a dreadful thing if there were any power in this country of strength enough to oppose with effect the general wishes of the people. Next to that would be the peoples wishing for themselves an object almost as surely destructive to them as anything which the worst Machinations of their worst Enemies could devise.' (4 April 1780, *Burke Correspondence*, Vol. IV, pp. 218–22.) Rockingham chided himself that although he had authorised Zouch and Croft to show his letters around so that his opinions might be well known he ought to have taken steps to make his views known more effectively. (Rockingham to Lord John Cavendish, post 23 March 1780, RI–1884, Wentworth Woodhouse MSS.)

[69] Even then the Rockinghams divided the meeting. They were unhappy at accepting triennial Parliaments, even though Sir George Savile spoke in their support (Lord John Cavendish to Rockingham, 28 March 1780, R–140–68, ibid.; C. Wyvill, *Political Papers*, Vol. I, pp. 148–64.)

[70] He confided to Shelburne that '*Discretion & Correctness have not predominated*'. (2 April 1780, Lansdowne MSS; Rockingham to Burke, 31 March 1780, *Burke Correspondence*, Vol. IV, p. 216.)

[71] Shelburne, of course, approved of the Plan. (C. Wyvill, *Political Papers*, Vol. IV, p. 131.) Yet Rockingham was prepared to look at parliamentary reform. In a memorandum he condemned the geographical distribution of seats which gave the sea ports 112 Members at Westminster R–28–7. *n.d.* Wentworth Woodhouse MSS).

[72] See, for example, Richmond to Shelburne, 16 January 1780, 8 March 1780, Lansdowne MSS.

[73] The Wiltshire committee refused to appoint delegates to the London conference, as Shelburne wished, and left it to the county meeting of 29 March to decide upon the line to be adopted. The meeting ignored Shelburne's parliamentary reform proposals and decided against joining the association. (Shelburne to Awdry, 13 March 1780, Awdry MSS 109/814; 26 March 1780, .C. Wyvill, *Political Papers*, Vol. I, pp. 131–6; Shelburne to Rockingham, post-28 March 1780, RI–1886, Wentworth Woodhouse MSS.)

[74] *The Parliamentary History*, **XX**, pp. 1376–82.

[75] Ibid., **XXI**, pp. 1–73.

[76] Ibid., pp. 74–83.

[77] Ibid. There can be no doubt that Savile and Wyvill were working together and in close consultation in an attempt to render reform rather more extensive than Burke envisaged (J. Bunce, op. cit., pp. 167–9).

[78] *The Parliamentary History*, **XXI**, pp. 111–37.

[79] Lord North to George III, 6 March 1780, Fortescue, Vol. V, p. 27.

[80] *The Parliamentary History*, **XXI**, pp. 193–217.

[81] Ibid., 233–77.

[82] Burke to an unidentified recipient, *post*-20 March 1780, *Burke Correspondence*, Vol. IV, pp. 214–15.

[83] Rockingham to Shelburne, 9 April 1780, Copy RI–1887, Wentworth Woodhouse MSS.

[84] Fox to Portland, 10 April 1780, Portland MSS.

[85] *The Parliamentary History*, **XXI**, pp. 340–67; T. Thoroton to the Duke of Rutland, 6 and 7 April 1780, *H.M.C. Rutland*, Vol. III, pp. 26–8.

[86] George III to Lord North, 7 April 1780, Fortescue, Vol. V, p. 40; Lord North to George III, 7 April 1780, ibid., pp. 39–40.

[87] 11 April 1780, ibid., pp. 41–2.

[88] By 61–41. *The Parliamentary History*, **XXI**, pp. 414–57.

[89] George III thought his illness an opposition ruse. (To North, 14 April 1780, Fortescue, Vol. V, pp. 43–4.) The Opposition thought the opposite: 'the House was getting very full & we should have been a majority once more, I believe, but we are very much out of luck'. (Lord Frederick Cavandish to Lady Spencer, 14 April 1780, Althorp MSS.)

[90] 'A comparison of the names of members voting with the Opposition on 6 and 24 April shows that nearly forty who supported Dunning on the first occasion deserted him on the second', including sixteen who voted with

the Government. (I. R. Christie, *The End of North's Ministry*, p. 22; *The Parliamentary History*, **XXI**, pp. 494–533.)

⁹¹ Lord Frederick Cavendish to Lady Spencer, 22 April 1780, Althorp MSS.

⁹² Lord Frederick Cavendish to Lady Spencer, 15 May 1780, ibid.

⁹³ *The Parliamentary History*, **XXI**, p. 619.

⁹⁴ Camden MSS.

⁹⁵ J. Bunce, op. cit., pp. 178–9.

⁹⁶ He deplored the 'very many well meaning men . . . running wild in *adopting speculative propositions as remedies*, and which are *by no means certain in their effects*'. (Rockingham to Lord Effingham, 1 May 1780, RI–1892, Wentworth Woodhouse MSS, printed Albemarle, Vol. II, pp. 408–9.)

⁹⁷ *The Parliamentary History*, **XXI**. The minority figure does the radicals more than justice. To support the committment of Sawbridge's bill was little more than an acceptance of further discussion. With Associators breathing down their necks some moderate MPs, including the Cavendishes, were in the minority. (Lord Frederick Cavendish to Lady Spencer, 18 May 1780 Althorp MSS.)

⁹⁸ Richmond asked Burke for a copy of his speech but Burke refused to comply with his request. (Burke to Richmond, *post*-8 May 1780, *Burke, Correspondence*, Vol. IV, pp. 235–8). Instead, he sent Richmond a copy of his letter to the Chairman of the Buckinghamshire County Committee of 12 April (ibid., pp. 226–9). Burke's letter repays careful inspection because it was a bitter and sarcastic attack upon Richmond's consistency. Richmond's conversion to parliamentary reform had been a slow and gradual process but his mind on the subject of universal suffrage had been made up by November 1779 (Walker King to Burke, 5 November 1779, ibid., pp. 165–8).

⁹⁹ *The Parliamentary History*, **XXI**, pp. 687–8.

¹⁰⁰ For a discussion of Richmond's thought at this time and of its development see A. Olson, op. cit., pp. 49–54; Richmond to Rockingham, 12 June 1780, RI–1900, Wentworth Woodhouse MSS.

¹⁰¹ Ramsden MSS, *n.d.*

¹⁰² M. P. Ludgershall, 1774–80, a soldier who was loosely attached to the Opposition. His hatred of the American war became almost uncontrolled in 1778. In 1779 and 1780 he became more passionate in his opinions, especially with respect to religion in general and catholicism in particular. He had become President of the Protestant Association in November 1779.

¹⁰³ On this subject see the still useful J. P. de Castro: *The Gordon Riots*, (Oxford 1926) as well as G. Rudé, 'The Gordon Riots; a Study of the Rioters and their Victims' (*Transactions of the Royal Historical Society*, 5th Series, **VI** (1956), pp. 93–114).

¹⁰⁴ Lord Frederick Cavendish to Lady Spencer, 9 June 1780, Althorp MSS.

¹⁰⁵ Manchester to Rockingham, 8 June 1780, RI–1899, Wentworth Woodhouse MSS, printed Albemarle, Vol. II, pp. 416–18; Richmond to Rockingham, 12 June 1780, RI–1900.

[106] C. Cone, op. cit., p. 351; Burke to Loughborough, 15 June 1780, *Burke Correspondence* Vol. IV pp. 247–50.

[107] Rockingham to Richmond, 11 July 1780 (Copy in Lady Rockingham's hand), RI–1909, Wentworth Woodhouse MSS.

[108] J. Norris, op. cit., pp. 103–4.

[109] For Burke's attitude see the letters in the *Burke Correspondence*, Vol. IV, pp. 254–8.

[110] As Charles Jenkinson put it: 'The strange Convulsions We have had of late in this Country have produced an Effect the very reverse of what might have been expected; They have strengthened the Government & restored the Country to a State of Tranquillity which it has not for a long time experienced'. (To J. Boulin, 20 July 1780, B.M. Add. MSS 38307, f. 195. Liverpool Papers.)

[111] R. Rigby to Lady Spencer, 26 March 1780, Althorp MSS.

[112] George III to Thurlow, 6 February 1780, Fortescue, Vol. V, pp. 2–5. On 14 April Fox and North had met in an attempt to establish a mutual disposition to negotiate but nothing came of it. (Robinson to Jenkinson, 16 April 1780, ibid., pp. 44–5.)

[113] It is extraordinarily difficult to reconcile the harsh anti-Rockinghamite strictures of Professor Guttridge (*English Whiggism and the American Revolution*, pp. 130–1) with the researches of Professor Christie which he cites. ('The Marquis of Rockingham and Lord North's Offer of a Coalition', June–July 1780', *English Historical Review*, **LXIX** (1954), pp. 388–407.)

[114] Richmond realised this and warned Rockingham of it at once. 'If You was drawn in to talk of Measures and Persons and did not say You must consult with Lord Shelburne the Duke of Grafton and Lord Camden, it was evident You had broke with them. This Point they have ascertained and You may be sure they will take Care to let Lord Shelburne and the others know that You have negotiated without naming them. If by this they keep up the Disunion their great Point is gain'd'. (Richmond to Rockingham, 9 July 1780, RI–1906, Wentworth Woodhouse MSS.)

[115] 9 July 1780, Lee Papers, printed Albemarle, Vol. II, pp. 420–1.

[116] As Jenkinson noticed, there were no meetings of Opposition leaders, Rockingham clearly assuming that he could make decisions to which all would agree. (Charles Jenkinson to John Robinson, 22 July 1780, Abergavenny MSS.)

CHAPTER 20

[1] The Dutch, in spite of their treaty obligations, had omitted to furnish Britain with military assistance against Spain and had never ceased trading with the Bourbon powers. Russia, for her part, was not only unwilling to enforce international rules pertaining to neutral shipping in war-time but, during the first half of 1780, was negotiating with Holland for an Armed Neutrality as a means of protecting neutral shipping in wartime.

[2] I. R. Christie, *The End of North's Ministry*, pp. 36–8.

[3] 'I think it a *wicked* measure in the *advisers*', he wrote to Portland on 1 September (Portland MSS). Professor Christie Prints one half of his letter (op. cit., pp. 44–5). The half that he does not print reveals the extent of Rockingham's worry about the Associations. 'I think *a little time* would have weakened their *machinations*.'

[4] 1 September 1780, Portland MSS.

[5] See the letters of Rockingham to his wife on 21 August, a 15 September 1780, RI–1918, 1922, Wentworth Woodhouse MSS. Rockingham to Savile, 17 September 1780, RI–1928, ibid., printed *H.M.C. Foljambe*, Vol. II, pp. 154–7.

[6] For Savile's uninhibited expression of his views see *The Remembrancer*, Vol. X (1780), pp. 242–6. For Rockingham's polite reception of Savile's views see his restrained letter to Savile, 17 September 1780 (loc. cit.), and compare this with the more frank comments in his letter to Portland on 22 September 1780, Portland MSS. Both the candidates subscribed £1,500, the rest coming from smaller donations from about 100 gentlemen. Rockingham gave nothing (R139–37. Wentworth Woodhouse MSS).

[7] There are some very friendly letters from Rockingham to Sir Lawrence Dundas in the Zetland MSS as early as 5 and 6 December 1778 of a non-political but still fairly intimate character.

[8] Eliot, formally a ministerialist had come out against the American War as early as 1776, and was thus not inclined to fill his boroughs with ministerialists. Rockingham was slow to take advantage of this situation, however. Although as far back as August he and Portland had fixed upon the names of three likely Members, they were unable to find a fourth, and when the election came only one of Rockingham's friends was accommodated by Eliot. Rockingham had treated the whole matter far too casually and Portland reprimanded him. He had 'very sincerely to lament your long silence, not only from apprehensions of the effect it may have upon Eliot's mind, but from the embarrassments which it has occasioned & may still create in his Parliamentary arrangements'. Portland to Rockingham, 3 September 1780, Portland MSS.

[9] Hedon was a difficult borough to hold and Rockingham was not inclined to go to the trouble and expense of defending it against an attack by Lord Sandwich between the two elections.

[10] R. Sykes wrote to Lord Fitzwilliam 3 May 1784: 'My father always brought in one member, and could have brought in any Man except Hartley, we have done with him for ever'. (Box R 1603 Fitzwilliam MSS Northamptonshire County Record Office.) Hartley's failure is a salient reminder that national issues were still rare in 1780 and that a sitting Member could not be dislodged by them alone. As late as 1790 Sykes was still grumbling to Fitzwilliam that in Hull 'The Whig Interest is very low . . . D. Hartley was the ruin of it' (Box X512, ibid.).

[11] Keppel was defeated in trying to retain his seat at Windsor but won a spectacular victory at Surrey, one of the two counties to go to the polls in 1780. See his letter of 9 September describing to Rockingham his defeat at

Windsor and of 26 describing the canvass at Surrey (RI–1925, 1930, Wentworth Woodhouse MSS).

[12] These conclusions are similar to those of Professor Christie (op. cit., pp. 213–18). My overall total is slightly higher than his. However, my estimate of Rockingham's connection is two smaller than his. I prefer to regard Baker, Barrow, Clayton and Ludlow as Independents. On the other hand, I include Sir John Pennyman and Lord John Cavendish.

[13] Lord John Cavendish has been included with the Rockingham group because of his dependence upon the Marquis for his seat and for their close friendship.

[14] It should be clear, however, that Fox was not an electoral patron and that he was not a borough monger in any sense. Fox's group owed everything, then, to his personal qualities. It was of course, his stand against the American war which attracted men to him. Thus it would be more accurate to say that rather than 'saving' the Rockingham Whigs, the American War created Charles James Fox's reputation.

[15] *The End of North's Ministry*, p. 116.

[16] On this subject see P. Underdown, 'Edmund Burke: The Commissary of his Bristol Constituents', *English Historical Review* (1954).

[17] Burke knew this. See his letters to Portland of 3 September 1780, (*Burke Correspondence*, IV, pp. 266–75) and to Rockingham of 7, 8 September (ibid., pp. 275–8).

[18] Burke's opinion on the tactical circumstances in which parliamentary reform might be justifiable is interesting. He wrote to Joseph Harford 'As to *some* remedy in the present State of the representation, I do by no means object to it. But it is an Affair of great difficulty; and to be touched with great delicacy; and by an hand of great power. Power and delicacy do not often unite. But without great power, I do not hesitate to say, it *cannot* be done. By power, I mean the executive power of the kingdom', loc. cit.

[19] The most important discussion of Burke's place in the Rockingham party in 1780 is N. C. Phillips, 'Edmund Burke and the County Movement', (loc. cit.). While accepting the importance of his experiences of 1780 in Burke's life, I feel that a longer view of Burke's career suggests that 1780 was part of a more gradual development and was perhaps less abrupt break in Burke's life than Phillips suggests. It is nearer the truth, I think, to take the years 1780–84 as providing the crucial change.

[20] I. R. Christie, op. cit., pp. 159–62.

[21] Ibid., pp. 221–6. These included Rutland, 6; Abingdon, 4; Shelburne, 7; Lowther, 7; Grafton, 3; Townshend, 2; Sir G. Warren, 3.

[22] Rockingham to Savile, 17 September 1780, loc. cit.

[23] *The Political Memoranda of Francis, Fifth Duke of Leeds*, ed. O. Browning (1884), pp. 35–6.

[24] On this subject, see J. Tyler; 'Lord North and the Speakership, 1780' (*Parliamentary Affairs*, **VIII** (1955), pp. 363–78). There is material on this subject in R.22, Wentworth Woodhouse MSS. Rockingham would have been quite ready to take party advantage of Montagu's election. (Rockingham to Montagu, 22 October 1780, R162–6, ibid.)

[25] *The Parliamentary History*, **XXI**, pp. 793–807 Lord North was so disappointed by the outcome of this incident that he once again begged the King to release him. (24 October 1780. Fortescue, Vol. V, pp. 142–3.)

[26] *The Parliamentary History*, **XXI**, pp. 817–44 November 1780.

[27] Lansdowne MSS.

[28] On 20 January 1781 Britain broke off diplomatic relations with Holland after several months of deteriorating relations. Holland, thereupon, sought Russian protection and Britain was in some danger of war on two further fronts. (See I. R. Christie, op. cit., pp. 243–8.)

[29] George III to Lord North, 25 January 1781, Fortescue, Vol. V, p. 189.

[30] I. R. Christie, op. cit., pp. 248–50.

[31] Ibid., p. 255.

[32] *The Parliamentary History*, **XXI**, pp. 1223–92. For George III's pleasure at this outcome see his letter to North, 27 February 1781 (Fortescue, Vol. V, p. 199).

[33] Christie, op. cit., p. 257. On the previous day the loan had been voted in the Committee of Ways and Means by 169–111.

[34] Ibid., p. 257.

[35] D. Hartley to G. Estraed, 19 February 1781, D/EHy.F.89. Hartley MSS.

[36] Christie, op. cit., pp. 257–8. On 21 March both the Contractors Bill and Crewe's Act had been thrown out, the former by 120–100, the latter by 133–86.

[37] *The Parliamentary History*, **XXII**, pp. 140–1, 204–18, 358–70; C. Wyvill, *Political Papers*, Vol. I, pp. 317–18. Rockingham had attempted somewhat half-heartedly to put pressure on the deputies so that they would water down their radical proposals. (I. R. Christie, *Wilkes, Wyvill and Reform*, p. 129.)

[38] *The Parliamentary History*, **XXII**, pp. 336–7.

[39] *The Parliamentary History*, **XXII**, pp. 435–516. The very length of the King's reply to North's account of the debate as well as its contents indicates a certain unease (13 June 1781, Fortescue, Vol. V, p. 247).

[40] Burke to Portland, 17 August 1781, *Burke Correspondence*, Vol. IV, pp. 366–7.

[41] Burke to R. Champion, 2 September 1781, ibid., pp. 369–70.

[42] On Yorktown, see R. G. Adams; A View of Cornwallis's surrender at Yorktown', *American Historical Review*, **XXXVII** (1931–2); W. B. Willcox, 'The British Road to Yorktown: a Study in Divided Command', ibid., LII (1946); W. B. Willcox, 'Rhode Island in British Strategy, 1780–1', *Journal of Modern History*, **XVII**.

[43] The only attempt to assess public reaction to Yorktown is the brief survey of the press in S. Lutnick, op. cit. (pp. 187–91).

[44] Because Rockingham refused to co-operate with Shelburne on the reform of the constitution Shelburne refused to co-operate with Rockingham on American affairs (Fitzmaurice, Vol. II, p. 82).

[45] Rockingham to Portland, 19 November 1781, Portland MSS. I

should like to acknowledge that the following account of the political impact of Yorktown is necessarily indebted to Professor Christie's masterful account *The End of North's Ministry*, pp. 267–369).

⁴⁶ *The Parliamentary History*, **XXII**, pp. 681–751. It was Dunning in the Commons who drafted the amendment, not a Rockinghamite.

⁴⁷ Sir Walter Rawlinson to Sandwich, 27 November 1781, Abergavenny MSS.

⁴⁸ *The Parliamentary History*, **XXII**, pp. 802–31.

⁴⁹ Germain to George III, 16 December 1781, Fortescue, Vol. V, pp. 314–15.

⁵⁰ George III to Stormont, 22 December 1781, ibid., pp. 317–18; George III to North, 26 December 1781, ibid., pp. 326–7.

⁵¹ The divisions both in the ministry and the Opposition are dealt with fully in I. R. Christie, op. cit. (pp. 276–83). Writing to George III on 19 December 1781 Stormont reported Rockingham's speech in a debate to postpone the third reading of the Land Tax in which Rockingham spoke. 'The general scope of his speech was that there must be a change of Men, Measures and System' (Fortescue, Vol. V, p. 316).

⁵² Henry Dundas had been MP for Edinburghshire since 1774 and the Lord Advocate of Scotland since 1775. He was a competent lawyer and a powerful debater. Although ambitious and something of an intriguer Dundas had a frank and engaging manner which made him more popular than most members of the Government. He was clearly a man with a future.

⁵³ North reported to the King that he was 'apprehensive, that many persons whom he may send for may vote against him, so little can he depend upon the House' (25 February 1782, Fortescue, Vol. V, p. 373).

⁵⁴ Lord North to George III, 8 March 1782, ibid., pp. 380–1.

⁵⁵ Rigby knew of North's decision in advance: 'Lord North is this instant going down to the House to give the Thing up'. (Rigby to Lady Spencer, 20 March 1782, Althorp MSS.)

CHAPTER 21

¹ Fortescue, Vol. V, pp. 374–5.

² George III to North, 28 February 1782, ibid., pp. 375–6.

³ 8 March 1782, ibid., pp. 380–1.

⁴ George III to Lord North, 9 March 1782, ibid., p. 382.

⁵ E.g. Shelburne to Rockingham, 14 February 1782, RI–1984, Wentworth Woodhouse MSS.

⁶ It was common gossip that the King would never agree to the appointment of Fox to a senior office (e.g. George Selwyn to Lord Carlisle, 13 March 1782, *H.M.C. Carlisle*, p. 592).

⁷ B. M. Egerton MSS 2232, f. 45. Thurlow Transcripts.

⁸ Ibid., f. 47.

⁹ Rockingham's 'Memorandum of his Negotiations with Lord Chancellor

Thurlow Over the Formation of a New Ministry' is in the Wentworth Woodhouse MSS (R.97) and, inaccurately, in Albemarle (Vol. II, pp. 451–3). There is no truth in Walpole's assertion (*Last Journals*, Vol. II, p. 516) that Thurlow did not have the King's authorisation and approval to conduct these negotiations.

[10] 13 March 1782, Fortescue, Vol. V, pp. 385–6.

[11] 12 March 1782, RI–1988, Wentworth Woodhouse MSS.

[12] R97–14, ibid.

[13] 'Memorandum of the Negotiations', ibid.

[14] Much to his own alarm and, even, distress. 'What affects me so much is, that *I am* as it were a Condition *sine qua non*. I well know the Handle and the use which will be made of it, & I much fear to the detriment of all our Friends. I confess too, I feel, that it brings on a *Sort of* Declaration from *me*, that I *would act* in that Station, when in the most solemn *Truth*, I feel, that the Joy of my Heart would be to see, *that Office*, & the *Governing Part of this Country* lodged *in such Hands*, as *I well* would govern this Country in *Such Principles* as *Your Grace* & *Myself* & *All our Friends* have acted—& that *I* might be perhaps, an useful Supporter to them' (Rockingham to Richmond, c. 12 March 1782, Ramsden MSS).

[15] *Leeds Memorandum*, pp. 61–2.

[16] Thurlow to Rockingham, 14 March 1782, RI–1993, Wentworth Woodhouse MSS, printed Albemarle, Vol. II, pp. 455–6.

[17] Albemarle, Vol. II, p. 458.

[18] Rockingham to Thurlow, 18 March 1782, Albemarle, Vol. II, p. 460.

[19] Memorandum of Georgiana, Lady Spencer, Althorp MSS (misdates the meeting 17 March).

[20] Lord North to George III, 18 March 1782, Fortescue, Vol. V, pp. 394–7.

[21] *The Parliamentary History*, **XXII**, p. 987.

[22] Althorp MSS. Also in the Althorp MSS is a Memorandum of Lady Spencer written on 20 March commenting, presumably on Rigby's information: 'That the King has determined not to send for Lord Rockingham but that Lord Shelburne is to be at the Queen's House tomorrow at 10 o'clock. That he will tell the King, nobody is so proper to be at the head of his Majesty's affairs as Lord R. but that if Lord R. is *unreasonable* the Country must not be driven to Anarchy on that account; that *some* popular Measures are necessary'.

[23] Fitzmaurice, pp. 87–8; L. Mitchell, *Charles James Fox and the Disintegration of the Whig Party*, 1782–94 (Oxford 1971), p. 11.

[24] Ibid., p. 88.

[25] Ibid., pp. 88–9.

[26] Shelburne to George III, 24 March 1782, Fortescue, Vol. V, p. 407, and enclosures, pp. 407–8.

[27] Ibid., p. 409.

[28] Lady Spencer's Memorandum, Althorp MSS.

[29] Rockingham to Richmond (25), March 1782, Ramsden MSS.

[30] Lady Spencer's Memorandum, Althorp MSS.

[31] Rockingham to Shelburne, 26 March 1782, RI–2011, Wentworth. Woodhouse MSS.

[32] George III to Shelburne, 26 March 1782, Fortescue, Vol. V, pp. 412–3.

[33] Of the eleven members of the Cabinet, I place Rockingham, Fox, Cavendish and Keppel as firm Rockinghamites; even though Keppel later stayed in office under Shelburne it is an exercise of retrospective wisdom to regard him as anything other than a Rockinghamite in the spring of 1782. I regard Shelburne, Dunning (Lord Ashburton), Grafton and Camden as Shelburnites. Of the remaining three, Thurlow was a King's man, Conway was allied to no group and Richmond was making the transition from Rockingham to Shelburne. My estimate of the Cabinet is thus slightly different from those of Dr Cannon (*The Fox–North Coalition, 1782–4*, p. 3, N4) and A. S. Foord (*His Majesty's Opposition*, p. 373.)

[34] R–155–1, Wentworth Woodhouse MSS (this is a long 'speech' in Burke's hand which Rockingham was to deliver to George III). See also the 'Memoranda for Consideration' written by Burke for Rockingham's benefit (*Burke Correspondence*, Vol. IV, pp. 423–4).

[35] Fortescue, Vol. V, p. 412 (misdated 26th).

[36] *The Fox–North Coalition*, p. 2.

[37] George III to Thurlow, 5 April 1782, Fortescue, Vol. V, pp. 443–4; George III to Shelburne, 7 April 1782, ibid., pp. 446–7.

[38] Lord Ossory was not clear over responsibility for patronage. (See his letter to Fox, 3 May 1782, B.M. Add. MSS 47579, f. 85, Fox Papers.)

[39] George III to Shelburne, 3 April 1782, Fortescue, Vol. V, p. 441.

[40] Shelburne to George III, 3 April 1782, ibid., p. 440.

[41] 5 April 1782, ibid., Vol. V, pp. 442–3. *See also* Cannon, op. cit., p. 5 n. 1.

[42] Shelburne to George III, 28 April 1782, ibid., pp. 494–5.

[43] Shelburne to George III, 29 April 1782, ibid., pp. 502–4.

[44] George III to Shelburne, 29 April 1782, ibid., pp. 504–5. It should not be overlooked that 'history' was on the side of the Rockinghams in the sense that the Cabinet was gradually coming to play a more formal and indispensable role in business. About 1779, for example, cabinet minutes summarising decisions were presented to the King (I. R. Christie, *Myth and Reality*, pp. 11–12).

[45] Lord Charles was later compensated by being brought to the Privy Council. (See the letters between Shelburne and the King, 13, 15 and 16 May 1782, Fortescue, Vol. VI, pp. 19, 23–5.)

[46] R–125, 12, 18, Wentworth Woodhouse MSS.

[47] The act had many loopholes, the most obvious being the possibility that jobs might be given to friends or relatives of voters. Further, to reduce the electorate of small and medium size boroughs might weaken the direct influence of the ministry, but it would throw open the borough to a patron who might be well disposed to Government. It would do nothing to eliminate corrupt practices (B. Kemp; 'Crewe's Act', *English Historical Review*, **LXVIII** 1953).

[48] Lord Ossory to Fitzpatrick, 3 May 1782, B.M. Add. MSS 47579, f. 85, Fox Papers.

[49] George III to Shelburne, 10 April 1782, Fortescue, Vol. V, p. 451; 12 April 1782, ibid., pp. 452–5.

[50] Fox to Fitzpatrick 12 April 1782, B.M. Add. MSS 47580, f. 71. Fox Papers, *Fox's Memorials*, Vol. I, pp. 314–5.

[51] Fox to Fitzpatrick, 15 April 1782, B.M. Add. MSS 47580, f. 77. Fox Papers, *Fox's Memorials*, Vol. I, pp. 315–16.

[52] George III to Rockingham, 28 April 1782, Fortescue, Vol. V, p. 496.

[53] *The Parliamentary History*, **XXII**, pp. 392–3.

[54] ibid., pp. 1356–61, 1376–7.

[55] 'Many retrenchments that had appeared to be indispensable, while he was in Opposition, were abandoned when he spoke from the Treasury Bench. Some abuses owed their prospective toleration to the personal respect that, he said, he felt for the Individuals who presided over the office or department. Others were perpetuated from deference to prejudice, or popular predilection. The Ordnance might be left to the Duke of Richmond's vigilant frugality. Lord Ashburton extended his protection to the Duchy of Lancaster' (N. Wraxall, *Historical Memoirs*, p. 444).

[56] R.119, 120, 132, 219, Wentworth Woodhouse MSS. Lord John Cavendish on 18 June obtained eleven resolutions anticipating reforms of the land, house and window taxes. *The Parliamentary History*, **XXII**, pp. 115–21).

[57] Op. cit., p. 446.

[58] In December 1781 pressure from the Quintuple Alliance—an association of the committees of the five metropolitan constituencies (London, the City of London, Westminster, Middlesex and Surrey)—upon parliamentary politicians began to revive the issue of parliamentary reform.

[59] Richmond to Rockingham, 11 May 1782, RI–2076, Wentworth Woodhouse MSS, part printed in Albemarle, Vol. II, pp. 481–3.

[60] Richmond to Shelburne, 21 March 1782, Lansdowne MSS, cited A. Olson, op. cit., pp. 190–1.

[61] William Pitt was MP since January 1781 for Lowther's constituency of Appleby. The son of the Elder Pitt he had already created a considerable impression by his support for economic reform in the House and parliamentary reform in the country.

[62] There is a convenient account of this famous debate in J. Ehrman, *The Younger Pitt* (1969), pp. 70–1.

[63] Richmond to Rockingham, 11 May 1782, loc. cit.

[64] *The Parliamentary History*, **XXIII**, pp. 826–75.

[65] Ibid., pp. 1266–8.

[66] Portland to Rockingham, 25 April 1782, RI–2059, Wentworth Woodhouse MSS.

[67] Shelburne does not appear to have been much interested in Irish affairs (see e.g. Shelburne to Pery, 18 May 1782, *H.M.C. Emly*, p. 168). For his hostility to concessions see his letter to the King, 10 April 1782 (Fortescue, Vol. V, p. 449). He told Portland that the Irish troubles should not be exaggerated (29 April 1782, Fitzmaurice, Vol. II, p. 143).

[68] Fox to Grattan, 27 April 1782, *Fox's Memorials*, Vol. I, p. 410; Fox to Fitzpatrick, 28 April 1782, ibid., p. 412.

[69] Shelburne to George III, 10 April 1782, loc. cit.

[70] *The Parliamentary History*, **XXIII**, pp. 23–30.

[71] Lord Aldborough to Fitzwilliam, 7 April 1782, Fitzwilliam MSS.

[72] 4 April 1782, *H.M.C. Charlemont*, pp. 56–8.

[73] Lord Aldborough to Fitzwilliam, 18 April 1782, Fitzwilliam MSS.

[74] RI–2075, Wentworth Woodhouse MSS.

[75] E.g. James Brown to Lord Buckinghamshire, 27 June 1782, *H.M.C. Lothian*, pp. 415–16. Portland claimed that during his Vice-Royalty he was able to connect to his party no less than one sixth of the Irish Commons. (Portland to Lord Northington, 18 September 1783, B.M. Add. MSS 38716 ff. 102–4 Northington Papers; See also, J. C. Beckett, 'Anglo-Irish Constitutional Relations in the later Eighteenth Century', *Irish Historical Studies*, **XIV** 1964–5.)

[76] Oswald was a rich merchant and a government contractor and had for some years been attached to Shelburne.

[77] Tom Grenville was the son of George Grenville and MP for Buckinghamshire. A Foxite Whig since 1780.

[78] The cabinet minute can be found in B.M. Add. MSS 47559, f. 9. Fox Papers.

[79] George III to Shelburne, 7 May 1782, Fortescue, Vol. VI, p. 10.

[80] For the cabinet minute see B.M. Add. MSS 47559, f. 21, Fox Papers.

[81] J. Cannon, op. cit., p. 17, N4.

[82] *Grafton Autobiography*, pp. 321–3.

[83] Ibid., pp. 324–5. While there can be no doubt of Fox's anger, it is, to say the least, doubtful if he would have resigned on this issue. To have done so would have been a confession of his own failure to persuade his cabinet colleagues of the soundness of his views. To have done so as an individual would have looked like pique. Finally, would Fox have precipitated a political and possibly a constitutional crisis while Rockingham was on his death bed?

[84] Fitzwilliam to Lady Charlotte Dundas, *n.d.* early 1782, Ramsden MSS.

[85] Henry Duncombe to Lady Rockingham, 31 July 1782, ibid. Burke wrote, simply; 'I have lost, & the public have lost, a friend'. (To Loughborough, 17 July 1782, *Burke Correspondence*, Vol. V, pp. 19–20.)

[86] Although he did not wish Fox to resign at once. (Shelburne to George III, 30 June 1782, Fortescue, Vol. VI, pp. 68–9.) The King realised that it might be difficult to get rid of Fox although he did not want him to remain. (The King to Shelburne, 1 July 1782, ibid., p. 70.)

[87] The evidence adduced by L. Mitchell (op. cit., pp. 21–2) to argue that Fox considered that he had a chance of the succession is much too flimsy to be accepted.

[88] Memorandum of Richard Fitzpatrick, B.M. Add. MSS 47582, f. 162, Fox Papers.

[89] Fox to John Lee, *n.d.* (but internal evidence dates it 4 July 1782) Lee Papers.

[90] R. Fitzpatrick to Lord Ossory, 3 July 1782, *Fox's Memorials*, Vol. I, p. 459.

[91] In the debate in the Commons on 9 July 1782, *The Parliamentary History*, **XXIII**, p. 162.

[92] *Charles James Fox* (1972), p. 149.

[93] E.g. Viscount Sackville to William Knox, 9 July 1782, *H.M.C. Various*, Vol. VI, pp. 185–6.

[94] Richmond to Lady Spencer, 6 July 1782, Althorp MSS.

[95] Burke to Fox, 3 July 1782, *Burke Correspondence*, Vol. V, pp. 5–6.

[96] For the debates on 9 and 10 July see *The Parliamentary History*, **XXIII**, pp. 152–201.

[97] Shelburne to the Duke of Marlborough, 8 July 1782, B.M. Add. MSS 34418, ff. 484–5, Auckland MSS.

[98] *The Speech of the Right Honourable Charles James Fox . . . to the Electors of Westminster*, 17 July 1782, p. 31.

CHAPTER 22

[1] A. Olson, op. cit., p. 32. This author's account of the Rockinghams is unduly severe (pp. 32–7). The Rockinghams are criticised for low attendance on occasions and on issues which attracted a low attendance! The impression is given that the party did secede from Parliament in 1772 (p. 34). Isolated quotations are extracted from the correspondence of Richmond and Burke to suggest constant and universal pessimism. Finally, the author exaggerates differences within the party over America. Richmond was always a law unto himself and Burke toed the party line.

[2] Close scrutiny of the letters of George III to Bute of 10 January, 3 May and 12 July 1766 (Sedgwick, op. cit., pp. 241–54) reveals that there must have been correspondence other than these three surviving letters.

[3] For evidence of this claim see my own *The Whig Party and the French Revolution* (1967), Appendix One, Chapter One and pp. 233–6; L. G. Mitchell, op. cit., p. 254, et. seq.

[4] See the Introduction to *Whig Organisation in the General Election of 1790* (University of California Press, 1967) and his paper 'The Financing of the Whig Party Organisation, 1783–93', *American Historical Review*, **LXXI** (1966).

Index

Abdy, Sir Anthony (1720–75) 249, 429, 480, 564–5, 574, 597
Absentee Tax, 1773 303–8, 381
A'Court, William (1708–81) 227, 430, 479, 565, 597–8
A'Court Ashe, Pierce (1734–68) 480
Adair, James (1743–98) 574
Adams, George (1731–89) 480, 564–5, 596, 598
Adams, Sam 308
Admiralty Board 386
Admiralty Courts 330, 333
Aislabie, William 564
Albemarle see Keppel
Albemarle Street 56, 81, 86
Almon, John 65, 69, 281, 509
Althorp, Lord see Spencer, George John
Amherst, Sir Jeffrey, 1st Lord (1717–1797) 233, 235, 331, 392, 568, 623
America
    Reaction to Stamp Act 138–9, 231, 533
    Reaction to Repeal of Stamp Act 156, 200–1, 556
    Reaction to Townshend Duties 202, 232–3
    American Issue in Development of Rockingham Party 230
    America as an issue in 1768 233–4, 248, 257, 567–8
    America as an issue in 1770 287
    America as an issue in 1773–74 308–14, 592–4
    America as an issue at election of 1774 319
    British Policy 1774–5 325–7, 331–2, 337–8
    The American War 315, 319, 322, 325–9, 333–4, 336–59, 367–8, 371–6, 380–9, 399, 405, 431, 436, 439–40, 452, 462–3, 598, 601–4, 617–18
    See also, Grenville, George, Independence, Saratoga

Ancient Constitution, The 267
Ancram, Lord see Kerr
Anderson, Francis Evelyn (1752–1821) 431
Anderson-Pelham, Charles (1749–1823) 431
Anglican Church 290
Anne, Queen 14, 16, 224, 496
Annual Register, The 175
Anson, Thomas (1695–1773) 227, 430, 438, 564–5, 596
Archer, Andrew (1736–78) 479, 564
Armytage, Sir George (1734–83)
Ashburnham, Sir William (1739–1823) 52, 479
Astley, Sir Edward (1729–1802)
Aufrère, George (1715–1801) 564
Augusta, Princess Dowager (1719–72) 26, 96–8
Aylesbury 248

Baker, Sir William (1705–70) 52, 115, 137, 479, 506, 555, 563–6, 596
Baker, William (1743–1824) 430, 634
Barne, Miles (1718–80) 481
Barré, Isaac (1726–1802) 125, 147–8, 153, 369, 407, 416, 564, 586
Barrington, William, 2nd Vct (1719–1793) 241, 503, 613
Barrow, Charles (1707–89) 227, 430, 563–5, 597–8, 634
Basset, Sir Francis (1715–69) 564
Bathurst, Benjamin (1691–1767) 481
Bathurst, Henry, 2nd Vct (1714–94) 366, 369, 395
Beauchamp-Proctor, Sir William (1722–73) 238, 240, 481, 564
Beauclerk, Aubrey (1740–1802) 563–4, 596
Beckford, William (1709–70) 197–8, 582
Bedford, Duke of see Russell
Bedford Whigs
    Attitude to Bute 76–7
    Conflict with Grenville, 1763 77–8

Bedford Whigs—*cont.*
  Opposed to 1st Rockingham Ministry 130–1, 133, 146, 159, 179, 193, 534–5
  Wooed by Chatham 188, 192–3
  Wooed by Rockinghams 193
  And Land Tax 199–200
  And Union of Opposition 1767 204, 206
  Enter Chatham Ministry 211–14, 561, 567
  In office 216–17, 221–2, 228, 234–5, 253, 256, 260, 287, 339, 379, 395, 400, 604–5
Bengal 298, 589
Bentinck Family 215
Bentinck, Lord Charles Edward (1744–1819) 226–7, 328, 429, 563–4, 596
Bentinck, John Albert (1737–75) 479, 563–4
Bentinck, William Henry Cavendish, 3rd Duke of Portland 190, 193, 215–16, 236–7, 252, 261, 298, 326, 348, 353, 35&, 378, 413, 423, 429, 460–2, 464–6, 562, 595, 617, 633, 640
  His Connection 222, 226, 317–18, 320, 429–30
Benyon, Richard (1746–96) 430
Bertie, Peregrine (1723–86) 481
Bertie, Lord Robert (1721–82) 536
Berwick 575
Beverley 317, 428
Bill of Rights Society 240, 251, 285, 582
Blackett, Walter 478
Blaquière, Sir John 303, 306
Bodmin 251
Bombay 298
Bootle, Wilbraham (1725–96) 478
Boston (Lincs) 308
Boston (Mass.) 325–6, 329, 338, 598–600
Boston Port Bill 311, 313, 325–6, 593
Boston Tea Party 308–9, 311, 313–14, 592
Botetort, Lord (1717–70) 233, 568
Boulton *see* Crabb Boulton
Bourbons 387, 391–2, 400–1, 440
Bouverie, Edward (1738–1810) 564
Braddyl, Wilson 429
Brand, Thomas (1717–70) 562
Brett, Sir Peircy (1710–81) 480

Brickdale, Matthew (1735–1831) 596
Bridgeman, Sir Henry (1725–1800) 429, 479
Bridges, Sir Brook (1733–91) 564
Bristol 248, 318–19, 381, 433–4, 575, 603, 617, 619
Briton, The 69
Broadbottom 446–55, 497
Brooke, John 9, 19, 86, 191, 193, 219, 221, 233, 496, 498, 503–4, 542, 548, 557, 560
Brudenell, George Bridges (1725–1801) 480
Brudenell, Robert (1726–68) 536
Brydges, James, 3rd Duke of Chandos (1731–1809) 591
Buckinghamshire 248, 252, 261, 273, 318, 429, 574
Bullock, John (1731–1809) 430, 480, 564
Bunbury, Sir Thomas (1740–1821) 430
Burgoyne, John (1723–92) 359, 361, 374, 392–3, 430, 441, 536, 612, 623
Burke, Edmund (1729–97) 19–20, 200, 227, 228, 389, 392, 412, 475–6, 563–4
  Early Life and Writings 176–7, 258–259, 547
  1st Rockingham Ministry 147–8, 152, 154, 176–8, 548
  Short Account 258, 262, 577
  Distaste for Chatham 188, 190
  Role in Rockingham Party (1766–1770) 194, 196, 211, 259–62, 561, 577–8
  East India Company (1767) 198
  1768 election 227
  1769 session and Petitioning Movement 240, 243, 248–9, 255, 259–60, 568, 572–5
  Observations on a Late State of the Nation 262–3
  Thoughts on the Causes of the Present Discontents 257, 263–4, 268–70, 277, 577–9
  Idea of Party 262–70, 474–6, 580, 610
  Impact of *Thoughts* 270–1, 579–80
  Anti-Chathamite strain in Idea of Party 263, 270–7
  Reformulation of Whiggism 263–4
  On Bute Myth 264

Burke, Edmund—*cont.*
On America 1770–71 273–4, 277, 279
On Rights of Juries 1771 281–2
Demoralisation in 1771–72 287–8, 291–2
On East India Company 1773 301
On Irish Absentee Tax 1773 308, 310–11, 592
On America 1773 308, 310–11, 592
Speech for Conciliation 1774 314
MP Bristol 318, 381, 433–4, 596, 617 619
On America 1774 323, 327–8, 597, 600–1
Conciliation Proposals (1775) 332–5, 344, 603, 607
Yearns for activity (1775–6) 341–2
American Policy, similar to Chatham's 344–5
Opposition to War 345–7
On Reaction to Declaration of Independence 348
On Secession 1776–77 348–50, 352
On Civil List 1777 352
Letter to the Sheriffs of Bristol 354–5
On Shelburne 356
Demoralisation 1777 356–7
American War placed within Rockinghamite framework of ideas 358, 363, 365, 367, 373–4, 379, 393
On Ireland 1779 381–2, 422
On Keppel 1779 384, 386, 620
On Economic Reform 404–5, 410–411, 413, 416–7, 420, 626–7, 630, 634
And Gordon Riots 422
Negotiations of 1780 424
Election of 1780 428
1780 in Burke's career 434
1781 session 437–40
And Rockingham-Shelburne Ministry, 453, 455, 458–9, 464, 466–7, 639–40
Burke, William (1729–98) 227, 555, 564–7, 596
Burrell, Peter (1723–75) 480
Burton, Bartholomew (c. 1695–1770) 52, 479, 564
Burton, Richard (1723–92) 479
Bute, Lord *see* Stuart

Bute Myth
Attitudes to Bute's early elevation 33–4, 63–5
Changing attitudes towards Bute 1763–65 64–6, 87–8
Status of Bute Myth in 1766 184–5, 198
Status of Bute Myth in 1767 554–5, 560
Status of Bute Myth in 1768 229
Function of Bute Myth 229, 324, 403, 473, 475, 567
Butler, John (1707–66) 52, 479, 563
Butterfield, Sir Herbert 10, 124, 548–9
Byng, George (1735–89) 318, 429, 438, 597

Calcraft, John (1726–72) 481, 584
Calvert, John (1726–1804) 52, 479
Calvert, Nicolson (?1724–93) 564
Cambridge 575
Camden *see* Pratt
Campbell, David (1736–77) 481
Campbell, J. *see* Lorne, Marquis of
Cannon, John 9, 453, 496
Carlisle 317, 318
Carlisle, Lord *see* Howard
Carlisle Peace Commission 366–8, 377–8, 388
Caroline, Queen 96, 98
Carolinas 399, 436, 439–40
Cavendish Family 50–3, 222–3, 226–8, 413, 429, 431
Cavendish, Lord Frederick (1729–1803) 53, 100, 188, 429, 479, 563–4
Cavendish, Lord George (1727–94) 53, 188, 429, 479, 506, 563–4, 597
Cavendish, George Augustus Henry (1754–1834) 429
Cavendish, Lord John (1732–96) 51, 53, 177, 188, 190, 211–12, 225, 259, 317, 328, 342, 347, 349–51, 354, 389, 427, 444, 466, 479, 506, 551, 560, 563–4, 566, 572, 595, 597, 611, 617, 634
Cavendish, Richard (1703–69) 53, 276, 429, 479, 564–5
Cavendish, Lord Richard (1752–81) 429, 596–7
Champion, Richard 596

Charlemont, James Caulfield, 1st Earl (1728–99) 462
Charles II 14
Charlestown 423, 426, 440
Charterhouse 115
Chatham 623
Chatham, Lady 235
Chathamites 273, 279, 290, 347, 357, 388, 409
Chatsworth 251
Chester 416
Chichester 623
Choiseul 35
Cholmley, Nathaniel (1721–91) 52, 225, 317, 481, 564–5, 596
Cholmondeley, Thomas (1726–79) 478, 564
Christie, Ian 9, 13, 429, 432, 543, 632–3
Cider Tax 59–62, 71, 79, 82–3, 99, 130, 168–9, 509–10
Civil List 274–5, 354, 403–4, 406, 417, 457, 459
Clare, Lord *see* Nugent, Robert
Claremont 54, 115, 121, 125, 134
Clayton, Sir Kenrick (c. 1715–69) 480, 564
Clayton, Sir Richard (1740–99) 227, 597, 598
Clayton, Sir William (c. 1718–83) 430, 564, 634
Clerke, Sir Philip Jennings (1722–88) 407, 423, 431, 438, 457–8, 635
Clive, Lord Robert (1725–74) 478
Codrington, Sir William (1719–92) 227, 481, 563–4, 597–8
Coercive Acts 311–13, 315, 333, 345, 598
Coke, Edward (1758–1837) 430
Coke, Thomas William (1754–1842) 430
Coke, Wenman (1717–76) 52, 479, 564–5, 596–8
Colebrooke, Sir George (1729–1809) 227, 480, 564–5
Colonial Agents 138–9
Committee on American Papers 151, 539
Conciliation Commission 339–40
Conciliatory Proposition 331, 559–60, 602–3
Congress 326, 330, 336, 344, 598–9, 602, 604

Connolly, Thomas (1737–1803) 227, 563, 597
Constitutional Society, The 285
Continental Association 326, 599
Contractors Bill 407, 423, 457–8
Conway, Henry Seymour (1719–1795)
  Dismissed from regiment 1764 87, 91
  1st Rockingham Ministry 122, 124, 134, 140, 142, 145–8, 151, 160, 171–2, 174, 181–3, 184–5, 545–6
  Chatham Ministry 190, 196–8, 201, 204–8, 213–14, 217, 549–50, 557, 559–62
  Opposes American War 347, 353, 369, 403, 444
  Rockingham-Shelburne Ministry 446, 452, 458
Cooke, George (1705–68) 134, 146, 232, 238, 481
Corn Embargo 195–6
Cornish, Sir Samuel (c. 1715–70) 563–565, 596
Cornwall, Charles Wolfran (1735–89) 436
Cornwall 251, 416, 575
Cornwallis, Charles, 1st Marquis (1738–1805) 388, 399, 460
Corsica 236
Country Politics 16, 228, 230, 271, 323, 402–8, 474, 497
County Movement 1779–85 407–15
Court-Country 15–16, 495
Coventry, Thomas (1713–97) 478, 481, 564
Coventry, Lord 153
Coventry 575
Coxe, Richard Hippisley (1742–86) 227, 430, 597–8
Crabb Boulton, Henry (1709–73) 481, 564
Crewe, John (1742–1829) 407, 419, 423, 430, 457–8, 635, 638
Cruger, Henry (1739–1827) 596
Cumberland 249, 252, 317, 575
Cumberland, HRH William Augustus (1721–65) 26–7, 38–40, 42–3, 47–48, 58–9, 70–2, 81, 85, 96–101, 473, 502–4
  Leader of Newcastle Whigs 1764–65 95, 98, 102, 116, 520

Cumberland—*cont.*
Negotiates during Regency Crisis
1765 98–100, 521–2
Negotiates Newcastle-Rockingham
Whigs into Office 103, 107–9,
116–17, 163, 173, 523
In Rockingham Ministry 1765 115–
119, 122, 125–7, 129, 131–4, 138,
158
Death 120, 132–3, 141, 158–9, 174–5
Curwen, Henry (1728–78) 226–7, 564–
565, 596

Dartmouth *see* Legge
Dashwood, Sir Francis (1708–81) 124,
188, 503
Davers, Sir Charles (1737–1806) 431
Declaratory Act 1766 144–5, 147, 151,
153–4, 156, 203, 234, 274, 309,
311, 313–14, 361–2, 367, 387
Dempster, George (1732–1818) 225,
317, 429, 555, 563–4, 597–8
Denbigh, Lord (1719–1800) 165–6
Denis, Peter (1713–78) 481, 564
Derbyshire 251, 254, 261
Dering, Sir Edward (1732–98) 481,
564
Devon 251, 433, 574–5
Devonshire House 59
Devonshire, William, 4th Duke (1720–
1764) 38, 43–4, 48, 54–7, 59, 70, 72,
75, 77, 90, 113–16, 500, 502–4,
513–14, 519
Devonshire, William 5th Duke (1748–
1811) 304–5, 410
Dickinson, John 232
Dissenters 291, 588
Divine Right 16
Dodd, John (1717–82) 52, 479, 564
Dominica 155
Dowdeswell, William (1721–75) 112,
227–8, 316, 464, 478, 529, 563–4,
597–8
Cider Tax 60
General Warrants 83
1st Rockingham Ministry 123, 140,
142, 145, 148, 169–70, 544, 551,
558
Opposes Chatham Administration
190, 194, 196
Land Tax 199–200

Dowdeswell Memorandum 1767
209–10, 560–1
Economic Reform 403–5
America 233–4
Opposes Grafton Ministry 235–6,
243, 245, 247–50, 255–6, 572–4,
578
Position in Rockingham Party 259–
261, 277–8
Opposes North Ministry 275, 280,
282–5, 290, 292, 301, 311, 328,
585
Downe, John Dawnay 3rd Vct (1728–
80) 225, 563–4, 596
Dublin 424
Dudley 603
Dummer, Thomas Lee (1712–65) 53,
479, 563–4
Duncombe, Henry (1728–1818) 428,
464
Dundas, Charles (1751–1832) 428
Dundas, Henry (1742–1811) 442, 456,
636
Dundas, James (1721–1780) 428
Dundas, Sir Lawrence (1710–81), 428,
633
Dunning, John (1731–83) 312, 365,
369, 386, 417, 419, 438, 441, 452,
457, 620, 630, 636
Dunning's Resolutions, April 1780
417–18, 419, 457, 630
Dyson, Jeremiah (1722–76) 146, 148,
173–4, 196, 536

East India Company 191, 197–8, 215,
260, 298–302, 308–9, 325, 405,
555–6, 589–90
Economic Reform 374, 376, 402–21,
437–9, 457–9, 625, 627–30
Eden, William (1744–1814) 361, 366,
370–1, 379, 605, 616
Edgecumbe, George, 3rd Lord (1720–95)
189–91, 220–1, 224, 473, 552–3
Effingham, Thomas Howard, 3rd
Earl (1747–91) 614
Egerton, Samuel (1711–80) 481, 564
Egremont *see* Wyndham
Elections 15, 17, 29, 215
Election of 1768 199, 214–15, 217, 220,
222–8, 231, 237–8, 268
Election of 1774 315–21
Election of 1780 414–15, 420, 423–35

Eliot, Edward (1727–1804) 428, 633
Elliott, Sir Gilbert (1722–77) 128–9, 196, 536
Ellis, Welbore (1713–1802) 158, 536, 564
Essex 249, 251, 433, 575
Exeter 251, 575
Eyre, Samuel 1729–95) 564

Falkland Islands 279–80, 321, 583–4
Family Compact 35, 561
Feathers Tavern Petition 290–1
Fenwick, Thomas (1729–94) 226, 318, 566
Fetherstonehaugh, Sir Matthew (1714–1774) 277, 479, 563–4, 596
Financial Crisis 1763 79
Finch, Savile (1736–88) 225, 317, 428, 480, 564–5, 597
Fisher, Brice (d. 1767) 52, 479, 563
Fitzherbert, William (1712–72) 480
Fitzmaurice, Thomas (1742–93) 480
Fitzpatrick, Richard (1748–1813) 466
Fitzmaurice, William, 2nd Earl of Shelburne (1737–1805) 27, 97, 119, 125, 159, 181, 201, 213, 217, 231, 234, 235, 279, 302, 345–6, 351, 355–7, 362, 368–71, 373, 382, 393–4, 400–1, 409, 415, 422–425, 432, 436, 497, 510, 515, 529, 555–7, 561–2, 567, 601, 608, 617, 622, 628, 632
  And George III 401, 435, 446–56, 637
  Rockingham-Shelburne Ministry 458–63, 639
  Succeeds Rockingham 464–8
Fitzroy, Augustus Henry, 3rd Duke of Grafton (1735–1811) 283, 310, 324
  And Young Friends 49–50, 53, 55–8, 90, 97, 115, 117, 166, 506, 509
  Secretary of State in 1st Rockingham Ministry 121
  America 153–5
  And William Pitt 1765–66 121, 124–125, 145, 160–1, 541–2
  Resignation April 1766 170–1, 545
  Formation of Chatham Ministry 177, 181–2, 183, 550
  Attempts to conciliate Rockingham Whigs 189–90, 552–3

Townshend Duties 557–8
  Negotiations of 1767 205–6, 207–8, 560, 567
  Relations with Bedfords 211–13
  Relations with Chatham 217–18
  Grafton Ministry
  Grafton as defender of monarchy 217, 559, 562
  Election of 1768 213, 224
  Grafton's Administration 231–7, 239–44, 252–6, 571, 567–9
  Supports North Ministry 287, 338, 587
  Opposes North Ministry 345, 351–2, 355, 391, 393, 429, 432, 436, 605, 608, 617
  Rockingham-Shelburne Ministry 448–9, 451–2, 458, 463
Fitzroy, Charles (1737–97) 53, 479
Fletcher, Henry (1727–1807) 226–7, 318, 429, 597
Flood, Henry (1732–91) 382, 426
Florida 47
Foley, Andrew (1748–1818) 430
Foley, Edward (1747–1803) 430
Fonnereau, Philip (1739–97) 478
Fonnereau, Thomas (1699–1779) 478
Fonereau, Zachary (1706–78) 478
Foord, A. S. 19, 56, 230
Forester, Brooke (1717–71) 52, 479, 564
Forester, Cecil (1721–74) 481, 564
Fox, Charles James (1749–1806) 20, 259, 323, 430, 634
  Royal Marriages Act 290
  Opposes American War 335, 346–354, 358–9, 361, 363–5, 368–70, 373–4, 380, 382–7, 385–6, 439–443, 602
  Negotiations of 1779 387, 389–91, 430
  Negotiations of 1780 423–4, 464
  And Petitioning Movement 1780 413–14, 418–21, 434
  Rockingham-Shelburne Ministry 452, 458–68, 640
  And Prince of Wales 472
  Political Connection 430–1
  Heir of Rockingham 414
Fox-North Coalition 472
Fox, Henry (1705–74) 88
  Becomes Leader of House of Commons 1762 42–4, 51, 88, 502–4

Fox, Henry—*cont.*
And Massacre of Pelhamite Inno-
cents 54–5
And Resignation of Bute 61–3, 100,
131, 510
France 35, 41, 104, 195, 351, 355, 357,
360, 367–8, 371–4, 376–7, 379,
386–7, 391–2, 615, 617–18
Frankland, Sir Thomas (1718–84) 428,
596–7
Franklin, Benjamin (1706–90) 332,
351, 463, 592, 599–600
Frederick, Prince of Wales (1707–51)
26, 30, 498, 578–9
Frederick the Great 31, 38, 170, 195
Free Ports Bill 155, 539–40
Fuller, Richard (1713–82) 480, 597
Fuller, Rose (1708–77) 126, 137, 290,
313, 320, 564, 596

Gage, General 316, 325–7, 599, 601–2
Gage, Lord (1718–92) 52, 479
Galway, Lord (1725–72) 478
Gascoigne, Sir Thomas (1745–1810)
428
Gazetteer, The 283, 608
General Warrants 68, 70–1, 73, 84–7,
89–91, 99, 130, 164, 512, 517
George II (1683–1760) 18, 21, 26, 28,
30, 476, 498–9
George III (1737–1820) 14, 18, 20, 21,
25, 51, 80, 84, 118–19, 126, 228,
230, 265
Heir to Throne 25–30, 498–9
Early months of reign 31–2
Appointment of Bute to Secretary-
ship 32–4
Attitude to Peace 35
Resignation of Pitt 35–6
Resignation of Newcastle 38–40, 502
Installation of Bute Ministry 40–1
Dismissal of Devonshire 43–4, 505
Massacre of Pelhamite Innocents 504
Resignation of Bute 61–3
And Wilkes 69–71
And Grenville 73–5, 76, 86–7
Relations with Bute during Grenville
Ministry 74–5
Negotiates with William Pitt 75–7,
103–7, 523–4
Regency Crisis of 1765 95–101, 520–
521

Reconciliation with Newcastle Whigs
101–2
Intentions in Summer 1765 102–3, 128
Relations with Rockingham 117,
128–30, 162
Assistance for 1st Rockingham Minis-
try 122–3, 128
George III and Cumberland in 1st
Rockingham Ministry 132
Relations with Pitt during 1st
Rockingham Ministry 134, 159–
160, 166–71, 183, 541–6
Rockingham and Repeal of Stamp
Act 141, 149, 152, 162–7, 175,
543
Rockingham and Office-holders
128–9, 157–8, 173, 530
Grafton's Resignation 172–3
Fall of Rockingham Ministry 173–5,
546–7
Formation of Chatham Ministry
177–84, 185, 541–3, 546, 553
Negotiates with Bedford Party 192–
193, 213
Negotiations of 1767 205–8, 559
Role in Politics in 1761 Parliament
217–18
Supports Grafton Ministry 231, 235
Fall of Chatham Ministry 234–5
Influences ministers over Middlesex
Election 238, 241, 248, 254–7,
569, 571
Royal Marriages Act 289–90, 298
Irish Absentee Tax 306, 314
American War 315, 322, 325–6,
330, 337–9, 348, 353–5, 364–79,
598–600, 604–6, 610
Negotiates with elements in opposi-
tion 367, 369–71, 374–5, 376
Reliance on Lord North 386–8,
393–5, 399–401, 406, 412, 427,
618–21
1780 Session of Parliament 417, 419,
423–6
Fall of North 441–5
Establishment of Rockingham-Shel-
burne Ministry 446–56, 637
Economic Reform 458–9
Parliamentary Reform 459–60
Ireland 461–2
Chooses Shelburne to succeed Rock-
ingham 465–8

George III—*cont.*
　Events of 1783–4 vindicate George
　　III's conception of politics 472
Georgia 138, 326, 556
Germain, Lord George *see* Sackville,
　Lord George
Gilmour, Sir Alexander (1737–92)
　53, 479
Glasgow 603
Glorious Revolution 14, 16, 118, 228–9,
　265, 267, 495
Gloucester, Duke of 174, 289
Gloucester 412, 629
Gloucestershire 433
Glyn, John (1722–79) 240
Gordon, Lord Adam (1726–1801) 536
Gordon, Lord George (1751–93) 421–
　422, 631
Gordon Riots 421–3
Gower *see* Leveson-Gower
Gower connection 444, 447, 449, 455,
　624
Grafton, Duke of *see* Fitzroy
Grampound 428
Granby, Marquis of 101, 181, 358, 576,
　610
Grantham, Lord (1695–1770) 190, 551
Grattan, Henry (1746–1820) 382, 426,
　461
Gregory, Robert (1729–1810) 430
Grenville, George (1712–70) 62, 66–9,
　71, 77, 79–80, 86, 101, 120, 129–
　130, 158–9, 179, 217, 219, 221–2,
　228, 262, 272–4, 278, 283, 287,
　403, 475
　Leader of House of Commons 1771–
　　1772 37–8
　Secretary of State 1762 41–2, 503
　1st Lord of Admiralty 1762–63 42
　Formation of Grenville Ministry 63,
　　66–8, 510
　Relations with George III 73–6, 86–
　　87
　Attitude towards Wilkes 69–71, 79–
　　80, 83–5, 512–13, 515–16
　Negotiations to reconstruct the minis-
　　try August 1763 75–7
　Friction with Bedford Whigs 77–8
　Stamp Act 91, 136–7, 156, 519–20,
　　531–3
　Conception of Empire 138, 531–2
　Regency Crisis of 1765 96–8, 102–3

Last days of Grenville ·ministry 100–
　103, 107, 522
Reconciliation with Temple 100,
　105–6
Contests Charterhouse Governor-
　ship with Rockingham 115
Opposes Rockingham Ministry 110,
　120, 124, 129–31, 133, 134–5,
　146, 159, 184, 185
Opposes Repeal of Stamp Act 141,
　148, 151–2, 155, 534–5
On Land Tax 1767 199–200
On America 1767 201–4, 557
Union of Opposition 204, 209,
　211
Negotiations of 1767 206–8
Breach with Rockinghams late 1767
　212–14, 561
On Nullum Tempus 216
Petitioning Movement 1769 233,
　236–7, 241, 246, 248, 255, 568
Grenville Whigs (after Grenville's
　death) 339
Grenville, James (1715–83) 106, 125,
　481
Grenville, Thomas (1755–1866) 430,
　463, 639
Grey, Booth (1740–1802) 318, 429,
　566
Grey, Lord (1737–1819) 20, 226, 479,
　564–5
Grifin-Grifin, Sir John (1719–97) 481
Grosvenor, Sir Thomas (1734–95) 478

Habeas Corpus 353–4
Halifax, Lord (1716–71) 70, 74, 153,
　510, 515
Hamilton, William Gerard (1729–96)
　177, 536, 547
Hampshire 413
Hanbury, Capel (1707–65) 126, 480,
　563–4
Hanbury, John (1744–84) 430, 596–8
Hanover 27, 499
Hanoverian Mercenaries 343
Hanoverian Succession 118, 228, 242,
　265
Harbord, Harbord (1734–1810) 227,
　430, 480, 563–5, 597–8
Harcourt, George (1736–1809) 188,
　303

Hardwicke, Philip, 1st Earl (1690–1764)
    20–1, 38, 41, 46–8, 50, 56–7, 58–9,
    61, 70, 74–5, 79, 85–6, 90, 115–16,
    253, 287, 500–1, 503, 507, 512
Hardwicke, Philip, 2nd Earl (1720–90)
    88, 162, 173, 183, 551
Harrison, John (1738–1811) 431
Hartley, David (c. 1730–1813) 317, 362,
    438, 597, 633
Hartley, Winchcombe Henry (1740–
    1794) 430, 439
Harvey, E. (1718–78) 174
Hastings, Warren 589
Havannah 47
Hawke, Sir Edward (1710–81) 231,
    567
Hay, George (1715–78) 89, 158
Hay, Thomas (1733–86) 227, 566,
    597–8
Hayes 71, 91, 100, 105, 125, 372
Heathcote, Sir Gilbert (c. 1725–85)
    481, 564
Hedon 317, 428
Henniker, John (1724–1803) 478
Hereford 575
Herefordshire 250, 574
Hertford, Lord (1718–94) 304–5, 591
Hertfordshire 575
Hervey, Frederick Augustus, 4th Earl
    of Bristol (1730–1803) 235, 383
Hervey, John (1696–1764) 563
Hewett, John (1721–87) 227, 479, 481,
    564–5, 597
Higham Ferrers 317, 428
Hillsborough Lord (1718–93) 158, 213,
    231, 304, 379, 394–5, 515, 546, 591,
    605
Holland 426, 437, 632
Honeywood, Philip (1710–85) 481, 564
Hopkins, Richard (c. 1728–99) 506
Hotham, Beaumont (1737–1814) 226,
    318, 429, 536, 597
Hotham, Sir Richard (1722–99) 430–
    431
Howard, Frederick, 5th Earl of Carlisle
    (1748–1825) 379, 455–6
Howard, Henry, 14th Earl of Suffolk
    (1721–83) 149, 153, 248, 252,
    261, 378, 575, 605, 634, 639
Howe, Richard (1726–99) 338, 350,
    361, 364, 605, 609, 612, 622
Hudson 613

Hull 317, 428, 633
Hunt, George (1720–98) 478, 480
Huntingdon, Lord 124

Impartial Administration of Justice
    Act 312, 594
Indemnity Bill (1766–67) 191, 196
Indians 312, 365, 380-2
Independence, American, 326, 344,
    348–9, 351–3, 355–6, 361–2, 367–8,
    371–3, 374, 378, 400, 423, 440–1,
    452, 609, 615, 622
Independents 270, 272–3, 323, 417,
    436
Inglewood Forest 215
Invasion Scare of 1779 391–2, 623
Ireland 302–8, 374, 376, 381–2, 394,
    399–400, 402, 426, 436, 438, 460–
    462, 605, 639

Jacobitism 17, 26, 473, 496
Jamaica 155
Jarrett, Derek 9, 10, 520–1, 567
Jebb, John 407
Jenkinson, Charles (1729–1808) 146,
    151, 379, 394–5, 400, 405–6, 436,
    456, 465, 536, 618, 632
Jennings, George (1721–90) 478, 480,
    564
Johnstone, Governor (1730–87) 349,
    363, 369, 597, 609
Junius 253, 562, 576
Junto 496
Juries, Rights of 280–2

Kent 251, 277, 574–5
Keppel, Augustus (1725–86) 190, 349,
    356, 382–6, 423, 429, 452, 564–5,
    597, 619–20, 634
Keppel, George, 3rd Earl of Albemarle
    (1724–72) 190, 211, 261, 561
    Albemarle Connection 1768 222,
    227, 420
Keppel, William (1727–82) 429, 563–
    565, 597
Keppel trial 382–6, 443
Kerr, W. H., Lord Ancram (1710–75)
    48, 479
King's Friends 264
Kingston, Jamaica 155
Kinnoul, Thomas Hay, Earl of (1710–
    1787) 53, 57

Knatchbull, Sir Wyndham (1737–63) 8, 478
Knox, William (1732–1810) 262

Ladbroke, Sir Robert (?1739–1814) 481, 564
Lancaster 566
Lancashire 575
Land Tax 67, 260, 600
Land Tax, reduction 1767 199–200
Lascelles, Edward (1740–1820) 478
Lascelles, Edwin (1713–95)
Lawrence, Laurence (?1723–98) 564
Lee, John (1733–93) 261, 425, 431, 466, 620
Leeds 603
Legge, H. B. (1755–1810) 51–2, 56–7, 60–1, 81, 88, 90, 116, 479, 563
Legge, William, 2nd Earl Dartmouth (1731–1801) 140, 142, 287, 325, 332, 337–8, 551, 559, 592, 600–1, 604–5
Legh, Peter (1707–92) 481
Leicester House 25, 26, 27, 29, 40, 498
Lennox, Charles, 3rd Duke of Richmond (1735–1806) 98, 173–4, 183, 190, 208, 212, 214, 252, 272, 277–9, 285–7, 290–1, 300, 304–5, 309, 312, 328–9, 345–6, 353, 357–8, 359, 364, 368, 371–3, 389–91, 409, 420–3, 434, 438, 448, 452, 459–460, 464–6, 474, 578, 582–3, 584, 601, 606, 608, 612, 613, 631
Richmond's connection in 1768 222, 227
Lennox, Lord George (1737–1805) 221, 227, 563–5, 597
Leveson Gower, Lord Gower (1721–1803) 181, 206, 213, 395, 432
Lewes 566
Lexington 233, 336–7, 348, 604
Lichfield, George Henry, Lord (1718–1772) 124
Lincolnshire 249, 575
Lister, Thomas (1752–1826) 431
Liverpool, Lord (1770–1828) 19
Liverpool 251, 261, 435, 575, 603
Lloyd, Richard (1730–1810) 564
London 248, 277, 319, 412, 433, 575, 639
Long, Dudley (1748–1829) 429
Long, Sir Robert (1705–67) 481

Lorne, Marquis of (1723–1806) 536
Lottery Act 1771 405
Lowther, Sir James, 5th Bt (1736–1802) 215–16, 318, 432, 441, 446, 449, 595
Lucas, Thomas (1724–84) 430
Ludlow, Lord (1730–1803) 227, 431, 598, 634
Lumley, George Augustus Lumley Saunderson, Lord (1753–1807) 597–8
Luther, John (1739–86) 564
Luton Hoo 87
Luttrell, Henry Lawes (1737–1821) 241, 571–2
Lyttleton, Lord (1709–73) 97, 102–3, 125

Macaulay, Catherine 270–1
Mackenzie, Stuart (?1719–1800) 100, 102, 104–5, 108, 124, 132, 134, 172, 179, 181, 188, 551
Madras 298
Maitland, James Vct (1759–1839) 430
Major, John (1698–1781) 478
Malton 318, 428, 434
Manchester 603
Manchester, Duke of *see* Montagu
Manners, Lord Robert (1717–82) 536
Mansfield, Lord *see* Murray, William
Marlborough, Duke of (1739–1817) 455–6, 562
Massachussets Bay Regulating Act 311–12, 313, 367, 593
Massachussets 326, 331, 600
Massacre of Pelhamite Innocents 54–5, 57, 67, 114, 120, 125, 164, 507–8, 511, 530
Massacre of St George's Fields 239, 241, 570
Maudit Israel 35, 501
Mawbey, Sir Joseph (1730–98) 478
Medlicott, Thomas (1728–95) 564
Mellish, Sir Joseph (1717–90) 52, 479, 564
Merchants and American Revolution 334–5, 347, 596
Merchants and Repeal of the Stamp Act 139–40, 142, 145–6, 152, 154–155, 185, 533–5

Meredith, Sir William (1725–90) 90, 137, 188, 190, 198, 225, 247, 251, 274, 287, 290, 317, 389, 480, 564–6, 596, 613

Metham, Sir George (1716–93) 53, 479, 563

Mexborough, Lord (1719–78) 564

Meynell, Hugo (1735–1808) 53, 479

Middlesex By-election 1769 240

Middlesex By-election 1779 407, 627

Middlesex Election 1768–69 237–9, 244–5, 248–9, 251, 256, 321, 571

Middlesex Journal, The 283

Middlesex and Petitioning Movement 1769 243, 248, 251

Middlesex Radicalism 1779–80 407, 413, 416, 627, 639

Middlesex and Wilkite Rioters 242

Middleton, George Brodrick, 3rd Vct (1730–65) 51–2, 479, 506, 563

Militia 248

Milles, Richard (1735–1820) 481, 564

Minchin, Humphrey (1727–96) 429

Minorca 440

Molyneaux, Thomas (?1724–76) 536

Monckton, Edward (1744–1832) 430

Monson, George (1730–76) 564

Monson, John, 2nd Vct (1724–74) 189–90, 552

Montagu, Frederick (1733–1800) 225, 317, 349, 423–4, 428, 435–6, 513, 564–5, 597

Montagu, George, 4th Duke of Manchester (1737–88) 288–9, 328, 342, 345, 353, 357, 369, 422, 424, 455, 629

Montagu, John, 4th Earl of Sandwich (1718–92) 79, 153, 213, 374, 378, 383, 386, 394–5, 432, 439–40, 442–3, 448, 515, 619–20

Morgan, Charles (1736–87) 564

Morgan, John (1710–67) 481

Morgan, Thomas (1702–69) 481

Morning Chronicle, The 608

Morning Intelligencer, The 383

Morpeth 575

Mostyn, Sir Roger (1734–96) 481, 564

Murray, James (1727–99) 227, 564–5, 597

Murray, William (1705–93) 1st Lord Mansfield 112, 196, 281–2, 339–340, 405, 525–6, 606

Musgrave, George (1740–1828) 226–227, 597

Mutiny Bill of 1765 91, 137, 556, 558

Namier, Sir Lewis Bernstein 9, 13–14, 19, 20–1, 46, 53, 56, 500–1

'Namierite' History 13–14, 19–21

Navigation Acts 326, 329

Nesbitt, Arnold (1721–79) 480

Nesbitt, John (1745–1817) 564

Newcastle 412, 433, 575

Newcastle, Duke of *see* Pelham Holles

Newcastle Whigs:
  Dilemma over Peace Preliminaries 39–40, 42–6, 50–1
  Lists of 51–3, Appendix
  Attitude to Opposition 53–4, 507, 511, 513–15
  Continuity of 56–7
  Young Friends and 56–8, 60
  Relations with Pitt 1763 57–9, 67–8, 71–3, 76–9, 89–92, 505–6, 516–517
  Suspicions of Bute 63–6, 77–8, 83, 86–8, 514–15, 518
  Size of 219–20, 223–4, 509, Appendix
  And Cider Tax 60–1
  Opposition to Grenville 67
  On Wilkes 70–1, 79–80, 512–13, 516
  Wildmans and Newcastle's Party 81–3
  On General Warrants 84–5
  Situation in recess of 1764 85–6, 88–89
  On Conway's dismissal 87–8
  Townshend's plan for strengthening Newcastle Whigs 88
  In session of 1765 90–1
  Newcastle Whigs and Regency Crisis 97–8
  Significance of Regency Crisis in history of Newcastle Whigs 101–2
  Newcastle Whigs accept secondary role to Pitt, 1765 101–3, 110, 523
  Party conception of themselves 68
  See also Pelham-Holles

Newfoundland 35

New Hampshire 233
New York 350, 378, 440, 556, 558, 609
Noel, Thomas (1705-88) 564
Norfolk 249, 572
Norris, John (1740-1811) 52, 479, 564-6, 597
Northamptonshire 249
North Briton, The 69-70, 503, 513-14
North, Frederick, Lord (1732-92) 20-1, 80, 478, 546
  Coming to power 255-7
  Establishment of ministry 272-3, 277-8, 287, 297, 580, 587
  Early American Policy 273
  Relations with George III 272, 580
  Falkland Islands Crisis 279-80, 583-584
  Printers' Case 283, 587
  Feathers Tavern Petition 291
  Regulating Act 1773 298-302, 308, 405
  Irish Policy 1773 303-5, 306
  Coercive Policy in America 308-14
  Conciliation Policy in America 331-332, 348, 360-1, 363, 366-8, 371, 374, 385-6, 402, 425, 432, 602-603, 615-18
  Impact of Saratoga 360-1, 363-4, 369-71
  Wishes to resign 364, 374-5, 378-9, 394-5, 399-402, 419, 618
  Legal Promotions of 1778 371, 616
  Military Strategy after Saratoga 377, 399, 618
  Ireland 1778-9 380-1
  Keppel Affair 1778-9 383-4
  Defence of American War, 1779 388-9, 624
  Negotiations of 1779 389-91, 624-5
  State of Ministry in late 1779 394-5, 624
  Session of 1780 417, 419
  Gordon Riots 421-2
  Negotiations of 1780 422-5
  Election of 1780 427, 434-5
  Session of 1781 437-9
  Fall of the Ministry 1782 440-51, 636
Northington, Robert Henley, Lord (c. 1708-72) 75, 104, 122-4, 140, 150, 153-4, 155, 162, 175-6, 179, 181-3, 196, 206, 212, 559, 575

Northumberland 99-100, 101, 124, 129, 182, 188
Norton, Sir Fletcher (1716-89) 123, 146-8, 289, 435, 453, 536, 564
Norwich 433, 603
Nottingham 412, 603, 629
Nottinghamshire 575
Nugent, Robert, Lord Clare (1709-1788) 148, 318
Nullum Tempus 215-16, 217

Octennial Act 303
Office-holders dismissed for votes in Parliament 54-5, 87-8, 125-7, 130, 163-7, 518-19, 542
Offley, John (1717-84) 52, 479, 564-6, 597
Onslow, George (1731-1814) 48-9, 53, 56, 115, 188, 479, 506, 513
Onslow, George (Col.) (1731-92) 52, 283, 479
Orkney and Shetland 428
Osbaldeston, Fountayne Wentworth (1696-1770) 225, 317, 563-5, 597
Oswald, James (1715-69) 128, 536
Oswald, Richard 463, 639
Oxford 575

Page, John (1696-1779) 480, 564
Palliser, Sir Hugh (1723-96) 383-6, 619-21
Palmer, Sir Thomas (1702-65) 481
Palmerston, Henry Temple, 2nd Vct (1739-1802) 478
Parker, John (1735-88) 431
Parliamentary Reform 242, 267, 276, 408-15, 582
Party
  Anti-Party feeling 19
  Continuity 14, 46, 48-51, 219-24, 431-2, 481-3, 496, 508
  Disappearance of Party in early 18th century 16-17, 19
  Element in English Political Life 229-30
  Ireland, Party in 461-2
  Organisation of in 1780s 476
  Origins of 14
  Two Party System, absence of 15, 495

Party—*cont.*

Types of Party 431–3
See also Newcastle Whigs, Rockingham Whigs
Peace of Paris 35, 42, 47–9, 51–3, 57, 69, 219, 507
Pelham, Henry (1696–1754) 18, 25
Pelham, Thomas (1728–1805) 49, 506
Pelham-Holles, Thomas, 1st Duke of Newcastle (1693–1768) 18, 20, 21, 30, 50–1, 95, 121, 128, 219, 309
In reign of George II 25, 28
In new reign 32–3, 63–4, 499–500
Relations with City of London 32, 38, 40–1, 79, 499, 510
Election of 1761 32, 499, 500
Attitude to Peace Terms in 1761 ·35
Isolation after Pitt's resignation 37–38, 501
Resignation, May 1762 38–9, 48, 54, 502
Post-Resignation dilemma 39–40, 502
Drift into Opposition 41–2, 47, 473, 502–3
Uncertain line on Peace Preliminaries 42–5, 46–8
On Devonshire's dismissal 43–4, 504–5
Debates on Peace Preliminaries 50–1
On Massacre of Pelhamite Innocents 54–5
Subsequent strategy 57–8
Relations with Pitt 1763 57–9, 68, 71–3, 75–9, 89–92, 505–6, 516–517
On Cider Tax 60–1
On Bute 67–8, 73–4, 100, 102, 518
On Wilkes issue 70–1, 512–13
Attitude to Wildmans 81
On General Warrants 84–5
On Conway's dismissal 87–8
Personal disasters of 1764 85, 90, 116, 519, 528
Decline of leadership in 1765 119–121, 473
Newcastle and Merchants 533–4
Newcastle and the Regency Crisis 1765 97–8
Newcastle and Cumberland 102, 132

Negotiation of 1st Rockingham Ministry 108–9
Relations with Rockingham 111–13, 115, 125–7, 526–7, 530, 534
Lord Privy Seal in 1st Rockingham Ministry 120–1
Wishes to reverse Massacre of Pelhamite Innocents 125–7, 530
Attitude to George III 129, 163
Repeal of the Stamp Act 140, 142–3, 150, 152–4, 536
Fall of Rockingham Ministry 183–4, 541
Edgecumbe Crisis 190
Decline of Influence in the Party 194
Land Tax, 1767 199–200
On relations with factions 208, 211, 561
Lists of 1766–67 220–2
Newcastle Connection in 1768 222, 225–6, 320
Death 236
See also Newcastle Whigs
Pelhams 18, 46, 50, 65–6, 162, 228–30, 268, 271, 404, 468, 473–4, 476, 496, 499
Pennant, Richard (1736–1808) 564
Pennyman, Sir James (1736–1808) 317, 428, 596–8, 634
Penton, Henry (1736–1812) 480, 564
Perth, 317, 429
Perceval, John, 2nd Earl Egmont (1711–70) 108, 123–4, 128, 140, 155, 162, 181, 515, 546
Petitioning Movement, 1769 241–53, 260, 277, 285, 324, 412, 573–4, 576
Petitioning Movement, 1779–85 407–415
Philadelphia 326, 378
Pigot, George, 1st Lord (1719–77) 564
Pigot, Hugh (1722–92) 430
Pitt-Newcastle Coalition 25, 27, 36, 162, 497
Pitt, John (1706–87) 481
Pitt, Thomas (1737–93) 478
Pitt, William (1759–1806) 460, 465, 468, 472, 639
Pitt, William, the Elder (1708–78) 18, 25, 29, 46–7, 49, 56–7, 73, 110, 112–13, 115–17, 119–22, 124, 129–30, 430

Pitt, William, the Elder—*cont.*
Political Ideals 31, 33–4, 68
Pitt and Leicester House 27–8
Pitt and Cumberland in 1750s 27
Pitt and Newcastle in Wartime
    coalition 497, 499
Pitt and Bute 30–4, 499–500
Pitt and Peace, 35, 50–1
Resignation 35–6, 501
Enduring grudge against Newcastle
    46–7, 50, 159–60
Relations with Newcastle Whigs in
    1763 57–9, 67–8, 71–3, 76–7,
    78–9, 89–91, 505–6, 516–17
Cider Tax 59–60
Attitude to Charles Yorke 72–3, 78–
    80, 514
Negotiation with court in August
    1763 75–7, 86
General Warrants 84–6, 514
Regency Crisis 99–102
Negotiation of June 1765 103–7
Attitude to 1st Rockingham Minis-
    try 125, 133–5, 158–62, 167–71,
    537, 541–2, 544–5
American Policy 143–5, 147–8, 152,
    155, 535
Attitude to George III 134, 159–60,
    166–7, 174, 541–3, 546
Formation of Chatham Ministry
    177–82, 183–5, 549
The Cabinet—the best of all parties?
    180–1
Anti-Party Crusade 180-2, 192–3,
    204
Health 181, 550
Peerage 181
Alienates Rockingham Whigs 188–90
Alienates Bedford Whigs 192–3
Chatham Ministry, mentioned, 76,
    220, 229, 260, 266, 481, 563
Failure of Prussian Alliance 195
Corn Embargo 195–6
East India Company 1767 196–9
American policy 201–2, 205
Negotiations of 1767 205–6
Bedford Whigs enter ministry 212–
    213
Cabinet divisions, early 1768 216–17
Chatham aloof from ministry 216–18
End of Chatham Ministry 231–2,
    234–5, 568

Later Career of Chatham 255, 257,
    272, 275–82, 284–7, 301–2,
    307–8, 311–12, 314, 581–7, 592,
    595
Relations with Rockinghams 1775–
    1777 328–31, 335, 344–5, 355–8,
    361–2, 363–4, 369, 371–3, 601–2
Conciliation Proposals with America
    329–31, 333, 355, 603
On Secession of 1776–77 351–3
Rumoured offer of a ministerial post
    in 1778 366
Death 373, 617
Place Bills 267, 402, 404
Plan of Association, March 1780 414–
    415, 629
Plumb, J. 13
Plumer, William (1736–1822) 227,
    431, 480, 564–5, 597
Plumptre, John (1711–91) 52, 227, 318,
    479, 564–5, 597
Plymouth 433, 623
Pocock, Sir George (1706–92) 536
Poland 195
Ponsonby, William, 2nd Earl of
    Bessborough (1704–93) 190, 304–
    305, 591
Poole, Sir Francis (1681–1763) 52, 479
Popham, Edward (1711–72) 481
Portland *see* Bentinck
Powlett, Lord Harry (1720–94) 480,
    563
Portsmouth 384, 392, 596, 623
Pownall, Thomas (1722–1805) 273, 564
Poynings Law 307, 461
Praed, Herbert Mackworth (1718–
    1803) 480, 481
Pratt, Charles, 1st Lord Camden (1714–
    94) 58, 72, 75, 80, 99, 104, 117,
    178, 181, 206, 213, 217, 231, 235,
    253, 281–2, 329, 345, 352–3, 357,
    372–3, 391, 400, 419–20, 448–9,
    451, 458, 509, 513, 576, 585, 607–8,
    623–4
Price Chase (1731–77) 536
Printers Case 283–4, 285
Private Subscriptions, Troops raised by
    363, 392, 623
Privy Council 307, 423
Protestant Association 421
Protestant Dissenters 291, 588
Protestant Succession 18

Prussia 99, 130, 170, 195
Prussian Subsidy 1762 38–9
Pryse, J. B. (1739–74) 481

Quartering Act 556–7
Quartering Act, 1774 312, 594
Quebec Act 312–13, 594, 607
Quebec 311, 594, 609, 639

Ramsden, Sir John (1755–1839) 428
Rashleigh, Philip (1729–1811) 564
Rawlinson, Abraham (1738–1803) 429
Rawlinson, Sir Walter (1734–1805) 430
Reading 412
Rebow, Isaac (1731–81) 564
Regency Bill of 1751 26
Regency Bill of 1765 96–7
Richmond *see* Lennox
Richmond 428
Rigby, Richard (1722–88) 141, 211, 213, 232, 450, 624
Robbins, Caroline 19
Roberts, John 52, 479
Robinson, John (1727–1802) 25, 319, 321, 379, 394–5, 427, 434, 437, 497
Rochford, Lord 605
Rockingham Ministry 1765–66 55, 90, 95, 108–9, 110–75, 176, 237, 524–5
    Prospects 119–23, 528–9
    Major Appointments 123–4
    Lack of ideological coherence 124–5, 132, 133–5, 246, 157, 541–2, 544–5
    Relations with William Pitt 124–5, 133–5, 157, 246, 541–2, 544–5
    Reinstatement of dismissed office holders 125–7
    Relations with George III 128–30, 133–5, 149, 157–8, 162–8
    American Policy 130, 133, 135, 136–56, 154–6, 537, 539–40
    Role of ministry in development of Rockingham party 220, 473, 563
Rockingham Whig Party
    Place in history of Party 19–21, 475–476, 641
    Uniqueness 20, 219–20, 223–4, 228–229, 432, 473–5
    Continuity 20–1, 46, 48–51, 219–24, 431–2, 481–3, 496, 508

Rockingham Whigs—relationship to Pelhams 219–20, 223–4, 496
    Country element 16, 228, 230, 271, 323, 402–8, 474, 496–7
    Reformulation of Whiggism 229
    Origins of Rockingham Party 56–7, 473
    Coming to power of 1st Rockingham ministry 108–10, 119–23
    Divisions among 123–4, 133–5
    Relations with Pitt 124–5, 158–62
    Relations with George III 128–30, 162–7
    Rockingham Party in 1765 174
    Downfall of ministry ascribed to Bute 135, 182–5
    Rockingham Whigs in Chatham ministry 184–5, 191
    Suspicions of Chatham ministry 187–8, 191
    Edgecumbe affair 190–1, 194, 220, 224, 552–3, 563
    Systematic opposition to Chatham ministry 191–2
    Innocence and virtue in opposition 193–4
    Relations with Bedford 193
    Rockinghams as a party in 1766 194–5
    Corn Embargo 196
    East India Company 197–9, 555
    Land Tax 199–200, 555–6
    Townshend duties 203–5, 558–9
    Union of Opposition 204–5, 558–9
    Negotiations of 1767 206–09
    Dowdeswell Memorandum 209–10
    Growing exclusiveness of Rockingham party 210–11
    Relations with Bedford Whigs 211–12
    Weakness of position in 1767 and 1768 212–15
    Nullum Tempus 215–16
    Rockinghams as a party in 1768 219–23
    Rockinghams and Election of 1768 224–8
    Issues and the development of the Rockingham party 230
    Rockingham Whigs and the merchants in 1768 566
    Rockingham Whigs and America 1768 233–4

Rockingham Whig Party—*cont.*
Attitude to Wilkes 1768 239–41
Petitioning Movement of 1769 242–252
Failure to gain office in January 1770 255–7
Union of the Opposition in 1769 237, 243, 245–7, 255, 257
Rockingham Whigs and Edmund Burke 259—63, 268–71
Failure to unsettle North 273, 276–7, 279, 282, 284–5, 286–7
On America 1770 273
Falkland Islands 279, 286, 584–5
Printers Case 284, 286, 586
Rockinghamite Ideology after Burke's *Thoughts* 286–7, 578
Civil List 274–5, 581
Relations with Chatham 275–6, 280–7, 301–2, 307–8, 581–3, 591
Secession discussions of 1772 287–9, 291–3, 298, 582, 588–90
Abiding suspicions of Bute 233, 244, 288
Royal Marriages Act 289, 588
Feathers Tavern 290–1
India 1773 298–302, 311, 590
Ireland 1773 302–8, 590–2
America 1773–4 308–14, 592–4
Rockinghams as 'Friends of America' 309–11, 313–14
Rockinghams and Election of 1774 316–20
Rockinghams as a party, 1774 320–322, 327
Rockinghamite ideology 323, 606–7
Rockinghams and Whig Tradition 324
Rockinghams and Defence of Liberty 324
Rockinghams and America 1774–5 327–8
Rockinghams and Chatham 1775 328–31, 333, 344–5, 609
Rockinghams and North's Conciliation 331–2, 602
Rockinghams lack mercantile support 334–5, 347
Opposition to War 340–1, 343, 346–347, 350–1, 602–3
Unpopularity of Rockingham party 347

Secession of 1776–77 347–49, 351–4, 610–11
Civil List 1777 354
Relations with Chatham 1777, 354–358, 361–2, 363–4, 369, 371–3, 611–13, 616–17
Dislike of Shelburne 355–6
Opening of 1777–78 Session 358–9
Session of 1778 363–5, 373–4
Raising troops by private subscription 363
Carlisle Peace Commission 367–8
Rockinghams and American Independence 371–2
Rockinghams and negotiations with North ministry 375
Rockinghams in session of 1779 380–389
Ireland 381–2, 389
Keppel affair 382–6, 388–9, 619–21
On America 1778–79 386–9, 621–2
Prerogative of appointment 369, 387–8, 424–5, 448–9
Good relations with Shelburne late 1779 393–4
Rockinghams and origins of Economic Reform 402–6 581, 625–6
Rockinghams and Economic Reform 406–10, 627–30
Rockinghams and Yorkshire Movement 408–15, 438
Divisive effects of the movement upon the party 415, 420–1
Split with Shelburne in 1780 420–423, 435, 439
Gordon Riots 422–3
Negotiations with North 1780 422–5, 632
Effect upon relations with Shelburne 424–5
Effect upon relations with George III 424–5
Size and Structure of Rockingham Party in 1780 431–5
Fox's place in Rockingham Party 431
Rockingham Whigs and American Revolution 431
Continuity in Rockingham party 431–2
Development of Rockingham Party by 1780 431–2

Rockingham Whig Party—*cont.*
Rockingham Whigs and Election of 1780 427-31, 433
Session of 1781 437-8
Rockinghams and Yorktown 439-441
Rockinghamite strategy and the downfall of North 441-7
The Establishment of the Rockingham-Shelburne Ministry 446-456, 637-8
Failure to establish a party administration 454-6, 471
Divisions on Parliamentary Reform 459—60
Divisions on Ireland 460-1, 471, 639
The Rockingham Whigs and Party in Ireland 461-2, 471
Rockinghams and peace with America 462-3, 471
Rockingham party after Rockingham's death 464-8
Interpretation of events in 1782 placed within 'Bute Myth' framework 471-2
Rockingham, Marquis of *see* Watson-Wentworth
Rockingham Club, York 111, 566
Rous, Sir John (1750-1827) 444
Royal Marriages Act, 1772 289-90, 321
Rudé, George 243, 568, 572
Rushout, Sir John (1738-1800) 481
Russell, John, 4th Duke of Bedford (1710-71) 37, 74-5, 103, 141, 149, 166, 184, 192-3, 503, 510, 523, 544
Russia 195, 426
Rutland, Duke of 410, 432, 449, 629
Ryder, Nathaniel (1735-1803) 479
Rye 623

St Lucia 41, 503
St John, St Andrew (1759-1817) 430
Sacheverell Trial 496
Sackville, Lord George (1716-85) 133, 145, 171, 232, 287, 339, 358, 361, 364, 369-70, 374, 379, 386, 394, 441-2, 536, 551, 605, 609, 612, 615
Sandwich *see* Montagu
Saratoga 359-64, 366, 374, 377-8, 392, 425, 612-13, 615

Saunders, Sir Charles (1713-75) 190, 317, 480, 564-5, 597
Savile, Sir George (1726-84) 52, 60, 83-4, 111-12, 216, 228, 243, 246, 250, 261, 284, 290, 292, 316-17, 349, 352-3, 358, 416-17, 421, 428, 438, 479,·526, 564-5, 597, 630, 633
Savile's Relief Act 1778 421-2, 433-4, 464
Sawbridge, John (1732-95) 413, 420, 631
Scarborough, Richard Lumley Saunderson, Earl of, (1725-82) 189-90
Scawen, James (1734-1801) 227, 479, 564-5, 597
Scudamore, Charles Fitzroy (1713-82) 53, 479
Scudamore, John (1727-96) 250, 430, 480, 564
Sedgwick, R. R. 496
Sergison, Thomas (1701-66) 563
Seven Years War 25, 29, 57, 195, 230
Seymour, Henry (1729-1807) 236
Shelburne *see* Fitzmaurice
Shelley, John 51-2, 189, 479
Sheridan, R. B. (1751-1816) 430, 466
Shropshire 575
Silk Riots, May 1765 100
Simpson, Sir Edward (1699-1764) 563
Skipwith, Thomas (1735-90) 431, 596
Sloper, William Charles (1731-1813) 429
Sons of Liberty 138, 533
South Carolina 556
Southwark 251, 433, 575
Spain 35-6, 38, 47, 104, 135, 195, 280, 321, 383, 386, 391-2, 583-4
Spencer family 429
Spencer, Lord Charles (1740-1820) 455, 562, 638
Spencer, George John (1758-1834) Lord Althorp 429
Stanhope, Sir William (1702-72) 564
Stanley, Hans (1721-80) 158, 536
Stanley, Thomas (1749-1816) 431
Staunton, Thomas (1706-84) 478
Stevens, Richard 481, 564
Stewart, John Shaw (1739-1812) 431
Stowe 245
Strange, Lord (1717-71) 164-6, 536
Structural explanations 13-16, 495

Stuart, John, 3rd Earl of Bute (1713–92)
47, 49–51, 53, 59, 82, 88, 97, 99–
101, 104, 106–8, 113–14, 116, 119,
124, 157, 169–70, 179, 183, 187–8,
195, 210, 217, 224, 430
Early Political Career 26
Early association with George III
26–7, 498
Bute and Princess Augusta 26–7
Character 27
Bute and German War 27–8
Plans for new reign 28–30, 182, 498
Bute and Pitt 30–1
Bute and Newcastle 32
Bute as Secretary of State 32–4,
500–3
Bute and Peace 35–6
Role in Pitt's resignation 36–8
Role in Newcastle's Resignation 38–
41
1st Lord of the Treasury 40–1
Importance of the Peace Issue 42
Appointment of Fox, a turning point
in Bute's relations with George
III 503
Bute and Massacre of Pelhamite
Innocents 54, 505
Resignation 61–3, 511
Bute's role in formation of Grenville
ministry 63–4, 567
Rumours of his continuing influence
64–6
Constitutional issue of his situation
65–7
Bute and the Grenville ministry 86–
87, 475, 515
Attitude of Rockingham ministry
towards Bute 128–30, 130–3,
146, 157
Bute during the Rockingham Minis-
try 149, 163–4, 172–3, 183–4,
540–2, 641
Rockingham's belief in his influence
1766–68 188, 216, 473, 562, 567
Bute in Burke's *Thoughts* 229, 264–
265
Stuarts 16
Sturt, Humphrey (1725–86) 481
Sugar Act 1764 531–2
Sullivan, Lawrence (1713–86) 481,
555
Sussex 55, 126, 127

Talbot, William, 1st Lord (1710–82)
124
Tea Act 1773 309–10, 313
Tea Duty 308–9, 313–14, 333, 367,
580–1
Tempest, John (1710–76) 481
Temple, Richard Grenville, 2nd Earl
Temple (1711–79) 31, 36–7, 59,
75–6, 79, 86, 88, 97–107, 113, 129,
134, 149, 160, 179–81, 184, 206,
276, 512–13, 523–4, 541, 549, 550
Temple, George, 4th Earl Temple
(1753–1813) 448–9
Thatched House Tavern 245, 260, 285
Thirsk 428
Thirty-nine Articles 290
Thomas Peter 9
Thomlinson, John (1731–67) 563
Thompson, Beilby (1742–99) 317, 428,
563, 597
Thompson, Edward 568
Thrale, Henry (1728–81) 564
Thurlow, Edward, 1st Lord (1731–
1806) 369, 371, 375, 395, 400,
423, 447–52, 457–8, 616, 624, 637
Thynne, Henry (1735–1826) 562
Tobago 440
Tollemache, Wilbraham (1739–1821)
429
Tories 21, 30, 61, 65, 104, 221, 473–4,
475, 497, 499
Tory Party 14–19, 341
Townshend, Charles (1725–67) 57, 84,
90, 99, 101–3, 121, 128, 145, 162,
181, 183, 197–8, 201–4, 232–4,
273–4, 308–10, 508, 536, 546,
556–8, 561
Townshend, 'Spanish' Charles (1728–
1810) 52, 479, 506
Townshend, John (1757–1833)
Townshend, Thomas, Snr (1701–80)
51, 479
Townshend, Thomas, Jnr (1733–1800)
50–1, 59, 160, 232, 358, 506
Townshend, George, 4th Vct (1725–
1827) 122, 162, 303
Tracy, Thomas (1716–70) 480, 564
Treasury 17, 25, 131, 272
Treasury Board 36, 39, 63
Trecothick, Barlow (1718–75) 139–40,
142, 146, 244
Treise, Sir Charles (1728–80) 481

Triennial Act 15

Tuckfield, John (1719–67) 481, 564

Tudway, Clement (1734–1815) 481

Tufnell, George (1723–98) 480, 564

Turner, Charles (1727–83) 317, 427, 566–7, 597

Undertakers 303

Upper Ossory, John, 2nd Earl of (1745–1818) 305, 430

Ushant 382–4, 442

Vane, Frederick (1732–1801?) 564

Vanneck, Sir Gerard William (1743–1791) 429

Verney, Ralph, 2nd Earl (1714–91) 177, 227, 248, 318, 555, 563–5, 595, 597

Verney connection, 1768 222–3, 227

Vernon, George Venables (1709–1780) 564

Vice-Admiralty Courts 155

Villiers, George Bussy (1735–1805) 50, 53, 479, 506

Vincent, Sir Francis (?1717–75) 478, 481

Virginia 138, 436, 533, 598

Viry, Count 32

Volunteer Movement 382, 426, 460

Wales 416

Warley 623

Walpole, Edward (1706–84) 480

Walpole, Horace, 4th Earl of Orford 91, 96, 132, 272, 282, 312, 365, 497, 500, 574, 607

Walpole, Horatio (1752–1822) 429

Walpole, Richard (1728–98) 429

Walpole, Sir Robert (1676–1745) 17–18, 65, 229, 268, 502

Walpole, Thomas (1727–1803) 50–1, 125, 171, 188, 429, 479, 506

Walsh, John (1726–95) 478

Walsingham, Robert (1736–80) 564–5, 597–8

Warren, Sir George (1735–1801) 480

Washington, George 377, 440

Watson, Derek 9, 56, 145, 566

Watson, Thomas (1701–66) 480, 563

Watson-Wentworth, Charles, 2nd Marquis of Rockingham (1730–82) 20, 57, 75, 92, 101–2, 219, 503

On Massacre of Pelhamite Innocents 55

Attitude to William Pitt 79, 113, 115–16

Wealth 111, 525

Pelhamite connections 111, 113, 525–7

Builds electoral empire 111, 526

Country Whiggism of 112, 118, 323

Attitude to Bute 113–14

Attitude to Devonshire's dismissal 113–14

Relationship to 'Young Friends', 115–16

Position in Newcastle Whigs in 1763 115

Contests Governorship of Charterhouse with Grenville 115

Offered Admiralty in August 1763 115

Position in Newcastle Whigs in 1764–65 116

Takes over leadership of Newcastle Whigs 111, 117–19, 515

Qualifications for leadership 117, 118

Relations with George III 117, 124–125, 141, 149, 152, 157–8, 162–7, 175, 530, 543

Relations with Newcastle 125–7, 140–1, 530

Optimism at outset of 1st Rockingham ministry 130–1

Attitude to Pitt, 1765–66 124–5, 131, 133–5, 157–62, 171–2, 184–5, 531, 541–2, 544–5

Reaction to death of Cumberland 132–3

American policy 136–8, 142–5, 154, 535

Rockingham and merchants 139–140, 142, 145–6, 533–5

Rockingham and the 'revolt' of the office holders 141, 146–7, 149–151, 163–7, 172, 210, 530, 543, 560

Hostility to Bute 171, 530, 543, 545

Ascribes fall of ministry to Bute 175, 182–5

Watson-Wentworth—*cont.*
Ascribes establishment of Chatham
ministry to Bute 176, 183–5,
187, 188, 550, 551, 554
Allows his men to remain in Chatham
ministry 184–5, 188, 551
Suspicions of Grenville 185, 188,
193, 553–4
Edgecumbe Crisis 190–1
Identifies Chatham with Bute 193–4,
473
Rockingham as prospective 1st Lord
of the Treasury 193
Rockingham as party leader, 1766
194–5, 208–9, 210–11
Search for Union of the Opposition
194–5, 209
Tactics on East India Company
affairs 197–200
Interprets political events within
'Bute myth' framework 197–8,
200
Rockingham's tactical errors in 1767
negotiations 206–8, 561
Problems of a Bedford alliance 211–
212
Breach with Grenville 212
Secret influence explains isolation of
Rockingham Whigs 214, 554
Lists of Rockingham party 1766–67
220–2
Rockingham connection in 1768
222, 225, 565
Relations with Cavendish family 223
Opinion on election of 1768 227–8
On America 1768 234
Rockingham and Petitioning Move-
ment of 1769 249–50, 574
And Charles Yorke's death 253–4
Defeat of Union of the Opposition
256–7
Rockingham and City politics 243–
244, 582
And Burke's Party Theory 258–64,
268–9, 578–9
Failure of Rockinghams in early
1770s 272, 293
Relations with Chatham 274–5, 276,
285–7, 581–2, 585
Illness 277–8, 578
Falkland Islands issue 279–81, 584
Printers Case 281–2

Hostility to Parliamentary Reform
276, 284, 582
Religious Toleration 290–1
Secession discussions of 1772 292–3
India 1773 301–2, 589–90
Ireland 1773 303–6, 590–2
America 1773–4 307–10, 592–4
Rockingham's leadership of party
1768–74 328
As a speaker 597–8
America 1774–5 327–8, 600
Relations with Chatham 1774–5
328–31, 335, 601–2, 608
Rockingham's leadership 1775 335
Rockingham's inactivity 1775–6
340–2
Secession, 1776–77 348–502, 606
Retreat from the Declaratory Act
351
Hopes for defeat of British arms, late
1776 357
Redefines party labels 606–7
Relations with Chatham 1778 366
Leader of opposition after Chatham's
death 375–6, 390–1
Motives of Irish Policy 1778–80 382,
401–2
On Office conditions 389–91, 474
On Private regiments 392
Relations with Burgoyne 392–3
Attitude to George III 393, 467
View of political scene, late 1779
401
Rockingham and Petitioning Move-
ment of 1780 408–9, 410–15,
630–2, 635
On Parliamentary Reform 1780
408, 412, 414–15, 629–31
On MP as a representative 412
On Economical Reform 408–15, 417
And Gordon Riots 423
Attitude to George III 425
Rockingham connection in 1780
election 427–9
Health after 1780 election 435
Conditions for taking office 422–5,
448–9, 636–7
On Parliamentary reform 1782 460
Death of Rockingham 463–4, 476–7
His influence on Rockingham party
473–4, 476–7
See also Rockingham Whigs

Weddell, William (1736–92) 225, 227, 317, 428, 563–5, 597
Wedderburn, Alexander (1733–1805) 146, 260, 278, 351, 371, 379, 564, 574, 616
Wendover 318
Wenlock 429
West, James (1703–72) 52, 126, 479, 564–6
West, James (1742–95) 563–5, 596
West Florida 440
West Indies 47, 154–5, 378, 386, 399
Westminster 412–13, 426, 575, 639
Westminster Association 420
Weymouth, Thomas Thynne, 3rd Vct Weymouth (1734–96) 213, 231, 235, 375, 385, 394–5, 447, 449, 584, 591, 605, 624
Whately, Thomas (c.1728–72) 245, 568
Whichcot, Sir Thomas (1700–76) 478
Whig Interpretation 13, 15, 16, 29, 476
Whigs, Old 28–30, 38–40, 42–5, 162, 496
Whig Oligarchy 17–18
Whig opposition to Walpole 17–18
Whig Party of 17th century 14–19, 495
Whig Party of 19th century 476
Whig tradition 299–300, 307–8, 381, 473–6
White, John (1733–68) 51–2, 190, 225, 479, 564–5
Whitmore, William (1714–71) 564
Wicklow 382, 413
Wigan 318, 430
Wildmans 56, 81–3, 223, 517
Wilkes, John (1725–97) 69–72, 78–9, 81, 83–5, 512–13, 106, 179, 231, 237–45, 249, 270, 273, 275, 285, 301, 308, 320, 404, 478, 512–13, 569, 571, 592
Wilkinson, Andrew (1697–1784) 52, 479, 563
Wilkites 270, 273
William III 16
Wiltshire 575, 630
Winchelsea, Daniel Finch, 8th Earl of (1689–1769) 123
Window Tax 169, 544
Windsor 634
Winnington, Sir Edward (1749–1805) 430
Winterton, Lord (1734–88) 52, 479, 564–5

Wolverhampton 603
Wood, Robert (1717–71) 536
Woodall, Henry 281, 608
Woodley, William (1728–93) 563
Worcester 433, 573, 575
Worcestershire 60, 248, 573
Wraxall, Sir Nathaniel (1751–1831) 405, 459
Wray, Sir Cecil (1734–1805) 250
Wyndham, Charles, 2nd Earl Egremont (1710–63) 37, 41–2, 74–5, 115, 503–4, 510
Wyndham, Percy O'Brien (1723–74) 564
Wyvill, Christopher (1740–1822) 407–415, 417, 460, 627–30

Yonge, Sir George (1733–1812) 480
York, City 55, 111, 114, 317, 410–12, 427–8, 566
Yorke, Charles (1722–70) 47, 51, 56–8, 70–3, 78–80, 84, 89–90, 102, 104, 116–17, 128, 227–8, 282, 480, 503, 505, 512–14, 551, 553, 564–5, 596
    Attorney General 1765–66 122–4, 172
    On America 140, 145, 147
    Death 73, 253–4
Yorke, Sir John (1728–1801) 55, 227 253–4, 369, 480, 564–5
Yorkshire 55, 111–12, 114, 249–50, 252, 260, 277, 306, 328, 334, 410–411, 413–14, 416, 428, 526, 566, 574
Yorkshire Movement 1779–85 407–15, 438, 627–30
Yorkshire Petition 408, 410–15, 628–9
'Young Friends' of the Duke of Newcastle
    Namier's interpretation 46, 48–50
    And Peace Preliminaries debates 51, 506, 509
    Status in Newcastle Party 51–4, 56–58, 60, 67, 507–8
    Organisation of 55–6
    And Cider Tax 60–2
    And Bute Myth 66
    Opposition to Grenville ministry 67, 70
    Wildmans 81–3
    In early 1765 90–1
    And Regency Crisis of 1765 97–8, 521
    In June 1765 107–9